MARITIME PLACE NAMES

Inland Washington Waters

MARITIME PLACE NAMES

Inland Washington Waters

RICHARD W. BLUMENTHAL

Inland Waters Publishing Co.

Maritime Place Names
Inland Washington Waters
Richard W. Blumenthal

Copyright © 2012 by Richard W. Blumenthal

All rights reserved. No part of this book may be reproduced or transmitted in any form or by any means, electronic or mechanical, including photocopying or recording, or by any information storage and retrieval system, without permission in writing from the author, except where permitted by law.

Printed in the United States of America
by Inland Waters Publishing Co., Bellevue, WA

ISBN-10: 0988326205
ISBN-13: 978-0-9883262-0-0
First edition published 2012
Cover design by Magicgraphix.com

Photographs used by permission of and copyright by Washington State Department of Ecology. The photos may be found at https://fortress.wa.gov/ecy/coastalatlas/
U.S. charts courtesy of NOAA.
Admiralty charts courtesy of Library Archives Canada.

To George & William.
When they learn to read,
I hope they'll develop
an interest in this subject.

Other books by Richard W. Blumenthal

*The Early Exploration of Inland Washington Waters.
Journals and Logs from Six Expeditions, 1786-1792.*
McFarland, 2004

*With Vancouver in Inland Washington Waters.
Journals of 12 Crewmen, April-June 1792.*
McFarland, 2007

*Charles Wilkes and the
Exploration of Inland Washington Waters.
Journals from the Expedition of 1841.*
McFarland, 2009

ACKNOWLEDGEMENTS

As the editor of several books, I found it very convenient to have my own editor. Having another pair of eyes to review the material, correct the sentence structure or spelling, ask the tough questions when the meaning is unclear, challenge dates and historical information, and, in general, keep me honest, is critical to the accuracy and completeness of any text. My editor is Alan Parsons, to whom I owe a great deal. Thank you, Alan, for your patience and long hours of examining this information.

Thanks to Ray Waldmann who also reviewed the text and provided many meaningful comments.

Thanks to Greg Lange whose family purchased property in the San Juans in the 1960s. As a result, he became interested in place names and over the years has documented his research on 3x5 index cards, enough to fill four boxes. Greg graciously provided access to his material that I found incredibly useful. Based upon his interests and research in the mid-1980s, he began providing input to the Washington State Board on Geographic Names and served on the State Board for several years in the early 1990s. Thank you, Greg, for the time you spent compiling this information and for allowing me to review it.

Thanks to Theresa Trebon, an author, archivist, and historian with the Swinomish Tribe in La Conner. Theresa's familiarity with the early history of Skagit and Island Counties has been extremely valuable.

Thanks to Dr. Scott Harrison. While searching for the meaning of some of Charles Wilkes' place names around Fidalgo Island, Scott encountered Horatio Hale's *Ethnology and Philology*, which became part of the 23 volumes of material ultimately published by the U.S. Exploring Expedition. Wilkes presented us with about 130 place names for which he left no reason; they were not contained in his *Narrative*. But these names, seemingly Indian in origin, were included on his charts which were published after the *Narrative*. Dr. Harrison found better than 30 listed in Hale's material. While it seems extraordinary that Wilkes would have arbitrarily borrowed names from Hale, the numbers support that theory. We may never know the origin of any of these 130 names. I offer Hale's names in this text without any actual knowledge as to their source.

Thanks to the Washington State Department of Ecology who graciously permitted my use of their shoreline photos. These amazing pictures may be found at https://fortress.wa.gov/ecy/coastalatlas/ and include high-resolution photos of the entire shoreline of the state.

Finally, special thanks to Gary Fuller Reese who is responsible for the Tacoma Public Library place name database. Cites to this database are shown in this manuscript as "TPL website." Gary and I exchanged hundreds of emails over the past ten years regarding maritime places and early settlers. Whenever I had questions, he was always very helpful. And, of course, his work on the database has been invaluable.

INTRODUCTION

According to Charles Wilkes who explored our waters in 1841: "Nothing can exceed the beauty of these waters, and their safety: not a shoal exists within the Straits of Juan de Fuca, Admiralty Inlet, Puget Sound, or Hood's Canal, that can in any way interrupt their navigation by a seventy-four gun ship. I venture nothing in saying there is no country in the world that possesses waters equal to these," (*Narrative* 305). George Davidson, author of the *Pacific Coast Pilot*, supported this opinion: "Washington Territory has a climate excelled only by that of California. We know not where to point to such a ramification of inland navigation, save in the British possessions to the northward. For depth of water, boldness of approaches, freedom from hidden dangers, and the immeasurable sea of gigantic timber coming down to the very shores, these waters are unsurpassed, unapproachable," (*Report* 416). Having cruised in these waters for nearly 60 years myself, I wholeheartedly agree with these observations. Even though I have encountered a couple of shoals and rocks in deference to their opinions about hidden dangers, they are certainly not wrong with respect to the beauty of our inland waters. One simply has to hop on any of our ferries to enjoy the experience firsthand.

When I started this project, I thought it might be interesting to examine some old nautical charts, catalog the place names, and identify the first appearance of each name. Focusing on the islands in San Juan and Island Counties, and with my three previous books on inland Washington maritime history as primary sources, I thought it would be relatively easy to bring it all together under one cover and identify the names, dates, and the reasons for the names. Besides, chasing down the charts gave me a good excuse to take a short winter vacation to the British Columbia Archives in Victoria, where many of the original Admiralty charts are located. Obviously, the project grew. I began, and expected to end, with a quick analysis of the San Juans. After mentioning the project to several friends, they encouraged me to enlarge the scope and direct the analysis southward into Puget Sound.

Early on, before the mid-1800s, attributing a place name to an individual was relatively easy. There were few explorers in our inland waters, and they left journals and/or charts to document their activities. After the mid-1800s, it became more difficult to identify who named what. The fact that American and British surveyors were in our waters at the same time led to names on charts that could not necessarily be attributed to the country originating the chart. I think that in many cases they shared notes. For example, the British might have discovered and named a rock. The Americans may have picked up on this information and reflected it on their rough chart. Because of timing, the American chart may have preceded the British. So, just knowing on which chart a particular name appeared first does not necessarily have any relationship to who named it. Such was the case between Richards of the British Admiralty and the U.S. Coast Survey team led by Davidson and Alden. Further, it is generally impossible to determine who on the Coast Survey or which of Richards' surveyors was responsible for a particular name. Thus, in most cases, I simply attributed the name to either the U.S. Coast Survey or to Richards.

Throughout this analysis, I "keyed" on the current name of a particular location, i.e., what appears on today's NOAA charts. Thus, information on *Seno de Padilla*, as named by the Spanish, can be found under the current name of Padilla Bay. I did not differentiate between subtleties of Centre Reef vs. Center Reef, or Roche Harbour vs. Roche Harbor, or Canal de Arro vs. Canal de Lopez de Haro vs. Haro Strait. Nor did I single out such names as Spiedens vs. Spieden's vs. Spieden Island. In all of these cases,

Introduction

I simply listed the name, Center Reef, Roche Harbor, Haro Strait, and Spieden Island respectively, as it is shown on current nautical charts.

Following the place name, where the information is available, I identified the earliest chart that reflected the name. The entry in brackets refers to the List of Charts found in Appendix B and may be referenced for a complete description of the chart. This bracketed entry is followed by the chart number and the date shown on the chart. In the case of the Spanish, Vancouver, and Wilkes charts, the date is also the year in which the place was named. Thereafter, it was either the year in which the chart was published or published with corrections. Admiralty charts are a bit confusing in this regard. All include the date in which the chart was initially published. This is located at the bottom center of the chart. Following this date, if applicable, is the date of large corrections. Additionally, small corrections if listed are shown at the lower left side of the chart. Small corrections use roman numerals to identify the month. Thus, VI 86 is June 1886. Where large and/or small corrections are identified on the Admiralty chart, I chose the latest date reflected on the chart. Finally, I identified the individual who named it. For example: "Spieden Island [7a] #145, 1841, Wilkes; [7c] #144, 1841, Wilkes." Spieden Island appears on charts #145 and #144 dated in 1841. This was the first appearance of the name on maritime charts. Wilkes was responsible for the name; the full title of the charts may be found in the Table of Charts under [7a] and [7c]. I did not include an individual's name on later Admiralty or U.S. charts, as it was unclear who was actually responsible for the name. I stopped researching charts from after about 1900. The reason was that after 1900, more often, places began to be named for the earliest settler rather than by an early explorer. Charts might take years to catch up to such information. And, I felt that knowing more about this individual or family was more important than documenting the chart that first reflected the name.

While working on this exercise, I learned a great deal. The most eye opening was that while we know much with respect to the history of place names, there is still much that we don't know. I have included about 200 names in this text for which I can find no information. With this in mind, here are my purposes:

- Build a folio of all inland Washington maritime names listed on current NOAA nautical charts,
- Identify information that is certain (e.g., data from original charts or journals of the explorers),
- Include information that represents the best opinion of previous authors, fully cited as to the source, and
- Include some speculation or guesses, but noted as such.

Regarding nautical charts, I indicated all maritime names above. I offer this caveat: I ignored most creeks, streams, rivers, and beaches. Although some hills and mountains are named on our charts, I excluded many of those that were off the water, but probably I have missed some of the intended maritime names. So, I think of this as an ongoing project, one that may have no end. And considering the fact that current names keep changing and new names arise, the project indeed has no end! With respect to "fully cited" as referenced above, I offer this note: For quotes from Vancouver, Charles Wilkes, and their men, I directed the reader to the original source material. Recognizing that this material is very difficult to obtain, transcriptions of these quotes may also be found in my three previous books.

The Washington State Board of Geographic Names was created by state law in 1973. Its purpose was to cooperate with local, state, and federal agencies to establish, change, and determine appropriate names for geographical features in the state. Because of a sunset law, the State Board was automatically terminated in 1982 before legislative action could be passed to continue it. Although the State Board continued to meet informally and make recommendations, twelve months passed before it regained legal authority. Because of budget restrictions, the State Board was eliminated entirely in 2010 but was again reformed in late 2011. Actually, two groups were formed: the Committee on Geographic Names and the Board on Geographic Names. The Committee is comprised essentially of the same members as the original Board before it was eliminated. The purpose of the Committee is to make recommendations on names to the Board.

Introduction

Approved changes are advanced to the Washington State Department of Natural Resources, which acts as the Board on Geographic Names, for final approval. Interested parties may review petitions for name changes and contribute opinions at the DNR website: http://www.dnr.wa.gov/BusinessPermits/Topics/OtherInteragencyInformation/Pages/bc_geog_agendas_minutes.aspx

The U.S. Board on Geographic Names was created in 1890 and in its present form by Public Law in 1947. Its purpose is to maintain uniform geographic name usage throughout the Federal Government. The intent is to standardize names, fix inconsistencies and contradictions, and correct spelling issues, but not to regulate names. The U.S. Board established a database in the late 1970s. The database, Geographic Name Information System, or GNIS, was populated with existing names at that time. As such, the Board did not officially "adopt" these names, and, as a result, there is no way to identify when the name originated. Around 1980, the database not only listed new names but the date in which a name was adopted was included as well. In addition, "variant names" were also included. As I discovered in one writing (Washington State Board file on Boundary Pass), not only are there variant names but unapproved variant names as well, all of which are listed in the database. "These may include former names or spellings, names derived by the application of policies other than those approved by the Board, misspellings, and names misapplied to the subject of the decision," (from the U.S. Board database at http://geonames.usgs.gov/). Beginning in 2010, the database also included "Decision Cards" (electronic note cards) which provide a brief amount of information for the reason for a particular name. And in 2012, "case files" were included which provide much more information. The database identifies several types of places where people once lived or currently live. These include census, civil, locale, and populated places. In this text, I do not differentiate and simply call all by the term "community" to encompass all of the definitions. Additionally, where the database is used as a reference, I simply note the cite as "GNIS files." The database may be found on the Internet (http://geonames.usgs.gov/).

In addition to maritime names listed on nautical charts, I discovered a large number of names in the GNIS which are not listed on current charts. The fact that these names are in the database means they have been formally recognized by the U.S. Board. That they are not reflected on current charts is likely the result of a lack of space. Regardless, these names are also included in this text.

I encourage and welcome reader input, criticisms, corrections, comments, and your first-person stories regarding grandparents or great-grandparents who shaped our early history. While this text is not intended as a "page-turner," my purpose is to establish a reference of maritime place names and create a medium to update and really nail down our early history. My hope is that perhaps in twenty or thirty years, one of my kids or grandkids can raise this torch again in the form of a new edition.

Please reach me through:
InlandWatersPublishing.com
Richard W. Blumenthal
September 2012

BIOGRAPHICAL INFORMATION

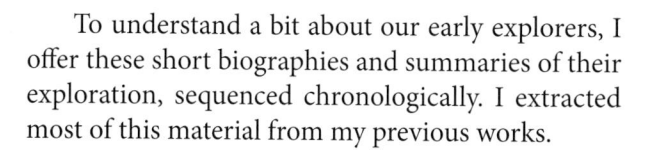

To understand a bit about our early explorers, I offer these short biographies and summaries of their exploration, sequenced chronologically. I extracted most of this material from my previous works.

John Meares

Although John Meares was not actively involved in inland water exploration or the naming of locations, his saga is still of interest. His activities nearly precipitated a war between Great Britain and Spain, and the resolution of this conflict caused the British Admiralty to dispatch George Vancouver on his voyage. From 1785 to 1795, Nootka on the western side of Vancouver Island was an extremely active location in the business of fur trade. John Meares was one of the participants. Born in 1756, he entered the British Navy in 1771 and was promoted to lieutenant after seven years of service. When the Treaty of Paris was signed in 1783, naval prospects for most junior officers declined. Meares, along with many others, transferred to the merchant navy. He retained his commission as a lieutenant and was placed on half-pay as a reservist. In February 1795, he was restored to active duty and promoted to commander. He died February 6, 1809.

Meares' adventures on the Northwest Coast began in 1785 in Calcutta. Inspired by Captain Cook's descriptions of the potential for fur trade, and with an interest in finding the famed Northwest Passage between the Pacific and Atlantic Oceans (a feat for which the British Parliament offered a reward of £20,000), Meares organized the Bengal Fur Society, including as one partner, Sir John Macpherson, the governor-general of India. In his first expedition, Meares sailed aboard the *Nootka* (200 tons) and another partner, William Tipping, also a reserve lieutenant in the Royal Navy, sailed aboard the *Sea Otter* (100 tons). The ships departed India in early March 1786. They planned to trade along the Northwest Coast and rendezvous in Prince William Sound. Unfortunately, Tipping and the *Sea Otter* were lost at sea. Because he arrived late in the season and was unable to fill out a cargo of skins, Meares decided to winter in Snug Corner Cove, Prince William Sound, rather than risk the loss of his crew to the pleasures of the Sandwich Islands. Ultimately surrounded by ice frozen to the hull and overheads below the deck covered with an inch of frost, the crew began to fall ill from the cold, from scurvy, and from smoke emitted by fires below deck to retard the formation of ice. Twenty-three sailors died as a result. By mid-May 1787, the ice released its grip on the *Nootka,* and with the assistance of Nathaniel Portlock and George Dixon who happened upon him, Meares departed for China on June 22, stopping over in the Sandwich Islands for provisions along the way. He arrived in Macao on October 20, 1787.

While the initial voyage was not successful, it helped Meares to organize a second. In January 1788, he purchased the *Felice Adventurer* (230 tons) and the *Iphigenia Nubiana* (200 tons) with Mr. William Douglas in charge. The ships departed on January 22, 1788, under the Portuguese flag. Because the Portuguese were one of the few countries that had trading rights with China, Meares could avoid high port costs. *Felice* reached Nootka on May 13, 1788 and anchored in Friendly Cove, almost ten years after Capt. Cook discovered it. Meares erected the first building on this land. He also constructed the first ship by Europeans on the Northwest Coast, the forty-eight-foot schooner, *Northwest America*, mostly from lumber stored aboard *Felice*. Meares launched it on September 19, 1788. While some of his crew were active in these pursuits, Meares sailed *Felice* south in search of the Northwest Passage and for fur trade. During this journey, Meares briefly entered the Strait of Juan de Fuca and then explored the West Coast of Washington as far south as the Columbia River.

Biographical Information

Unfortunately, he did not discover the Columbia River, leaving that to Robert Gray in 1792.

Felice returned to Nootka on July 26, 1788, but *Iphigenia* was yet to arrive. In early August, Meares sailed for Clayoquot Sound for more trading. Along the way, he encountered the sloop *Princess Royal* and Capt. Charles Duncan from London. After exchanging pleasantries, the ships continued in their separate directions. *Felice* returned to Nootka on August 24, and Meares was pleased to be joined by *Iphigenia* two days later. The two vessels were also joined in Friendly Cove by the American sloop *Lady Washington* commanded by Robert Gray on September 17. Meares left for China in *Felice* on September 24 with the season's spoils. With a stop in the Sandwich Islands for provisions, he anchored in Macao December 5, 1788. *Iphigenia* and *Northwest America* departed Nootka October 27 and wintered in the Sandwich Islands.

While in China, Meares organized a third expedition by forming a partnership with past competitors, the Associated Merchants Trading to the Northwest Coast of America. They purchased the *Argonaut* under the command of James Colnett and with the *Princess Royal*, now under the command of Thomas Hudson, departed in the spring of 1789.

Iphigenia and *Northwest America* returned to the Northwest Coast. *Iphigenia* arrived April 20 and *Northwest America* on April 24, 1789. At Nootka, they found the American ship *Columbia* commanded by John Kendrick. *Lady Washington*, consort to the *Columbia*, under the command of Robert Gray, arrived several days later. *Northwest America* was dispatched north for trade on April 28. On May 5, the Spanish warship *Princessa*, commanded by Estéban José Martinez, arrived with orders from the Viceroy of New Spain, Manuel Antonio Flores, to establish a permanent colony and take possession of the territory. With the additional support of the *San Carlos*, commanded by Gonzalo López de Haro, which arrived May 14, Martinez ignored England's claim and seized *Iphigenia*. Douglas was charged with illegally entering Spanish territory. In a surprise turnaround, Martinez suddenly found the papers of *Iphigenia* in order and released her in late May. However, Martinez forced Douglas to sign a document effectively giving title of the *Iphigenia* to the Spanish for payment of previously rendered assistance. Douglas was allowed to depart June 1 and headed northward to trade for furs and to warn *Northwest America* to avoid Nootka. Failing to locate *Northwest America*, Douglas left for China in the early autumn. *Northwest America* returned to Nootka June 8 and was seized by the Spanish the following day. The crew was transferred to the Spanish warship. Martinez made repairs to *Northwest America* and renamed it *Santa Gertrudis la Magna*, intending to keep it for use in trade and exploration. After repairs, Martinez dispatched it south into the Strait of Juan de Fuca for exploration.

Princess Royal arrived in Nootka mid-June 1789. Hudson claimed he was merely repairing his ship and Martinez allowed him to do so. Hudson stayed long enough to have a conversation with Robert Funter, captain of the *Northwest America* and to learn of the seizure of that ship as well as the *Iphigenia*. Hudson departed on July 2. The following day, James Colnett in the *Argonaut* arrived off Nootka and the ship was seized. On July 14, Martinez dispatched the *Argonaut* including Colnett and his crew to San Blas, Mexico. San Blas is located on the Pacific side, about 125 miles south of Mazatlan. On July 27, the *Princess Royal*, renamed the *Princesa Real*, and crew, also sailed for Mexico, escorted by Capt. López de Haro in the *San Carlos*. The crew of the *Northwest America* was transferred to the *Columbia*, now under the command of Robert Gray, after Gray and Kendrick exchanged ships, for passage to China. The *Columbia* eventually became the first American ship to circumnavigate the globe.

As a footnote to this Spanish activity, two other American ships became involved. The *Eleanora* under the command of Simon Metcalfe and the *Fair American* commanded by Metcalfe's young son, Thomas Humphrey Metcalfe, were both involved in the fur trade. Martinez captured *Fair American* and took the ship and crew to Mexico. The Spanish released the ship shortly, and the young Metcalfe departed for Hawaii to join his father, who barely eluded the Spanish. Fate, however, prohibited the reunion. Anchored off the islands, natives murdered the crew and captain of *Fair American*.

Iphigenia reached Macao October 4 where Douglas related to Meares his treatment by the Spanish. Upon the arrival of the *Columbia* on November 17, 1789, they became fully aware of the Spanish activity. The Spanish had now taken possession of the *Northwest America*, the *Argonaut*, and the *Princess Royal*.

The new Viceroy, the Conde de Revilla Gigedo, apparently disapproved of Martinez's actions. Reviewing Colnett's numerous letters regarding his crew's treatment at the hands of the Spanish, the Viceroy agreed to release the *Argonaut* and crew as well as the *Princess Royal*. The Viceroy directed Capt. Manuel Quimper to sail north on the *Princess Royal*, meet Colnett in Nootka, and surrender the ship. The ships departed in July 1790. Along the way, Quimper explored a portion of the Strait of Juan de Fuca and Colnett continued his fur trading along the coast. Upon arrival at Nootka, Quimper's entrance was delayed by fog and bad weather. After six days trying and short of supplies, he finally turned south and returned to Monterey. When the Viceroy learned that the *Princess Royal* was not released, he ordered Quimper to take her to Manila. Along the way, Quimper anchored in Kailua Bay on Oahu in March 1791, to trade for supplies. Colnett, also returning to China, coincidentally discovered the ship and Quimper surrendered the ship to him. *Princess Royal* was now back in the hands of the Associated Merchants Trading to the Northwest Coast of America.

As a result of the Spanish activity, Meares departed China in December 1789, and arrived in London in April 1790. Several months earlier, London had already become aware of the Nootka incident, and some amount of "letter-writing" had already occurred between London and the Spanish. Armed with the latest information from Meares, Parliament requested King George III to authorize a mobilization for war. Conversations between the English and Spanish governments continued through the summer and early fall. King Carlos IV finally decided that Spain could not win a war with England and authorized his chief negotiator, the Conde de Floridablanca, to yield. The first Nootka Convention was signed October 28, 1790. The Spanish agreed to release the British ships and men and to provide Great Britain equal trading rights along the Northwest Coast as well as in the Pacific Ocean and South Seas. The second Nootka Convention was signed February 12, 1793, and provided for Meares to be paid damages. The third Nootka Convention was signed January 11, 1794, and required the mutual abandonment of Nootka Sound.

José Maria Narvaez

In 1786, the French naval officer and explorer La Pèrouse returned from the Alaska Coast and stopped at Monterey. He provided information to the Spanish regarding Russian settlements in the area. The Spanish became concerned that the Russians intended to migrate south. In 1788, the Spanish sent two ships north commanded by Estéban José Martinez and Gonzalo Lopez de Haro to learn more about the Russian activities. The vessels returned to San Blas, Mexico and reported their findings to the Viceroy, Manuel Antonio Flores. After considering the information, Flores ordered Martinez and de Haro to take possession of Nootka and prevent Russian encroachment on Spanish territorial rights. However, for several years, the English had already used Nootka in their fur trade activities, and, in fact, had established a settlement of their own. While the Spanish were aware of Cook's voyage, they were apparently unaware of the trade it had generated. Martinez arrived at Nootka on May 5, 1789, aboard *Princesa*; de Haro and the *San Carlos* arrived a week later.

As referenced earlier, Martinez took possession of the *Northwest America* and appointed José Maria Narvaez (1768-1840) at command. Narvaez was born in Cadiz, Spain. Beginning in 1784, he spent three years in the Caribbean and then was ordered to San Blas. In 1788, he explored the Northwest Coast with Martinez and then returned to Nootka with him the following year. Narvaez departed Nootka June 21 and returned on July 5. While he observed the Strait of Juan de Fuca, he did not enter far. He simply confirmed the existence. An account by Narvaez has not been found, but the Martinez journal referenced the voyage. Martinez left Nootka, arriving in San Blas, Mexico December 1789, and, thus, eliminated any Spanish presence at Nootka. Believing a settlement to

Biographical Information

be important, Juan Francisco Bodega y Quadra, the senior naval officer at San Blas and supported by the current Viceroy, Juan Vincente de Güemes Pacheco de Padilla Horcasitas y Aguayo, Conde de Revilla Gigedo, appointed Lieutenant Francisco de Eliza to the command of *Conceptión* as well as Commandant of Nootka. Salvador Fidalgo and Manuel Quimper accompanied him in the *San Carlos* and the smaller *Princesa Real* (*Princess Royal*).

Manuel Quimper

The three ships sailed on February 3, 1790. *Princesa Real* was commanded by Manuel Quimper, an ensign in the Spanish navy. Also aboard was Estéban Mondofía, the first pilot, and Juan Carrasco, the second pilot ("pilotin"). On April 4, the two larger vessels arrived at Nootka; the *Princesa Real* arrived on April 7. Lopez de Haro, a pilot on the *Concepción* commanded by Eliza, transferred to the *Princesa Real*.

On May 31, Quimper set out with forty-one men. Two months were allowed for his exploration, and half of this time was spent in Clayoquot Sound. Departing Clayoquat, they coasted along the southwestern side of Vancouver Island, and on June 28 they anchored in Pedder Bay, seven or eight miles west of Victoria.

On July 4, *Princesa Real* anchored off New Dungeness. The following morning, Quimper directed Carrasco in the longboat to explore the land to the east toward Port Discovery. Carrasco sailed as far as Point Wilson and the entrance to Admiralty Inlet. He did not attempt to navigate the inlet, as there was insufficient time. Carrasco viewed the San Juan Archipelago from afar, but he believed it to be part of the mainland.

On July 18, *Princesa Real* returned to the Vancouver Island side of the strait and anchored off Royal Roads. On July 21, the vessel returned and anchored off the Washington Coast. The following morning, they hauled the anchor and worked their way west along the coast, eventually anchoring in Neah Bay on July 26. Quimper attempted to return to Nootka but was turned back because of weather. He sailed for Monterey and, after taking on supplies there, departed for San Blas, Mexico.

Francisco de Eliza

Following Quimper's exploration of 1790, the viceroy ordered another examination of the inland waters. He dispatched *San Carlos* from San Blas February 4, 1791, under the command of Ensign Ramon Saavedra. Saavedra carried instructions to Eliza written by Bodega y Quadra for Eliza to prepare one of the ships and continue the exploration. Quimper's diary and a chart of the Strait of Juan de Fuca were also enclosed. *San Carlos* reached Nootka on March 26, meeting up with Eliza's *Concepción* and the schooner *Santa Saturnina*. Eliza took command of *San Carlos* with Juan Pantoja y Arriaga as the first pilot. José Antonio Verdia was the second pilot. *Santa Saturnina* was commanded by José Maria Narvaez, with the Pilot Juan Carrasco. Both Narvaez and Carrasco had been with Quimper the previous year.

San Carlos and *Santa Saturnina* departed Nootka May 4, 1791. After surveying Clayoquot Sound, Eliza ordered Narvaez to complete the survey of Barkley Sound, while *San Carlos* continued on to Esquimault, anchoring on May 29. Narvaez arrived at Esquimault June 11. On June 14, *Santa Saturnina* and the longboat, commanded by Pantoja, entered Haro Strait and explored into the British Columbia Gulf Islands. That evening, they anchored off the southeast point of Patos Island. On June 16, they worked part way down the eastern side of Orcas Island, perhaps reaching Clark and Barnes Islands, but were hindered by torrential rains. They retraced their path and returned to Esquimault on June 24.

Eliza crossed the Strait of Juan de Fuca and anchored in Bahia Quimper (New Dungeness) June 29 and Puerto de Quadra (Discovery Bay) the following day. On July 1, *Santa Saturnina* departed with the longboat, commanded by the Second Pilot Don José Verdia. While Narvaez did not leave a log, his chart indicated his route and anchorages in this second expedition. They headed east, entered Rosario Strait, then Guemes Channel, and anchored in Bellingham Bay. From there, they passed east of Lummi Island and anchored in Birch Bay. Continuing north, they explored Boundary Bay and eventually worked up to Texada Island in British Columbia before returning.

Eliza departed Discovery Bay July 26 and reached Neah Bay August 11. On the evening of the 14th, the vessels separated. *San Carlos* arrived at Nootka on August 29. However, Carrasco (who was then commanding the *Santa Saturina*) battled weather conditions and finally turned south, arriving in Monterey for supplies on September 15 and ultimately at San Blas on November 9.

Alcalá-Galiano and Cayetano Valdéz

Alejandro Malaspina (1754-1810) was born in Mulazzo, Italy. As an Italian in the service of Spain, he led a scientific expedition to the Pacific Coast from 1789-1794. With his two vessels, the *Descubierta* and the *Atrevida*, equipped with the most modern scientific and navigational instruments available, he spent the summer of 1791 exploring the Alaska coastline. Returning to Spain in 1794, he became embroiled in Spanish politics and was imprisoned as a result. Ultimately, he was deported to Italy and his journals and records were filed away to be forgotten until 1885 when they were finally published.

Prior to receiving an account of Eliza's findings, the Viceroy ordered Francisco Antonio Mourelle to form another expedition to explore Northwest waters. The expedition was ready to depart December 1, 1791, but, unfortunately, Mourelle was ill and unable to leave. By this time, Carrasco arrived in San Blas, Mexico and provided information regarding Eliza's surveys. In addition, Malaspina also returned. In view of this additional information, Malaspina suggested the loan of two of his officers in lieu of Mourelle and the use of two new schooners, the *Mexicana* and *Sutil*, both recently constructed at San Blas. The Viceroy accepted the suggestion and the vessels were commanded by Dionisio Alcalá-Galiano and Cayetano Valdéz y Flores Bazán. Each vessel, forty-six feet, ten inches in length, carried a crew of seventeen plus officers.

Both Galiano (1760-1805) and Valdéz were aboard initially with Malaspina but left the expedition in Mexico. Galiano was responsible for creating some excellent charts of the eastern Vancouver Island waters. He died at the Battle of Trafalgar. Valdéz (1767-1835) was recommended to his post by his uncle, Antonio Valdéz y Bazán, Spain's Minister of Marine and Captain General of the Navy. Seriously wounded at Trafalgar, he was subsequently appointed Governor and Captain General of Cadiz. He became involved in politics, was imprisoned for his ideas, and exiled to England. In 1833, he was restored to Spain by Isabel II and appointed Captain General of the Navy. Posted to Cadiz as the Controller, he died there in 1835.

They sailed on March 8, 1792, and arrived at Nootka on May 13. They departed Nootka on June 5 and reached Neah Bay the following day. From Neah Bay, they departed for Esquimault on June 8, and on the 10th anchored at the southeast point of Lopez Island. The following morning, the vessels sailed up Rosario Straight. They passed through Guemes Channel and into Bellingham Bay. On June 12, the vessels departed Bellingham Bay through Hale Passage and that evening observed two small boats which appeared to be European in origin. Later that evening, they observed lights on board the *Discovery* and *Chatham* under the command of George Vancouver, anchored in Birch Bay. On June 13, the Spanish schooners entered and explored Boundary Bay. Departing the next day, they were met by the *Chatham*, commanded by Lieutenant Broughton, who presented his compliments to the Spanish and offered to render assistance. Galiano and Valdéz continued minor explorations and then anchored near Point Grey. On June 22, they were surprised to see George Vancouver in a long boat sailing south. Vancouver stopped and suggested that the two expeditions should work together. The Spanish agreed, and on June 24, the four ships proceeded north.

George Vancouver

In terms of Northwest maritime history, George Vancouver was perhaps the most noteworthy of the early explorers. Not only was he the first to accurately chart the inland waters of Washington and British Columbia, but he was the first to circumnavigate Vancouver Island. Born June 22, 1757, in King's Lynn, Norfolk, he was the sixth and youngest child of Bridgety and John Jasper Vancouver. He sailed on board *Resolution* during Capt. James Cook's second (1772-1774) and third (1776-1779) voyages, the latter of which brought the explorers to the Northwest Coast of Washington. Upon Cook's death in Hawaii, Vancouver returned to London in 1780. Commissioned as a lieutenant in late 1780, Vancouver served aboard several ships including, in 1784, the *Europa* under Alan Gardner.

Based upon a suggestion by Gardner, Vancouver was appointed second in command to Capt. Henry Roberts to explore the Northwest. Vancouver immediately began fitting out the H.M.S. *Discovery*, newly purchased by the government. During this period, Capt. John Meares filed with Parliament a notification of the Spanish seizure of English property and ships and the imprisonment of English crews at Nootka Sound. Because of these Spanish actions, England prepared for war. The officers and men assigned to *Discovery* were reassigned elsewhere, including Roberts, who was sent to the West Indies. Vancouver resumed service under Gardner.

Because of the show of force, Spain capitulated and signed the Nootka Convention on October 28, 1790. As Roberts had not yet returned from the West Indies, the Admiralty promoted Vancouver to Commander on December 15, 1790, and selected him to lead *Discovery* on the Northwest expedition. The twofold purpose now was to receive restitution from Spain for the territories seized and to make an accurate survey of the coast. Vancouver's orders were signed by Chatham, Hopkins, Hood, and Townshend on March 8, 1791. Besides *Discovery* with its complement of one hundred twelve men, the armed tender *Chatham* accompanied Vancouver. Commanded by Lieutenant William Broughton, the *Chatham* carried forty-five men.

Vancouver ultimately returned to London on October 20, 1795. Until his death on May 10, 1798, Vancouver prepared his journal which was actually completed shortly after his death by his brother, John, with the assistance of Peter Puget. It was initially published in three folio volumes and an atlas in 1798. A second edition was published in 1801 in six volumes, without the atlas.

John Work

John Wark, as his name was recorded in birth records, was born about 1792 in the North of Ireland. He joined the Hudson's Bay Company in 1814 where the spelling of his name was altered. For the first eight years he was stationed at Hudson Bay, primarily at the York Factory. The Company sent him to the Northwest in 1823 where he rose through the ranks, first as a clerk, then as a Chief Trader in 1830, and then to Chief Factor in 1846. In 1849, he was appointed District Manager of Fort Simpson, and in 1860 he became Chief Factor in Victoria. He died in 1861 and was buried at the Quadra Street Cemetery in Victoria. Hubert Bancroft wrote in *Native Races of the Pacific States*, II, 464: "To none of the Hudson's Bay company's officers is posterity more indebted than to John Wark, whose journals of various expeditions, nowhere else mentioned, fill a gap in history. He was a man of strong rather than graceful physique. His mind, like his frame, was constructed for practical use and endurance. His strict integrity commanded universal respect, and his kindly disposition won all hearts." The British honored him with the names 'Wark Point' in Victoria Harbor, 'Wark Channel' in Observatory Inlet, and 'Wark Island' in Graham Reach (Walbran 522, 523). In 1850, Work's oldest daughter, Jane, married Dr. William F. Tolmie, also a Chief Factor of the Hudson's Bay Company. One of their sons, Simon Tolmie, became a BC Premier. His second daughter, Sarah, married Roderick Finlayson (*see* Mount Finlayson).

Work left a series of journals that described early life and hardships in the Northwest. The particular journal I used and quote from in this text was dated November and December, 1824, where Work was in a party ". . . for the purpose of discovering the entrance of Fraser's River, and ascertaining the possibility of navigating that River with boats, and also examining the coast between Fort George [Astoria] and Fraser's River as far as practicable," (Work 200).

The party departed Fort George on November 18, 1824, and reached Eld Inlet on Puget Sound on December 5. From there, they worked along the eastern continental shoreline toward Nisqually, through The Narrows, Admiralty Inlet, Port Susan, and into the Swinomish Channel. By December 12 they arrived at Boundary Bay. They completed their exploration of the Frasier River and departed on December 20, essentially retracing their northward path by following the eastern shoreline. They arrived back at Fort George on December 30, 1824.

To make the quotes more understandable, I have taken the liberty of adding parenthetical information in brackets. In addition, because he described some places on the northward as well as the southward journey, I have included both. John Work's journals are of significance, as they add to the body of knowledge of our inland waters between the major explorations of Vancouver and Wilkes. It is interesting to note the place names used by him and his knowledge of our waters. John Work notes that he either had or had seen Vancouver's 1792 chart, as he referenced it on several occasions. It is unfortunate, through lack of clarity, that his exact location cannot be determined at all times. But that does not diminish the importance of the document.

Charles Wilkes

Charles Wilkes is perhaps the most important of the early explorers whose work shaped the description of Puget Sound country as we know it today. He was born April 3, 1798, in New York City. He was the youngest of three sons and one daughter of John de Pointhieu Wilkes and Mary Seton. Upon the death of his mother in 1801, Wilkes was cared for by various female relatives and friends among whom was his aunt, Elizabeth Seton, canonized by Pope Paul VI in 1975 as the first Roman Catholic American saint and for whom Seton Hall University was named. Educated at various boarding schools, Wilkes entered the merchant service in 1815, and during the course of the next few years he saw service on several ships. On January 1, 1818, he received an appointment as a midshipman in the U.S. Navy and was assigned to the *Independence* in Boston commanded by Capt. William Bainbridge. He then saw duty on the *Guerriere* (1818-1819), *Franklin* (1821-1822), *Waterwitch* (1822-1823), and *O'Cain* (1823). Returning to New York, he prepared for his lieutenant's examination and was promoted on April 28, 1826. Just two days earlier, he married Jane Renwick, a childhood friend. For the next several years, he continued his studies, mostly in hydrography. At one time he was tutored by Ferdinand Hassler, the first superintendent of the U.S. Coast Survey. Later, he studied with Nathaniel Bowditch, author of the *New American Practical Navigator*.

The United States Exploring Expedition of 1838-1842 (known as the U.S. Ex. Ex.) was authorized by an Act of Congress in 1828. The resolution allowed the President to send a public ship to explore the Pacific Coast, islands, harbors, shoals, and reefs. However, a special appropriation was not included. Wilkes volunteered for duty with the expedition and drew up a list of required instruments. Unfortunately, with a lack of funding, interest waned.

Wilkes was next assigned to the *Boston* (1830), transferred to the *Fairfield* (1830-1831), and was then placed on leave awaiting orders, a typical event in the peacetime navy. He renewed his academic interests and in 1833 took charge of the Depot of Charts and Instruments in Washington D.C., the predecessor to the Navy Hydrographic Office and today's Navy Oceanographic Office.

On May 14, 1836, Congress passed an appropriation to the Naval Appropriation Bill authorizing the president, then Andrew Jackson, to "send out a surveying and exploring expedition to the Pacific Ocean and South Seas." The Honorable Mahlon Dickerson, Secretary of the Navy, was responsible for outfitting the expedition. He requested that Wilkes prepare an equipment list and arrange for the necessary purchases in Europe. Wilkes left in August 1836 and returned the following January finding the preparations for the expedition in disarray. Although hoping for an assignment, he decided to distance himself from the chaos and spent the next year in survey activities along the East Coast.

Wilkes was not the first choice for command. Thomas ap Catesby Jones resigned in disgust over delays from the Secretary of the Navy. The command was then offered to Commodore Shubrick who declined. Then, it was offered to Captains Kearney and Gregory who also declined. On March 20, 1838, Secretary of War Joel R. Poinsett offered command of the expedition to Wilkes. President Van Buren approved the selection on April 20. Needless to say, there was a considerable protest with the command assigned to such a junior officer in the Navy. Of Wilkes' approximately 40 contemporaries, 38 had

Biographical Information

more sea experience. However, because this was intended to be an exploration as opposed to a military expedition, some of the resentment declined. Wilkes immediately set out to select his officers, crew, scientists, and to outfit the ships.

J. K. Paulding, the new Secretary of the Navy, identified the objectives in a letter dated August 11, 1838: ". . . purpose of exploring and surveying the sea, as well to determine the existence of all doubtful islands and shoals, as to discover and accurately fix the position of those which lie in or near the track of our vessels in that quarter, and may have escaped the observation of scientific navigators."

Wilkes had at his disposal the sloops of war *Vincennes* and *Peacock* and the brig *Porpoise*. *Vincennes*, launched in 1826, drew 700 tons and was 127 feet in length; *Peacock* 559 tons, 118 feet in length and was originally constructed in 1828; *Porpoise*, launched in 1836, drew 224 tons and was 88 feet. *Peacock* was lost in 1841 off the Columbia River bar, but all hands were saved. As a replacement, Wilkes purchased the merchant brig *Oregon* at 250 tons and 85 feet in length. In addition, the store ship *Relief*, 468 tons, 109 feet and the tenders *Sea Gull*, 110 tons, 73 feet and *Flying Fish*, 96 tons 70 feet in length, were subsequently added. *Sea Gull* was lost with all hands off the Chilean Coast in mid-1839.

The squadron departed the U.S. East Coast on Saturday, August 18, 1838. The ships sailed to South America and surveyed the coast. In late February 1839, they departed for their first Antarctic expedition. By July, the fleet headed for the Western Pacific where a survey commenced, followed by a second Antarctic expedition early the next year. By March 1840, the ships began exploration of Australia and New Zealand, followed by Fiji in May, and Hawaii in September. Departing Hawaii on April 5, 1841, the *Vincennes* and *Porpoise* arrived at Cape Flattery on April 29, surveyed Puget Sound, and departed Washington waters in early August. The autumn was occupied by surveys of the Columbia River and San Francisco Bay. By mid-November, Wilkes returned to Hawaii but departed ten days later for West Pacific surveys.

Wilkes returned to the East Coast on June 10, 1842, with a wealth of data and scientific information, including geological, botanical, zoological, anthropological, and other materials. Even with the accomplishments, the return was anticlimactic. The congressional attitude was unfriendly, the public, indifferent. Further complicating the situation were charges and countercharges between Wilkes and his officers regarding the treatment of the men. A court martial was convened, and Wilkes was found guilty of a single charge, that of proscribing punishment more severe than allowed. Although reprimanded, on August 1, 1843, he was placed in charge of the extensive collections and made responsible for documenting the findings. The collections were initially displayed in the Patent Office in Washington D.C. in 1840 and later moved to the Smithsonian in 1857. During the intervening years, Wilkes published his *Narrative* in early 1844 in five folio volumes and an atlas, but he spent the next seventeen years supervising the publication of nine atlases and fifteen additional volumes devoted to specimens collected by scientists and information from his crew.

Wilkes was promoted to commander on July 13, 1843, and to captain on September 14, 1855. Wilkes' wife died in 1848. In 1854, he married Mary Lynch Bolton. He returned to active duty in 1861 during the Civil War. While in command of the *San Jacinto*, Wilkes intercepted the British mail steamer *Trent* and took prisoner two Confederate Commissioners en route to England. While American reaction was euphoric, England was outraged. To avoid war with Great Britain, President Lincoln released the prisoners. On September 8, 1862, Wilkes received an acting appointment to rear admiral. During the following two years, he continued to alienate his superiors. At another court martial, he was found guilty on April 26, 1864, of disobedience of orders, insubordinate conduct, disrespectful language, disobedience to a general order or regulation, and conduct unbecoming an officer. He was given a three-year suspension and a public reprimand. However, late that year, President Lincoln reduced the penalties. In August 1866, Wilkes was promoted to rear admiral and placed on the retired list.

In 1865, Wilkes purchased property in North Carolina and established an iron works. Despite his frantic attempts, the endeavor was unsuccessful and he was forced to sell in 1874. During the early 1870s, he became involved again with the navy to finish the volumes on hydrography and physics, the latter of which was never published. Discouraged and in poor health, Wilkes died in his home in Washington D.C. on February 7, 1877. He is interred at Arlington National Cemetery.

In Vol. II of Wilkes' List of Charts, he left us with 17 charts of inland Washington waters. The list contains page numbers, but there are no individual chart numbers. The individual chart numbers that I included in this text were added from NOAA reprints in the early 1960s. I include a list below cross referencing his Vol. II page number to the current NOAA chart number:

Page	Chart	Description
76	144	Straits of Juan de Fuca
77	145	Archipelago of Arro, Gulf of Georgia, and Ringgold's Channel
78	146	Admiralty Inlet, Puget Sound, and Hoods Canal
79	147	Inlets in Puget Sound
80	148	St. Juan and Scarborough Harbours, and Port Discovery
81	149	New Dungeness Roads & Budds Harbours
82	150	Ports Townsend and Lawrence
83	151	Ports Ludlow and Gamble
84	152	Suquamish and Colsee-ed Harbours
85	153	Scabock and Hooetzen Harbours, and Tzu-sa-ted Cove
86	154	Case's and Carr's Inlets
87	155	The Narrows & Commencement Bay
88	156	Ports Orchard & Madison
89	157	Ports Susan, and Gardner and Apple and Pilot's Coves
90	158	Deception Passage, Holmes' Harbour, and Penn's Cove
91	159	Birch Bay, Drayton's Bay, and Point Roberts Anchorage
92	160	Strawberry, and Argus Bays, Hornet's Harbour &c

In the Northwest, an interested reader may find paper copies of Wilkes' charts at the Museum of History and Industry as well as the Northwest Collection at the University of Washington. Copies of the NOAA charts are available electronically on the NOAA website. And electronic copies of the actual charts may be found on the Harvard University web site at: http://pds.lib.harvard.edu/pds/view/12012229?n=1&imagesize=1200&jp2Res=.125&printThumbnails=trueIn addition, many of the British charts may be found at Library Archives Canada at http://www.collectionscanada.gc.ca/index-e.html

Henry Kellett

Henry Kellett was born in 1806 in Clonabody, Tipperary, Ireland. He joined the British Navy in 1822. After spending five years in the West Indies, he served on survey vessels in Africa and later the East Indies. In 1845, he was appointed Captain of the H.M.S. *Herald* and commissioned to survey waters on the American West Coast. He was reassigned in 1848 to search for the missing Arctic explorer Sir John Franklin. He made three voyages through the Bering Strait and performed considerable hydrographic work there. Kellett was promoted to rear admiral in 1862 and had subsequent commands in the West Indies and China. He retired to Clonabody where he died in 1875.

Interestingly, Kellett did not provide a journal of his exploration in Washington and British Columbia. Although it was customary for the commander of an expedition to do so, he did not. The Admiralty reassigned Kellett to join other ships in the search for Sir John Franklin's Expedition, which was lost in the Artic. However, the story of Kellett's exploration in Washington waters was not entirely lost, as Berthold Seemann, a naturalist appointed to the *Herald*, undertook the task. His efforts were severely compromised. Not only did he not participate in the exploration, but journals from the various other officers and the commander were lacking. According to Seemann (ix), "That portion of Capt. Kellett's journal relating to the first volume is entirely wanting, and cannot, in the absence of its author, be procured." Seemann was forced to rely on the information provided by other officers, some of whom did not see fit to do so; others provided their information so incomplete as to make it useless. Regardless, it is the only source of information available to my knowledge of his inland Washington surveys, but the detail regarding time spent in the Northwest is deficient. Thus, in this text, the few quotes attributed to Kellett's exploration were really written by someone else who was not even aboard.

Robert A. Inskip

Robert Inskip was a naval instructor. He entered the British Navy in 1836 and was attached to the H.M.S. *Fisgard* on station in the Northwest from 1843-1847 where he set up a midshipman's school. Inskip conducted a number of surveys of Puget Sound and, without knowledge of Wilkes' activities, derived his own names. He returned to England, became a chaplain, and continued service as an instructor. In 1857 the Admiralty built the *Illustrious*, a two-decker cadet training vessel. Inskip was appointed the chief naval instructor. He held that position until he retired in 1871. He died in 1900.

George H. Richards

Admiral Sir George H. Richards was born in 1820 and entered the Royal Navy in 1833. He served aboard the *Rhadamanthus* for two years. Promoted to midshipman in 1835, he served for five years aboard *Sulphur* under Capt. Beechey and later under Capt. Edward Belcher to explore and survey in the Pacific, and then he transferred to the *Starling* to continue survey activities as Senior Executive Officer under Capt. Kellett. He returned to England in 1842 and was promoted to lieutenant. He served aboard *Philomel* surveying the Falkland Islands and the Southeast Coast of South America and was involved in the conflicts with Uruguay. As a result of his activities, he was promoted to commander in 1845. Richards departed in 1847 on the *Acheron* for survey duty in New Zealand. Returning home in 1851, he volunteered for duty in the Arctic for the search of Sir John Franklin. While on this duty, he traveled over ice more than 2,000 miles and spent seven months away from the ships on survey activities. Returning home in 1854, he was promoted to captain. In 1856, he was given charge of the *Plumper* to survey Vancouver Island and the British Columbia Coast. In addition, he was appointed the Queen's Commissioner with Capt. Prevost for settling the Washington boundary issues. He spent seven years surveying these waters. The *Plumper* was found to be small and defective. By 1859, the *Hecate* was sent from England as a replacement. In 1863, he left his surveying duties to Capt. Pender and returned to England where he was appointed Hydrographer of the Admiralty, a post which he held for ten years. He was appointed rear admiral in 1870 and retired from service in 1874. He was knighted in 1877 and promoted to admiral retired in 1884. For the balance of his life, Richards was a Managing Director of the Telegraph Construction and Maintenance Company which laid some 76,000 miles of submarine cable throughout the world. He eventually became chairman of the company where he served until his death in 1896.

George Davidson

Davidson was born in Nottingham England in 1825. He came to the U.S. in 1832 with his parents who settled in Philadelphia. A student in Central High School, in 1843 he studied under Alexander Dallas Bache, Benjamin Franklin's great grandson. Bache was appointed the Superintendent of Coast Survey and in 1845 selected Davidson as his clerk. Unhappy with a desk job in Washington D.C., by 1850 Davidson was on the West Coast establishing accurate latitude and longitude values for prominent points on the coast. Off and on for the next fifteen years, Davidson spent time charting inland Washington waters.

One of Davidson's accomplishments was the *Report: The Superintendent of the Coast Survey showing the progress of the Survey during the Year 1858*. This was reissued in 1862 as the *Directory for the Pacific Coast of the United States, report to the Superintendent of the U.S. Coast Survey*. In 1869, this evolved into the *Pacific Coast Pilot* which he reissued again in 1889. The 44th edition was issued in 2012! All can be found on the NOAA website. Throughout this text, I have included "landscapes" of our inland waters taken from the early editions of the *Pacific Coast Pilot*. These were replaced by actual pictures as time went on.

It is impossible to adequately summarize Davidson's accomplishments in two short paragraphs. A quote from the NOAA website probably says it all (http://www.history.noaa.gov/cgsbios/biod1.html): "Davidson combined the skills of hydrographer, geodesist, geographer, astronomer, seismologist, civil engineer, historian, and teacher for the good of the world scientific and engineering community, the citizens of the United States, and, in particular, the development of the West Coast states."

James S. Lawson

Born in Philadelphia in 1828, Lawson attended Central High School with Davidson and also studied under Alexander Dallas Bache. In 1848, he became clerk to Bache in the Coast Survey and was assigned duty on the Pacific Coast in 1850 under Davidson. For almost 46 years, Lawson worked tirelessly on triangulation and topographic surveys up and down the coast. He died in 1893 after a very short illness. Lawson left a wonderful accounting of the Coast Survey activities which can be accessed on the NOAA web site.

James Alden, Jr.

Born in 1810 in Portland, Maine, Alden was appointed midshipman in 1828. His early career consisted of desk jobs and one tour in the Mediterranean. In 1838, he was transferred to the Wilkes expedition and served to the end of the exploration in 1842. During 1841, he was involved in survey activities in inland Washington waters. Following the Wilkes expedition, Alden was assigned to various ships until detached from duty in 1849 when he was assigned to the Coast Survey. After limited East Coast surveys, he transferred to San Francisco, took command of the U.S.S. *Active,* and began West Coast hydrographic surveys until 1860. During the Civil War, Alden saw service commanding several ships and was promoted to captain in 1863 and then commodore in 1866. Promoted to rear admiral in 1871, Alden continued in active duty eventually commanding the U.S. European Fleet in 1873. He died in San Francisco in 1877.

Following Davidson, Lawson, and Alden, the next major survey activity in our waters occurred over a ten year period beginning about 1887. Much of this work was led by J. J. Gilbert who created a series of t-sheets and Descriptive Reports of the shoreline of the entire Puget Sound country. The t-sheets, or topographic sheets, concerned themselves with topography of the land only. In most cases, hydrography was ignored. The t-sheets not only gave us an extremely accurate survey of our shorelines, but they identified the towns and settlers present at that time. Even though shoreline hazards were identified, e.g., reefs and rocks, they were not meant for navigation. About 120 were created. The Descriptive Reports, about 40 of which were prepared, contained written observations of the terrain and shore side features. In addition, many pictures were taken and included in these reports. A web site recently made these t-sheets and Descriptive Reports available and may be found at http://riverhistory.ess.washington.edu/tsheets/framedex.htm

SURVEY ACTIVITIES

The actual job of surveying, the difficulties and the hardships faced by the men, require some explanation. The basic steps involve reconnaissance, triangulation, topography, and hydrography. Obviously, these steps were accomplished in greater detail and accuracy as time progressed and newer techniques and instruments were developed.

The first step, reconnaissance, involved a preliminary review of the area to be surveyed in order to select sites for use as primary triangulation stations and base lines. Stations selected needed to be accessible, meet the criteria of a strong triangulation network, and hopefully had direct line-of-sight to surrounding stations. Without all of these being present, the station was of limited value. Base line sites were selected based upon the distance between base lines, flatness of the terrain, amount of grading and clearing necessary, ease of connection with triangulation, and accessibility. Generally, triangulation sites selected were major points of land with a permanent prominent mark or locations where a signal could be erected. Once primary stations were selected, secondary and tertiary triangulation stations would also be identified as required.

When reconnaissance was complete, primary triangulation began. This included clearing lines of sights and potentially building scaffolds or tall signals to permit viewing over obstructions. All of this was accomplished while fighting off insects and dangerous animals, encountering miserable weather conditions including rain and fog which obstructed sights, dealing with hostile Native Americans, and suffering through disease, just to mention a few hardships. The intent was to develop a series of connected triangles which adjoin or overlap each other. All angles were carefully measured from the fixed stations.

Triangulation was followed by topography. This involved a thorough survey of land features including heights. The primary tool was a plane table or flat drawing board attached to a tripod. An alidade, a tool used for measuring horizontal and vertical angles, was used from various locations to determine positions and heights of various objects. Resultant measurements were plotted on the plane table, and ultimately a topographic map of the shoreline was developed.

Hydrography is the final step in preparing a chart. It produces a topography of the ocean floor. Surveys were normally undertaken in a long boat with up to six men rowing. The boat would also have a coxswain, a leadsman, one or more men taking angles using a sextant, and someone to record the data. One primary objective of the hydrographic survey was to located hazards to navigation.

PLACE NAMES

Active Cove

Active Cove [13a] #2689, 1859, Richards
Located on the west side of Patos Island, Richards named it for the U.S. survey ship *Active*, a wooden paddle steamer commanded by James Alden. She was built in New York in 1849 and named the *Gold Hunter*. Schooner rigged, she was sailed to San Francisco and hauled freight on the coast. The U.S. Government purchased her in 1853 from the Pacific Mail Steamship Company and converted her at Mare Island to a survey ship. In the 1860s, she returned to hauling freight, mail, and passengers along the coast. She sank off Mendocino in 1865 (Walbran 11).

Adelaide
It is located on the eastern shoreline of Puget Sound, about five miles north of Tacoma, perhaps a half mile north of Dumas Bay. When the post office opened in 1886, the area was named for Miss Adelaide Dixon, the postmaster's daughter (Meany, *Origin* 1).

Adelma
The small community is located along the eastern side of Discovery Bay. *See also* Adelma Beach. The hill above the water was referred to by settlers as Adelma Heights. The origin of this name is unknown. The name ultimately morphed into simply Adelma.

Adelma Beach
It is located on the eastern side of Discovery Bay. In 1850, three men jumped ship; the local Indians brought them ashore to Discovery Bay. John Tukey, James Keymes, and James Woodman homesteaded along the eastern side of the Bay, with Keymes in the middle, Tukey on the north, and Woodman on the south. Keymes and Tukey married Indian women. Later settlers referred to the Keymes property as Keymes Beach. It was reflected as Keymes Landing on [22]. Still later, the adjacent neighbors began calling their property "Adelma Beach" supposedly after a nearby hill, "Adelma Heights" (Information obtained by Mrs. Burns, Director of the Jefferson County Historical Society from Keymes' stepdaughter and Mrs. Bailey whose parents owned Adelma Beach, reported to the Washington State Board on Geographic Names in 1980). Mrs. Burns also reported that although Keymes Beach is more historically correct, the name Adelma has the predominant use. The Washington State Board on Geographic Names settled the name issue in favor of Adelma Beach in Docket 247 on September 12, 1980. The U.S. Board on Geographic Names followed later in the year noting the variant Keymes Beach (from Washington State Board Files).

Admiralty Bay [11] #654, 1858, U.S. Coast Survey
Located on the western side of Whidbey Island, it takes its name from the inlet.

Admiralty Head [10] #51, 1854, U.S. Coast Survey
Located on the western side of Whidbey Island, Wilkes originally named this Red Bluff [7a] in 1841 for the reddish color of the soil on the bluff. Wilkes did not include this name in his *Narrative*, but it is shown on his chart. According to Davidson, the name was changed because "It has now no marked color to suggest the appellation." Davidson continued: "Admiralty Head, abreast of the entrance

Admiralty Head - Agate Beach

Admiralty Head

to Port Townshend, is a perpendicular cliff 80 feet high, falling on the eastern side to a low, pebbly shore, which runs 2 miles to the E. NE. and strikes the high cliffs on the eastern side of the inlet," (Davidson, *Report* 440, 443). The current name is from Admiralty Inlet. The Salish name for the head was simply "head" (Hilbert et. al., 355).

Admiralty Inlet [6] 1792, Vancouver
After passing through the Strait of Juan de Fuca, Admiralty Inlet is the primary passage for entry to Seattle, Tacoma, and Olympia. In 1790, Quimper's pilot, Juan Carrasco, discovered and named it Ensenada de Caamaño. Quimper reflected it on his chart as Boca de Caamaño [1]. In 1791, Eliza stated, "Touching the description of the strait, I refer to that of Don Manuel Quimper as I found all the points he had explored to be as he said, except the Ensenada de Caamaño, which is a boca . . ." (Wagner 153). However, both Pantoja and Eliza reflected it on their charts [2] and [3] as the Ensenada de Caamaño. Vancouver named it in 1792 for the Board of Admiralty. On Vancouver's chart, the "A" in Admiralty Inlet is placed off Port Townsend. The "t" in Inlet is placed near Elliott Bay. Davidson wrote: "This inlet may be described as a vast canal, commencing at the southeast extremity of the Strait of Juan de Fuca and running in a general SE. by S. direction for 60 miles to the south end of Vashon's island. It has for that length an average width of 3½ miles, and then branches into a multitude of arms, which cover an area of about 14 by 22 miles. Their general direction is SE.¾ S., and they comprise what is called Puget's Sound," (*Report* 439). The U.S. Board on Geographic Names addressed the boundaries of the inlet in 1917 and severely restricted them over what Vancouver intended. The Board decided: "That part of Puget Sound from the Strait of Juan de Fuca to the lines: (1) From southernmost point of Double Bluff, Island County, to the northeast point of Foulweather Bluff, Kitsap County, Wash. (2) From northwest point of Foulweather Bluff to Tala Point, Jefferson County, Wash," (*Decisions*). The file on Admiralty Inlet from the U.S. Board includes some interesting comments: "As represented on chart No 6450 sent herewith, one would suppose that Admiralty Inlet and Puget Sound were independent bodies of water but generally the former is considered as part of the latter. An old edition of Rand McNally Atlas restricts the name Puget Sound to a small section of 12 miles south of Tacoma. The new edition (1914) agrees with our charts 6450 and 6400. Vancouver's map applies the name to a restricted area at the head waters near the present site of Olympia, and shows Admiralty Inlet as extending from the Strait of Juan de Fuca to and beyond where Seattle now stands." Armed with that information, one wonders about the evolution in the change of boundaries from what Vancouver intended (from U.S. Board files).

Adolphus Island [7a] #145, 1841, Wilkes
As shown on Wilkes' chart, it is located northeast of Waldron Island and to the east of Bare Island. However, it does not exist. Its appearance on the chart is attributed to a disgruntled crew member, William May, in 1841, as he surveyed the area. Wilkes did not include this name in his *Narrative* (Meany, *Origin* 2). Davidson noted: "On some recent maps two islands, called Adolphus and George, are laid down close to the Skipjacks, but in 1853 we examined the vicinity and satisfied ourselves that they did not then exist," (*Report* 428).

Agate Bay
Located immediately west of Crescent Bay on the Strait of Juan de Fuca, the name was likely descriptive.

Agate Beach
Located on the eastern corner of Outer Bay, southwestern side of Lopez Island, it was on the south side of the narrow neck of land between Barlow Bay and Outer Bay. It was likely named for agates on the beach; it was referenced in Mason (15).

Agate Passage [7d] #146, 1841, Wilkes; [7q] #156, 1841, Wilkes

Located off the eastern side of Bainbridge Island, Wilkes honored crew member Alfred T. Agate in 1841 (Meany, *Origin* 2). Davidson wrote: "At the SW. part of the bay [Port Madison] is the very narrow entrance to Port Orchard. The channel is somewhat crooked, but it has 3 and 4 fathoms water in it. On the western side of this entrance are some white patches of beach, formed by clam shells. In 1857, an Indian village was situated here, and an Indian sub-agency," (*Report* 445). In 1977, there was a proposal to change the name to Agate Pass in order to align it with other feature names, e.g., Agate Pass Bridge, Agate Pass Loop Road. Because the current name had such a lengthy history, the proposal was denied.

Agate Point

Agate Point

Located on the northern end of Bainbridge Island, and at the entrance to Agate Pass, the point was named for Agate Passage. In the 1860s, William DeShaw settled on the point and built a trading post and a dock. He traded merchandise with the Indians for fish and logs. He married Princess Mary Telase, granddaughter of Chief Seattle and second daughter of Princess Angeline (Bowen et al., VI: 99). Shaw was very friendly with the Indians who lived across the water at the Port Madison Reservation. Unfortunately, when he replaced Capt. Meigs, owner of the Port Madison Mill as the sub-agent for the U.S. Government administering the reservation, one of his first tasks, as ordered by the Governor of Washington Territory, was to tear down Old Man House. Disheartened, DeShaw proceeded in 1870 with the destruction and funded the first home for the Indians in Suquamish out of his own pocket (Warner 59, 60; Carlson 27, 28). He died in 1900. The Salish name for the point was "a squeaking sound" (Hilbert et. al., 225).

Aguayo, Islas de [3] 1791, Eliza
See Clark Island.

Ala Spit [7e] #158, 1841, Wilkes
See Ben Ure Spit.

Alden Bank [11] #654, 1858, U.S. Coast Survey

Located northeast of Sucia Island, it was named for James Alden. The name also shows on the 1859 Admiralty chart [13a]. *Report* (485) lists it as Shoal. *Directory* (132) called it Alden's shoal and indicated that it was discovered by the U.S. Coast Survey in 1853; [11] lists it as Aldens Bank.

Alden Point [13a] #2689, 1859, Richards
Located on the west end of Patos Island, it was named by Richards for James Alden (Meany, *Origin* 3).

Alderbrook

Located east of The Great Bend on Hood Canal, the resort hotel, golf course, and small stream were all named for the red alder trees growing nearby (TPL website).

Aleck Bay

It is located at the southern end of Lopez Island west of Watmough Head. According to the GNIS files for Aleck Rocks, the name Aleck was reported by McLellan and Meany, apparently after an early settler. McLellan wrote: "The average depth of water in McArdle Bay and Hughes Bay is about 30 feet. Aleck Bay is somewhat larger and deeper, being more than half a mile long and averaging about 60 feet in depth. Aleck Bay trends northwesterly and approximately follows the strike of the rock formations." Lange indicated that the bay first appeared on chart #6380 originally published January 1912, corrected to July 7, 1919.

Aleck Rocks
It is located off Aleck Bay. The U.S. Board on Geographic Names approved the name in 1925 over the variant The Rock (Mason 21; *Decisions*). According to the GNIS files, the name was reported by McLellan and Meany, apparently after an early settler. McLellan noted: "The larger of the two islands is sometimes known as Fish-trap Island." The U.S. Government owns the rocks.

Alger Bay [22] #6450, 1909
See Elger Bay.

Alegria Island
It is located on the southwestern side of West Sound, south of Double Island. The name was proposed by Gretchen and Wallace Gudgell who purchased and lived on the island from 1973 to 1992. *Alegria* means "joy or contentment in Spanish." Gretchen is the granddaughter of industrialist Henry J. Kaiser of shipbuilding, hospital, aluminum, steel, and automobile manufacturing fame. The Washington State Board on Geographic Names approved the name in September 1978. Apparently, this information was not submitted to the U.S. Board on Geographic Names until later, as two years elapsed before it was approved. Variants were Double Island, Dudley Island, Little Double Island, and Little Island (from the Washington State Board, GNIS files). Mike Brown, a retired Microsoft employee, owns the island. According to an email from Gretchen, Brown donated the island to the Nature Conservancy. *See also* Double Island.

Alice Bay
See Samish Island.

Alice Bight
Located on the eastern side of Burrows Island, the origin of the name is unknown.

Alki Point [10] #51, 1854, U.S. Coast Survey
Located at the western end of West Seattle, Wilkes named this Point Roberts in 1841 [7a], [7d], [7m], perhaps honoring one of the crew members named Roberts: Abraham, Humphrey, Owen, or William. The Denny party called the point New York as the Terrys originated from there. Later, they added an Indian name and it became New York-*Alki*. As Emily Denny explained: "*Alki* is an Indian word pronounced

Alki Point

with the accent on the first syllable, which is *al* as in altitude; *ki* is spoken as *ky* in silky. Alki means 'by and by.'" Eventually New York was dropped entirely (Meany, *Origin* 4; Denny 41). According to Shaw (2), *Alki* holds some additional meanings including: after a while, soon, presently, directly, and in a little while. Thus, the combination of New York-*Alki* presumably meant that they felt the settlement would sometime grow to the size of New York or become as important as New York. The U.S. Coast Survey renamed it Battery Point in 1856 (Davidson, *Report* 446). The point supposedly was the landing spot of the first settlers in Seattle. David T. Denny and John N. Low arrived on September 25, 1851, accompanied by Olympia resident, Lee Terry. While Denny built a cabin, Low returned to Portland for the families. In 1849, John Holgate explored the Duwamish area. He selected land on the river but was unaware of the legal requirement to physically file a claim. He left to retrieve his family located in Trenton, Ohio. Upon returning in 1851, he discovered Luther Collins on the land. Collins arrived in June 1851 and had filed the correct paperwork for the 640 acre parcel. There is some speculation that his party didn't actually arrive until September. Holgate selected another landsite, south of Doc Maynard's property on Beacon Hill. Collins was accompanied by his friends, Henry Van Asselt, Jacob Maple, and Jacob's son Samuel, who all filed on September 14, 1851, almost two weeks before Denny, Terry, and Low arrived at Alki. Jacob and Samuel's Duwamish land would eventually become Georgetown and Boeing Field (Denny 41-

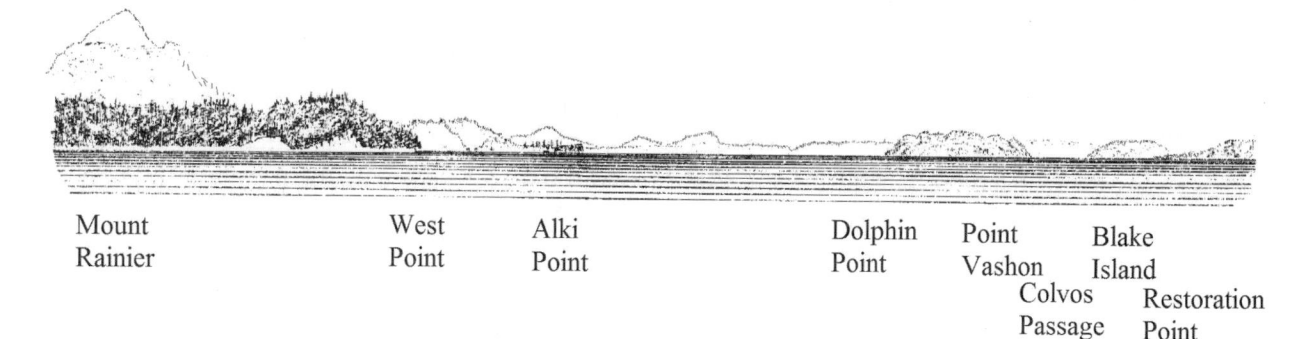

Mount Rainier   West Point   Alki Point   Dolphin Point   Point Vashon   Blake Island   Colvos Passage   Restoration Point

47; *Seattle Times*, September 28, 2001; *The Duwamish Diary, 1849-1949* 5-10). Van Asselt's land along the current Airport Way became the community of Van Asselt. The U.S. Board on Geographic Names chose the current name over Point Roberts in 1895.

Allan Island [7a] #145, 1841, Wilkes; [7m] #160, 1841, Wilkes

This island is located off the southern side of Burrows Island. In 1841, Wilkes honored Capt. William Henry Allen who died during the 1812 battle between the *Argus* and *Pelican* (Meany, *Origin* 4, 5). Microsoft billionaire Paul Allen purchased Allan Island in 1992 for $7.4 million. After purchasing the Sperry Peninsula on Lopez Island, Allan Island was put on the market in 2006 for $25 million. As of 2012, the property remained unsold despite a price reduction to $13.5 million.

Allan Pass

Located between Allan and Fidalgo Islands, the name likely came from Allan Island.

Allen, Point [7a] #145 1841, Wilkes
See Camano Head.

Allen Bank [19] #662, 1867, U.S. Coast Survey

Located off the northern end of Vashon Island, the U.S. Coast Survey named it in 1857. Davidson did not disclose for whom it was named (Davidson, *Report* 448).

Allen Point

Located on the eastern shoreline of Carr Inlet, Wilkes originally named it Kaskuse Point [7h] in 1841. He left no reason for the name. Wilkes did not include this name in his *Narrative*, but it is shown on his chart. The point received its current name for Fannie A. Allen, as listed on the 1915 Kroll Atlas of Pierce County (Reese, *Origins* 14).

Allshouse's Islet [7d] #146, 1841, Wilkes; [7h] #154, 1841, Wilkes
See Raft Island.

Allyn

Located at the head of Case Inlet, it was platted in 1889 and named for Judge Frank Allyn from Tacoma who actively promoted the area (TPL website).

Amah Point [7h] #154, 1841, Wilkes

From Wilkes' chart, this appears to be the northern entrance to Mayo Cove on the western side of Carr Inlet. Wilkes left no reason for the name; it appears only on his chart. The name is neither reflected on current charts nor recognized by the U.S. Board on Geographic Names.

American Camp

American Camp was located on the site of the original Hudson's Bay Company farm at the south end of San Juan Island, and it was there as a result of the boundary dispute. To summarize briefly, the governments of Great Britain and the U.S. agreed in 1818 upon a midwestern boundary between Canada and the U.S. It ran from the Lake of the Woods (in Northern Minnesota) to the summit of the Rockies along the 49th parallel. However, they failed to address the western boundary. In 1824, the British proposed to extend the boundary along the 49th parallel to the Columbia River where it would then follow the river to the Pacific Ocean. The Americans rejected this proposal. The two governments argued for the next twenty years. In 1846, they agreed to extend the border between the United States and Canada at the 49th parallel. The treaty further defined the far western border with such lack of clarity that no one could determine where the boundary was. The English argued for Rosario Strait; the Americans argued for Haro Strait. Further discussions ensued, until Lyman Cutler killed a pig owned by Charles Griffin who was running Bellevue Farm for the Hudson's Bay Company, and the arguments escalated. For a number of reasons, the Americans ultimately landed army personnel at American Camp. They were led by Capt. George E. Pickett ostensibly to protect the American settlers, although Pickett had more difficulties dealing with ornery Americans selling whiskey to the Indians than he ever did with the British. Regardless, there were some tense situations and the Americans built an earthen redoubt (French for fortification and known locally as Robert's Gopher Hole) as a gun emplacement for protection. These activities were supervised by an engineer, Lieutenant Henry M. Robert. Robert graduated fourth in his 1857 West Point class and arrived on San Juan Island in 1859. He spent his career in the civil engineering ranks and was promoted to Chief of Engineers in 1901 with the rank of Brigadier General. He retired later that year. Robert was most famous for his parliamentary book *Robert's Rules of Order*, first published in 1876 (McDonald 30-32; Richardson, *Pig* 75). In 1862, Robert Firth replaced Charles Griffin. Firth was born in 1830 in the Orkney Islands, an archipelago north of Scotland. He began working for the Hudson's Bay Company and arrived in Victoria in 1851. In 1857, he returned home to marry Jessie Grant. The couple found themselves next on San Juan Island in charge of Bellevue Farm. Ultimately, the U.S. and England agreed to arbitrate the boundary issue. The Americans won, and the military from both sides vacated the island leaving two wonderful parks. Firth became an American citizen and homesteaded a portion of the farm raising wheat, oats, potatoes, and sheep. They raised eight children. Jessie died on San Juan Island in 1889. Robert died in 1903 (McDonald, Lucile. "San Juan Island Diary of the '60's." *Seattle Times*. Nov. 6, 1960. Magazine Section p 4). His name is spelled Furth on t-sheet #2300 from the Washington State University digital collection, (http://kaga.wsulibs.wsu.edu/cdm-maps/sanjuantsheet.html) The homestead was near the water about halfway between Deadmans Bay and Pile Point. Interestingly, the name American Camp was not recognized by the U.S. Board on Geographic Names until I raised the issue in early 2012. American Campsite was in the database with American Camp as a variant. According to park literature, the campsite is within American Camp. The change will now list American Camp as the primary name and American Campsite as a variant. Additionally, as old topos used both names, American Campsite will also be listed in the database with no variant. In his 1897 survey and Descriptive Report #2301, (http://riverhistory.ess.washington.edu/tsheets/reports/t2301.pdf, p 7, 8), J. J. Gilbert wrote: "The old fort was on the crest of the hill 210 feet above the level of the sea. The outline of the old earth works is still well marked. Two of the buildings used as officers quarters remain, and also some of the old barracks. These old barrack buildings were originally put up by the Hudson Bay Co. which had a post located here. They are peculiar in that they were built without nails, the siding being dovetailed into the studding."

Amsterdam Bay
It is located on the western side of Anderson Island. The Netherlands-American Manufacturing Company owned land there in 1924 (Reese, *Origins* 15).

Anaco Beach
Located east of Flounder Bay on Fidalgo Island, the origin of the name is unknown.

Anacortes [21] #6300, 1895
It is located on the northeastern end of Fidalgo Island. Amos Bowman, born in Ontario in 1840, attended universities in Ohio and New York, and he graduated with a degree in mining and civil engineering from the College of Mines at Freiberg, Germany. After traveling in Europe, he made his way to California in 1868 where he was placed in charge of the state geological survey. Impressed with the land in Skagit County from previous visits, he purchased land in Anacortes in 1876 or 1877 and moved his family from California. He named the town after his wife, Anna Curtis but altered the spelling to give it a Spanish flair. Bowman died in his home in 1894 (Meany, *Origin* 7; *An Illustrated History*, 611, 612). The first settlers in the area were likely Richard and Shadrack Wooten who arrived in 1865 and settled on Fidalgo Bay (http://www.liveanacortes.com/AboutAnacortes/History/tabid/868/default.aspx).

Anderson Cove

Located on the eastern side of Hood Canal, eight miles south of Seabeck Bay, the area was first settled by William Anderson with his Indian wife Mary. Their homestead included the land from Anderson Cove to the community of Holly. The Andersons supported themselves by farming and fishing. Anderson, from Holland, came to Port Gamble and could not speak English. Learning both English and the Chinook jargon at the same time, his new tongue became a combination of the two. In the early 1880s, the Indian Department insisted that unless married to a White man, all Indian women must return to the reservation. Upon hearing this, Anderson decided to formally wed Mary. He headed to Seabeck for a marriage license unaware that they could only be obtained at Port Madison, the county seat. Harry Schafer was tending bar the day Anderson arrived. Listening to his plans, Schafer decided to play a joke on Anderson and retrieved a road tax receipt from a dusty cigar box, wrapped it in tinfoil, and presented it to Anderson as his license. Full of joy, Anderson headed back to Holly. He and Mary then set out for the Skokomish Reservation where the preacher, Myron Eells, would marry them. At the alter, Anderson handed over the "license." Eells read the road tax receipt and had the unfortunate task of explaining the joke. Mary, furious, turned him away, saying she didn't want to see him again. Anderson left with a heavy heart, but about three weeks later, in December 1883, he returned to the reservation with the proper license, and they were wed (Clayson 101-104).

Anderson Cove

It is located on the southern side of Port Washington Narrows. John P. Anderson, about 14 years old, jumped ship at Port Blakely about 1879. John worked around the Bremerton area, homesteaded a quarter section, and cut timber on Dyes Inlet. Bremerton High School was built on his homestead. He later sent to Sweden for his sister Anna, who settled in Seattle. The 16-year-old Ellen Noren arrived in Seattle from Sweden in 1888 and was employed as a domestic for a wealthy family. John and Ellen met through John's sister and were later married. John then sold the homestead and purchased 40 acres from the Kimball family, in the area which later was known as Anderson's Cove. John and Ellen's eight children were born at the cove (Perry, *Year* 61, 67).

Anderson Island [7d] #146, 1841, Wilkes; [7i] #147, 1841, Wilkes

Located at the southeastern end of Puget Sound, near Nisqually, Wilkes honored Alexander Caulfield Anderson, Chief Trader of the Hudson's Bay Company in 1841. Anderson was born in Calcutta in 1814 and died near Victoria in 1884. At Nisqually, Wilkes wrote (*Narrative* 304): "Soon after we anchored, I had the pleasure of a visit from Mr. Anderson, who is in charge of the fort, and Capt. M'Niel. They gave me a warm welcome, and offered every assistance in their power to aid me in my operations." Wilkes honored both gentlemen with local place names. In 1846, Inskip named this Fisgard Island [24] for the H.M.S. *Fisgard* stationed at Nisqually from 1844-1847 (Meany, *Origin* 7, 8). After Fort Nisqually closed, Anderson moved back north and held many important positions with the Hudson's Bay Company as well as the colonial government of Vancouver Island. His son, James Robert Anderson (1841-1930), was born at Nisqually. Schooled in Victoria, he lived there permanently from 1858 until his death. He was very involved in BC politics. Christian Christensen from Denmark was the first settler on Anderson Island, arriving in the early 1870s. He settled on Amsterdam Bay, cleared the land, built a cabin, and sold cordwood to passing steamers. Christian's cousin, Helda, arrived from Denmark in February 1872 and the couple soon married. Christian died about 1887. Helda with her seven children married another islander, August Lindstrom. Unfortunately, Lindstrom later committed suicide. Helda died on the island in 1933. John and Ann Ekenstam and their seven children were the second family to arrive, in February 1879. They settled on the south shore (Heckman; Cammon 216, 217).

Anderson Point

Located north of Olalla on the western side of Colvos Passage, the origin of the name is unknown.

Andrews Bay [13h] #2689, 1888
Located north of Bellevue Point on the western side of San Juan Island, Wood (83) speculated it was named for a local family. Unfortunately, the family cannot be identified with certainty. The township plats of San Juan County, c. 1875 did not reflect anyone by that name as owning land there, although an island old-timer remembered a family named Andres who lived there. Another possibility was B. S. Andrews who was part of the citizen's group to get American soldiers stationed on the island. Still another was a 33-year-old farmer from Tennessee, William Andrews, who lived near the bay. Andrews sold liquor to the Indians and the soldiers at English Camp. He was brought before an American Justice of the Peace for his activities but acquitted. Capt. George Bazalgette, the Commander of English Camp, entered a second complaint which resulted in Andrews' banishment from the island in 1862. The name is shown on the 1894 t-sheet #2194 at http://kaga.wsulibs.wsu.edu/cdm-maps/sanjuantsheet.html but a property owner is not identified.

Andrews Island
See Low Island.

Angeles, Port [2] 1791, Pantoja; [3] 1791, Eliza
Located on the Strait of Juan de Fuca, Eliza named it *Puerto de Nuestra Señora de Los Angeles* in 1791 (Wagner 153). Historians disagree on the first settler in Port Angeles. It was either Angus Johnson with his 1857 claim or Alexander Sampson, a sailing captain, whose claim dated to 1856. Sampson, born in Duxbury, Massachusetts in 1802, worked and traded along the inland waters for some time and observed the natural spit at Port Angeles. He purchased lumber from a local mill, selected a donation claim on 320 acres of land, and built a home at the base of the spit. Along with farming at Port Angeles, Sampson served as the lighthouse keeper at Tatoosh Island at Cape Flattery from 1868 to 1893. Sampson died February 2, 1893, in Port Angeles. Victor Smith was appointed as the Collector of Customs in Port Townsend. He arrived in July 1861. Because of his eccentric nature, he soon antagonized the locals. With a strong belief that the British intended to join with the Confederacy and attack the U.S. on the Northwest Coast, he recommended moving the Customs House to Port Angeles and fortifying that location. He felt its proximity to Esquimalt and the port of Victoria would permit settlers to keep a close eye on British affairs there. As a result of his views, President Lincoln signed an order to move the Customs House in 1862. The order also created the "Second National City" after Washington D.C. Smith built the new Customs House near Valley Creek in Port Angeles. In December 1863, the Smiths lost everything. A massive mudslide in the Olympics formed a dam on the creek creating a huge reservoir of water behind it. As the rain continued to fall, the dam burst. A wall of water several feet high washed through the town and floated the Customs House into the Strait of Juan de Fuca. Smith was removed in 1864, but it required another couple of years to relocate the Customs House back to Port Townsend (Fish, *Tracks* 89; McCurdy, *By Juan* 56, 58).

Angeles Point [7c] #144, 1841, Wilkes
Located east of Port Angeles on the Strait of Juan de Fuca, it was first named Davila by Quimper in 1790. It does not appear on his chart but does appear on Eliza's in 1791 [3]. Quimper named it after Juan Herrera Davila, a captain in the Spanish Navy (Blumenthal, *The Early Exploration* 24). Wilkes renamed it in 1841 for the nearby Port Angeles and wrote: "There is a small harbor within Point Angeles, but its mouth is barred by a sand spit, which does not permit any but a vessel of small draft of water to pass in," (Wilkes, *Narrative* 305). On his charts, he spelled it Angelos. Kellett reflected it as P. Angelos on his 1847 chart [8a].

Annapolis
It is located on the southeastern shore of Port Orchard, opposite Bremerton. John Mitchell arrived in Port Orchard in 1865 and settled on 151 acres. A portion of this land became Annapolis, and another portion became Retsil, just northeast of the community of Port Orchard. Near his homestead, he met George Diggs who was living with Elizabeth, the Indian mother of their three children. Within two years, Elizabeth moved in with Mitchell. They later had three children of their own. Mitchell logged and worked at the Port Orchard Mill at Enetai. He filed the plat in 1890 and

named the community for Annapolis Maryland (TPL website). Mitchell died in 1896; Elizabeth continued to live on the land, and in 1920 her daughter Elizabeth joined her. The daughter lived in the cabin until shortly before her death in 1960 (Perry, *Year* 82-86). Mitchell Point was named for him.

Annas Bay [7d] #146, 1841, Wilkes
Located at the Great Bend in Hood Canal, Wilkes left no reason for the name (Meany, *Origin* 8). Homer Morrison speculated that Anna was Anna Rogers who married Lieut. Augustus L. Case following the expedition. Case led the survey work in Hood Canal.

Apostolos, Mount
See Mount Valerianos.

Apple Cove Point
Located on the western side of Admiralty Inlet a mile north of Kingston, it was likely named for Appletree Cove, with the tree omitted. The Salish name for the point was "a whisper" (Hilbert et. al., 190).

Appletree Cove [7d] #146, 1841, Wilkes; [7o] #157, 1841, Wilkes
Located on the western shore of Admiralty Inlet about seven miles south of Point No Point, Wilkes named this in 1841 ". . . from the numbers of that tree which were in blossom around its shores. This cove answers well all the purposes of a temporary anchorage," (Wilkes, *Narrative* 303, 304). On his chart, he called it Apple Cove. There is some controversy about the name since Wilkes may have observed dogwood, not apple trees (Meany, *Origin* 8). However, an early settler, Benjamin Bannister, recalls cutting down the crab apples around the cove. In 1874, Bannister homesteaded 200 acres there. Born in 1849 and employed as a machinist, he shipped out of England aboard the *Niagra* at age twenty-two. After 135 days at sea, he landed in San Francisco in February 1873 where he jumped ship, deciding that life aboard a sailing vessel was not in his best interest. He headed for Puget Sound, arriving at Port Madison later that year. There were numerous Indian tribes in the area, and Bannister counted Jim Sealth, son of the Chief, and Chief Jacobs of the Suquamish Tribe as close friends. He married and raised seven children. Initially, Bannister made his living selling shakes and shingles to Seattle builders but later turned to farming. Benjamin Bannister's daughter, Mrs. Josephine Bannister Stevenson, continued to live in the area for many years. She died in 1989 at the age of ninety-two (Bowen et al., II: 110, 111).

Aquarium
Located on the northeastern side of Vashon Island, it was originally named Vermontville by settlers from Vermont (Hitchman, 319). Henry P. Fish, first postmaster, chose to name the community Aquarium in 1892, perhaps for its connection to the water. He sold, and the community was renamed Glen Acres in 1914, although Aquarium endured (Vashon Island Beginnings, http://www.historylink.org/).

Arbutus Point [13a] #2689, 1859, Richards
See Madrona Point

Arcadia [23] #6460, 1905
The community is located at the southern entrance to Hammersley Inlet. Wilkes recorded the name Cook Point on his chart [7d], honoring crew member John Cook in 1841 (Meany, *Origin* 56). Wilkes did not include this name in his *Narrative*, but it is shown on his chart. Arcadia Point is unnamed on current charts, but it is a recognized name by the U.S. Board on Geographic Names. Locals named it for a region in Greece (Hitchman 8). After the area was well logged, the community grew out of the resultant stump farm and was platted in 1859. James Pickett, the son of George Pickett and his wife Morning Mist, a Haida princess, was an early resident. George Picket was of San Juan Island Pig War fame, as well as his charge on Gettysburg. In later life, James worked for the *Portland Oregonian* but died of typhoid at age thirty in Portland (Fredson, *Oakland to Shelton* 30; Thomas 3). The Salish name for the area was "rainy place" (Hilbert et. al., 281).

Argus Bay [7a] #145, 1841, Wilkes; [7m] #160, 1841, Wilkes
See Burrows Bay.

Argyle [13k] #2689, 1900
It is located at the northern end of Griffin Bay, on the eastern side of San Juan Island. According to one story, a Scot named McDonald named it after his

home county. Hitchman wrote (8) that it was named after Argyll Scotland. Meany (*Origin* 9) suggested that it was perhaps for its namesake in either Wisconsin or Nova Scotia. Or perhaps it took its name from the Argyle Milling Company founded in 1886. Clarence M. Tucker came to San Juan Island to build and operate the mill in 1866. It was a large structure, modern for its time and powered by steam. It was also set up so that mechanically it could be adjusted to crush or grind any product. In later years, it operated sporadically until 1909 when it shut down entirely. Tucker went on to serve as county treasurer and went to work for the San Juan County Bank where he rose to its vice-presidency. In 1921, Thomas Davis, a rancher, purchased the mill and disassembled it for the lumber (Garrett, Anita. "Grist Mill Symbolized Argyle's Ambitions." *Seattle Times*. Dec. 3, 1961 p 8).

Argyle Island
See Little Island.

Argyle Lagoon & Creek
Located off the community of Argyle on the eastern side of San Juan Island, it was originally named Jones Lagoon for Fred Jones, an early homesteader (Lange). The entrance to the lagoon is locally known as Argyle Creek.

Argyle Shoal
Located on the eastern side of San Juan Island, ¾ mile due east (true) from Dinner Island, it is unnamed on current charts. It was first referenced in the 1903 *Pacific Coast Pilot* (153): "Argyle Shoal with 10 feet over it and marked by kelp, lies about ¾ mile ENE from the eastern point of Dinner Island; a buoy (spar, red and black horizontal stripes) is placed in 18 feet close to and westward of the shoal." Use of the name continued in various editions of the *Pacific Coast Pilot* through 1963, but it was mysteriously removed in the 1968 edition. It is not clear if this name even rose to the point of being a local name. The U.S. Board on Geographic Names did not acknowledge the name until I reviewed the history with them. In mid-2011, the Board formally recognized it. Observing modern charts, there is no buoy nearby and the end of the shoal is marked "Rk 0⁵" meaning at low tide, there is five feet of water covering the rock. Wood (84, 166) asserts that the rock was named New Shoal and initially appeared on the first edition (1865) of Admiralty chart #611. It was apparently named New Reef on the 1914 edition of the U.S. Navy Department Hydrographic chart #1769. The name was changed to Argyle Shoal by the Admiralty and appeared on the 1938 edition of their chart #2840.

Ariel Point [7a] #145, 1841, Wilkes; [7d] #146, 1841, Wilkes; [7p] #150, 1841, Wilkes
See Nodule Point.

Ariels Point [7d] #146, 1841, Wilkes
See Double Bluff.

Arletta
Located on the Great Peninsula on the northern side of Hale Passage, settlement began about 1880. Locals built a school in 1886 and a post office in 1893 with Mrs. George Powell as postmistress. One theory on the name was that Mrs. Powell combined the names of her daughter, Arla, with her friend Lucetta Castle (*History* I: 58). According to Meany (*Origin* 9), it was a combination of her daughter and Valetta, a city on the Island of Malta. A third source attributes the name to Mrs. Powell's two daughters, Arla and Letta or Letty (Phillips 8).

Armitage Island
It is located near the eastern entrance to Thatcher Pass. The name was reported by McLellan and Meany. According to the GNIS files, McLellan apparently found reference to the name on an 1875 "Soil Survey Map." It may have been for an early settler. The U.S. Board on Geographic Names approved the name in 1925.

Aroo, Canal de
See Haro Strait.

Arro, Canal de [7c] #144, 1841, Wilkes
See Haro Strait.

Arrow Point
Located at the entrance to the community of Manzanita on the western side of Bainbridge Island, Albert Lord platted the community and named it for arrow heads found there. An artist, landscape architect, and engineer, Lord subdivided the point in 1906 into 33 small waterfront lots which surrounded a community park (Battle Point park) (Bowen et al., VI: 99).

Arrowhead Beach
It is located on either side of Brown Point, east of Utsalady. The name likely came from the presence of arrowheads in the sand.

Arthur, Port
Located on the eastern side of Whidbey Island, on the southwestern side of Penn Cove, it was named for Arthur Phinney by his brother John, who platted the land in 1895 (Hitchman, 237). The name is not reflected on current charts.

Atlanta
Located near William Point on Samish Island, it was platted and named by a Confederate veteran, George Washington Lafayette Allen, on June 12, 1883 (Meany, *Origin* 10). He intended it as a refuge for persecuted Confederates. *See also* Samish Island.

Austin
Located on the southwestern side of Whidbey Island in Mutiny Bay, Thomas Harvey Marshall settled there, built a store, and opened a post office in 1902. He named it for his son, Austin Marshall (Cherry I: 118).

Avalon Island
See O'Neal Island.

Ayock Point [7d] #146, 1841, Wilkes
Located on the western side of Hood Canal, Wilkes spelled this Ayoch's Point in his 1841 *Narrative* (322) but Ayocks Point on the chart. He left no reason for the name (Meany, *Origin* 11). The U.S. Board on Geographic Names approved the name in 1941 over the variant, Aycock Point (*Decisions*).

Ayres Point [7d] #146, 1841, Wilkes
Located at the southeastern side of Hood Canal, Wilkes honored crew member John Ayres in 1841. Wilkes did not include this name in his *Narrative*, but it is shown on his chart (Meany, *Origin* 11). In 1985, residents in the area proposed changing the name to Bald Point, a local name, the result of a forest fire perhaps in the 1920s that denuded the entire hillside. Because of objections from the Mason County Historical Society, and their recognition of the historic name from the U.S. Exploring Expedition, the Washington State Board on Geographic Names denied the request. The U.S. Board followed in 1986 (from Washington State Board Files).

Baada Point [20f] #654, 1853, U.S. Coast Survey
Located at the eastern entrance to Neah Bay, Wilkes originally named this Village Point [7c] in 1841 (Meany, *Origin* 11). Wilkes did not include this name in his *Narrative*, but it is shown on his chart. In his 1847 chart [8a], Kellett simply reflected "Village" for the point. On his 1849 chart [9a], he showed it as "Classet Village." The U.S. Coast Survey later referenced the name Ba-ad-dah [20f] as did Davidson (Davidson, *Report* 416). During the 1850s, Davidson noted that the large village of "Mukkaws" was within a mile of Koitlah Point. Wilkes pegged it very close to Baada Point. The U.S. Board on Geographic Names changed the spelling from Baadah to Baada in 1934 as it was ". . . the best and simplest spelling for this name." Another variant was Baaddah. Differences in spelling were attributed to an inability to spell the guttural Makah language (GNIS files).

Baby Island

Baby Island
Located off the eastern side of Whidbey Island, near the eastern entrance to Holmes Harbor, some charts

Baby Island - Baker, Mount

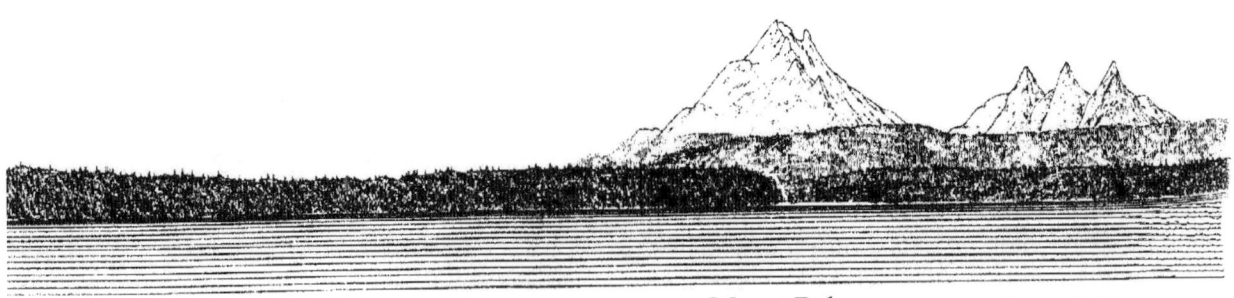

Mount Baker   Cascade Range
Sandy Point   Lummi Bay

show this as Hackney Island [21]. In 1975, Robert P. Campbell of the Automobile Club of Washington submitted a proposal to the Washington State Board on Geographic Names to change the name from Hackney Island to Baby Island to conform with local usage. In its review, the Board heard from Ivan Little, a Langley resident. Mr. Little wrote: "Received your inquiry about Baby Island and have since talked to other people about it, and none of them know who Hackney was. It has been Baby Island ever since I came here in 1906. Probably acquired the name of Baby Island from common usage. No one knows how come it was named Hackney on the maps. He might have been one of Capt. Vancouver's men. There was some buildings on it, in a very run-down condition, when I first remember it. Indians dug clams and dried them there." The Board approved the name change on December 10, 1976, as part of Docket 213. The U.S. Board followed in 1977 (from Washington State Board Files). Early Tulalip Indians and later Whites used the area as a picnic spot. After World War I, Darrell Scott purchased it. Scott, a veteran, actually camped on the island as early as 1910. He built a fishing lodge with cabins for sportsmen and operated it until 1937. Future owners attempted to control erosion by erecting bulkheads but none succeeded (Cherry II: 212). At low tide it is connected to Rocky Point. Even as late as 1959, a couple of houses and a water tower remained on the island. Today, some foundations are all that is left. In 1993, the Tulalip Indian Tribe purchased the island for $127,400 (http://oldcamano.net/babyisland.html). The Salish name for the island was "wrinkled" (Hilbert et. al., 359).

Baileys Bay
See Cultus Bay.

Bainbridge Island [7d] #146, 1841, Wilkes
Located on the western side of Admiralty Inlet, this island was named by Wilkes in 1841 for Capt. William Bainbridge who commanded the *Constitution* in the battle with *Java* during the War of 1812 (Meany, *Origin* 12). Davidson wrote: "Bainbridge island lies between Port Orchard, Port Madison, and Admiralty Inlet. It is 8 or 9 miles long by 2½ in breadth, and its general direction is SE. by S. A few loggers' huts stand on the western side and the Madison saw-mill at the north end. On the SE., part of it is indented by two small harbors," (*Report* 445).

Bainbridge Reef [23] #6460, 1905
Located in the western entrance of Rich Passage on the southern end of Bainbridge Island, it likely took its name from the island.

Baird Cove
Located a mile southeast of Johnson Point and about four miles northwest of Nisqually Head, it was purchased in 1905 by Edmund Baird, a friend of Claude Poncin who owned an estate nearby. During the 1920s, Baird managed the Yesler Estate and was Secretary Treasurer of the Poncin Corporation (Palmer, 2; TPL website).

Baker, Mount [6] 1792, Vancouver
Located east of Bellingham in the Cascade Range, Vancouver named it for crew member Joseph Baker who first observed it (Vancouver 222). Baker wrote: "We lay in sight of two remarkable high Snowy Mountains, the North^{mt} of which bore N 3 E & was named Mount Baker, I having been the first person who saw it, the day after we enter'd the straits," (Blumenthal, *With Vancouver* 148).

In 1790, Quimper named it *Gran Montaña de Carmelo* [1] (Blumenthal, *The Early Exploration* 24). Davidson wrote: ". . . and in the back ground the snow-covered, double summit of Mount Baker, 10,900 feet in height, with the mouth of the crater distinctly visible behind the peaks, and at times emitting vast volumes of smoke. The elevation of the line of perpetual snow upon this mountain is 3,145 feet," (Davidson, *Directory* 139).

Balch Cove
See Glen Cove.

Balch Passage
Located between Anderson and McNeil Islands, the current name is for Capt. Lafayette Balch (1825-1862) who established a store and founded the town of Steilacoom in 1850. Balch, from Maine, shipped lumber from the Northwest to San Francisco on the brig *George Emery* and returned with supplies for his store (Meany, *Origin* 13). Inskip named this Ryder Channel [24]. *See also* Steilacoom.

Bald Bluff [13c] #2689, 1865, Richards
Located on the western side of Blakely Island, it was listed on the 1854 U.S. Coast Survey chart simply as Peak [10].

Bald Bluff
See Windy Bluff.

Bald Hill [13m] #2689, 1904
Located near Argyle on the eastern side of San Juan Island, south of Friday Harbor, it was likely named for its appearance. The name is neither reflected on U.S. charts nor is it recognized by the U.S. Board on Geographic Names. It is shown on [13m] as well as t-sheet #2301 from 1897 on http://kaga.wsulibs.wsu.edu/cdm-maps/sanjuantsheet.html. McLellan noted it: "The isthmus between Friday Harbor and North Bay has the form of an elevated ridge known as Bald Hill, with an altitude of 321 feet. Bald Hill is composed entirely of glacial materials and a gravel quarry is located on its northern side near the shore of Friday Harbor." Current charts show it as 399 feet. It was settled by George Wright in 1885. According to the February 17, 1906 issue of *The San Juan Islander*, Wright, born in Ontario in 1862, died in an accident on his farm in 1906. While trying to move logs from the hillside to the water: "His skull was crushed, evidently by a number of logs rolling over him and it is thought that his death must have been almost instantaneous." This is likely Richard's Park Hill [13a]. The reason for the Admiralty rename between 1859 and 1904 is unknown.

Bald Island
Located in Skagit Bay, north of Hawk Point, the name perhaps originated based upon its appearance.

Bald Peak [10] #51, 1854, U.S. Coast Survey
See Eagle Cliff.

Bald Point
See Ayres Point.

Baldwin Point
Located on McNeil Island at the northern end of Still Harbor, it was named for Margaret Baldwin who once owned the land (TPL website).

Ballow
Located on the eastern side of Harstine Island, the community was first settled in 1880 by Edward S. and Margaret Ballow. The post office was established in 1894 and closed in 1926 (TPL website). Hitchman (13) wrote that the name came from the Indian word *Bala* which referred to a mythical monster that created the Olympic Mountain Range.

Bangor
Located on the eastern side of Hood Canal, five miles north of Seabeck Bay, Bangor is a restricted Naval site, home to Trident submarines. The land was originally owned by George King in 1875. The adjacent spit carries his name [22]. J. H. Stevens, a later owner, named the area for Bangor, Maine. In 1944, the Navy began construction of an ammunition depot, displacing 1,100 residents. The population grew significantly afterwards to accommodate military needs (Bowen et al., IV: 105; TPL website).

Bare Island [11] #654, 1858, U.S. Coast Survey
Located north of Waldron Island, the U.S. Coast Survey named the island for its appearance (TPL website). Richards on [13a] named it Penguin Island in 1859. This is one instance where the American name was adopted over the British name. Later Admiralty charts [16c] reflected the name Barren Island. *See also* Skipjack Island.

Barlow Bay
It is located off the southwestern side of Lopez Island, inside Mackaye Harbor. Arthur "Billy" Barlow settled there in 1856. In 1854, Barlow deserted from a survey vessel in His Majesty's Service and with three other companions, paddled a canoe from Esquimalt to New Dungeness. He and his wife ultimately reared a family of nine. One son, Sam, was a long-time Puget Sound pilot (Walsh 12, 13). Sam regularly made the Seattle, Smith Island, Richardson, and Friday Harbor round trip on the *Rosalie*. Later, he ran a boat on Joshua Green's Black Ball Ferry Line on the Anacortes-Friday Harbor run. On foggy days, Sam stationed a deckhand on the bow, lead line in hand, to keep track of the depths. However, Sam generally navigated by tooting his horn. He would adjust his course depending up the length of time for the return echo (Mason 51).

Barnacle Rock
Located off Flint Beach on the southern end of Lopez Island, it is unnamed on current charts but the name is recognized by the U.S. Board on Geographic Names. McLellan noted: "Between Aleck Bay and Iceberg Point there are a number of small rocky islands and reefs. The largest of these, which is situated in the small bay midway between Iceberg Point and Aleck Rocks, has an area of about two acres and is known as Barnacle Rock."

Barnacle Rock Beach
Located southeast of Buck Bay in East Sound opposite Barnacle Rocks, Lange found this local name referenced in a UW Friday Harbor Labs publication. It was a 1960s collection site.

Barnacle Rocks
Located southeast of Buck Bay off Barnacle Rock Beach, Lange found this local name in a 1930s publication.

Barnes Island [7a] #145, 1841, Wilkes
Located in Rosario Strait on the eastern side of Orcas Island, in 1841 Wilkes honored a War of 1812 naval hero who has not yet been identified (Meany, *Origin* 14). Wilkes did not include this name in his *Narrative*, but it is shown on his chart.

Barnum Point
Located on the northern end of Port Susan at the entrance to Triangle Cove, it was named for Sterling Barnum, the first land owner. It is still owned by descendents of his family (Prasse 32).

Baron Point
Located on the northern shore of Totton Inlet near the entrance to Little Skookum Inlet, the origin of the name is unknown.

Barrel Point
See Pear Point.

Barren Island
See Bare Island.

Barren Island [16c] #601, 1921
Located north of Pearl Island in Spieden Channel, the name is descriptive. Richards first named this Bare Island on chart #2840 [14a] in 1861 and then continued with the name on chart #602 in 1865 [16a]. For whatever reason, the Admiralty changed the name to Barren Island in 1921 on [16c]. The U.S. Government owns the island.

Barrons Bay [7d] #146, 1841, Wilkes; [7q] #156, 1841, Wilkes
See Yukon Harbor.

Barstow Point
Located at the head of Penn Cove, Capt. Benjamin Barstow settled there and opened a trading post on the point in 1853. The Whid-Isle Inn was built on the site in 1907 by Judge Still. At various times, the inn was a store, a post office, and a girls' school. It was later renamed The Captain Whidbey Inn and is a bed-and-breakfast today, as well as operating a full service restaurant (Evans, Elizabeth Wright. "Early Charm Retained at Old Inn on Whidbey." *Seattle Times*. Sep. 12, 1965. Magazine Section p 6). The name is not recognized by the U.S. Board on Geographic Names.

Bartow
See Suquamish.

Basalt Point [20i] #6410, 1856, U.S. Coast Survey
Located two miles north of Port Ludlow, the U.S. Coast Survey provided the current name in 1856 for the basalt rock found there (Davidson, *Directory* 140). Wilkes originally named this Point Kanawi

in 1841 [7d], [7f], [7p]. On his charts, the spelling appears to be Kauawi. He left no reason for the name (Meany, *Origin* 14).

Bass Point
Located on the western side of Port Washington Narrows, the origin of the name is unknown.

Battery Point
See Alki Point.

Battle Point
Located on the western side of Bainbridge Island, it was the site of a battle between Chief Kitsap and northern Indians (Warner 61).

Battleship Island
Located to the northwest of Henry Island, Wilkes named it Morses Island [7a] in 1841 honoring crew member William H. Morse. Wilkes did not include this name in his *Narrative*, but it is shown on his chart. It was renamed Battleship Island for its shape. Many sources credit the name to an event in 1907 when Theodore Roosevelt visited Roche Harbor. According to the story, his purpose was to place monuments at American and British Camps. The battleship *Wyoming* was involved in the ceremonies. A British battleship was also expected. When the *Wyoming* crew observed Battleship Island from a distance, they prepared a salute, as the island looked like a battleship. Approaching closer, they discovered their error and cancelled the salute. But the observation and name remained. Based upon the research of Richard Walker, once editor of *The Journal of the San Juan Islands* and current editor of the *North Kitsap Herald*, no one can recall Roosevelt's visit. The only evidence is two entries in the register of the Hotel de Haro. One from 1906 is extant; the second from 1907 was apparently stolen. The 1906 entry, made in pencil, was originally undated. Someone later added a note with the date (Davis 31). According to an email, Mr. Walker wrote: "I have not been able to find evidence that President Roosevelt visited Roche Harbor in 1906 or 1907. On the date in the hotel register, the president was at home in Oyster Bay, according to presidential historian John Morton Blum, who edited the president's daily diaries. I talked to the employee who said he put the signature and date in there to replace a page that had been stolen. So, the signature in the register is not authentic, which is evident by a comparison of the signature to a copy of the president's signature," (Walker, Richard; June 6, 2011 email to author). Indeed, based upon my own review of back issues of *The San Juan Islander*, San Juan County's primary newspaper, there was no mention of a Roosevelt visit in either 1906 or 1907. Contrast that with Roosevelt's visit in 1903. The May 28 edition of the paper devoted more than half of page 2 to the itinerary. He spent Friday night in Tacoma May 22. The next morning, he boarded the steamer *Spokane*, visited the Navy yards in Sinclair Inlet, and landed in Seattle for a speech. He reboarded the *Spokane* and gave a speech in Everett before returning to Seattle for the night. The next day, Sunday, he relaxed, had only a few meetings, and dined at the Harvard Club. Late that evening, he boarded a train for the return trip to the East Coast. There was no mention of a visit to the San Juans. The most intriguing piece of information in the 2006 Washington State Board's Morse Island file is a 1925 letter from Professor Edmund Meany to the U.S. Board in which Meany supported the name change from Morses to Battleship Island. In his final paragraph, Meany wrote: "In closing may I venture to telling of an interesting incident in regard to Battleship Island. In 1904, through the help of President Roosevelt and others I conducted a successful ceremony on San Juan Island during which we erected a monument at American Camp and another at British Camp to commemorate the joint occupancy of that Island. Among others directed from headquarters to participate was Commander (Admiral) V. L. Cottman who proceeded to the Islands with the *Monitor*, then known as the *Wyoming*. He had told me that he did not believe that the British officers would comply with their promise to send a battleship from Esquimalt to participate in our ceremonies. I relied upon the promise and told him to not be surprised if he found a British battleship among the islands when the hour came. In passing from American camp around to British camp on a misty morning Commander Cottman received a notice 'battleship ahead, sir.' He said 'I gave orders for the saluting crews to go to their stations and in another moment would have fired the salute for that

British battleship which Meany was so sure would appear. Just in time we discovered it was an island.' Commander Cottman in relating his experience to me made this statement. 'Meany if I had given the order to fire that salute I could never live it down the rest of my days in the Navy, saluting an island for a battleship.' " The October 15, 1904 edition of *The San Juan Islander* devoted a full column on the front page to the planning for this upcoming event. The next week's paper devoted half of the front page to the activities which took place. In *Origin* (15), Meany wrote: "It is so named because of its resemblance to a battleship." McLellan agreed with Meany's observation. About the island, McLellan wrote a 1925 letter to Meany: ". . . presents a remarkable likeness to a modern battleship in its appearance, that it is locally known by no other name than Battleship Island," (from Washington State Board Files, Morse Island). It is unfortunate that Meany did not relate the name to Commander Cottman's experience, but that 1904 event indeed seems to be the genesis of the name. The Battleship Island name became official by a 1925 decision from the U.S. Board on Geographic Names in part from Messrs. McLellan's and Meany's letters supporting the change. According to Wood (85), the name first appeared on chart #6381 in 1914. This is strange, as it had not yet been adopted by the U.S. Board. In 2006, Stafford-Ames Morse, a relative of William H. Morse, submitted an application to change the name back to the original. At its May 11, 2007 meeting, the Washington State Board denied the proposal (files from the Washington State Board).

Bay Shore
Located near the head of Hammersley Inlet, it was named for its location (TPL website).

Bay View
See Cromwell.

Bay View
Located inland from Useless Bay on the southern end of Whidbey Island, it was first settled by Robert H. Millman in 1890 with his wife Octavia and their three sons. At that time, they could take a boat through the marsh to the head of Useless Bay. Later, a series of dikes and fill created some very productive farm land (Cherry II: 138). The name is likely descriptive.

Bay View
It is located on Padilla Bay about two miles east of the northern entrance of the Swinomish Channel. It was perhaps named for its unobstructed view of Fidalgo and Guemes Islands. The community formed in 1892 around the logging camp of Powell and Hernden. William J. McKenna and his wife purchased land in the area and built a saloon, small hotel, store, and a home for themselves. Mrs. McKenna became the first postmistress. Within a few years, the community grew to 11 logging camps, a shingle mill, another hotel, a second store, and a blacksmith. By 1900, there were 40 buildings, a Methodist Church, and a railroad (McDonald, Lucile. "Padilla Bay." *Seattle Times*. July 1, 1962. Magazine Section p 4,5). A variant listed in the U.S. Board on Geographic Names database is Bayview. According to Board information, Bay View may represent a misspelling (Project Ph 5905, Jan. 27, 1960).

Bazalgette Point [14c] #2840, 1872
Located on the southeastern side of Roche Harbor, San Juan Island, it was named by Capt. Pender in 1868 for Capt. George Bazalgette, the Commander of English Camp, 1860-1867, during the Pig War (Meany, *Origin* 16). Bazalgette was born in Nova Scotia in the late 1820s. Commissioned as a 2nd lieutenant in 1847, he saw duty on the North America and West Indies stations. He was promoted to 1st lieutenant in 1848 and was posted in numerous places, including the War in China where he was promoted to captain in 1858. In late 1858, Bazalgette was transferred to British Columbia where as a member of the Royal Marines, he was involved in some survey work and in guarding road building activities for a couple of years until being transferred to San Juan Island. When relieved by Capt. Delacombe in 1867, Bazalgette returned to Plymouth, England and served three more years. He retired from active duty in 1870 but accepted a position at an Exeter recruiting station where he served until 1872. He was promoted to major immediately following his retirement. He died in 1885 (http://www.royalengineers.ca/Bazalgette.html).

Beach

Located on the eastern side of Lummi Island near the ferry landing, it was named by and for Wade H. Beach who opened the first post office in his home in 1882 (http://www.lummi-island.com/history.html).

Beach Haven

Located on the northwestern side of Orcas Island, about two miles south of Point Doughty, the origin is unknown.

Beacon Tombolo

See Cypress Head.

Beals, Point [7d] #146, 1841, Wilkes; [7g] #155, 1841, Wilkes

Located on the eastern side of Vashon Island, Wilkes honored crew member Artimus W. Beals in 1841. Wilkes did not include this name in his *Narrative*, but it is shown on his chart.

Beans Point [23] #6460, 1905

Fort Ward was located near the point on a 375 acre site. Construction began in 1899 and was mostly completed by 1911. In 1935, it was used as a state run children's camp and converted to a park in 1958 (*An Historic* 9, 10). The Salish name for the point was "looking plain or conspicuous" (Hilbert et. al., 226). *See also* Blakely Harbor.

Beaverton Cove

Located north of the marina in Friday Harbor and east of the UW Friday Harbor Labs, the origin of the name is unknown (Soland, Leslie; Oct. 10, 2010 email to author). The local name is not listed on the U.S. Board GNIS database. Another local name used by the Friday Harbor Labs is Station Cove.

Beckett Point [9a] #1911, 1849, Kellett

Located on the eastern side of Discovery Bay, Wilkes originally named it Sandy Point in 1841 [7b]. Wilkes did not include this name in his *Narrative*, but it is shown on his chart. Kellett renamed it Beckett Point in 1846, stating that it was the local name for the Indian stockade built there (Meany, *Origin* 16; TPL website).

Bee

Located on the southern shore of McNeil Island, the name was selected for the beekeeper in the community (TPL website; Hitchman 17).

Beef Harbor [22] #6450, 1909

There are two very small harbors located in Hood Canal north of Seabeck Bay. On older charts, the one to the northeast was labeled Beef Harbor. On newer charts, this was renamed Big Beef Harbor. Its companion to the southwest is labeled Little Beef Harbor. Jacob Hauptly, born in Switzerland in 1830, came to the United States at age ten. In later years, he worked his way west, arriving in Port Gamble in 1862. Amos Brown hired him at his logging camp at Ducaboos. After a short time, Hauptly began selling supplies to logging camps. He boarded with the Ninemire family in Seabeck for a year and then returned to Brinnon. Locals elected him Justice of the Peace in 1866 and constable of Ducaboos precinct in 1869. In 1872, he sold his property to Elwell Brinnon, Mrs. Ninemire's brother, and returned to Seabeck to establish a slaughterhouse. He died at the home of his daughter in Seattle in 1928 (Bailey 100). The Beef Harbor name may have been connected with Hauptly's slaughterhouse.

Bell Island

It is located between Orcas and Shaw Islands, just east of Crane Island. The origin of the name is unknown. McLellan referenced it in 1927: "Bell Island is located near the northeast extremity of Wasp Passage and midway between Orcas and Shaw islands. Though rocky, it is moderately wooded, and its maximum elevation is 40 feet. Bell Island has an area of 3.67 acres." But perhaps Lange discovered its earliest reference in May 10, 1901 correspondence from R. K. McLachlan to John Murray, Surveyor General in Olympia: ". . . a small island in front of my place (locally known as Belle Island)."

Bell Point [16b] #602, 1869, Pender

It is located on San Juan Island between Garrison and Westcott Bays. According to Wood (86), it was possibly named for William H. Bell, an assistant surgeon on the H.M.S. *Hecate* and *Plumper* in the 1860s. Although John Bell served as a paymaster aboard the *Thetis* under Capt. Kuper, Lieutenant Daniel Pender named several points in the area after medical personnel. Hanbury was possibly named for Ingham Hanbury, an assistant surgeon at Garrison Bay 1865-1870, and White Point possibly for Charles W. White, Surgeon on the H.M.S. *Phaeton* in 1853 and a surveying officer on the *Satellite* in 1857-1860.

Belle Rock [10] #51, 1854, U.S. Coast Survey
Located in the middle of Rosario Strait east of Decatur Island and named by the U.S. Coast Survey, Davidson indicated: "We discovered and named this danger in 1854, and while placing a signal upon it noticed that the tide rose nearly 1½ foot while the current was yet running ebb at the rate of 3 miles an hour," (*Directory* 128). They left no reason for the name.

Bellevue Harbor
See Griffin Bay.

Bellevue Island [10] #51, 1854, U.S. Coast Survey
See San Juan Island.

Bellevue Point [18] #654, 1866, U.S. Coast Survey
Located on the western side of San Juan Island between Andrews Bay and Deadman Bay, the name first appears on U.S. Coast Survey chart of 1866, likely for the Hudson's Bay Company Bellevue Farm located on the south end of the island.

Bellevue Prairie
Located near Griffin's Bellevue Farm on the south end of San Juan Island, Lange discovered the reference to the name in an 1859 memoir of George Gibbs, an early settler.

Bellingham
Located on Bellingham Bay, the community name was taken from the bay. The earliest settlement was Whatcom followed by Sehome and Fairhaven [20a]. Sehome was formed on land owned by Messrs Vail and DeLancy and platted by E. C. Fitzhugh, James Tilton and C. Vail in 1858. It was named for Chief Sehome of the Samish tribe. Fitzhugh married a daughter of the Chief. Fairhaven was incorporated in 1890 by Daniel J. Harris. He named it from the Indian name *See-see-lich-em* which meant "safe port" or "quiet place" — thus, fair haven (Hitchman 87). Davidson referenced Fairhaven Bay in the 1889 *Pacific Coast Pilot* (571). All of the shoreline communities became part of Bellingham in 1903 (TPL website).

Bellingham Bay [6] 1792, Vancouver
Located off the mainland, Vancouver named it in 1792 and honored Sir William Bellingham, Knight, controller of the British Navy's storekeeper account (Meany, *Origin* 17). In 1791, Eliza named this Gaston. It is not reflected on his chart but appears on Pantoja's [2] (Blumenthal, *The Early Exploration* 47). Kellett maintained the name Gaston and used it for the northern portion of Bellingham Bay on [8a]; he labeled the southern portion using Wilkes' name. According to Davidson: "In some recent maps the northern portion is called Gaston bay, and for the southern part the original name is retained; but Vancouver's designation is that universally adopted on the western coast," (*Report* 438). The U.S. Coast Survey included Gaston Bay on [10]. In 1841, Wilkes wrote: "Bellingham Bay is 12 miles in length, northwest and southeast, and 4½ miles in width. Point Francis and Point William, which embrace the bay, are but 7 miles asunder. There is good anchorage in Bellingham Bay, in from 4 to 20 fathoms water. At its northern and southern ends are extensive mud-flats. The shores surrounding these are low and marshy; but towards the centre the land rises and forms a bluff," (Wilkes, *Narrative* 308, 309).

Bellingham Channel [10] #51, 1854, U.S. Coast Survey
It is located between Cypress and Guemes Islands. "The breadth of Rosario Strait at Belle Rock is 3½ miles; but it is soon contracted by James island on the western side, and opens into a channel N.NE. called the Bellingham Channel, which is about 2 miles wide at its entrance," (Davidson, *Report* 432). It was named by the U.S. Coast Survey in 1854 (Davidson, *Directory* 136).

Bells Beach
It is located on the eastern shores of Whidbey Island. Born in Scotland, Elizabeth Hendry lost both parents by the age of sixteen. She immigrated to the United States searching for her uncle and only relative located somewhere in British Columbia. To pay her passage, she indentured herself for a year to a Penticton, B.C. dentist, but she spent most of her time deflecting the advances of his teenage son. She finally located her uncle who settled the balance of her debt. Soon after, she met the aristocratic son of a British family who was managing a horse ranch. He wooed and married the teenage girl. However Elizabeth found her new husband to be an abuser, gambler, and an alcoholic. Two children later, she fled to Port Angeles. Her

husband pursued, abducted her children, and placed them in an orphanage. In Port Angeles, Elizabeth met David Bell who also had an unusual childhood. His mother had died when he was five. He moved with his father to Minnesota and studied for the clergy. Disillusioned, he became estranged from his father and while still a teen, he ran away, ultimately settling in Seattle. Over the years, he set up a business and became very successful. On a trip to Port Angeles, he met Elizabeth. He located the orphanage and retrieved her children. David and Elizabeth married in 1914. David began building a house in Lake Forest Park (north end of Seattle) for his family. One day, a stranger greeted him and David found himself looking at his father! The reunion went well. Bell Sr. assisted with the construction of the house. In thanks, David purchased a farm in Kenmore for him. During the next fifteen years, David and Elizabeth had four children in addition to Elizabeth's two, and his business continued to prosper. Looking for more elbow room for his children to grow, David searched and finally located land near Saratoga on Whidbey Island. He pestered the owner for two years without success. But he purchased the property upon the owner's death. They built a summer home and added cottages for a fishing resort. During the 1930s Great Depression, David lost his business as well as his Lake Forest Park home. But they held the Saratoga property where they permanently moved. They platted the property and began selling parcels, reserving waterfront sites for their six children and upland sites for the seventeen grandchildren. Today, the property is an exclusive housing community where many of the Bell children, grandchildren, and great grandchildren continue to live (Cherry II: 290, 291).

Belspeox Point
Located at the southwestern end of Squaxin Island, about a mile south of Potlatch Point (due east from the southern end of Hope Island), it is the transliteration of an Indian name meaning "Where there are seagulls." The name was originally applied to the cove south of the present Belspeox Point. However, the Squaxin Tribe recommended in January 1982 that it be applied to its current location in an effort to ". . . simplify navigation around the island as well as preserve the history of the tribe." This was the first of six names recommended by the tribe. The others were Palela Bay, Salmon Point, Seafarm Cove, Tuckapahwox Point, and Tucksel Point. With respect to Salmon and Tucksel Points, the tribe recommended corrections to the current names. The Washington State Board on Geographic Names approved all six names on Docket 280 at its June 11, 1982 meeting. All names were approved by the U.S. Board on Geographic Names on March 22, 1983 (from files of Washington State Board).

Ben Muir Island
See Ben Ure Island.

Ben Nevis
Located on Shaw Island, it is the highest hill on the island at 380 feet. It was reflected on NOAA chart #18434 (Mar. 13, 1983) as Ben Nevis Peak. Another variant was Mount Ben Nevis. Early settlers took the name from the highest peak in Great Britain which is 4,406 feet. It is located southwest of Inverness, Scotland. Because "Ben" in the Gaelic language means "mountain peak or summit," it apparently seemed duplicative to also include the word "peak" or "mount" in the name. The Washington State Board on Geographic Names agreed with the proposal, and the U.S. Board followed on April 9, 1992, Docket 350. An island road to the north of the peak is called Ben Nevis Loop (from Washington State Board Files).

Ben Ure Island
Located in Deception Pass, Wilkes first named this Little Tenif Island in 1841 [7e]. According to Hale (577), Tenif is a Waiilatpu name meaning "teeth." The Waiilatpu family includes the Willatpoos or Cayuse tribes who lived in Eastern Washington and Oregon. Somehow, the name Big Tenif was used on an 1890 hydrographic sheet as well as Admiralty chart #2689. When the light was installed on the island, both Ben Muir and Ben Ure were used in the Notice to Mariners. This raised immediate questions among locals as to the correct name. Apparently, the name Ben Muir was offered from a steamship master who operated in the area. Later, the then-present owner, who was more familiar with its history, corrected the name to Ben Ure. In 1913, the U.S. Board on Geographic Names addressed the several different variants and

settled on the current name (GNIS files). Variants in the GNIS database include Ben Muir and Big Tenif. An early settler, Ben Ure, lived (or stayed at times) on the island as well as at Ben Ure Spit. He went broke at farming and ranching, apparently losing his cattle herd to rustlers in the late 1850s or early 1860s. In 1890, he applied for a survey of the island, which was completed in 1895. The plat referenced it as "Ure's Island." He decided that smuggling was more to his liking and did well with rum, opium, woolens, and Chinese. He built a dance hall and saloon, drawing in both loggers and seamen to part with their money. Finally arrested in 1902, at age 72, Ure spent five days in jail. He returned to the island, repented, and died in 1908 (Neil 193). Notwithstanding a potential date conflict here, the tract book reflects that Ure purchased the island in 1908.

Ben Ure Spit
Located on the northeastern side of Whidbey Island, Wilkes originally named this Ala Spit in 1841 [7e] (Meany, *Origin* 2). Wilkes did not include this name in his *Narrative*, but it is shown on his chart. The Salish name for the spit was "shut up or closed up" (Hilbert et. al., 361). Hale (294) cited the Polynesian *Ala* meaning "awake or watchful." A letter is included in the Washington State Board files from La Conner historian Carroll F. Anderson, relating a couple of stories of Ben Ure. They are worth repeating. When questioned as to the proper name, he wrote: "Ben Ure Spit is correct — could have been named Ala spit in the early days but I doubt it. I do not believe that Ben Ure ever lived on Ben Ure Island — he could have stayed over night on the island once in a while. He was married to an Indian woman, who warned him from the island and from Ben Ure Spit by lantern light as a signal when the coast guard boats were in the area of Deception Pass. One night the coast guard nailed him and started to tow him to Port Townsend. They left him in his boat as it was a little rough that night. Ben Ure poured half the whiskey out of a barrel and stuck an oar in it and placed the lantern on same and in the morning the coast guard found Ben had left with his boat. He stayed in the hotel in La Conner one night after being quite drunk and had left a suitcase on the dock next [to] the La Conner Hotel. The next morning the suitcase was still on the dock with its contents of some $2,500 dollars in gold. He probably smuggled more than a thousand Chinese into this country in a twenty-five year period. Many went to California." Ben Ure Spit became official by a September 10, 1976 decision of the Washington State Board on Geographic Names, Docket 211. The U.S. Board approved the name the following month (from Washington State Board Files). *See also* Ben Ure Island.

Bertodano Cove [9a] #1911, 1849, Kellett
As drawn on Kellett's chart, the cove is located along the Strait of Juan de Fuca south of Kulakala Point (southeast of Dungeness). There is really no cove there. The reason for its appearance as well as the name is unknown.

Beverly Beach
Located on the eastern side of Homes Harbor, Whidbey Island, the source of the name is unknown. It is recognized as an official name by the U.S. Board on Geographic Names. Although it appears on a 1949 Metsker Map, it is not reflected on charts.

Big Beef Harbor
See Beef Harbor.

Big Cove
Located off the western shoreline of Totten Inlet about a mile south of the entrance to Little Skookum Inlet, the origin of the name is unknown. According to the TPL website, the name first appeared on the Metsker 1969 Atlas of Mason County.

Big Fishtrap
A bay between Dover and Dickenson Points on Dana Passage, slightly larger than Little Fishtrap, it was named for the wood and brush traps used by the Indians to catch fish (Palmer, 4).

Big Rock
Located south of Fisherman Bay on the western side of Lopez Island at Rock Point, Lange found it on the 1938 Admiralty chart #2840. It also appears on the current NOAA chart #18434. Its name is descriptive.

Big Slough
Located on the Nisqually Reach at the Tolmie State Park, the name is perhaps descriptive.

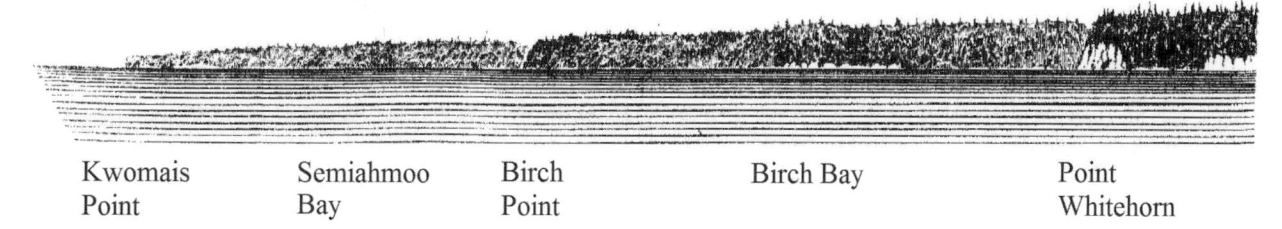

Kwomais Point · Semiahmoo Bay · Birch Point · Birch Bay · Point Whitehorn

Big Skookum Inlet
See Hammersley Inlet.

Big Tenif Island [7e] #158, 1841, Wilkes
See Strawberry Island.

Big Tenif Island
See Ben Ure Island.

Big Tykel Cove
Located on the western side of Budd Inlet about three miles south of Cooper Point, it was named after the George Tykel family who settled there. Originally named Tykle Cove, in 1993, the Washington State Board on Geographic Names addressed using the name Tykel, as that was consistent with how the original landowner spelled his name. It wasn't until the March 13, 1997 Board meeting that the current name was agreed upon. The U.S. Board followed later in the year. Variants included Big Tykle Cove, Big TyKels Cove, Ty Kels Cove, and TyKel Cove (from Washington State Board files).

Bill Point [7q] #156, 1841, Wilkes
Located on the southerly entrance to Eagle Harbor, Wilkes may have named this for eagles in the area in 1841. It is unnamed on current charts, but the name is recognized by the U.S. Board on Geographic Names. Wilkes did not include this name in his *Narrative*, but it is shown on his chart. In its place is the community of Creosote [22], the site of a creosote plant which was established in 1905. When the post office was opened two years later, the community was called Eagle Harbor. But the name was changed to Creosote in 1908. The post office closed in 1956 (TPL website). In 1987, the point became an EPA clean-up site, part of the superfund. The organizer and original manager, a Mr. Rood, died on the Titanic (Marriott 85; Warner 49).

Bill Point [7o] #157, 1841, Wilkes
See Mission Beach.

Bilouxi
Located on the northwestern side of Vashon Island near Point Vashon, the community was named by the early settler Ruth Kellogg for her hometown in Mississippi (Haulman).

Biological Hill
Located on the eastern side of San Juan Island, inland of Point Caution, Richards named it Sheep Hill [13a]; he likely observed sheep grazing there. In 1927 McLellan wrote: "In the vicinity of Point Caution there is a rocky wooded elevation which is here called Biological Hill. It has an altitude of 440 feet. The slopes of Biological Hill are gentle in all directions, but in places the nearby shores are somewhat precipitous. The covering of soil is very scanty and the conifers occur in scattered patches on those areas which were especially favored with soil. The grounds of the Puget Sound Biological Station are located on the eastern slopes of Biological Hill, near the shore of Friday Harbor."

Birch Bay [6] 1792, Vancouver
Located on the mainland north of Bellingham Bay, Vancouver wrote of the bay in 1792: "On the islands some few small oaks were seen, with the Virginian juniper; and at this place the Weymouth pine, Canadian elder, and black birch; which latter grew in such abundance, that it obtained the name of Birch Bay," (Vancouver 315). Galiano and Valdéz referenced it that same year as the *Ensenada del Garzon* (Wagner 249). However, it was likely named earlier by the Spanish as the same name appeared on Eliza's 1791 chart [3]. The name does not appear, however, in Eliza's account of the 1791 exploration.

Birch Point [11] #654, 1858, U.S. Coast Survey
Located at the northern side of Birch Bay, the U.S. Coast Survey likely named it for the bay. Wilkes called it Red Bluff [7l] in 1841. Richards named it South Bluff in 1859 [13a].

Bird Rock [14a] #2840, 1861, Richards
Located west of Crane Island, Richards left no reason for the name. For whatever reason, the Admiralty changed it to Bird Island on [14b] but the name later reverted to the original.

Bird Rock [7b] #148, 1841, Wilkes; [7c] #144, 1841, Wilkes
Located about a mile east of Neah Bay, in 1841, Wilkes referenced this name only on his charts.

Bird Rocks [7a] #145, 1841, Wilkes
Located in the middle of Rosario Strait east of Decatur Island, Wilkes named these in 1841 for the nesting seabirds (Meany, *Origin* 20). In 1927 McLellan wrote: "Bird Rocks are situated in Rosario Strait about half a mile to the southwest of Belle Rock. The rocks are three in number and they are lined up in a northeast and southwest direction. They appear to be a part of the same submerged ridge or reef that forms Belle Rock. Bird Rocks have a combined area of about 3.75 acres and the two most southern islands have elevations of about 40 feet. The northern island is much lower and it extends northward as a low reef. Bird Rocks contain neither soil nor vegetation but they serve as the nesting-place for large numbers of sea-fowl. The waters surrounding Bird Rocks and Belle Rock are noted for their strong tide-rips and these small rocky islands are seldom visited."

Bishops Point
It is located on the eastern side of Indian Island opposite Mystery Bay. The 1860 Jefferson County census lists William Bishop, a 27-year-old farmer from England, living in the Port Townsend precinct. The 1870 census lists what appears to be two Bishop families, that of William (age 37 from England) and that of James (age 30 from New York). Their relationship is unknown. William's family included his wife Anna and five children. James and his wife Ann had one child. Both families are listed as living in the Chemicum precinct, which is where other Indian and Marrowstone Island residents were listed. Bishops Point is perhaps named for one of these families. In 1875, Dennis Haight with his wife Susannah and two small daughters, Kate and Laura, homesteaded 150 acres on the east side of Indian Island about a quarter mile south of Bishops Point. Dennis and his wife were both mysteriously murdered in 1878. Lorens Hoff (*see* Oak Bay) discovered their bodies in the barn. Hoff found their young daughters, Kate and Laura, alive in the farmhouse. Haight had recently sold some timber for $600. Townsfolk suspected that the money was stolen and that the Haights were killed to cover-up the crime. Neither the killers nor the money were ever found. Port Townsend families raised their children (Bean 4, 5). In 1876, James Anderson married Emelia Johanson. Anderson then purchased the Haight property where he lived for many years with his wife and family. Anderson's early mentor, Hoff, died in 1890, his wife Emelia in 1908, and James Anderson died in 1932. Until 1966, descendants of James and Emelia continued to live on the original homestead (*With Pride* 203, 204).

Biz Point
Located on the western side of Fidalgo Island, in 1900, the crew of the tug *Biz* landed there and painted the name BIZ PT on a boulder that could be seen from the water. It gained local acceptance. The road leading to the point is named Biz Pt Rd. The Washington State Board on Geographic Names approved this name in their September 10, 1976 meeting, Docket 209. The U.S. Board followed the following month. Variants are Langley Point, which was the name used on nautical charts since the 1890s, and Point Sares (from Washington State Board Files). *See also* Sares Head.

Bjorgen Creek
The creek begins at North Kitsap High School and flows into what locals call Nesika Bay, near Lemolo. In 1997, Jens Knutson Bjorgen's (1874-1959) great grandson, George A. Bjorgen, submitted an application to the Washington State Board on Geographic Names to name it. Jens was born in Norway. About 1900, he and his wife Lena homesteaded in the area east of Poulsbo. They raised 11 children on their farm. Water came from an artesian well which fed the creek and continues to do so today. Two of his grandchildren own property neighboring the creek. The Suquamish name for the creek was "*Aatacac*" which means "camping ground." In its June 27, 1998 meeting, the Washington Board approved the name, Docket 368. The U.S. Board followed in September (from Washington State Board Files).

Black Creek [7d] #146, 1841, Wilkes
See Skokomish River.

Black Point
Located on the western side of Hood Canal, this is the southern entrance to Pleasant Harbor. Wilkes reflected two names on his chart in 1841 [7j]. Boston Point is shown on the outside of the harbor and Slik is shown as the inner point. On current charts, both are combined into Black Point.

Black Rock [10] #51, 1854, U.S. Coast Survey
Located off the southeastern side of Blakely Island in Rosario Strait, it was named in 1854 (*Directory* 130), likely named for its appearance.

Blaine [20j] #6399, 1857, U.S. Coast Survey
Located on the Washington/British Columbia border, Meany (*Origin* 22) indicated that it was named in 1885, but yet it appeared on the U.S. Coast Survey chart of 1857 [20j]. Brokenshire (24) stated that it was named in 1892. Both agree that the community was named for James Gillespie Blaine who ran for President in 1884 against Grover Cleveland. Meany added that James, Cornelius, and George Cain selected the name. The Cain brothers built the first store in the community in 1884. James was elected as the first mayor when the community incorporated in 1890. In 1884, he recorded the first plat for the town and used the name Blaine (http://www.historylink.org).

Blair Waterway
One of the waterways in Commencement Bay (from west to east, Thea Foss, Middle, St. Paul, Puyallup, Milwaukee, Sitcum, Port Industrial-now Blair, and Hylebos). In 1948, the Port of Tacoma requested the U.S. Board on Geographic Names to change the name of this waterway from Wapato Waterway to the Port Industrial Waterway. The early name originated from Wapato Creek which flowed into Commencement Bay. When the waterway was enlarged, Wapato Waterway became the obvious name. Rationale for the name Port Industrial Waterway was that the waterway served both the Port of Tacoma as well as the Industrial District. While the U.S. Board balked at the name, they later approved it. The Washington State Board on Geographic Names approved Blair Waterway in its June 7, 1974 meeting, Docket 184. The name honored Archie E. Blair, who in 1954 became the Port Commissioner of Tacoma. The U.S. Board approved the change later that month (from Washington State Board Files).

Blake Island

Blake Island [7d] #146, 1841, Wilkes; [7q] #156, 1841, Wilkes
Located south of Bainbridge Island, Wilkes likely honored George Smith Blake in 1841 who was responsible for the U.S. Coast Survey from 1837-1848 (Meany, *Origin* 22). William Pitt Trimble was born in Cynthiana, Kentucky in 1865. Educated in the public schools of Kentucky and Cincinnati, Ohio, he attended a prep school in Paris for three years. He returned, enrolled in the University of Cincinnati, and graduated with a law degree in 1887. He practiced briefly and traveled extensively, arriving in Seattle in 1894 where he opened a law office. Rapidly, he became involved in numerous business and real estate interests and was one of the wealthiest men in Seattle. In 1897, he married Cannie (Cassandra) Ford (b. 1871), the daughter of an attorney in Kentucky (Hunt, vol 3 419-421). In 1900, he built a 12 room home on the island with two floors and five fireplaces on the main floor. The living room alone was 35 by 40 feet. While living there, Trimble commuted to Seattle on his 50 foot yacht. Trimble even created a post office on the island, naming it Trimble Island. He was the postmaster. The family also had homes in Seattle, New York, and Washington D.C. In 1929, Trimble lost most of his

fortune to the stock-market crash. Shortly after, his wife Cannie drowned when her auto slid off a dock into Elliott Bay. He never again returned to the island. In 1936, he traded the island for a building owned by the United National Corporation in Tacoma. With his fortune continuing to decline, he retired to a small home on Capitol Hill and died in 1943 at the age of 80. During World War II, the island was home to several anti-aircraft gun emplacements and a few soldiers who lived in the mansion. Some claim that the soldiers made a mess of the home, or perhaps it was simply vandalized after the war. In the late 1940s, two Manchester teenagers, Don Winslow and Keith Williams, ran their sixteen-foot homemade boat to the island. As it was cold, they started a fire in one of the fireplaces. Later that evening, a glow was observed above the island. The mansion was no longer (*Seattle Times*, July 28, 2008). In early 1959, the state purchased (traded timber for) 355 acres on the island to complement the 120 acres already owned as school land. Later in the year, the state set aside the entire island as a park. In 1961, Tillicum Village was developed by Bill Hewitt, a Seattle caterer. Trading a 320 foot public pier and a 180 foot float for the concession to the Village, it opened in 1962. (www.historylink. org, Daryl C. McClary). The Salish name for the island was "bullhead" (Hilbert et. al., 233).

Blakely, Port

The community is located on the northern side of Blakely Harbor, east side of Bainbridge Island. It takes its name from Blakely Harbor. The U.S. Board on Geographic Names addressed the spelling, Blakely vs. Blakeley, in 1916. According to one letter in the GNIS files: "An examination of correspondence with Commander Johnston Blakely on file in the Navy Department discloses the fact that he spelled his name both ways. In fact, the Superintendent of the Naval Records and Library reports that on the same day he signed two letters, one as J. Blakely and one as J. Blakeley." Regarding this issue, Edmund Meany wrote to the Board and indicated that the first settlement in the area surrounded the Port Blakely Mill. Thus, the predominate spelling was with a single "e."

Blakely Dome

See Blakely Peak.

Blakely Harbor [7d] #146, 1841, Wilkes

Located on the southeastern side of Bainbridge Island, in 1841, Wilkes honored Capt. Johnston Blakely of the *Wasp* which was lost at sea during the War of 1812 (Meany, *Origin* 22). Reuben Bean was the first homesteader. He arrived in 1852, a widower with eight children, and claimed 148.5 acres in 1854. In 1859, a Tongass Indian slit his throat. A patent for the land was then issued to his children, because of the murder. The homestead ran from the harbor to Beans Point on Rich Passage (Price 16; Perry, *Port Madison* 6; Rhoades 35). Beginning in 1863, William Renton began buying land around the harbor including the Bean homestead. The lumber mill was completed in 1865 (Bowen, VI: 31). Davidson referenced the mill in the 1889 *Pacific Coast Pilot* (611): "At the inner end of the harbor is one of the largest sawmills of the country; it has an average daily output of over two hundred thousand feet of lumber and has reached an output of three hundred and fifty thousand feet of lumber in one day. The mill is under the north shore. Here also is an extensive ship-building establishment. Between 1881 and 1887 there were built here twenty-two vessels (including a United States revenue-cutter), aggregating nine thousand three hundred and sixty-nine tons; the largest vessel was seven hundred tons burden; and at this writing there are three vessels on the stocks." William Renton, born in Pictou, Nova Scotia in 1818, emigrated to the U.S. at age eighteen. In 1841 he married Sarah Silva, a widow with three children, in Philadelphia, where they lived until 1849. The Rentons moved to San Francisco in 1850. William immediately got into the timber business. As Captain of the bark *Alabama*, he headed north into Puget Sound country in 1852 and returned to San Francisco with a load of lumber. Renton, impressed with the potential of the Northwest, met Charles C. Terry who was developing Alki Point. Terry persuaded Renton to build his mill on the point. Constructed in 1853,

Renton rapidly discovered Alki Point unsuitable due to its exposure. In 1854, with a new partner Daniel S. Howard, he moved the mill to Port Orchard. His wife and three children visited from San Francisco occasionally until 1857, when the oldest daughter, Mary Ann, fell in love with a mill hand, David Livingston. They married in Olympia. Renton's first grandchild, the first in Port Orchard, was born in 1858. Mill problems continued to plague Renton and he sold the Port Orchard mill (Price 1-11). In 1863, he searched for a better site and discovered Port Blakely. By mid-year, Renton began acquiring land around the harbor including Reuben Bean's homestead. Before long, he accumulated more than 700 acres. Completed in 1865, the mill produced 20,000 feet of lumber a day and by 1879, 90,000 board feet daily. While still small compared to Port Madison, Seabeck, and Port Gamble, Port Blakely grew to fifty-nine Whites and a few Indians. A hall, jail, general merchandise store, and post office were constructed. In 1872, the first school was built. And in 1873, Renton built a hotel with seventy-five rooms. The hotel was managed by Daniel J. Sackman, husband of Renton's daughter Elizabeth. By 1882, the population reached 500. Five years later, the mill alone employed 1,200 men. The 1888 fire destroyed the mill. Renton reconstructed at a cost exceeding $250,000 and started business again within six months. Recognizing that the long-term growth of the company depended upon a ready source of timber, land acquisition continued. Surrounding the mill, the company purchased 32,000 acres. By 1882, they purchased 22,000 acres in Mason County, and it ultimately grew to more than 100,000 acres. Today, that land is managed by the Port Blakely Tree Farms (Price). Sarah Renton died in 1890 at the age of 74. Despondent, and also in ill health, Renton, for whom the city is named (he invested heavily in the Renton Coal Company mine in 1873 but never actually visited the city) sold his interests to nephews John and Jim Campbell in 1891 and retired from the lumber business. He died the same year (Price 118; Bowen et al., VI: 32). The Port Blakely mill was again sold in 1902 to David E. Skinner and John W. Eddy who came from Michigan in 1900. As president of the company, Skinner remained in San Francisco while Eddy managed the business in Port Blakely. The mill continued to expand but burned a second time in 1907, destroying about half of the plant. Economic conditions delayed rebuilding for two and a half years. The business foundered until the war. The boom was short-lived, however, and after the war, the timber industry declined once more. The mill closed permanently in 1923. Skinner started the Alaska Steamship Company soon after (Price 159, 170-173). Blakely Harbor was also home to the Hall Brothers Shipyard. Isaac and Winslow G. Hall started the yard in 1874 at Port Ludlow. Another brother, Henry Knox, joined them in 1875. They constructed thirty-one ships, ten of which were used in Hawaii for the sugar cane business. Capt. Renton at Port Blakely made some enticing offers to the Halls in the late 1870s. When Pope and Talbot purchased the Port Ludlow Mill in 1878, their expansion plans included that land used by the Halls. Thus, the Halls finally decided to take Renton up on his offer and relocated to Port Blakely in 1879 (Isaac died that same year). Over the years, the yard continued to turn out larger and better ships. Winslow died in 1898 at age sixty-five. By 1901, Hall Brothers launched hull number 100, the 626 ton *Gamble*, which was quickly followed the next year by the 1,237 ton five-masted schooner, *H. K. Hall*. An important character throughout the history of the yard was George Monk, who started work at the company in Port Ludlow in 1873, at age twenty-eight. He married Anna Saunders in 1892 and ultimately spent twenty-seven years with the yard, the latter portion as superintendent. In 1900, at age fifty-five, Monk joined the Moran Brothers Shipyard in Seattle. His son, Edwin G. Monk, learned the business at his father's elbow and acquired an excellent reputation in later years as a designer of modern power boats (Price 70-86).

Blakely Harbor
Located on the northern side of Blakely Island, the name came from the island.

Blakely Island

Blakely Island

Blakely Island [7a] #145, 1841, Wilkes

Located east of Lopez Island and bordering Rosario Strait on its eastern shore, in 1841 Wilkes spelled the name with an extra "e" for Capt. Johnstone Blakeley, captain of the *Wasp* who captured the H.M.S. *Reindeer* during the War of 1812 and was later lost at sea. In 1859, Richards dropped the "e" [13a]; Richards' spelling has remained to the present. Paul Hubbs ran sheep on the island. Along with his wife Sasha (one of several), he was shown on the 1870 census as the sole occupant, somehow having received the "exclusive privilege to the island." The 1880 census continued to show Hubbs on the island but without a wife. However, he may not have been the first to actually live on the island. John and Mary Reed logged there in the 1860s; their daughter Isabelle was born on the south end in 1867. The record is unclear regarding Hubb's activities on the island. There is some indication that he sold it to Edward C. Gillette about 1874 (Richardson, *Pig* 217-223). In the late 1870s, Harrison Coffelt and his brother-in-law, William H. Vierick built a mill in Thatcher Bay. Taking advantage of the water flowing from Spencer Lake into the bay, they added a reciprocal saw powered by water. It was operational by 1879. At that time, the two families owned the entire shoreline of Thatcher Bay and the property up to Spencer Lake. Coffelt bought out Vierick in 1888. Coffelt sold to Theodore Spencer in 1892. Spencer moved his family from Lopez to a homestead on Spencer Lake in 1889, but Coffelt remained for a few years to run the mill, which closed in 1942 (Roe, *Blakely* 16-19). In 1889, Gillette sold the land that he actually owned on the south end of the island to Richard H. Straub, a school teacher. Straub and his wife Jane Elizabeth settled on land near J. C. Burns, a railroad man. Burns' wife Pauline was part of the Lanterman family of Decatur Island. Eventually, bad blood developed between Straub and the Burns/Lanterman families, culminating in Straub's ouster as the local teacher. Leon (also spelled Leone) Lanterman from Decatur cast the deciding vote. It was particularly galling to Straub, as Lanterman didn't even live on Blakely. Unfortunately, Straub's wife also died suddenly about the same time in mid-1895. At the end of that summer, Straub got his revenge. As explained in the September 5, 1895 edition of *The Islander* (p 2): "San Juan county has been brought into unenviable prominence within the past week by the commission within its borders of one of the most atrocious crimes in the history of the state. Mr. Leon Lanterman, who had born a most excellent reputation for integrity and worth, has been foully murdered by a man of more than twice his years, and apparently for no other reason than that Lanterman, as a school director, would not consent to the engagement of the murderer Straub to teach the district school. There can be no doubt that the fearful crime was deliberately planned and committed with all the malice that the law deems essential to conviction of murder in the first degree. The terrible deed was committed by an assassin of the worst type, a coward who had not the nerve to face his unarmed victim, and who, not satisfied with one cold blooded murder, wrought with equal diabolism to kill his victims young half brother and his sister, a wife and mother, both entirely defenseless and as free from thought of trouble as a babe in arms." The follow-up story on page 3 contained some more detail. Lanterman and his half brother Ralph Blithe were assisting Pauline in bringing in the potato crop. Irving Parberry, a 17-year-old friend of Straub stalked them from an adjoining field and began insulting Lanterman "in a scurrilous manner, calling him all sorts of vile and obscene names." When Lanterman walked to the fence, Straub jumped up and instantly shot him. Straub turned his attention to Blithe who fell down and acted dead. Next Straube fired at and wounded Pauline Burns, but she was able to make it to the small house, gathered her ten-year-old son, and rowed to Mr. Spencer's. Blithe crawled away and escaped. Straub and Parberry, now fearing for their own lives, rowed to Friday Harbor and turned themselves over to Sheriff Newton Jones. The County dropped charges against Parberry when he agreed to testify on behalf of the prosecution. Straub was tried and convicted. According to the April 29, 1897 issue of *The Islander*: "Richard H. Straub, the Blakeley island murderer, was hanged here on Friday last, April 23rd, at 11:15 o'clock." The grisly detail was also provided: "A second later Straub's body was hanging in the air. Death must have been instantaneous and Straub's neck must have been broken, as there was not the slightest movement of the body, merely his toes fluttering a trifle." He was buried where the Marine Laboratory stands at Friday Harbor. This was the only hanging in San Juan County (Richardson, *Pig* 217-223). After the mill closed in 1942, the Spencer family remained until 1946 when they sold to Dr. Lloyd W. and Margaret Hines. Hines apparently had big plans but eventually sold in 1954 to Floyd Johnson who was a salesman for a Cessna dealership in Portland. Over the next half dozen years, partnerships to develop the land came and went, but slowly an airstrip was hacked out of the western side of the island, a marina dredged, piers constructed, and about 170 lots platted, improved, and sold (Roe, *Blakely* 51-63; McDonald, Lucile. "Picturesque Log Buildings left by Pioneers Are Curiosities on Rugged Blakely Island." *Seattle Times.* Aug. 13, 1961, Magazine Section p 8).

Blakely Island Shoal
Located off the western side of Blakely Island, in 1854 it was originally named Entrance Shoal on Admiralty chart #2689 [13c]. It likely takes its name from the island.

Blakely Lake
See Horseshoe Lake.

Blakely Peak
It is the highest hill on Blakely Island. McLellan wrote: "Blakeley Dome, the highest elevation on the island, occurs near the north east margin with an altitude of 1060 feet." The U.S. Board on Geographic Names adopted the current name in 1925. Hitchman (23) suggested that the name came from the island.

Blakely Rock [23] #6460, 1905
Located a half mile north of Restoration Point on Bainbridge Island, it likely takes its name from Port Blakely. Davidson referenced the name in the 1889 *Pacific Coast Pilot* (610). The U.S. Board on Geographic Names addressed the spelling, Blakely vs. Blakeley, in 1916. *See also* Port Blakely.

Blanchard
See Herron.

Blind Bay [13a] #2689, 1859, Richards
It is located off the northern side of Shaw Island. According to Hitchman (23), it is named because it can only be seen directly from the north.

Blind Island
It is located in Blind Bay off the northern end of Shaw Island. In the late 1800s, the John Fox family, which included John Jr. and his married sister, first settled the island. While John and his son were fishing in Alaska in 1905, John's wife left him and sold the house. John and his son returned, rebuilt, and lived on Blind Island for many years. At the death of John Jr., around 1960, the state took over the three-acre island and created a marine park (McDonald 185; Bailey and Nyberg, *San Juan Islands* 80). Lange indicated that the name first appeared on chart #6380 published in 1912, corrected to July 7, 1918. Hitchman (23) indicated that it was named for the bay.

Blind Island
Located off the southeastern end of Lopez Island off the entrance of McArdle Bay, the origin of the name is unknown. The U.S. Government owns the island.

Blossom Point [7o] #157, 1841, Wilkes
Located on the northern entrance to Appletree Cove, Wilkes used the descriptive name for the crab apple trees he observed along the shoreline in 1841. Wilkes did not include this name in his *Narrative*, but it is shown on his chart. The name is neither reflected on current charts nor recognized by the U.S. Board on Geographic Names.

Blowers Bluff [21] #6300, 1895
Located on the eastern side of Whidbey Island, a mile south of Oak Harbor, it was originally called Fords Point for the early settler. After the Fords left, the bluff was renamed to honor Alvah D. Blowers, a prominent man on Whidbey Island who was president of the local bank, was involved in a large mercantile business, and managed the local newspaper (TPL website).

Blunts Island [7a] #145, 1841, Wilkes
See Smith Island.

Blyn
First mentioned in the 1934 *Pacific Coast Pilot*, it was once a logging town on the southwestern side of Sequim Bay. Named for Capt. Marshall Blyn, a land inspector for the government, locals established a post office in 1890, which closed in 1907 (TPL website).

Boat Channel [14c] #2840, 1872
Located between Turn Island and the eastern side of San Juan Island, it is unnamed on current charts. But the name is recognized by the U.S. Board on Geographic Names.

Boat Harbor [21] #6300, 1895
It is located on the eastern side of Guemes Island. Although the name appeared on charts from the 1890s (e.g., t-sheet #1794 at http://riverhistory.ess.washington.edu/tsheets/framedex.htm), locals from as far back as the 1880s apparently only knew it by the name Square Bay. This was some of the information collected by the Washington State Board on Geographic Names which denied the proposal to change the name to Square Bay in its September 10, 1976 meeting, Docket 210. The U.S. Board followed in October. Another variant was Square Harbor. The origin of any of these names is unknown (from Washington State Board Files).

Bodega y Quadra, Puerto de la [1] 1790, Quimper
See Discovery Bay.

Bodega, Boca de [2] 1791, Pantoja
See Boundary Bay.

Bodega, Punta de la [3] 1791, Eliza
See Boundary Bay.

Bolin, Point [7q] #156, 1841, Wilkes
Located at the southwesterly end of Agate Passage, Wilkes honored crew member Jacob Bolin in 1841 (Meany, *Origin* 215, 216). Wilkes did not include this name in his *Narrative*, but it is shown on his chart. The Salish name for the point was "dusty point." A large and small rock is located on the point and named elk and wolf respectively. According to the Indian legend, the transformer turned both of them to stone. It appears that the smaller rock is chasing the larger (Hilbert et. al., 198).

Bolton Peninsula [7d] #146, 1841, Wilkes
It is located in Hood Canal. Wilkes wrote: "Colsee-ed Harbor [Quilcene] is separated from Dabop Bay by Bolton Peninsula." He perhaps honored crew member William F. Bolton in 1841 (Wilkes, *Narrative* 325; Meany, *Origin* 24).

Bonilla, Islas de [3] 1791, Eliza
See Smith Island.

Boston Harbor
Located at Dofflemeyer Point at the eastern entrance to Budd Inlet, C. D. Hillman purchased the 320 acre Dofflemeyer claim, platted the property, and named it Boston Harbor. A Seattle real estate developer, he attempted to sell the plots (Meany, *Origin* 25). According to the TPL website, the community was named for the Boston Harbor Railroad, Steamship & Land Company. The website goes on to say that local names included Harriman and Hillman.

Boston Point [7j] #153, 1841, Wilkes
See Black Point.

Boulder Island
Located off the southeastern side of Lopez Island in Rosario Strait, in 1859 Richards originally named it Kellett Island for Henry Kellett [13b]. Meany (*Origin*, 25) claimed the island was named by the U.S. Coast Survey in 1858. I am unable to confirm with Davidson's writings. The name is likely descriptive. Lange indicated that the name first appeared on chart #6380 published in 1912, corrected to July 7, 1918. In 1927, McLellan wrote: "Boulder Island is located at the south entrance to Watmough Bight. It has an area of 6.9 acres and its maximum elevation is 79 feet. Boulder Island is almost circular in outline, although a narrow rocky point projects from the south side of the island. It is rocky throughout and contains only a scanty growth of vegetation." The U.S. Government owns the island.

Boulder Reef [11] #654, 1858, U.S. Coast Survey
It is located off the northern end of Sinclair Island. "It is covered with kelp, which is, however, generally kept under the surface of the water by strong currents. A huge erratic granite boulder is seen at ordinary tides inside of the outer point of the reef . . ." (Davidson, *Report* 433). Davidson continued: "The revenue cutter *Jefferson Davis* and the steamship *Panama* have been upon it since we discovered it in 1854." The Admiralty chart of 1859 [13a] reflects the name Panama Reef. The name selected by the U.S. Coast Survey survived.

Boundary Bay [18] #654, 1866, U.S. Coast Survey
Located at the Canadian Border, its western boundary is Point Roberts. The eastern boundary is more difficult to determine as it merges with Semiahmoo Bay. Eliza named both Boundary and Semiahmoo Bays as *Boca de Bodega*. It is not reflected on his chart, but it is shown on Pantoja's [2]. Eliza also used the name *Punta de la Bodega* [3] for a point in Boundary Bay. It is difficult to place this point as they believed Point Roberts was an island and charted it as *Isla de Lángara* [3]. Off to the eastern side of Boundary Bay, Eliza noted on his chart *Boca de Floridablanca* [3]. Galiano/Valdéz called this entire area *Boca de Floridablanca*. Wilkes originally named the current Boundary and Semiahmoo Bays as Draytons Bay in 1841 [7a], [7l] (*see also* Drayton Harbor). He honored crew member Joseph Drayton (Meany, *Origin* 72). The U.S. Coast Survey reflected both bays as Mud Bay in 1862 [17] but changed the name in 1866 to Boundary Bay [18]. Ultimately, with a 1952 decision by the U.S. Board on Geographic Names, Boundary Bay was split; the eastern portion was named Semiahmoo Bay (*see also* Semiahmoo Bay).

Boundary Channel
See Haro Strait.

Boundary Pass
The exact location of this pass was subject to months of discussions and negotiations between interested U.S. parties as well as Canadians. The file from the Washington State Board on Geographic Names runs 56 pages! In fairness, several boundary issues were discussed including the Strait of Georgia, Haro Strait, Rosario Strait, and a minor adjustment to the name of the Strait of Juan de Fuca. Each of these will be addressed in its proper spot. However, with each of these bodies of water, the specific issue was their boundaries, i.e., where does a pass or strait begin, and where does it end? Early on, the boundaries were not very exacting. Boundary Pass was defined as follows: "A channel between Patos Island, United States, and Saturna Island, Canada; connects Haro Strait with the Strait of Georgia . . ." The Canadian and American positions were later clarified in a February 2, 1978 meeting: "No agreement was reached on the boundaries of this feature. Gene Little [Executive secretary, Washington State Board] reported that the Washington State Board would like to define Boundary Pass as a line between East Point (Saturna Island) and Alden Point (Patos Island). Don Orth [Executive Secretary, U.S. Board] agreed with this viewpoint. However, Don Pearson [Canadian Permanent Committee on Geographical Names] and Peter Browning [Canadian Hydrographic Service] did not. The sailing directions used by Canada indicate that the west limit of boundary Pass lies between Monarch Head (Saturna Island) and the west end of Skipjack Island, and the east limit lies between the west end of Alden Point in a general northwesterly direction to a light on Rosenfeld Rock. They also indicate that Boundary Pass is an extension

of Haro Strait." After 18 months of discussions, late in 1978, the parties reached an agreement as follows: "Boundary Pass lies between Haro Strait and the Strait of Georgia, encompassing the area from Stuart Island to Patos Island. The southern limit is between Turn Point (Stuart Island) and Point Fairfax (Moresby Island). The northwest limit is between Pelorus Point (Moresby Island) to Wallace Point (North Pender Island), thence to Tilly Point (South Pender Island), thence from Teece Point to Taylor Point (Saturna Island). The north limit is between East Point (Saturna Island) and Alden Point (Patos Island). The southeastern limit is between Alden Point (Patos Island) and Point Hammond (Waldron Island), thence from Sandy Point (Waldron Island) to Charles Point (Stuart Island)." This decision had the effect of reducing the size of Haro Strait and increasing the size of Boundary Pass. This was affirmed in 1979 by the U.S. Board (from Washington State Board Files).

Bowman Bay
It is located on the northwestern side of Deception Pass. The Bay was originally named Reservation Bay and was shown on hydrographic surveys dated 1887. Amos Bowman founded Anacortes in 1876. He and his wife Anna Curtis purchased 186 acres, built a wharf and a store, and started a newspaper. Because of extensive local use of the name instead of Reservation Bay, the Washington State Board on Geographic Names approved Bowman Bay in its December 10, 1976 meeting, Docket 209. The U.S. Board on Geographic Names followed in early 1977 (from Washington State Board Files).

Bowman Cove
Located on the northern shoreline of Totten Inlet, nearly opposite Burns Cove, it was named for Wava V. Bowman who owned the waterfront land as shown on the 1962 Metsker Map. It is about a quarter mile west of Hurley Cove.

Bowman Creek
See Cascade Creek.

Boxer Cove [7a] #145, 1841, Wilkes; [7m] #160, 1841, Wilkes
See Short Bay.

Boy Scout Point
See Cypress Head.

Brace Point [19] #662, 1867, U.S. Coast Survey
Located on the Seattle shoreline, four miles south of Alki Point, the U.S. Coast Survey named the point in 1856 but left no reason (Davidson, *Report* 448). The Salish name for the point was "horned snake." Apparently a monster lived there and appeared like a huge snake with the antlers and forelegs of a deer (Hilbert et. al., 69).

Brackenridge Passage [7i] #147, 1841, Wilkes
Located between Fox and McNeil Islands, Wilkes named this in 1841 for crew member J. D. Brackenridge (Meany, *Origin* 26). The name is neither reflected on current charts nor recognized by the U.S. Board on Geographic Names. Inskip called it Bruce Channel [24] in 1846 for one of the naval officers in the Bruce Baronetcy (Reese, *Origins* 22). The Bruce of Downhill Baronetcy started in 1804 for the Rev. Henry Bruce. The title of Baron is part of the English peerage system in which the queen (or king) bestows titles of nobility. In ascending order, the ranking of the titles are baron (the lowest), viscount, earl, marquis, and duke.

Bramblebluff [7k] #152, 1841, Wilkes
Located about halfway between Frenchmans and Whitney Points at the western entrance to Quilcene Bay, Wilkes spelled this Bramble Bluff on his chart in 1841. The name may have been descriptive.

Brant Island
Located in Portage Bay off Bellingham Bay, the origin of the name is unknown.

Brant Point
Located on the northeastern side of Portage Island in Bellingham Bay, the origin of the name is unknown.

Breezy Point
Just north of Lowell Point on Camano Island, it was likely named for the windy conditions on Saratoga Passage. The local name is not reflected on current charts, but there is a light placed there: Fl R 4 sec 15ft "2." This means that the light flashes red every four seconds. It is mounted 15 feet in the air and has the number "2" marked on it. The name can be found on a 1958 Camano Island tourist map at http://www.oldcamano.net/resorts57.html

Breidablik

Adjacent to Vinland on the eastern side of Hood Canal, Breidablik is the home of Baldur, the Nordic God of Love and Beauty. Most early settlers were Scandinavian; two of the earliest, the Nels Hansons and Olof Wistrands, arrived in 1886. They established a post office in 1892. Mr. Ole M. Able, who lived near Lofall, chose the name. The following year, Max and William Vetter constructed a school on a lot owned by Gilbert Paulson. After the logging industry declined, the settlers established dairy farms, fruit orchards, and chicken farms. The old schoolhouse still stands (Carson 65).

Bremerton

Bremerton

It is located on the southwestern portion of Port Orchard, in Sinclair Inlet. In 1875, Andrew Williams purchased a 168 acre homestead along Point Turner. His land included the site for the future naval shipyard. He remained for 15 years and slowly logged. In 1891, William Bremer purchased a portion of the homestead. He platted it and named it Bremerton. Also, that same year, another town was platted on the opposite side of the shipyard, southwest of Bremerton, and named Port Orchard. In 1893, Port Orchard was incorporated with some adjoining land as Charleston. This land was above the naval yard and west of Point Turner. Bremerton and Charleston finally merged in 1927 (Bowen et al., III: 21-24; *With Pride* 242). Bremer died in 1910 (Meany, *Origin* 27). The history of the early shipyard is of interest. As naval ships grew in size and number, the major West Coast seaport at Mare Island in San Francisco Bay could not accommodate repairs. Congress authorized a commission in 1866 and again in 1890 to select a replacement site. In 1877, Lieutenant Wyckoff, on board the coast survey steamer *Yukon*, observed the Bremerton shoreline and envisioned a great navy yard. In 1891, the navy made a final decision regarding the yard and from a congressional appropriation purchased 190¼ acres at fifty dollars per acre. During 1892, the navy constructed a wharf and cleared a portion of the land for home sites. The navy also constructed a dry dock, completed in 1895, at a cost of $610,000. It measured 650 feet long by seventy wide and included land-based repair facilities (Bowen et al., III: 21-24; *With Pride* 242).

Bretland

Located on the eastern shoreline of Camano Island, the land was first purchased by Oliver F. Gerrish in 1872. It changed ownership 16 times before being purchased by Alfred L. Bretland in 1911. Bretland barged in lumber for his home and filed a plat on the property in 1912. For some reason, the name Cornell appeared on Metsker Maps and some USGS maps of the area. In its March 13, 1987 meeting, the Washington State Board on Geographic Names addressed both names and approved Bretland, Docket 322. The U.S. Board followed in 1989 (from Washington State Board Files).

Brigantine Bay

It is located in Lopez Sound on the western side of Decatur Island inside Trump Island. In 1968, Robert H. Kinnaird purchased 625 acres on the northwestern side of Decatur. Late that year, he petitioned the U.S. Board to name this previously unnamed feature. He chose the name because "It relates to the nautical orientation of the San Juan Islands and in particular to Stephen Decatur, the distinguished U.S. Naval Commodore for whom the island is named." The Board adopted his proposal early the following year (GNIS files).

Brinnon

Located on the western side of Hood Canal, a mile north of Pleasant Harbor, Elwell P. Brinnon first settled in the area in the mid-1860s. Brinnon started his career as a mill fireman at Seabeck and was one of the first loggers at Union, and at Tahuya on the north side of the canal across from Union. When the government established the Skokomish Indian reservation, Brinnon sold his property west of Union and moved to Brinnon, claiming land at the mouth of the Duckabush River. He married Kate, the sister of the Clallam chief Chetzemoka. Ultimately, he owned almost all of the property in the lower Dosewallips Valley. As more settlers arrived, Brinnon sold his first claim to Tom Pierce and took out another three miles to the south, near the mouth of the Dosewallips River. Pierce, from East Machias, Maine (1832-1918) arrived in Seabeck in 1859 and was one of the earliest loggers in Brinnon. His wife Mary Ellen was the first White woman in the area. Town folk established the post office in 1888. At that time, Julius and Jessie Macomber ran a store. Jessie selected the name in honor of its first settler (Bailey, *Brinnon* 95-100). Brinnon died in 1896.

Brisco Point [7h] #154, 1841, Wilkes
Located at the southern end of Harstine Island, its naming honored crew member William Brisco in 1841 by Wilkes. Wilkes did not include this name in his *Narrative*, but it is shown on his chart. The Salish name for the point was "far offshore rocks" (Hilbert et. al., 295).

British Camp
See English Camp.

Broad Spit [22] #6450, 1909
Located on the western shore of Dabob Bay on the Bolton Peninsula, Wilkes originally named this Pilash Point in 1841 [7d] although it appears to be labeled Pildsh on his chart (Meany, *Origin* 27). The current name is descriptive.

Broken Point [13a] #2689, 1859, Richards
Located on the northern end of Shaw Island, it was named for its descriptive shape.

Broughton Point [13a] #2689, 1859, Richards
Located on the southeastern side of Cypress Island, south of Deepwater Bay, it was named Broughton Point by Richards who honored Lt. William Broughton, Commander of the *Chatham*, consort to Vancouver's *Discovery* in 1792 (Meany, *Origin* 27). The name is neither reflected on current charts nor recognized by the U.S. Board on Geographic Names. This appears to be the same location as McLellan's Olivine Hill.

Brown Cove
Located on the southern shoreline of the Little Skookum Inlet, it was likely named for Mary F. Brown who owned acreage on the eastern side of the cove as shown on the 1962 Metsker Map (http://www.historicmapworks.com/Map/US/29572/Page+010++Totten+Inlet++Skookum+Inlet++Kamilchie++Deer+Harbor/Thurston+County+1962/Washington/).

Brown Island [14a] #2840, 1861, Richards
See McConnell Island.

Brown Island [7a] #145, 1841, Wilkes
Located on the eastern side of San Juan Island at the entrance of Friday Harbor, in 1841 Wilkes honored crew member John G. Brown (Meany, *Origin* 28). Wilkes did not include this name in his *Narrative*, but it is shown on his chart. Friday Island is a local name used on real estate and other San Juan Island literature.

Brown Point
It is located on the northern side of Camano Island. The 1860 Island County census lists Richard Brown, age 23, from Brunswick, a laborer at the Grennan and Craney Mill. Although his post office was listed as Coveland, Brown Point is perhaps named for him. Alternatively, the 1870 census lists several people named Brown (relationship unknown) living in the Camano Island precinct.

Brown Point [7d] #146, 1841, Wilkes; [7i] #147, 1841, Wilkes
See Dofflemeyer Point.

Brown Point [7d] #146, 1841, Wilkes
It is located on the eastern side of the Toandos Peninsula. Although there were a dozen plus men named Brown on the 1841 expedition, Wilkes did not disclose which one was honored, if any, or if the name was simply descriptive. Wilkes did not include this name in his *Narrative*, but it is shown on his chart.

Brown Rock
Located a half mile west of Deer Point on the southeastern end of Orcas Island, the name was likely descriptive. It was likely first shown on t-sheet #1952 from 1889 (http://kaga.wsulibs.wsu.edu/cdm-maps/sanjuantsheet.html).

Browns Cove
See Nellita.

Browns Point
See Sandy Point.

Browns Point [23] #6460, 1905
It is located at the northern entrance to Commencement Bay. In 1841, Wilkes named it Point Harris [7d], [7g] honoring crew member Alvin Harris. Wilkes did not include this name in his *Narrative*, but it is shown on his chart. In 1903, a lighthouse was built on the point. The first keeper was Oscar Brown. The community and point were named for him (*History* I: 56). The Salish name for the point is "a cape" (Hilbert et. al., 75). The U.S. Board on Geographic Names in 1959 approved the current name over the variants including Brown Point, Point Brown, and Point Harris.

Browns Point
See Sandy Point.

Brownsville
Located on the western shores of Port Orchard, it was first settled by the Louis Peterson and Solomon Brown families. The first post office was built on Peterson's property in 1888; the community was named after Solomon (Bowen et. al., IV: 122).

Bruce Channel [24] #1947, 1849, Inskip
See Brackenridge Passage.

Brush Island
See Cliff Island.

Buck Bay [13j] #2689, 1894
Located off Orcas Island on the eastern side of East Sound behind Olga, Richards originally named this Stockade Bay [13a], perhaps for the presence of a stockade used by local Indians for protection against northern Indians. The current name is likely for the animal, similar to Deer Bay, Deer Point, Buck Mountain, Doe Bay, etc. It appeared as "Stockade or Buck Bay" on [13j].

Buck Island
See Geese Islets.

Buck Lake
See Day Lake.

Buck Mountain
There are two Buck Mountains on Orcas Island. One is east of the community of Eastsound, and the other is on the southeast end of the island. Lange found a 1941 reference to the name: "Once when I was on the islands I tried to find out something about a Peer Gynt ride reputedly made by one Charlie Beale on the back of a wild buck which is supposed to have given Buck Mountain its name."

Buckeye Shoal [13k] #2689, 1900
Located east of Sinclair Island, it was named for the 60-foot *Buckeye* built in 1890 in Seattle. In April 1895, the *Buckeye* left Friday Harbor headed for Bellingham and foundered on the shoal (Lange). The April 4, 1895 issue of *The Islander* reported that the *Buckeye* was swamped in Bellingham Bay, apparently due to a shifting load. There was no mention of Buckeye Shoal in the article. The *Buckeye* was owned by Andrew Newhall. It was repaired and back in service in the summer. The July 25, 1895 edition reported that the *Buckeye* was disabled and had lost all but one blade of her propeller. Perhaps this was the encounter with Buckeye Shoal.

Buckhorn
The community is located on the northern shore of Orcas Island. Following WW I, the Buckhorn Lodge was established, likely named for its proximity to Buck Mountain. It became popular in the 1950s as it was the first place on Orcas to sell hard liquor by the glass. The lodge disbanded perhaps in the 1960s, and the property was subdivided and sold off. As such, the Washington State Board on Geographic Names addressed a name change from Buckhorn Lodge to Buckhorn. In its December 10, 1976 meeting, Docket 211, the Board approved the name. The U.S. Board followed in early 1977 (from Washington State Board Files).

Budd Inlet [7d] #146, 1841, Wilkes; [7i] #147, 1841, Wilkes
Located at the southern end of Puget Sound, Wilkes honored crew member Thomas A. Budd in 1841 (Meany, *Origin* 30).

Budd's Harbor [7n] #149, 1841, Wilkes
See Sequim Bay.

Buffingtons Lagoon
Located on the eastern side of Harstine Island, it was the site of the Buffington and Sutton Lumber Company mill (TPL website).

Bull Town
See Seabold.

Bulls Head [7f] #151, 1841, Wilkes
Located at the southern end of Port Ludlow, it is the peninsula forming the northeast entrance to the inner harbor. Unnamed currently, Wilkes presumably named it for its shape in 1841.

Bumstead Spit
It is located on the eastern side of Lummi Island, due east of Lovers Bluff. According to the 1910 Whatcom County census, the extended family of George and Cordelia Bumstead lived on the island. The spit was likely named for them.

Bung Bluff [7h] #154, 1841, Wilkes
Located at the southern end of Herron Island, Wilkes left no reason for this 1841 name. Wilkes did not include this name in his *Narrative*, but it is shown on his chart. The name is neither reflected on current charts nor recognized by the U.S. Board on Geographic Names.

Buoy Bay
It is located off the southeastern shore of Orcas Island between Doe Bay and Deer Point. In 1979, the 11 homeowners around the bay met to discuss a potential name for the bay. In their filing they stated: "1. In the beginning, over 20 years ago, when our group of residents began settling the area and building their summer homes which will eventually become their retirement homes, small anchor buoys were placed by each family for moorage of boats. These buoys have become a recognized feature of this bay. 2. The residents here feel that the stunning natural beauty of the bay and its surrounding setting always lifts up or 'buoys' the spirit." At its December 14, 1979 meeting, the Washington State Board on Geographic Names approved the name. The U.S. Board followed in 1980 (from Washington State Board Files).

Burke Bay [22] #6450, 1909
Located immediately south of Brownsville in Port Orchard, the origin of the name is unknown. The name is reflected on the 1881 t-sheet #1637 of Port Orchard.

Burley
Located at the northern end of Carr Inlet, the original land owner was Henry W. Stein. The Co-operative Brotherhood purchased the 291 acre tract from him in 1898. Over several years, locals built a blacksmith shop, a two story building which served as a dormitory, dining room and office space, a school and a library, as well as a sawmill. A socialist operation, it failed within ten years. The members liquidated, and the land and buildings were sold off, generally to the original settlers (Bowen et al., V: 116-118). According to Reese (*Origins* 23), there are a couple of stories about the name. The first was that a post-Brotherhood settler chose the name. The second is that the Brotherhood manufactured cigars and named the area for a kind of tobacco from Burley, Kentucky.

Burley Lagoon [23] #6460, 1905
Located off the community of Burley, it takes its name from the community.

Burner Point
According to Wilkes' chart, he named two points on the western entrance to Port Ludlow in 1841. The most easterly point was Syral [7f], perhaps a couple hundred yards from the westerly point which he named Tit Point [7f]. Tit Point marks the entrance to the marina, near where the current gas dock is located. Wilkes did not include either name in his *Narrative*. Syral has been renamed Burner Point on current charts and was apparently the site of a sawmill burner (U.S. Board on Geographic Names). Tit Point is neither reflected on current charts nor recognized by the U.S. Board on Geographic Names. Wilkes left no reason for either name. In 1967, Pope and Talbot developed the Port Ludlow property into a major resort. A large marina now occupies the northern shore of the bay with extensive public and private moorage. The resort property also features a hotel, restaurant, beach club, and a golf course. Burner Point and the harbor are protected by a totem

pole, carved by David Boxley, from a 720-year-old western red cedar. The pole was commissioned by Pope and Talbot and erected in June 1995.

Burns Cove & Point [23] #6460, 1905
Located on the southern side of Totten Inlet, Jolson and Henry Burns settled in the area in the 1870s. The cove and the point were both named for the Burns family (Palmer 10, 11). The Salish name of the cove was "gooseberries" (Hilbert et. al., 282).

Burns Landing [23] #6460, 1905
Located on the northern side of Totten Inlet, this also could have been named for the Burns family who settled on the southern side of the inlet.

Burrows Bay [13a] #2689, 1859, Richards
It is located off the western side of Fidalgo Island, between that and Burrows and Allan Islands. Wilkes originally named this Argus Bay in 1841 [7a], [7m] for the *Argus* commanded by Capt. William Henry Allan (Meany, *Origin* 32). Richards' name selection is a mystery. Why he would have replaced the American ship (*Argus*) with a name which honored an American naval hero (Lt. William Burrows) is unknown. The U.S. Board on Geographic Names approved Richards' name over Wilkes' in 1891.

Burrows Island [7a] #145, 1841, Wilkes; [7m] #160, 1841, Wilkes
Located off the western side of Fidalgo Island, Burrows and Allan Islands collectively were named *Islas Morros* in 1792 by Galiano/Valdéz. In 1841, Wilkes honored Lt. William Burrows who served on the *Enterprise* during the War of 1812 (Meany, *Origin* 32). The State of Washington Park and Recreation Commission owns about three quarters of the 450 acre island.

Burrows Pass
Located on the northern side of Burrows Island, it takes its name from the island.

Burton
Located on Vashon Island in Quartermaster Harbor, the first settler was Lars Hansel who filed on 137.9 acres in 1869. He was also the first settler on Vashon Island. The community was named by Mrs. M. F. Hatch after the town where she previously lived, in McHenry County, Illinois (Meany *Origin* 32).

Burton

Another story suggested that it came from her birthplace in England, Burton-In-Kendall (Hitchman 32). The Salish name for the area was "old houses" for the Indian village that was there (Hilbert et. al., 238).

Bush Point [11] #654, 1858, U.S. Coast Survey
Located on the western side of Whidbey Island, Wilkes originally named this Point Leavitt in 1841 [7a], [7d] perhaps for crew member David Leavitt (Meany, *Origin* 32). The U.S. Coast Survey provided its current name in 1855. Davidson wrote: "About 5 miles on this course is passed, on the eastern shore, a low point, with one or two clumps of trees and bushes, to which has been given the name Bush Point," (Davidson, *Report* 443). The first White settler in the area was Andrew Deming who established a farm in 1865 and grew hay. In 1875, he married an Indian girl, Catterina, and they raised six children (Cherry II: 243).

Bushoowah-ahlee Point
It is located on the western side of Snyder Cove on Eld Inlet, on the Evergreen State College campus. Originally named Squaw Point, in 2010, the college and Squaxin Indian Tribe submitted a request to the U.S. Board on Geographic Names to change the name to Bushoowah-ahlee Point, as the current name was extremely offensive. According to information provided to the Board, the original Salish name was *Blcuwa'3ale* (Indian spelling) which has no English equivalent. The proposed name is the Roman spelling. The U.S. Board approved the change in its September 2011 meeting.

Butler
See Gorst.

Butler Cove [23] #6460, 1905
Located on the western side of Budd Inlet southwest of Olympia Shoal, it was named for John L. Butler who settled there on a 321.6 acre claim about 1850. Butler was born in 1827 in Boston. In the 1850s, northern Indians from Alaska and British Columbia, the Tlingit, Tsimshian, and Haida, discovered a labor market in Puget Sound. These Indians found good employment and excellent wages from the Hudson's Bay Company at Nisqually, at various sawmills, and on farms. In 1854, a group arrived led by their chief Tsus-sy-uch. Tsus-sy-uch, from southeast Alaska, was the result of a union of a Tsimshian father and a Tongas Tlingit mother. For several weeks, the small party stayed at Fort Nisqually looking for work. They eventually met John Butler and contracted with him to clear part of his farm. Since Butler also worked on various boats in the sound, he was absent much of the time. Thus, James Burt, who managed Butler's farm, was to oversee the work. When the Indians were finished, Tsus-sy-uch requested pay from Burt. Although the reasons are unclear, on May 7, 1854, language became heated as Burt refused to pay. The dispute escalated to the point where Burt, in the presence of Butler, shot and killed Tsus-sy-uch. The remaining Indians departed to Nisqually and waited for justice. Both Butler and Burt were arrested for the murder (Whites in the area accepted it as such after hearing accounts of the event). But, they were later released. Burt left the territory. Butler remained and was never punished. The Indians decided to return home. But because of the fear of hostilities, they were escorted to Victoria. Three years later, the Indians finally exacted their revenge with the murder of Isaac Ebey in August 1857. Ebey's head was removed and taken back to Alaska. Some connect Ebey's death to the murder of another chief in Port Gamble in 1856. Regardless, Ebey was still dead. On January 20, 1860, Capt. Charles Dodd, Commander of the Hudson's Bay Company steamer *LaBouchere* bartered successfully with the Indians for the head and it was returned to Ebey's family. Today, Butler Cove is a quiet residential neighborhood. The Olympia Golf and Country Club also shares part of the original homestead (http://www.squaxinislandmuseum.org/index.html?culture/history.html~mlrcContent).

Butterball Cove
Located on the Nisqually Reach, the origin of the name is unknown.

Buttonhole Island
It is located off the eastern shore of Cypress Island. Speaking of the Cone Island Group, McLellan wrote: "The most western member of the group is little more than a small thin jagged rock which rises about eight feet above tide. Because the side of this island is perforated by a small hole, it is commonly known as Buttonhole Island." The name is not recognized by the U.S. Board on Geographic Names.

Bywater Bay
The bay is formed by Hood Head and the mainland on the western side of Hood Canal. The origin of the name is unknown.

Caamaño, Ensenada de [1] 1790, Quimper
See Admiralty Inlet.

Cactus Islands [13a] #2689, 1859, Richards
Located north of Spieden Island, Richards chose the name because of the cacti growing there (TPL website). Walter and Othelia Beals first settled the islands in 1912 (McDonald 186). "A species of cactus also grew on Yellow and Low Islands, along with other islands that lack fresh water," (McLellan). The cactus is the Prickly-Pear *Opuntia Mill* (Lange). There are two islands in this group, each has a single owner.

Caldwell Point
It is located at the western entrance to West Sound. A miner by the name of H. Patrick squatted on the point originally. William Caldwell bought him out for $6. The price included a boat ride for Patrick to Port Townsend. Caldwell, from Connecticut, was a ship's carpenter and worked at the Hall Brothers yard in Port Ludlow. He filed for his homestead in 1882 (Lange). Caldwell is listed on the 1887 San Juan County census as age 61, with he and his wife Clara having three children ages 12, 22, and 29, all born in Connecticut.

Caledonia & Caledonia Beach

The community and beach are located between Browns Point and Dash Point, north of Commencement Bay. According to data submitted to the Washington State Board on Geographic Names, the name has long been in local use. Caledonia, the Latin name for Scotland, was introduced by Matthew McDowell when he purchased the land in 1905. About 150 homes occupy the land today. At its September 17, 1993 meeting, Docket 359, the Washington State Board on Geographic Names approved both names. The U.S. Board followed in early 1995. *See also* Dash Point.

Callam

See Sekiu.

Calset Point [9a] #1911, 1849, Kellett

See Kalset Point.

Cama Beach

Located north of Lowell Point on the western side of Camano Island, the origin of the name is unknown.

Camano City

Located on the western side of Camano Island, it was the site of either the Camano Commercial Company or the Camano Land & Lumber Company. The company owned the sawmill and wharf where steamers stopped (Prasse, Karen. Stanwood Area Historical Society. E-mail to author, May 2, 2010).

Camano Head

Located at the southerly end of Camano Island, Wilkes originally named this Point Allen in 1841 [7a], [7o]. Because of Vancouver's name for Port Gardner, most assume that Wilkes honored Sir Alan Gardner, including Meany (*Origin* 5). Vancouver served under Gardner in 1784 and named Port Gardner [6] off Everett for him. In the description of Point Allen, Davidson wrote in the 1889 *Pacific Coast Pilot*: "This point is known to steam-boat captains as Camano Head." This is the first formal usage of the new name. In 1910, the U.S. Board on Geographic Names queried officials from Snohomish and Island Counties. Learning that the accepted local name was Camano Head, the Board thus changed the name.

Camano Island [8a] #1917, 1847, Kellett

Located in Saratoga Passage, Wilkes first named it M'Donough Island [7a] in 1841 for master commandant Thomas MacDonough of the *Saratoga* during the War of 1812 (Meany, *Origin* 33). Kellett renamed it in 1847 in honor of the Spanish explorer, Don Jacinto Caamaño, the brother-in-law of Francisco de Eliza. Born in Madrid in 1759, Caamaño served at San Blas in Mexico in 1789. In 1792, Caamaño led the final Spanish voyage of exploration, examining the Northwest Coast from Bucareli Bay in Southwest Alaska to Nootka Sound. Following this expedition, he was posted in the Philippines until 1807. He later served at various posts between Mexico and Peru and died in Equador about 1820. His grandson, Jose Placido Caamaño became president of the Republic of Ecuador in 1883 (Wikipedia). Eliza, who explored the Strait of Juan de Fuca in 1790, originally applied the name *Boca de Caamaño* to Admiralty Inlet, but Vancouver unknowingly renamed it. The U.S. Board on Geographic Names approved the name in 1910.

Camp Lagoon

It is located immediately north of Onamac Point on the western side of Camano Island. In 1931, a Mr. Major dredged the area and built 15 cabins. The name is descriptive (http://www.oldcamano.net/resorts94.html).

Camp Grande

Located near Rocky Point on the western side of Camano Island, the origin of the name is unknown. The camp with its fifty cabins was built by Charlie Brown in 1828 (http://www.oldcamano.net/resorts94.html).

Camp Point [7b] #148, 1841, Wilkes

It is located on the southeastern side of Discovery Bay. The name is neither reflected on current charts nor recognized by the U.S. Board on Geographic Names. Wilkes left no reason for the 1841 name, although it could have been for the remnants of an Indian camp in the neighborhood.

Camp Point [7i] #147, 1841, Wilkes

Located on the eastern shoreline of Totten Inlet, it is located at the entrance to Gallagher, across the inlet from Skookum Inlet. Wilkes did not include this name in his *Narrative*. Unfortunately, the name shown on his chart is unclear, but it appears to be Camp Point. The name is neither reflected on current charts nor recognized by the U.S. Board on Geographic Names.

Camp Sealth
Located on the western side of Vashon Island and named after Chief Sealth, the land was acquired initially for the Camp Fire Girls. The camp is comprised of 400 acres and a mile of waterfront along Colvos Passage. Camp Fire was founded in 1910. Northwest clubs originated in Federal Way and Kirkland in 1911. By 1920, there were 1,200 members. In 1921, the Seattle-King County Council of Camp Fire Girls affiliated with the Community Chest which later became United Way. With community funds, the Council purchased 186 acres on Vashon Island. Additional purchases occurred later. Originally a resident camp for Washington State girls, it turned coed in 1975. Most campers arrived by water on the *Virginia V*, which made the run throughout the summer from 1922 to 1970. The camp serves children from 4 to 18 (http://wikipedia.org).

Cannery Point
Located on the southern shore of Hammersley Inlet, it was perhaps the location of a fish cannery.

Canoe Island [15a] #611, 1865, Richards
It is located off the eastern edge of Shaw Island; Richards provided no reason for the name. Dr. and Mrs. Warren Austin founded French Camp there in 1969. The camp teaches children about the French language and culture in a "summer-camp" atmosphere (http://www.canoeisland.org/about-us/history-and-philosophy.html). In the late 1800s, the island was a military reservation. According to the Apr. 14, 1898 issue of *The San Juan Islander* (p 3), Judge I. J. Lichtenberg of Lopez Island secured a lease of the island, perhaps to run sheep.

Canoe Island
See Pass Island.

Canoe Pass
Located in Deception Pass, between Fidalgo and Pass Islands, it was likely named either because of its size or because it was the preferred route for canoes.

Cap Sante

Cap Sante [21] #6300, 1895
Located on the northern end of Fidalgo Island, it was originally named Lawrence Head in 1841 by Wilkes [7m]. Wilkes did not include this name in his *Narrative*. The name appears on [21] and the Admiralty chart [13j] as *Capsante*. In early 1976, Anacortes residents submitted a name change to the Washington State Board, from *Capsante* to Cap Sante. Locals provided a wealth of support for the change including a letter from William F. Gallagher dated August 11, 1976. He provided details of late 1800s and early 1900s newspaper articles referencing Cap Sante (two words). He also wrote: "An early resident of Anacortes has in her possession a picture given her by a descendant of the Curtis family who had one of the first homes on Cap Sante. The descendant was told that the picture was of a promontory of the same name on the St. Lawrence River in the Province of Quebec, where the Curtis family resided before coming to Anacortes. The promontory here reminded them of their former home so that the name was used here. 'Cap' is used as part of promontory names in this French area of Quebec Province." While this story seems unlikely, there is in fact a city of Cap-Santé on the St. Lawrence, about 25 miles from Quebec City. The Washington State Board approved the change in its September 10, 1976 meeting, Docket 210; the U.S. Board followed later in the year. A variant was Rocky Point (from the Washington State Board files).

Capp Island
See Cayou Island.

Capstan Rock [23] #6460, 1905
Located on the eastern side of Hood Canal directly across from Ayock Point, it may have been named for its shape.

Careen Creek [13a] #2689, 1859, Richards
The creek empties into Fisherman Bay on the western side of Lopez Island. Richards provided no reason for the name, although the nautical term applies to the act of beaching a boat at high tide and allowing it to lay over as the water recedes. This permits work to be done on the bottom, but it obviously needs to be finished by the next high tide, twelve hours later.

Carlisle
According to McLellan: "Along the west shore of the island [Lummi], about two miles south of Point Migley, a low sandy point extends out to the westward to form Village Point. The village of Carlyle is located on this point." The Lummi Island Packing Company established a salmon cannery on Village Point in 1896. The name was later changed to the Carlisle Packing Company, owned by Frank Wright. The generally accepted spelling of the local name is Carlisle, although Carlyle is frequently used.

Carlson Bay
It is located on the western side of Anderson Island, a half mile southeast of Treble Point. It was named after Charlie Carlson, an early settler, who owned the land around the bay, according to Washington State files and the U.S. Board GNIS database. Reese (*Origins* 28) indicated that it was named for Falk and Clara Carlson who settled there in 1881. At its March 10, 1995 meeting, the name was approved by the Washington State Board on Geographic Names. The U.S. Board approved it later in the year (from Washington State Board Files). Variants were Carson Bay and Sleepy Lagoon.

Carlyon Beach
Located on Squaxin Passage across from Hope Island, the land was originally developed by Fred Carlyon. He operated a fish camp/resort from 1927 to 1959 (Palmer 13).

Carr Inlet [7d] #146, 1841, Wilkes; [7h] #154, 1841, Wilkes
One of the major branches in Puget Sound, Carr Inlet is the most northeastern. Wilkes honored crew member Lieut. Overton Carr with the name in 1841 (Meany, *Origin* 37).

Carr Point [7b] #148, 1841, Wilkes
See Contractors Point.

Carrasco, Isla de [1] 1790, Quimper
See Protection Island.

Carrel River [1] 1790, Quimper
See Pysht River.

Carrol, Point
See Marrowstone Point.

Carson Bay
See Carlson Bay.

Carter Point [7a] #145, 1841, Wilkes
Located on the southern end of Lummi Island, in 1841 Wilkes honored crew member William Carter (Meany, *Origin* 38).

Cascade Bay [13a] #2689, 1859, Richards
Located off Orcas Island on the eastern side of East Sound, it was named by Richards for a waterfall which cascaded from nearby Cascade Lake into the bay.

Cascade Creek
Cascade Creek on Orcas Island flows from Summit Lake and Mountain Lake into Buck Bay. It was originally called Bowman Creek after John H. Bowman who settled on the creek in 1872 and gained his patent in 1879. Bowman sold to Edward P. Newhall (McDonald, Lucile. "Orcas Island Gets a New Checkup." *Seattle Times*. June 16, 1963. Magazine Section p 11).

Cascade Lake
The lake took its name from the falls. When Robert Moran purchased the property in 1905, he dammed the lake for hydroelectric power. In the 1920s, McLellan wrote: "Cascade Lake, with an elevation of 350 feet, drains to the westward directly into Cascade Bay. This water is now used to furnish power for a large electric generating plant."

Cascade Range of Mountains
The mountain range runs along Western Washington from its northern to southern border. In 1792, Vancouver viewed the mountains surrounding Puget Sound country and frequently described them as "covered with eternal snow" or "rugged snowy mountains" or "high craggy mountains" (Vancouver 214, 221, 227). And Vancouver named both Baker and Rainier, which had previously been observed and named by Quimper. In 1823, the Scottish botanist David Douglas traveled to Oregon Territory to collect plants. In his journal (221, 252, 257), he specifically mentions the Cascade Mountains and perhaps was the earliest to actually provide a name for them. According to Hitchman (39), Douglas apparently selected the name based upon seeing the waterfalls along the Columbia River. It is not known if Wilkes knew of Douglas, but it is very coincidental as Wilkes used the same name in 1841. He wrote: "The head of the bay has an extensive mud-flat, where several small streams enter, among them the Pugallop, which takes its rise in the Cascade Range of Mountains," (Wilkes, *Narrative* 319). Perhaps he picked it up while at Nisqually or from his travels to the Columbia River. Certainly by 1858 the name was common as evidenced by Davidson: "On the east the face of Whidbey island is very steep; it is about 250 feet high and appears flat, as does the whole country eastward to the sharp-cut outline of the Cascade range, stretching its serrated ridge northward where the snow-peak of Mount Baker is distinctly seen; and to the southward where the higher peak of Mount Rainier attracts the eye," (*Report* 415). But obviously, Davidson would have had access to all of Wilkes' material and likely would have maintained the name. The U.S. Board on Geographic Names approved the name in 1907 and defined its boundaries in 1953: "limited on the south by the gap south of Lassen Peak and extending northward into British Columbia," (*Decisions*).

Case Inlet [7d] #146, 1841, Wilkes; [7h] #154, 1841, Wilkes
Located on the northwestern side of Puget Sound, the naming by Wilkes honored crew member Augustus L. Case in 1841. Case was born on 1812 in Washington D.C. and appointed midshipman in 1828. He served in the Mexican-American War and Civil War. Promoted to Rear Admiral in 1872, he died in 1893. Case led much of the survey work in Hood Canal (Meany, *Origin* 39).

Case Shoal [7k] #152, 1841, Wilkes
Located in Suquamish Harbor in Hood Canal, Wilkes named this Case Bank in 1841 in honor of crew member Augustus L. Case. Wilkes did not include this name in his *Narrative*, but it is shown on his chart.

Casey, Fort
With the construction of the Naval Shipyard in Bremerton, a board of engineers recommended establishing coastal defenses to better protect Admiralty Inlet. Sites selected by the engineers included Point Wilson, Marrowstone Point, Admiralty Head on Whidbey Island, and Deception Pass. The War Department approved their plan and Congress appropriated funds for Point Wilson, Marrowstone Point, and Admiralty Head. Fort Casey on Admiralty Head honored Brigadier General Thomas Lincoln Casey, the late chief of the Corps of Engineers. Construction began in 1897 and troops arrived in 1902. The fort was deactivated in 1953 (*With Pride* 261-263).

Castle Island [13a] #2689, 1859, Richards
Located off the southeastern end of Lopez Island, Richards provided no reason for the name. According to Meany (*Origin* 40), it was reflected as Old Hundred Island on the United States Coast Survey report, 1855, chart 44. The U.S. Government owns the island.

Castlenook
Located on the northern side of Fox Island, west of Ketners Point, it was the site of the North Commercial Company, a fishery established in 1871 by B. F. Tayler. The packing house employed twenty men who processed more than 3,000 dogfish daily. Dogfish are a species of shark. The name resulted because they travel and hunt in packs. All parts were used. They obtained machine oil from the livers, the skin of the sharks was used as sandpaper, and the heads, fins, and tails were used to make glue. They

packed the meat in barrels and shipped it to, among other places, France. The Castlenook fishery lasted only four years (Perisho 12).

Cattle Pass
Located between Cattle Point on San Juan Island and Lopez Island, the name does not appear on current charts but is the local name for the pass from Middle Channel to San Juan Channel. McLellan referenced the name Cattle Point Narrows which was evidently dropped for the more popular Cattle Pass.

Cattle Point

Cattle Point [13a] #2689, 1859, Richards
The point is located on the southeastern end of San Juan Island. In the mid-1800s, Chief Factor James Douglas organized a Hudson's Bay Company farm on the south end of San Juan Island. On December 13, 1853, Charles John Griffin, sent by Douglas to run the farm, took possession of 1,300 sheep and possibly some cattle and offloaded the animals at the point. Wood (88) found a reference to the pasture land at the point where the Hudson's Bay Company used to run their stock. Middleton (36) spoke of a shipwreck in 1857 and the cattle were forced to swim ashore. The U.S. Government owns the land.

Cattle Point Narrows
See Cattle Pass.

Caution, Point [13a] #2689, 1859, Richards
Located on the eastern side of San Juan Island (just north of Friday Harbor), Richards apparently selected the name as a warning because of strong currents in the vicinity. A becalmed sailing vessel could experience some great difficulties if caught in these currents (Wood 89).

Cayou Cove
Located on the northeastern side of Deer Harbor, it is the local name for the homestead of Louis Cayou.

Cayou Island
Located at the southern end of Lopez Sound off the eastern side of Lopez Island, it was originally named Rum Island. In 1981, the Washington State Board on Geographic Names entertained a proposal to change it to Capp Island honoring George Lloyd Capp who died the previous year in a wood cutting accident. Capp worked for the U.S. Fish and Wildlife service for environmental and habitat preservation programs. According to data provided to the Washington Board, the Rum Island name first appeared on a 1973 USGS quad, and the field cartographer apparently picked up the name as local usage while surveying in the area. In soliciting comments on this proposal, an alternative arose: to name the island after Henry Thomas Cayou. Henry was born in 1869 in Deer Harbor, the first son of Louis and Jennie Cayou. Jennie was a Lummi Indian. Henry was noted as an inventor of fish traps, a master of setting them, and for his reef netting skills. J. J. Gilbert, in his 1897 Descriptive Report #2300, described the process of using fish traps (http://riverhistory.ess.washington.edu/tsheets/reports/t2300.pdf, p 4): "Piles are driven from eight to 20 feet apart and a net stretched between them. At the end is a square enclosure with a net all around and closed at the bottom. This net is hoisted to the surface with its catch of fish and the fish are lifted out by means of a dip net, manipulated by means of blocks and windlass." When fish traps were outlawed in Washington in 1934, Henry moved to Oregon to continue with fish traps there. But as Oregon soon after also outlawed the traps, he returned to the San Juans and fishing. He served as a San Juan County commissioner for 27 years. He died in 1959 at the age of 90. Henry's father Louis initially settled in Deer Harbor, the first permanent White settler in western Orcas Island, and was employed by the Hudson's Bay Company to provide meat to Victoria. In its September 11, 1981 meeting, the Washington Board approved the name Cayou Island, Docket 270. The U.S. Board followed later in the year. Another variant was Grass Island (from Washington State Board Files).

Cedar Head Light
See Cypress Head.

Cedarhurst
Located on the northwestern side of Vashon Island, early settlers named it for the trees (Haulman).

Cedrona Bay
A local name for a bay on the Hale Passage side of Fox Island, it is about a mile and a half southeast of Ketners Point.

Cement, Mt.
Located on Waldron Island, it is the 612 foot hill behind Point Disney. The origin of the name is unknown.

Cemetery Island
See Gossip Islands.

Center Island
Located in Lopez Sound off the western side of Decatur Island, it was named because of its location in the center of the sound (Hitchman 42). Peter Grott homesteaded on the south end of Center, and J. L. Abrams purchased the north end. In 1899, C. E. Olney purchased Grott's land and the H. F. Schaldach family bought the entire island in 1926 (McDonald 186, 190).

Center Reef [13a] #2689, 1859, Richards
Located in Spieden Channel, north of San Juan Island, Richards possibly named it for its location in the channel.

Cepeda, Peninsula de
See Point Roberts.

Chadwick Hill
Located on the southeastern end of Lopez Island, it was named for Sampson Chadwick, born in 1847 near Toronto, Canada. Chadwick's father deserted the family, and his mother died when he was ten. Sampson moved to New York as a child and was raised by his uncle. He began a career of repairing watches and at age 17 and joined the Union Army. According to one story of questionable accuracy, after the Civil War, he learned that his father was mining gold on the Fraser River. At age 25, he found his father on an impoverished farm in British Columbia. The elder Chadwick died while his son was still there. According to another story, Chadwick worked in a hotel in San Francisco. Regardless, he worked his way to the Northwest and found a job on San Juan Island as a member of the occupying troops. After the settlement of the Pig War, he moved to Lopez about 1873 and tended sheep for William Keddy, a British sheep farmer, cut cord wood for passing steamers, and hunted deer. His contract with Keddy was to care for 200 sheep on Lopez. As pay, he would receive half of the wool and half of the increase in new lambs. The contract was for a two-year period. He settled on Watmough Bay and built a rough cabin, infrequently walking to the Lopez store for supplies. Along the way, he would kill several deer and take their hides to trade for groceries. On the return trip, he would take the venison home. In 1877, he wed Adelia Bradshaw, daughter of Charles M. Bradshaw. Adelia had moved from Dungeness to Long Island in 1876 to care for the wife of Hezekiah Davis. When Mrs. Davis died, Adelia married Chadwick. Together, they built a new home on the bay and raised six children, three of whom lived past childhood. Chadwick died in 1924 (http://freepages.history.rootsweb.ancestry.com/~lopezislandhistory/8_families_chadwick.html). The U.S. Board on Geographic Names approved the name in 1925 (*Decisions*).

Chambers Creek
Located on the eastern shoreline of Puget Sound, a couple miles north of Steilacoom, it was named after Judge Thomas M. Chambers. He settled on what was originally called Steilacoom Creek and built a sawmill in 1852 (Meany, *Origin* 42; *A History* 93). Inskip referenced this as Chudley River [24].

Chapman Bay
Located in Henderson Inlet immediately north of Woodward Bay, the origin of the name is unknown.

Chapman Cove
Located near the head of Hammersley Inlet, it was originally called Swindall Cove for Mr. Calvan Swindel and John Swindel who settled there in 1855 on a 160 acre donation claim. Even though Swindle died in the late 1860s, his name appeared on an 1879 U.S.C. & G.S. field survey sheet. A Mr. Chapman settled on the estate about 1871 after Swindel (GNIS files for Hylebos Creek).

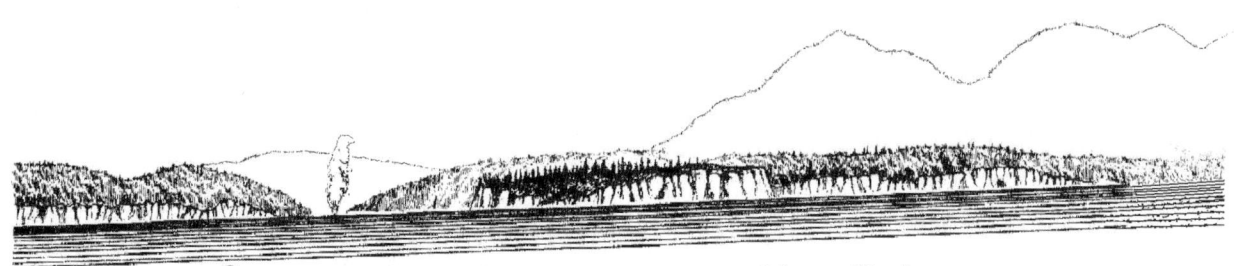

Cape George   Discovery Bay   Protection Island   Mount Chatham

Charles Island [13a] #2689, 1859, Richards
Located off the southwestern side of Lopez Island, Richards honored Capt. James Charles Prevost (TPL website). Prevost was born in Bedhampton, Hampshire, England in 1810. At age 13, Prevost joined the navy, and by 1880 reached the rank of admiral. He performed survey work under Richards on Northwest inland waters. When Richards was recalled to England, Prevost became the Boundary Commissioner for England in negotiations over the Pig War. He died in London in 1891 (http://wikipedia.org).

Charles Point [14a] #2840, 1861, Richards
Located at the northeastern end of Stuart Island, Richards named this for James Charles Prevost (TPL website).

Charleston [23] #6460, 1905
See Bremerton.

Chautauqua
See Ellisport.

Chatham, Mount [18] #654, 1866, U.S. Coast Survey
Located west of Discovery Bay in the Olympics, the U.S. Coast Survey named this in 1855 for the H.M.S. *Chatham*, the consort to Vancouver's *Discovery* (Davidson, *Directory* 119). The 4-gun survey brig, 80 feet in length, was named after the Earl of Chatham, 1st Lord of the Admiralty from 1788-1794. She was launched in Dover in 1788 and departed in 1791 on Vancouver's voyage of exploration. Commanded by Lieutenant William Broughton, he served until 1792 when he returned to England with dispatches from Vancouver. For the balance of the voyage, Peter Puget commanded the *Chatham*. She continued naval service until 1830 when sold in Jamaica.

Chatham Point [13a] #2689, 1859, Richards
See Clark Point.

Chaunceys Island [7a] #145, 1841, Wilkes
See Lopez Island.

Chebaulip
See Tacoma.

Cherry Point [21] #6300, 1895
Located on the eastern mainland three miles south of Birch Bay, M. J. Cherry owned land on the point as early as 1924. The 1915 Pierce County Directory also referenced Joseph Cherry as living in the area (TPL website).

Chetzemoka Park
Located in Port Townsend near the Point Hudson Marina, the name honored a local Indian. Because the pioneers had great difficulty in pronouncing Indian names, they substituted English names. One, Chetzemoka, was known as the Duke of York. His older brother, King George, was the reigning chief among the Clallams. After his brother King George drowned, Chetzemoka was soon recognized as the new leader. Chetzemoka's first wife, See-Hei-Met-Za, was known as Queen Victoria, his second, Chill-lil, was Jenny Lind. Chetzemoka was born about 1808 and greeted the first White settlers at Port Townsend in 1851. His father Lah-Ka-Nim, who they called Lord Nelson, was a Skagit Indian, and his mother Quah-Tum-A-Low was a Clallam. Chetzemoka recalled his father's stories of Vancouver's arrival in 1792. Lah-Ka-Nim, though a boy at the time, had even managed to acquire a knife from one of Vancouver's men. In 1870, Chetzemoka moved to the reservation. With Queen Victoria and Jenny

Lind, he had two sons and four daughters. All of the daughters married White men. The Chetzemoka Park in Port Townsend as well as a bronze plaque near the seventh tee of the Port Townsend Elks Golf Course honor his assistance. Chetzemoka died June 21, 1888 and was buried in the Laurel Grove Cemetery in Port Townsend (*With Pride* 130, 131; McCurdy, *By Juan* 36, 37, 126).

Chibahdehl Rocks [20f] #654, 1853, U.S. Coast Survey
Located two miles east of Cape Flattery, the word is a corruption of the Quillayute Indian word *Chi-chi-a-quil* meaning "standing rocks" (TPL website; Hitchman 45, 46). At the March 8, 1985 meeting of the Washington State Board on Geographic Names, the committee addressed and passed a proposal to change the name from Chibanbehl to Chibahdehl. This resolved the spelling differences between nautical charts and U.S. Forest Service Maps. The U.S. Board followed in 1986 (from Washington State Board Files).

Chicken Rock
Located near Cattle Point, it was the local name for a rock upon which a small boat encountered while loaded with chickens (McDonald, Lucile. "Rabbit-Hunters 'Take Over' Historic Site." *Seattle Times*. Nov. 20, 1960. Magazine Section p 7).

Chico Bay
Located on the southwestern side of Dyes Inlet, it was named in 1889 by B. S. Sparks and honored Chief Chico, who owned the adjacent land. The chief died in 1909 at 105 years of age (Phillips 26; Middleton 38).

Chimacum & **Chimacum Creek** [22] #6450, 1909
Located on the western side of Port Townsend, it was the site of the principle village of the Chimacum Tribe, from which several names arose. The U.S. Board on Geographic Names made the name of the creek and the community official in 1941 and corrected the spelling from Chimikim (GNIS files). The creek flows through the Chimacum Valley and enters Port Townsend at the community of Chimacum. The Chimacums lived from northern Hood Canal to Discovery Bay, but their principal village was at Chimacum Creek near Irondale. The Snohomish who lived near Everett intermarried with the Barkley Sound Indians located on the west coast of Vancouver Island. When visiting each other, they often passed Port Townsend and were generally harassed by the Chimacums, numbering about 400, who robbed them and took slaves. According to one account, around 1822, the combined forces of the Snohomish and Barkley Sound Tribes annihilated all of the Chimacums except for two young girls. One girl was taken prisoner by the Snohomish and the other by the Barclay Sound Indians. Both girls ultimately returned and married Port Townsend men (*With Pride*, 193-195).

Chimacum Portage
Located at the head of Port Townsend, it separated Port Townsend from Oak Bay. It was frequently used as a portage by Indians to avoid the rougher water on the outside of Marrowstone Island. *See* Portage Canal.

China Cove
It is a local name for the cove inside the port marina at Friday Harbor (Soland, Leslie; Oct. 10, 2010 email to author).

Chinom Point [7d] #146, 1841, Wilkes
Located on the eastern side of Hood Canal, about eleven miles south of Seabeck, Wilkes did not include this name in his *Narrative*, but it is shown on his chart where he spelled it Tchinom (Meany, *Origin* 46). In 1927, George Asch (1873-1941) and Dale Asch (1878-1972) homesteaded 113 acres of land including 4,000 feet of beach. Their two children rode horses six miles to Holly to attend primary school. For high school, they rowed a boat north of Holly and caught the school bus to Silverdale. George's eldest son, George, Jr., who was a civil/mechanical engineer, retired to Fawn Island in the entrance to Deer Harbor.

Chinook [9a] #1911, 1849, Kellett
According to Kellett's chart, this is located at Adelma in Discovery Bay. Kellett provided no reason for the name.

Chittendon Locks

Chittenden Locks

Located between the Seattle ship canal and Shilshole Bay, the locks permit transit from fresh water (Lakes Washington and Union) into Puget Sound. Hiram M. Chittenden was born in New York in 1858. After graduation from West Point, he was commissioned as a 2nd Lieutenant in the Army Corps of Engineers. He ultimately rose to Brigadier General in 1910. During the early 1900s, H. M. Chittenden with the Army Corps of Engineers was responsible for construction of Fort Warden behind Point Wilson. He later designed and oversaw the construction of the locks which were completed in 1916. He died in Seattle in 1917 (http://wikipedia.org).

Christensen Cove & Creek

Located halfway down the western side of Vashon Island, it was named after Nels G. Christensen, the founder of the West Pass Transportation Company. He was a steamboat captain and lived on the bay at the mouth of the creek. Christensen was born in Denmark in 1872, the week before Christmas. When he was only six weeks old, his family moved to the United States. By age four, his family settled in Seattle. In 1897, Nels and his brother opened a grocery store at First and Battery. That same year, he married Margaret Baunsgard. In 1902, Margaret's brothers purchased 100 acres of land on the western shore of Vashon Island. Six years later, Nels and Margaret purchased 23 acres of this land. Nels purchased a barge, loaded it with lumber and their family possessions, and pitched a tent on board. A boat towed the barge to Lisabuela in 1908 where the family built a home. Nels commuted to Seattle to continue running the grocery store, but because the local steamboat service proved to be a bit irregular, Nels, along with a neighbor, John Holm, purchased a 60-foot gas launch for $5,000. The boat was named *Virginia Merrell* which they shortened to simply *Virginia*. Their first trip to Seattle was on September 10, 1910. Holm sold his interests to Morris Shain who designed a second boat, *Virginia II*, which Christensen built in his front yard in 1912. Two years later, Nels purchased the steamer *Typhoon* which he renamed *Virginia III*. *Virginia II* and *III* began making daily round trips between Seattle and Tacoma along Colvos Passage which was locally called West Pass. In 1918, the steamer *Tyrus* became *Virginia IV*. In 1922, he built the *Virginia V* on the other side of Colvos Passage at Maplewood. Until 1970, one of *Virginia V's* summer runs was to carry children from Seattle to Camp Sealth on Vashon Island. At its March 14, 1980 meeting, the Washington State Board on Geographic Names selected Christensen over Jod Creek. Apparently no one could remember the origin of Jod or how it even got on a map (from Washington State Board Files).

Christmas Island

See Harnden Island.

Chuckanut Bay [21] #6300, 1895

Located south of Bellingham Bay, in 1791 Eliza named this *Puerto del Socorro* [1] or Port Relief. In 1852, Henry Roeder gave the bay its current name after an old Indian name (Meany, *Origin* 47). Davidson referenced it in the 1889 *Pacific Coast Pilot* (571). He wrote: "This bay is the recession of the eastern shore of Bellingham Bay, and is over two miles long north-northwest and south-southeast, by one mile deep. It has well marked points at the north and south with a large islet close to the northeast of the latter point. This South Point lies north fifty-two degrees east (N.52°E.) three miles from the North Point of Eliza Island. The greater part of the shore-line is sandstone, and the land rises to thirteen hundred feet in half a mile and then drops sheer two hundred feet. The stone is of good quality, and is extensively quarried for building purposes."

Chuckanut Island [21] #6300, 1895
Located south of Bellingham Bay, it took its name from Chuckanut Bay.

Chuckanut Point [21] #6300, 1895
Located south of Bellingham Bay, it took its name from Chuckanut Bay.

Chuckanut Rock [21] #6300, 1895
Located south of Bellingham Bay, it took its name from Chuckanut Bay.

Chuckanut Village
Located south of Bellingham Bay, it took its name from Chuckanut Bay.

Church Island
See Indian Island.

Church Point
It is located on the northern shore of Hammersley Inlet. In November 1881, John Slocum, age 40, operated a logging camp on Hammersley Inlet with his two half brothers. A Squaxin tribal member, Slocum was killed in an accident. His half brothers departed to Olympia for a casket. While they were gone, the body began to stir. Soon, Slocum began talking. He asserted that God had resurrected him to bring a message to the Indian people: to believe in the man named Jesus. Slocum and his followers built a church at what is now known as Church Point. He began to minister to tribal members. Several years later, John became ill. His wife Mary retired for a private prayer. Suddenly, she began shaking all over. Returning to John, she shook over his head and he regained his health. Mary, thus, was known "as the bearer of 'the shake' which is believed to bring healing to those who are physically or spiritually ill." This is one of several stories of the founding of the Indian Shaker Church. The others are similar in nature. In the late 1800s, the President of the United States issued an executive order which removed Church Point from the Slocum family and deeded it to a ship captain. Virtually 100 years later, in June of 1995, the Squaxin Tribe bought back the point (http://www.squaxinislandmuseum.org/index.html?culture/history.html~mlrcContent).

Chudley River [24] #1947, 1849, Inskip
See Chambers Creek.

City of Seattle Rock
Located along the southern shoreline of Guemes Channel about a half mile west of the ferry terminal to Guemes Island, the rock is about 500 feet off the Fidalgo Island shoreline. At low tide, it is nine feet underwater. It is first mentioned in the 1903 *Pacific Coast Pilot* (161). Given the propensity to name rocks after the name of the ship that encountered it, this perhaps was named for the Steamer *City of Seattle*. There were two vessels with that name: a steam ferry built in Portland in 1888 and an Alaska steamship launched in Philadelphia in 1890 (Wright 357, 374; Kline, and Bayless 2, 3, 27, 28).

City Waterway
See Thea Foss Waterway.

Clallam
See Sekiu.

Clallam Bay [8a] #1917, 1847, Kellett
Located on the Strait of Juan de Fuca, it was first named *Ensenada de Rojas* by Quimper in 1790 [1] for José de Rojas, the *Conde de Casa-Rojas*, a Spanish rear-admiral (Meany, Origin 47). Kellett reflected the name Callam on his charts (both [8a] and [9a]), for the Indian tribe. The U.S. Board on Geographic Names altered the spelling to the present in 1896. From then, the name evolved such that today the term Clallam is used to describe the population (including Native Americans) of Clallam County. "Klallam" has been adopted by some of the Salish Indians (e.g., the Lower Elwha Tribe), while others (Port Gamble and Jamestown Tribes) use the spelling "S'Klallam."

Clallam Point [13a] #2689, 1859, Richards
See Diamond Point.

Clallam River
Emptying into Clallam Bay, the river was named for the bay.

Clam Bay
Located on Rich Passage, south of Middle Point, it was likely named because of an abundance of clams.

Clam Island
Located in Miller Bay on Port Madison, this was the local name for a small island that occasionally

poked above the water at low tide. It was named for the prolific number of clams (McDonald, Lucile. "Miller's Bay Ponders Development Plans." *Seattle Times*. Mar. 29, 1964. Magazine Section p 2,3).

Clark Island

Clark Island [7a] #145, 1841, Wilkes
Located in Rosario Strait on the eastern side of Orcas Island, in 1841, Wilkes perhaps honored Midshipman John Clark who died in Perry's Battle of Lake Erie in 1813. Wilkes did not include this name in his *Narrative*, but it is shown on his chart. In 1791, Eliza named the combination of Clark and Barnes Islands as *Islas de Aguayo* after one of names of the Viceroy of New Spain, whose full name was Juan Vincente de Güemes Pacheco de Padilla Horcasitas y Aguayo, Conde de Revilla Gigedo (Meany, *Origin* 48). The May 28, 1896 issue of *The Islander* reported a Mr. Wm. Reilley as living on the island. Today, the 55-acre Clark Island is a marine park.

Clark Point [7a] #145, 1841, Wilkes
Located on the northerly end of Guemes Island, in 1841 Wilkes honored crew member Levin Clark (Meany, *Origin* 48). Wilkes did not include this name in his *Narrative*, but it is shown on his chart. Richards renamed it Chatham Point in 1859 [13a] in honor of the H.M.S. *Chatham*, consort to *Discovery* and George Vancouver. Later Admiralty charts, beginning in 1888 [13h], acknowledged the earlier name by using both names: "Clark or Chatham Point," and then reverted simply to Clark Point [13j] thereafter.

Classet [6] 1792, Vancouver
See Cape Flattery.

Classic
Located in Honeymoon Bay, Holmes Harbor on the eastern side of Whidbey Island, it was the site of a post office and boat landing. The origin is unknown. According to the GNIS files for Honeymoon Bay: "To be noted that the name Classic, still shown at this feature on chart 6450, but not on the new quadrangle, was reported by the 1960 C&GS field party as obsolete. Has not been used in at least 40 years since the former p.o. of that name was closed. The only surviving trace of the former community name is the occasional use of the name Classic Road." Classic Road runs east-west and connects highway 525 to Honeymoon Bay Road. While at one time the name appeared on chart #6450, it was reported by CG&S field officers to be obsolete. The name was removed from the chart and is no longer recognized by the U.S. Board on Geographic Names.

Clements Reef [13a] #2689, 1859, Richards
Located north of Sucia Island, Richards provided no reason for the name.

Cliff Island [14a] #2840, 1861, Richards
Located in Wasp Passage and one of the Wasp Islets, Richards likely named it for its appearance. In 1896, Thomas Paxson quarried a limestone ledge on the island, but it was also occupied the previous year by a Mr. Wakefield and W. Tift (Richardson, *Magic* 69; Lange). In 1895, J. J. Gilbert wrote in his Descriptive Report #2229 (http://riverhistory.ess.washington.edu/tsheets/reports/t2229.pdf, p 11, 12): "Cliff Island was wholly unoccupied until late in 1895 after the survey when the Everett Smelter Co. opened a limestone quarry at the point abreast of Knob Island, and the limestone is being shipped in large quantities to the smelter in Everett." Brush Island was a local name mentioned in the November 21, 1895 issue of *The Islander*: "Mr. W. D. Tift, of Brush Island, was in town Tuesday." The following week, the paper reported that "Mr. T. T. Paxson, of Brush Island, was in town yesterday." Additionally, the paper reported "Mr. A. J. Paxson came over from Brush Island Saturday evening and returned Sunday evening." The February 20, 1896 issue reported: "The tug *Occident* with a scow load of lime rock from the Brush Island quarry, ran onto a reef, near Fussel's place on Decatur island at high tide on Wednesday morning . . ."

Cliff Point
It is located on the western shoreline of Henderson Inlet about a mile from the entrance. The name is perhaps descriptive as the shoreline rises to 100 feet immediately above the water.

Cline Spit
Located west of the Dungeness River on the Strait of Juan de Fuca, it was named for Elliot Henry Cline who arrived in New Dungeness in 1852, a year after the first settlers. The spit is below the bluff where the settlement began and juts out a short distance from the mainland shoreline to the northward. Cline platted the town site in 1865 (Fish, *Tracks* 154; Keeting 1).

Clinton
Located on the eastern side of Whidbey Island on Saratoga Passage, this was the site of the first settlement in south Whidbey. Around 1875, Edward C. Hinman arrived and soon took over the post office established by John Phinney four miles to the north. Hinman named the area for his hometown of Clinton County, Michigan. He built a dock, opened a general store, and cut cord wood for the steamers (Cherry II: 1). Edward's brother Henry arrived a few years later. Henry initially settled at Browns Point (Sandy Point) where he and his wife raised two daughters. Eventually they moved to Clinton (Cherry I: 84). Phinney Ridge in Seattle was named for John Phinney (Hitchman 228).

Cluster Islands
According to McLellan: "Near the north shore of Echo Bay, to the south of Ewing Island and the north arm of Sucia Island, there are a number of knob-shaped islands and reefs called the Cluster Islands, some of which are covered at high tide. The most western member of the Cluster Islands is known as Wiggins Reef. The most eastern member is called Stony Reef." Wiggens and Stony Reefs are not recognized by the U.S. Board on Geographic Names.

Coal Bay
See Colby.

Cod, Cape
The point is located at the southern entrance to Hammersley Inlet. The origin is unknown.

Coffin Rocks
Located near the western entrance of Deception Pass off Sharpe Cove, they may have been named as a burial place for Indians.

Col-see-ed Harbor [7d] #146, 1841, Wilkes; [7k] #152, 1841, Wilkes
See Quilcene Bay.

Colby [23] #6460, 1905
Located on the western shore of Admiralty Inlet, west of Blake Island, there are a couple of versions on the origination of the name. Meany (*Origin* 51) suggested that coal was found on a nearby creek. Thus, the community of Coal Bay was born and later shortened to Colby. However, as there never has been coal in Colby, the second story is more plausible. The name was a corruption of either the name of the Indian chief who camped with his tribe near Colby and Harper or simply the Salish name of the area (Hilbert et. al., 51). William H. Morgan established a store and post office in 1884. He sold out to his brother-in-law, Joseph Squire Grant, Sr. the following year. The Hardings arrived with their 12-year-old daughter Georgeina, in 1887. With no dock, the boat landed at a log float and a young boy ferried passengers to the beach in a rowboat. This boy, Tom Grant, son of Joseph Squire Grant, married the Harding girl in 1898 (Bowen et al., V: 97-102).

Colchester
Located on the western shore of Admiralty Inlet, halfway between Colby and Manchester, the name is a combination of the two (Phillips 29).

Cole Point [24] #1947, 1849, Inskip
Located on the southeastern side of Anderson Island, it was named in 1846 by R. N. Inskip honoring Edmund P. Cole, master of the *Fisgard* (Meany, *Origin* 52).

Columbia Beach
Located on the eastern side of Whidbey Island on Saratoga Passage, E. A. Ramstad honored Everett's Norwegian-American Columbia College (Cherry I: 115). Hitchman (54) suggested it was chosen by early settlers for "Columbia, the gem of the ocean," an early nickname for the U.S.

Colville, Point [13a] #2689, 1859, Richards
Located on the southeastern side of Lopez Island off Rosario Strait, Richards likely honored Andrew W. Colville, a Hudson's Bay Company employee and a company governor from 1852 to 1856 (TPL website).

Colville Island [13a] #2689, 1859, Richards
Located off the southeastern end of Lopez Island, Richards honored Andrew W. Colville, a Hudson's Bay Company employee and a company governor from 1852 to 1856 (TPL website). In 1854, the Coast Survey [11] named this S West Island, Southwest, South west, or S.W. Island, and even continued the name on the 1862 [17] and 1866 charts [18]. According to Davidson: "Off this point [Watmough Head] lie several rocky islets, with deep water among them and a rushing current. The outer one, named South west island, is about 50 feet high, rocky, flat-topped, destitute of bush or tree, narrow, and about one-third of a mile in length, east and west," (*Directory* 128). The Admiralty name endured. The U.S. Government owns the island.

Colvos
The community is located on the western side of Vashon Island, near Point Peter. It was named for the passage (Haulman).

Colvos Passage [7d] #146, 1841, Wilkes; [7g] #155, 1841, Wilkes
Wilkes wrote: ". . . bounded by Vashon Island on the east, and the Indian Peninsula on the west: it is 12 miles in length by half to a mile in width. Throughout its length the water is very deep, with a few places where an anchor can be dropped. The shores are bold, and the largest class of vessels may approach close to them," (*Narrative* 318). Wilkes honored crew member George W. Colvocoresses in 1841. Colvocoresses was born on the Greek island of Scio in 1816. As a young boy of 5, he was taken hostage by the Turks during the siege of Scio. His father was able to pay a ransom, and George was shipped to Baltimore aboard the brig *Margarita*. Educated in Vermont, George entered the Navy in 1832 at the age of sixteen. Eventually promoted to captain, he retired in 1867. In 1872, he was murdered in Bridgeport, Connecticut (Meany, *Origin* 55; Blumenthal, *Charles Wilkes* 156). Locals refer to the passage as West Passage, to differentiate from East Passage on the other side of Vashon Island. West Passage is not recognized by the U.S. Board on Geographic Names.

Colvos Rocks [7d] #146, 1841, Wilkes; [7f] #151, 1841, Wilkes; [7p] #150, 1841, Wilkes
Located three miles north of Port Ludlow, Wilkes named this for crew member George W. Colvocoresses in 1841 (Meany, *Origin* 55).

Command Point
It is located on the western shoreline of Colvos Passage. The origin of the name is unknown. The Salish word for the point was "a small sized net" (Hilbert et. al., 221).

Commencement Bay [7d] #146, 1841, Wilkes
Located north of The Narrows, Tacoma surrounds the bay. Wilkes named it in 1841 because his surveys of our inland water commenced at that location. Wilkes wrote: "On the 15th of May, the *Porpoise* left Nisqually, and anchored the first night near the point where the surveys were to begin, but outside of the Narrows. The first bay at the bottom of Admiralty Sound was termed Commencement Bay," (Wilkes *Narrative* 479). Davidson commented during their early survey activities: "There are no settlements upon it, but in 1857 we found some deserted fishing stations," (Davidson, *Report* 449).

Commencement City
See Tacoma.

Cone Hill [7a] #145, 1841, Wilkes
See Eagle Cliff.

Cone Islets [7a] #145, 1841, Wilkes
Located off the eastern shore of Cypress Island, in 1841 Wilkes likely named them in 1841 for their shape (Wilkes *Narrative* 309).

Constance, Mount
See Fauntleroy Cove.

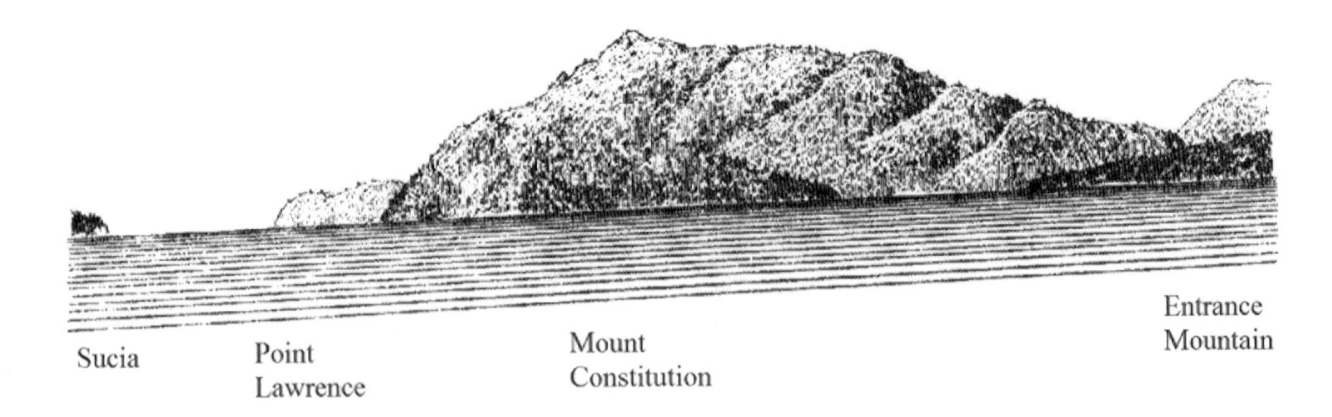

Sucia — Point Lawrence — Mount Constitution — Entrance Mountain

Constitution, Mount [7a] #145, 1841, Wilkes
Located on the eastern side of Orcas Island, in 1841 Wilkes honored the U.S. frigate *Constitution* during the War of 1812 (Meany, *Origin* 175). At 2,409 feet, Mount Constitution is the tallest peak in the San Juans.

Contractors Creek
Located along the western side of Discovery Bay at Contractors Point, the name likely came from the point.

Contractors Point

Contractors Point
Located on the western side of Discovery Bay, it was originally named Carrs Point by Wilkes [7b] in 1841 honoring crew member Lieut. Overton Carr (Meany, *Origin* 39). In 1847, Kellett renamed it Vancouver Point [9a]. An 1890 map of the City of Port Townsend reflected the name of Contractors Point for Beckett Point on the eastern shore, likely an error. According to the table attached to Descriptive Survey #1124 (http://riverhistory.ess.washington.edu/tsheets/reports/t1124.pdf), James Lawson wrote that the local name was Contractors Point. In the GNIS files for Adelma Beach, a surveyor wrote that the point was occupied at one time by a large road-building company and the current name resulted from their presence.

Cook Point [7d] #146, 1841, Wilkes; [7i] #147, 1841, Wilkes
See Arcadia.

Cooks Cove
Located off Guemes Island, west of Southeast Point, the origin of the name is unknown.

Coon Bay
Located in Hood Canal, two miles south of Foulweather Bluff, it was likely named for raccoons.

Coon Hollow
Located two miles north of Rosario in East Sound, Orcas Island, it was likely named for raccoons.

Coon Island
Located southeast of McConnell Island near Wasp Passage, it was likely named for raccoons.

Cooper Point [7d] #146, 1841, Wilkes; [7i] #147, 1841, Wilkes
Located at the tip of the peninsula dividing Eld and Budd Inlets, Wilkes reflected this in 1841 as Point Cooper in his *Narrative* and on one chart [7d] and Cooper Point on the other chart [7i]. He honored crew member John Cooper (Meany, *Origin* 217).

66 ♦ Maritime Place Names - Inland Washington Waters

Cooper Point

The U.S. Board on Geographic Names approved the name over the variant Cowper Point in 1892.

Cooper Point [7d] #146, 1841, Wilkes; [7i] #147, 1841, Wilkes
Located at the tip of the peninsula dividing Eld and Budd Inlets, Wilkes reflected this in 1841 as Point Cooper in his *Narrative* and on one chart [7d] and Cooper Point on the other chart [7i]. He honored crew member John Cooper (Meany, *Origin* 217). The U.S. Board on Geographic Names approved the name over the variant Cowper Point in 1892.

Cooper Point [16b] #602, 1869, Pender
Located on the eastern side of Henry Island, west of Pole Island, it was named by the Admiralty for Lieut. Henry T. M. Cooper, a Royal Marine stationed at Garrison Bay, 1863-1866 (TPL website). The name is neither reflected on current charts nor recognized by the U.S. Board on Geographic Names.

Coopers Point [7h] #154, 1841, Wilkes
Located at the northern end of Herron Island in Case Inlet, Wilkes may have honored crew member John Cooper in 1841 although it is extremely unusual that Wilkes would name two points in the neighborhood for the same man. Ezekiel Cooper also served on the cruise. Wilkes did not include this name in his *Narrative* but shows it on his chart. The name is neither reflected on U.S. charts nor is it recognized by the U.S. Board on Geographic Names.

Cormorant Passage [24] #1947, 1849, Inskip
Located between Ketron Island and the mainland, it was named in 1846 by R. M. Inskip after the H.M.S. Paddle Sloop *Cormorant*, stationed at Fort Nisqually from 1844 to 1850 (Meany, *Origin* 57).

Cornet & **Cornet Bay**
Located off the northern end of Whidbey Island in Deception Pass, the community and the bay were named for John Cornet who settled there with his Indian wife in the early 1860s. In 1876, he was accidentally shot and died (Meany, *Origin* 57).

Cottonwood Island
See Sinclair Island.

Cougar Point
Located on the eastern shoreline of Totten Inlet, the origin of the name is unknown. It is not reflected on current charts.

Cougar Spit
It is located on the eastern shore of Hood Canal, about a mile north of Musqueti Point. It was named for a cougar that was chased by dogs in the early 1900s into Hood Canal, swam across, and exited the water at the spit. In 2005, Brad Lambert, owner of the spit, identified that current charts showed the location incorrectly. The name for that particular location is Mustakmwode. The name of Cougar Spit should be moved 0.8 miles to the north. At its December 1, 2006 meeting, the Washington State Board on Geographic names agreed. The U.S. Board followed early the next year (from Washington State Board Files).

Coulter Creek
The creek flows into the head of Case Inlet. It was named by A. H. Sylvester, a U.S. Forest Supervisor, in honor of the surveyor Waldo Coulter (TPL website).

Richard W. Blumenthal ♦ 67

Coupeville

Coupeville

Coupeville [21] #6300, 1895
Located on the southern shores of Penn Cove, Whidbey Island, Capt. Thomas Coupe sailed through Deception Pass in the *Success* and became the town's earliest settler, filing his claim on November 20, 1851 (Neil 32). Much literature credits Coupe as the first to sail a ship through the pass; perhaps the first reference was Wright (40), who wrote: "While in the coasting trade with the bark *Success*, Captain Coope sailed the vessel up through Deception Pass, a feat never before or since undertaken by a similar vessel without the aid of steam power." However, this credit must go to Wilkes' Commander Cadwalader Ringgold, of the *Porpoise*, 224 tons and eighty-eight feet in length, who transited the pass on June 26, 1841. According to the journal of Acting Master George T. Sinclair: "Got underway about 8 AM & with a light wind from the SSE & on the last of the flood tide, passed thro Deception Passage without the least difficulty. By half past nine we were snug at anchor under Deception Island with broad Pacific once more open to us. Altho Vancouver says that this passage cannot be used & we have used it, yet he is not so far out in his suppositions as would at first appear, but few vessels would venture thro for it is really frightful to look at the passage, when the Tide is at its strength, yet as I have before said, at a proper time of Tide, there is no real danger," (Blumenthal, *Charles Wilkes* 184). Thomas Coupe was born on the Isle of Man in 1818. He arrived in the United States at age twelve and began a career at sea. In 1852, he purchased an interest in the ship *Success* and hauled Northwest lumber to San Francisco. After filing a 320 acre land claim on Whidbey, which comprised the entire eastern portion Coupeville, Coupe sent for his wife Maria and their four children. In 1854, the family built the first frame house in Coupeville which still stands on the bluff at the east end of town. Coupe continued to sail, carrying cargo to San Francisco and even to France. He established a ferry service between Port Townsend and Whidbey Island. Coupe's son, Capt. George M. Coupe, was born in New York in 1849 and came to Whidbey Island with his parents. He piloted ships on Puget Sound for fifty years beginning on a ferry service between Port Townsend and Whidbey Island in the sloops *Mary Ellen* and *Ketereauch*. His father had initially established this service (Wright 185). George died in 1938. The Salish name for the area was "where there are snakes" (Hilbert et. al., 360). John Alexander also arrived on Whidbey Island in 1851 with his wife and three sons, William, fourteen; John Jr., twelve; and Joseph, two. They came from Portland on board the *Exact* with the Denny party. During the wagon train journey west, Alexander's leg became infected from an accident, and near death, he instructed the men (there was no physician) to amputate. They removed it with a carpenter's saw. The Alexanders migrated to Coupeville and found two other families, the Coupes and the Lovejoys. Alexander filed a claim adjacent to the Coupe's, which formed the western portion of the town. Another son, Abram, was born February 12, 1852, the first White child born in Coupeville. Alexander built a blockhouse on his land in 1855. It was moved to its present location in 1930 and still stands next to the historical museum just up from the wharf. Alexander's peg leg ultimately caused his death in 1858. While beachcombing, he broke it in some driftwood. Unable to walk, he crawled home in freezing rain and died from pneumonia four days later. Alexander's widowed wife Francis married Capt. Robert Fay, one of John Alexander's closest friends. They opened an inn together along the waterfront and ran it for years. Later, her son took it over, enlarging it to become the State Hotel. It burned in 1968 and is now the site of the Island County Historical Museum, built in 1989. Capt. Fay was a Government Agent and died in 1872. His wife Frances died in 1902 (Neil 17-19, 32, 33, 36).

Cove
Located on the western side of Vashon Island, the community was likely named for its appearance.

Coveland
See San de Fuca.

Cowlitz Bay [13a] #2689, 1859, Richards
Located on the southwestern side of Waldron Island, it was named after the Hudson's Bay Company barque *Cowlitz* (Meany, *Origin* 59). One of the oldest houses in San Juan County was constructed above Cowlitz bay in the 1860s by John E. Brown. Originally from Ohio, he spent time carrying mail in Alaska before settling on Waldron. He obviously possessed some outstanding carpentry skills and built a very fine cedar log cabin and a barn. He paid Chinese and Indian laborers twenty-five cents a day to dig a ditch a half mile in length and forty feet in depth in places to drain a marshy lake on his property. Once drained, he attempted to burn out some of the stumps and unfortunately caught most of the rich peat soil on fire rendering it almost useless. He died before patenting his homestead (Ludwig 4, 5). Sinclair A. McDonald, from Gainsville, Georgia was Brown's neighbor. He left his wife and children and headed for the California gold rush in 1849. Failing to strike it rich, he prospected on the Fraser River before settling on Waldron. McDonald purchased the Cowan/Oldham claim for $350 on October 10, 1870. Within a few years, he built a log cabin and several outbuildings, one of which was used for the post office. McDonald lived there until 1905 (Ludwig 4, 5). Much of the waterfront in the bay is owned by the Nature Conservancy.

Cowper Point
See Cooper Point.

Coyle
Located on the eastern side of Hood Canal on Fisherman Harbor, it was named for the former resident George Coyle when the post office was opened in 1908 (Meany, *Origin* 60).

Crab Island
Located at the southern end of Lopez Sound, off the peninsula separating Hunter from Mud Bay, the name is likely descriptive. McLellan referenced this as Crab Rocks.

Crabapple Creek
The 1½ mile creek flows into Apple Tree Cove. The name was approved by the Washington State Board on Geographic Names in its May 11, 2007 meeting. The name came from the crabapple trees that grow in the area. The U.S. Board followed later in the year (from Washington State Board Files).

Craft Island
Located on the eastern shoreline of Skagit Bay east of Ika Island, the origin of the name is unknown. In 1962, the U.S. Board on Geographic Names chose the name Craft Island over the variant Delta Rocks, as Craft was in "undisputed local usage."

Crandall Spit
It is located on the western side of March Point. Davidson referenced it in the 1889 *Pacific Coast Pilot* (564). He wrote: "The Northeast point of the entrance is named Crandall Spit, and a *fixed white light* lens lantern is shown at an elevation of eight feet above the water from a white post placed about fifty yards inside the low-water mark." According to the 1910 Skagit County census, the Crandall family lived in the Fidalgo precinct. Headed by Alice, age 57, she had six children ranging from 20 to 33 years of age. Their relationship to Crandall Spit is unknown.

Crane Island [13a] #2689, 1859, Richards
Located between Orcas and Shaw Islands, Walter P. Cadwell settled on the island in 1879 and likely named it for the bird or something that appeared like a crane, for example, a blue heron (McDonald 187). Caldwell operated a small fruit and vegetable farm. He sold in 1906 to J. C. Hammond for $5,200. When Hammond died, his daughter sold it in 1938 to a local theater operator in Bellingham, John Baillargeon.

Crane Point [20g] #647, U.S. Coast Survey
Located on the western side of Indian Island, Wilkes named this Midille Point in 1841 but left no reason for the name. Wilkes did not include this name in his *Narrative*, but it is shown on his chart [7p]. The origin of the current name is likely from the bird.

Crauford Channel [24] #1947, 1849, Inskip
See Pitt Passage.

Striped Peak   Crescent Bay   Olympic Mountains

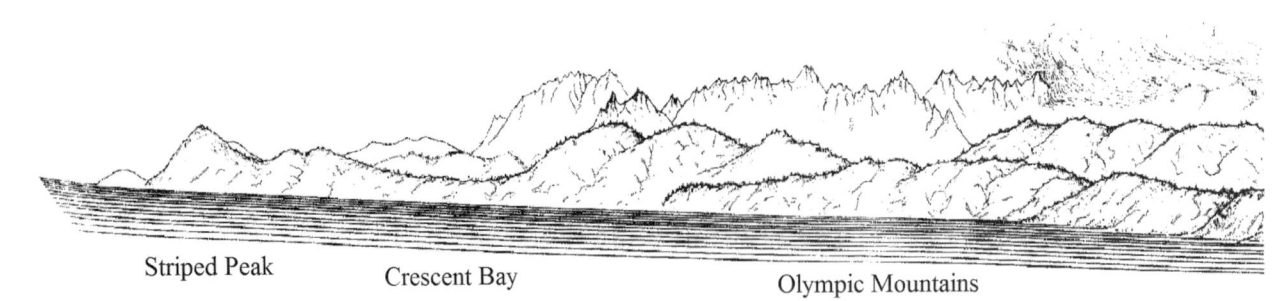

Craven Peninsula [7a] #145, 1841, Wilkes; [7d] #146, 1841, Wilkes; [7p] #150, 1841, Wilkes
Located on Admiralty Inlet, east of Port Townsend, this is a combination of Indian Island and Marrowstone Island. Wilkes named it in 1841 for crew member Thomas T. Craven (Meany, *Origin* 60). Although the name is recognized by the U.S. Board on Geographic Names, it does not appear on current charts.

Craven Rock
Located on the eastern side of Marrowstone Island, the name came from the Craven Peninsula.

Creosote [22] #6450, 1909
See Bill Point.

Crescent, Port [21] #6300, 1895
Located on the Strait of Juan de Fuca 14 miles west of Port Angeles, the name likely came from the bay. The original community hoped for a Union Pacific Railroad terminus. But the 1893 depression put an end to those thoughts. Jim Frank homesteaded along Crescent Bay. At the beginning of the boom, about 1889, he sold the town site to John and Harry Lutz and C. F. Clapp. The developers formed the Port Crescent Improvement Company and platted the town. Later, the Puget Sound Sawmill & Shingle Company began logging in earnest. Booms were towed to Bellingham. The death knell was sounded by about 1916 when the mill moved to Port Angeles. Soon after, the town was abandoned.

Crescent Bay [8a] #1917, 1847, Kellett
Located on the Strait of Juan de Fuca 14 miles west of Port Angeles, Kellett perhaps named it for its appearance.

Crescent Beach
Located at the head of East Sound, it likely was named for its shape.

Crescent Harbor
Located off the easterly side of Whidbey Island, east of Oak Harbor, Wilkes originally named this Duncan's Bay in 1841 [7a], [7e] in honor of an officer who served on the *Saratoga* during the War of 1812. Dr. Richard Lansdale, an early settler in the area, named Crescent Harbor around 1852 for its curved shoreline (Meany, *Origin* 61). The U.S. Board on Geographic Names made it official with the current name in 1910. The first settlers were William and Ruthinda Wallace who arrived in 1851. Ruthinda was the first White woman on the island. Her daughter, Polowna, born in 1851, was the first White child born on the island (Neil 13, 241).

Crescent Head
It is located on the western side of Crescent Bay. In his 1926 survey and Descriptive Report #4182, H. A. Cotton wrote (http://riverhistory.ess.washington.edu/tsheets/reports/t4182.pdf, p.5): "It is recommended that the name 'Crescent Head' be given to the western point of Crescent Bay. This head of land is prominent when viewed from along shore and therefore should be named." The name is not recognized by the U.S. Board on Geographic Names.

Crescent Rock [21] #6300, 1895
Located on the Strait of Juan de Fuca west of Port Angeles, the name likely comes from the bay.

Crockett Lake
Located on the western side of Whidbey Island near Keystone, it was named for the earliest settlers in the neighborhood, Samuel B. and Walter Crockett (Meany, *Origin* 61).

Cromwell
Located on the northern side of Hale Passage, west of Wollochet Bay, the first settlers called it Little Norway after their origin. John B. Cromwell

established the first post office in 1903 and changed the name (*History* I: 58). A railroad worker and real estate agent, Cromwell served as the postmaster of Tacoma in 1899. He died in 1937 (TPL website). East Cromwell formed to the east and in Wollochet Bay. The small community of Bay View formed further into the bay on the western side.

Crowlie, Point [7d] #146, 1841, Wilkes
It is located at the Great Bend in Hood Canal, at the community of Union. Wilkes named it in 1841 for Lieut. Charles E. Crowley who was at the Battle of New Orleans in late 1814 and early 1815 (Meany, *Origin* 217). The name is neither reflected on U.S. charts nor is it recognized by the U.S. Board on Geographic Names. The name is shown on t-sheet #1560b.

Crown Island
See Fortress Island.

Crystal Springs [22] #6450, 1909
Located on the southwestern side of Bainbridge Island, the Ninningers settled first. They sold to the Warren Gazzam family in 1905. When Jack Nibbe left Point White in 1905, Mrs. Gazzam moved the post office into her home. Warren Gazzam was the president of the Kitsap County Transportation Company and constructed a large stone house overlooking Port Orchard. The stone house was later converted to a hotel and vacated in 1939 (Marriott 101). The Salish name for the area was "partly covered" (Hilbert et. al., 226). The origin of the current name is unknown. *See also* Point White.

Crystal Springs Lake
See Gazzam Lake.

Cuesta, Rio [1] 1790, Quimper
See Lyre River.

Culver Point
See Minnesota Reef.

Cultus Bay [19] #662, 1867, U.S. Coast Survey
Located at the southern end of Whidbey Island, it was named for the Chinook word "worthless" (Meany, *Origin* 61). The 26-year-old Robert Bailey from Virginia settled in Cultus Bay in 1852, becoming the first recorded White landowner on the south

Cultus Bay

end of Whidbey. Having lived there and traded with the Indians for a couple of years, he finally filed his claim on September 1, 1852. He and his son both married Snohomish Indian women who wintered at a village called *Digwadsh* on the original sand spit which has now become Sandy Hook. Robert established a trading post and built a home, where he died in 1889. Early locals called it Bailey's Bay. Shortly after Bailey arrived, Zacheus Lewman started a fish business on the other side of the Indian village. The Indians caught the salmon and Lewman packed them in barrels. The company folded within a few years when the Indians were relocated to the Tulalip Indian Reservation. William Jewett homesteaded on land neighboring Bailey's in 1868. When Bailey's daughter Laura reached the age of seventeen in 1889, she married William Jewett. William and Laura's granddaughter lived on the property until 1981. Josiah Collins, a Seattle Fire Chief during the 1889 fire, and a banker named Brownell, started the Collins-Brownell Sportsmen's Paradise in the bay. Joshua Green eventually took over the private hunting club. In the early 1900s, the Sea Products Fertilizer Company erected a plant on the Cultus Bay spit. The owners rendered fish oil from salmon and dogfish. The plant operated until the mid-1950s, leaving, some say, a stink that can still be smelled at low tide! (Cherry I: 57-59; Cherry II: 69-71; Neil 107). Fish oil rendering plants were not the only offenders regarding offensive smells, as canneries had similar problems. The Oct. 12, 1899 issue of *The San Juan Islander* (p 2) eloquently reported on one: "Blaine people are considerably incensed against the cannery companies there for dumping all the fish offal from the canneries into the water where there is not tide enough to carry it away and it is allowed to drift upon the beaches and become a most atrocious stench in the nostrils both of the just and the unjust. …they [the town folk] have a right to demand that the public health shall not be jeopardized nor private property injured and homes rendered almost inhabitable by accumulations of stench-breeding filth that could very easily be daily disposed of at slight expense." Today the Cultus Bay spit is home to the Sandy Hook Yacht Club Estates consisting of homes on a dredged channel.

Cummings Point [7d] #146, 1841, Wilkes
Located on the western side of Hood Canal near the Hamma Hamma River, Wilkes honored crew member W. H. Cummings in 1841 (Wilkes, *Narrative* 322).

Curley Creek
The small creek flows into Admiralty Inlet between South Colby and Harper, east of Blake Island. Charts well into the 1900s reflected the name as Gurley, consistent with its appearance on [19]. However, the Washington State Board on Geographic Names determined in 1996, Docket 359, that the name was a typographical error because of the long-supported local usage of the name Curley. The U.S. Board followed later in the year. It was: "named for Curley, a Suquamish Indian who was famous among the Indians as 'a good man of speech in the Indian language,'" (from Washington State Board Files).

Cushman Point [23] #6460, 1905
See Hunter Point.

Cutts Island
Located on the eastern shoreline of Carr Inlet, Wilkes originally named this Silipo Island in 1841 [7h]. He left no reason for the name. Wilkes did not include this name in his *Narrative*, but it is shown on his chart. Peter Puget named it Crow Island and wrote: "The Tide prevented our making any considerable Progress before Breakfast to which we Stopped on a Small Island about 6 Miles from Last Nights sleeping Place—This Island was called after its only Inhabitants, an astonishing Quantity of

Cutts Island

Crows," (Puget 197). It was named after Richard M. Cutts, a member of the U.S. Coast Survey. In 1877, he did some hydrographic work in Puget Sound (Reese, *Origins* 35). The island, about 500 by 1,000 feet in size, has a 2,000 ft sand spit which is exposed at low tide. It is currently a State Marine Park. Variant names include Dead Man's Island and Dead Mans Island. Consistent with Puget's name, the Salish name for the island was "crows" (Hilbert et. al., 317). On December 10, 1976, the Washington State Board on Geographic Names formalized the name, Docket 213. The dispute was between Deadmans Island and Cutts Island. There was no information in the file regarding Wilkes' original name. The U.S. Board similarly approved Cutts Island in early 1977 (from Washington State Board Files).

Cypress Dome
See Cypress Lake.

Cypress Head
Located on the eastern side of Cypress Island, it appears as a small islet in Bellingham Channel and is connected to Cypress Island by a tombolo. A tombolo is an area of land which is attached to the mainland or another island by a sand spit or bar. A light was placed on the previously unnamed head in 1909. The Boy Scouts purchased 127 acres of land there in the 1930s. Over the years, the head was variously known as Beacon Tombolo, Boy Scout Point, East Point, and Lighthouse Point, as well as Cedar Head Light. In 1992, because of the campground on the Head, the State Department of Natural Resources

Cypress Head

felt it reasonable to name the location as a guide to boaters. The Washington State Board on Geographic Names agreed to the name in 1993, Docket 359; the U.S. Board on Geographic Names followed in 1995 (from Washington State Board Files).

Cypress Island [6] 1792, Vancouver
It is located on the eastern side of Rosario Strait. It was named *San Vincente* by Eliza in 1791, one of the many names of the Viceroy of New Spain (Meany, *Origin* 62). According to Vancouver: "With a tolerably good breeze from the north, we weighed about three in the afternoon, and with a flood tide, turned up into Strawberry bay, where, in about three hours, we anchored in 16 fathoms, fine sandy bottom. This bay is situated on the west side of an island, which, producing an abundance of upright cypress, obtained the name of Cypress Island." He continued: "The island of Cypress is principally composed of high rocky mountains, and steep perpendicular cliffs, which, in the center of Strawberry bay, fall a little back, and the space between the foot of the mountains and the sea-side is occupied by low marshy land, through which are several small runs of mostly excellent water, that find their way into the bay by oozing through the beach," (Vancouver 294, 297). Vancouver thought these trees to be cypress, but they are more likely Rocky Mountain Junipers which are members of the Cypress family, according to Meany (*Origin* 62). Alternatively, Vancouver may have seen lodgepole pine which grows in patches on the island. The tree is easily confused for cypress. The prime example is the 1,000 square mile area known as Cypress Hills in southwestern Saskatchewan. Early fur traders confused the cypress for the lodgepole pine which are prolific there. Settlement came slowly to Cypress Island because of its rugged terrain, poor soil, and minimal flat land. Humphrey P. O'Bryant claimed land on April 12, 1866, but soon relocated to Guemes Island. He might have been followed by Edward Hammond who proved up his Eagle Harbor claim in 1887. He left a cabin built from 12 inch shiplap boards and square nails. Deepwater Bay was home to several large fish pens and the Secret Harbor School, a private school for troubled boys, founded in 1949. In the 1970s, a developer acquired 3,000 of the 5,500 acres on the island and submitted plans for a large housing development, condos, a golf course, and marina. Environmentalists and public pressure halted the project and the state purchased the property. With additional purchases, including the site of the school, by 2005, the state owned 90% of the island. It has officially been designated as an aquatic reserve. The school moved its program to the mainland in 2008 (McDonald, Lucile. "Rugged Cypress Island Stands High." *Seattle Times* Jul. 17, 1960. Magazine Section p 4).

Cypress Lake
Located on Cypress Island, the U.S. Coast Survey referenced it in 1854 [10] (Davidson, *Report* 432). Davidson wrote: "A high white cliff is seen to the south of the harbor [Strawberry Bay], from the shores of which rise rapidly the Lake mountains, to an elevation of 1,525 feet, and among whose peaks

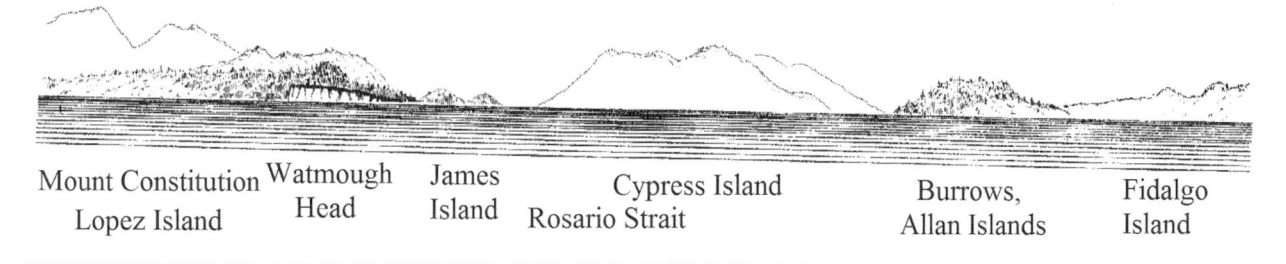

Mount Constitution   Watmough   James   Cypress Island   Burrows,   Fidalgo
Lopez Island   Head   Island   Rosario Strait   Allan Islands   Island

we found two large sheets of fresh water. These peaks are very noticeable from the Strait of Fuca, and being connected by comparatively low ridges of other hills on the island, they present a saddle-like appearance from the southward and westward." McLellan wrote: "The central portion of Cypress Island is elevated and Rocky. It is composed of a group of rock domes which merge into each other. The highest of these, known as Cypress Dome, is located about a mile to the east of Tide Point and has an elevation of 1530 feet." According to the Washington State Board on Geographic Names file on Cypress Lake, the peak referenced above is actually 1,530 feet in height and is called Cypress Dome. The lake was previously known as Phebe Lake, Phoebe Lake, Big Lake, The Lake, and Clear Lake, but there is no information on the source of these names. As Cypress Lake was most commonly used by locals, the State Board chose it as the official name in 1993, Docket 359. The U.S. Board on Geographic Names followed in 1995 (from Washington State Board Files).

Cypress Reef [13b] #2689, 1861, Richards
Located north of Cypress Island, Richards likely named it for the island.

Cypress Rock
See Towhead Island.

Dabob Bay
Located in the northwestern portion of Hood Canal, Wilkes originally named this Dabop Bay in 1841 [7d]. He left no reason for the name (Meany, *Origin* 62). Bright (130) indicated that *Dabob* was a Twana Indian name but the meaning was unknown. In 1941, the U.S. Board on Geographic Names applied the local Dabob Bay to both the bay and community over Wilkes' name. According to the GNIS files, the name Dabob first appeared on a 1910 Map of Puget Sound by Anderson Map Company. However, Dabop continued to be used and appeared as late as the 1934 *Pacific Coast Pilot* (264). The 1942 *Pilot* (343) reflected the current name.

Dabop Bay [7d] #146, 1841, Wilkes
See Dabob Bay.

Dadah Point [7d] #146, 1841, Wilkes
Located on the eastern side of Hood Canal, about a mile south of Dewatto Bay, Wilkes left no reason for the name (Meany, *Origin* 62). Wilkes did not include this name in his *Narrative*, but it is shown on his chart. While it is difficult to tell, this may be today's Long Point.

Daisy Bluff [7b] #148, 1841, Wilkes; [7n] #149, 1841, Wilkes
Located on the western side of Protection Island, Wilkes named it in 1841, likely for the flower. Wilkes did not include this name in his *Narrative*, but it is shown on his chart. The name is neither reflected on current charts nor recognized by the U.S. Board on Geographic Names.

Dalco, Point [7g] #155, 1841, Wilkes
Located on the southeastern side of Vashon Island, Wilkes left no reason for the 1841 name (Meany, *Origin* 62). The U.S. Coast Survey reflected it as Dales Point on [19].

Dalco Passage [23] #6460, 1905
Located between the southeastern side of Vashon Island and Point Defiance, it was reflected in Wilkes' *Narrative* but not his charts. He left no reason for the name (Meany, *Origin* 62).

Dales Point [19] #662, 1867, U.S. Coast Survey
See Point Dalco.

Dallas, Mount [13a] #2689, 1859, Richards
Located at the western side of San Juan Island, Richards honored Alexander Grant Dallas, Governor of the Hudson's Bay Company west of the Rockies. Dallas was born in British Guyana in 1816. He married Jane Douglas, the second daughter of Chief Factor and ultimately Governor of Vancouver Island, James Douglas. Dallas represented the Company in Western Canada from 1857-1861 and gradually took over from his father-in-law. He was involved in the boundary dispute with the United States. He returned to Scotland in 1864 and continued as a Company advisor until 1866. He died in 1882 at age 66 (Walbran 129). At 1,086 feet, Mount Dallas is the tallest peak on San Juan Island.

Dallas Bank [17] #27, 1862, U.S. Coast Survey
Located off Protection Island, Davidson reported that the U.S. Coast Survey named it (*Directory* 119) for Alexander Grant Dallas (Hitchman 64).

Damrock Point
See Rocky Point.

Dana Passage [7d] #146, 1841, Wilkes; [7i] #147, 1841, Wilkes
Located off the southern end of Harstine Island in Puget Sound, Wilkes honored crew member James Dwight Dana in 1841 (Meany, *Origin* 68). Dana was born in Utica, NY in 1813. Schooled at Yale, he taught there for a short time before the Wilkes expedition. He was Wilkes' geologist, mineralogist, and zoologist on the voyage. At the end of the voyage, he returned to New Haven and spent part of the following 13 years preparing reports of his explorations. He married Henrietta Frances Silliman, the daughter of his professor and mentor. In 1850, he was appointed as Professor Silliman's successor as Professor of Natural History and Geology at Yale College. He held the position until 1892. He died in 1895.

Danger Rock
It is located on the eastern side of San Juan Island, just northeast of Pear Point. The name is likely for the hazard to navigation that it presents.

Danger Rock [13a] #2689, 1859, Richards
Located off the southern end of Waldron Island, it was named apparently because of the difficulties navigating around it, particularly in a becalmed sailing vessel.

Danger Shoal [13a] #2689, 1859, Richards
Located in Spieden Channel, north of San Juan Island, Richards named it presumably for its danger to navigation.

Darlington
Located between Everett and Mukilteo, it was named for D. G. Darling who settled near Marysville in 1901 and raised chickens (TPL website).

Dash Point [23] #6460, 1905
Located on the eastern shoreline north of Tacoma, early Indians inhabited the surrounding area. Settlers began purchasing the land in the early 1900s. Cabins and tents were erected on the beachfront for vacationing Tacoma settlers. James and Linna Churchill, the first permanent residents in 1907, ran a store and dance hall. Churchill was a real estate agent, justice of the peace, and mayor of the point.

He established the post office in 1912. Richard P. Milne built the first house on the point in 1907. He worked for the *Tacoma Ledger* (*History* I: 56; http://risingphoenixds.org/history_dash.php). The U.S. Board on Geographic Names approved the name for the community in 1959 over the variants including Caledonia and Olympic Heights.

Davidson Rock [13a] #2689, 1859, Richards
Located off the southeastern end of Lopez Island, Richards honored George Davidson. The U.S. Coast Survey discovered and named the rock Entrance Rock in 1854 (Davidson, *Directory* 128). Entrance Rock was not reflected on any chart until 1862 [17], but the U.S. Coast Survey changed it to Davidson Rock on their 1866 chart [18]. According to Davidson: "S. 83° E from it [Colville Island], at a distance of half a mile, lies Entrance Rock, possibly bare at the lowest tides. A patch of kelp exists upon and around it, but the kelp is generally run under the surface of the water by the strength of the current. We discovered this rock in 1854," (*Report* 430, 431).

Davila [3] 1791, Eliza
See Point Angelos.

Davis Bay [13a] #2689, 1859, Richards
See Shoal Bight.

Davis Bay
It is located off the southwestern side of Lopez Island. Hezekiah Davis was born in 1802 near Niagara Falls. When old enough, he ran the family logging camp and sawmill. He married Katerine Uline in 1823 in Ontario, Canada. Two of their five sons, Alonzo and Clark, headed west in the early days. Alonzo returned to Ontario in 1853 and described the land in the Northwest, ultimately convincing his father to sell out and move west, although it took seven years. In 1860, the family left Ontario, worked their way west, and landed at Dungeness where they secured a farm. Hezekiah worked as a scaler at the Port Discovery mill and Katherine taught school. Their 4th child, Clark, squatted on land on the southwestern side of Lopez Island, intending to claim it. But even though he built a small cabin, he didn't remain. James, Hezekiah's 5th child, married Amelia Culver in 1864.

In 1869, they settled on Clark's land in Davis Bay and filed a homestead claim on it. James imported cattle from Texas and supplied beef to the solders at English Camp. Later, he raised Percheron horses and ran a dairy. In 1902, James and Amelia sold the homestead to James Ernest Davis, the first White boy born on the island and James and Amelia's 5th child. James and Amelia retired and moved to Victoria. By then the homestead occupied 210 acres. A portion of the land was also deeded to another son, Herbert and his wife Mary. The couple married in 1897. Herbert was the Master of the steam tug *Roche Harbor*; Mary was the daughter of William Crook who owned English Camp. In 1907, they returned and purchased a home in Port Stanley. Herbert died in the 1930s; Mary was killed in an automobile accident near Garrison Bay in 1959 (*see also* English Camp). It is unclear if Davis Bay was named for Clark, or more likely, James and Amelia. But it certainly was named for a member of the Davis family (McDonald, Lucile. "The Pioneer Davis Family of Lopez Island." *Seattle Times*. Mar. 6, 1960. Magazine Section p 8).

Davis Point
Located on the southwestern side of Lopez Island, it was named for the Davis family. The local name was Jack Sherer's Point for the Englishman John Sherer who squatted there for 25 years.

Davis Slough
Located at the northern end of Port Susan, it was named for Ruben J. Davis who settled in Utsalady on Camano Island in 1858 (Joergenson XVI).

Davison Head
Located on the northern end of San Juan Island along Spieden Channel, it was named for the first landowner, A. W. Davison. According to Wood (89), it first appeared on U.S. chart #6381 in 1901. It also appeared on the 1921 Admiralty chart [16c].

Day Lake
It is a small lake southeast of Buck Mountain on Orcas Island. In 1927, McLellan wrote: "Buck Lake, Killebrews Lake, and the Twin Lakes also contain a considerable volume of water. The large bogs occurring on Mount Constitution Range and in other localities in the map-area are capable of retaining a remarkably large volume of water. The water derived from the relatively heavy precipitation which falls on Mount Constitution Range is naturally conserved so efficiently that numerous streams issue from all sides of the range at all seasons of the year. Orcas Island is abundantly supplied with water." It was named after Oscar Day who settled there (Lange).

Days Island [7d] #146, 1841, Wilkes
Located just south of The Narrows, Wilkes honored crew member Stephen W. Days in 1841. Wilkes' naming method is apparent here as he named the adjacent Fox Island for assistant surgeon J. L. Fox. Days was a hospital steward (Meany, *Origin* 64). The Salish name for the island was "itching back" (Hilbert et. al., 326). The U.S. Board on Geographic Names approved the name over the variant Day Island in 1962 (GNIS files).

Dead Mans Island
See Treasure Island.

Dead Mans Island
See Cutts Island.

Dead Mans Point
See Skiou Point.

Deadman Bay
Located off the southern end of Guemes Island west of Cooks Cove, the origin of the name is unknown.

Deadman Bay [13h] #2689, 1888
Located on the western side of San Juan Island just south of Bellevue Point, Meany (*Origin* 69) claimed that it was the location of the first White grave on the island. Wood (90) stated that it was the location where a man's body had washed ashore. Alternatively, another longtime resident recalled that a Chinese cook had murdered another man with a knife at that location.

Deadman Island
Located off Davis Point on the southwestern side of Lopez Island, today it is a National Wildlife Refuge owned by the Nature Conservancy. The origin of the name is unknown. The U.S. Board on Geographic Names approved the name in 1925. According to the GNIS files, the name was reported by McLellan. A variation was Dead Man Island.

Deadman Island

It is located on the southwestern end of Fidalgo Island in Skagit Bay, a mile north of the southern entrance to the Swinomish Channel. With its smaller neighbor, Little Deadman Island, both were originally named Tokano Islets [7e] by Wilkes in 1841. Wilkes did not include this name in his *Narrative*, but it is shown on his chart. He left no reason for the name. In 1908, USC&GS t-sheet #2856 listed the two islands as Tonkon. On some charts, all three names can be found. The U.S. Board on Geographic Names addressed the multiple names in 1960. In their evaluation, they found that Deadman was used on the 1943 and 1951 USGS Deception Pass quadrangle maps, but Tonkon was used on chart #6376 since it was first issued in 1945. However, since Deadman and Little Deadman were in local use and residents did not use the name Tonkon, the U.S. Board opted for the Deadman/Little Deadman names. The names came from the fact that both islands were used as Indian burial grounds (GNIS files).

Deans Spit
See Samish Island.

Decatur
Located on the western side of Decatur Island, the community was named for the island (Meany, *Origin* 64). It was spelled Decautur on a topographic map, perhaps the only instance of this spelling. Accordingly, the Washington State Board on Geographic Names corrected the spelling in their March 13, 1995 meeting (from Washington State Board Files).

Decatur Head

Decatur Head
Located on the eastern side of Decatur Island, it was originally named Round Head on [13d]. The current name comes from the name of the island.

Decatur Island [7a] #145, 1841, Wilkes
Located to the east of Lopez Island and south of Blakely Island, in 1841 Wilkes honored Capt. Stephen Decatur, U.S.N. Decatur was born in Maryland in 1779 and raised in Philadelphia. He entered the navy at age 19 and rapidly advanced. Noted for his heroism during the Barbary Wars and the War of 1812, he was at age 25 the youngest man to reach the rank of captain in U.S. naval history. Decatur was killed in a duel with Commodore Barron on March 22, 1820. His second was his good friend Commodore William Bainbridge (Meany, *Origin* 64, 65). By 1870, there were only a few settlers on Decatur Island, including John P. Reed (Reads Bay) and his Indian wife Mary, Edward Jensen, H. Bockman from Germany, and Benjamin Smith from New York. Reed built the first home on the island in the early 1870s; it became the election precinct for both Blakely and Decatur Islands. *See also* Reads Bay.

Decatur Reef [22] #6450, 1909
Located off the southeastern end of Bainbridge Island, the reef was named for the U.S. sloop-of-war *Decatur* which struck the reef in 1855. The ship, named after Stephen Decatur, was defending Seattle during the 1855-1856 Indian Wars. The tide refloated the ship early the following morning (Pelly 22). Davidson mentioned the name of the reef but did not identify who named it (Davidson, *Report* 447).

Deception
See Dewey.

Deception Island [13a] #2689, 1859, Richards
Located outside (west) of Deception Pass, Wilkes originally named this *Ketslum* Islet [7a] in 1841. According to Hale (574), *Ketslum* is an Iakon Indian term meaning "people." The family inhabited the Oregon Coast; the particular language observed by Hale was the lower Killamuk. Davidson included a footnote (*Directory* 128) to indicate that the U.S. Coast Survey named the island in 1854.

Deception Pass

Deception Pass [6] 1792, Vancouver
Located between Fidalgo and Whidbey Islands, the pass was originally named *Boca de Flon* in 1790 by Manuel Quimper [1]. While the Spanish did not explore it, they saw the channel from a distance (Meany, *Origin* 65; Wagner 111). Joseph Whidbey explored the area around Whidbey Island for Vancouver in 1792. When Whidbey reached the northern end of Saratoga Passage (along the eastern shores of Whidbey Island) he encountered a waterway, according to Vancouver: ". . . where it then ceased to be navigable for vessels of any burthen, in consequence of the rocks and overfalls from 3 to 20 fathoms deep, and a very irregular and disagreeable tide. On meeting these impediments, the party returned . . ." (Vancouver 287). On this excursion, Whidbey failed to discover Deception Pass. Several days later, Vancouver dispatched Whidbey to explore the western coastline of Whidbey Island. The small boats entered Deception Pass, and it was not long before Whidbey determined that he was exploring old ground. Upon reporting back, Vancouver felt he was "deceived," hence the name. Recognizing Whidbey's accomplishment, Vancouver honored him with the name of the island. Davidson said (*Report* 431): "On the eastern side of the entrance [of Rosario Strait] is a small wooded islet called Deception island, at the mouth of Deception pass, an intricate and very narrow 3-fathom channel, 3 miles long, running between the north end of Whidbey island and the south end of Fidalgo island. In 1841 the United States brig *Bainbridge* passed through it from the eastward. It is the *Boca de Flon* of Quimper, 1790, but is now known only by the apt designation given above." Davidson erred above. It was not the *Bainbridge*; it was the U.S.S. *Porpoise* commanded by Lieut. Cadwalader Ringgold, part of the Wilkes Expedition. This error was continued in the 1862 *Directory*. Of this excursion, Wilkes wrote in 1841: "The brig moved, on the 18th of June, to the northern outlet of Possession Sound, through Deception Passage. This was not believed by Vancouver to afford a passage for vessels; but, although narrow, it is feasible for those of small size," (Wilkes, *Narrative* 482). The Salish name for the pass was "dangerous" (Hilbert et. al., 349).

Deep Bay
See Fox Cove.

Deepwater Bay

Deepwater Bay [13a] #2689, 1859, Richards
Located off the eastern side of Cypress Island, Richards perhaps named it for the depths found.

78 ◆ Maritime Place Names - Inland Washington Waters

Deepwater Bay
See Inati Bay.

Deepwater Point
Located on the northern shoreline of Totten Inlet opposite Burns Cove, the origin of the name is unknown.

Deer Creek
See Rendsland Creek.

Deer Harbor

Deer Harbor [13a] #2689, 1859, Richards
An indent into the far southwestern side of Orcas Island, both the harbor and community were named for the abundance of deer in the area. According to Lieut. R. C. Mayne: "Deer abound more in Orcas than any of the other islands. During our stay, upwards of thirty were shot," (Lange). In 1859 the Hudson's Bay Company sent four deer hunters to Orcas Island to supply meat to Victoria. Two, William Bradshaw and Louis Cayou, age twenty-six, from Kentucky, settled in the harbor. Both married Indian women. Cayou and his wife, Jennie, age fourteen, raised a large family. One son, Henry, lived in the islands for ninety years (*see* Cayou Island). J. T. Stroud established the first post office and a store in Deer Harbor in 1893. He married Mary A. Cobble of Tennessee and they raised four girls (McDonald 81). The Cayou Quay Marina is located at the northwestern side of the harbor.

Deer Harbor
It is located at the northern entrance to Little Skookum Inlet off Totten Inlet. The name is likely from the animals in the area.

Deer Lagoon

Deer Lagoon [19] #662, 1867, U.S. Coast Survey
Located at the southern end of Whidbey Island off Useless Bay, it was named by the U.S. Coast Survey likely for the deer in the neighborhood (Davidson, *Report* 444). South Whidbey's second permanent settler, Edward Oliver, arrived in 1858. Oliver hailed from Virginia, and at age twenty-eight he married Melvina Sooy. Together they raised four children. He logged on Deer Lagoon and homesteaded the land to the west. The small lake on the west side of Useless Bay was named after Oliver. Melvina died in 1886. Oliver remarried the following year to an Indian Princess, Goh-toh-litsa or Jane Johnson, the widow of William T. Johnson. They raised six additional children. In 1906, he sold twenty-five acres of land to William and Christine Dow whose ten children spent much time playing with the Oliver's children (Neil 108; Cherry I: 62, 63; Cherry II: 138).

Deer Point [13a] #2689, 1859, Richards
Located on the southeastern side of Orcas Island, it was likely named for the local deer.

Defiance, Point [7d] #146, 1841, Wilkes; [7g] #155, 1841, Wilkes
Located west of Tacoma at the eastern entrance to The Narrows, Wilkes named this in 1841 for the

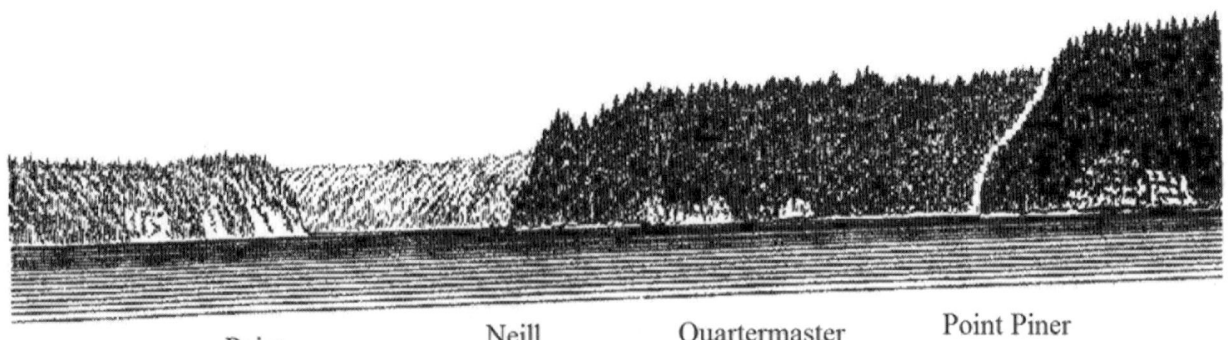

Point Defiance   Neill Point   Quartermaster Harbor   Point Piner

protection provided to southern Puget Sound. Wilkes wrote: "This narrow pass [The Narrows] seems as if its natural facilities intended by nature to afford every means for its perfect defense," (*Narrative* 304). The Salish name for the point was "closed face" referring to the fact that the point runs almost to the opposite shore (Hilbert et. al., 327).

Delacombe Point [16b] #602, 1869, Pender
Located on San Juan Island on the eastern side of Mosquito Pass at the southern entrance to Garrison and Westcott Bays, Richards named it for Capt. William A. Delacombe who replaced Capt. George Bazalgette as the Commander of the Royal Marines in English Camp in 1867 (*English Camp* 13). Commissioned as a 2nd lieutenant in 1850, Delacombe was promoted to captain in 1862. He moved to English Camp five years later with his wife and three children. He returned to Victoria in 1872 and then to England the following year. He was promoted to major in 1875, and then lieutenant colonel upon his retirement in 1876. He died in 1902 (Lange).

Delano Beach
Located on the western side of Carr Inlet, George Delano and his wife built a hotel there in 1891 (Reese, *Origins* 36).

Delta Rocks
See Craft Island.

Demock, Point [7a] #145, 1841, Wilkes
See Rocky Point.

Dennis Shoal [7a] #145, 1841, Wilkes
Located south of Burrows and Allan Islands, Wilkes provided no reason for this 1841 name. Wilkes did not include this name in his *Narrative*, but it is shown on his chart. The U.S. Coast Survey called it Denis Rocks on [10], [11], [17] and [18]. Richards on [13a] and subsequent Admiralty charts maintained Wilkes' name and spelling, a convention which endured on later U.S. charts.

Des Moines
Located on the eastern shoreline of Admiralty Inlet, south of Seattle, the earliest settler was John Moore who homesteaded 154 acres along the water in 1867. Moore went insane and in 1879 was committed to an asylum. Fountain O. Chezum later acquired his land. Chezum sold it in 1889 to F. A. Blasher. Also in 1889, John W. Kleeb and Orin Watts Barlow platted the town site. When they acquired Blasher's land, they named the community after his home town in Iowa. By 1890, Des Moines was home to several hotels, a chair factory, a tin factory, a boat yard, a school, churches, numerous shingle and lumber mills, and had a population of 216. The Panic of 1893 nearly destroyed the community. It again recovered and by 1920 the population reached 751. Ten years later it was 2,000 (http://www.historylink.org).

Despond, Bay of [23] #6460, 1905
See Jarrell Cove.

Detroit
See Grapeview.

Devereaux Lake
Located between the end of Hood Canal (Lynch Cove) and Case Inlet (Allyn), Wilkes reflected this as Kellums Lake [7d] on his chart honoring crew member John Kellum. Wilkes did not include this name in his *Narrative*, but it is shown on his chart. The origin of the current name is unknown.

Devils Head [23] #6460, 1905
Located on the southern end of the Indian Peninsula, on the western shore of Drayton Passage, Wilkes named it Park Point in 1841 [7i] honoring crew member David Park. Wilkes did not include this name in his *Narrative*, but it is shown on his chart. In 1846, Inskip named it Moore Bluff [24] for one of ". . . those young gentlemen who were most forward in assisting me in the work," (Meany, *Origin* 68). Davidson referenced it (1889 *Pacific Coast Pilot*, 625), writing: "This is a bluff about eighty feet above the water, and covered with trees that reach a height of 100 feet. There are trees under the bluff down to the very narrow sand beach." Davidson did not indicate that it was named by the U.S. Coast Survey.

Dewatto Bay
See Dewatto River.

Dewatto River
Located on the eastern side of Hood Canal, the Indians called it *Du-a-ta* for the location where evil spirits come out of the Earth (Meany, *Origin* 69). The U.S. Board on Geographic Names addressed a creek vs. river issue and adopted the current name in 1961. The name also gave rise to Dewatto Bay and the community of Dewatto. While the locals logged the area for a number of years, Dewatto was not settled until Jack Wilson, Alexander Dillman, and their Indian wives arrived in the 1870s. In 1883, John Green settled at the head of the bay. Six years later, the Pfundt family arrived. Christian Frederick Pfundt, born in Germany in 1848, married Catherin Jennewier in St. Louis in 1876. They migrated to Tacoma in 1885 and then to Dewatto in 1889 where they homesteaded 160 acres two miles south of the bay. Henry Fletcher, his wife, and their seven children joined Pfundt. The sternwheeler *Josephine* transported the group to Dewatto and landed in what was reported as four feet of snow. They found their cabin, previously built, with a stove-in roof from the heavy snow load. The group moved into a tent and rebuilt the cabin, living there for the next two years. Fletcher soon moved his family across Hood Canal to Lilliwaup and in 1896 to the Hoh River (Bowen et al., IV: 66; Eells 26).

Dewey
Located at the northeast end of Deception Pass on Fidalgo Island, the community was originally named Deception from its proximity to the pass. In 1889, F. J. Carlyle and George Loucke platted it as Fidalgo City. After the Spanish American War, the community was renamed Dewey which honored the hero of the 1898 battle of Manila Bay during the Spanish-American War (Meany, *Origin* 69). In 1976, the USGS identified a map where the community of Gibraltar was incorrectly placed. The proponent recommended replacing the name with Dewey. The Washington State Board on Geographic Names agreed with the suggestion in its December 10, 1976 meeting, Docket 211; the U.S. Board on Geographic Names followed in early 1977 (from Washington State Board Files).

De Wolf Bight
Located on the Nisqually Reach, the origin of the name is unknown. This is an unusual name. There was a Samuel J. De Wolf who was a part of our Northwest history and perhaps the bight was named for him. De Wolf was the master aboard the *Brother Jonathan* which carried supplies and passengers between Northwest ports and San Francisco. Deeply overloaded, she departed San Francisco in the summer of 1865 and wallowed northward in a heavy gale. On the northern California Coast, unable to make headway, she turned around and headed for Crescent City to anchor in calmer water and wait out the storm. Unfortunately she struck a rock. The description provided by Wright (132, 133) came from Jacob Yates, the quartermaster on watch. "We ran till 1:50, when she struck with great force, knocking the passengers down and starting the deck planks. The captain stopped and backed her, but could not move the vessel an inch. She rolled about five minutes, then gave a tremendous thump, and part of the keel came up alongside. By that time the

wind and sea had slewed her around until her head came to the sea, and she worked off a little. Then the foremast went through the bottom until the yard rested on the deck. Captain De Wolf ordered every one to look to his own safety, and said that he would do the best he could for all. The greatest confusion reigned on board. The steamer was poorly equipped with life-saving apparatus, and the helplessness of the passengers increased when the nature of the injuries received became apparent. The vessel was impaled on a hidden ledge, and a jagged point had pierced the hull and held her so that all efforts to back off were futile. The sea was beating heavily on the port quarter, and the vessel veered around until she came head to the wind. The obstruction on which she had lodged must have been wedge-shaped, as in swinging, the bottom of the ship burst open and the foremast skipped down through the opening." Only 19 survived out of nearly 200 passengers, one of whom was Victor Smith (*see also* Port Angeles).

Diamond Hill [13a] #2689, 1859, Richards
Located at the southwestern entrance to East Sound, Richards left no reason for the name of the 1,020 foot hill. According to the November 25, 1897 issue of *The Islander* (p 3): "If a hoarse horse laugh has any effect on feeble-minded persons, no doubt little work will be done on Diamond mountain looking for a diamond lead. The report that an aged Indian found a diamond there a great many years ago is discredited by well-informed people. Old timers prospected it thoroughly during the Fraser river rush." Perhaps the rumor gave rise to the name.

Diamond Lake
Located on Diamond Hill, it was originally called Martin's Lake after Edward Martin of West Sound. He had a mining claim nearby (Lange).

Diamond Point [13a] #2689, 1859, Richards
Located at the southwestern entrance to East Sound, Richards named both the hill and the point.

Diamond Point
Located on the western entrance to Discovery Bay, Wilkes named it North Bluff [7b], [7n] in 1841 for crew member James North. Kellett renamed it Challam Point in 1849 [9a], but Richards corrected the spelling to Clallam in 1859 [13a] (Meany, *Origin*

Diamond Point

47). The U.S. Coast Survey maintained that name on [19] but spelled it in the 1889 *Pacific Coast Pilot* (534) as both Clallam and Challam. It was changed to Diamond Point by a 1941 decision of the U.S. Board on Geographic Names. Although there was a marine hospital in Port Townsend, in the 1870s a separate "pest-house was situated in the dense woods about two miles west of town [Port Townsend]. Here the unfortunate patient was kept under the care of a volunteer nurse, usually an old sailor, and a doctor visited the sufferer when he could spare the time," (McCurdy, *By Juan* 147). Unfortunately, because of a lack of care, many died. In 1878, Congress passed the National Quarantine Act which prohibited ships from bringing infectious diseases into the United States. The intent of the station was to provide an isolation hospital for passengers found suffering from an infectious disease or who were suspected of carrying one. Among other diseases, the list included influenza, cholera, malaria, smallpox, yellow fever, diphtheria, and leprosy. On June 13, 1893, Congress appropriated funds for a quarantine facility to be located on Diamond Point. The federal government purchased 156 acres of private land at the point and began building. The first structures, a wharf and three hospital buildings, were completed and the facility opened by year's end. The following year, a disinfection plant, a warehouse, and support buildings were constructed. It ultimately grew to 27 buildings during its 43 years of operation, including a detention facility, the surgeon's house, attendants' houses, disinfecting house, water storage facilities, etc. All vessels arriving from foreign ports were required to stop. Until 1899, when a new facility was built on the Columbia River, it handled ships on the entire Oregon/Washington Coast. In 1936, a new quarantine station opened at Point Hudson and Diamond Point closed. The marine hospital in Port Townsend had already moved from Port Townsend to Beacon Hill in Seattle in 1933. Title to Diamond Point passed through a number of owners until 1956 when the 56 acre spit was acquired by the Diamond Point Land Company which later developed the real estate (McCurdy, *By Juan* 100, 101; Roe 10-13). Even today, some of the old buildings remain, including the hospital and nurses quarters which are now private residences. In 1989, the Surgeon's House, also a private residence, was placed on the National Register of Historic Places.

Dickenson Point [7d] #146, 1841, Wilkes; [7i] #147, 1841, Wilkes

There are two points on the peninsula separating Budd and Henderson Inlets. According to Wilkes' charts [7i], he named the easternmost Point Dickenson in 1841. The spelling on [7d] is the same, but Wilkes placed the name such that it is unclear which point he intended to name. There is some controversy with the spelling and for whom the point is named. It could have been for the Secretary of the Navy Mahon Dickerson and Wilkes misspelled it on both charts, or it could have been for crew member Thomas Dickenson. Chart #6460 [23], 1905, reflects the name on the westernmost point and appears to spell it Dickenson. Wilkes did not include this name in his *Narrative*, only on his charts (Meany, *Origin* 69). The Salish name for the point was "where they jump" (Hilbert et. al., 310). The U.S. Board on Geographic Names settled on the current name in 1838 by throwing out Dickerson Point.

Dickerson Peninsula [7a] #145, 1841, Wilkes; [7d] #146, 1841, Wilkes
See Quimper Peninsula.

Dickerson Point
See Dickenson Point.

Dilworth
The community is located on the eastern side of Vashon Island. The name honored the Rev. R. B. Dilworth who settled on the island in 1884 (TPL website, Haulman).

Dines Point
Located on the eastern side of Whidbey Island in Holmes Harbor, Wilkes originally named this Pt. Maury in 1841 [7e], presumably honoring crew member William L. Maury. Wilkes did not include this name in his *Narrative*, but it is shown on his chart. The origin of the current name is unknown.

Dinner Island [13a] #2689, 1859, Richards
Located in North Bay on the eastern side of San Juan Island, Richards did not leave a reason for the name. Meany (*Origin* 69) reported that the crew from a British vessel stopped on the island to eat dinner. It henceforth became know as Dinner Island. Lange uncovered two alternative stories: The island was a stopping spot for American soldiers on their way from American Camp to Bald Hill for target practice. Another alternative came from the Jensen family who lived to the south on San Juan Island. They raised rabbits on Dinner Island. As such, when food became scarce, there was always dinner waiting for them there. After the 1906 earthquake in San Francisco, Dinner Island was reported as missing. A few days later, it was reportedly back in place (Richardson, *Magic* 77). In mid-1907, Charles Tutt visited Friday Harbor in his 116 foot ketch *Anemone*, "the largest and finest private yacht which has ever visited this port," according to the July 6, 1907 *The San Juan Islander* (p 1). Mr. Tutt was the president of United States Smelting Company in Denver and owned other mining interests in Colorado, Oregon, California, and Mexico. According to the article: "It may be of interest to the ISLANDER's readers to know that Mr. Tutt is a property owner in this county, having purchased what is known as "Dinner Island" in Griffin Bay, quite a number of years ago." This apparently occurred while he was getting a shave in a local barber shop when a man came in and mentioned to the barber that he was selling the island. Mr. Tutt discussed it with him and, sight unseen, made the purchase. The purchase actually happened in 1896 according to the August 20 issue of *The Islander*: ". . . he purchased, on Tuesday last, of Mr. J. L. Farnsworth, a small piece of land known as Dinner island . . ." Today, William Potts of Medina, WA, President of Precor, owns the island.

Discovery, Point
See Mill Point.

Discovery Bay [6] 1792, Vancouver
Located along the Strait of Juan de Fuca, Quimper first named it in 1790 [1] *Puerto de la Bodega y Quadra* after the commandant of the naval station at San Blas. Bodega y Quadra (1744-1794) was born in Peru and received his early training in Spain. He was posted to Mexico in 1774, where the following year he joined an exploration on the Northwest Coast commanded by Bruno de Hezeta. In 1779, Bodega again explored and charted along the Alaska Coast. He was next assigned to Cuba and then to Spain, but he returned to Mexico in 1789 where he commanded the naval station at San Blas. In 1792, he met Vancouver at Nootka Sound. Having suffered from chronic headaches for years, in 1793, Bodega finally requested a leave from his duties. He died less than a year later in Mexico City. Quimper wrote: "At 4 I sent the longboat with the pilot and the canoe with the second pilot to make a plan of the port which had been discovered to the south of the Isla de Carrasco [Protection Island] and to put up a cross in the most conspicuous part of it. At 9:30 they came back and told me that they had planted the Holy Cross on a sand point [Contractors Point] in front of the port, the most southerly and westerly one which can be seen when entering the mouth. There is a stream of delicious water in it which comes down apparently from a mountain behind it. The port, they said, can hold many vessels by reason of its size and shelter. The country although somewhat high is level. I have named it Quadra." Vancouver wrote: "Thus we proceeded without meeting any obstruction to our progress; which, though not rapid, brought us before noon abreast of the stream that discharges its water from the western shore near 5 miles within the entrance of the harbour; which I distinguished by the name of Port Discovery, after the ship," (Wagner 114; Vancouver 228). Seemann (107) wrote: "Several streams of good water fall into it, the holding ground is very good, the shores are generally steep, and there is no danger in working in or out. A few ruined villages and burial-places are seen on the shore; and the pathless woods, preventing in almost every direction any ingress into the country, render the scene rather monotonous." The evolution from Port Discovery to Discovery Bay is unclear. Kellett maintained Vancouver's naming, as did Richards, Wilkes, and Alden. In 1978, the National Ocean Survey requested the evaluation of returning to Vancouver's original naming. In its meeting of December 8, 1989, the Washington State Board on Geographic Names voted to retain the name Discovery Bay, Docket 235. The U.S. Board followed in 1979. Variant names included *Kiu-la-tsu-ko*, Port Discovery, Port Discovery Bay, *Puerto de Quadra,* and *Puerto de la Bodega y Cuadra* (from Washington State Board Files). H.M.S. *Discovery* was 95 feet in length and carried ten 4-pounders and ten swivels. She was built in 1789 by Randall and Bent on the Thames River. Following the exploration, *Discovery* was used as a bomb vessel from 1795 to 1808, and a as a prison ship from 1808 to 1834. She was broken up at Deptford in 1834.

Disney, Point [7a] #145, 1841, Wilkes
Located on the south end of Waldron Island, Wilkes named it in 1841 for crew member Solomon Disney. Wilkes did not include this name in his *Narrative*, but it is shown on his chart. James E. Riley from South Dakota was mining sandstone on Stuart Island when locals discovered sandstone on Point Disney. Riley moved his operation to Waldron about 1906 and began taking out material. George Savage and George Scofield, both from Tacoma, learned of the mine and discovered that Riley did not own the shore lands in front of the quarry. Savage and Scofield took out a forty-five year lease on the land and simply displaced Riley. Initially, they blasted tons of rock off the cliff to create a shelf at the edge of the water below the steep bluff. There, they set up machinery and a wharf. The cliff was blasted by digging three foot square "coyote" holes about sixty feet into the solid rock. Then, a "T" was dug thirty feet on either side, packed with powder, fused, and lit. The quarry employed from 100 to 150 men hired for the dangerous task of blowing off a large section and cutting it into six-by-six by twelve-inch blocks after it slid to the beach below. Many of the blocks were used to pave Yesler Way as well as other streets in Seattle. The development of concrete replaced the stones a few years later, and the quarry operation ended in 1909. Three of the coyote

holes apparently still exist on the Point Disney cliffs (Lovering 37; Bailey and Nyberg, *San Juan Islands* 143). The entire point, 207 acres, is owned by the Nature Conservancy. An adjacent 217 acre parcel is owned by the San Juan Preservation Trust.

Dockton
Located on the western side of Maury Island, the Puget Sound Dry Dock Company named the community about 1891 (Meany, *Origin* 70). The Salish name for the area was "launching things into the water" (Hilbert et. al., 237).

Doe Bay [13k] #2689, 1900
Located off the eastern side of Orcas Island, the bay was named for the deer in the area. The community of Doe Bay took its name from the bay. Regarding the community, the name was originally spelled Doebay (one word). John G. Viereck was one of the earliest settlers, arriving about 1870. He established the first post office in 1880 and died in 1899 of small pox causing a quarantine of both Doe Bay and Olga. In 1976, locals submitted evidence to the Washington State Board on Geographic Names and recommended duplicating the name of the bay (two words). Some felt the name change was unnecessary as there was already evidence of similar situations, e.g. East Sound and the community of Eastsound. However, the Washington Board agreed on Doe Bay for the community in their September 10, 1976 meeting, Docket 211. The U.S. Board followed in December (from Washington State Board Files).

Doe Bay Mountain
See Mount Pickett.

Doe Island
Located in Doe Bay on the eastern side of Orcas Island, the name was reported to Roy McLellan who passed it along to the U.S. Board on Geographic Names. The Board formalized the name in 1925. The Island is a Washington State Park.

Dofflemeyer Point [23] #6460, 1905
Located on the mainland, it is the eastern entrance to Budd Inlet. Wilkes named this Browns Point [7d], [7i] in 1841 honoring crew member James Brown (Meany, *Origin* 70). Wilkes did not include this name in his *Narrative*, but it is shown on his charts. An early name was Allen's Point for James and Jane Allen who settled on 160 acres in 1854. Isaac and Susan Dofflemeyer settled on a 320 acre claim in 1852. The point was ultimately named for them (Palmer, 1). The Salish name for the point was "house pits" referring to the building techniques of Indian homes (Hilbert et. al., 307). The U.S. Board on Geographic Names chose the current name over the variant Dofflemyer's Point, in 1891.

Dogfish Bay [19] #662, 1867, U.S. Coast Survey
See Liberty Bay.

Dogfish Bay
See Honeymoon Bay.

Dogfish Bight
Located on Nisqually Reach, the name is for the prolific dogfish found there (Palmer, 21).

Dogfish Point
Located on the western shore of Samish Bay, it was perhaps named for the dogfish.

Dolphin Bay
Located on the eastern side of East Sound, Orcas Island, across from Entrance Mountain, the community and bay were locally named for a dolphin installed for mooring purposes in 1903. A dolphin is a grouping of piling, from 3 to perhaps a couple dozen, cabled together for strength. The most obvious examples are the dolphins used by the Washington State Ferry System at each landing. Jefferson D. Moore, who later was the postmaster in Olga, established the Dolphin Bay Post Office in his house in 1908 and used the name Dolphin. The bay also became known by the same name. Over the years, the community disappeared but the name was retained. In 1973, locals proposed eliminating the community name Dolphin from all maps and charts. The Washington State Board on Geographic Names approved the change in its September 10, 1976, Docket 209. The U.S. Board followed later that year (from Washington State Board Files).

Dolphin Point [19] #662, 1867, U.S. Coast Survey
Located on the northwestern side of Vashon Island, it was named by the U.S. Coast Survey in 1857 (Davidson, *Directory* 144) for porpoises that were prolific in the area (Hitchman 73).

Dosewallips River
Located on the western side of Hood Canal two miles north of Pleasant Harbor, it was named from the Twana Indian word *Dos-wail-opsh* which was the title of a mythical Indian chief who was changed into a mountain at the head of the river (Hitchman 73). The name became official in a 1941 decision of the U.S. Board on Geographic Names, which selected the current name from the variants: Dusewallips, Dosewallips, and Dosewallups (*Decisions*). According to the GNIS files, the name first appeared on an 1872 G.L.O. Township Plat. John Clements (1838-1902) arrived in Port Gamble in 1856. At the end of five years working for the mill, he returned to East Machias to marry. He returned to Port Gamble, but it was five years later before his wife joined him. He was one of the first ox-team loggers in Brinnon, arriving around 1870. He established a farm which ultimately became the Dosewallips State Park (Bailey 102, 105).

Dot Island [21] #6300, 1895
It is located in Padilla Bay. According to Meany (*Origin* 71), the name first appeared on U.S. chart #6300 corrected to 1904. But it actually appears on the first issue. It is now a National Wildlife Refuge. *See* Hat Island.

Dot Island
Located near the southern entrance of the Swinomish Channel, a half mile north of Goat Island, the name may be descriptive. It is not reflected on current charts.

Dot Rock [13a] #2689, 1859, Richards
Located off the southeastern shore of Decatur Island in Rosario Strait, the name is likely descriptive.

Double Bluff [19] #662, 1867, U.S. Coast Survey
Located at the southwestern end of Whidbey Island, Wilkes originally named this Ariels Point [7d] in 1841 for the American vessel *Ariel* which saw action during the War of 1812 (Meany, *Origin* 71). The U.S. Coast Survey provided the current name in 1855 (Davidson, *Report* 443). Davidson later wrote: "This is a mesa promontory one mile wide and one and a half miles long, lying between Mutiny Bay on the west and Useless Bay on the east. The cliffs are three or four hundred feet in height, and the greater part of the surface back from the face is covered with trees, but near the water it is destitute of trees, except one large clump which marks it conspicuously in going up the sound," (1889 *Pacific Coast Pilot* 595).

Double Bluff

Double Heads
See Jackson Cove.

Double Hill [13a] #2689, 1859, Richards
Located in central Orcas Island near the head of East Sound, it describes two small peaks near the town of Eastsound. McLellan referenced the name Double Hill Range for this feature. Today's charts reflect two features: Double Hill and Lookout Hill. *See* Lookout Hill.

Double Island [14a] #2840, 1861, Richards
Located in West Sound, Richards gave this name to the combination of Double Island and its neighbor, Alegria Island (Meany, *Origin* 71). The islands are linked at extreme low tides. The U.S. Board on Geographic Names approved the name Alegria for the smaller southern island and left the name Double for the northern island in 1980. *See also* Alegria Island. Mike Brown, a retired Microsoft employee, owns the island.

Double Point [7b] #148, 1841, Wilkes
Located on the eastern side of Discovery Bay, directly across from Contractors Point, Wilkes likely named it in 1841 because of the appearance of two points. The name is neither reflected on current charts nor recognized by the U.S. Board on Geographic Names. Wilkes did not include this name in his *Narrative*, but it is shown on his chart.

Dougall Point [7d] #146, 1841, Wilkes; [7h] #154, 1841, Wilkes

Located at the northern end of Harstine Island, Wilkes spelled this with only one "l" as did the U.S. Coast Survey in 1867 [19]. Wilkes left no reason for the name (Meany, *Origin* 71). He did not include this name in his *Narrative*, but it is shown on his chart.

Doughty, Point [7a] #145, 1841, Wilkes

Located near the northern end of Orcas Island, Wilkes named it for crew member John Doughty. Wilkes did not include this name in his *Narrative*, but it is shown on his chart. Richards gave this point two names: Nob Point and Bill of Orcas but provided no reason. In 1866, the U.S. Coast Survey on [18] reverted back to Point Doughty for which it is now currently known. The land on the point is owned by the State of Washington.

Douglas Channel [13a] #2689, 1859, Richards
See President Channel.

Dover Point [23] #6460, 1905

Located on Dana Passage near Boston Harbor, the origin of the name is unknown.

Drayton Bay [7a] #145, 1841, Wilkes; [7l] #159, 1841, Wilkes
See Boundary Bay.

Drayton Harbor [7l] #159, 1841, Wilkes

Located at the Canadian boundary, Wilkes reflected this in 1841 as Drayton Cove on his chart. He honored crew member Joseph Drayton (Meany, *Origin* 72). It was originally named by José Mariá Narvaez in 1791 as part of the Eliza Expedition and is reflected as *Boca de Florida Blanca* on Eliza's chart [3]. In 2007, an attempt was made through the Washington State Board on Geographic Names to change the name of Drayton Harbor to Blaine Harbor. The proponent argued: "Identification, less confusion, tourism. The public best identifies a name with a geographic feature." Proponent further stated: "The name is old but irrelevant since Blaine surrounds the harbor." The Board denied the proposal in its September 21, 2007 meeting (from Washington State Board Files).

Drayton Passage [7d] #146, 1841, Wilkes; [7i] #147, 1841, Wilkes

Wilkes wrote: "Anderson's and M'Niel's Islands are separated from the Indian Peninsula by Drayton's Passage," (*Narrative* 322). He honored crew member Joseph Drayton in 1841 (Meany, *Origin* 72).

Driftwood Cove

Located in Colvos Passage nearly opposite Fern Cove on Vashon Island, the origin of the name is unknown but presumably descriptive.

Dry Creek
See Rendsland Creek.

Dtokoah Point [20f] #654, 1853, U.S. Coast Survey

Located immediately east of Baada Point on the Strait of Juan de Fuca, the origin of the name is unknown.

DuPont

It is located at the southeastern end of Puget Sound, just north of Nisqually on what was Hudson's Bay Company land. The Federal Government purchased the land in 1869. The E. I. du Pont de Nemours and Company of Wilmington, Delaware acquired the property from various owners in 1906 to build an explosives plant. Éleuthère Irénée du Pont de Nemours (1771-1834) was born in Paris. He was an assistant to Antoine-Laurent de Lavoisier, considered by some to be the father of modern chemistry. One of his many discoveries was that of nitrate extraction and manufacture, a skill du Pont learned well. He married Sophie Dalmas (1775-1828) in 1791, and narrowly escaping death during the French Revolution, he immigrated with his entire family to the U.S. in 1799. Settling in Delaware, he founded one of the largest and most successful American companies, which is still the second largest chemical company, behind BASF, in terms of market capitalization, and fourth behind BASF, Dow Chemical, and Ineos, with respect to revenue. The number of discoveries includes neoprene, nylon TyVek, Corian, Teflon, Mylar, Kevlar, Lycra, Freon, etc. But early on the company produced gunpowder and by the mid-1800s became the largest supplier of gunpowder to the U.S. military. The Eleutherian Mills site on the Brandywine Creek near Wilmington was declared a National Historic Landmark in 1966 and is now a museum. The explosives plant in Puget Sound was one of many scattered around the U.S. Early workers lived in one of the 58 tar paper houses on Fort Nisqually land. Some of this land is now part of the DuPont Golf Course. For forty-five years, all property remained under the control of the corporation, but in 1951, DuPont sold the houses to the occupants who then incorporated the town of DuPont. In 1976, the company closed the plant and sold its remaining 3,200 acres to Weyerhaeuser. By 1985, with a decline in forest industry products, Weyerhaeuser began building a master planned community on the land using their Quadrant subsidiary (*A History* I: 57; www.dupontmuseum.com).

Duck Harbor [7o] #157, 1841, Wilkes
See Tulalip Bay.

Duck Lake
Located on Cypress Island, it was named for the ducks attracted to the lake (TPL website).

Duckabush
Located on the western side of Hood Canal, immediately south of Pleasant Harbor, the community and river came from the Indian name *do-hi-a-boos* which means "reddish face." Apparently, the hillside behind the community has a reddish appearance (Meany, *Origin* 72).

Dudley Island
See Alegria.

Dugualla Bay
Located on the eastern side of Whidbey Island in Skagit Bay, it is opposite Goat Island. The name is Indian for "houses in the inlet" or "shut in houses" (Hilbert). The U.S. Board on Geographic Names responded to a spelling issue in 1941, Dugula on [21] vs. Dugualla and selected the present name. Dugualla first appeared on an 1870 Map of Puget Sound and Cowlitz Valley by Colton (GNIS files).

Dumas Bay
It is located on the eastern shoreline of East Passage, about five miles north of Tacoma. It was apparently named for an early settler (Aug. 24, 2011 email to author from Gary Reese).

Duncan Rock [6] 1792, Vancouver
Located north of Tatoosh Island, Vancouver wrote (217): "We followed the *Chattam* between Tatooche's Island and the rock, hauling to the eastward along the southern shore of the supposed straits of De Fuca. This rock, which rises just above the surface of the water, and over which the surf breaks with great violence, I called Rock Duncan, in commemoration of that gentleman's discovery." Vancouver named it for Capt. Charles Duncan of the merchant ship *Princess Royal*, who discovered the rock in 1788 and provided information to Vancouver on the Northwest Coast (Meany, *Origin* 73). Davidson reported: "This is a small low black rock rising above the highest tides, but always washed by the western swell, which breaks over it. Deep water is found close around it," (*Report* 413).

Duncan's Bay [7a] #145, 1841, Wilkes; [7e] #158, 1841, Wilkes
See Crescent Harbor.

Dungeness

Dungeness [6] 1792, Vancouver
Located along the Strait of Juan de Fuca, it was discovered and named by Quimper in 1790 [1]. He wrote: "I named the bay and the port 'Quimper.'" In 1792, Vancouver wrote: "The low sandy point of land, which from its great resemblance to Dungeness in the British channel, I called New Dungeness," (Wagner 112; Vancouver 222). According to Meany (*Origin*, 188), the name is derived from dune and "*naess*" or cape. Concerning the area, in 1841 Wilkes wrote (*Narrative* 312): "New Dungeness Roads is the best temporary anchorage for vessels, as they are well

protected from the prevailing winds, easy of access, and if need be, water may be filled up. It is probable that here, in future, pilots for Admiralty Inlet may be obtained, and supplies in any quantities that may be required." Wilkes also called it New Dungeness Point [7c], [7n] and New Dungeness Roads [7n]. Davidson wrote: "On the inside [of Dungeness Spit], one mile from the eastern extremity, another narrow sand spit makes 1½ mile southward towards the main shore, forming a large inner shoal bay, with a narrow opening, through which the water passes as over a rapid at low tide. Abreast of this point is a small stream, affording an abundance of fresh water, but boats must obtain their supply at low tide, and come out when the tide has sufficiently risen. The western side of this stream is a bluff 60 feet high, and upon it is a large village of the Clallums," (*Report* 420). By a 1964 decision of the U.S. Board on Geographic Names, the "New" was dropped from Dungeness Bay, Dungeness Spit, and the community of Dungeness. However, the light is still called the New Dungeness light (GNIS files). According to the files for Dungeness: " 'New' is to be retained as part of the name of the light." No further information was provided. The original community formed on the west side of the Dungeness River at what was called Old Town. Because of a lack of access on the water, it slowly migrated to the east side of the river. The first settlers at New Dungeness did not arrive until almost sixty years following Vancouver's visit. Capt. Thomas Abernethy, B. I. Madison, J. C. Brown, John Donnell, and Elisha McAlmond boarded a barkentine in Boston. (A barkentine is a ship with three or more masts rigged with square sails on the forward most mast, and fore and aft sails typical of modern sailboats on the remaining masts.) Upon arriving in San Francisco, Donnell got "gold fever," left the party, and headed for the California hills. The remaining four departed for Puget Sound in 1850 and anchored in New Dungeness to replenish their water. The following spring, this group, along with another friend, Jim Connelly, staked out claims. Elliot Henry Cline arrived in 1852 and platted the town site in 1865. Early settlers logged, and many planted potatoes. In 1860, Hezekiah Davis established a store (*see also* Davis Bay). Others followed his lead, and soon hotels, saloons, and more stores served the town. New Dungeness was originally settled on the bluff above Cline Spit, west of the Dungeness River. Locals constructed a pier on the spit, but in 1890 the bay began to silt around the dock. With continued shoaling, its usage became dangerous. Settlers decided that the flat area to the east of the Dungeness River was a more appropriate spot for the growing community. In 1891, C. F. Seal constructed a 4,300-foot dock. Most townsfolk living in what became "Old Town" soon migrated to the new center for shipping traffic. Old Town declined as New Dungeness grew. A post office and school were erected in 1892. The school is now a Washington State Historic Site. A covered bridge, built across the Dungeness River, allowed settlers to move between the two towns (Keeting 1; Roe 15; Fish, *Tracks* 154-163).

Dungeness Bay
The bay fronts the community of Dungeness on the Strait of Juan de Fuca. *See also* Dungeness.

Dungeness Shoal [13a] #2689, 1859, Richards
It is located off the Dungeness Spit. The name is neither reflected on U.S. charts nor is it recognized by the U.S. Board on Geographic Names.

Dungeness River
It flows into Dungeness Bay and the Strait of Juan de Fuca.

Dungeness Spit
Except for its continual growth through the years, Dungeness Spit appears today much as it did 200-plus years ago: sand covered with driftwood, and birds. It extends five and a half miles into the Strait of Juan de Fuca, and it is the longest natural spit in the world and is still growing. The government built a lighthouse which became operational on December 14, 1857, two weeks prior to that of Cape Flattery. The first keeper, Henry Blake, was twenty-nine years of age. The original tower was eighty-nine feet in height. The government reduced this to sixty-seven feet in 1927. According to one story, percussion from the firing of Canadian guns at Esquimalt cracked the tower. The remedy was to cut the top off. The light was originally located about 800 feet from the end of the spit (Roe 15; Fish, *Tracks* 159). Today, it is more than a half mile! A story passed down

through the years epitomized the hardships faced not only by settlers but by the Native Americans as well. On September 21, 1868, 18 Tsimshian Indians from Fort Simpson, BC, stopped at Dungeness Spit. Night was falling and the weather deteriorating. They chose to wait until morning to cross the Strait of Juan de Fuca. The group, who had been picking hops near Puyallup for several weeks, consisted of men, women, and children, including one pregnant woman. Unknown to them, a band of 26 Clallam Indians were observing. The Clallams attacked in the middle of the night and clubbed and speared to death all of the Tsimshians but for the pregnant woman. Feigning death, but badly wounded, she eventually made it to the water and then crawled/floated to the lighthouse, about a mile away. Henry Blake opened the door to this woman and took her in. His wife cleaned her up and cared for her until she was well enough to board a Hudson's Bay Company steamer and return home. All of the Clallams were captured, imprisoned by the reservation, and put in hard labor. About 1920, E. A. Brooks noticed an older Indian man come ashore. Brooks was then the lighthouse keeper at Dungeness. He wandered down to the water's edge and the two talked for awhile. The Indian eventually broached the subject of the 1868 massacre and how a pregnant woman was saved. Brooks was very familiar with the story, as that section of the spit has been locally known as Graveyard Spit ever since the event. The old Indian admitted that he was that baby. Brooks told him that Henry Blake's son Richard lived in the area and would like to meet him. When the massacre occurred, Richard was about three but likely remembered the story well from retellings. Unfortunately, the meeting never took place (Hanify, Mary Lou. "The Massacre at Dungeness Spit." *Seattle Times*. July 11, 1965. Magazine Section p 3).

Duntze Island [24] #1947, 1849, Inskip
See McNeil Island.

Dutcher Cove
Located about two miles south of Vaughn on the Key Peninsula, it was originally known as Reynolds Bay as reflected on the 1889 Atlas of Pierce County. It was likely named for the settler Eli Dutcher who married Mary Ellen Smith in 1889 (TPL website).

Duwamish Bay
See Elliott Bay.

Duwamish Head [22] #6450, 1909
Located at the northern end of West Seattle, Wilkes referenced this in 1841 as Point Rand in his *Narrative* (316) but with two names: Point Rand and Point Moore on his charts [7d], [7m]. Wilkes left no reason for the names. The U.S. Coast Survey provided the current name in 1856, likely for the Indian tribe (Davidson, *Directory* 142).

Duwamish River
It flows into Elliott Bay at Seattle. In 1824, Work wrote (213): "We this day proceeded through a fine channel formed, as the others, by the main land and an island [Vashon]. Passed an opening on the E. side in the morning and on the same side a bay into which flows the Linananimas River [flows]." Davidson referenced the name but did not specifically state that the U.S. Coast Survey named it (Davidson, *Report* 446). It was named for the Duwamish Indians. Based upon the perception that it was in fact named by the Coast Survey, the U.S. Board on Geographic Names approved the name in 1895. In 1959, the Board received a proposal for an alteration in the location of the Duwamish River. The proponent wrote: "For the Duwamish, beginning at the outer Harbor Line (U.S. Pierhead Line) in Elliott Bay and proceeding south and up-river, East Waterway and West Waterway to their confluence above West Spokane Street; Duwamish Waterway from this point to the head of the existing project of the U.S. Corps of Engineers; Duwamish River from the point on up-river to this junction with Green River at Renton junction." The Board approved this proposal in early1960. Variants include D'Wamish River, Dewampsh River, Dwamish River, and Linananimis River (GNIS files).

Dyes Inlet [7d] #146, 1841, Wilkes; [7q] #156, 1841, Wilkes
Located north of Bremerton, Wilkes honored crew member John W. W. Dyes in 1841 (Meany, *Origin* 74). Wilkes wrote (*Narrative* 317): "The main entrance to Port Orchard is through Rich's Passage: this lies between the south end of Bainbridge Island

and the Great Peninsula, trending in a northwest direction 2 miles in length, by half a mile wide, when it takes a sharp turn to the southwest, of one mile. Properly speaking, Rich's Passage is a part of Port Orchard, but as there were so many branches, I thought it necessary to give the arms which lead into it different names, reserving the name given by Vancouver to the largest; the others we called Dye's, Sinclair's, and May's Inlets." In 1941, the U.S. Board on Geographic Names settled on the current name from the variants including Dye Inlet, Dye's Inlet, and Port Washington Bay (GNIS files).

Dyke Point [24] #1947, 1849, Inskip
See Hyde Point.

Eagle Cliff [21] #6300, 1895
Located on the northern end of Cypress Island, Wilkes originally provided the name Cone Hill [7a] in 1841. The U.S. Coast Survey renamed it Bald Peak in 1854: "When in the narrowest part of Rosario strait, a very marked perpendicular rocky peak is seen to the north over the low point of Cypress, and soon shows rising abruptly from the water's edge to a height of 750 feet. It is called Bald Peak," (Davidson, *Report* 433). The U.S. Board on Geographic Names changed the name in 1893.

Eagle Cove [13a] #2689, 1859, Richards
Located two miles west of Cattle Point on the southern end of San Juan Island, it was likely named for eagles in the area.

Eagle Creek [22] #6450, 1909
It is located along the western side of Discovery Bay, likely named for birds in the area. According to the table attached to Descriptive Survey #1124 (http://riverhistory.ess.washington.edu/tsheets/reports/t1124.pdf), James Lawson wrote that the Coast Survey named the creek.

Eagle Harbor [7d] #146, 1841, Wilkes; [7q] #156, 1841, Wilkes
Located on the eastern side of Bainbridge Island, Wilkes perhaps named this in 1841 for Henry Eagle of the *Eagle* during the War of 1812, or, more likely, for the presence of eagles in the area, particularly

Eagle Harbor

since the entrance points were named Wing and Bill (Meany, *Origin* 74, 75).

Eagle Harbor
Located on the eastern side of Cypress Island, it was likely named for the presence of eagles in the area.

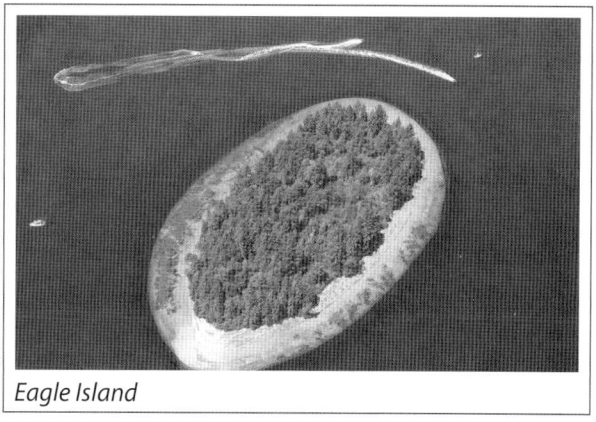

Eagle Island

Eagle Island [24] #1947, 1849, Inskip
Located in Balch Passage between McNeil and Anderson Islands, the island was named by Inskip,

perhaps for its residents. Alternatively, the name honored the H.M.S. *Eagle* which visited Nisqually in 1834 (Meany, *Origin* 75; Reese, *Origins* 38). On Wilkes' 1841 chart [7i], he drew Ned as the same size as the adjacent Tom Islet. In reality, Tom is Eagle Island; Ned is merely a small (currently unnamed) rock to the west. In addition, between the two islands, Wilkes wrote the words Pepper Corns. He provided no reason for any of these names (Wilkes, *Narrative* 322). The ten acre island today is a state park.

Eagle Point [13a] #2689, 1859, Richards
Located on the south end of San Juan Island, a couple miles west of Cattle Point, it was likely named for eagles in the area.

Eagle Point [13a] #2689, 1859, Richards
Located at the northeast end of Matia Island, it was likely named for the presence of eagles.

Eagle Point
Located on the southern side of Hammersley Inlet, it was likely named for the presence of eagles.

Eagle Point [21] #6300, 1895
Located west of Clallam Bay on the Strait of Juan de Fuca, Meany (*Origin* 74) stated that it was named for an eagle's nest in a nearby tree.

Eagledale
Located on the southern side of Eagle Harbor, Bainbridge Island, it was originally named Teelan. In 1881, Capt. Saddler bought land near the creosote plant and started a brick yard which was productive for only about five years. Glen Reeve settled in 1884 and opened his home as a schoolhouse. Apparently, town folk didn't care for the name. So, in the 1920s, they held a contest for a new name. Ed Severson submitted the winning name (Marriott 83, 84).

East Bay
It is located on the eastern side of Budd Inlet. According to the Chief Administrative Officer of the Thurston County Commissioners, it is "the historical and common name" for its location. The Washington State Board on Geographic Names adopted this name in their April 11, 1985 meeting, Docket 292. The U.S. Board followed later in the year (from Washington State Board files).

East Bluff [7b] #148, 1841, Wilkes
See Cape George.

East Cromwell
See Cromwell.

East Oro Bay
Located on the southern end of Anderson Island, it was named for its proximity to Oro Bay. It is the northeastern portion of Oro Bay.

East Passage
It is located between Vashon Island and the mainland.

East Point [13a] #2689, 1859, Richards
Located on the eastern side of Cypress Island, north of Deepwater Bay, Richards likely selected the name for its location. *See* Cypress Head.

East Point [7d] #146, 1841, Wilkes; [7e] #158, 1841, Wilkes
Located on the eastern side of Whidbey Island, Wilkes named it in 1841 for its location (Meany, *Origin* 75). Wilkes did not include this name in his *Narrative*, but it is shown on his chart. In 1959, the U.S. Board on Geographic Names addressed the name differences between charts and topo maps and approved the current name over the variant of Fox Spit.

East Sound [13a] #2689, 1859, Richards
There are two large inlets indenting the southern portion of Orcas Island: East Sound and West Sound. East Sound was originally named Ironsides Inlet [7a] in 1841 by Wilkes for *Old Ironsides*, the nickname of the U.S. frigate *Constitution* (Meany, *Origin* 75). Richards renamed it for its position on Orcas (TPL website).

East Waterway
See Harbor Island.

East Waterway
Located south of Everett, the U.S. Navy has a facility located there.

Eastern Bank [21] #6300, 1895
Located between Hein and Partridge Banks, it may have been named for its location.

Eastsound

Located at the head of East Sound, the community took its name from the sound. In the late 1860s, Charles W. Shattuck, born in Massachusetts in 1830, moved into a tent at the head of East Sound eventually building a small cabin and store which grew to a larger store, dance hall, post office, and his home. With the Pig War boundary dispute complete, he filed for a homestead which included half of the present town of Eastsound. By 1877, he established a post office and named it East Sound (two words). In the mid-1890s, locals changed it to Eastsound (one word). Shattuck sold to Walter Sutherland in 1887. Sutherland remodeled the building and converted part of it into a hotel. The hotel is still in service today and is called Outlook Inn. Perhaps Sutherland was responsible for the name change when he became postmaster in 1887. His son Luther later replaced him. Shattuck's neighbor, Ephraim Langell, arrived in 1870. He filed for the other half of the land around the community of Eastsound. Langell, from Nova Scotia, worked the Cariboo gold rush and then wound up on Orcas Island. He initially worked at the Port Langdon lime quarry and then settled in Eastsound. He married Rosa Houp in Victoria. Their daughter, Belle, was the first White child born on Orcas. Six more children followed, one of whom, William, was the first curator of the Orcas Historical Museum. At Eastsound, Langell planted an orchard of prune, apple, and cherry trees. When not working in the orchard, he logged and cut firewood for the several lime quarries around East Sound. The beach on the property was known by the local name of Langell's Beach (Richardson, *Pig* 194, 195; Richardson, *Magic* 50; Splitstone 32; *The San Juan Islander*, July 13, 1907, p 8). The Orcas Island Historical Society museum resides in Eastsound. The Society restored four pioneer cabins and relocated them to the village. The museum includes Pig War cannon balls, a pioneer doctor's medical bag, and the rowboat used by Ethan Allen as well as his collection of Indian objects. *See also* Mail Bay.

Ebey's Landing

Davidson wrote: "Between Admiralty Head and Point Partridge there is a slight receding of the shore to the northward, and at two and two-thirds miles from the Light-house there is a breaking down of the cliff to a low sag in the land, which is free from woods for a mile. This is known as *Ebey's Landing*, and a boat can land on the beach in ordinary weather. Small schooners can anchor off the landing in ten to fifteen fathoms of water one-third of a mile from the shore; but the bottom drops off suddenly to thirty and forty fathoms in a little over half a mile," (1889 *Pacific Coast Pilot* 590). Isaac Ebey left his wife Rebecca and two small boys and departed his hometown of Plumb Grove, Missouri in 1848. With a short trip to the gold fields in California, he ended up in San Francisco, where with several other men, including Edmund Sylvester, the founder of Olympia, purchased the brig *Orbit*. They loaded her with supplies and set sail for the Northwest. After arriving in Tumwater, Ebey sold his share of the ship to Michael Simmons. During the summer of 1850, Ebey paddled a canoe around Puget Sound searching for mill sites and farmland. He explored the Puyallup River, the Seattle area including the Duwamish and Lake Washington, and finally Whidbey Island where he claimed the property originally settled by Thomas Glasgow in 1848 (*see also* Whidbey Island). After a considerable period of time, Ebey was reunited with his family in late 1851. Rebecca traveled with her Missouri neighbors, John, Thomas, and James Davis (her brothers), the Walter Crockett and Cochran families, all of whom ultimately settled near Ebey's claim on Whidbey. The family decided to remain in Olympia through the rainy season, thus, they did not actually arrive on the Whidbey homestead until March 1852. In 1853, at age 30, Rebecca died after a difficult pregnancy and birth of a daughter (probably from tuberculosis). In 1855, Isaac married Mrs. Emily Sconce, a widow from Portland. Unfortunately, the marriage lasted barely two years when Ebey was murdered by northern Indians. *See also* Butler Cove, Whidbey Island.

Ebey Slough

Located north of Everett, it was named for Colonel Isaac Ebey. The name first appeared as Ebey's Slough on t-sheet #1681 dated 1884. It next appeared as Ebeys Slough on the Coast and Geodetic Survey chart #6448, Everett Harbor and Approaches, published in 1909. Two years later, the name appeared on a

1911 USC&GS topo. In 2011, the City of Marysville petitioned the U.S. Board on Geographic Names to change the name to Ebey Estuary as they believed "the current part of the name, 'Slough,' does not provide an accurate description of the waterbody." Referred back to the Washington State Board on Geographic Names for consideration, in its May 2012 meeting, the Washington State Committee denied the request. Presumably, the Washington State Board will follow this recommendation. *See also* Butler Cove, Whidbey Island.

Echo Bay [13k] #2689, 1900
It is the largest bay off Sucia Island and is located on the eastern side. According to J. J. Gilbert in his 1888 Descriptive Report #1870 (http://riverhistory.ess.washington.edu/tsheets/reports/t1870.pdf, p 7): "Echo Bay, named for the very fine echo at a point near its head, is a good safe harbor, free from dangers."

Echo Bay
Located on the Hale Passage side of Fox Island, it is the local name for the bay that includes Tanglewood Island (Edgers 107). The name may be descriptive.

Echo Bay Island
See Justice Island.

Echo Point
Located on the eastern side of Lummi Island just north of the ferry terminal, the origin of the name is unknown.

Edgewater
The community is located on the eastern side of Possession Sound, between Everett and Mukilteo. It was named because of its location (Meany, *Origin* 76).

Edison
Located on Samish Bay, east of Samish Island, it was first settled in 1869 by Ben Sampson. The name was suggested in 1876 by the first postmaster, Edward McTaggart, for "The Wizard of Menlo Park [NJ]" (*An Illustrated History*, 233).

Edith Point
Located on the western side of Fidalgo Island, about a mile north of Langley Bay and a mile east of Allan Island, the origin of the name is unknown.

Ediz Hook

Ediz Hook [9a] #1911, 1849, Kellett
A three-mile sand spit that forms the port of Port Angeles, Kellett provided the name. Davidson indicated: "The Hook is covered with coarse grass, and in many places with driftwood, showing that the sea sometimes washes over it." He continued: "The bay was first discovered by the Spaniards, and by them made known to Vancouver in 1792. We first heard of its present name, False Dungeness, in 1852, when at Cape Flattery, from traders there," (*Report* 419, 420). Ediz comes from the Indian word *I'e'nis* meaning "good beach" (http://www.historylink.org). Today, it is home to Coast Guard Station Port Angeles. The Air Station has numerous helicopters that perform search and rescue activities, as well as several Coast Guard cutters.

Edmonds [22] #6450, 1909
Located on the eastern shoreline of the mainland, a few miles north of Seattle, it was first settled by Pleasant Ewell in 1866. He cleared a portion of the

land in the heart of the current city and built a log cabin. On March 25, 1870, he sold to Jacob D. Fowler, Nat B. Fowler, and Morris H. Frost, from Mukilteo, for $200 (Humphrey 79; Swift 12). George Brackett, one of twenty children, was born in 1841 in New Brunswick. He worked in the timber industry in Maine and New Brunswick. In 1869, Etta Jones Brackett, his wife, and George, Jr., accompanied him to California and then to the Pacific Northwest. He logged in the Ballard, Magnolia Bluff, and Bothell areas for several years. While paddling a canoe north of Seattle one day, continuing his search for good timber, he encountered rough water. He quickly pulled into shore, beached the canoe, and began wandering through the forest. Amazed at the virgin timber which grew to the shoreline, he made plans to purchase this property but delayed two years before taking any action. In 1872, he bought the Elwell land site from Frost and the Fowler brothers for $650. Two years later, when he completed his work in Ballard and Bothell, he moved to Edmonds with Etta, the only White woman for miles around. Their daughter Fannie was the first White child born in the area. By 1876, Brackett organized a logging camp and constructed a small wharf at the foot of Bell Street. The original pilings were removed in 1988. Brackett drew up a plat in the mid-1880s and applied for a post office, naming the town after Vermont Senator George Franklin Edmunds. The Post Office Department somehow changed the name to Edmonds. Wilkes named the point just south of town Point Edmund. It is perhaps a coincidence that the two names were identical. Regardless, the U.S. Board on Geographic Names addressed Edmunds vs. Edmonds in 1897. Based on input from the then-current postmaster, the Board favored the current name. The city was incorporated in 1890 with Brackett as its first mayor (Satterfield 14-16; Swift 17). In late 1890, Brackett sold 455 of his accumulated 550 acres for $36,000 to the Minneapolis Realty and Investment Company, a land developer. The new owner, James Bishop, speculated that the planned arrival of the Great Northern Railway would cause a significant boom, but he could not keep up with the payments. Although the railroad came in 1891, Bishop could not capitalize and went bankrupt in 1893. Brackett took his land back. The Investment Company previously started construction of the Bishop Hotel which Brackett sold to Mr. and Mrs. W. S. Stevens on April 16, 1894. Ownership passed through many hands over the years. The hotel was finally demolished in 1975 (Satterfield 18, 36, 367). The Allan M. Yost family arrived in 1890. Yost, born January 19, 1856, in Pennsylvania, married Amanda C. Roth in 1875. Yost moved to Kansas in 1883 and farmed. Losing virtually everything, he continued west, arriving in Edmonds with nine dollars in his pocket. Yost quickly found work in his trade as a carpenter and soon sent for his wife and eight children. Over the years, he opened a shingle mill, erected a wharf, and established a phone company, an automobile company, and a bus company. By the late 1800s, the city had three logging camps, nine shingle mills, two sawmills, three general stores, a hotel, and a number of saloons. As the cedar forests disappeared, the shingle mills slowly went out of business. The last mill, the Quality Shingle Company, closed on June 1, 1951. Construction began on the Edmonds breakwater in 1961. The first expansion was completed in 1968, the second in 1984, and a third in 1989. Yost died in 1915, and Brackett died in 1927 at the age of 86 (Cloud 14; *An Illustrated History*, 951, 959).

Edmund, Point [7d] #146, 1841, Wilkes
See Edwards Point.

Edmund Group [7a] #145, 1841, Wilkes
See Matia Island.

Edwards
See Otis.

Edwards Island
See Harbor Island.

Edwards Point
Located along the mainland at Edmonds, Wilkes originally named this Point Edmund [7d] in 1841 but left no reason for the name. He did not include this name in his *Narrative*, but it is shown on his chart. Edwards Point became official by decision of the U.S. Board on Geographic Names over Point Edmund in 1897.

Eglon

Located on the western shoreline of Admiralty Inlet, three miles south of Point No Point, early settlers originally named both the creek and community Silver Creek, after Charles and Jessie Silver who homesteaded 160 acres in 1891 (Bowen et al., II: 88). The property changed hands over the years. The name was chosen for that ancient land between Canaan and the Mediterranean Coast (TPL website). The Salish name for the area was "abundant little red crab" (Hilbert et. al., 190).

Eld Inlet [7d] #146, 1841, Wilkes; [7i] #147, 1841, Wilkes

Located at the southwestern side of Puget Sound, Wilkes honored crew member Henry Eld in 1841 (Meany, *Origin* 78). The U.S. Board on Geographic Names addressed the Mud Bay variant in 1937 and selected the current name (GNIS files). *See also* Henderson Inlet.

Eldon

Located on the western side of Hood Canal at the mouth of the Hamma Hamma River, it was named for a logger who worked there around 1900 (Hitchman 81).

Elger Bay

It is located off the west side of Camano Island. It was perhaps named after Martha J. Alger who owned land in the area in 1872, as Algers Bay is a variant. In addition, there was an Alger's Bay School in the 1920s (Prasse, 92). Algers Bay appeared on the 1899 version of chart #6450. GNIS files imply it also appeared on the first issue of the chart in 1891. Despite this, the U.S. Board on Geographic Names relied on the memory of J. F. Pratt. Mr. Pratt, who was a surveyor with the C&GS wrote to the Board in 1892, that an "Old Settler" provided him the name of Elger's Bay. The Board settled on the current name in 1895 (GNIS files).

Elgin

Located on the western side of Carr Inlet, the first area post office was run by Ludinca Minter (*see* Minter Creek). In 1892 or 1893, William Kernodle became postmaster and moved the office to the west side of the bay. He named the new community after Elgin, Illinois (Meany, *Origin* 78; Slater 29).

Eliza Island [7a] #145, 1841, Wilkes

Located to the east of Lummi Island and almost in the entrance of Bellingham Bay, Wilkes honored Juan Francisco de Eliza y Reventa, 1759-1825. Eliza entered the Spanish Navy in 1773. He saw duty in the expedition against Algers as well as the American Revolution at Florida. He was sent to San Blas, Mexico in 1789 and led an expedition in 1790 aboard the *Concepción* to Nootka Sound. That summer, he dispatched Salvador Fidalgo to the Alaska Coast and Manuel Quimper to the Strait of Juan de Fuca. In 1791, Eliza led an expedition into inland waters, reaching as far as Texada Island. He returned to San Blas in 1792 and was appointed to the command of the naval facility from 1795-1801. He was transferred to Cadiz, Spain in 1803 where he continued to serve the navy (Meany, *Origin* 78). Lange identified the possibility that Wilkes may also have named it for his sister. With a great deal of monetary backing, Illinois Senator Eugene Canfield purchased it in 1889. He immediately constructed a wharf, drained part of the land for cultivation, built a warehouse, a farmhouse with fourteen rooms, and three dozen other structures on the island. One was the poultry house, some 530 feet in length. Canfield bought 9,000 chickens intending to create the Northwest chicken capital. Business declined and he was soon gone. In 1899, the Pacific American Fisheries Company purchased the island for $3,500 and set up a storage area for fish trap piles. The traps were outlawed in the 1930s and the island economy declined again. The U.S. Navy used the island in 1940 for bombing practice. In the late 1940s or early 1950s, Black Cat, Ltd. ran a fur operation using the pelts of cats. Between 500-1,000 cats were killed each month (McDonald 182, 183; McDonald, Lucile. "Eliza Island." *Seattle Times*. May 1, 1960. Magazine Section p 2).

Eliza Rock

Located to the south of Eliza Island, its name likely came from the island.

Ellinore, Mount

See Fauntleroy Cove.

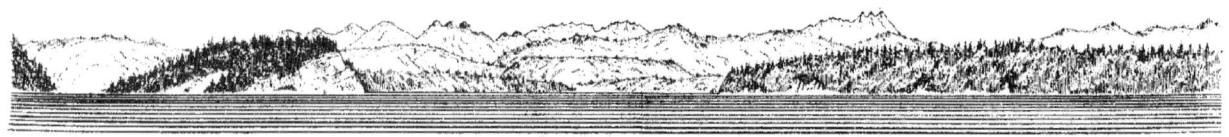

Possession Point   Possession Sound   Elliot Point

Elliot Point [7d] #146, 1841, Wilkes; [7o] #157, 1841, Wilkes

Located on the mainland at Mukilteo, Wilkes may have honored crew member Samuel Elliott in 1841. The U.S. Board on Geographic Names removed a "t" in 1997; likely there was a question on the correct spelling of Elliott's name. While Wilkes reflected it on his chart and journal (several times) as Elliott, consistent with how Samuel Elliott spelled it himself, Wilkes wrote it in his muster with a single "t." Other crew members spelled it both ways. *See also* Elliott Bay.

Elliott Bay [7d] #146, 1841, Wilkes; [7m] #160, 1841, Wilkes

According to Meany (*Origin* 78), the bay was named for Rev. J. L. Elliott, the chaplain during Wilkes' Exploration. There were two other Elliotts on the cruise, Midshipman Samuel Elliott and a first class boy, George Elliott. It is unlikely Wilkes would have bestowed a name for George Elliott. That leaves Samuel or the Rev. According to Howard Hanson (*The Naming of Elliott Bay* 28-32), there is some Wilkes material that Meany apparently did not review. Wilkes wrote: "So many reports and facts having been communicated to me respecting Mr. Elliot the Chaplain that I came to the conclusion that it was my duty to suspend him which I reluctantly did this day [April 2, 1841] by letter he having applied to leave the ship which I should have been inclined to grant if we had been anywhere but at Honolulu. The charges made against him are willfully & maliciously slandering the officers of the squadron particularly those of this ship [ ], falsehood, prevarications and lying also his indecent and ungentlemanly conduct towards Mrs. Smith . . ." In fact, Rev. J. L. Elliott resigned and quit the cruise in October 1841 as a result of the controversy. From this information, it seems extremely unlikely that Wilkes would have honored him with any place name. The dilemma is that Wilkes also named Elliot Point. It also seems unlikely that he would have named two places 20 miles apart for the same gentleman. Thus, it is unclear who Wilkes intended to honor for either point. Regarding Elliott Bay, Wilkes wrote (*Narrative* 316): "The anchorage is of comparatively small extent, owing to the great depth of water, as well as to the extensive mud-flats; these are bare at low water. Three small streams enter at the head of the bay, where good water may be obtained. I do not consider the bay a desirable anchorage; from the west it is exposed to the prevailing winds, and during their strength there is much sea." Acting Master George Sinclair also had some thoughts regarding Elliott Bay: "There is a large Bay nearly opposite to Port Orchard into the head of which a small river discharges itself. I was sent to examine this Bay & found it much too extensive to pull round it in one day. I however saw enough of it to convince us that it is not of much importance, the water being very deep in the outer part & shoaling very suddenly to three miles from the back of it at which distance a mud bank commences & fills the whole back of the Bay," (Blumenthal, *Charles Wilkes* 178). Davidson wrote: "Through the centre of the bay the depth ranges from 88 to 40 fathoms. On the north side of Battery Point [Alki Point] a vessel anchoring in 20 fathoms cannot have a greater scope of chain than 35 fathoms without being to close to the shore. When we anchored there in 13 fathoms and veered to 25 fathoms of chain the vessel's stern was in 2½ fathoms." He went on to say: "On this side of Battery Point is the deserted town of Alki, (the Indian phrase for 'by and by'). The town has had several names, but there is nothing about it to command trade," (Davidson, *Report* 446). Davidson also mentioned the name Duwamish Bay. Ezra Meeker didn't think much of Elliott Bay either. In 1853 he wrote: "It was not much of a town, probably 20 cabins in all with a few new frame houses. The timber was scarcely beyond the reach of the mill and there was not the semblance of a street. The lagoon presented an uninviting appearance and scent where the filling with sawdust and slabs had begun. The mill was the life of the place." He later clarified and referenced it as an "ill-smelling lagoon" (Conover, C. T. "Just Cogitating: Ezra Meeker Made and Wrote Puget Sound History." *Seattle Times*. Apr. 9, 1961. Magazine Section p 6). The U.S. Board on Geographic Names addressed the variant of Duwamish Bay in 1895 and selected the current name.

Ellis Cove & Creek
Located at Priest Point north of Olympia, the area was logged by Isaac Ellis in 1856. Ellis Creek flows into the cove (TPL website).

Ellisport
It is located in Tramp Harbor on the eastern side of Vashon Island. According to http://www.historylink.org — when the post office opened in 1888, settlers gave the name of Chautauqua to the community. Chautauqua was a non-profit institution founded in 1874 in New York as an educational experiment and because of its success, expanded to include academic subjects, the arts, physical education, and music. The movement gave rise to "mini-Chautauquas" around the country. Edward E. Perry was the first postmaster. The Rev. Ellis settled there in 1879 and founded the community. The name was changed in 1912 (Meany, *Origin* 79).

Elwha River [8a] #1917, 1847, Kellett
Flowing into the Strait of Juan de Fuca near Port Angeles, Kellett provided the name in 1847. *Elwha* is an Indian name meaning "elk."

Elwha Rock
The famed rock is located in Harney Channel, just east of Grindstone Harbor. It is always underwater, but apparently not far enough, as the ferry Elwha discovered by depositing some green and white paint upon it (and holing the boat!). The ferry was built in 1967 and named after the Elwha River, which was, in turn, named after the Indian village located at the mouth. The name means "elk." The press had wonderful fun reporting the accident. Headlines included: "Ferry Hits Reef; Steering Failure Blamed"; "Why was the Elwha off course?"; "Ferry Crash Blamed On Tour Given Woman"; "Ferry Chief Lambasts Skipper As 'Irresponsible' "; "Ferry Often Makes Passes Near Shore, Area Residents Say"; and another, "Elwha Joyride." Even before repairs were made, which cost $200,000, the skipper 'retired' and the General Manager of the Ferry System, Nick Tracy, was fired. On October 2, 1983, the Elwha started its initial westbound trip of the morning by passing close to shore near Grindstone Harbor. The Elwha's skipper, Billy Fittro, was apparently attempting to show off for a couple of women who lived nearby. On its 5:00 P.M. run from Anacortes, one of the women, Peggy Warrack, was on the bridge in the wheelhouse. According to the skipper's testimony, the woman asked for a closer view of her home. The skipper complied, and the 382 foot ferry hit the rock at full speed, 17½ knots. Passengers and on-shore observers stated, "It sounded like thunder. It tore full bore into that reef and never slowed down . . ." Another Grindstone Harbor resident said, "When it hit, it was just like an earthquake. Glass shook in the windows, dishes rattled in the cupboards." The damage took out one of Elwha's two rudders, ripped the hull with a 1½ to 2 foot gash, and opened a 5 foot seam along the keel. Proceeding on its run, the ferry eventually lost steerage entirely and was doing doughnuts in mid-channel according to one observer. In 1989, Greg Lange submitted a proposal to the Washington Board on Geographic Names to name this feature Elwha Rock. Mr. Lange cited a strong tradition to name reefs after the ship that first hit them and local support for the change. Even though the ferry system opposed the name, the Board approved it in its December 8, 1989 meeting, Docket 342. The U.S. Board followed in 1990 (from Washington State Board Files). The song written to commemorate the event goes something like this:
Out in Friday Harbor where the jazz bands play,
You can take a ferry out there almost any time of day.
You can cruise through Grindstone's Harbor,
And when the ferry docks,
You pour a long, tall cool one,
Called Elwha on the Rocks.
With the Lady in the wheelhouse,

You can cruise along the shore.
You can blow the ferry's whistle,
As you pass by her front door.
You can blame it on the steering,
If the ferry rams the dock,
And we'll pour a long, tall cool one,
Called Elwha on the Rocks.
We love our ferry system,
It's always in the news;
We're changing to computers,
Cuz computers don't drink booze . . .

The drink consisted of equal parts Meyer's Rum Crème and Meyer's Rum, on ice.

Elwood Point
Located on the western side of Ostrich Bay in Dyes Inlet, the source of the name is unknown.

Enetai
Located on the western side of Port Orchard, north of Bremerton, it was the site of Capt. William Renton's sawmill in 1854. Renton moved from Alki Point to Enetai Beach (local name), and then he sold in the early 1860s to J. Coleman and A. K. P. Glidden. The community, which was originally named Port Orchard, swiftly grew with hotels, saloons, and the company store (Bowen et al., III: 2, 3). *Enetai* is Chinook for "across, opposite, or on the other side," (Hitchman 84).

Enetai Creek
The Enetai Creek flows into Port Orchard and was named for the community of Enetai. According to the description on 2003 information submitted by the Manette History Club to the Washington State Board on Geographic Names, it is approximately 1½ miles long, 6 feet wide, and 6 inches deep. The Board approved the name, and the U.S. Board followed in 2006. It had numerous early names including Croxton's Creek, Dee Creek, Howerton's Creek, Jensen's Creek, McMicken Creek, and Micam Creek.

English Boom
Located about a mile southeast of Brown Point, Camano Island, it was named for the English Logging Company or English Lumber Company that boomed their logs in that location. The company was sold in 1945 to the Puget Sound Pulp and Timber Company and the booming grounds fell into disuse. It is now the site of the English Boom Historical Park (http://redmondlibrary.blogspot.com/2010/05/english-boom-historical-park-camano.html).

English Camp

English Camp
Located in Garrison Bay on San Juan Island, it was the site of the British garrison during the Pig War. American and British tensions on San Juan Island ran high. The British claimed the island and established a sheep and cattle ranch (Bellevue Farm) at the south end. American settlers were verbally hostile to this intrusion by the Brits and ignored the British claims. One settler, Lyman Cutler, even established his own small farm in the middle of Bellevue Farm and planted potatoes. John Griffin, an officer of the Hudson's Bay Company responsible for Bellevue Farm, owned a pig. One day, Cutler found the pig routing out and eating his potatoes, and this wasn't the first occasion. Cutler shot the pig, and thus began the "Pig War", initially a war of words, but it escalated rapidly. Because the Americans stationed troops on San Juan Island, the British followed suit and dispatched a single company of the Royal Marines Light Infantry in late March 1860 commanded by Capt. George Bazalgette. The British built some twenty structures. Relations between the American and British commanders were good, and troops frequently socialized with each other. Capt. William A. Delacombe replaced Bazalgette in 1867. In 1871, the parties agreed to submit their boundary claims to arbitration. In late October 1871, the Emperor of Germany placed the boundary at Haro Strait

(Richardson, *Pig* 143-151). The British left Garrison Bay on November 18, 1871. William Crook was born in Yorkshire, England in 1836 and arrived in the U.S. at age 16. He first lived in New Orleans and then migrated to Canada where he married Mary Forrest. Slowly, the couple worked their way west via Nebraska and Wyoming, and they arrived on San Juan Island in 1874. Coincidentally, the Pig War was winding down and the British were departing. Crook was fortunate to claim the camp, along with the buildings. One washday, the stove heating the hot water overheated and the barracks caught fire. They then moved into one of the cottages on the hillside. Mary died in 1899. The Oct. 26, 1899 *San Juan Islander* reported: "Mrs. Wm. Crook, who suffered a stroke of paralysis at her historic old home at English Camp a few days ago, died Monday afternoon. She had improved enough to be able to sit up and converse with her family and friends, although she had an attack of pneumonia and suffered much from pleurisy." William died in 1901. Their son James (1873-1967) spent 88 of his 90 years there. Jim, as he was known, tended the English cemetery on the hillside above the camp. He kept the fence painted and the weeds to a minimum. Seven British soldiers are buried there, victims of drowning, sickness, suicide, or accidental shooting. For his continued actions, the Canadian Government paid him $10 annually. Later in life, Jim's sister, Mary Davis (*see also* Davis Bay), cooked and cared for him. She had an unfortunate accident in her Model A Ford in 1959 and died. Jim's other sister, Rhoda Anderson, cared for him after Mary's death. The State of Washington purchased 87 acres of his homestead in 1963, including some land on Mt. Young, for $106,000. Jim retained a 200 feet swath along the bay and some other land. It became a National Park in 1966 with legislation signed by Lyndon B. Johnson and included more than 500 acres. Following Jim's death in 1967, Rhoda remained on the homestead until her death in early 1971 (Washington Rural Heritage website; McDonald 62-64, 78; McDonald, Lucile. "Historic Acres to Be a State Park." *Seattle Times*. Dec. 15, 1963. Magazine Section p 7). Four buildings as well as the formal gardens have been reconstructed and preserved. The blockhouse stands near the edge of the bay. On the open parade ground is a commissary, a storehouse, a barracks, and a masonry ruin nearby (*English Camp* 13). In 1991, the National Park Service recommended changing the name. In their submittal, they noted: "The British Marines occupied this area during the time of joint occupation. This was due to the boundary dispute between British-controlled Canada and America. The National Park Service has taken a course of action to change the name from English Camp to British Camp to reflect that the troops stationed here were from throughout Britain, and not just England." Previous to this request, in 1986 the Park Service changed all the signage to British Camp, before the Washington State Board even addressed the matter. The file on this subject includes numerous letters from locals, both for and against the change, and runs 113 pages. One letter strongly argued that the proper name is Royal Marine Camp, as that is what it was called by the British Admiralty. Eventually, the Board relied on the long and heavy use of the name English Camp and denied the request to change it, Docket 348 (from Washington State Board Files). But for their embassies, English Camp was the last spot in the United States where the British flag flew as a symbol of sovereignty.

Enriquita [24] #1947, 1849, Inskip
See Pitt Island.

Enterprise Bay
Located between False Bay and Kanaka Bay on the western side of San Juan Island, the origin of the name is unknown.

Entrance Mount [13a] #2689, 1859, Richards
Located on the eastern side of Orcas Island and overlooking East Sound, it was likely named as the "entrance" to East Sound.

Entrance Rock [17] #27, 1862, U.S. Coast Survey
See Davidson Rock.

Entrance Shoal [13c] #2689, 1865
See Blakely Island Shoal.

Erie, Mount [7a] #145, 1841, Wilkes
Located in the middle of Fidalgo Island, Wilkes named the peak in 1841 honoring Commodore Oliver Hazard Perry and his victory over the British in the Battle of Lake Erie during the War of 1812 (Meany, *Origin* 176).

Burrows, Allan Islands   Fidalgo Island   Mount Erie   Deception Pass   Whidbey Island

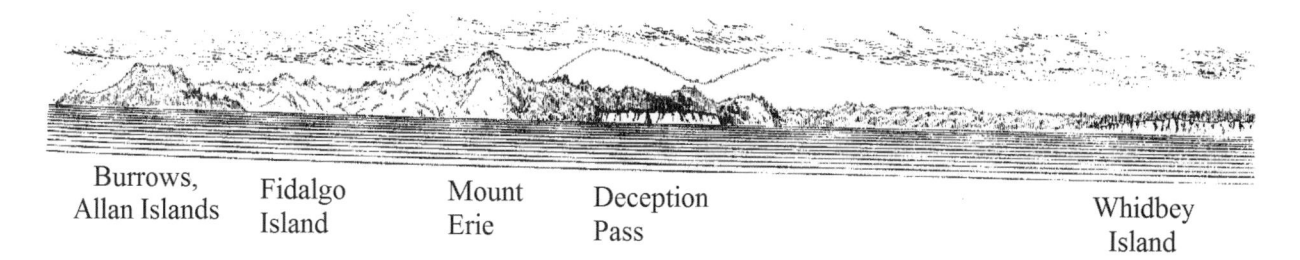

Erlands Point

Located at the southern end of Dyes Inlet with Chico Bay to its west, it was originally named Steve's Point for Steve Wilson, an Indian, who was involved in the construction of a Catholic Church. Knute and Marie Erland later purchased property on the point and began camping on it in 1912 (TPL website). Currently, the U.S. Board on Geographic Names recognizes the name Erland Point for the cape and Erlands Point for the community. Nautical charts reflect simply the name of Erland. As the descriptor "point" is not also present, one would assume that this name applies only to the community, as the point is left unnamed. Topographic maps show the name Erlands Point. I suspect that when the Washington State Board on Geographic Names addresses this inconsistency, the name Erland will disappear.

Eureka Beach

Located on the eastern side of San Juan Island north of Point Caution, it was the site of the Eureka Lime Works. According to Lange and Wood (139), it had a hotel, saloon, wharf, warehouse, two kilns, and a post office. The community was named Werner after John C. Werner, the general superintendent of the lime company. About 20 families lived there until the 1890s when the operation shut down. Neither local name is reflected on current charts; it is shown as abandoned on http://kaga.wsulibs.wsu.edu/cdm-maps/sanjuantsheet.html on the 1895 t-sheet #2231. According to the December 24, 1896 issue of *The Islander* (3): "Mr. A. Newhall, owner of the mail steamer Buckeye, has purchased the cordwood that has been piled at Eureka for several years past and is now using it on the steamer. There are about 250 cords and most of it is sound and dry." An 1894 Descriptive Report #2231 on Washington Sound referenced the area (http://riverhistory.ess.washington.edu/tsheets/framedex.htm): "From Pt Caution to Signal "Shed," a distance of 1½ miles, the shores are rocky and bold, and the water deep close to the shoreline. There are no reefs in this stretch. Signal "Shed" is the gable end of the large warehouse on the wharf at Eureka Limekiln. This Limekiln has been abandoned and the buildings are fast falling to decay. It was the largest of the many plants at one time in operation among these islands. There are two substantial kilns and a number of vacant houses beside a good wharf and large warehouse," (from Washington State files, Avalon Island).

Ev Henry Point

Located on the southwestern entrance to Fossil Bay, it is a local name which honored Everett Henry. Another local name, mentioned in the May 16, 1895 edition of *The Islander* was Fossil Point. J. J. Gilbert noted the name of Fossil Point in his 1888 Descriptive Report #1870 (http://riverhistory.ess.washington.edu/tsheets/reports/t1870.pdf, p 8). *See* Sucia.

Evans, Point [23] #6460, 1905

It is located on the western side of The Narrows. The origin of the name is unknown.

Evans Cove

Located off the southern end of Orcas Island, a half mile east of Pole Pass, the origin of the name is unknown.

Evans Rock [23] #6460, 1905

Located off Point Evans in The Narrows, it likely took its name from the point.

Everett

Located on the eastern shores of Port Gardner, Everett was named in 1890 for the young son of Charles L. Colby, a wealthy financier from New York. Colby was investing in land purchases with Henry Hewitt, Jr. in the Everett area, and ultimately

Everett

included John D. Rockefeller in the partnership. The group built a shipyard, nail factory, paper mill, a street railroad, hotels, mines, and the smelter. Everett was incorporated in 1893. Rockefeller ultimately sold all of his land holdings to Frederick Weyerhaeuser in 1900 for $5.4 million (Clark 19-23). When Everett Colby grew up, he graduated from Brown University and Harvard Law. He became a state senator in Olympia and in 1917 Chairman of the U.S. Food Administration (Brokenshire 74).

Ewing Cove
It is located between Ewing and Sucia Islands and was likely named for the U.S. Survey Schooner *Ewing*.

Ewing Island [13a] #2689, 1859, Richards
Located off the eastern side of Sucia Island, it was likely named for the U.S. Survey Schooner *Ewing* (Meany, *Origin* 82).

Fair Harbor
Located on the western side of Case Inlet behind Reach Island, Hitchman (87) suggested it was named because the narrow channel provides only a fair harbor.

Fairhaven [20a] #6376, 1856, U.S. Coast Survey
See Bellingham.

Fairhaven Bay [20a] #6376, 1856, U.S. Coast Survey
See Bellingham.

Fairmount
Located at the head of Discovery Bay, it was named by Thomas Borger for his home in Pennsylvania (*With Pride* 153).

Falk Bay
See Murden Cove.

False Bay [13a] #2689, 1859, Richards
Located on the southwestern side of San Juan Island, the large bay is essentially dry at low water, the result of river silt from the south end of the island, and thus is Richards' reason for the name. Wood (91, 92) explained that later U.S. charts changed the name to Kanaka Bay, and indeed it appears on Admiralty charts beginning with [13i] in 1892. The 1862 U.S. Coast Survey on [17] reflected the name of Foul Bay, clearly an error which was corrected four years later on [18].

False Bay [13b] #2689, 1861, Richards
See Swifts Bay.

False Dungeness
See Ediz Hook.

Fauntleroy Cove
Located along the Seattle shoreline, four miles south of Alki Point, the U.S. Coast Survey named the cove in 1857 (Davidson, *Report* 448). Meany (*Origin* 83, 84) indicated that Davidson honored the survey brig *R.H. Fauntleroy* which in turn he named for Lieut. Robert Henry Fauntleroy. Davidson married Fauntleroy's daughter Ellinore in 1858. Also, in 1857, Davidson named several Olympic peaks for his future wife, her sister, and her two brothers. Thus, we have Mount Ellinore, Mount Constance, and The Brothers. In 1968, the U.S. Board on Geographic Names received a proposal from Mrs. Thomas Horn to change the name of The Brothers to Brother Kennedy Mountains to commemorate the Kennedy brothers. The Washington State Board thanked Mrs. Horn for her suggestion but politely declined the change.

Fauntleroy Point
Located on the northeastern side of Decatur Island, it likely honored the survey brig *R.H. Fauntleroy* which George Davidson named for Lieut. Robert Henry Fauntleroy, his father-in-law.

Fawn Island [14a] #2840, 1861, Richards
Located in Deer Harbor, Orcas Island, Richards likely named it for the abundance of deer in the vicinity. McLellan referenced that the name had been changed to Fisherman Island, but it apparently didn't last.

Fern Cove
Located along the western side of Vashon Island, the U.S. Coast Survey named it in 1857 because of the plant life (Davidson, *Report* 448).

Fern Point
Located on the western side of Lummi Island north of Village Point, the origin of the name is unknown.

Ferncliff
It is located on the eastern side of Bainbridge Island a half mile north of Yeomalt. Hitchman (89) indicated that the descriptive name was chosen by a pioneer named Lowman. It is mentioned in the 1942 *Pacific Coast Pilot* (257) although it is spelled Ferncliffe. The name is not reflected on current charts, but it is recognized by the U.S. Board on Geographic Names.

Fidalgo
See Dewey.

Fidalgo, Boca de [1] 1790, Quimper
See Rosario Strait.

Fidalgo Bay
Located off the northeastern side of Fidalgo Island, the name likely came from the island (Meany, *Origin* 85). The Salish name for the bay was "protected place where there is calm water" (Hilbert et. al., 351).

Fidalgo City [21] #6300, 1895
Located on Fidalgo Island near Dewey, it merged with Gibraltar in 1893 (Meany, *Origin* 85).

Fidalgo Head
It is located on the far western side of Fidalgo Island. In 1841, Wilkes named it Raindeer Point [7m]. Wilkes did not include this name in his *Narrative*, but it is shown on his chart. The current name does not appear on any pre-1900 U.S. or Admiralty charts. But the name, like that of Fidalgo Bay, likely came from the island.

Fidalgo Island [8a] #1917, 1847, Kellett
It is located on the eastern side of Rosario Strait. Wilkes originally named it Perrys Island in 1841 [7a], [7m] for Commodore Oliver Hazard Perry who fought in the Battle of Lake Erie during the War of 1812. Wilkes also named Mount Erie, the highest peak on the island (Meany, *Origin* 85). In his attempt to restore Spanish names, Kellett replaced *Boca de Fidalgo* with Rosario Strait and moved the name Fidalgo to the island. Manuel Quimper was the originator of the name [1] in 1790 after Salvador Fidalgo, a naval officer who at that time was exploring Alaska (Wagner 111).

Filucy Bay
Located off the eastern side of the Great Peninsula, northwest from Anderson Island, Wilkes originally named this Titusi Bay [7i] in 1841. He left no reason for the name although perhaps it was his understanding of the name of the Indian woman who lived on the bay. It is reflected on his chart but not in his *Narrative*. In 1846, Inskip called this Turnours Bay [24] for Nicholas Turnour, Captain of H.M.S *Clio* from 1864-1868 (Meany, *Origin* 85). The Canadian trapper Pierre Legard and his wife the Haida Indian Princess Filucy were the first settlers in the bay. They built a cabin in the 1830s. Joe Shettleroe arrived in 1859. A man named French and his Indian wife Soldier Sally helped him in the logging business. Joe donated land at the head of the bay for the first school which was completed in 1885. Henry Mahncke homesteaded in the bay in 1886; the following year, William Sipple joined him. Sipple ran a carpentry and boatbuilding business on the old Legard site. His shed still stands on the bay (Bailey and Nyberg, *Gunkholing in South Puget Sound* 226; Slater 2, 76). The U.S. Board on Geographic Names addressed variant names in 1941: Filuce Bay, Longbranch Bay, Tetusi Bay, Titusi Bay, and Turnours Bay, and selected the current name (*Decisions*). According to the GNIS files, the name Filucy first appeared on an 1891 map by Fred G. Plummer. Over the years, the other variants were also used on various maps and charts. In 1951, Myron L. Frost, a landowner on the bay, provided some additional information to the U.S. Board. His interesting theory was that Wilkes' men named the bay Felucca which was a type of boat used on the Mediterranean. They were unsure how to spell the word, and hence, it became Feluce. Mr. Frost believes that when Wilkes' material was published, Feluce was transcribed in error as Titusi. The Board thanked him for his thoughts (GNIS files).

Finch Point
See Yeomalt Point.

Finlayson, Mount [13a] #2689, 1859, Richards
Located on the south end of San Juan Island, the 295 foot hill was named for Roderick Finlayson, Chief Factor of the Hudson's Bay Company. Born in 1818 in Scotland, he migrated to Canada in 1837. Finlayson immediately began working as a clerk for the Hudson's Bay Company upon his arrival and saw most of his service in Victoria where he was assigned in 1843. The following year, he was placed in charge of the Victoria Station. He married John Work's daughter Sarah in 1849. He held various positions in the Hudson's Bay Company until his retirement in 1872. He was also active in politics, serving as a member of Vancouver Island's Colonial Legislative Council and Mayor of Vancouver among other positions. Finlayson died in Victoria in 1892 at the age of 74. According to Walbran (178), he was "practically the founder of Victoria." Paul K. Hubbs, the customs inspector for San Juan Island, established a farm on a portion of the mountain. He named it Floraville for his wife Flora ("Cattle Point, on San Juan Island." *Seattle Times*. Mar. 6, 1960. Magazine Section p 9). *See also* Jakles Lagoon.

First Beach
It is located between Baada and Dtokoah Points on the Strait of Juan de Fuca. Further to the east are Second Beach and Third Beach. All were named in sequence because they were respectively, the first beaches south of the Indian Village of La Push (Parratt 48).

Fisgard Island [24] #1947, 1849, Inskip
See Anderson Island.

Fish Creek [15a] #611, 1865, Richards
Located on the southeastern end of San Juan Island, Richards likely named it for the Hudson's Bay Company smokehouse located there in the 1850s. According to Wood (92, 93), the name creek is a misnomer because of differences in American vs. British usage of the term. The British meant "A comparatively narrow inlet, of fresh or salt water, which is tidal throughout its course." In U.S. usage, a creek is a freshwater stream. Although there is no freshwater entering Fish Creek, the name survived. Wood also referenced the name God's Pocket attributed to the bay. It is reflected on a map entitled "South-East San Juan Island in Pig War Days," (Richardson, *Pig* 117). According to Lucile McDonald, it was a hiding place for smugglers ("Rabbit-Hunters 'Take Over' Historic Site." *Seattle Times*. Nov. 20, 1960. Magazine Section p 7). Another name for the bay was Illinois Inlet named by Walter Muenscher, honoring the Illinois State Representative at the Puget Sound Marine Station.

Fish Creek

Fish Point
Located at the eastern end of the Lummi Reservation on the northwestern side of Bellingham Bay, the source of the name is unknown.

Fish Point
Located on the northeastern side of Samish Island, named for the squatters who lived and fished there (http://www.samishisland.net/documents/historicdocuments/SamishHistoryHopleyClift.html).

Fisherman Bay

Fisherman Bay [21] #6300, 1895
Located off the western side of Lopez Island, Richards reflected this on earlier Admiralty charts as Lagoon. *See also* Lopez.

Fisherman Harbor [22] #6450, 1909
Located off the southern side of the Toandos Peninsula on Hood Canal, the secluded cove provided refuge for fishermen looking to get out of the weather on the canal and thus acquired the name.

Fisherman Island
See Fawn Island.

Fishermans Cove
Located on the mainland on Hale Passage east of Lummi Island, it is home to the ferry terminal. In 1990, to resolve spelling differences, the U.S. Board on Geographic Names addressed Fisherman vs. Fishermans. The Board approved the current name at its November 14, 1991 meeting, Docket 348 (GNIS files).

Fishermans Point
Located on the eastern entrance to Quilcene Bay, Wilkes named this Rose Point [7k] in 1841 (*Narrative* 324). He left no reason for the name, although it is likely descriptive.

Fishery Point
Located on the northwestern side of Waldron Island, it was likely named for the occupation of the early residents.

Fishing Bay [13a] #2689, 1859, Richards
Located at the head of East Sound, Orcas Island, Wilkes named it Morses Cove [7a] in 1841 for crew member William H. Morse. Wilkes did not include this name in his *Narrative*, but it is shown on his chart. Richards named it for good fishing found by his crew (Hitchman 92).

Flag Point [7p] #150, 1841, Wilkes
See Walan Point.

Flagler, Fort
Fort Flagler, at Marrowstone Point, was named in honor of General D. W. Flagler. Surveyed in 1896, construction began the following year. Troops arrived in 1902. Activities at Fort Flagler subsided after the end of World War I but increased during World War II. Deactivated in 1953, the Washington State Parks and Recreation Commission acquired the 806 acre property (*With Pride* 256-258).

Flagstaff Point
It is connected to the western end of Kiket Island by a sand spit. The origin is unknown.

Flapjack Point
Located on the western shore of Eld Inlet, the origin of the name is unknown.

Flat Creek [9f] #1911, 1874
Located on the western side of Lopez Island, it perhaps took its name from Flat Point. It may also appear on [9e].

Flat Point

Flat Point [13a] #2689, 1859, Richards
Located on the northwestern side of Lopez Island, it was likely named for its appearance.

Cape Flattery   Fuca Pillar   Tatoosh Island Lighthouse

Flattery, Cape
"This cape forms the southern head of the entrance of the Strait of Juan de Fuca. It has a bold, wild, jagged sea-face, about 100 feet high, much disintegrated by the wearing action of the ocean; rises in a mile to an irregular hill of 1,500 or 2,000 feet in height; is cut up by gorges and covered with a dense growth of fir and almost impenetrable underbrush from the edge of the cliffs to the summit," (Davidson, *Report* 414). It was first named *Punta de Martinez* in 1790 by Quimper [1] for Estéban José Martinez, an explorer on the West Coast who took possession of Nootka Sound in 1789 to prevent Russian encroachment. The name is reflected on Quimper's chart but not in his journal. It is, however, noted in Eliza's journal (Wagner 182). Its present name was given by Capt. James Cook. According to his journal entry for March 22, 1778: "I continued to stand to the North with a fine breeze at West, and West North West, till near seven o'clock in the evening, when I tacked to wait for day-light. At this time, we were in forty-eight fathoms water, and about four leagues from the land, which extended from North to South East half East, and a small round hill, which had the appearance of being an island, bore North three quarters East, distant six or seven leagues, as I guessed; it appears to be of a tolerable height, and was but just to be seen from the deck. Between this island or rock, and the Northern extreme of the land, there appearing to be a small opening, which flattered us with the hopes of finding an harbour. These hopes lessened as we drew nearer; and at last, we had some reason to think, that the opening was closed by low land. On this account I called the point of land to the North of it Cape Flattery." Vancouver wrote in 1792: "About noon, we reached its south entrance, which I understand the natives distinguish by the name of Classet," (Vancouver 216). Davidson explained this naming: "On recent English charts it is called Cape Classet, because, in 1792, Vancouver stated that as the name given by the Indians to distinguish it, but in a marginal note it is called 'Cape Flattery' " (Davidson, *Report* 414).

Flattop Island [7a] #145, 1841, Wilkes
Located to the northeast of Spieden Island, Wilkes presumably chose the name in 1841 for its appearance (Meany, *Origin* 87). Wilkes did not include this name in his *Narrative*, but it is shown on his chart. The U.S. Government owns the 54 acre island.

Fleming Beach
The July 14, 1906 of *The San Juan Islander*, p 8, contained the following note: "Many of the purse seiners have established their camp for this season at Fleming's Beach. There are eleven or twelve 'outfits' there and twenty or more at Eagle Cove." The referenced property belonged to Thomas Fleming, born in Glasgow, Scotland in 1819 and arrived on San Juan Island in 1863 via Australia and San Francisco. He and his wife Mary plus eleven children homesteaded land overlooking Kanaka Bay on the southwestern side of the island (http://wagenweb.org/sanjuan/obits.htm). A picture of the homestead appears in Vouri, *San Juan Island*, p 57. Although the local name did not become permanent, the Fleming family lived on the homestead for years. Mary died in 1902. When Thomas died in 1908, the property was passed to his son Archibald.

Fletcher Bay [22] #6450, 1909
Located on the western side of Bainbridge Island, both the bay and community were named for William Fletcher who settled there with George Allep in 1869. They logged the land with their Indian wives and large families (*An Historic* 10). Hitchman (92) noted the variant of Greek George's Bay which appeared on

the 1881 t-sheet #1637, perhaps for Allep. The Salish name for the bay was "bitten into." The name refers to a monster living in the bay that attacked anyone who crossed its mouth (Hilbert et. al., 226).

Flint Beach
Located on the southern end of Lopez Island, it is the small bay between Iceberg Point and Aleck Bay. It was likely named for the Flint family. Three Flint brothers settled on Lopez in 1869, along with the James Davis family, Charles Anderson, and John Shearer who was the first coroner and probate judge in San Juan County (http://freepages.history.rootsweb.ancestry.com/~lopezislandhistory/history_of_lopez_island.html).
The 1885 San Juan County census lists the Flint family as nine members from ages 1-39.

Flon, Boca de [1] 1790, Quimper
See Deception Pass.

Florence
It is located up the Stillaguamish River. Henry Marshall settled in the Stanwood area in 1864, and late that year he filed a claim three miles up the Stillaguamish River. In 1866, James Perkins purchased the Marshall claim and opened a hotel. In 1884, F. E. Norton built a store and established a post office, naming the town after his old sweetheart (Essex 1, 2; Phillips 51).

Florence Island
Located on the eastern shore of Port Susan and bounded by Hat Slough and the Stillaguamish River on the north, east, and southern sides, the drained marshland is now used for productive farmland. It was named in 1883 for the pioneer daughter of F. S. Norton (Hitchman 93). The relationship of F. S. Norton to F. E. Norton who named Florence is unknown, although Hitchman may have been in error.

Floridablanca, Boca de
See Boundary Bay.

Flounder Bay [13h] #2689, 1888
Located off the western side of Fidalgo Island, in 1841 Wilkes originally named it Sanfords Cove [7a], [7m] for either quartermaster Thomas Sandford or Passed Midshipman Joseph Sanford (Blumenthal, *Charles Wilkes* 82). Wilkes reflected the latter name in his muster table as Joseph Sandford but spelled it both ways in his *Narrative*. The cove was more likely named for Joseph as he was involved in survey duties in the area. Peter Puget had some interesting comments regarding camping near the bay: ". . . we brought up the Night on the Continental Shore on a narrow Spit of Low Sandy Soil on which was immense Quantities of Drift Wood this however is to be found on every Beach. behind this Neck of Land is a Large Lagoon with some Remnants of Huts where the Indians must have been very recently—Here we passed a most uncomfortable Night tormented by Musquito's & Sand Flies, which however was in some measure forgot in the morning by a large Supply of Strawberries and Wild Onions, which were found growing Spontaneously close to the Tents," (Puget 213). Flounder Bay originally was a log pond for rafts destined for the E. K. Wood Mill, which started in 1923 and went out of business in the 1950s. In the 1960s, real estate developer Harry Davidson dredged the bay and sold home sites (Bailey and Nyberg, *San Juan Islands* 218, 219). The 600 foot drying shed originally used by the mill still sits on the west side of the bay. It is currently in use by the marina for boat repairs and storage.

Flower Island [21] #6300, 1895
Located off the northeastern side of Lopez Island, north of Spencer Spit, the origin of the name is unknown. The U.S. Government owns the island.

Flower Island
See Picnic Island.

Floyd Cove
Located off McNeil Island in Pitt Passage, Joseph E. Floyd owned land there and was the postmaster of Meridian from 1903-1915 (Reese, *Origins* 44).

Fonte Bank [8d] #1917, Sept. 25, 1865
See Hein Bank.

Forbes Point [6] 1792, Vancouver
Located on the easterly side of Whidbey Island, between Oak and Crescent Harbors, Vancouver reflected this name on his chart but not in his journal. He left no reason for the name. Wilkes originally named this Kalamut Island [7a], [7e] in

1841 (*Narrative* 316) for the Indian name *Cal-a-met* which means "stone or rocky ground" (Hitchman 141). Alternatively, according to Hale (586), it was a Nez Perce name meaning "pipe." The Nez Perce Indians lived primarily in Idaho. Wilkes believed Kalamut to be an island, or perhaps a tombolo, rather than a point. Current marine charts are confusing with respect to the point. Some reflect Forbes Point as the entire point which extends from the City of Oak Harbor. Other charts reflect the name solely as the southeast tip, with the southernmost tip named Maylor Point. The Salish name for the point was "flea" (Hilbert et. al., 360).

Fords Point
See Blowers Bluff.

Fortress Island
Located in the southern end of Lopez Sound, the U.S. Coast Survey named it for its appearance (TPL website). McLellan indicated that this was shown on Admiralty charts as Crown Island. At a bit over three acres, it rises to 100 feet in the center. The U.S. Government owns the island.

Fosdick, Point [7d] #146, 1841, Wilkes; [7g] #155, 1841, Wilkes; [7h] #154, 1841, Wilkes
Located at the southwestern entrance to The Narrows, Wilkes honored crew member Stephen Fosdick (Meany, *Origin* 218). Wilkes did not include this name in his *Narrative*, but it is shown on his charts. Archibald Menzies, who explored the area with Peter Puget on the Vancouver expedition, wrote: "We pursued our Southerly direction with a strong flood tide in our favor & about two in the afternoon we came to another arm leading off to the Westward which we enterd & found a very strong tide against us. At this time we were at a loss how to account for this as it evidently appeard to be the flood tide by rising on the shore, though we afterwards found that it was occasioned by a number of Islands round which the Tide had reverted / & as it was very strong against us we disembarkd on the Point to dine till it should slacken a little," (Menzies 33).

Fossil Bay

Fossil Bay
Located off the southern side of Sucia Island, it was named for the fossils found in the eroded shoreline surrounding the bay.

Fossil Point
See E. V. Henry Point.

Foster Point [13a] #2689, 1859, Richards
Located in the southern portion of Orcas Island, about two miles east of the ferry terminal, Richards left no reason for the name. It may have been named for Major George Foster, a retired British officer. He came to the West Coast in 1859 and purchased property in Esquimalt. He held various political positions on Vancouver Island, including a member of the House of Assembly of Vancouver Island. He was also a Colonel of the Volunteer Rifle Corps on the island. He returned to England about 1870 and died in 1887 (Walbran 187).

Foulweather Bluff [6] 1792, Vancouver
Located along the western shoreline of Admiralty Inlet, Vancouver named this in 1792. He wrote: ". . . the shores of which terminating in a high perpendicular bluff point, was, in consequence of the change we experienced in its neighbourhood, called Foulweather Bluff." Vancouver went on to say: "This promontory is not ill named, for we had scarcely landed, when a heavy rain commenced, which continuing the rest of the day, obliged us to remain stationary," (Vancouver 237, 243). Wilkes renamed it Suquamish Head [7d] in 1841, an alteration of the Indian name *Suk-wa-bish*. The name Suquamish was later moved to Port Madison by a 1915 decision of

Foulweather Bluff - Francis, Point

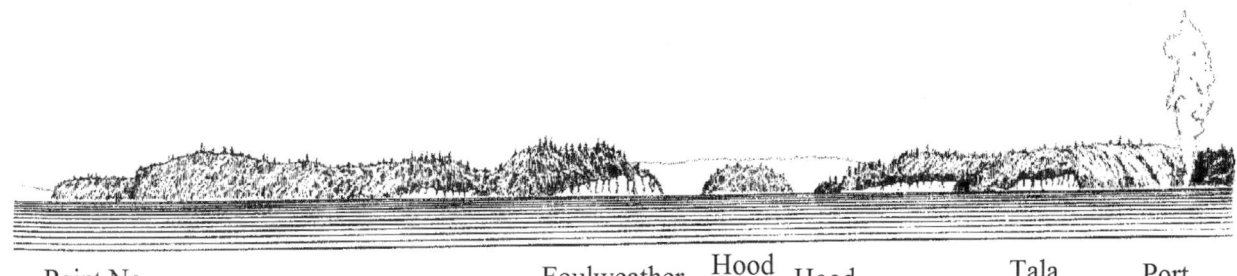

Point No Point — Foulweather Bluff — Hood Head — Hood Canal — Tala Point — Port Ludlow

the U.S. Board on Geographic Names (Blumenthal, *Charles Wilkes* 90). Davidson wrote: "On the western side of the last mid-channel course we pass Foulweather Bluff, which is perpendicular on its N.NW. face, and about 225 feet high, with heavy firs upon its summit. It slopes towards the east to a bluff 40 feet high, but is steep on the side next to Hood's Canal," (*Report* 444). The Salish word is "mica or sand containing mica" (Hilbert et. al., 190).

Foulweather Bluff

Fourmile Rock [22] #6450, 1909
Located in Elliott Bay north of Magnolia Bluff, the origin of the name is unknown. The Salish name was simply "rock or boulder" (Hilbert et. al., 61).

Fourth of July Beach
Located on the eastern side of San Juan Island at the northern part of American Camp, the origin of the local name is unknown.

Fox Cove
Located on the western side of Sucia Island, opposite Fossil Bay, it may have been named by Henry Wiggins who raised foxes on Sucia Island. J. J. Gilbert noted the name of Deep Bay in his 1888 Descriptive Report #1870 (http://riverhistory.ess.washington.edu/tsheets/reports/t1870.pdf, p 4, 6), perhaps in contrast to Shallow Bay to the north. Fox Cove, however, is anything but deep! It is about a fathom throughout. According to his chart, there was one family living in the bay.

Fox Island [7d] #146, 1841, Wilkes; [7g] #155, 1841, Wilkes; [7h] #154, 1841, Wilkes; [7i] #147, 1841, Wilkes
Located south of The Narrows in Puget Sound, Wilkes honored crew member J. L. Fox. The bridge to the island was built in 1954. In 1846, Inskip named the island Rosario [24] for the wife of Capt. Duntze of the *Fisgard* (Meany, *Origin* 92, 93). John Swan was the first settler to actually move to the island. Appointed as an Indian Agent, he built a log cabin on the north end in 1856 and supervised the non-hostile south-sound Indians who were moved to the island. Swan remained after hostilities declined (Edgers 7).

Fox Point
Located on the eastern end of Fox Island, the name was likely from the island.

Fox Spit
See East Point.

Fragaria
Located on the western shoreline of Colvos Passage, Ferdinand Schmitz of Seattle named the community in 1912 with the genus name of strawberries which grew there (Meany, *Origin* 93).

Francis, Point [6] 1792, Vancouver
Located on Portage Island at the northern entrance to Bellingham Bay, Vancouver noted the point on his chart but did not reference it in his journal. He left

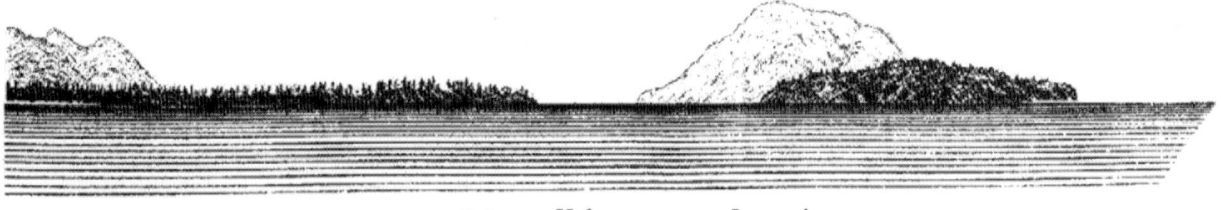

Sandy Point　　　Point Francis　Hale Passage　Lummi Peak

no reason for the name. In 1841, Wilkes spelled it Frances [7a], as did the 1865 U.S. Coast Survey on [10] and later charts; Admiralty charts conformed to this spelling as well. In 1976, the Washington State Board on Geographic Names received a request to formally spell it Frances and to apply the name to the entire island. In its March 11, 1977 meeting, Docket 210, the Board corrected the spelling to Francis and approved the name of Portage Island. The U.S. Board followed later in the year (from Washington State Board Files).

Freeland
Located at the head of Holmes Harbor on the eastern side of Whidbey Island, Freeland was settled in the early 1900s as the Free Land Association, a socialist cooperative. James P. Gleason owned most of the land around the harbor and sold five acre parcels to members for ten dollars down. The experiment in living lasted only a few years. By 1903, members began accepting work in local logging camps, and the wholesale store failed; fewer and fewer things were being done on a cooperative basis (Cherry II: 152).

Freeman Island [7a] #145, 1841, Wilkes
Located on the northwestern side of Orcas Island, Wilkes named it for crew member J. D. Freeman. Wilkes did not include this name in his *Narrative*, but it is shown on his chart (Meany, *Origin* 93). The U.S. Government owns the island.

Frenchmans Point
Located on the western shoreline of the entrance to Quilcene Bay, the origin of the name is unknown.

Freshwater Bay [8a] #1917, 1847, Kellett
Located west of Port Angeles, Kellett likely named it because the Elwha River flows into it.

Freshwater Creek
See Snohomish River.

Friday Harbor

Friday Harbor [13a] #2689, 1859, Richards
The harbor is located on the eastern side of San Juan Island. The Kanaka Joseph Pa'ilie, known to everyone as Joe Friday, lived there in the 1860s. When the British searched for locations to site English Camp, they pulled into the harbor, encountered Joe, and asked him for the name of the place. Joe did not understand English well and thought they asked for his name, which he gave them (Meany, *Origin* 94). An alternative story was that he was asked, "What bay is this?" He thought they said, "day," to which he responded. Hannah Sandwith Jensen wrote (*Told by the Pioneers* 187): "A Kanaka named Friday had settled on a claim, called squatting, which bordered the little harbor which now bears his name. It was first known as Friday's Place. On his property was the finest spring on the island. A number of years ago the spring was piped to a fountain which is located between the ferry landing and the wharf on the main street of Friday Harbor. The Sandwith family bought Friday's place and the Friday family bought land out in the country from Victoria." Lucile McDonald told

of a July 1905 issue of *The San Juan Islander* which reported the death of what locals believed to be Joe Friday. They estimated his age at 75. He and his wife apparently had three children. His son John was killed in a logging accident on Vancouver Island about 1902. At that time, his wife and two daughters were living in Victoria ("San Juan Island Had Man Friday." *Seattle Times*. Nov. 3, 1963. Magazine Section p 3). Indeed, the July 15, 1905 issue contained a front page article: "A venerable Kanaka named Friday, a relative of the man for whom Friday Harbor was named, was found dead just outside of his cabin on Peter Lawson's ranch, near Andrew's bay, last Monday morning. It is supposed that his death resulted from heart failure due to extreme old age. Some of the early pioneers of the island say that the old man was here when they came and that he must have been upwards of 100 years old at the time of his death." According to McDonald's article, later pioneers apparently believed the man to be *the actual* Friday.

Friday Island
See Brown Island.

Fridays Creek
This used to flow directly into Friday Harbor just north of the ferry terminal. Now it is diverted into a fountain/pond at the head of the public dock. It takes its name from the harbor (McDonald 64-67). It is a local name.

Fritz Point [7a] #145, 1841, Wilkes
Located on the western side of Orcas Island, just to the north of Jones Island, Wilkes honored crew member James Fritz. Wilkes did not include this name in his *Narrative*, but it is shown on his chart (Meany, *Origin* 94). It is unnamed on current charts.

Frolic Straits [7a] #145, 1841, Wilkes
See Upright Channel.

Frost Island [7a] #145, 1841, Wilkes
Located off the eastern shore of Lopez Island, Wilkes honored crew member John Frost in 1841. Wilkes did not include this name in his *Narrative*, but it is shown on his chart (Meany, *Origin* 94).

Frye Cove
It is located on the western side of Eld Inlet at the Frye Cove County Park, north of Flapjack Point. George W. Frye once owned the land (TPL website).

DE FUCA'S PILLAR.

Fuca pillar
Located about a mile southeast of Tatoosh Island, Davidson wrote: "From the top of the island (Tatoosh) a leaning rocky column, about 75 feet high and one-third of that in diameter, is seen to the southeastward close under the face of the cape. It is sometimes called Fuca's pillar," (*Report* 412). Davidson later corrected the height in the 1889 *Pacific Coast Pilot* to 140 feet. Speaking of de Fuca, Meares (272) stated in 1788: "He describes a great headland or island with an exceeding high pinnacle rock placed near it, which is, in all probability, the very island or headland whereon our friend Tatootche has his town and fortress; and as to the pinnacle rock, we have had ocular demonstration of its being placed in the entrance of this sea, as well as the great island or headland which we have particularized in the voyage of the *Felice* in that latitude." While Vancouver was aware of the same story, he did not see the rock: ". . . nor did we observe the Pinnacle rock, as represented by Mr. Mears and Mr. Dalrymple, in order to identify these as De Fuca's straits, or any other rock more conspicuous than thousands along the coast, varying in form and size; some conical, others with flat sides, flat tops and almost every other shape that can be figured by the imagination," (Vancouver 216, 217). Puget related: "But no distinguishable Spiral Rock or Pillar made its appearance, to my knowledge, however Mr. Baker & Menzies say, that after rounding Green Island, a Rock of that Description came in Sight for a Minute or two—" (Puget 188, 189). Thus, for years, various explorers either saw it or didn't see it and denied its existence. Wilkes finally located the pillar and provided a drawing. Unfortunately he did not specify its exact location, but he seems to place it about a mile south of Tatoosh Island, consistent with current charts. Four hundred years after its supposed naming, the U.S. Board on Geographic Names received

a proposal to correct its location as it "appears to have been misplaced on the Cape Flattery 15 quadrangle (1965)." There were differences in location between USFS, USGS, and NOS maps at that time. After deliberating, the Board concluded that after 400 years, the pillar would have been seriously eroded, perhaps completely so. In his February 12, 1985 letter to the Board, Mr. Harry M. Majors, Editor of *Northwest Press* wrote: ". . . the Board should keep in mind that it is being asked to deliberate, not on the mythical fuca pillar of 1592, nor the Meares-Duncan pinnacle of 1788, nor the Wilkes pillar of 1841, but instead the Fuca Pillar that was designated during the 1850s by George Davidson and published thereafter in various editions of the Coast survey charts and coast pilots." The U.S. Board approved the change in its February 13, 1986 meeting, Docket 293.

Fudge Point
It is located on Harstine Island, south of McMicken Boulder. The origin of the name is unknown, although it has been in use since 1910. In 1976, the Washington State Board on Geographic Names addressed an issue with the location of the point. Some maps incorrectly showed it a couple miles north of the McMicken Boulder (from Washington State Board Files).

Fukuzawa Creek
The small creek flows into Apple Tree Cove. It was named for the Yoko and Tushisaburo Fukuzawa family who settled in Kingston in the 1920s and raised strawberries. During WW II, they were sent to a relocation camp but returned to their farm after the war. The Washington State Board on Geographic names approved the name in its May 11, 2007 meeting. The U.S. Board followed later in the year (from Washington State Board Files).

Gallagher Cove
Located on the southern shoreline of Totten Inlet, it was named for John J. Galliher, an early settler (Palmer, 29).

Galliher Point
Located at the southern end of the Swinomish Channel, it was referenced by Davidson in the 1889 *Pacific Coast Pilot* (602): "*Galliper Point Light.-*This is a *fixed red light* shown from a lantern upon a white post nine feet high and six feet above high water. It is placed on the starboard side of the channel (in entering to La Conner) upon a low point of the main land, one-quarter of a mile from La Conner, and is about ten feet from the edge of the channel. The point is covered at high tide." The name is not referenced in the 1903 *Pacific Coast Pilot*. Perhaps the light was removed. Looking at an 1892 chart of the Swinomish, there is a significant bend in the channel opposite what would be the entrance to Shelter Bay. The channel was obviously straightened when dredged by removing some of the point. The original light was likely near where the red light "16" appears on current charts. The Point was named for the early settler, Milas Galliher. Based upon the reference by Davidson in 1891, the U.S. Board on Geographic Names adopted the name but corrected the spelling. It is unnamed on current charts, but the point is recognized by the U.S. Board on Geographic Names.

Gamble, Port [7d] #146, 1841, Wilkes; [7f] #151, 1841, Wilkes
Located near the entrance to Hood Canal on the eastern shoreline, Meany believed that Wilkes honored Lieut. Thomas Gamble in 1841 (with Meany incorrectly reporting his name as Robert Gamble), a War of 1812 figure who was wounded aboard the U.S. frigate *President* during the battle with the H.M.S. *Belvidere* (Meany, *Origin* 226, 227). Gamble recovered from his injuries but died at age 31. From an unpublished paper by Homer Morrison of Poulsbo, WA, there were a number of military heroes in the Gamble family. How Meany singled out Thomas Gamble is unknown, as there were three other brothers who also served in the War of 1812. About the port, Davidson wrote: "After passing Foulweather Bluff keep closer to the eastern shore than the western, to avoid the strong current passing round the low point which makes out from Hood's Head. Run for the saw-mill plainly in sight on the western side of the entrance to the bay, and when within a mile of it approach the eastern bluff within the third of a mile, in about 10 or 15 fathoms, gradually drawing closer in shore, and passing between the outer white and inner black can buoys." He went on to describe the mill: "The saw-mill here is the largest

and most effective in this part of the territory, cutting at the rate of six or seven millions of feet of lumber per year. Attached to it are lath, shingle, and planning machines. A large quantity of the lumber and rough spars for masts are carried to Australia and the Sandwich Islands," (*Report* 452, 453). The Puget Mill Company at Port Gamble was the oldest continually operating lumber mill in North America. It began production in 1853 as the Puget Mill Company and closed on November 30, 1995. The founders, from East Machias, Maine were born into the lumber and shipping business from their fathers, William Pope and Deacon Peter Talbot. Andrew Jackson Pope and Frederic Talbot arrived in San Francisco in 1849. With two other partners, Lucius Sanborn and J. P. Keller, they began operating barges on the bay. They turned a profit almost immediately. Sanborn sold his share back, and the three partners branched into the lumber business. In the early 1850s, Frederic's older brother, W. C. Talbot, arrived on the bay with his brig, the *Oriental*. En route, W. C. met Cyrus Walker in Panama and thought enough of the young man to hire him. Shortly after, Frederic decided to return to the East Coast and W. C. took his place as a partner in the company. They initially shipped lumber from Maine, but that became impractical due to the distance. They heard of the huge timber in the Northwest and decided to see for themselves. While A. J. ran the business in San Francisco, W. C. Talbot loaded his new ship, *Julius Pringle* with lumber, tools, foodstuffs, and trade goods and arrived in the Strait of Juan de Fuca in July 1853. Keller and Cyrus Walker also accompanied Talbot to help build the mill. When Keller died in 1862, Walker replaced him as partner. During the next sixty years, Walker became manager and superintendent of the Puget Mill Company (Bowen et al., II 128-132). The *Julius Pringle* worked its way into Discovery Bay. From there, Talbot set off in a small sailboat and Walker in an Indian canoe to explore Puget Sound in search of an appropriate mill site. They first stopped at Port Townsend and then Port Ludlow, where W. P. Sayward, another lumberman from Maine, was already building a mill. They cruised the western shores of Hood Canal as far as Hazel Point but found nothing to their liking. Returning along the eastern shore, they "discovered" Port Gamble and decided to build the mill there for its accessibility, protected waters, and proximity to the Strait of Juan de Fuca (Bowen et al., II 128-132). Within the next couple months, they roughed in the mill and covered it with cedar shakes. They unloaded *Julius Pringle* and sailed her to Yesler's steam mill in Seattle to pick up a load of piling and lumber for San Francisco. Talbot returned to Port Gamble to review the progress and then headed back to San Francisco (Carlson 1-8). Within a few months, production exceeded 2,000 feet of lumber a day. With improvements and new equipment, the figure rose to 15,000 by early 1854. During 1854, the mill produced three and a half million feet of lumber, by 1864 — fourteen million, and by 1884 — forty-five million under the watchful eye of Cyrus Walker. During the 1880s, Walker also managed mills at Port Ludlow and Utsalady, as well as a mercantile business and flour mill (*Port Gamble Story*, 1853-1953). See also Teekalet.

Gardiner
Located along the western side of Discovery Bay, it was founded in 1906 by Herbert Gardner. Originally named after himself, he altered the spelling slightly to avoid duplication with another town in the state. Gardner and his wife owned and logged 2,500 acres along the shoreline. Then they planted orchards and built cabins along the beach for fruit pickers that they employed (*With Pride* 155).

Gardner, Port [6] 1792, Vancouver
Vancouver originally named all of the waters on the east side of Whidbey Island as Possession Sound. He also named the smaller eastern arm Port Susan, and the western arm Port Gardner. It is unclear where Vancouver meant for the western arm to begin, although, on his chart, the 'P' in Port Gardner is located off the southern entrance of Penn Cove, and the 'r' is placed near East Point on Whidbey Island. Today, Port Gardner is relegated to the water off Everett.

Garrison Bay [16c] #602, 1921
Located off the western side of San Juan Island, south of Roche Harbor, it was named for the British Garrison ensconced there beginning in 1860. *See also* English Camp.

Garzon, Ensenada del
See Birch Bay.

Garzon, Pta y Laguna del [3] 1791, Eliza
See Birch Bay.

Gaston, Seno de [2] 1791, Pantoja
See Bellingham Bay.

Gazzam Lake
Located on the southwestern side of Bainbridge Island, it was named after the Warren Gazzam family. It was also known as the Crystal Springs Lake. *See also* Crystal Springs.

Gedney Island [7a] #145 1841, Wilkes; [7d] #146, 1841, Wilkes; [7o] #157, 1841, Wilkes
Located on the eastern side of Whidbey Island in Possession Sound, Wilkes likely honored Jonathan Haight Gedney in 1841, a New York inventor and friend (Meany, *Origin* 95, 96). But Robert A. Brunjes (2), who lives on the island, believes that it was named for Lieut. Thomas R. Gedney, commander of the *Washington*, who captured the Spanish slave ship *Amistad* in 1839. Passing Gedney, Archibald Menzies commented (44): "In the afternoon we both weigh to follow the Boats up the arm to the Northward but did not proceed far when we came to again near an inland [sic] in mid-channel for the night during which it raind very heavy. Some dogs had been left on shore on this Island whose yellings were heard several times in the night." Peter Goutre or Goutrie, also known as French Peter, was the first to homestead on Gedney in 1863. As a result of the 1855 Treaty of Point Elliott, the government purchased his Tulalip Bay homestead and he moved to Gedney. He was murdered in 1875, supposedly for his money. His body was found slumped over a log on the beach with his dog standing guard. The homestead was later sold for $525 to John Davis; the dog fetched $1.13. Peter Goutre was buried near the present clubhouse. In 1870, the Hat Island Sand and Gravel Company formed and began transporting material to the mainland. As a result, locals then, and even now, refer to it as Hat Island, although some believe it carries the name because of its shape. John Davis logged Goutrie's land. In 1918, August Greyerbiehl purchased 153 acres of the Davis land and built a summer home, a few cabins for rent, and a wharf. During WW I, the north end of the island was used for bombing practice by Paine Field fighters. John Macintosh purchased 367 acres in 1961, including the Goutrie homestead. Macintosh formed a development company and began to sell lots. While lot sales flourished, very few homes were built. Ultimately, Macintosh went out of business and the assets were turned over to the community. Through the early 1970s, with no water and intermittent power, growth was minimal. As these problems were finally fixed, growth boomed in the 1980s with more than 170 new homes (Brunjes 1-12). In 1943, the U.S. Board on Geographic Names addressed the names Gedney vs. Hat, and based upon the input of locals, they determined that the island was known by both names but Hat was probably in greater use. Seeing no compelling reason for a change, the Board retained Wilkes name. In 1979, the Washington Board on Geographic Names received a proposal to change the name to Hat Island. The proponent indicated that the name Hat was used by all locals. In its meeting on September 12, 1980, the Board rejected the proposed change but agreed to include Hat as a secondary parenthetical name. Thus on official publications, it would show as "Gedney (Hat) Island." The U.S. Board rejected that notion indicating its policy to approve one name only. Thus, the official name remained Gedney.

Geese Islets [7a] #145, 1841, Wilkes
Located off Middle Channel at the southeastern end of Lopez Island, Wilkes likely chose the name in 1841 because of the presence of geese. Wilkes did not include this name in his *Narrative*, but it is shown on his chart. The islets are comprised of Whale Rocks, Long Island, Buck Island, and Mummy Rocks (Meany, *Origin* 96). The U.S. Government owns Buck Island and Mummy Rocks.

George, Cape [9a] #1911, 1849, Kellett
Located at the eastern entrance to Discovery Bay, Wilkes originally named it East Bluff in 1841 [7b]. Wilkes did not include this name in his *Narrative*, but it is shown on his chart. Kellett honored Vancouver in 1847 when he renamed it (Meany, *Origin* 36).

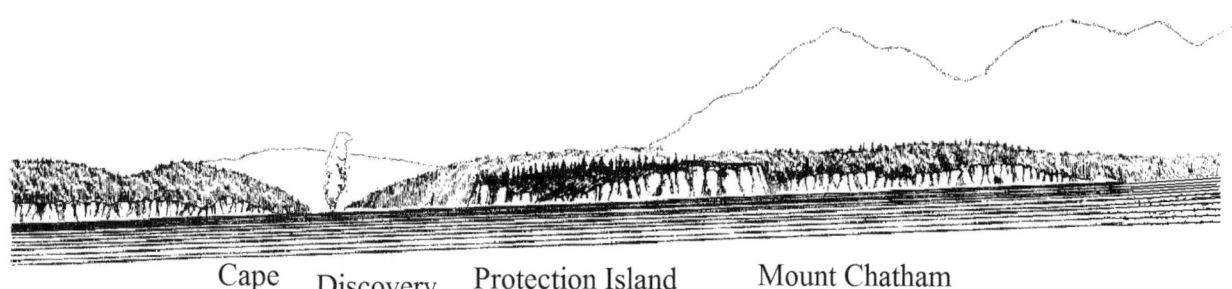

Cape George — Discovery Bay — Protection Island — Mount Chatham

George, Point [14c], #2840, 1872
It is located on the southwestern side of Shaw Island. The origin of the name is unknown.

George Island
See Gossip Islands.

Georgetown
Located in South Seattle, Julius Horton, Dexter's brother, purchased property on the Duwamish River in 1869. He platted it in the 1880s, naming it Georgetown for his son who was then studying to become a doctor. Seattle annexed Georgetown in 1910 (*Duwamish Diary* 38, 45).

Georgia, Strait of [6] 1792, Vancouver
Vancouver originally named this the Gulph of Georgia. Richards altered it to the present name on [13d]. Vancouver honored George II who ruled from 1727 to 1760 (Meany, *Origin* 96). The southern boundary of the strait is a line between Pt. Thompson (Orcas Island) and Pt. Migley (Lummi Island). It was originally named *El Gran Canal de Nuestra Señora del Rosario la Marinera* by Eliza [3].

Gertrude
The community was located on the shores of Still Harbor, McNeil Island. Originally named Sunne by the first postmaster, Charles Julin, town folk later changed it for the island in the harbor. The post office operated from 1900 to 1936. At its peak, there were 400 people living there (Reese, *Origins* 48).

Gertrude Island [24] #1947, 1849, Inskip
Located off the northern side of McNeil Island, it was named Gertrudis by R. N. Inskip in 1846 for Gertrude Duntze, the daughter of Capt. John A. Duntze of the H.M.S. *Fisgard*. Duntze surveyed in Canadian waters with Inskip from 1843-1847 (Meany, *Origin* 96). The Salish name for the island was "small island" (Hilbert et. al., 321).

Gettysburg [21] #6300, 1905
Located west of Port Angeles on the Strait of Juan de Fuca, it was named in 1897 for Robert N. Getty, a logger from Pennsylvania, who established a hotel, store, and landing (TPL website). It is mentioned in the 1903 *Pacific Coast Pilot* (131).

Gibbs Point [22] #6450, 1909
See Kalset Point.

Gibraltar [21] #6300, 1895
Located near Dewey on Fidalgo Island, it was a short-lived town founded by Legh R. Freeman. It consolidated with Fidalgo City in 1893. In 1976, the Washington State Board on Geographic Names received information to correct the location on AMS (Army Map Service). In its December 10, 1976 meeting, Docket 211, the Board agreed to relocate the name about one mile east. The U.S. Board followed in early 1977 (from Washington State Board Files).

Gibson Point [7d] #146, 1841, Wilkes; [7i] #147, 1841, Wilkes
Located on the southeast end of Fox Island, Wilkes honored crew member James H. Gibson in 1841. In 1846, Inskip named this Patterson Point [24] for Lieut. George Patterson of the H.M.S. *Fisgard* (Meany, *Origin* 97). The Salish name for the point was "fern promontory" (Hilbert et. al., 321).

Gibson Spit
It is located at the western entrance to Sequim Bay. The 1860 Clallam County census lists George Gibson, age 35, in the Dungeness Precinct. The spit is perhaps named for George.

Giffin Rocks
Located two miles north of Rosario in East Sound, Orcas Island, they were named for William R. Giffin who settled along the shoreline east of the rocks. He was born in 1873 in Ohio and was involved in the oil delivery business in the early 1900s in Seattle, Mt. Vernon, and Chehalis. He relocated to Orcas Island in 1910, had an oil distribution service, and was later a realtor in East Sound. Giffin married in 1893. He and his wife raised five children. In 1990, the U.S. Board on Geographic Names agreed to modify the spelling as it appeared on the 1980 NOAA chart #18430 from Griffin to Giffin (from Washington State Board Files). McLellan mentioned a stream flowing from the western slopes of the Mount Constitution Range and emptying into East Sound near Giffin Park.

Gig Harbor

Gig Harbor (bay and community) [7d] #146, 1841, Wilkes; [7g] #155, 1841, Wilkes
Located on the mainland opposite Point Defiance, Wilkes left no reason for the 1841 name. While some sources indicate Wilkes surveyed it himself in the captain's gig (hence the name), there is no evidence that he did so, nor is there any reference in his *Narrative*. He only stated that the harbor: ". . . has a sufficient depth of water for small vessels," (Wilkes, *Narrative* 319). In 1867, Samuel Jerisich rowed a small boat from British Columbia waters with a couple of friends. As soon as Jerisich saw Gig Harbor, he knew he needed to look no further for a home. But for an Indian village at the head of the bay, no one else was nearby. The men rowed back to British Columbia, and Jerisich returned with his wife Annie, a Canadian Indian. They built a one-room, split-cedar-board cabin on the west side of the bay. Jerisich fished and farmed a small plot of land. For sixteen years, the Jerisich family lived in solitude in the harbor. In 1883, Joseph Goodman, his wife, and their five children arrived, followed the next year by Dr. Alfred M. Burnham with his family from Minnesota. In addition, Burnham encouraged his midwestern friends to follow. Burnham platted the town in 1888. That same year, John Ross and his wife settled there. Their son, John Ross, Jr. was perhaps the first White boy born in the area. The following year, Frank Hall, A. S. Prentice, and James Parker, all friends of Burnham from Minnesota, formed the Gig Harbor Mill Company on the west side of the harbor. Hall also started a store. George Atkinson moved to the harbor. He previously managed the Tacoma Mill Company. With his experience, he became the first manager of the mill. They sold lumber primarily to Chile. But when a revolution started there, sales evaporated and the company folded. Two shingle mills also operated in Gig Harbor, both on the west side. They burned after a few years and were not rebuilt (Evans 1-9). The Salish word for the harbor was "trout" (Hilbert et. al., 221).

Gilberton
Located south of Brownsville in Port Orchard, it was settled in 1888 by Thor and Olive Gulbranson and their four children. They received a patent to the homestead in 1895. The family changed their name in 1909, and the name of the community followed (Hitchman 250).

Glen Acres
See Aquarium.

Glen Cove & **Glencove**
Located on the western side of Carr Inlet, the bay Glen Cove was originally named Balch Cove for Capt. Lafayette Balch (*see also* Steilacoom). The community of Glencove also took the name Balch when the post office was established in 1891. Two sources credit the loggers Harry Winchester and Nick Peterson for the name after the resort on

Long Island, N.Y. (Meany, *Origin* 97; *History* I: 60). According to Reese (*Origins* 50), Christine O'Neill indicated that her father, as the postmaster, changed the name of the community in 1896.

Glen Cove
Located midway down the western shoreline of Port Townsend, it was the site of Fort Townsend, erected by Major Granville O. Haller as a result of hostilities with northern Indians. By 1859, with increasing border hostilities, General Harney ordered Haller and his men back to Fort Steilacoom, leaving the pioneers to fend for themselves. In 1874 Fort Townsend was rehabilitated with additional buildings, barracks, officer's quarters, etc. But by 1895, with the Indian threat essentially gone, the fort was again abandoned and the War Department turned it over to the Interior Department. During World War II, the property was used as an enemy-munitions defusing station. Washington State Parks Department took custody of the site in 1953 (McCurdy, *By Juan* 113-117). The origin of the name is unknown.

Glendale
Located on the eastern side of Whidbey Island on Saratoga Passage, its earliest settler was an Indian named Leonard who built a house on the beach and dock. About 1900, James and Jane Peck with their three children purchased the Leonard land, built a store, a cabin, and enlarged the dock. In 1906, the second eldest son, Ernest, then thirty, married and brought his wife to the cabin. Their daughter was named Edna Glen, and in her honor they named the area Glendale. The Pecks ran a logging business supplying cordwood for the steamers and shingle bolts. In 1911, the Peterson brothers bought out the Pecks and built a large building which housed a store and post office. Dorlesca Peterson, wife of William, was the daughter of Henry Hinman (Cherry II: 60, 61). *See also* Clinton.

Glover, Point [7d] #146, 1841, Wilkes; [7q] #156, 1841, Wilkes
Located on the southern side of Rich Passage, Wilkes honored crew member John Glover in 1841 (Meany, *Origin* 219). Wilkes did not include this name in his *Narrative*, but it is shown on his charts.

Goat Island
Located in Skagit Bay at the southern entrance to the Swinomish Channel, the name originated for goats kept on the island. From 1909 to 1947 it was a military reservation. Now it is run by the Washington State Department of Game (Hitchman 106). The Salish name for the island was "crosswise" (Hilbert et. al., 350).

God's Pocket
See Fish Creek.

Goldendale
See Silverdale.

Goldsborough Creek
The eight mile creek flows into Oakland Bay at Shelton. It was named for Maj. Hugh A. Goldsborough who settled on the creek in 1853. He left before obtaining title to the property (TPL website). In its December 11, 1981 meeting, Docket 267, the Washington State Board on Geographic Names resolved a naming issue between federal and local maps and selected the current name. The U.S. Board followed in 1982 (from Washington State Board Files).

Goodman Creek
See Minter Creek.

Goodnough Creek
The creek, pronounced "Good-nuff," flows into Henderson Bay near Purdy. The Purdy Clubhouse Association, a non-profit community group, petitioned to name the creek after the club's benefactor, Wiley C. Goodnough. Goodnough was born in Tennessee in 1885 and died in Purdy in 1953. He donated land for the club and helped to build the clubhouse. In its December 10, 1982 meeting, Docket 274, the Washington State Board on Geographic Names approved the name. The U.S. Board followed the next year (from Washington State Board Files).

Goose Island [14a] #2840, 1861, Richards
Located at the southeast end of San Juan Island near Cattle Point, Richards likely chose the name because of the presence of geese. Currently owned by the Nature Conservancy, it was a military reserve between 1884 and 1923.

Goose Point
Located on the eastern side of Sequim Bay, Wilkes originally named this Spak Point [7n] in 1841. Wilkes did not include this name in his *Narrative*, but it is shown on his chart. The current name was likely descriptive. The U.S. Board on Geographic Names approved the name in 1960 over the variants Goose Spit and Spak Point. The site apparently has been favored by locals for years as a spot for hunting geese.

Goose Rock
Located in Cornet Bay at Deception Pass, it was possibly named for its "roast goose" appearance or as a nesting spot for the birds. A variant is Goose Peak.

Gooseberry Point
Located on the mainland at the ferry terminal to Lummi Island, it was named for the wild gooseberries that grew there (Hitchman 108).

Gorden, Point [7d] #146, 1841, Wilkes; [7q] #156, 1841, Wilkes
See Restoration Point.

Gordon Island [7a] #145, 1841, Wilkes
As shown on Wilkes' chart, it was located north of Waldron Island and to the east of Bare Island. However, it does not exist. Its inclusion is attributed to a disgruntled crew member, William May in 1841 (Meany, *Origin* 99). See also Adolphus Island.

Gordon Point [24] #1947, 1849, Inskip
Located on the eastern shoreline of Puget Sound at Steilacoom, Wilkes originally named this Qulam Point [7i] in 1841. He left no reason for the name. Wilkes did not include this name in his *Narrative*, but it is shown on his chart. Capt. R. M. Inskip named this in 1846 honoring George Thomas Gordon who commanded H.M. steam sloop *Cormorant* (Meany, *Origin* 99). Gordon entered the navy in 1818 and was ultimately promoted to Admiral in 1877. He died in 1887 (Walbran 212).

Gorst
Located at the southwestern end of Sinclair Inlet, it was originally named Butler for Penn Butler who settled there in 1887. It was renamed for Samuel and Mary Gorst who purchased land from the Port Blakely Mill and settled there in 1897. Gorst Creek flows into Sinclair Inlet through the small community (Hitchman 109).

Gosnell Creek [23] #6460, 1905
See Mill Creek.

Gossip Island [14c] #2840, 1870
See Gossip Islands.

Gossip Islands [14e] #2840, 1906
McLellan wrote: "Two small rock islands, called the Gossip Islands, are located at the entrance of Reid Harbor on Stewart Island. They have a combined area of 1.75 acres and rise but a few feet above sea level. The larger of these two islands is sometimes known as George Island." The name Gossip Island appeared on the 1870 Admiralty chart [14c]. Somehow it morphed into Gossip Islands by 1906 [14e] (or perhaps earlier) and later returned to Gossip Island. The 1894 t-sheet #2193 clearly shows two islands and labels both as Gossip Islands. This is the first appearance on U.S. charts. Despite the appearance on the t-sheet, Hitchman (109) indicated that there were three islands in the grouping, Cemetery, Gossip, and Happy. Ignoring a few rocks nearby, I can only locate two islands and thus believe McLellan was more correct. Hitchman also stated that Richards provided the name for the Indian custom of eating, drinking, and gossiping during the salmon season. Because the name does not appear earlier than 1870, and Richards left the Northwest in 1863, without more information I would be unable to credit him with the name, but it would at least be reasonable to credit it to British surveyors. Current U.S. charts label the larger island Gossip I and leaves the smaller island unnamed. The topo for Stewart reflects the name "Gossip Island" for the larger and "Cem" for the smaller. The State of Washington owns both Gossip and Cemetery Island. The U.S. Board on Geographic Names includes the names Gossip Islands, Gossip Island, Cemetery Island, and Happy Island. I believe the database is in error with respect to Happy Island.

Gourd Island [7a] #145, 1841, Wilkes
See Patos Island.

Governors Point
Located on the mainland at the southeastern entrance to Bellingham Bay, the origin of the name is unknown.

Graham Point
It is located on the western side of Pickering Passage where the bridge between the mainland and Harstine is located. This appears to be what Wilkes in 1841 called Kopo Point [7h]. He left no reason for the name. Wilkes did not include this name in his *Narrative*, but it is shown on his chart. According to the TPL website, it was named for a local settler.

Gran Montaña de Carmelo [1] 1790, Quimper
See Mt. Baker.

Grandmas Cove
Located on the southwestern side of San Juan Island near Eagle Cove, it was likely named for Grandma McCrae, whose family owned a nearby farm in the late 1800s.

Granite Beach
Mentioned in the November 7, 1895 issue of *The Islander*, it was located near Doe Bay on the eastern side of Orcas Island. It is not a recognized formal name.

Grant
Located on the western shoreline of Pickering Passage, north of the Harstine Bridge, the community was named in 1900 for the school teacher and postmistress, Mary Grant (Meany, *Origin*, 101).

Grant, Mount
See Sugarloaf Mountain.

Grapeview
Located on the western shoreline of Case Inlet, behind Stretch Island, it was first settled in 1885 by the three brothers, Tom, Albert, and John Malaney. The town grew quickly over the next five years and included graded streets, three sawmills, a newspaper, several merchandise and hardware stores, a hotel, three restaurants, plus more. Early settlers called the area Detroit after its Michigan counterpart, but when the post office opened in 1890, the first Postmaster, Walter O. Eckert, named it for the grapes that grew nearby (Hitchman 111).

Grass Island
See Cayou Island.

Grave Island [23] #6460, 1905
See Tanglewood Island.

Gravel Point
A local name for the point located at the light at the south end of Blakely Island. The entire hillside is gravel (Soland, Leslie; Dec. 20, 2011 email to author).

Graveyard Spit
Dungeness spit runs from the southeast to the northwest. Graveyard Spit is that portion that runs north and south. It is formed (as is the entire spit) by sand eroding from nearby hills combined with summer northeast winds which well up against the side of the hook. It is a local name. *See also* Dungeness Spit.

Grays Marsh
Located three miles southeast of Dungeness, it was first settled by Capt. William H. Gray in the 1870s. Gray sold the quarter section to Alfred H. Anderson in 1909. Apparently, at the time of the sale, the names were combined into Graysmarch and the property has been locally known by that name ever since (http://www.olypen.com/grysmrsh/GMhistory.html). Grays Marsh is the only name recognized by USBGN. The 1870 Clallam County census listed Gray at 60 years of age.

Great Bend, The
Located near the southern end of Hood Canal, the name applies to the turn point in Hood Canal only. In 1985, the U.S. Board on Geographic Names addressed a 1985 NOAA chart #18448 which incorrectly reflected the name extending into the eastern extension of the canal past Sisters Point. The Board approved of correcting the chart in its April 10, 1986 meeting, Docket 304 (from Washington State Board Files).

Great Peninsula [7d] #146, 1841, Wilkes
See Indian Peninsula.

Green Cove
It is located on the eastern shoreline of Eld Inlet, nearly opposite Flapjack Point. It was named for the green trees reflecting off the water (TPL website).

Green, Point

Green, Point [7d] #146, 1841, Wilkes; [7h] #154, 1841, Wilkes
Located on the mainland at the western entrance to Hale Passage, Wilkes honored crew member Daniel Green in 1841 (Meany, *Origin* 103). Wilkes did not include this name in his *Narrative*, but it is shown on his charts.

Green Point [13a] #2689, 1859, Richards
Located on the western side of Fidalgo Island, Richards named it for the color of the vegetation growing there (Hitchman 113).

Green Point [10] #51, 1854, U.S. Coast Survey
Located on the Strait of Juan de Fuca between Ediz Hook and Dungeness, the U.S. Coast Survey likely named this for its appearance.

Green Point [13a] #2689, 1859, Richards
Located on the eastern end of Spieden Island, Richards' reason for this name is unknown.

Greenbank
Located on Whidbey Island on the western side of Holmes Harbor, it was named by Calvin Philips in 1906 after his home in Greenbank, Delaware (Meany, *Origin* 103). Philips arrived in the Northwest in 1890 and settled in Steilacoom. As a Seattle realtor, he was asked to sell 10,000 acres of land in that area. He was able to sell half of it within the first month, and he bought 1,500 acres fronting Holmes Harbor where he built a hotel and store (Neil 203). His home, barn, and several cabins and outbuildings remain today. Philips died about 1947, the oldest "Social Chairman" of the Rainier Club (Apr. 20, 2012 letter from great grandson, Peter Philips, President of Philips Publishing). The community was once home to the world's largest loganberry farm, Mogen David. The Greenbank store has been run by the Coupe family since it opened in 1904.

Griffin Bay [13a] #2689, 1859, Richards
Located off the southeastern portion of San Juan Island, Richards honored Charles John Griffin, an official of the Hudson's Bay Company who was in charge of the Bellevue Farm. Lange found a reference from an 1859 memoir of George Gibbs that it was named Bellevue Harbor in 1854.

Griffin Rocks
See Giffin Rocks.

Griffiths Point
Capt. James Griffiths was an early settler on the land south of Mystery Bay on Marrowstone Island. He purchased waterfront property in Port Townsend and several acres in 1855 on the west side of Marrowstone. Griffiths was partially responsible for supporting his mother and step-father in Wales. He frequently sent money to them. One day, while watching passengers disembark from a ship that had just landed, he was startled to see his parents. His mother and her husband, Frank Knight, settled on Griffiths' Marrowstone land, while Griffiths continued investing in nearby land to ultimately accumulate 181 acres. It was locally known as Griffiths Point. Griffiths' stepfather Frank died and was buried on the land in the early 1870s. His mother moved to Seattle in 1872 where she died eleven years later. Griffiths eventually married in 1874 and moved to Seattle but continued to lease the Marrowstone property. The land stayed in family hands until the last child, Sarah Griffiths Parker, died in 1967 (Bean 8, 9).

Grindstone Harbor
It is located on the southern end of Orcas Island in Harney Channel. During the Pig War, Paul K. Hubbs, was stationed on San Juan Island as the Customs Inspector. In 1868 he moved to Orcas, settling in Grindstone Harbor. He obtained an exclusive permit to run sheep on Blakely Island and owned the only

grindstone on Orcas — hence the name. As a result, settlers and Indians alike visited, always accompanied by knives or an ax that needed sharpening. Hubbs eventually erected a small store, the first on the island. Some years later he closed the store and adopted a nomadic life, wandering the islands and living off the land (Splitstone 32; Richardson, *Pig* 180).

Griswold
Located in Blind Bay on Shaw Island, it is a local name for a historic location named after George Griswold. The history is confusing. Either Griswold established the post office about 1891-1892 or Mrs. Cynthia Hix moved the post office there from Maple in 1890. On t-sheet #2230 from 1895 (http://kaga.wsulibs.wsu.edu/cdm-maps/sanjuantsheet.html), the name is spelled Griswald. The t-sheet reflects the post office.

Guemes Channel [13a] #2689, 1859, Richards
Located between Fidalgo and Guemes Islands, it took its name from the island. In 1841, Wilkes named it Hornet Harbor [7a], [7m] for the *Hornet*, a ship under the command of Captain James Lawrence.

Guemes Island [2] 1791, Pantoja; [3] 1791, Eliza
Located north of Fidalgo Island, it appears on both Pantoja's and Eliza's 1791 charts. It was named for Juan Vincente de Güemes Pacheco de Padilla Horcasitas y Aguayo, Conde de Revilla Gigedo, the Viceroy of New Spain. In 1841, Wilkes renamed it Lawrence Island [7a], [7m] for Capt. James Lawrence who died during the battle between the *Chesapeake* and *Shannon* during the War of 1812 (Meany, *Origin* 99). Lawrence made famous the battle cry, "Don't give up the ship." Kellett restored the original name [8a]. Allen Kittle was possibly the earliest settler on Guemes Island in 1862 but did not remain long before moving to Sinclair Island. The first more permanent settler was James Mathews who married an Indian woman and planted an orchard in 1865 along the northwestern shore. The location is reflected on current charts as "Indian Village" (recognized by the U.S. Board on Geographic Names) — the site of a Samish village. The Samish Indians refused to relocate to Bellingham, as required by the 1855 Treaty of Point Elliott. They continued to live on Guemes and were resettled about 1872 to March Point. With continued homesteading pressures there, they obtained land on the northwestern side of Guemes again where they constructed a 480 foot longhouse. Nine families lived there until the early 1900s. Because of an apparent error in administering homestead laws, the protective status of the land disappeared in 1903. Unable to pay back taxes, they lost the land and moved about 1912. About 1866, Humphrey P. O'Bryant purchased the claim of a French trapper for $40 and settled in next to Mathews.

Guerriere Bay [7a] #145, 1841, Wilkes
See West Sound.

Gull Harbor
Located off the northeastern shore of Budd Inlet, in 1841 Wilkes originally named it Wepusec Inlet [7i]. He left no reason for the name. Wilkes did not include this name in his *Narrative*, but it is shown on his chart. Apparently, at low tide, the resultant mudflat appears like a seagull in flight (TPL website). Alternatively, according to Palmer (32), it was named for the many gulls which frequent the area.

Gull Reef [14a] #2840, 1861, Richards
Located between Johns and Spieden Islands, the reef is a feeding spot for seagulls, which may have been Richards' reason for the name.

Gull Rock [7a] #145, 1841, Wilkes; [7c] #144, 1841, Wilkes
See Pole Island.

Gull Rock
Located off Fidalgo Island near the western entrance to Deception Pass on the south side of Sharpe Cove, the name was likely descriptive.

Gull Rock [7a] #145, 1841, Wilkes
Located to the northeast of Spieden Island, Wilkes perhaps named it because it was a nesting place for seagulls (TPL website).

Gun Point
Located on the northern shore of Whidbey Island, a half mile west of the Deception Pass Bridge, the origin of the name is unknown.

Gurley Creek [19] #662, 1867, U.S. Coast Survey
See Curley Creek.

Guss Island [16b] #602, 1869, Pender
Located in Garrison Bay, San Juan Island, Richards named it for August Hoffmeister who owned 160 acres just south of English Camp, as well as land in Victoria, and a sheep ranch on Henry Island. He also ran a store for the British while they were in Garrison Bay (Meany, *Origin* 106). Wood (98) noted the possibility that the original name was Gus's Island. According to the later convention of removing apostrophes, it became Guss. According to Archibald Fleming (*Told by the Pioneers* 52): "Gus Hoffmaster had 100 head of cattle and 500 sheep on Spieden Island (near San Juan) and 300 sheep on Henry Island. Hoffmaster had the contract of furnishing beef to the English camp. Times were good when the military camps were on the island. Boats would bring excursion parties over from Victoria on the fourth of July, and everyone had a good time, even though the territory was held jointly by the two governments." Mary Davis, who lived at English Camp with her brother, related the early days of the island, ". . . Indian tree burials were there and a mysterious circle of stones, 12 feet across, with an upright stone in the center. Indian women used to circle the island in their canoes 'calling their dead'," (McDonald, Lucile. "Historic Acres to Be a State Park." *Seattle Times*. Dec. 15, 1963. Magazine Section p 7). The U.S. Government owns the island.

Guthrie Camp
See Macklin.

Guthrie Cove
Located in Harney Channel east of Grindstone Harbor, James Guthrie homesteaded in the early 1870s. He married an Alaskan Indian in 1877. In 1990, the U.S. Board on Geographic Names addressed a name change from Guthrie Bay to Guthrie Cove to conform to local usage. The change was approved in its April 9, 1992 meeting, Docket 350 (from Washington State Board Files). The 1887 San Juan County census spelled the family name Gurthie. At that time, James was 55, his wife Agnes was 40, and their three children were 6, 9, and 13.

Hackney Island [21] #6300, 1895
See Baby Island.

Hadlock, Port

Hadlock, Port [22] #6450, 1909
Located near the southern end of Port Townsend, the community received its name from the first major land owner, Samuel Hadlock. Hadlock was born in 1829 in Hudson, New Hampshire. About 1850, he reached California and became involved in milling, lumber, and mining ventures. He married Susan Lawrence in 1864. She died in Port Hadlock in 1873. With experience from running a sawmill in Tacoma, he arrived in Port Townsend in 1870, representing the interests of several financial investors. He purchased the 400 acres around Port Hadlock and by 1885 established a shipping center, dry dock, and shore side facilities. When the Washington Mill Company burned at Seabeck in 1885, he convinced the company to relocate to Port Hadlock, adding more settlers to his small town. The mill was reorganized in 1890. The owner, William J. Adams, dispatched Edward P. Blake to run the business. However, the mill closed in 1907 because of depressed lumber prices. It employed 125 men at its peak. Shortly after closing, Adams learned of a process to make alcohol from sawdust. He erected a massive building, purchased machinery, hired a manager, and began distilling alcohol. The plant closed in 1913 after a year and a half of operation. It was purchased in 1978 by Ray Hansen. Over a nine-year period, and four million dollars later, he converted it into a resort and hotel. Samuel Hadlock died in the town in 1912 at the age of eighty-three (Roe 83; Fish, *Tales of Port Hadlock* 3, 4). Although the name of the

Lummi Bay   Hale Passage, North entrance   Lummi Peak

community was shortened to Hadlock by local use, the Washington State Board on Geographic Names received a proposal in 1990 to restore the original name. In their December 1990 meeting, Docket 349, the Board approved Port Hadlock. The U.S. Board on Geographic Names followed in 1991.

Haida Point [14a] #2840, 1861, Richards
Located on the western side of West Sound, Orcas Island, Richards named it for nearby Indian battles.

Hale Passage [7a] #145, 1841, Wilkes
Located off the eastern side of Lummi Island, Galiano/Valdéz named it *Canal de Pacheco* for the Viceroy of New Spain. In 1841, Wilkes honored crew member Horatio Hale with the name. Hale's mother Sarah wrote the poem "Mary Had a Little Lamb" and was instrumental in getting Thanksgiving Day recognized as a national holiday. Wilkes did not include this name in his *Narrative*, but it is shown on his chart. Hale was left behind to study the Indians after Wilkes departed. He was the author of the first book on the Chinook jargon (Meany, *Origin* 107; Wagner 249). The U.S. Board on Geographic Names changed the name from Hales to Hale in 1891.

Hale Passage [7d] #146, 1841, Wilkes
Located between the mainland and Fox Island, Wilkes honored crew member Horatio Hale in 1841 (Meany, *Origin* 107).

Halftide Rocks [15a] #611, 1865, Richards
It is located in Griffin Bay off the southeastern side of San Juan Island. The implication of Richards' naming was that at high water this rock was submerged and as the tide dropped the rocks were slowly uncovered (Hitchman 116). An 1897 USC&GS report refuted this theory. Wood (98) quotes the log of the H.M.S. *Plumper*, August 4, 1858: "Half tide Rock on with a low Black point." Wood found the name on an 1858 Fair Chart by the Officers of the H.M.S. *Plumper*. Richards used the name West Rock on [13c], but Halftide Rocks endured. J. J. Gilbert of the Coast Survey supported the log of the *Plumper*. In his 1897 survey and Descriptive Report #2301, he wrote: "One half mile SW from Low Point is Halftide Reef. The name does not appear appropriate for it shows above high tide, just a few points of rock. At low tide an extensive reef is visible," (http://riverhistory.ess.washington.edu/tsheets/reports/t2301.pdf, p 6).

Hall Island [13a] #2689, 1859, Richards
It is located off the southwestern side of Lopez Island. Lange speculated that it was named for Matthey Hall, a Royal Engineer. The U.S. Government owns the island.

Hallets Cove [7f] #151, 1841, Wilkes
It is located at the southern end of Port Ludlow. Wilkes left no reason for the 1841 name. He did not include this name in his *Narrative*, but it is shown on his chart. The name is neither reflected on U.S. charts nor is it recognized by the U.S. Board on Geographic Names.

Hamma Hamma River
Emptying into Hood Canal on the western side eight miles south of Pleasant Harbor, the name is a corruption of the Twana name *Du-hub-hub-bai*, which referred to the Hub-hub rush that grew along the river (Hitchman 117). The name became official by a 1941 decision of the U.S. Board on Geographic Names when the variant, Hamahama, was discarded.

Hammersley Inlet [7d] #146, 1841, Wilkes; [7i] #147, 1841, Wilkes
Located at the southwestern side of Puget Sound, Wilkes honored crew member George W. Hammersly in 1841 (Meany, *Origin* 107, 108). Wilkes' *Narrative*

(321) spells it Hammersly, but both of his charts spell the name Hammersley, which is what is in use on current charts. The U.S. Board on Geographic Names approved the name in 1937 by ignoring the variants Big Skookum Inlet or simply Big Skookum. Skookum means "strong" in the Chinook language. Hilbert (274) indicated that the local use of this name was increasing. *See also* Henderson Inlet.

Hammond, Point [7a] #145, 1841, Wilkes
Located on the north end of Waldron Island, Wilkes named it in 1841 for crew member Henry Hammond (Meany, *Origin* 219). Wilkes did not include this name in his *Narrative*, but it is shown on his chart.

Hanbury Point [16b] #602, 1869, Pender
Located at the southeastern entrance of Mosquito Pass on San Juan Island, Pender named it for Ingham Hanbury, the assistant surgeon at English Camp (*English Camp* 12, 13; Wood 98).

Handle Heads [7j] #153, 1841, Wilkes
See Jackson Cove.

Hankin Point [13c] #2689, 1865
It is located on the eastern end of Shaw Island. Lange speculated that it was named for Lt. Philip James Hankin. Hankin arrived on the West Coast as a mate aboard the H.M.S. *Plumper* in 1857 and was promoted to lieutenant the following year. He returned to England and served under Commander Anthony Hoskins aboard the H.M.S. *Hecate*, which arrived in Esquimalt in 1860. He left the service in 1864 in England but again returned to the West Coast. He served in various political positions in British Columbia and England (Walbran 225, 226).

Hannon, Point [7d] #146, 1841, Wilkes
Located at the northwest entrance to Hood Canal off Hood Head, Wilkes left no reason for the 1841 name. The 1934 *Pacific Coast Pilot* (262) stated that it was known by the local name, Whiskey Spit.

Hansville
Located on the western shoreline of Admiralty Inlet, on Norwegian Point, three miles south of Foulweather Bluff, it was named for Hans Zachariasen who settled in the area in the early 1880s (Hitchman 117). He fished and operated a passenger service from Seattle to Port Townsend.

Happy Island
See Gossip Islands.

Harbor Island
It is located at the head of Elliott Bay off Seattle. The Indian name for the mouth of the Duwamish was *Ts-ekas* which means "muddy." An early local name was Edwards Island (Hitchman 118). In 1909, the Puget Sound Bridge and Dredging Company began to fill it in with spoils from the Duwamish River and the Jackson Hill and Dearborn Street regrades. When completed, it was 350 acres and at that time the largest artificial island in the world. The name was chosen for its location to Elliott Bay. The channels on either side of the island were named East and West Waterway.

Harbor Rock [14a] #2840, 1861, Richards
Located north of Fish Creek at the southeastern side of San Juan Island, it was the turn point for entering Griffin Bay from the south according to Wood (99). Wood found the name on an 1858 Fair Chart by the Officers of the H.M.S. *Plumper*. McClellan called it Kelp Rock.

Harbor Rock [14a] #2840, 1861, Richards
Located west of Haida Point in West Sound, Orcas Island, Richards left no reason for the name.

Harbour Rock [14d] #2840, 1872
Located near Cliff Island in Wasp Passage, it is one of the several currently unnamed rocks. No reason was provided for the name.

Hardwick Point
Located on the eastern side of Sequim Bay, Wilkes originally named this Takup Point [7n] in 1841. Wilkes did not include this name in his *Narrative*, but it is shown on his chart. Hitchman (298) wrote that the name was a corruption of the Indian word *T'kope* which meant "white," appropriate for the two-foot layer of clam shells on the point. Hardwick Point became official in a 1960 decision by the U.S. Board on Geographic Names over the variants Hardwick Spit, Takup Point, and White Point. The Hardwick family was the first to settle in the area (GNIS files).

Harmon, Point [7d] #146, 1841, Wilkes; [7g] #155, 1841, Wilkes

Located on the southern shoreline of Commencement Bay, Wilkes honored crew member John Harmon in 1841. Wilkes did not include this name in his *Narrative*, but it is shown on his chart. Although the historical name is recognized by the U.S. Board on Geographic Names, it is not reflected on current charts.

Harmon's Landing

See Harper.

Harnden Island

Located between Fossil and Mud Bays on Sucia Island, it was named for the Harnden family. Capt. William Harnden and his wife lived on the island from 1918 and raised five girls there. Harnden was born in Wisconsin, and in 1889, the family, including his 12 other brothers and sisters, moved to Mountain View in Whatcom County. There he met a neighbor, Gertrude Wilson, whom he married in 1896. During their courtship, Harnden would row 60 miles to visit Gertrude. For more than 15 years, Harnden worked on the west coast of Vancouver Island, fishing and piloting a mail boat. The family returned to Camano Island about 1914 where Harnden logged. In 1918, they moved into an abandoned cookhouse at the limestone quarry in Fossil Bay. There, they built the 48 foot *Tulip King*, an excursion boat that took tours through the islands. During the off-season, Harnden kept busy on log patrol, logging, raising sheep and turkeys, and substituting for lighthouse keepers on Patos and Stuart Islands. The house burnt down in 1929, so the family built a house on a barge in Mud Bay and remained until 1942. Ultimately, they relocated to North Beach on Orcas Island. Capt. Harnden died there in 1962 at age 89. In 1973, the U.S. Board on Geographic Names approved the name Wilkins Island in Docket 172. Variants were Christmas Island, Harndon Island, and Herndon Island. Wilkins Island came from Chris Wilkens who lived on the small island during the summers of the late 1960s and later retired there. He died in late 1972 or early 1973. Wilkens provided his own name for the island: Christmas Island. He felt that living there was like Christmas every day. The last two names were misspellings of Harnden's name. His daughter, Shirley Guilford, confirmed the spelling in correspondence to the Washington State Board. The Board ultimately changed the name and approved Harnden Island in 1976, Docket 209. The U.S. Board on Geographic Names followed later in the year (from Washington Board). *See also* Sucia.

Harney Channel [13b] #2689, 1861, Richards; [14a] #2840, Nov 26, 1861, Richards

Located between Orcas and Shaw Islands, the channel was named for U.S. Brig. Gen. William S. Harney who became involved in the Pig War by stationing troops on San Juan Island. It is not clear if the name appeared first on [13b] or [14a]. While [14a] provides an exact publishing date, [13b] simply indicates "corrections to 1861."

Haro Strait [1] 1790, Quimper

According to Quimper in 1790: "At midday the Bahia de Quimper [New Dungeness] bore S 75° E, the middle of the channel, more to the north, to which I gave the name 'Lopez de Haro' . . ." (Wagner 117). Gonzalo Lopez de Haro was Quimper's pilot. Quimper also named Gonzales Point on the outskirts of Victoria for him. Davidson's comments regarding the strait are enlightening (*Report* 437): "The experience of three season's surveying in this immediate locality has not increased our relish for navigating these channels in sailing vessels. With plenty of wind no navigation could be better, but in a calm vessels will frequently be jammed close to rocks, with only a few fathoms inside of their positions, but 40 or 50 outside, and a swirling current that renders towing with boats utterly impossible. Frequently, too, boats have been nearly swamped by the tide rips that exist through them. Off East Point [Saturna Island], as an instance, a five-oared whale boat entirely failed in trying to hold her own against the current, which we judged to be *rushing* (the only term applicable) at the rate of 7 miles per hour. Throughout the Canal de Haro the roar of the conflicting currents can be heard for miles, and the main current runs frequently 6 miles per hour." In 1953, the U.S. Board on Geographic Names set the boundaries on the Haro Strait. At that time, the southern boundary was a line between Gonzales Point off Victoria to Cattle

Point on San Juan Island. The northern boundary was a line between Saturna Island and Patos Island. In 1977, the Washington State Board again addressed the boundaries of various bodies of water. As a result of redefining Boundary Pass, the northern boundary of Haro Strait changed significantly (*see* Boundary Pass). Ultimately, after a year of negotiations with the Canadians and others, the parties reached an agreement and the Washington State Board approved it in its September 8, 1978 meeting, Docket 222 (from Washington State Board Files). The revised boundaries for Haro Strait: "The S end is formed by a line between Seabird Point (Discovery Island), British Columbia and Cattle Point (San Juan Island), Washington; The W boundary is formed by a line extending from the N shore of Discovery Island through Chatham Island to Cadboro Point (Vancouver Island); the N boundary is formed by a line from the N tip of Saanich Peninsula (Vancouver Island) through Harry Point (Piers Island) to Kanaka Bluff (Portland Island) and then from the N tip of Portland Island to Reynard Point (Moresby Island) and from Point Fairfax (Moresby Island), British Columbia, to Turn Point (Stuart Island), Washington; the E boundary is formed by a line extending from the S tip of Stuart Island to McCraken Point (Henry Island) to Mitchell Bay (San Juan Island)," (from U.S. Board database). Variants are Boundary Channel, Boundary Pass, Canal de Aroo, Canal de Haro, Canal de Arro, Canal de Lopez de Aro, and Canal de Lopez de Haro.

Harper
Located on the western shore of Admiralty Inlet, west of Blake Island, it was originally known as Harmon's Landing after the first settlers, George and Jennie Harmon. When clay was discovered in the hillside above, Frederick Harper established the Harper Brick and Tile Company in 1899. It employed 60 men at its peak. They dug clay near what is now Harper Park, hauled it to town, and manufactured bricks. They loaded the finished product aboard scows beached at low tide. When the tide floated the scows, they were towed to various locations on Puget Sound. Only one local house of bricks was built from clay bricks from the mine, that of the Coates family in 1925. It still stands (Bowen et al., V: 108).

Harriman
See Boston Harbor.

Harrington Lagoon
Located on the eastern side of Whidbey Island one mile south of Snatelum Point, it was named for Pearl and Ada Harrington, and Pearl's brother Hal, who settled on 300 acres there about 1917 and began clearing off the logged lands (*Island County Times*, March 24, 1922). Hal died in 1941, Pearl in 1952, and Ada in 1976.

Harris, Point [7d] #146, 1841, Wilkes; [7g] #155, 1841, Wilkes
See Browns Point.

Harstine Island [7d] #146, 1841, Wilkes; [7i] #147, 1841, Wilkes; [7h] #154, 1841, Wilkes
The largest island in South Sound, Wilkes honored crew member Henry J. Hartstein in 1841. On his muster table, Wilkes spelled the name Hartstein but spelled it Hartstene on the charts and in his *Narrative*. The local spelling is Harstine (Meany, *Origin* 110). In 1942, the U.S. Board approved the spelling Harstene Island and included the community of Harstene in its decision. In 1995, the Washington State Board, at their meeting on June 9, 1995, Docket 364, reevaluated and settled on the spelling Harstine Island, consistent with a hundred years of local use. The U.S. Board followed in 1996. Regarding the community of Hartstene, according to October 11, 1995 correspondence from Kathryn Ransdell, Chairman of the Island Name Change Committee, she provided a photocopy of a USCGS map dated 1911 with the name Harstine for the community. Ransdell wrote: "There certainly is NO site named 'Hartstene' existing on Harstine Island. We trust the U.S. Board on Geographic Names will either delete this site, or rename it 'Harstine'," (from Washington State Board Files). Ms. Ransdell apparently forgot about Hartstene Pointe, incorporated in 1970 by the Quadrant Corporation. Located on the north end of the island, the 215 acre private community includes Dougall Point. Regardless, the community of Hartstene continues to be recognized by the U.S. Board. Ferry service began to the island in 1922. The *Island Belle*, a sixteen by forty-foot scow was

powered by a ten-horse Fairbanks-Morse engine. County run, she carried three cars and crossed Pickering Passage just north of the bridge, which was completed in 1969 (Hitchcock 39-42).

Haskuse Point [7h] #154, 1841, Wilkes
See Allen Point.

Hat Island
See Gedney Island.

Hat Island [21] #6300, 1895
Located off the eastern side of Guemes Island in Padilla Bay, Wilkes originally named it Peacock Island in 1841 [7m] for the *Peacock*, one of the ships that accompanied him on the exploration. In the summer of 1841, she foundered on the Columbia River bar. Wilkes did not include this name in his *Narrative*, but it is shown on his chart. Individual names for Hat, Dot, Huckleberry, and Saddlebag are shown on [21]. In 2010, the Washington State Parks Commission transferred ownership of Huckleberry to the Samish Island Nation.

Hat Slough
Located on the eastern shoreline of Port Susan, Henry Marshall, Willard Sly, George Nevils, James Hatt, and perhaps John Silva settled in the Stanwood area in 1864. Hat and Nevils Slough were named for these early men. Hatt logged in Port Susan for the Utsalady mill.

Hautboy Island [7a] #145, 1841, Wilkes; [7m] #160, 1841, Wilkes
See Strawberry Island.

Hawk Point
Located in Skagit Bay, east of Ika Island, the origin of the name is unknown.

Hawley
It is located on the northern shore of Eagle Harbor. Originally logged by Asa Fowler, it was first settled by James Ryan in 1877 who moved into Fowler's abandoned logging camp near Wing Point (Bowen et al., IV: 43). Riley M. Hoskinson and his son Stuart settled near Ryan in 1878. Hoskinson established a weather bureau. For twenty-one years, he gathered and dispatched information to Washington D.C. Hoskinson farmed and sold produce in Port Madison and Port Blakely during this time. In 1881, locals built a school which was followed by a church the next year. In 1890, Charles and Cynthia Williams established a post office with Cynthia (Mrs. Ryan's daughter) as the first post-mistress. Cynthia named the entire Winslow area Madrone for the tree. A Mr. Hawley purchased the claim in 1924, and the community was ultimately named for him (Marriott 77-80). See Eagle Harbor.

Hazel Point [6] 1792, Vancouver
Located on the southeastern end of the Tonados Peninsula in Hood Canal, Vancouver named it: "From this station, which I called Hazel Point in consequence of its producing many of those trees . . ." (Vancouver 239). Wilkes renamed it Suqualus Point in 1841 [7d] but left no reason. Wilkes showed this as Suqualus Point [7d] on his chart, but Squaller's Point in his *Narrative*. Blumenthal (*Charles Wilkes* 105, 110) did not discover this and believed the names to be separate locations. This is perhaps understandable, as Wilkes provided one name on his chart and a fuzzy description of the same place in his *Narrative* (322): "Hood's Canal branches off from Admiralty Inlet at Suquamish Head [Foulweather Bluff], where it is 2 miles wide. Its direction is south-southeast, 5 miles; it then turns to the south-southwest, 6 miles; thence to Squaller's Point, southeast 6 miles, turning again to the west-southwest, 3 miles, to Nukolowap Point [Oak Head], the south point of Toandos Peninsula, which divides the north branch from the Canal."

Heath Bay [24] #1947, 1849, Inskip
Located off Steilacoom, it was named for Joseph Thomas Heath who in 1844 leased 640 acres from the Hudson's Bay Company north of Fort Nisqually on a previously abandoned farm. He cleared a portion of the land, raised cattle and sheep, and grew wheat, potatoes, and peas (TPL website).

Hedley Spit
Located on the northeastern end of Bainbridge Island, it's the natural spit that extends from Point Monroe. Once called Jack Spit, it was named for an early settler (Hitchman 121).

Hein Bank [17] #27, 1862, U.S. Coast Survey
Located about six miles southwest of Cattle Point, San Juan Island, the shoal area was originally named Fonte Bank by the British in 1865 [8d]. Lange speculated that the British may have named it for the Spanish Admiral Bartholomew de Fonte who in 1640 discovered the Northwest Passage and allegedly sailed through the strait located at latitude 53° north and met a ship from Boston sailing in the opposite direction. According to Meany (*Origin* 112), the current name may have originated from A. D. Bache, Superintendent of U.S. Coast Survey, for Samuel Hein, Esq., the general disbursing agent. Davidson wrote (*Directory* 128): "Bearing W. ½ S. from Smith's island, and eight miles distant, is another field of kelp nearly a mile in extent. We came unexpectedly upon it at night, in 1854, during a heavy blow, with rain. It was not then marked on any chart. Next morning we sounded through it, and found the depth of water very uniform at 5 fathoms. Recent partial examinations show that this field marks the NE. portion of the bank lying nearly north and south, with a length of 4 miles, and a breadth of 1½ mile within the limits of the 20-fathom line. We have named it the Hein bank." A further note in the 1869 *Pacific Coast Pilot* (204) reinforces the fact that they named the bank in 1854.

Heke Point [7p] #150, 1841, Wilkes
See Kinney Point.

Helix Point [7b] #148, 1841, Wilkes
See Mill Point.

Henderson Bay
Located on the northern end of Carr Inlet, Wilkes originally named this Puki Cove [7h] in 1841. He left no reason for the name. Wilkes did not include this name in his *Narrative*, but it is shown on his chart.

Henderson Inlet [7d] #146, 1841, Wilkes; [7i] #147, 1841, Wilkes
Located at the southern end of Puget Sound, Wilkes honored crew member James Henderson in 1841 (Meany, *Origin* 113). During 1936 and 1937, the U.S Board on Geographic Names addressed local names for Henderson Inlet (South Bay), Totten (Oyster Bay), Hammersley (Big Skookum), and Eld Inlets (Mud Bay). On Feb 3, 1937, the then-acting Director of the USC&GS wrote to the Board in response to these name changes: ". . . you are advised that this office strongly recommends the retention of the present names. The present names as shown on the charts have historical significance, they have been charted without deviation or change since the first charts of this area were printed and map usage appears to be well established in favor of these names. It is considered that it would be a mistake of policy to change these names . . ." The Board denied the proposed changes (GNIS files).

Henry Island [7a] #145, 1841, Wilkes; [7c] #144, 1841, Wilkes
Located east of San Juan Island, in 1841 Wilkes honored his nephew, Midshipman Wilkes Henry who was killed by natives in Fiji July 24, 1840. As a result of the massacre, Wilkes took the Fiji chief named Vendovi captive (Meany, *Origin* 113). For whatever reason, Wilkes also honored this chief with an island of his own. Lange speculated that Wilkes could have named Henry Island after his older brother, Henry Wilkes. Henry H. Edwards was perhaps the earliest settler on the island. He acquired the first land patent in 1878 but gave it up in 1885. In 1886, Henry Perkins homesteaded in Open Bay but died the following year. John Izett claimed most of the northern end of the island. Born in Scotland in 1831, he received early training as a ship's carpenter. He arrived in the Northwest in 1854 and worked in the lumber mill at Utsalady and built ships around Puget Sound for the next 20 years (Wright 94). He was a customs officer in Roche Harbor beginning in 1882. In 1905, William Schultz bought 229 acres of land and eventually accumulated 120 more, about a third of its total acreage. He was the superintendent of the Roche lime plant. When he retired to the island, he became involved in fishing and sheep ranching. He died in 1925 (McDonald 148, 149).

Hermosa Point
Located at the northern end of Tulalip Bay, the origin of the name is unknown. The word means "beautiful" in Spanish.

Herrera, Pta de [1] 1790, Quimper
On both Quimper's and Eliza's 1791 charts, this is shown on the southwestern side of the San Juan archipelago. It was not mentioned in any of the Spanish journals. It is only possible to guess at its actual location. Various sources have placed it at Eagle Point, Bellevue Point, or Pile Point. It was likely named after Juan Herrera Davila, a captain in the Spanish Navy (Wood 149). There is another entry on Eliza's chart to the east of Herrera; all that is legible is *Boca de S . . .* A search in his journal has not shed any light on this location, but it could be Cattle Pass.

Herron
Located on the eastern side of Case Inlet on the peninsula opposite Herron Island, the community was originally called Blanchard for George Blanchard, who built a sawmill in the 1890s. The post office was established in 1894 as Blanchard. The name changed in 1913 for the island (Reese, *Origins* 55).

Herron, Point [7d] #146, 1841, Wilkes
Located on the northeastern side of Port Washington Narrows, east of Bremerton, Wilkes honored crew member Lewis Herron in 1841. Wilkes did not include this name in his *Narrative*, but it is shown on his chart.

Herron Island

Herron Island [7d] #146, 1841, Wilkes; [7h] #154, 1841, Wilkes
Located in Case Inlet, Wilkes honored crew member Lewis Herron (Meany, *Origin* 113). Peter Puget named it Wednesday Island and spent a night there in 1792. He wrote: "By Noon we had reached the Continental Shore that now trended about West & pursued it for Ten Miles to an Island, where we were glad to stop and erect our Tents to avoid a threatening Squall from the SE. About two it came on with Thunder Lightening & a heavy Gust which continued without Intermission all the Afternoon. The Rain fell in perfect torrents; we therefore were obliged to remain in our Quarters Till Next Morning Thursday May 24th," (Puget 202, 203). The Salish name for the island was "where the tide goes far out" (Hilbert et. al., 268).

Heyer, Point [7d] #146, 1841, Wilkes; [7g] #155, 1841, Wilkes
Located on the eastern side of Vashon Island, Wilkes honored crew member Henry R. Heyer in 1841 (Meany, *Origin* 220). Wilkes did not include this name in his *Narrative*, but it is shown on his chart. The Salish name for the point was "hidden spring." The name relates to the story of a young Salish girl who was given in marriage to a man she didn't like. Friends hid her, and an old woman carried water to her in a basket. The basket was transformed into a spring (Hilbert et. al., 236).

Hicks Bay [13m] #2689, 1904
Located on the southeastern side of Lopez Island, it was named for Louis D. Hix who owned the land in 1891 (Cardel, *Who* 42).

Hidden Inlet
It is located on the western side of Lopez Island, west of Jones Bay. In the early 1900s, there were three canneries located along the inlet, one of which was the Hidden Inlet Packing Company. The origin of the local name is unknown. It is mentioned at http://freepages.history.rootsweb.ancestry.com/~lopezislandhistory/Lopez%20Island%20-%20History.doc

Higgins Cove
Located on the northern shore of Anderson Island, west of Otso Point, it was named for Robert and Nella Higgins. The couple retired to the island after Robert's career as an engineer for the Northern Pacific Railroad (Reese, *Origins* 56).

Hika Island [21] #6300, 1895
See Ika Island.

Hilcome, Point #148, 1841, Wilkes
See Koitlah Point.

Hillman
See Boston Harbor.

Hoballa
Located on the northern shoreline of Hammersley Inlet, a mile west of Church Point, a post office opened there in 1906 and closed in 1917. According to the TPL website, the name was selected by Ed Miller, a retired sea captain. He said the Indian name meant "shut up" or "hush up."

Hoffman Cove
Located on the southern end of Shaw Island, Delbert Hoffman settled there in 1891. Hugh Park was first to settle on the land. His land was auctioned when he shot himself in 1885. Louis Hix purchased it in 1888 for $1,250. *See also* Hix Bay, Parks Bay. Hix sold to Hoffman about 1891 (http://depts.washington.edu/fhl/CedarRockManagementPlan.pdf). Hoffman became a citizen in 1896 and was a boat builder who crafted boats ranging from small motorboats to larger cannery tenders. He also spent time repairing the fish boats of the Island Packing Company (Richardson, *Magic* 66; Lange). The name likely first appeared on t-sheet #2230 from 1895 http://kaga.wsulibs.wsu.edu/cdm-maps/sanjuantsheet.html

Hogan Point
Located on the western end of McNeil Island at the south end of Pitt Passage, the source of the name is unknown.

Hogum Bay
Located on the Nisqually Reach, the land was called Hogum and the bay Hogum Bay. When tracks were being laid for the Northern Pacific Railroad, a small group of people bought up the land. As a result, they were called hogs by other locals who later attempted to purchase the land (Meany, *Origin* 114).

Hole in the Wall
A narrow channel located at the southern end of the Swinomish Channel. It was likely named for its appearance. The Salish name was "facing toward aperture" (Hilbert et. al., 350). Davidson referenced

Hole In The Wall

the name in the 1889 *Pacific Coast Pilot* (602): "This position is locally known as Hole in the Wall, and is nearly one mile south from La Conner."

Hole in the Wall
Located at Cape Flattery on the Makah Indian Reservation at the mouth of Flattery Creek, it is a cave worn from years of pounding by the Pacific surf (Hitchman 125).

Holly
It is a community located on the eastern side of Hood Canal, nine miles south of Seabeck Bay. William Anderson was the first to settle here with his Indian wife Mary. *See* Anderson Cove. Holly was named by Robert Wyatt in 1895 for a holly tree located near the post office (Meany, *Origin* 115).

Holmes Harbor [7a] #145, 1841, Wilkes; [7d] #146, 1841, Wilkes; [7e] #158, 1841, Wilkes
Located off the eastern side of Whidbey Island, Wilkes honored crewmember Silas Holmes in 1841 (Meany, *Origin* 113).

Home
It is a community located on the western side of Carr Inlet. Joe Faulkner first settled Home in the 1870s. Beginning in 1870, George Meigs purchased land and logged it for the Port Madison mill. In 1896, the Oliver Verity, the B. F. Odell, and the George H. Allen families purchased 26 acres of the land for $182. Within two years, the group filed Articles of Incorporation for the Mutual Home Association on February 2, 1898. The area soon became a refuge for radical activists, anarchists, and socialists, where the

only rule was: "Do anything you want, as long as it doesn't offend your neighbor." The twenty-six original acres expanded to 217 acres by the time Home was platted in 1901. Apparently, the living arrangements did not appeal to everyone as the courts dissolved the Association on September 10, 1919 (Retherford Vol. I & III). It is interesting to note that when Meany collected the information, likely prior to 1919, he reported (*Origin* 115) a different perspective for the name. According to the postmaster at Lake Bay, the name originated "for the friendly attitude toward all." It was precisely unfriendly behavior and arguments that caused the dissolution of the association. The U.S. Board on Geographic Names approved Home over the variant Home Landing in 1980.

Honeymoon Bay
It is located off the eastern side of Whidbey Island in Holmes Harbor. In 1909, Minnie Spencer and Freeman Plum honeymooned in a tent in the harbor. The small bay was named in their honor (Cherry, II). In 1962, the U.S. Board on Geographic Names addressed differences between charts and topo maps (which used the name Dogfish Bay) and approved Honeymoon.

Hongking
Located on the eastern side of Quartermaster Harbor, Chinese fishermen established the community in the early 1880s. It was abandon in 1885 (Hitchman, 125). The name is not reflected on current charts and is designated a historical location by the U.S. Board on Geographic Names.

Hoo-et-zen Harbor [7d] #146, 1841, Wilkes; [7j] #153, 1841, Wilkes
See Jackson Cove.

Hood Canal [6] 1792, Vancouver
A western extension off Admiralty Inlet, the canal runs 55 miles. In 1792, Vancouver wrote: "Early on sunday morning [May 13, 1792] we again embarked; directing our route down the inlet, which, after the Right Honorable Lord Hood, I called Hood's Canal," (Vancouver 243). In a later edition of Vancouver's journal, the name was altered to Hood's Channel. Samuel Hood was born in 1724 and entered the navy in 1741 as a captain's servant. Receiving titles and promotions over the years, by 1796 he was created Viscount Hood (see Brackenridge Passage for information of peerage titles). He was promoted to Admiral of the Red in 1805 (Meany, *Vancouver's Discovery* 109-113). With respect to ranks, large fleets in the 1700s were comprised of three squadrons. In battle the white led, with the red in the middle, followed by the blue in the rear. The commander of the fleet was the admiral in the red squadron. The lowest rank of admiral was rear-admiral of the blue; the next higher rank was rear-admiral of the white, and then rear-admiral of the red, vice-admiral of the blue, vice-admiral of the red, vice-admiral of the white, admiral of the blue, admiral of the white, and admiral of the red. The Royal Navy's highest rank was admiral of the fleet. During Vancouver's time, the position was held by John Forbes, followed in 1796 by Richard Howe for whom Vancouver named Howe Sound. The U.S. Board on Geographic Names selected the singular Hood and addressed the boundaries of Hood Canal in 1932. They wrote: "Western arm of Puget Sound, extending from Tala Point, Jefferson County, and Foulweather Bluff, Kitsap County, to Clifton, Mason County, Wash," (*Decisions*).

Hood Head [19] #662, 1867, U.S. Coast Survey
Located on the western shore of Hood Canal about five miles south of Port Ludlow, its name comes from the canal. Vancouver wrote: "On the flood returning, we resumed our route, and found our supposed high round island connected with the main by a low sandy neck of land, nearly occupied by a salt-water swamp," (Vancouver 238). Davidson mentioned the name but not the origin: ". . . and passing a high round wooded peninsula on the west side of the channel, and connected to the main by a narrow neck of low sand beach. It is frequently mistaken for an island, and is called Hood's Head," (Davidson, *Report* 451).

Hood Point [19] #662, 1867, U.S. Coast Survey
Located about four miles south of Seabeck on the eastern side of Hood Canal, Wilkes named this Sandy Point [7d] in 1841, likely for its appearance (Wilkes, *Narrative* 323). Hitchman (126) suggested that the current name came from Hood Canal because of an overabundance of Sandy Points in Puget Sound country.

Hoodsport
Located on the western side of Hood Canal near The Great Bend, it took its name from the canal.

Hope
A small community located on the Hale Passage side of Fox Island, a mile and a half southeast of Ketners Point, the origin of the name is unknown.

Hope Island [7d] #146, 1841, Wilkes; [7i] #147, 1841, Wilkes
Located on the western side of Harstine Island in Puget Sound, Wilkes left no reason for the 1841 name. Meany indicated that the local name was Johns Island for the early settler John Gilmore (Meany, *Origin* 116). Following Gilmore, the Louis Schmidt family of Olympia Brewing fame purchased Hope Island in 1896. They sold to the Munn family who in turn sold it to the State of Washington in 1990 for three million dollars (Bailey and Nyberg, *South Puget Sound* 283). The Salish name for the island was "small island" (Hilbert et. al., 283).

Hope Island [7a] #145, 1841, Wilkes; [7e] #158, 1841, Wilkes
Located on the eastern side of Whidbey Island, just east of Deception Pass, Wilkes left no reason for the 1841 name.

Hope Reef
It is located in the southern end of Griffin Bay, San Juan Island, about a quarter mile off shore and halfway between Half Tide Reef and North Pacific Rock. The name is shown on t-sheet #2301 from 1897 (http://kaga.wsulibs.wsu.edu/cdm-maps/sanjuantsheet.html). J. J. Gilbert noted its name in his 1897 and Descriptive Report #2301 (http://riverhistory.ess.washington.edu/tsheets/reports/t2301.pdf, p 6). He wrote: "Two hundred meters SE from Half Tide Reef is a small reef which is bare only at extreme low tide. A schooner named the *Hope* once struck on it and gives it a name." McLellan wrote: "It is awash only at the lowest tides."

Horcasitas, Boca de [3] 1791, Eliza
See San Juan Channel.

Horn, Cape [23] #6460, 1905
The point is located at the northern entrance to Hammersley Inlet opposite Cape Cod. The origin is unknown. The Salish name for the cape was "dug out on one side." It referred to nets that the Indians stretched across the inlet to catch ducks (Hilbert et. al., 275).

Hornbecks Spit
Located in Eagle Harbor west of Wing Point, it was named for John C. Hornbeck who built sailing ships there beginning in the 1860s (TPL website).

Hornet Harbor [7a] #145, 1841, Wilkes; [7m] #160, 1841, Wilkes
It is now Guemes Channel, named for the *Hornet*, commanded by Capt. James Lawrence during the War of 1812. According to Wilkes in 1841: "There is a connection between Penguin and Hornet Harbors on the north, through Levant Passage . . ." (Wilkes, *Narrative* 310). Richards on [13a] renamed it Guemes Channel honoring the Viceroy of New Spain, whose full name was Juan Vincente de Güemes Pacheco de Padilla Horcasitas y Aguayo, Conde de Revilla Gigedo.

Horsehead Bay

Horsehead Bay
Located on the eastern shores of Carr Inlet, Wilkes originally named this Ihikum Cove [7h] in 1841. He left no reason for the name. Wilkes did not include this name in his *Narrative*, but it is shown on his chart. The current name is likely for its appearance.

Horseshoe Bay
Located off the western portion of San Juan Island, east of Delacombe Point, it was likely named for its shape. According to Wood (100), it first appeared on U.S. chart #6381 in 1901. It also appears on the 1921 Admiralty chart [16c].

Horseshoe Lake
Referenced by McLellan who called it Blakely Lake, it is the northernmost lake on Blakely Island. It may have been named for its shape.

Hoska Island
See Tanglewood Island.

Houston Island [13c] #2689, 1865
See Ram Island.

Hoypus Point [7e] #158, 1841, Wilkes
Located on the eastern side of Deception Pass, on the northern end of Whidbey Island, Wilkes spelled it *Hoipus* on his chart. Wilkes did not include this name in his *Narrative*. According to Hale (582), *Hoipus* is a San Raphael Indian name meaning "chief." The San Raphael family lived in the area north of San Francisco. *See also* Yokeko Point.

Huckleberry Island [21] #6300, 1895
See Hat Island.

Hudson, Point

Hudson, Point [6] 1792, Vancouver
Located a mile south of Point Wilson, Vancouver does not specifically mention the name in his journal, but it is clearly included on his chart. Wilkes wrote (*Journal* 58): "At 10.30 got under weigh and beat out of Port Discovery and rounded the point called by Vancouver Point Wilson and went in and anchored. Roads in 10 fathoms water sandy bottom. This is a beautiful Bay and has a long level beach with a Pond of Freshwater backing it and a run into the Bay where the vessels may be supplied – the Point a low sand one called Hudson's Point is bold to and may be passed about a ¼ of a mile . . ." Meany (*Origin* 220) incorrectly gave Wilkes credit for the name in honor of crew member William L. Hudson. Blumenthal (*Charles Wilkes* 15) similarly errored. Early on, the marina area was simply swampy lowland. It was dredged by the Puget Sound Bridge and Dredging Company in 1931.

Hudson, Point & Bay
Located a half mile east of Blind Island on the northern end of Shaw Island, the point and Hudson Bay to the west were named for Henry H. Hudson who settled there and ran pigs and cows on his farm and developed an orchard (Lange). Hudson and his family departed San Juan County in early 1899 for New York where the family had large business interests (*San Juan Islander*, Feb. 23, 1899, p 3).

Hudson Cove
Located on the eastern side of Totten Inlet, the origin of the name is unknown.

Hughes Bay
Located off the southern end of Lopez Island, west of Watmough Head, the bay was originally known as Huggins Bay after Thomas Huggins, an early settler. It is unclear if Benjamin Hughes also settled in the bay or if he purchased Huggins' land. Hughes, a retired blacksmith from Ireland, was shown on the 1880 census as 80 years old.

Hulls Island [7a] #145, 1841, Wilkes
See Orcas Island.

Hummel Lake
Located east of Fisherman Bay, it was named for the early Lopez settlers, Robert and Edwin Hummel (TPL website). The lake frequently froze during the winters and locals enjoyed skating on it (*The Islander*, Dec. 3, 1896, p 3).

Humphrey Head [21] #6300, 1895
Located on the northeastern side of Lopez Island, the Admiralty originally named it Separation Point [13j]. It was named for William Humphrey who was born in 1838. He emigrated in 1862 and settled in Estherville, Iowa. He married Annie Graham in 1866. The family moved to Lopez in 1877 at the southern side of Shoal Bay, homesteaded 166 acres (and cleared 50 of those acres), planted an orchard with 500 trees, and raised wheat, hay, and chickens.

Humphrey Head

The Humphreys were the first settlers on the north end of Lopez. William died in 1902 and was buried in the Lopez cemetery (Bailey, *San Juan Islands* 57; http://freepages.history.rootsweb.ancestry.com/~lopezislandhistory/1901.html).

Hungerford Point
It is located at the northern entrance to Hammersley Inlet. The 1892 Thurston County census listed a Hungerford family in the Arcadia precinct. H. C., age 45, and his wife Mary, age 38, lived there with their two children.

Hunot Point [7e] #158, 1841, Wilkes
See Snee-oosh Point.

Hunter Bay [13h] #2689, 1888
The bay is located on the eastern side of Lopez Island at the south end of Lopez Sound. In 1911, Thomas Gourley led a religious cult to the bay called the "Come-Outers." Originally from the Ballard area, there were more than 130 adults and children in the group. They initially lived in tents but soon built cabins and a cookhouse that doubled as a chapel. Gourley left within five years, and by 1922 most of the members also departed. During prohibition, the cookhouse was home to a still. The bay was named for the final elk on Lopez Island hunted and killed by the Indians (TPL website).

Hunter Point
Located on Squaxin Passage and the northern entrance to Eld Inlet, the Alfred A. Hunter family purchased property near the point in 1887. They ran a hotel and sold firewood to local steamers (TPL website). The Salish name for the point was "wet foot" (Hilbert et. al., 299). The U.S. Board on Geographic Names addressed the variants in 1938 including Cushman Point [23], named for Elizabeth Cushman who purchased land there in 1865, and Hunters Point (*Decisions*). According to the GNIS files, Cushman Point first appeared on an 1878 U.S.C. & G.S. field survey sheet No. T-1672. However, the more popular local name endured.

Hurley Cove
Located on the northern shoreline of Totten Inlet, nearly opposite Burns Cove, the origin of the name is unknown. It is about a quarter mile east of Bowman Cove.

Hyde Point [7d] #146, 1841, Wilkes; [7i] #147, 1841, Wilkes
Located on the eastern side of McNeil Island, Wilkes honored crew member William Hyde in 1841. Wilkes did not include this name in his *Narrative*, but it is shown on his chart. In 1846, Inskip named this Dyke Point [24] for Lieut. Charles Dyke of the *Fisgard* (Meany, *Origin* 118).

Hygedith [8a] #1917, 1847, Kellett
Located on the eastern side of Clallam Bay, Kellet used this name for the Indian village located there.

Hyland Spit
This is the local name for the spit that protects Miller Bay in Port Madison (McDonald, Lucile. "Miller's Bay Ponders Development Plans." *Seattle Times*. Mar. 29, 1964. Magazine Section p 2,3).

Hylebos Creek [23] #6460, 1905
Originating near Milton, it flows into the Hylebos Waterway in Commencement Bay. It was named for Reverend Peter F. Hylebos who arrived in Tacoma about 1870 and served at the Steilacoom Catholic Church and St. Leo's Parish in Tacoma (TPL website). He also founded the St. George's School for Boys on the creek and administered primarily to Puyallup Indian children (Hilbert et. al., 249). Variants included East Hylebos Creek and Hylebo Creek which were discarded in a 1938 U.S. Board on Geographic Names decision (GNIS files).

Hylebos Waterway
Located in Commencement Bay, it was named for the Hylebos Creek (TPL website).

Iceberg Island
Located off the southwestern side of Lopez Island, the name was taken from the point as offered by Roy McClellan who wrote: "Iceberg Island is located about 700 yards to the northeast of Iceberg Point, being the most eastern member of the Geese Islet group. It has an area of 3.5 acres and an elevation of about 50 feet. The shores of Iceberg Island are bare and rocky." The State of Washington owns the island.

Iceberg Point [18] #654, 1866, U.S. Coast Survey
It is located on the southwestern side of Lopez Island. In 1859, Richards originally named it Jennis Point [13a] but left no reason. The U.S. Coast Survey provided its final name in 1866. Admiralty charts waffled on the name into the 1900s by calling it Jennis or Iceberg Point. The U.S. Board on Geographic Names finally decided upon the current name in 1891. The U.S. Coast Guard owns the point.

Idlewild
See Newhall's Point.

Ihikum Cove [7h] #154, 1841, Wilkes
See Horsehead Bay.

Ika Island
Located in Skagit Bay, east of Goat Island, the origin of the name is unknown. The Salish name for the island was "large head." The name is a transliteration of the Indian word (Hilbert et. al., 350). The U.S. Board on Geographic Names approved the name in 1941 over the variants of Hika Island [21] and Hyka Island (*Decisions*). According to the GNIS files, the name Ika first appeared on a 1910 Map of Puget Sound by Anderson Map Company.

Illahee
Located south of University Point on the eastern side of Port Orchard, the word is Chinook jargon for "country, land, or place where one lives" (TPL website).

Illinois Inlet
See Fish Creek.

Inati Bay [21] #6300, 1895
Located on the southeastern side of Lummi Island, it is Chinook jargon for "across, beyond, or opposite." It apparently relates its position with respect to Point Francis. The origin of the name is unknown, but it was used in the 1889 *Pacific Coast Pilot* and on charts since the 1890s. In 1976, the Washington State Board on Geographic Names received a proposal to change the name to Deepwater Bay, based upon local usage. The Board denied the proposal in its December 10, 1976 meeting, Docket 210. The U.S. Board followed in 1977 (from Washington State Board Files).

Indian Beach
Located north of Lowell Point on the western side of Camano Island, the origin of the name is likely the result of an Indian campground.

Indian Cove [13a] #2689, 1859, Richards
Located on the southeastern side of Shaw Island, the name came from the site of an early Indian village.

Indian Cove
It is located off the northern side of Harstine Island, a mile northeast of Jarrell Cove. The origin of the name is unknown.

Indian Hole
Located at The Great Bend, it is part of Annas Bay. The origin of the name is unknown.

Indian Island
It is located at the head of East Sound in Fishing Bay, just west of Madrona Point. According to a July 2, 1942 article in *The Orcas Islander*: "The little islet lying out in the water a short distance from East Sound [the author references the community of Eastsound], has for years been known as Jap island. In view of the relationship with the Japs, at present, citizens decided that some other name, such as Victory island or MacArthur island, would be more appropriate." The follow-up article occurred on August 13, 1942: "In a recent issue of The Orcas Islander there appeared the suggestion that the name of the small island in East Sound bay, be changed from Japanese Island to Victory Island. Everyone seemed to be in accord with this suggested change." The author of this article also stated: ". . . that this small island is recorded by the U. S. Coast and Geodetic Survey, not as Japanese island but as Indian island." A November 18, 1981 article in the *Seattle PI* addressed the possibility of mining on the one-acre rock known, according to the PI, as Jap Island. That article prompted a Japanese

university student, Tatsumi Morishige, to inquire to the Washington State Board about the origin of the name and the history of the island. According to a January 30, 1982 letter from the Orcas Island Historical Society: ". . . at one time it was covered with dwarf pines and the winds had blown them till they were twisted and the tops resembled conical hats. They [locals] seem to think that is the only reason why it might have been named Jap Island . . ." Another theory was that pencil junipers grow on the island and resembled bonsai trees, thus giving rise to the name. Unfortunately, the files of the Washington State Board provided no further information. From a different Board file (Madrona Point), an early name for the island was Indian Island, according to McLellan. He wrote: "Indian Island, which has an area of 1.25 acres, is situated near East Sound village. It is located on the west side of Arbutus Point [Madrona Point] in the little harbor known as Fishing Bay. The island is low and rocky but it contains sufficient soil to support a limited amount of vegetation. At low tide, it is connected with Orcas Island by a broad sand bar." When J. J. Gilbert was in the neighborhood in 1889, he reflected the name of Church Island on the topo sheet (http://kaga.wsulibs.wsu.edu/zoom/zoom.php?map=uw181). None of these names, Church, Indian, Jap, MacArthur, or Victory Island are reflected on U.S. charts nor are they recognized by the U.S. Board on Geographic Names. But Indian Island is used on the web site (https://sites.google.com/site/indianislandproject/) which lists it as a marine health observatory. It is owned by the U.S. Government and as of this writing, apparently has no formal name. According to Joanne Johnston from the Orcas Island Historical Society, locals most favor the name Indian Island.

Indian Island
It is located on the eastern side of Port Townsend. The name became popular in the early 1900s for the Indians living in the area (Hitchman 133).

Indian Peninsula [7d] #146, 1841, Wilkes; [7i] #147, 1841, Wilkes
Wilkes wrote: "The Indian or Great Peninsula divides the waters of Admiralty Inlet and Puget Sound on the east, from those of Hood's Canal on the west. The extent of this tract is 45 miles in length by 25 in breadth; it is indented by numerous bays on the east and south, and several islands lie in close proximity to it, forming roadsteads and harbors." On [7d], Wilkes includes the name "Indian or Great Peninsula." On [7i], Wilkes lists "Indian Peninsula South end." Wilkes intended the peninsula to run from Foulweather Bluff on the northern end to Devils Head on the south (Wilkes *Narrative* 90; Meany, *Origin* 119). The southern portion is now known as the Key Peninsula.

Indian Point [14a] #2840, 1861, Richards
Located on the western side of West Sound, Orcas Island, Richards likely honored the local Indians.

Indian Point [7d] #146, 1841, Wilkes
Located at the southern end of Whidbey Island in Useless Bay, Wilkes originally named this Indian Head on his table of latitude/longitudes but showed it as Indian Point on his chart.

Indian Village
See Guemes Island.

Indianola

Indianola
It is located on the northern shore of Port Madison. By 1909, Tar-de-blue, mother of Chief Jacob, became sole heir of the property around Indianola. Alpheus Loughrey married her daughter Katie. Their son, Ernest A. Loughrey married Carrie, the daughter of William DeShaw. The Loughreys sold to the ex-mayor of Seattle, Ole Hanson. Ole named the area for a combination of Loughrey's Indian wife and his own name (Carlson, 30, 31; TPL website). In 1916,

Warren L. Gazzam purchased the property, formed the Indianola Beach Land Company, and sold individual lots. The very wide beach and shallow water in front of Indianola created some early problems for passenger and freight traffic. To accommodate, Gazzam built a 960 foot pier. To handle car/ferry traffic, locals built a new dock alongside the existing wharf, out to 1,080 feet. The Agate Pass Bridge opened in 1950; ferry service stopped the following year. By 1971, the wharf was in sad shape. Rebuilt at a cost of $34,000, it was shortened to 870 feet. The decking was again replaced in 1982 due to storm damage and refurbished again in 2004 (*Indianola*, 12-37). Today, the pier is used for fishing and for general loading and unloading. Overnight moorage is not permitted.

Inman Point [16b] #602, 1869, Pender
It is located on the northeastern side of Henry Island, at the entrance to Roche Harbor. It is neither named on current charts nor recognized by the U.S. Board on Geographic Names. Pender likely named it for Lieut. James Inman who served under Capt. Delacombe at English Camp (Wood 152).

Inner Passage [15a] #611, 1865, Richards
Shown on current U.S. and Canadian charts as Inner Passage, it is located between Salmon Bank and Cattle Point. However, Richards labeled it Inner Passage Not Recommended as a warning to mariners to avoid that area due to shoal waters. It is interesting how a warning because of dangerous waters became an accepted channel by simply modifying the name!

Inside Passage
While not an official name with the U.S. Board on Geographic Names, it has been in local use for years. It is generally defined as a ship passage with Puget Sound (Olympia) at its southern end and Skagway, Alaska at the northern terminus. The route runs through Puget Sound, inside Vancouver Island, inside the Queen Charlotte Islands, and through sheltered passages from there to Skagway.

Inskip Bank [24] #1947, 1849, Inskip
See Nisqually Bluff.

Iowa Rock
Located off the southern end of Lopez Island about a half mile east of Iceberg Point, it was named in 1909 by Dr. R. B. Wylie from the University of Iowa. Wylie was attending summer classes at the Puget Sound Marine Station in Friday Harbor and named it for the State of Iowa (Hitchman 134).

Irondale [22] #6450, 1909
It is located on the western shoreline of Port Townsend. After having several owners, the land was sold to the Puget Sound Iron Company, incorporated in 1879. Because of a large deposit of hematite ore discovered in the Chimacum Valley, the Company constructed furnaces, casting pits, rolling mills, cooling bed, and boiler houses; production began in 1881. Problems and an inferior product plagued the company for years and the plant closed in 1889. The Pacific Steel Company purchased the plant in 1901. Production ceased in 1904. At various other times, the plant would open and soon close. The final closure was in 1919 (Britton).

Ironsides Inlet [7a] #145, 1841, Wilkes
See East Sound.

Islandale
Located at the south end of Lopez Sound, Lange reported that it was named for a summer resort called Islanddale, established there in 1910. The post office, which opened in 1910, likely replaced the Edwards/Otis post office. The first postmaster was Samuel R. Pusey. Locals changed the name in 1912 or 1913 to Islandale and filed a plat under that name.

Issei Creek
The creek flows into Fletcher Bay on the western side of Bainbridge Island. The name means "first generation" in Japanese and is pronounced "issey." In its March 14, 1997 meeting, the Washington State Board on Geographic Names approved the name. The U.S. Board followed later in the year (from Washington State Board Files).

Itsania Ledge
See Itsami Ledge.

Itsami Ledge [7i] #147, 1841, Wilkes
Located at the entrance of Henderson Inlet, Wilkes called it a shoal in 1841 rather than a ledge. He left no reason for the name. Wilkes did not include this name in his *Narrative*, but it is shown on his chart. GNIS files contain some interesting 1892

correspondence from George Davison to the U.S. Board on Geographic Names regarding a variant, Itsania Ledge. Apparently, the 1880 Buoy List reflected the name Itsania Shoal, but by 1892 it had changed to Itsania Ledge. Davidson wrote: "I consider the Itsania Ledge of the Buoy list a typographical or clerical error of transferring m into ni, and the 'ledge' [ ] a misapplication of the term." The Board selected the current name in 1892.

Jack Island [7a] #145, 1841, Wilkes
Located off the northeastern side of Guemes Island, Wilkes provided no reason for the 1841 name.

Jack Island [7d] #146, 1841, Wilkes; [7i] #147, 1841, Wilkes
See Squaxin Island.

Jack Point [7p] #150, 1841, Wilkes
Located on the northeastern end of the spit at the entrance to Kilisut Harbor, Wilkes named this in 1841 but left no reason for the name. The name is no longer used. Wilkes did not include this name in his *Narrative*, but it is shown on his chart.

Jack Sherer's Point
See Davis Point.

Jack Spit
See Hedley Spit.

Jackson Cove
Located on the western shoreline of Hood Canal about five miles north of Pleasant Harbor, Wilkes in 1841 originally named this Hoo-et-zen Harbor in his *Narrative* but spelled it Hooetzen on the charts [7d], [7j]. He wrote: "Hoo-et-zen Harbor is the next. It lies on the west shore of the north branch, 3 miles above Sylopash Point, and forms a segment of a circle, three-fourths of a mile in diameter; its shores are rocky and elevated, except on the northwest side, where there is a sand-beach, with the usual mud-flat. Pulali Point lies on the east side, from which to the double heads the shore is a rocky bluff." The double heads above referenced appear to be two small "bumps" in the northern end of the cove, sticking out from the land. On the eastern shoreline, he included the label "Rocky Bluff" [7j], but this was likely more of a descriptor rather than a place name. The cove was named for R. E. DeJackson who homesteaded there (Hitchman 136). In 1918, Reginald Parsons donated 280 acres of the land to the Boy Scouts. Born in New York in 1873 to a wealthy family, his investments continued to grow after he arrived in Seattle in 1904. He became the first president of the Seattle Boy Scouts Council in 1916 and served five years. He died in 1955. The area is still known as Camp Parsons to thousands of scouts who enjoyed it.

Jakles Lagoon
Located on Griffin Bay on the eastern side of San Juan Island, it is one of three lagoons near American Camp. From east to west, they are Third Lagoon, Jakles Lagoon, and Old Town Lagoon. It was likely named for George Jakle, a soldier at the camp who later tended the Cattle Point Lighthouse. Early on, the lighthouse was simply a lantern tacked to a post. Jakle received frequent shipments of kerosene in five-gallon cans to use for the lantern. Jakle, who owned most of Cattle Point at the time, also raised sheep and farmed (http://www.thesanjuans.com/san-juan-island-places/sanjuan-parks-forest/jakles_lagoon_sanjuan_island.shtml). The Jan. 26, 1899 edition of the *San Juan Islander* spelled the name Jakles in a short note on the family: "Mrs. Geo. Jakles and daughter went to Seattle on the *Thompson* Saturday." Paul K. Hubbs sold his farm on Mt. Finlayson to John Franklin Bryant in 1868. Bryant drowned in an accident, and his widow remarried Jakle in 1871 ("Cattle Point, on San Juan Island." *Seattle Times*. Mar 6, 1960. Magazine Section p 9).

James Island [13a] #2689, 1859, Richards
See Satellite Island.

James Island [7a] #145, 1841, Wilkes
Located east of Decatur Island, in 1841 Wilkes likely honored Reuben James (circa 1776-1838), an American sailor who saved the life of Capt. Stephen Decatur (1779-1820) in Tripoli during the Barbary Wars. While attempting to set fire to the U.S.S. *Philadelphia* captured by the Barbary pirates in 1804, Decatur's crew fought hand-to-hand with the pirates. James took a blow from a sword intended for Decatur, thus saving his life. James served for many more years under Decatur (Meany, *Origin* 122, 123). According to Davidson: "James island consists of two heads a mile apart and 250 feet high, but connected

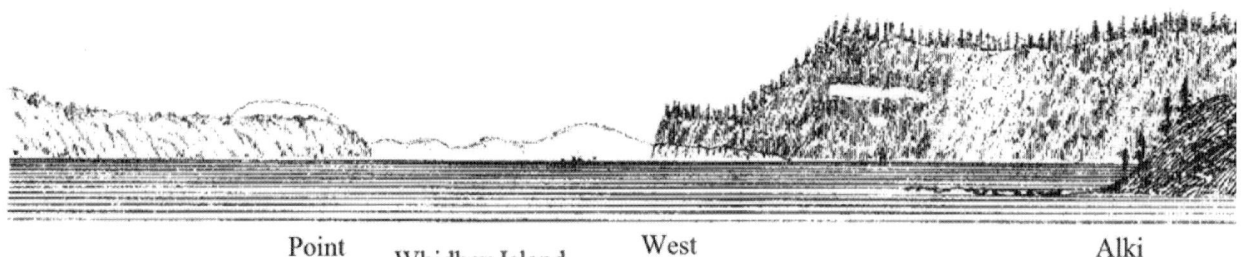

by a narrow ridge. The southern head is the higher, and not very heavily timbered. Close to the west of the ridge lies another head, connected with Decatur Island by a low sand beach," (*Report* 432).

Jamestown
Located three miles southeast of Dungeness, it was a Clallam Indian village named for Chief James Balch (Meany, *Origin* 123). Faced with forced relocation from the Dungeness Spit, the S'Klallam Tribe purchased 210 acres of land in 1874 and formed Jamestown.

Jap Island
See Indian Island.

Jarrell Cove
Located on the northern end of Harstine Island, it was first settled by Robert Jarrell in 1852. Born in Tennessee in 1828, Jarrell moved with his parents to Missouri in 1830. In 1849 he headed to the California gold fields and then migrated to Puget Sound in 1852 where he settled on Harstine. He built a house in Jarrell Cove about 1860 on 160 acres, logged the area, and planted an apple orchard and a garden. In 1878, at age 50, he married Philura who became the first postmistress on the island, a job she continued until she died in 1913. Robert died in 1894, just a couple weeks shy of his 66th birthday (Hitchcock 41, 42, 60-62). The Salish name for the cove was "hunting canoes" (Hilbert et. al., 295). The U.S. Board on Geographic Names approved the name of Gerald Cove in 1941 and Jarrell Cove in 1968. Other variants included Bay of Despond [23], which originated from an 1879 t-sheet #1528, Jarrells Cove and Jarrels Cove.

Jasper Bay
Located off the eastern side of Lopez Island opposite Ram Island, Lange speculated it was named for the jasper found there. Alternatively, there was a Jasper family listed in the 1880 census (http://freepages.history.rootsweb.ancestry.com/~lopezislandhistory/history_of_lopez_island.html).

Jeal Point
Located on the northern side of Boston Harbor in Budd Inlet, it was named for Herbert Jeal, age 49 according to the 1870 Thurston County census (Palmer 39).

Jeff Davis Harbor
See Neil Bay.

Jefferson, Point [7d] #146, 1841, Wilkes; [7q] #156, 1841, Wilkes
Located at the northern entrance to Port Madison, Wilkes named this as well as Points Monroe and Madison for those presidents in 1841 (Meany, *Origin* 220). The Salish name for the point was "bent knee" (Hilbert et. al., 191).

Jennis Point [13a] #2689, 1859, Richards
See Iceberg Point.

Jensen Bay
Located on the eastern side of San Juan Island, on Griffin Bay, it was named by J. J. Gilbert for the Jensen family who lived there about 1880 (Wood 108, 109). Mr. Gilbert surveyed in the area in 1897 and prepared Descriptive Report #2301 (http://riverhistory.ess.washington.edu/tsheets/reports/t2301.pdf, p 6). Gilbert spelled the name Jansen. Wood noted the interesting modifications of the name over the next 100 years. On charts, it was variously spelled Jansen, Jenson, and Jensen. The Norwegian Benjamin Jensen settled on San Juan Island in 1883. His sons, Joe, Albert, Frank, and Pete accompanied him. For a few months they lived at

San Juan Town but moved to the spit below Jensen Bay. As Benjamin had been a shipbuilder in Norway, he and his sons began building boats on the island along with farming. In 1905, the family purchased property on the southern end of Friday Harbor and built a shipyard. It celebrated its 100th anniversary in 2010 (McDonald, Lucile. "Noted Friday Harbor Shipbuilders." *Seattle Times*. Aug. 21, 1960. Magazine Section p 7).

Jerisich Park
Located on the southwestern side of Gig Harbor, it was named after the first settler, Samuel Jerisich, who arrived in 1867 (Evans 1, 2). *See* Gig Harbor.

Jetty Island
Located off the main boat harbor at Everett, it was an 1892 scheme by Henry Hewett, representing John D. Rockefeller to construct a bulkhead or dike to divert the water from the Snohomish River to the Everett waterfront. By building completely around Everett, a freshwater harbor would have been created, accessible to Puget Sound by locks. The intent was to control wood-boring shipworms, a blight on wooden boats. The worms died in freshwater. Even though Rockefeller withdrew his support during the financial Panic of 1893, construction finally began in 1896. However, the lock and dam were never built. Construction was doomed because the river's heavy sediment load would require extensive and ongoing dredging to maintain a channel for navigation. Regardless, the Army Corps of Engineers continued to dump onto the island until the late 1960s when locals began to protest its use as a dumping ground. In 1975, the *Everett Herald* coined the name Jetty Island (http://edmondscc.ning.com/profiles/blogs/840871:BlogPost:15641). In 1988, the Washington State Board on Geographic Names received a proposal to formally name it. Although there was some concern over the inconsistent use of the term "jetty," i.e., a jetty is connected to shore, the Board approved the name at its July 13, 1989 meeting, Docket 331. The U.S. Board followed later in the year.

Jod Creek
See Christensen Creek.

Joe, Point
Located on the western side of San Juan Island, about a mile northwest of Eagle Cove, the origin of the name is unknown.

Joemma Beach State Park
Located on the western side of the Key Peninsula, the park was named after Joe and Emma Smith who lived on the premises from 1917 to 1932 (State Parks website).

Joes Bay
See Von Geldern Cove.

Johns Island [7a] #145, 1841, Wilkes; [7c] #144, 1841, Wilkes
Located off the southeastern side of Stuart Island, Wilkes' reason for this name in 1841 is unknown (Meany, *Origin* 124). Lange speculates that Wilkes named it for his first son John, born in 1821. John was also the first name of Wilkes' father.

Johns Island
See Hope Island.

Johns Pass [13b] #2689, 1861, Richards
The passage between Stuart and Johns Islands, Richards' reason for this name is unknown. Presumably he extended Wilkes' name for the island to the pass.

Johns Point
On the southwestern side of Lopez Island, a peninsula is formed by Mackaye Harbor and Barlow Bay on the north and Outer Bay on the south. This peninsula was part of the original homestead of Billy Barlow who passed it down to his son Sam. Sam gave his son John the western end of the peninsula and it came to be known as John's Point. The point and peninsula were later purchased by John Troxell, who in 1902 married Eunice Davis, daughter of James and Amelia. John was a fish trap man who installed traps from lower Puget Sound into the San Juan Islands (Mason 50, 170).

Johnson Point [13a] #2689, 1859, Richards
Located on the southeast side of Sucia Island, Richards likely honored P. C. Johnson, passed midshipman aboard the steamer *Active* under Lieut. Alden (Meany, *Origin* 125). The Salish name for the point was "crooked promontory" (Hilbert et. al., 311).

Johnson Point [23] #6460, 1905
Located on the mainland at the eastern head of Henderson Inlet, Wilkes originally named this Point Moody [7d] [7i] in 1841 honoring crew member William Moody (Meany, *Origin* 125). Its current name could have been for P. C. Johnson, a crew member of James Alden. Or, according to Holt (17), it could have been named for Dr. J. R. Johnson who lived on the point. Ezra Meeker commented on a summer 1853 visit: "The tide turned, night overtook me, and I could go no further. Two men were in a cabin, the Doctor Johnson, heretofore mentioned, and a man by the name of Hathaway, both drunk and drinking, with a jug handy by, far from empty. Both were men that seemed to me to be well educated, and, if sober, refined. They quoted from Burns, sang songs and ditties, laughed and danced until late in the night, when they became exhausted and fell asleep." According to Palmer (39) it was named by Meeker for Doctor Johnson.

Joint Island
See Justice Island.

Jones Bay
Located off the southern end of Lopez Island west of Mackaye Harbor, Lange noted the first settler on the bay to be Robert Jones, a sailor from England. Jones was shown on the 1880 census as 41 years old and received a patent to his homestead in 1891. George Richardson also settled in the area in the early 1870s. A plat filed May 5, 1891 shows Richardson Bay and the "Jones addition."

Jones Bluff [7f] #151, 1841, Wilkes
According to Wilkes' chart, this is a bluff about a mile north of Port Ludlow. There were at least five crew members named Jones, plus a host of other historical figures, including Thomas ap Catesby Jones whose resignation led to Wilkes' assignment. Wilkes left no clue as to whom he honored. The name is neither reflected on U.S. charts nor is it recognized by the U.S. Board on Geographic Names.

Jones Island [7a] #145, 1841, Wilkes
Located off the western side of Orcas Island, Wilkes named this in 1841 for Capt. Jacob Jones of the *Wasp* who captured the *Frolic* in the War of 1812 (Meany, *Origin* 125). The earliest settler was Robert Kittles, Sr. who lived there with his Indian wife and children. Lange uncovered a reference to Saddle Island in an Oct. 6, 1846 log entry of the H.M.S. *Cormorant*. The 1895 t-sheet #2229 at http://kaga.wsulibs.wsu.edu/cdm-maps/sanjuantsheet.html reflected the name of Capt. Kittle and his farm at the south end of the island. In his 1895 Descriptive Report #2229, J. J. Gilbert wrote: "Jones Island has but one settler, a Capt. Kittles, he was living on Sinclair Island when I surveyed it in 1886 and in 1899, I found him living on Blakely Island. He now lives in the bay on the south part of Jones Id." The September 9, 1897 *Islander* (p 3) included an article about Robert Kittles, an acting mate aboard the steamer *Buckeye*. In Whatcom, returning to the boat on a dark evening, he jumped over a rail thinking it was a fence in front of the dock. Instead, it was the edge of a railroad trestle. He fell 38 feet to the tide flats and landed on a pile of logs. Although taken to the hospital, he was not expected to recover. The following week, *The Islander* reported that Mr. Kittles died. According to the article: "The steamer *Buckeye*, on which he was mate, made a special run Saturday evening for the purpose of bringing his body to Jones island, where it was laid to rest on Saturday (sic), beside the remains of his mother, who was buried there several years ago. At the time of his death, Mr. Kittles was a young man, about 30 years of age, who had always held the good will and respect of his many friends and neighbors. Deceased leaves a father, four brothers and one sister to mourn his loss." The June 23, 1898 edition of *The San Juan Islander* (p 3) spelled the name Kettles and reported the Mr. Kettles was very ill. He died in July 1899 at the age of seventy-three (*The San Juan Islander*, July 20, 1899, p 3). McLellan mentioned that the island was used as a fox farm in the 1920s. Today it is a wildlife reserve and state park.

Jones Lagoon
See Argyle Lagoon.

Jones Rock
Located between Cape Flattery and Tatoosh Island, it is awash at half tide. The origin of the name is unknown.

Jorgenson Hill
It is a 348 foot hill located on the eastern side of Indian Island, south of Bishops Point. The 1885 Jefferson County census lists three Jorgenson brothers from Norway. Two lived at the Ducaboos, the third in Port Ludlow. The census also lists J. Jorgenson from Indiana in the Irondale precinct. None of these men were listed in the 1887 census. The relationship, if any, of these men to Jorgenson hill is unknown.

Juan de Fuca, Strait of [6] 1792, Vancouver
There is a good deal of controversy regarding the first discoverer of the Strait of Juan de Fuca. The earliest story begins with Samuel Purchas (1577-1626), an English clergyman and author. In one publication, he related a note from Michael Lock (or Loc). According to the note, in 1596, Lock met Juan de Fuca in Venice. De Fuca, originally from Cephalonia, was the Greek, Apostolos Valerianos. He claimed forty years of service for Spain piloting ships in the West Indies. In 1592, de Fuca sailed north along the California Coast. When he reached 47 degrees of latitude, he entered a broad inlet and explored for more than twenty days. While de Fuca's story is intriguing, most historians agree that there is little evidence to support it. In a letter to the Washington State Board on Geographic Names dated February 12, 1985, Mr. Harry M. Majors, Editor of the *Northwest Press* stated the following: "There is a minor amount of controversy concerning the authenticity of this alleged 1592 voyage. Only one major historian of the Northwest Coast (Warren Cook) holds the opinion that the voyage may have an element of truth. The two greatest historians of the early voyages of exploration to the Northwest Coast (Henry Wagner and Frederic Howay) believe that the voyage is a hoax. I myself have examined all of the documentary material pertaining to this 'voyage', and after an extensive analysis I must concur with Wagner and Howay that the Fuca 'voyage', as with the 'voyages' of de Fonte and Maldonado (who also claimed to have sailed into a strait), are apocryphal," (from Washington State Board Files, Fuca Pillar). However, as it was written by a well-known author, the story was widely known. Capt. James Cook was skeptical of the story and wrote on March 22, 1778: "It is in this very latitude where we now were that geographers have placed the pretended Strait of Juan de Fuca. But we saw nothing like it; nor is there the least probability that ever any such thing existed." In de Fuca's defense, Cook was blown off the coast by a gale and entirely missed the strait. The first "re-discoverer" was Capt. Charles William Barkley (d. 1832) of the *Imperial Eagle*, in July 1787. Barkley, familiar with the description given by the Greek and recognizing its geographical features, applied the name in honor of its supposed original discoverer. According to the diary entry for July 1787 of Capt. Barkley's wife Frances Hornby Barkley (d. 1843), who was aboard during his West Coast adventures (Barkley's log is not extant): "In the afternoon, to our great astonishment, we arrived off a large opening extending to the eastward, the entrance of which appeared to be about four leagues wide, and remained about that width as far as the eye could see, with a clear westerly horizon, which my husband immediately recognized as the long lost strait of Juan de Fuca, to which he gave the name of the original discoverer, my husband placing it on his chart." Vancouver questioned the credibility of the discovery in his journal: "On these grounds, and on these alone, stands the ancient authority for the discoveries of John De Fuca; and however erroneous they may be, seem to have been acknowledged by most of the recent visitors to this coast, who as well as myself, (as is to frequently and injudiciously the case), have been led to follow the stream of the current report. By my having continued the name of De Fuca in my journal and charts a tacit acknowledgment of his discoveries may possibly, on my part, be inferred; this however I must positively deny, because there has not been seen one leading feature to substantiate his tradition: on the contrary, the sea coast under the parallels between which this opening is said to have existed, is compact and impenetrable; the shores of the continent have not any opening whatever, that bears the least similitude to the description of De Fuca's entrance; and the opening which I have called the *supposed straits of Juan de Fuca*, instead of being between the 47th and 48th degrees, is between the 48th and 49 degrees of north latitude, and leads not into a far broader sea or Mediterranean ocean. The error, however, of a degree in latitude may, by the

advocates for De Fuca's merits, be easily reconciled, by the ignorance in those days, or in the incorrectness in making such common astronomical observations; yet we do not find that Sir Francis Drake, who sailed before De Fuca, was liable to such mistakes," (Vancouver III 502). George Davidson wrote: "There is not a single statement in the so-called narrative of Juan de Fuca as given by Matthew Locke (Michael Lok), the elder, that applies to this strait. The whole story is a fabrication," (Meany, *Origin* 292). But Walbran stated (274): "The old seaman Juan de Fuca, whose real names was Apostolos Valerianos, a native of Cephalonia, who seems to have been in his own day neglected and misunderstood as he was afterwards doubted and ignored, and whose pretentions in regard to the exploration of these waters were long scoffed at by geographers, was undoubtedly the discoverer of the strait which bears his name." The controversy will likely never end! In describing the Strait, Davidson wrote: "The entrance to this strait from the Pacific lies between Cape Flattery and Cape Bonilla, on Vancouver island, which forms the northern shore. Its width is about 14 miles, and the bearing from Flattery to Bonilla NW. ¾ N. From this line the strait runs east for 40 miles with a uniform width of 11 miles. It gradually contracts to 8 miles between Beachy Head, on the north, and Striped Peak, on the south; changes its direction to E. by N. ½ N. for 15 miles; then expands to the northward, attaining a width of 18 to 20 miles, and divides into two ship channels, the Canal de Haro and Rosario Strait, leading through the Archipelago de Haro, northward, to the Gulf of Georgia. It is terminated on the east by Whidbey island; at the southeast it passes into Admiralty Inlet; and it is bounded on the south by the main land of Washington Territory, which forms the entire southern shore of the strait. From the ocean to Whidbey island the mid-channel distance is 84 miles," (Davidson, *Report* 414, 415). The U.S. Board on Geographic Names has an interesting history with respect to this name. In 1897, it approved Strait of Juan de Fuca. In 1932, it approved Juan de Fuca Strait; in 1953 it approved both Strait of Juan de Fuca and Straits of Juan de Fuca. In 1977, the Washington State Board on Geographic Names addressed the issue of the boundary for the Strait. After months of discussions with interested parties, including the Canadians, the boundary was finally settled. It is described on the U.S. Board GNIS database: "Extends east from the Pacific Ocean between Vancouver Island, Canada, and the Olympic Peninsula, Washington, to Haro Strait, San Juan Channel, Rosario Strait, and Puget Sound; its Pacific Ocean boundary is formed by a line between Cape Flattery – Tatoosh Island, Washington, and Carmanah Point (Vancouver Island), British Columbia; its north boundary follows the shoreline of Vancouver Island to Gonzales Point, then follows a continuous line east to Seabird Point (Discovery Island), British Columbia; Cattle Point (San Juan Island), Washington; Iceberg Point (Lopez Island); Point Colville (Lopez Island); and then to Rosario Head (Fidalgo Island); the eastern boundary is a continuous line extending south from Rosario Head along Whidbey Island to Point Partridge and south to Point Wilson (Quimper Peninsula); the Washington mainland forms the southern boundary of the strait." The boundary was approved by the Washington State board in its September 8, 1978 meeting, Docket 222. The U.S. Board followed in 1979 (from Washington State Board Files). Variant names included Fucas Straits, John de Fuca Strait, and Strait of Fuca.

Judd Bay

Located near the head on the northeastern side of East Sound, Orcas Island, it was named after the first homesteader, Corben Judd. Corben and his wife Elizabeth were shown as age 32 and 31 respectively on a San Juan County 1907 census (Lange). Apparently, it appeared as Judd Cove on a 1973 USGS map. In 1976, the Washington State Board on Geographic Names reviewed the name. At its September 10, 1976 meeting, the Board addressed name differences of Judd Bay vs. Judd Cove and approved the name Judd Bay, Docket 209. The U.S. Board on Geographic Names approved the name later that year (from Washington State Board Files).

Judd Creek

Flowing into Quartermaster Harbor on Vashon Island, it was named for A. W. Judd, a retired Methodist minister who settled and farmed on the north side of the creek (Hitchman 139).

Julia, Point [7f] #151, 1841, Wilkes
Wilkes wrote: "Port Gamble lies 6 miles within Hood's Canal from Squamish Head [Foulweather Bluff], on its eastern side; it is 2½ miles in length, north and south, and half a mile wide at its entrance. The channel lies through an extensive mud-flat, to the northward of its two points, Totten's on the west, and Point Julia on the east," (Wilkes, *Narrative* 323). Homer P. Morrison eloquently wrote: ". . . the two sandy points [Totten's Point and Point Julia], physically separated but visually similar, seem to mirror and reach out to each other across the water of the bay's [Port Gamble] narrow entrance." Mr. Morrison went on to explain the connection. Julia Rush Gamble was the daughter of Marine Corps Colonel John Marshall Gamble. She was also the niece of Lieut. Thomas Gamble for whom Wilkes named Port Gamble. Julia and George Totten were members of the same church in Brooklyn, where Julia's father was the Commandant of the Marines at the Brooklyn Navy Yard. Julia and George married on July 26, 1842, a month after the return of the expedition. It is highly likely that Wilkes knew of these connections, and thus explains the name.

Juniper Beach
Located on Camano Island on the western shoreline of Port Susan, the origin of the name is perhaps from the local trees.

Jupiter Hills [7d] #146, 1841, Wilkes
Located on the western side of Hood Canal between the Duckabush and Dosewallips, in 1841 Wilkes possibly named it for the Roman god Jupiter (Meany, *Origin* 125, 126; Hitchman 140).

Justice Island
It is located in Echo Bay, Sucia Island, on the northwestern end of South Finger Island. Together with South Finger, both were originally called South Finger Islands. In mid-1982, E.C. Investment Company purchased two thirds of the island for $78,000 from Laszlo and Susan Pal, owners from 1977. The company turned out to be a front for marijuana smuggling that existed on the East Coast and was expanding to the West Coast. The island was intended as temporary storage for drugs shipped from Columbia. The new owners were dismayed when, at closer inspection, they found a hundred boats anchored off their new island. Obviously, it could not be used for the intended purpose. When the drug ring was finally broken up, the island was part of the asset forfeiture of the gang leader, Robert Sterling. The island was seized in 1985 as part of a marijuana smuggling operation by the DEA (Operation Chuckanut). The federal government transferred the property to the State of Washington State Parks and used the name "Echo Bay Island" in the 1986 transfer. In 1990, the Washington State Board on Geographic Names received a proposal to name the island Echo Bay Island, and change South Finger Islands to South Finger Island. As part of Docket 350, the Board rejected the proposal. Given the island's history, the Board decided to consider several other alternatives including Justice Island, Joint Island, and Slammer Island, which were in local use. The argument for the name Joint Island was strong. According to proponents: "In Echo Bay are two long thin islands adjacent to one another, South Finger Island[s] and North Finger Island. To be anatomically correct, the small 3 acre island at the northwest end of South Finger Island is a joint." Dr. Wayne Thornburg purchased the other third of the Island in 1959. The Dr. was a Professor at the UW Medical School in the Anatomy Department and knew well the structure of the hand. As of the date of seizure, his brother was the owner of the property which he acquired through inheritance. Arresting and convicting the drug smugglers was a cooperative joint undertaking by federal, state, and local enforcement agencies from the Pacific to the Atlantic Coasts of the U.S. Nearly all the gang members of the smuggling operations, including the kingpin, Robert Sterling, ended up in the joint. And, finally, a marijuana cigarette is commonly referred to as a joint. The *Seattle Times* from December 19, 1981, and the *Seattle PI* from April 18, 1982, have articles on the arrests and convictions. The arguments for Justice Island were equally strong. The activities were led by the U.S. Marshal, Dept. of Justice; justice was meted out by the forfeiture of property and transfer to the Parks Department; justice was served by long prison sentences, and, finally, our symbol of justice, the bald eagle, nested on the island while the transfer was underway. The Park Rangers advocated Slammer

Island, as that is where the bad guys went! The Board eventually decided that Echo Bay Island lacked imagination and that Joint or Slammer Island were too flippant. Justice was strongly favored and was approved in late 1991 or 1992 (from Washington State Board Files). However, this decision never reached the U.S. Board until I forwarded it in October 2010. In its May 10, 2012 meeting, the U.S. Board approved Justice Island.

Kakeldy Beach
See Seola Beach.

Kakua [7k] #152, 1841, Wilkes
A location at the southern end of Suquamish Harbor in Hood Canal, Wilkes left no reason for the 1841 name. Wilkes did not include this name in his *Narrative*, but it is shown on his chart.

Kala Point [7a] #145, 1841, Wilkes; [7d] #146, 1841, Wilkes; [7p] #150, 1841, Wilkes
Located south of Port Townsend, Wilkes left no reason for the name. He did not include this 1841 name in his *Narrative*, but it is shown on his charts. He spelled it Kula Point on [7p].

Kalamut Island [7a] #145, 1841, Wilkes; [7e] #158, 1841, Wilkes
See Forbes Point.

Kalila Point [7h] #154, 1841, Wilkes
Located on the eastern shoreline of Case Inlet, about two miles south of Vaughn, Wilkes left no reason for the 1841 name. Wilkes did not include this name in his *Narrative*, but it is shown on his chart. The name is neither reflected on U.S. charts nor is it recognized by the U.S. Board on Geographic Names.

Kalset Point [9a] #1911, 1849, Kellett
Located on the western shore of Discovery Bay, Kellett spelled it Calset on his chart. It also appears on the U.S. Coast Survey chart of 1854 [10] as Calset; other charts [22] reflect the names Gibb or Gibbs Point. The U.S. Board on Geographic Names resolved the name conflict in 1941.

Kamilche
Located at the southern entrance of Little Skookum Inlet, the name is the Indian word for "valley" (Meany, *Origin* 127).

Kanaka Bay [21] #6300, 1895
It is located on the southwestern side of San Juan Island next to False Bay. In 1872, with the settlement of the boundary line, the British troops along with most of the Hudson's Bay Company operations immediately departed the island. In addition, most of the Kanaka herdsmen, as they were called then, who were brought in from Hawaii to handle the sheep, also departed. Many settled near Victoria or on Saltspring Island. Most of those who remained settled in a shantytown in Kanaka Bay (Richardson, *Pig* 160). The first Hawaiians were actually brought to the Northwest in 1810. In May of that year, Capt. Nathan Winship of the *Albatros* brought 25 Hawaiians to the Columbia River to establish a trading post. Hostile Indians and the weather caused them to pull out a few months later. In 1811, a small group became part of the Astor fur trade on the Columbia. The contract allowed the Hawaiians food and clothing and $100 in merchandise at the end of a three-year term. The pay increased to $10 per month for later workers. By the mid-1840s, approximately 300 Hawaiians were on the coast, working predominantly for the Hudson's Bay Company. In 1870, 15 out of 18 employees at Bellevue Farm on San Juan Island were Kanakas.

Kanawi, Point [7d] #146, 1841, Wilkes; [7f] #151, 1841, Wilkes; [7p] #150, 1841, Wilkes
See Basalt Point.

Kanem Point [7b] #148, 1841, Wilkes; [7n] #149, 1841, Wilkes
Located on the western end of Protection Island, Wilkes named it in 1841. Wilkes did not include this name in his *Narrative*, but it is shown on his chart. According to the Descriptive Survey #1124 (http://riverhistory.ess.washington.edu/tsheets/reports/t1124.pdf), James Lawson wrote: "Wilkes seems to have adopted many of the words of the Indian jargon as names of places and this may be one, Kanim – canoe. Or it may be the [ ] (Kanem) adopted by a formerly influential family among the Indians of this vicinity."

Kangaroo Point
There are two Kangaroo Points listed in the Federal GNIS database. Both are located on the eastern side of Orcas Island. The first is northwest of Lawrence Point and is entered in GNIS as "Kangaroo Point

(Historical)." The second is located south of Lawrence Point, halfway between the point and Doe Bay and is entered simply as "Kangaroo Point." The fact that there are two entries in GNIS is suspicious. As listed, their latitude and longitude make them about a mile apart on either side of Lawrence Point. Neither is reflected on current charts. About 1916, George Burke came to the Northwest and became caretaker for the S. J. Kraft estate which includes the present Sea Acre as well as all of Kangaroo Point. The nearest neighbors to the south were the Pattons. George worked for Kraft until about 1933 at which time he moved a half mile south and became caretaker of the Patton property. He tore down the house of the original homesteader, Robert Patenoster, and used the lumber for a new home which he erected perhaps 100 feet up the hill. The home still stands. George died about 1936. According to Harry Patton, now 89, who lives on the property, as a child, he enjoyed listening to his father's conversations with George about Australia (Patton, Harry, series of emails to author Feb. 2012). Hitchman (141) claimed that the Kangaroo Point name originated with George for his fond memories of Australia. Based on Harry Patton's emails, that information likely came from a member of the Patton family, either Harry's father Joe or one of the many relatives who still own the Patton property. *See also* Patton Cove. The Washington State Committee on Geographic Names is currently reviewing "Kangaroo Point (Historical)" to determine if the name should remain in the federal database.

Kansas Cove
Located on San Juan Island inside Turn Island, it was named by Walter L. C. Muenscher from the University of Kansas in honor of his home state and the students from there who attended the Puget Sound Marine Station (Wood 156; Hitchman 142).

Kashukud'dil Point [20f] #654, 1853, U.S. Coast Survey
It is located a mile east of Baada Point in Neah Bay. This may be Kellett's Scarborough Point. It is neither named on current charts nor is it recognized by the U.S. Board on Geographic Names.

Kayak Point
It is located on the mainland on the eastern shore of Port Susan. Formerly the site of a resort, it currently is a Snohomish County park.

Kellett Bluff [13a] #2689, 1859, Richards
Located on the south end of Henry Island, Meany (*Origin* 128) suggested that Lt. Cmdr. James Wood of the H.M.S. *Pandora* named it for Capt. Henry Kellett in 1847. This is suspicious for several reasons. First, it is very unusual for a subordinate officer to actually name anything. And with this name in particular, it smacks of an uncomfortably high degree of flattery or "apple polishing" to name something for ones' superior. More importantly, the name does not appear on any of Kellett's charts. It first appears on [13a] in 1859. As such, it is possible that Richards actually made the selection. The U.S. Government owns a 62 acre parcel on the point.

Kellett Island [13b] #2689, 1861, Richards
See Boulder Island.

Kellett Ledge [13a] #2689, 1859, Richards
It is located off the southeastern side of Lopez Island in Rosario Strait. According to Davidson (*Directory* 129), the U.S. Coast Survey named this in 1854 for Henry Kellett.

Kellog Island
It is located a mile up the Duwamish River from Harbor Island. In 1976, David Kellog queried the Washington State Board on Geographic Names to determine the origin of the name. Specifically, he wondered if it was named for his grandfather, David Kellog, who arrived in Seattle in 1861 and purchased land in the area. The Board could find no information on the origin of the name (GNIS files).

Kellums Lake [7d] #146, 1841, Wilkes
See Devereaux Lake.

Kellys Point
Located on the southwestern side of Guemes Island, it was first settled by Larry Kelly who arrived in the Northwest around 1872 following Confederate Army service during the Civil War. He settled on Guemes in the mid-1870s and was commonly known as the "King of Smugglers." In 1877, he married an Indian woman, Lizzie Kotz or Cootes, who was the 16-year-

Day Island Steilacoom Ketron Island Fox Island Point Fosdick

old daughter of Sheriff C. J. Cootes. Kelly was famous around the islands for supplementing his income by smuggling opium, wine, furs, and occasionally Chinese laborers seeking work in Washington or California. The human cargo was particularly profitable, as the Chinese living in British Columbia would pay one hundred dollars for transportation to the U.S. where they worked in the hop fields, canneries, mines, and railroads. When pursued by customs officials, Kelly was said to have dumped his cargo overboard, human and all. Kelly's sloop, *Katy-Thomas*, was built by Ashton Thomas and named for his wife Katherine. He had a second home on Sinclair Island where he kept another sloop, *Alert*. Kelly had serious difficulties with the law throughout his illustrious career. Despite numerous fines and some jail time, he continued smuggling. By 1886 he and Lizzie moved to Waldron. He and Lizzy raised six (some say nine!) children there; Kelly became a member of the school board. In the early 1890s, Lizzie began selling off property to make ends meet and finally left him for good in 1898. Kelly was still busy at his trade in 1904 when he was apprehended on a train carrying 60 pounds of opium. At the first opportunity, he leaped off the train while it was running full speed. He was picked up again lying unconscious by the side of the track. He provided a bond as bail but forfeited it and returned to his smuggling operations. He was again caught the following spring, this time with 60 pounds of opium. Before he could throw it overboard, he was in handcuffs. For that he spent one year in the penitentiary. In May 1909, Kelly served his last time at McNeil Island. After a year, old and tired at age sixty-five, Kelly contacted the Daughters of the Confederacy, a Confederate soldiers' retirement home in Louisiana where he moved and later died (McDonald 100-103; McCurdy *Criss-Cross* 191, 192; Turner 60-66).

Kennedys Lagoon
Located at the head of Penn Cove, Sheriff Kennedy settled there in the 1930s (Neil 119).

Ketners Point
Located on the northern end of Fox Island on Hale Passage, Wilkes originally named this Slavis Point [7h] in 1841. He left no reason for the name. Wilkes did not include this name in his *Narrative*, but it is shown on his chart. The Richard A. Ketner family purchased property on the point in 1892. Ketner worked in the insurance and lumber business in Tacoma. They camped on the property early on and finally built a home in 1894 (Perisho).

Ketron Island [7d] #146, 1841, Wilkes; [7i] #147, 1841, Wilkes
Located in southeastern Puget Sound, north of Nisqually, Wilkes honored William Kittson in 1841, an employee of the Hudson's Bay Company. He spelled it both Ketron and Kitron in his *Narrative* but reflected it as Ketron on both charts (Meany, *Origin* 129). Ownership of Ketron was first claimed by Capt. Warren Gove. He eventually lost his claim because he did not live on the property or develop it according to the terms of the Oregon Land Law (*History* I: 76). The Salish name for the island was "bad rocks" (Hilbert et. al., 326).

Ketslum Island [7a] #145, 1841, Wilkes
See Deception Island.

Ketsoth [8a] #1917, 1847, Kellett
Located near Pillar Point on the Strait of Juan de Fuca, Kellett used this name for the Indian village located there. The name is not recognized by the U.S. Board on Geographic Names.

Key Peninsula
The Key Peninsula is the southern portion of the Great or Indian Peninsula. It was previously known as the Longbranch Peninsula or Kitsap Peninsula or Lower Kitsap Peninsula. In 1980, the Washington State Board on Geographic Names received a proposal to change the name to the Key Peninsula. According to the information collected, the Key Peninsula Businessmen's Association had a naming contest. On January 28, 1931, they awarded Mr. R. M. Stone of Lake Bay $25 for his winning entry of the Key Peninsula. The name obviously had a long local use. At its December 23, 1980 meeting, the Board approved the name change, Docket 263. The name was meant to apply to that part of the peninsula located in Pierce County. The U.S. Board followed in 1981 (from Washington State Board Files).

Keymes Beach [22] #6450, 1909
See Adelma Beach.

Keyport
Located at the entrance to Liberty Bay, homesteading began in the 1860s. After completing a wharf in 1896, three of the early settlers, O. A. Kuppler, H. B. Kuppler, and Pete Hagen, chose the name after the resort in New Jersey, although according to another story, locals selected the name because the point was the key to Liberty Bay (Meany, *Origin* 130; Carlson 79-83; Phillips 71). In 1914, the Navy condemned and purchased 88 acres of land in Keyport as the Pacific Coast Torpedo Station. Original settlers were given a year to vacate. At its peak in the 1940s, 2,000 civilian personnel and additional navy personal worked at the site (Bowen et al., III: 12).

Keystone Harbor
Located on the western side of Whidbey Island in Admiralty Bay, it is the termination of the Port Townsend/Keystone ferry. It was originally called New Chicago, but the name was changed following the Panic of 1893 (Hitchman 144).

Kiapot Point [7n] #149, 1841, Wilkes
Located at the entrance to Sequim Bay, this is the end of the sand spit extending from the eastern shore. According to Hale (648), the name was Chinook for "needle." Wilkes did not include this name in his *Narrative*, but it is shown on his chart.

Kiket Bay
Located on the eastern side of Deception Pass between Hope and Kiket Islands, it was named for the island. The bay was created in the 1960s when the sand spit between Fidalgo and Kiket Islands was filled in. In 1987, the Washington State Board on Geographic Names received a proposal from a La Conner resident to name the previously unnamed bay. The Board approved the new name and the U.S. Board followed in 1989, Docket 330 (from files of Washington State Board).

Kiket Island [7e] #158, 1841, Wilkes
It is located at the easterly entrance to Deception Pass. At the time of Wilkes' exploration, Kiket presumably was an island. According to Descriptive Report #2856 (http://riverhistory.ess.washington.edu/tsheets/framedex.htm) of the Coast and Geodetic Survey (4): "Kiket Island, formerly an island, but now connected with the mainland by a sand spit is a very prominent land-mark and forms the southern shore of Similk Bay." In the early 1960s, Gene Dunlap, who owned it, began filling in the sand spit and improving the connection with Fidalgo Island so that he could build a road and a home on the island. According to Hale (582), the name was Nez Perce in origin meaning "blood." Hale also indicated (617) that it was a Salish Flathead name meaning "near." The Nez Perce tribe lived primarily in Idaho; the Flatheads lived around the upper Columbia in eastern Washington. But according to Hilbert (350), the name is a transliteration of the Indian name. In 2010, the island became a state park, managed jointly by the state parks and the Swinomish Indian Tribal Community.

Kilcome, Point #148, 1841, Wilkes
See Koitlah Point.

Kilisut Harbor [7a] #145, 1841, Wilkes; [7d] #146, 1841, Wilkes; [7p] #150, 1841, Wilkes
Located between Indian and Marrowstone Islands, Wilkes named this after the Clallam Indian term meaning "protected waters" in 1841 (Meany, *Origin* 131; Blumenthal, *Charles Wilkes* 88). Hitchman (220) indicated that the word was Chinook for "bottle, glass, or flint." The U.S. Coast Survey renamed it Long Harbor in 1854 on [10], but Wilkes' name endured.

Killebrews Lake
It is about a half mile north and a bit east of Grindstone Harbor on Orcas Island. It was named for John G. Killebrew who proved up his homestead in 1896 (Lange).

Killinas Lake
See Devereaux Lake.

Kimple Bay, Beach & Point
The bay, point, and Kimple estate are shown on t-sheet #2192 dated 1894 at (http://kaga.wsulibs.wsu.edu/cdm-maps/sanjuantsheet.html). McLellan also referenced all of these names. None are named on current charts. They are located about 1½ miles south of Point Doughty on the western shoreline of Orcas Island. It was named for David Kimple, originally from Russia. The 1889 census showed him as 42 years old, and his wife Mary was 41. They had five children (Lange). Only the beach and point are recognized by the U.S. Board on Geographic Names.

King Spit [22] #6450, 1909
See Bangor.

Kingfisher Cove
A local name for a small cove to the east of Miller Bay, on the northeastern entrance to Deception Pass (Harrison, Scott, Jan. 2, 2012 email to author).

Kingfisher Creek
The small creek flows through Kingston into Appletree Cove. In its May 11, 2007 meeting, the Washington State Board on Geographic Names approved the name. The U.S. Board followed later in the year (from Washington State Board Files).

Kings Point
Located on the southwestern side of Lopez Island, opposite Cattle Point, the origin of the name is unknown.

Kingston
Located on the western shoreline of Admiralty Inlet, W. S. and Caroline Ladd settled it in 1869. Michael King purchased the land in 1878. The community is named either for him or for William P. Kingston, who established a sawmill there in 1888. By 1890, the Puget Mill Company purchased all the land surrounding Kingston. A church and hotel were constructed in 1890, and the hotel continued to operate until 1949.

Kingston

The post office was built in 1906 and is still standing. The first school was built in 1895 and a second in 1903. The third school was built in 1909 which was used until 1952. From 1903 to 1915, the Kingston Shingle Company, built by Frank Newell, was the area's largest employer (Osborne, 111; TPL website). The Salish name for the area was "twisting a writhe to make it flexible" (Hilbert et. al., 190).

Kingston Creek
Taking its name from the community, the small creek flows through the city into Appletree Cove. In its May 11, 2007 meeting, the Washington State Board on Geographic Names approved the name. The U.S. Board followed later in the year (from Washington State Board Files).

Kinney Point
Located at the south end of Marrowstone Island, Wilkes originally named this Heke Point [7p] in 1841. He left no reason for the name. Wilkes did not include this name in his *Narrative*, but it is shown on his chart. The origin of the current name is unknown.

Kiowo Point [7l] #159, 1841, Wilkes
Located in Birch Bay, a mile to the southeast of Birch Point, Wilkes left no reason for the 1841 name. The name appears on his chart only and is very difficult to read. It may also be spelled Kuwo Point. It is not recognized by the U.S. Board on Geographic Names.

Kitsap Peninsula
See Key Peninsula.

Kiu-la-tsu-ko
See Discovery Bay.

Klachopis Point [20f] #654, 1853, U.S. Coast Survey
Located about a mile east of Neah Bay, Wilkes named it Sail Rock Point in 1841 [7b], [7c]. Evidently, the current name is closer to the original Indian name.

Klaholoh Rock [9a] #1911, 1849, Kellett
See Sail Rock.

Klahostah Rock
See Sail Rock.

Klas Rock [7f] #151, 1841, Wilkes; [7p] #150, 1841, Wilkes
Located two miles north of Port Ludlow, Wilkes left no reason for the 1841 name (Meany, *Origin* 133).

Klootchman Rock
One of several rocks north of Blowers Bluff near Oak Harbor, the origin of the name is unknown. The name is not reflected on current charts, but it is recognized by the U.S. Board on Geographic Names. Klootchman is Chinook jargon for "wife or female."

Koitlah Point [9a] #1911, 1849, Kellett
The westerly-most point in Neah Bay, it was first named *Punta de Rada* by Quimper in 1790 [1] (Wagner 127). In 1841, Wilkes named it Point Kilcome in his *Narrative*, but on his chart #148 [7b], he reflected the name Point Hilcome (Meany, *Origin* 135). Wilkes labeled it North Point on chart #144 [7c]. It was left to Kellett to provide the current name, although he spelled it Koikla. That spelling was retained on later Forest Service maps, while charts reflected it as Koitlah. In 1884, the Washington State Board on Geographic Names formally adopted the current spelling.

Kopo Point [7h] #154, 1841, Wilkes
See Graham Point.

Kosa Point [7i] #147, 1841, Wilkes
Located three miles north of Steilacoom on the southeastern Puget Sound shoreline, Wilkes left no reason for the 1841 name. The name is neither reflected on current charts nor recognized by the U.S. Board on Geographic Names. Wilkes did not include this name in his *Narrative*, but it is shown on his chart (Meany, *Origin* 136). According to Hale (610), *Kosa* is an Oregon Molele Indian name which means "small."

Kosa River [7g] #155, 1841, Wilkes
See Wilson Creek.

Kuhn Spit
Located south of Glen Cove on Port Townsend, it was named for Joseph Kuhn. Kuhn came to Port Townsend in 1866 and was admitted to the bar in 1870. He was involved in a number of activities and at one time was mayor of the city (TPL website).

Kulakala Point [7n] #149, 1841, Wilkes
Located southeast of Dungeness, Wilkes likely named it for the Indian word meaning "travel." Wilkes did not include this name in his *Narrative*, but it is shown as Kula Kala on his chart (Meany, *Origin* 136).

Kuwo Point [7l] #159, 1841, Wilkes
See Kiowo Point.

Kwaatz Point [7d] #146, 1841, Wilkes; [7i] #147, 1841, Wilkes
It is located on the eastern mainland side of the Nisqually Flats. Wilkes left no reason for the 1841 name (Meany, *Origin* 136). Bright (245) wrote that it was Lushootseed for "crooked promontory." The name is neither reflected on U.S. charts nor is it recognized by the U.S. Board on Geographic Names.

Kydaka Point [8a] #1917, 1847, Kellett
Located three miles west of Clallam Bay, Kellett left no reason for the name.

Kydikabbit Point [20f] #654, 1853, U.S. Coast Survey
Located a half mile west of Koitlah Point on the Strait of Juan de Fuca, the origin of the name is unknown.

La Conner [21] #6300, 1895
Michael Sullivan settled on the Sullivan Slough, some say in 1864, but other sources indicate that it was in 1868. He claimed land on the "back side" of La Conner. The slough was named for him. Over time, he accumulated 315 acres of land and diked much of it for crops. Born in Massachusetts of Irish immigrant parents, he was orphaned early in life. He shipped out from Boston as a cabin boy and landed in San Francisco, and he finally reached the Northwest in 1866 where he worked at the mill in Utsalady. In

La Conner - Lakebay

LaConner

1867, Alonzo Low (1845-1921) established a trading post and a post office using the name Swinomish. It is unclear if the building was on the west side of the Swinomish or on the east side, but most sources indicate that it was on the present site of the town. Low arrived in the Northwest at Alki Point with his parents and the rest of the Denny Party. Low remained about 14 months at La Conner then sold to a man named Clark and his Indian wife. Thomas Hayes took over the trading post next, perhaps in 1868. John S. Conner bought him out in 1869 or 1870 and set up a store in what is now the town of La Conner. Connor, born in Ireland but raised in Pennsylvania, achieved his teaching certificate at age 18. In 1862, he began farming in Missouri and met and married Louisa Ann Siegfried-Connor. In 1865, the family moved to Colorado where John opened a store and operated a hotel. In 1869, the family again moved and lived in Olympia for a year before purchasing the trading post in La Connor. It is unclear if the original post office was abandoned with Connor establishing a new one in 1870 or if the name was simply changed later. Either way, Conner renamed the town for his wife, using her first two initials as part of the name. Connor sold the store to the Gaches brothers in 1873. Much of the original town site was claimed by J. J. Connor, the cousin of J. S. Connor. History is unclear here. *An Illustrated History* (806) indicates that J. J. platted the town site in 1872, covering his 160 acres, and named it after his cousin's wife. J. J. ultimately sold his claim to J. S. who platted and began developing the town in earnest in the early 1880s. J. S. died in 1885, and his son, Herbert, one of his nine children, took over his affairs (Meany, *Origin* 137; Seebring 24; Bailey and Nyberg, *Gunkholing in the San Juan Islands* 196; TPL website; *An Illustrated History*, 102, 201, 202, 645-647, 668, 808). In 1972, the Washington State Board addressed the spelling of the community, one word vs. two words. The Washington State Board approved the two-word name in late 1982, Docket 280. The U.S. Board followed in 1983. Variants were L A Conner, LaConner, Laconner, and Swinomish (from Washington State Board Files).

Lagoon [13a] #2689, 1859, Richards
See Fisherman Bay.

Lagoon Point [11] #654, 1858, U.S. Coast Survey
Located on the western side of Whidbey Island, two miles north of Bush Point, the U.S. Coast Survey provided the name from a small lagoon that ran parallel to the shoreline behind the point.

Lakebay
Located on the western side of Carr Inlet, William and Sarah Creviston were the first settlers around 1876 or 1877. Sarah was the first schoolteacher, and their son Bill was the first White child born on the Key Peninsula. In 1884, the Carl Lorenz family arrived and built a mill and shipyard. Power for the mill came from the small lake nearby, Bay Lake, named by Mrs. Creviston. They named the community by reversing the words. Lorenz migrated from Germany to the United States in 1871 and settled in Orting in 1875 where he constructed a sawmill. After a flood wiped out the mill, the family moved to Lakebay and utilized the small stream for waterpower. Lorenz and his two sons successfully entered the boat business

on Puget Sound. They constructed the first steamship on the Key Peninsula, the *Sophia*, named after Carl's mother, and they transported supplies and people for years (Retherford III; *A History* 60; Meany, *Origin* 137; Slater 2, 19; TPL website). The Salish name for the area was "prairie" (Hilbert et. al., 317). In 1979, Lakebay residents asked the Washington State Board on Geographic Names to clarify the spelling of the name (Lake Bay vs. Lakebay) and the location. The proponents argued that it should be one word and relocated from the head of Mayo Cove to the head of Von Geldern Cove. The Board approved this request at its March 1980 meeting, Docket 255. Following the decision, residents of Home on the shores of Von Geldern Cove objected to the relocation aspect of the decision. They were concerned that Home would lose its identity. Follow-up action by the Board is unclear, but likely moving the location of Lakebay was later rejected (from Washington State Board Files).

Lakota
It is located on the mainland, about five miles north of Tacoma. The plat for the community was filed in 1913 by M. R. and Georgia W. Wood and Ellen Davies. The post office began operation in 1915 and closed in 1934. The origin of the name is unknown.

Landing Place [13b] #2689, 1861, Richards
Located on the southern end of San Juan Island just southeast of Eagle Cove, it was named simply to note the location where a ship's boat might land. On the larger scale chart #611 [15a], Richards clearly identified the boundaries of the HBC Farm adjacent to the small bay, implying that access to the farm was from the beach in the bay. U.S. charts reflected the name only briefly, and it has not been shown since 1928 (Wood 103). The name is not recognized by the U.S. Board on Geographic Names. In his 1897 survey and Descriptive Report #2301, J. J. Gilbert wrote (http://riverhistory.ess.washington.edu/tsheets/reports/t2301.pdf, p 14): "The next little bay eastward from Eagle Cove is a place used as a landing for Indians, the rocks in the bay affording some shelter. On the bluff are some Indian houses which are occupied during the salmon season. This landing was also used in early days by the Hudson Bay Co. whose station was but a short distance back."

Landmark
It is located less than a mile south of President Point. The local name is not recognized by the U.S. Board on Geographic Names. According to the 1934 *Pacific Coast Pilot* (255), there was an electric power plant located there at one time. The U.S. Navy also had a degaussing plant there. Large commercial and military ships were subjected to a huge AC current which demagnetized the vessel and reduced or even eliminated the magnetic properties of the ship itself and allowed the compass to work properly. The stations were also used to prevent a ship from setting off a magnetic mine.

Lane Spit
Located on the eastern side of Lummi Island, Frederick F. Lane first settled there in 1881. A graduate of Yale University, he prospected in California, continued in the Cariboo gold rush, and finally landed in Whatcom where he served as a county sheriff in 1859. He departed Washington but returned in 1866 and was rehired as sheriff. In 1868 he married Lellie Howen, a Sumas Indian. Two years later, they moved to Lummi Island where they raised 12 children. He died in 1909 from a logging accident. The family continued to reside on the spit until about 1929 (McDonald, Lucile. "Lummi Island Is Synonymous With Reef-Netting." *Seattle Times*. June 25, 1961. Magazine Section p 10, 11). J. J. Gilbert noted the name in his 1888 survey and Descriptive Report #1871 (http://riverhistory.ess.washington.edu/tsheets/reports/t1871.pdf, p 2). He wrote: "Mr. F. F. Lane, present postmaster, has lived there a great many years and it might be very properly designated Lanes Point." In 1990, U.S. Board on Geographic Names received a proposal to apply the name to the entire spit and retain the name of Lummi Point for the end of the spit. The Board pointed out that a similar proposal was rejected in 1976. However, in the May 8, 1992 meeting, the Board approved the change, Docket 350 (from Washington State Board Files).

Lang Bay
Located off the northern side of Hope Island in Skagit Bay, the origin of the name is unknown. The name is not reflected on current charts, but the small bay is marked by mooring buoys on the north side of Hope.

Lángara, Isla de [3] 1791, Eliza
See Boundary Bay.

Langdon, Port
Located in Buck Bay, near the eastern entrance of East Sound, George R. Shotter found limestone in 1863 along with five other Canadians including Daniel McLachlan. Shotter sold out early in 1875 to McLachlan and Robert M. Caines from Port Townsend (McDonald 89, 90).

Langley

Langley
It is located on the eastern side of Whidbey Island. Born in Germany in 1865, Jacob Anthes left his home in Gros Gerau at age fourteen seeking adventure and to avoid compulsory military service. He arrived on the south end of Whidbey Island in the fall of 1880 and was hired by a Seattle businessman to hold down a homestead. In those days, in order to retain property, an owner or owner's agent was required to reside on the land or the claim would not be met and the land would return to the government. During the following months, he explored the south end of the island and met the few settlers. In 1881, Joseph Brown from Browns Point (Sandy Point) strongly advised Anthes to begin purchasing land. At that time, Anthes was too young to file a homestead. He bought 120 acres about a half mile west of Langley from John Phinney for $100. With help from Seattle loggers, he cleared some of the area, sold cord wood to the steamers, and planted a garden. The following year, he sold potatoes to the nearby logging camps. In 1886, at age 21, he filed a homestead claim on 160 acres on land which adjoined Langley. In 1888, he started a small business in Seattle and met Leafy Weeks. The courtship was difficult as he frequently rowed the thirty miles from Langley to Seattle at night after a hard day's work. The following year, his business was destroyed by the Seattle fire, but he gained a wife. They honeymooned in Germany and returned to settle on his homestead. In 1890, he purchased the balance of the Phinney property in Langley and set out to create a town site. He convinced Judge J. W. Langley and others to form the Langley Land and Improvement Company. Anthes platted the town the following year and named it for the judge. The town of Langley was incorporated in 1913 (Cherry III: 1-8). The Salish name for the area was "where gooseberry bushes grow" (Hilbert et. al., 358).

Langley Bay
Located on the western side of Fidalgo Island, it was named for a pioneer settler (Hitchman 157).

Langley Point
Located on the western side of Fidalgo Island, it was named for a pioneer settler (Hitchman 157). According to Washington State Board on Geographic Names files, the name has appeared on nautical charts since the 1880s (Biz Point file). *See* Biz Point.

Lara, Ensenada de
See Lummi Bay.

Lawrence Head [7m] #160, 1841, Wilkes
See Cap Sante.

Lawrence Island [7a] #145, 1841, Wilkes; [7m] #160, 1841, Wilkes
See Guemes Island.

Lawrence Point [7a] #145, 1841, Wilkes
Located on the far eastern side of Orcas Island, in 1841 Wilkes honored Capt. James Lawrence of the *Chesapeake* during the War of 1812. Wilkes did not include this name in his *Narrative*, but it is shown on his chart (Meany, *Origin* 220). The entire point is owned by the State of Washington.

Lawrence, Port [7d] #146, 1841, Wilkes; [7p] #150, 1841, Wilkes
See Oak Bay.

Lawson Bluff [13a] #2689, 1859, Richards
Located on the west side of Sucia Island, it was likely named for Lieut. James S. Lawson of the U.S. Coast Survey.

Lawson Reef [18] #654, 1866, U.S. Coast Survey
Located about two miles west of the western entrance to Deception Pass, it was named for its discoverer, James S. Lawson, the primary topographer of the U.S. Coast Survey (Hitchman 159).

Lawson Rock [13a] #2689, 1859, Richards
Located off the southeastern side of Blakely Island near Thatcher Pass, it was named for Lieut. James S. Lawson of the Coast Survey (Hitchman 159).

Lay Inlet
Located on the eastern shore of Carr Inlet north of Raft Island, it was named for B. S. Lay, E. Lay, and M. R. Lay who owned land there (TPL website).

Leavitt, Point [7a] #145, 1841, Wilkes; [7d] #146, 1841, Wilkes
See Bush Point.

Legoe Bay
It is located on the western side of Lummi Island, south and east of Village Point. Hitchman (159) speculated that the name was selected by Christian Tuttle, an 1871 settler on the bay. Tuttle was born in Michigan in 1827. He deserted ship in California to search for gold there. With his partner named Shrewbury, they began a mining adventure but were attacked by Indians. Shrewbury and his wife were killed, but Tuttle and Shrewbury's two-year-old daughter Clara escaped. Having no idea what to do with a two-year-old child, Tuttle took her to a convent to be raised. After years of whaling and prospecting, he ended up on Lummi Island near Legoe Bay where he homesteaded 160 acres and took out a preemption claim on 160 more. Some years later, the nuns in California contacted him. The girl had reached 18 and could not remain in the convent unless she entered the order. Tuttle went to California, brought her back to Washington, and ultimately married her. They returned to Lummi where they raised six children (McDonald, Lucile. "Lummi Island Is Synonymous With Reef-Netting." *Seattle Times*. June 25, 1961. Magazine Section p 10, 11).

Leku Beach [7p] #150, 1841, Wilkes
Wilkes gave this name in 1841 to the sand spit which "closed" the south end of the Port Townsend Canal. He does not include this name in his *Narrative*, but it is shown on his chart. According to Hale (648), it is Chinook for "neck." Davidson wrote: "At the head of Port Townshend is a narrow channel opening into a large flat, bounded by a low, sandy beach, separating it from Oak Cove. The Indians frequently use this as a portage," (*Report* 441).

Lemolo
Located directly across the water from Keyport, the community is adjacent to the Port Madison Indian Reservation. The first loggers arrived in the 1860s. The first permanent settlers were Frank and Maria Johnson in 1887. Uno Brauer followed them two years later and purchased adjacent land. Brauer was an accomplished musician, artist, and ordained minister in the Baptist Church. By 1907 a wharf was built, followed by a store run by Mr. and Mrs. Andrew Jacobson. Andrew Madison Young platted the community in 1907. The name *Le-Mo-lo* means "wild and untamed or barbarous" (Carlson 86-89).

Lemos
See Waldron Island.

Leo Reef
Located off the northeastern side of Lopez Island, north of Flower Island, the origin of the name is unknown.

Leque Island
Located off the eastern side of Camano Island in Port Susan, it is surrounded by water from South Pass (on the east) and Davis Slough (on the west). It was named for the early Camano settler Nels P. Leque who worked at the Utsalady mill (Prasse 46).

Levant Passage [7a] #145, 1841, Wilkes
Located off the southeastern side of Guemes Island, it represents the channel between Guemes and Huckleberry Islands on the west and Hat and Saddlebag Islands on the east. Levant Passage leads into Penguin Harbor to the north. In 1841, Wilkes named it for the British ship *Levant* captured by the *Constitution* during the War of 1812. The name is neither reflected on current charts nor recognized by the U.S. Board on Geographic Names.

Lewhough, Point [7b] #148, 1841, Wilkes
It is located in Neah Bay just west of Baada Point. The name is neither reflected on current charts

nor recognized by the U.S. Board on Geographic Names. Wilkes did not include this 1841 name in his *Narrative*, but it is shown on his chart.

Libby Point
Located on the northern shore of Hammersley Inlet, the origin is unknown.

Liberty Bay [22] #6450, 1909
Located on the mainland west of Bainbridge Island, Wilkes originally named this Mays Inlet in 1841 honoring crew member William May (Wilkes, *Narrative* 317). Early settlers named it Dogfish Bay [19] for the prolific numbers of resident dogfish caught and rendered for oil which was used on logging skids. In 1893, Rep. C. H. Scott introduced a bill to call it Liberty Bay, which died in committee. Kitsap County representative F. E. Patterson introduced a bill in 1899 to change the name to Poulsbo Bay. For whatever reason, the House amended the bill and substituted Patterson for Poulsbo. The bill passed the House but died in the Senate (Meany, *Origin* 146). During 1905 and 1906, local residents petitioned the U.S. Board on Geographic Names to change the name from Dogfish to Liberty Bay. Some correspondence to the Board indicated that the name dogfish was actually the Indian name (translated) for "the waters." That claim, however, could not be substantiated. For whatever reason, the Board did not rule on the issue until 1914 when they adopted Liberty Bay (GNIS files). Interestingly, according to the 1903 *Pacific Coast Pilot* (140): "A narrow, unimportant inlet, Dogfish Bay, makes into the western shore about 4 miles at the southern end of Agate Passage."

Lighthouse Point
Located near the western entrance to Deception Pass on the north side of the pass, it was perhaps named for the light located there.

Lighthouse Point
See Cypress Head.

Lilliwaup Bay & **River**
Located on the western shoreline of Hood Canal five miles north of The Great Bend, the name is a Salish word meaning "inlet" (Middleton 123).

Limberry Point
Located on the eastern shore of Waldron Island, north of Mail Bay, the origin of the name is unknown.

Lime Kiln [13h] #2689, 1888
Located on the western side of San Juan Island just south of Bellevue Point, the community was named after lime that was burned there by the Henry Cowell Co. as part of the refining process called calcinations. In addition, the Lime Kiln post office, run by James McCurdy, existed there from 1879-1888 (Wood 103, 104). According to J. J. Gilbert and his 1894 Descriptive Report #2194 (http://riverhistory.ess.washington.edu/tsheets/reports/t2194.pdf, p 2): "This lime works has two kilns with a capacity of about 400 barrels per day. Only one kiln was in operation in 1894." (In contrast, Gilbert wrote that the capacity of Roche was about 3,000 barrels per day.) Cowell was listed in *The Islander* Oct. 1, 1896 (p 3) as E. V. Cowell, who at the time was living in Santa Cruz, CA but still owned the lime works.

Lime Kiln Point
Located on the western side of San Juan Island, it was the site of the San Juan Lime Company founded in 1860 by D. F. Newsom, E. C. Gillette, and Lyman Cutler of Pig War fame. Gillette sold to Augustin Hibbard in 1861. Hibbard also moonlighted as a bootlegger. In 1864, Hibbard bought out the other two partners. Cutler moved to Samish on the mainland in Whatcom County. According to the records, a school was built on his property in 1873 (*An Illustrated History*, 111). He died in May 1874, a footnote in the history of the Pig War, where fortunately the only fatality was a pig (Lange). While the name Lime Kiln Point State Park is recognized by the U.S. Board on Geographic Names, it is not reflected on charts. Lime Kiln Lt is recognized and is shown on charts, but Lime Kiln Point is not recognized or shown on charts.

Limestone Point
It is located on the northwest end of San Juan Island in Spieden Channel. Wood (104) stated that the name first appeared on the USC&GS Descriptive Report (1894). According to t-sheet #2231: "Limestone Point is a knob of limestone, on outward face of which is an abandoned quarry; the kiln and warehouse, now tottering with decay are in the angle of the beach."

Linananimis River
See Duwamish River.

Liplip Point [7a] #145, 1841, Wilkes; [7d] #146, 1841, Wilkes; [7p] #150, 1841, Wilkes
Located on the southeastern side of Marrowstone Island, Wilkes named it in 1841 for the Chinook word for "boiling" (Meany, *Origin* 147).

Lisabuela
Located on the western side of Vashon Island, Mr. Butts, the first postmaster, combined the names of two daughters, Elisa and Buelah (Meany, *Origin* 148). Cardel (*About* 64) claims that Butts was the second postmaster. According to the TPL website, the Postmaster General in Washington D.C. combined the same two names, but they were for workers in his office. Haulman offers an alternative story: When John Brink applied for the post office, he named it after his two daughters.

Little Beef Harbor
See Beef Harbor.

Little Belt Passage [7a] #145, 1841, Wilkes
See Middle Channel.

Little Boston
It is located on the eastern side of Port Gamble, south of Point Julia. On the opposite side of Hood Canal, Wilkes named the southern entrance to Pleasant Harbor, Boston Point [7j] in 1841. It is possible that Little Boston is somehow related (Phillips 80). "Boston Man" as opposed to "King George Man" was the term used by the Indians to differentiate Americans from the English. The Salish name is "noon, broad daylight" (Hilbert et. al., 190).

Little Deadman Island
It is located in Skagit Bay off the southeastern shore of Fidalgo Island and south of Deadman Island. *See* Deadman Island, Tonkon Islands.

Little Dewatto
Located on the eastern side of Hood Canal, the name for this bay likely came from Dewatto Bay, a mile to the north.

Little Double Island
See Alegria Island.

Little Fishtrap
A small bay between Dover and Dickenson Points on Dana Passage, it was named for the traps used by the Indians to catch fish. The U.S. Board on Geographic Names approved the local name in 1985, Docket 292 (from Washington State Board Files).

Little Island
Located off the eastern side of San Juan Island in North Bay, the name may have been descriptive. The name is shown on t-sheet #2301 from 1897 (http://kaga.wsulibs.wsu.edu/cdm-maps/sanjuantsheet.html). On the Descriptive Report that accompanied this t-sheet, J. J. Gilbert wrote (http://riverhistory.ess.washington.edu/tsheets/reports/t2301.pdf, p 2): "Westward from the bluff [Bald Hill] is a long gravel spit composed largely of material from the bluff. The spit extends to a small island, rocky and bare, and then makes an acute angle toward the shore. The spit encloses a large lagoon which, owing to the shallow outlet, never runs bare." McLellan wrote: "Little Island is a small rocky knob situated near the village of Argyle. It is no longer isolated for it is connected with San Juan Island by the long sand spits that enclose the Argyle Lagoon." Lange discovered a 1925 cite referring to this as Argyle Island.

Little Island
See Alegria Island.

Little Mountain [13a] #2689, 1859, Richards
There are two Mount Littles that appear on [13a]. One is located north of False Bay on the western side of San Juan Island. Charts show it as being 475 feet in height, and its size, in relation to Mt. Dallas at 1,036 feet, could have been the reason for the name. The second Mount Little is no longer named on charts. It was a 320 foot hill located east of False Bay. On later charts the taller Mount Little was renamed Little Mountain (Wood 160). Both are recognized by the U.S. Board on Geographic Names.

Little Norway
See Cromwell.

Little Patos Island
Located off the southwestern side of Patos Island, it takes its name from the island. McLellan wrote: "Little Patos Island is located near the southwest

shore of Patos Island and separated from it by the narrow waters of Active Cove. Little Patos Island is heavily wooded. The whole island is formed from the western extension of the resistant strata which follow along the southern shore of Patos Island. The maximum elevation on Little Patos Island is about 50 feet."

Little Skookum Inlet

Little Skookum Inlet

It is located off the western side of Totten Inlet. A variant of Hammersley Inlet is Big Skookum Inlet. Little Skookum Inlet is a carry-over. The name appeared in an 1879 hydrographic survey but was reflected as simply Skookum Inlet on other government publications including chart #18448, the 1905 edition of chart #6460 [23], and later editions of the *Pacific Coast Pilot*. In its March 13, 1981 meeting, the Washington State Board on Geographic names approved the current name (Docket 267) to conform to local usage. The U.S. Board followed later that year.

Little Sister

Located on the southern side of The Sisters, south of Clark Island, this island likely takes its name from the adjacent islands.

Little Sucia

Located off the western side of Sucia, this island likely takes its name from Sucia Island.

Little Tenif Island [7e] #158, 1841, Wilkes

See Ben Ure Island.

Little Tykel Cove

Located off the western side of Budd Inlet, about four miles south of Cooper Point, it was named after the George Tykel family who settled in the area. In 1997, the Washington State Board on Geographic Names changed the name of Big Tykle Cove to Big Tykel Cove. Somehow, the Board forgot about Little Tykel Cove. When the Board became aware of this discrepancy in 2008, they agreed to the current name for the sake of consistency (GNIS files).

Livingston Bay

Located on the northern end of Port Susan, it was named for Jacob and David Livingston who homesteaded there in 1862 (Prasse 45).

Lloyd, Point [7a] #145, 1841, Wilkes

See Upright Head.

Loa Point [7i] #147, 1841, Wilkes

Located on the western-mainland side of the Nisqually Flats, Wilkes possibly named it for the Hawaiian volcano Mauna Loa (Meany, *Origin* 149). The name is neither reflected on U.S. charts nor is it recognized by the U.S. Board on Geographic Names.

Lofall

Located on the eastern side of Hood Canal, three miles south of the eastern terminus of the Hood Canal Bridge, it was first settled by Helge and Sophia Lofall. With nine children in tow, they arrived in the Northwest in 1908. They moved to their property in Lofall in 1910, erected a store, a post office, and a dock. For years, Helge and his sons supplied fish to logging camps and surrounding stores. Sophia died in 1941, and Helge followed in 1950 at the age of ninety-eight (Bowen et al., IV 46, 47). In 1942, the U.S. Board on Geographic Names addressed the variants Lovfall and Loyfall and selected the current name (GNIS files).

Lone Rock [22] #6450, 1909
Located on the eastern side of Hood Canal a couple miles north of Seabeck, the name was likely descriptive.

Lone Tree Island
See The Sisters.

Lone Tree Point
It is located in Skagit Bay on the southwestern side of Fidalgo Island, inside Hope Island. According to Descriptive Report #2856 of the Coast and Geodetic Survey (5): "Lone Tree Point is so called on account of a lone fir tree which stands on the outer end of a spit forming the point and enclosing a small salt lagoon which bares at low water," (http://riverhistory.ess.washington.edu/tsheets/framedex.htm). The U.S. Board on Geographic Names approved the name Tosi Point in 1941, as Wilkes named it in 1841 [7e]. In its September 10, 1976 meeting, Docket 211, the Washington State Board approved the current name as the local name was extensively used. The U.S. Board followed later that year. Another variant was Tesi Point (from Washington State Board Files).

Lonesome Cove
Located on the northeastern end of San Juan Island along Spieden Channel a half mile west of Limestone Point, Wood (105) stated that it first appeared on a 1953 U.S. chart. It is a campground with some small-boat floats and cabins. The local owner apparently selected the name.

Long Bay
Located on the southeastern side of Guemes Island, due west of Huckleberry Island, the origin of the name is unknown.

Long Branch Bay
See Filucy Bay.

Long Branch Peninsula
See Key Peninsula.

Long Island [13a] #2689, 1859, Richards
Located off the southwestern side of Lopez Island, Richards left no reason for the name. J. J. Culpepper settled on Long Island and sold to Robert Firth for twenty dollars in 1874 (*see also* American Camp). Firth soon sold to Hezekiah Davis who obtained a patent in 1878. Davis' wife died in 1877; he remained a few more years and departed for Dungeness where he died in 1890. Hezekiah left the island to his son, Alonzo, who had been living in Dungeness since 1875 and ran a herd of Jersey cattle. His brother Hall ran Holsteins. The island has changed hands many times since and was once owned by D. R. Fisher of flour mill and Fisher Communications fame (McDonald 189; McDonald, Lucile. "The Pioneer Davis Family of Lopez Island." *Seattle Times*. Mar 6, 1960. Magazine Section p 8).

Long Point
Located on the eastern side of Whidbey Island about a mile east of Coopeville, the name is apparently descriptive (Hitchman 167). The U.S. Board on Geographic Names approved the name in 1941 over variants Snaklum Point and Watsak Point [21] (*Decisions*).

Long Point
Located on the eastern shore of Hood Canal about a mile south of Dewatto Bay, the origin of the name is unknown. This may be Wilkes' Dadah Point [7d].

Long Spit [22] #6450, 1909
Located at the head of Dabob Bay, separating Dabob Bay from Tarboo Bay, the name was likely descriptive.

Longbranch
The community is on Filucy Bay, east side of the Great Peninsula. It was named for the town in New Jersey (Meany, *Origin* 149).

Longbranch Peninsula
See Key Peninsula.

Lookout Hill
Located west of Eastsound on Orcas Island, the 680 foot hill was one of two hills originally named by Richards Double Hill [13a]. It was locally known as Lookout Mountain, so named by the owners of a resort there. McLellan wrote: "Near the northwest extremity of East Sound there is a small group of rocky hills known as the Double Hill Range, which trends in a northeasterly direction. Lookout Mountain, the highest point on the range, has an elevation of 680 feet." In 1925, the U.S. Board on Geographic Names approved the name Lookout Mountain (GNIS files). In its March 11, 1977 meeting, the Washington State Board settled the issue of mountain vs. hill and

approved the current name, Docket 216, to conform to local usage (files from the Washington State Board, Morse Island and Lookout Hill).

Lopez
Located near the entrance to Fisherman Bay, the community takes its name from the island. It was originally named Lopez Island, but locals changed it to simply Lopez sometime in the 1890s. Lange identified that the post office was operating in 1891 (and perhaps earlier) with Irene Weeks as the postmaster. Weeks was the sister of Hiram Hutchinson, originally from Vermont, who established a trading post there around 1870. Hutchinson came to the island in the early 1850s. Entering Fisherman Bay, he encountered some northern Indians attacking the Lummi Indians. Hutchinson helped to fight off the northern Indians, and the Lummi's rewarded him with a place to live where he later built the store. Weeks came to Lopez to help her brother in 1874. When he died, she inherited the store. Weeks died in 1926.

Lopez Hill
Located near the center of Lopez Island, at 480 feet it is the tallest hill on the island. The name reported by McLellan was Lopez Peak. However, in 1925, the U.S. Board on Geographic Names changed it to Lopez Hill.

Lopez Chain [18] #654, 1866, U.S. Coast Survey
Located at the southern end of Lopez Sound off the eastern side of Lopez Island, the U.S. Coast Survey gave this name to a string of islands which include Ram, Cayou, and Rim (*Directory* 129). It is difficult to determine from the chart if other islands were also included. According to Davidson: "Abreast of them [Bird Rocks in Rosario Strait], on the western side, is a narrow opening between two low rocky heads of Lopez and Decatur islands. Inside is a line of islets ranging from the north head, and making the channel run towards the south. This barrier is called the Lopez Chain, and the entrance the Lopez Pass," (*Report* 431).

Lopez de Haro, Canal de
See Haro Strait.

Lopez Island [8a] #1917, 1847, Kellett
It is located in the heart of the San Juans bordered by San Juan Channel on its western side and touching Rosario Strait on the east. In 1841, Wilkes originally named it Chaunceys Island [7a] for Capt. Isaac Chauncey who commanded the *Washington* in 1815 at the battle of Algiers. Kellett honored Gonzalo Lopez de Haro (Meany, *Origin* 150, 151).

Lopez Pass [18] #654, 1866, U.S. Coast Survey
Located between Decatur and Lopez Islands, Lopez Pass provides access from Rosario Strait into Lopez Sound. The U.S. Coast Survey named the pass in 1854 (*Directory* 129) likely honoring Lopez de Haro. Richards showed it as Maury Passage on his 1859 chart [13a]. He provided no reason for the name.

Lopez Sound [13a] #2689, 1859, Richards
Located off the eastern side of Lopez Island, Wilkes named this in 1841 the Macedonian Crescent [7a] for the *Macedonian*, a British frigate captured by Capt. Stephen Decatur during the War of 1812 (Meany, *Origin* 151). In 1854, the U.S. Coast Survey named it Lopez Bay (*Directory* 129) likely for the Spanish pilot Lopez de Haro. However, the name didn't make it onto any U.S. charts until 1866 [18], and by then the U.S. Coast Survey conformed the name to that of Richards' whose 1859 chart reflected it as Lopez Sound.

Lottie Bay
It is located near the northwestern entrance of Deception Pass to the east of Lighthouse Point. It is likely named for the steamer *Lottie*, which struck nearby rocks in a snowstorm in February 1882 and sank (Wright 350).

Lottie Point
Located to the east of Lottie Bay, the local name appears on some park and recreation maps but not on charts.

Lovejoy Point
Located in Coupeville, it was named for Capt. Howard B. Lovejoy. Lovejoy was Capt. Coope's friend and neighbor in the community. Born in Maine in 1805, Lovejoy arrived on Whidbey Island in 1853. He carried spars from Penn Cove to San Francisco to be used for some of the first docks there. In 1855 he married Calista Kinney, age 16 and daughter of another captain. They settled at Lovejoy Point, although he was at sea much of the time (Cahail). Lovejoy died in Coopeville in 1872.

Lovers Bluff
Located on the western side of Lummi Island at the southern entrance to Legoe Bay, the origin of the name is unknown.

Lovers Cove
Located on the western shoreline of Orcas Island about 3½ miles southwest from Point Doughty, the origin of the name is unknown.

Low Island [13a] #2689, 1859, Richards
Located between Orcas and Shaw Islands, it was named perhaps because of its flat appearance (TPL website). McLellan called it Andrews Island. The U.S. Government owns the island.

Low Island
Located off the western side of San Juan Island between Smallpox and Andrews Bays, it was likely named for its appearance.

Low Point [9a] #1911, 1849, Kellett
It is located at the mouth of the Lyre River which flows into the Strait of Juan de Fuca. Kellett likely named it for its appearance.

Low Point [14a] #2840, 1861, Richards
It is located on the eastern shore of San Juan Island on Griffin Bay. Wood (98) quoted the log of the H.M.S. *Plumper*, August 4, 1858: "Half tide Rock on with a low Black point." The low Black point ultimately became Low Point.

Lowell Point [7a] #145, 1841, Wilkes; [7e] #158, 1841, Wilkes
Located on the westerly side of Camano Island, Wilkes honored crew member James Lowell in 1841. Wilkes did not include this name in his *Narrative*, but it is shown on his chart. The Salish name for the point was "scorched face or scorched cliff" (Hilbert et. al., 373).

Lower Lynch Cove
Located on the northern shoreline of the Little Skookum Inlet, the origin of the name is unknown. It is about a mile to the east of Upper Lynch Cove.

Lower Kitsap Peninsula
See Key Peninsula.

Luana Beach
The community is located on Maury Island northwest of Point Robinson . Frank Hubell settled in the area in 1908 and named it after a former girlfriend (Haulman). In 1982, the Washington State Board on Geographic Names addressed the Luana vs. Luena spelling differences on government documents. The Board approved Luana in late 1983, Docket 285. The U.S. Board followed in early 1984 (from Washington State Board Files).

Ludlow, Port

Ludlow, Port [7d] #146, 1841, Wilkes; [7f] #151, 1841, Wilkes
Located on the northeastern side of Admiralty Inlet, in 1841 Wilkes honored Lieut. Augustus C. Ludlow who died aboard the *Chesapeake* in the battle with *Shannon* during the War of 1812. About the port, Wilkes wrote: ". . . though of small extent, offers many facilities for vessels, particularly those wishing to make repairs; it is situated at the mouth of Hood's Canal. From its locality and the extent of agricultural land in its neighborhood, advantages are afforded to settlers, and supplies, such as the country will produce, may be raised in abundance," (Wilkes, *Narrative* 314). Davidson wrote: "Abreast of Tala the width of the bay is three-quarters of a mile, but it gradually contracts to less than half mile at the saw-mill, at which vessels load. Inside of the saw-mill point is an excellent anchorage in 7 and 8 fathoms. About a mile from the mill is an ample water power, with a fall of 80 feet," (Davidson, *Report* 452). The mill referenced was owned by W. P. Sayword who arrived in the harbor in 1852, leased land from John Thorndike, and established the sawmill. It

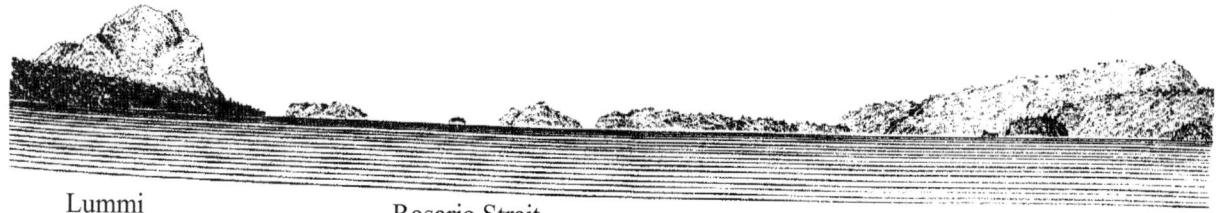

Lummi Peak   Rosario Strait, North entrance   Cypress Island

averaged 3,000 board feet of lumber early on but suffered constant equipment breakdowns. In 1858, Sayword finally leased it to Zachariah Amos, Arthur Phinney, and William Hook (Amos and Phinney Company). The Hall brothers started a shipyard in 1874 and launched thirty-one vessels from the harbor. Phinney died in 1877, and within a year the Puget Mill Company (Pope & Talbot) purchased the mill for $64,850. Under the management of Cyrus Walker (1827-1913), the owners erected a new mill. It opened in 1883 and boasted a daily capacity of 100,000 board feet and 120 men to run the operation. About the same time, Walker also branched into the ship building business near the Port Ludlow mill. In the summer of 1884 he launched the *Tyee*, then the most powerful tugboat in the United States. When the Port Gamble mill burned in 1885, Walker moved his home to Port Ludlow and built a mansion above the beach. Walker, at age eighty-five, wed William Talbot's thirty-seven-year-old daughter, Emily. The mill closed in 1890 because of depressed timber prices but reopened in 1897 when business improved. Walker moved to San Francisco in 1907 where he died in 1913. His mansion became the Admiralty Hotel in 1914. Over the years, the mill operated sporadically when lumber prices justified the expense. In the mid-1920s, with antiquated equipment, Pope & Talbot recognized the need to modernize. But because timber sales would not support the capital expense, they decided to sell all their holdings. In 1925, the Chas. R. McCormick Lumber Company of Delaware took over for $15 million. The depression struck soon after forcing McCormick out of business. The mill closed permanently on December 4, 1935. Pope and Talbot regained the property in 1938 by foreclosing against McCormick for unpaid debts. Walker's mansion was torn down in 1940. The mill site was ultimately cleared, and today there is little left to mark its location (McCurdy, *By Juan* 75, 76; Roe 94-97; *With Pride* 180; Campbell 24).

Lummi Bay
Located off the mainland east of Lummi Island, east of Sandy Point, it was named *Ensenada de Lara* by Galiano/Valdéz in 1792. The current name is from the Indian tribe that inhabited the area.

Lummi Island [10] #51, 1854, U.S. Coast Survey
It is located on the northeastern edge of Rosario Strait. In 1841, Wilkes named it McLaughlins Island [7a] honoring Dr. John McLaughlin, Chief Factor of the Hudson's Bay Company (Meany, *Origin* 152). The U.S. Coast Survey renamed it in 1853 for the Indian tribe that inhabited the area. The U.S. Board on Geographic Names approved the current name over Wilkes' name, in 1899.

Lummi Peak [10] #51, 1854, U.S. Coast Survey
Located on the southern end of Lummi Island, the U.S. Coast Survey named the 1,600 foot peak for the Indian tribe that inhabited the area.

Lummi Point [18] #654, 1866, U.S. Coast Survey
Located on the northeastern end of Lummi Island, at the end of Lane Spit, the U.S. Coast Survey named it for the Indian tribe that inhabited the area. *See also* Lane Spit.

Lummi Rocks [11] #654, 1858, U.S. Coast Survey
Located off the southwestern side of Lummi Island, the U.S. Coast Survey named it Lummi Rock in 1854 for the local Indian tribe that inhabited the area. Davidson indicated: "The rock nearly 100 feet high off the highest part of the ridge, and a third of a mile from shore, is the Lummi Rock, and a capital boat harbor is found on its northwest side," (*Report* 433). The name morphed into Lummi Rocks later.

Lydia Shoal
Located in Rosario Strait, a mile east of Obstruction Island, the origin of the name is unknown.

Lyle Point [23] #6460, 1905
Located at the southern end of Anderson Island, at the entrance to Oro Bay, Wilkes originally named this Turku Point [7i] in 1841. He provided no reason for the name. Wilkes did not include this name in his *Narrative*, but it is shown on his chart. The current name came from William Lyle who homesteaded there in the 1880s (Reese, *Origins* 69). Davidson mentioned the new name in the 1889 *Pacific Coast Pilot* (623).

Lynch Cove [7d] #146, 1841, Wilkes
Located at the far end of Hood Canal, in 1841 Wilkes honored Lieut. William Francis Lynch, U.S.N., who explored the Jordan River and Dead Sea. Wilkes wrote: "Lynch Cove is situated at the farthest point of the northeast branch. The land about it is low and marshy on the east; on the west it rises, and is sparsely covered with wood. At the head of this cove is also an extensive mud-flat. There is good anchorage, in 5 and 6 fathoms, between the two small sand spits, which lie on opposite sides of and form the cove," (Meany, *Origin* 153; Wilkes, *Narrative* 109).

Lyre River [8a] #1917, 1847, Kellett
Located along the Strait of Juan de Fuca about five miles west of Crescent Bay, it was first named Rio Cuesta by Eliza [3] in 1791 (Meany, *Origin* 153). However, it is reflected on Quimper's 1790 chart as well [1] but not mentioned in either of their journals. It was renamed by Kellett (*Directory* 116).

Mabana
Located on the western side of Camano Island, Niles "Peg Leg" Anderson started a lumber camp there. Nils apparently lost his leg to an accident. He named the town for his oldest daughter, Mabel Anderson, with a couple of extra letters for a more pleasant sound (Dean 41).

Macedonian Crescent [7a] #145, 1841, Wilkes
See Lopez Sound.

Mackaye Harbor [13a] #2689, 1859, Richards
Located off the southern side of Lopez Island, Richards left no reason for the name.

Macklin
Located on the northern side of Fox Island, it was originally named Guthrie Camp after Harry Guthrie. The name was changed to Macklin in the 1890s. Dr. John C. Donaway and Dr. Benjamin F. Allen lived there. Allen worked as the attending physician at the McNeil Federal Penitentiary and was Macklin's first postmaster in 1896 (Perisho 19).

Macs Cove
Located off the northern end of Whidbey Island west of the Deception Pass Bridge, it was named for A. O. McCormic from Seattle who used to row out of the cove.

Madison, Port

Madison, Port [7d] #146, 1841, Wilkes
Located along the western shore of northern Puget Sound, nearly opposite Seattle, Wilkes honored the fourth president of the U.S. (Meany, *Origin* 153). On current charts, Port Madison is the large body of water bounded by Point Jefferson on the north, Point Monroe on the south, and Agate Pass on the western side. Davidson wrote: "One mile west of it [Point Monroe] is the narrow entrance to a natural canal, upon which, in full view, are situated the Port Madison saw-mills," (*Report* 445). Current charts reflect the community on the eastern shore as Port Madison and the community on the western shore as West Port Madison. The small canal referenced by Davidson is unnamed. In the early 1850s, George A. Meigs (1816-1897), born in Vermont, established a sawmill at Port Madison. Soon, early loggers began work in the surrounding area to provide lumber for

the mill. By 1854, the mill turned out 40,000 feet of lumber each day. In 1856, Port Madison became the county seat of Kitsap, formed from portions of King and Jefferson counties. In 1859, Meigs' daughter Lillian was the first White child born in Port Madison. His only son, born two years later, died a month shy of his ninth birthday. By 1861, the mill produced 80,000 feet a day mostly because Meigs employed James M. Colman (the Colman Building) as an efficiency expert. Meigs and Chief Seattle became close friends. The Chief visited often for long conversations. When the Chief's health began to fail in 1866, he requested that Meigs attend the funeral and shake his hand before he was put to rest. When the Chief died, Meigs closed the mill and attended the funeral with many of the Port Madison residents. William DeShaw from Agate Point paid the burial expenses of $96.38, including the coffin, pants, coat, vest, shoes, shirt, and blankets (Carlson 25-28). The mill burned in 1868 but was rebuilt. In 1872, Meigs confronted a decline in readily available lumber. Several bad business decisions made by his partner, W. H. Gawley, forced Meigs to heavily mortgage the mill to the Dexter Horton Bank (which became Seafirst and ultimately Bank of America). Despite attempts to repay the loans over the next twenty years, the bank foreclosed in February 1892. The mill was closed and Port Madison became a ghost town. Gawley committed suicide as the mill neared bankruptcy (Bowen et al., VI: 6-12; Warner 8; Perry 19).

Madrona Beach
Located north of Onamac Point on the western side of Camano Island, the name perhaps came from the local madrona trees.

Madrona Peninsula
Located between Friday Harbor and North Bay, it was named in 1915 by Walter L. C. Muenscher for the madrona trees that line the shoreline (Wood 161). It is neither reflected on current charts nor is it recognized by the U.S. Board on Geographic Names.

Madrona Point
Located at the northern end of the Madrona Peninsula on the eastern side of San Juan Island, Wood (162) quoted Walter L. C. Muenscher: "A point on the north side of Madrona Peninsula opposite Brown Island." The name is neither reflected on U.S. charts nor is it recognized by the U.S. Board on Geographic Names.

Madrona Point
Located east of Bremerton, the point separates Ostrich and Oyster Bays. It was likely named for the madrona tree.

Madrona Point
Located in East Sound, Orcas Island, Richards initially named it Arbutus Point in 1859 [13a]. *Arbutus menziesii* is the scientific name for the madrona tree, the tree being named after Archibald Menzies who discovered the new species in our Northwest area in 1792 while with George Vancouver. It was changed to Tongue Point on a 1890s chart, but locals apparently chose to call it by its common name of Madrona Point particularly when the Harrison family built a lodge in the 1880s and named it the Madrona Inn. The tree is simply known as "arbutus" in British Columbia. It was also shown as Tongue Point on a 1958 USGS Quad which gave rise to a 1973 query to the Washington State Board on Geographic Names to standardize the name. The owner of the land at that time was the well-known Seattle businessman, Norton Clapp, who strongly suggested retaining the name Madrona. In its December 10, 1976 meeting, the Board approved the current name, Docket 209. The U.S. Board followed in 1977 (from Washington State Board Files). In 1989, the Lummi Tribe purchased the point using $2.2 million in appropriated U.S. Congressional funds. It was a park until 2007 when the Lummi Nation mysteriously closed it to the public.

Madrone
See Winslow.

Magnolia Beach
Located on the southern end of Vashon Island in Quartermaster Harbor, Charles A. Cook homesteaded there in 1878. When he filed a plat in 1902, he selected the name after his hometown in Iowa (Meany, *Origin* 157).

Magnolia Bluff [22] #6450, 1909
Located on the northern end of Elliott Bay, Davidson mentioned the name but does not specifically state that the U.S. Coast Survey named it (*Report* 446). Meany (*Origin* 157) credits the Coast Survey with the name in 1856. Apparently, Davidson confused magnolia trees, which do not exist there, with madronas.

Mahnckes Point
Located on the northern entrance to Filucy Bay, it was named after Henry Mahncke, a Tacoma baker, who purchased land and finally retired there in the 1880s (Reese, *Origins* 72).

Mail Bay
Located off the eastern side of Waldron Island, it gained its name as the location where mail was first delivered to Waldron (GNIS database). Ethan and Sadie Allen homesteaded south of the bay in 1895. Later, they purchased 440 acres from the Doucette brothers, including the entire waterfront in the bay, for $500. Both having been schoolteachers from Indiana, Ethan became the superintendent of schools for San Juan County in 1898, rowing frequently to check the twenty-seven schoolhouses. Interested in Indian artifacts, Ethan started a collection, contributed to by people in the islands as well as Canada. The collection grew to be one of the most important in the Northwest (Ludwig 21-26). Much of it is viewable at the Orcas Island Historical Museum in East Sound. According to the Apr. 7, 1898 issue of *The San Juan Islander* (p 3): "Mr. Ethan Allen, of Waldron, has been appointed by the board of county commissioners as county superintendent of schools to fill out the unexpired term of Miss Rhoda A. Lee, resigned. The Islander regards the choice as made as a most fitting and excellent one, and predicts that the people of this county will never have cause to regret the action of the board."

Mailman Point
Located in Oro Bay, Anderson Island, it was a drop-off point for mail.

Makak Point [7j] #153, 1841, Wilkes
Located at the southern end of Seabeck Bay, Wilkes charted it as Mukak Landing in 1841. He wrote: "Near its head [Seabeck Bay] is an extensive sand-flat, dry in places at low water. The watering-place can be approached by boats at half tide: the landing is on the south-east side, at Makak Point," (Wilkes, *Narrative* 324). The "watering-place" is now called Seabec Creek. Makak Point is neither reflected on U.S. charts nor is it recognized by the U.S. Board on Geographic Names.

Mal Abrigo [2] 1791, Pantoja
See Matia.

Manaco Beach
Located about halfway between Lowell and Onamac Points (Camano spelled backwards), Manaco is an anagram for Camano (Prasse, Karen. Stanwood Area Historical Society. E-mail to author, May 2, 2010). In the 1950s, there were numerous beaches or resorts along the Camano shoreline. I have generally excluded them from this text because few are named on maritime charts. Pebble Beach, Cama Beach, Indian Beach, Rockaway Beach, Sunset Beach, Camp Lagoon, Camp Grande, Maple Grove Beach, Tyee Beach, Tillicum Beach, Sunny Shore Acres, Mountain View Beach, and Juniper Beach are officially recognized by the USBGN. The rest are local names; however, it is worth listing them: From Camano Head north: Pebble Beach, Gary Beach, Irenella Beach, and Peterson's Beach. From Lowell Point north: Cama Beach, Manaco Resort, Camp Comfort, Indian Beach, and Camano Beach. From Onamac Point north: Rockaway Beach, Sunset Beach, Madrona Beach, Camp Lagoon, Camp Grande, and Maple Grove Beach. On Port Susan, from Point Allen north: Tyee Beach, Tillicum Beach, Sunny Shore Acres, Mountain View Beach, Long Beach, Sundin Beach, and Juniper Beach (http://www.oldcamano.net/resorts57.html).

Manetee
Located on the eastern entrance to the Port Washington Narrows, near Bremerton, the townsfolk named it after the first steamer to use their newly-built wharf (Meany, *Origin* 157).

Manchester
Located on the western shore of Puget Sound, west of Blake Island, Isaac Ellis settled on what

became downtown Manchester in 1871. Locals named the community Brooklyn, as they sought a large naval yard like that in Brooklyn, New York. Later, townsfolk selected the current name after its namesake in England. James and Mary Hall acquired the fifty-three acre Ellis homestead in the 1880s and built a house and small sawmill. A post office was established in 1893 but was discontinued later in the year. Samuel A. Denniston built the first general store about 1905 and became the first postmaster when the office re-opened in 1906. In 1908, a dock and school were built and a second school in 1912 (Bowen et al., V: 91).

Mane Cove [7h] #154, 1841, Wilkes
According to Wilkes' 1841 chart, he drew Reach Island in Case Inlet as a peninsula. Mane Cove represents the water on the inside or western side of Reach. Wilkes left no reason for the name. He does not include this name in his *Narrative*. The name is neither reflected on U.S. charts nor is it recognized by the U.S. Board on Geographic Names.

Manhait Point [7i] #147, 1841, Wilkes
There are two unnamed points on the northern end of McNeil Island. This is the eastern one. Wilkes left no reason for the 1841 name. Wilkes did not include this name in his *Narrative*, but it is shown on his chart. Inskip named it McCarthy Point [24], presumably for J. W. McCarty who settled on 160 acres nearby.

Manzanita, Manzanita Bay, Manzanita Creek
Located on the western side of Bainbridge Island, Anders Anderson was first to settle around 1885. *See also* Miemois Creek. Mrs. Margaret A. Wheeler became the first postmistress in 1900 and named the community for the madrona trees she thought were manzanitas. Presumably, the bay was named for the community although it was earlier known as Mosquito Bay (Bowen et. al., IV: 100-101; Marriott 106). In 1999 the City of Bainbridge Island Engineering Department proposed the name Manzanita Creek for the previously unnamed creek. The Washington State Board on Geographic Names approved the name in its March 2001 meeting, the U.S. Board followed later in the year. A variant was Clock-way-dupe which was the phonetic spelling of the original Suquamish name. It means "place that was chopped" (from Washington State Board files).

Manzanita
This is located on the southwest side of Maury Island. It is spelled Manzanita in the GNIS database as well as NOAA chart #18445, but Mansanita on chart #18448. The April 2012 reissue of chart #18448 corrected the spelling to conform to GNIS. According to Haulman, the property was originally owned by the Tacoma Yacht Club and named by them in 1892 for the madrona trees on the site. Manzanita is sometimes used to refer to madrona. The name is first referenced in the 1909 *Pacific Coast Pilot* (156).

Maple
Located on the western side of Shaw Island north of Parks Bay, this community was the site of the first post office on Shaw Island. Established in 1886, the first postmaster was Bert Tift (Richardson, *Magic* 67). The name is not recognized by the U.S. Board on Geographic Names.

Maple Beach
It is located on the eastern shoreline of Hood Canal, just south of Seabeck Bay. John Depenheuer, born 1887 in Germany, jumped ship in Philadelphia in 1911. He worked his way westward and arrived in the Seabeck area in 1913. Depenheuer bought five acres at Maple Beach for $400 and slowly over the years purchased more property. He and his wife Elisabeth logged, farmed, and built the Maple Beach Resort consisting of four cabins in the early 1930s. They rented the cabins to Seattleites for five dollars a night (Perry, *Seabeck* 190, 196).

Maple Cove
Located off the eastern side of Whidbey Island immediately south of Sandy Point, it was named for the prolific maple trees that once grew along the shoreline (Hitchman 175).

Maplewood
Located on the western shoreline of Colvos Passage south of Olalla, it was possibly named for maple trees which grow in the area.

March Point - Mariners' Cove

March Point

Mariners' Cove

March Point [13k] #2689, 1900
Located on the northern end of Fidalgo Island, Wilkes named it Sachem Point in 1841 [7m]. Wilkes did not include this name in his *Narrative*, but it is shown on his chart. *Sachem* is apparently a Massachusetts Indian name for "head chief." The current name honored Hiram Alfred March, who arrived in the Northwest in 1858. Born in Vermont in 1826, March worked as a stone mason in New York and Boston. He moved to California in 1853 and Washington in 1858. In 1859, he claimed 160 acres on Fidalgo Island and moved his family to the farm four years later. At various times he was a deputy sheriff, a contractor, a dairy farmer, Commodore of the Anacortes Yacht Club, and he became noteworthy for the cauliflower seed he raised in 1891. He died in 1905. The issue of the application came before the Washington State Board on Geographic names in 1976. Locals recommended applying the name to the entire point or peninsula, from Highway 20 northward, rather than simply the northern portion. In its September 24, 1976 meeting, the Board approved, Docket 211. The U.S. Board followed in late 1976 (*An Illustrated History*, 639; Washington State Board files).

Mariners' Cove
It is a small community of 169 lots, a few on Saratoga Passage, most on or overlooking man-made canals, on the eastern side of Whidbey Island about a mile southwest from Strawberry Point. The canals were dug with a cofferdam at the entrance such that it is possible to maintain a minimum water level inside. However, one must enter only above mid-tide. The canals and piers easily handle boats into the 50 foot range. The name is not reflected on current charts nor is it officially recognized by the U.S. Board on Geographic Names. In 1899, Hans and Katerina Olson settled in Milltown, a community on the east side of Skagit Bay. In 1906, the family purchased 60 acres of farmland at what would later become Mariners' Cove. Hans not only built a home and barns, but he began diking a portion of the land such that the resultant canal would maintain water even at low tide. Hans built a boathouse where small boats were stored in the winter. The dikes were destroyed during a 1935 windstorm. In 1921, Agaton and Berte Olson (no relation to the Hans Olson family) were awarded a contract by the state for ferry service between Utsalady on Camano Island and Oak Harbor on Whidbey Island. The termination on Whidbey was not actually in Oak Harbor, but rather at the Hans Olson homestead. Some of the old piling is still visible at the entrance to the Mariners' Cove canal, at a small point that was known as Olson's Landing (for Agaton and Berte). Initially, Agaton's fish boat, the *Rainbow*, simply towed a scow across Saratoga Passage, but because business was profitable for the Olsons, they built two ferries in 1924. The *Deception Pass* ran on the Yokeko Point to Hoypus Point route. The *Acorn* replaced Agaton's fish boat on the Utsalady to Oak Harbor run. *Acorn* was 65 feet in length with a 25 foot beam and was propelled by a 75 horsepower diesel. She could carry 16 cars along with foot traffic. In the early 1960s, a partnership formed between Bob Fisher, Charlie Reisdorff, Wayne Chapman,

and Milo Norton. Their vision of building a marina and summer resort began in earnest when the group purchased the 60 acre Olson farm in 1965. The canals were dredged and the dirt was used to form building lots. Interest was slow initially, and the first home was constructed in 1972. But over the years, the lots were all sold and homes now occupy most of them (*A History of Mariners' Cove*; Kline & Bayless 137).

Marrowstone Island
Located off Port Townsend in the northern portion of Admiralty Inlet, the name came from Marrowstone Point named by Vancouver in 1792.

Marrowstone Point

Marrowstone Point [6] 1792, Vancouver
The point is located at the northeastern end of Marrowstone Island. Vancouver wrote: "In most of my excursions I met with an indurated clay, much resembling fuller's earth. The high steep cliff, forming the point of land we were now upon, seemed to be principally composed of this matter; which, on a more close examination, appeared to be a rich species of the marrow stone, from whence it obtained the name of Marrow-stone Point," (Vancouver 235). Wilkes reflected this as Point Ringgold on his charts in 1841 [7a], [7d], [7p], but he did not show it in his *Narrative*. Wilkes honored crew member Cadwalader Ringgold, Commander of the *Porpoise*, who was responsible for leading much of the survey work in our inland waters.

Marshville
Located on the western side of Budd Inlet, it is now part of Olympia. It was named for Edwin Marsh who settled there in 1851 (Meany, *Origin* 159). The name is not reflected on current charts, but the historical name is recognized by the U.S. Board on Geographic Names.

Marthas Bay
Located on the southeastern end of Fidalgo Island to the north of Goat Island, the origin of the name is unknown.

Martinez, Punta de [1] 1790, Quimper
See Cape Flattery.

Marysville
Located north of Everett on the Ebey Slough, Truman L. Ireland and Louis Thomas settled in the area in the 1860s or early 1870s. John Stafford arrived shortly after. In 1874, James and Marie Comeford arrived and purchased the three claims from the Port Blakely Mill,, along with a fourth owned by William Renton, 1280 acres in all, for $450. Comford, in 1872, started as an Indian agent at the Tulalip Indian Reservation but was soon drawn to the Marysville area. James remained on the reservation and ran the trading post, but he also continued the logging operation started by the previous owners. In 1877, the Comefords moved to Marysville and within the next year opened a trading post and built a hotel, a small dock, and a warehouse. A post office soon followed. Comeford set aside 40 acres of his holdings and platted the town in 1889, naming it after his wife, according to one story (Humphrey 53; *An Illustrated History*, 346). Another source suggested that it was named either after the hometown of two of the early settlers, James Johnson and Thomas Lloyd of Marysville, California (Meany, *Origin* 160) or that Father Casimir Chirouse suggested naming the town after the Virgin Mary. It was incorporated in 1891 (Hitchman 178). By that time, the city was home to two shingle mills, a sawmill, two hotels, several stores, a livery stable, a meat market, a shoemaker, a blacksmith, several wharfs, schools (with 80 children enrolled), and churches. Local farmers did very well raising berries (*An Illustrated History*, 347).

Mason County
In 1854, David Shelton drafted a bill to organize Swamish County, named after the Indians in the area. It means "drifting." The Legislature approved

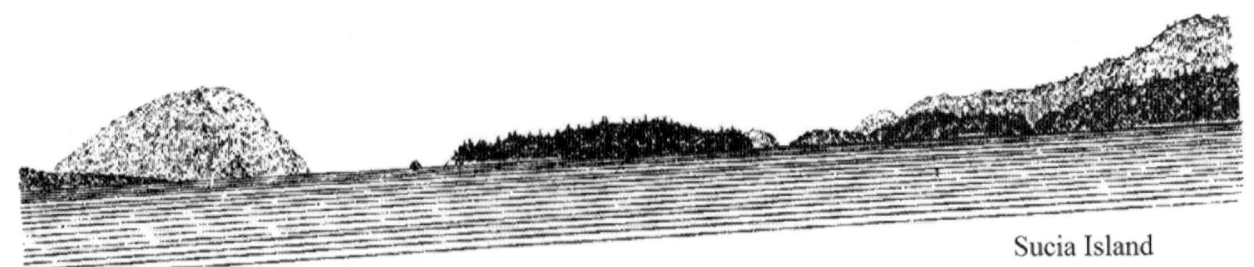

Lummi Island   *Matia Island*   *Sucia Island*

the new county. It included Eld and Totten Inlets all the way to the coast and north to the head of Case Inlet. It was signed by Charles H. Mason, Secretary of State. The name was changed ten years later to honor Mason who died in 1859 at age thirty-two (Fredson, *Oakland to Shelton* 8).

Massacre Bay [13a] #2689, 1859, Richards
Located off the western side of West Sound, Orcas Island, Richards found a nearby burial site where northern Haidah Indians had massacred more than 100 Lummi Indians in 1858 (Meany, *Origin* 161; Lange). *See also* Skull Island.

Massey Creek
The creek flows through Des Moines into Puget Sound. It was named after the Rev. Thomas J. Massey who founded the Des Moines United Methodist Church in 1885, and the name was in local use for years. In its March 8, 1990 meeting, Docket 340, the Washington State Board on Geographic Names approved the name. The U.S. Board followed later in the year. A variant was Rink Creek (from Washington State Board Files).

Mata [3] 1791, Eliza
See Matia.

Matia East
See Puffin Island.

Matia Island [8a] #1917, 1847, Kellett
Located east of Sucia Island, Pantoja in 1791 originally named the island *Mal Abrigo* [2] for "poor shelter." According to some sources, Eliza changed the name to Mata. But the new name does not appear on his chart or in his journal. In 1841, Wilkes [7a] named Matia and Puffin Islands the Edmund Group (Meany, *Origin* 161). Wilkes did not include this name in his *Narrative*, but it is shown on his chart. Lange speculated that Wilkes named it for his second son, Edmund Wilkes, born in 1833. Edmund was the first non-Morman family to settle in Utah. Kellett restored Eliza's name of Matia in 1847. Elvin Haworth Smith, a Civil War veteran and captain in the Union Army, settled on the island in 1892. He was not the first to live there, but he stayed the longest. He built a cabin in a small cove about a quarter mile east of Eagle Point. He fished in the harbor, farmed five acres of land, and raised sheep, chickens, and rabbits. Over the years, Smith became known as the hermit of Matia Island based upon his solitary habits. He journeyed weekly into Eastsound to pick up mail and supplies. Smith continued to live on the island for years, changing his life and habits little. In 1920, friends on Orcas noted that he had failed several weekly visits. They finally went to Matia to check on his health and found him nearly starved. A storm had broken up his rowboat, preventing him from leaving the island. He had been living off chicken eggs and slowly butchering

Matia Island

the hens. They brought him to Orcas to recover, and soon after he returned to Matia, but this time with a permanent house guest, an old war friend, George Carrier. Following one trip for mail and supplies in early 1921, the pair headed back to Matia in their small skiff, now powered by a two-and-a-half-horse motor. They never made it home. A few days later, a can of kerosene and part of their cargo was found on Sucia. That spring, some Indians near the Canadian border uncovered a portion of the skiff with the motor still attached (Richardson, *Pig* 245-254). In 1936, administration of Matia was assigned to the Department of Agriculture, thus closing it to homesteaders. It is currently a National Wildlife Refuge; however, limited public use is permitted as long as the wildlife is not threatened. At one point, somehow, "Matia Islands, one of" became a variant. The U.S. Board on Geographic Names addressed this in 1941 and approved the current name (GNIS files). According to the June 2, 1898 edition of *The San Juan Islander* (p 2): "Captain Smith of Maties Island was in town [Eastsound], Monday of last week." This provided another (local) variant.

Mats Mats [20i] #6410, 1856, U.S. Coast Survey
A small bay located north of Port Ludlow, the Indian name means "in and out" (TPL website).

Maury
Located on the eastern side of Maury Island, early settlers named the community for the island. It was the site of the Ogilvy farm and general store, a school named Maury ½ mile west, and a dock ¾ mile north of the store. All disappeared by the 1930s. In 1982, proponents submitted the name to give recognition to a name in local use as well as to correct its location on nautical charts. The Washington State Board on Geographic Names approved the proposal in its meeting of December 9, 1983, Docket 285. The U.S. Board followed in early 1984 (from Washington State Board Files).

Maury, Point [7e] #158, 1841, Wilkes
See Dines Point.

Maury Island [7d] #146, 1841, Wilkes; [7g] #155, 1841, Wilkes
Located southeast of Vashon Island, Wilkes honored crew member William L. Maury in 1841 (Meany, *Origin* 161). Wilkes wrote: "At extreme low water, Maury's and Vashon's Islands are joined by a sandbar," (Wilkes, *Narrative* 319). Wilkes' crew described a portage across the bar and implied that it was not passable by boat, even at high tide. These two observations seem to be describing two different places. Regardless, today Maury is not an island. It is connected by road to Vashon. Davidson commented: "Half way down on its eastern side [Vashon Island] lies a curiously shaped peninsula, formed by a narrow, low, sandy neck of land which makes out into the inlet, and then runs towards the south point of the island. The space between this peninsula and the island is an excellent harbor [Quartermaster Harbor] 4 or 5 miles long, and three-quarters of a mile wide, with 5 to 10 fathoms water in it," (Davidson, *Report* 449). The U.S. Board on Geographic Names modified Maurys Island to the current name in 1899. Another variant was Mori Island.

Maury Passage [13a] #2689, 1859, Richards
See Lopez Pass.

Maury's Point [7e] #158, 1841, Wilkes
See West Point.

Maxfield
See Nisqually.

Maxwelton
Located on the southern side of Whidbey Island in Useless Bay, it was settled by Luther L. Moore in 1863, the first landowner on the south end of Whidbey Island. He homesteaded 900 acres of land and sold to Mike and Mary Lyons in 1870. Peter Howard Mackie and his wife Ada Hally arrived in Seattle's Ravenna district shortly after the 1889 fire. Peter found immediate work as a carpenter. Like many others with large families looking for more land, they turned toward south Whidbey where Peter's brother, Theodore had built a home just north of Indian Point. Peter, Theodore, and two other brothers, Herbert and David, purchased the Lyons property in 1905. David named the land Maxwelton for their favorite Scottish song. The men planted oats, fruit trees, and a garden on 300 acres of the land. In addition to food from the crops, they fished and hunted deer, ducks, bear, and rabbits, all of which were plentiful on the island

(Cherry II). Meany (*Origin* 161) indicated that it was "named by the MacKee brothers 'in honor of the bonnie braes of Scotland.'" According to Hitchman (179), it was named by the McKee brothers from Maxwellton, Scotland.

Maylor Point
Located on Whidbey Island near Oak Harbor, Samuel and Thomas Maylor built a log cabin and established a farm. Born in County Cork, Ireland, the brothers immigrated to Boston in June 1849. They boarded a steamer for Panama, crossed the isthmus, boarded another ship, and arrived in San Francisco in August 1851. They then headed north to Astoria, walked to Tumwater, and built a small cabin at Steilacoom. Their stay was short-lived when they found that the soil would not support farming. They searched for better land, eventually settling on Maylor Point in 1853. In 1855, Samuel returned to Ireland. He wed Mary Barrett in December 1856. Two years later, the family, now including a young son, Paul, returned to Whidbey Island. Samuel was a gunsmith and found his skills in great demand. Mary died at age 31 during the birth of their third son in April 1861. Brokenhearted, Samuel headed back to Ireland with his family. In October 1862, he married Margaret Corcoran, a cousin of Mary's. The following year, he again pulled up stakes and departed for Oak Harbor. Ultimately, Samuel and Margaret had five children. Margaret died in 1891 after a long illness at age 47. Following Margaret's death, Samuel's health declined. His last four years were spent as an invalid, and he died in 1896. Descendants of the Maylors lived on the point until the navy requisitioned the property in 1941 to become part of the Naval Air Station (Neil 55; Juanita Maylor Bonnelle, *An Historical Sketch of the Life of Samuel Lindsay Maylor*, 1947). George Davidson wrote: "*Maylor's Spit Light* is a *fixed red light*, dioptric (lens lantern), shown from a white post eighteen feet high. It is twenty-five feet above the water. It is placed at the extremity of Maylor's Spit, and is kept on the starboard hand in entering." Despite Davidson's reference to this in the 1889 *Pacific Coast Pilot* (602), it wasn't until 1949 that the USBGN chose the current name over Maylor Spit.

Maynard
Located at the head of Discovery Bay, the community was named for the early settler Mrs. S. P. Maynard who managed a hotel there (TPL website).

Mayo Cove [23] #6460, 1905
Wilkes' chart is a bit confusing. There are three coves on the western shore of Carr Inlet: Von Geldern to the north, Mayo in the center, and Delano Beach to the south. Wilkes reflected only the two southern coves on his chart. He labeled Mayo Cove as Talie Bay [7h] in 1841 but left no reason for the name. Wilkes did not include this name in his *Narrative*, but it is shown on his chart.

Mays Inlet [7d] #146, 1841, Wilkes
See Liberty Bay.

McArdle Bay
Located at the southern end of Lopez Island west of Watmough Head, the origin of the name is unknown.

McArthur Bank [21] #6300, 1895
Located south of Iceberg Point in the Strait of Juan de Fuca, the origin of the name is unknown. There is a slight possibility that it was named for the whaleboat of the *McArthur*. As reported by Ensign C. P. Eaton: "It is my painful duty to report the death by drowning of Lieut. F. H. Crosby, Quartermaster (third class) John Freyer, and Seamen William Nehm, Alexander Smith, and Jens Gudmundson, while attempting to land through the surf near Jo Creek, about 17 miles north of Grays Harbor, on the west coast of Washington, about 8 A.M. Saturday, August 18 [1895]." While the survey ship *McArthur* was anchored a mile and a half offshore, her whaleboat attempted to land and erect a hydrographic signal. She was overturned in heavy surf (*U.S. Coast and Geodetic Survey showing The Progress of the Work during the Fiscal Year Ending with June, 1895*. Washington Printing Office. 1896). Alternatively, Lange speculated that it was named for Lt. Comdr. W. P. McArthur who was the first surveyor on the West Coast from 1848-1850. He died in 1850 and Alden replaced him.

McCarthy Point [24] #1947, 1849, Inskip
See Manhait Point.

McConnell Island

Located within the Wasp Islets group off the western side of Shaw Island, it was originally named Brown Island [14a] by Richards; he provided no reason. A local name arose in the 1880s for its first settlers, the McConnells. Vic McConnell lived with his mother, who was blind, along with five other brothers and sisters. His father died off Vancouver Island in a shipwreck. Vic McConnell was reputed to be a smuggler and developed quite a reputation in the community (Richardson, *Pig* 273). Professor Thomas Thompson later acquired the island. He took over the UW labs in Friday Harbor about 1930 (McDonald 169, 179). McConnell was approved by the U.S. Board on Geographic Names in 1925 by discarding the variants Brown Island and Wasp Island. Wasp was reflected on a 1920s County Land Classification Map (Washington State Board files, Morse Island).

McCrackin Point

Located on the northwestern end of Henry Island, it was named for the McCracken family who owned the land. This name appeared first on U.S. Coast Survey chart #6381, Roche Harbor and Approaches, 1901 (Wood 105).

McCurdy Point

Located on the north end of the Quimper Peninsula, the U.S. Coast Survey first named it Middle Point in 1854 [10] for its location, halfway between Points George and Wilson. It was renamed for the early pioneer, James McCurdy. William A. McCurdy arrived in Port Townsend aboard the *Franklin Adams* in 1857. He was a cousin of F. W. Pettygrove, a pioneer of Port Townsend. Trained as a ship's carpenter, he built ships for the government at Mare Island in California and worked in various shipyards around the Northwest. He married Johanna Ebinger from Portland, Oregon in 1868. The couple continued moving from place to place as his job required. But in 1871, they returned to Port Townsend where he built many of the Victorian homes on the bluff. Their son, James, was born in 1872. After schooling, he found work as an errand boy in the Port Townsend National Bank, where he later became president. He is very well known for his book on Northwest history, *By Juan de Fuca's Strait*. In 1893, James married Anna Tobena Laursen from Denmark. Their son, Horace W., known as 'Mac', was born in Port Townsend in 1899. He attended public schools, and at an early age he worked in William's shipyard. At age 16, Mac enrolled in the University of Washington but volunteered for the navy in his sophomore year in 1917. Following the war, he enrolled in the Massachusetts Institute of Technology and graduated in 1922 with a B.S. in Engineering. That same day, he wed his childhood sweetheart Sarah Catherine McManus. Mac immediately found work with the Puget Sound Bridge and Dredging Company and moved around as work required. In 1927, he became manager of the entire Dredging Department and settled in Seattle. By 1931, he was president of the company. His major projects included the first Lake Washington Floating Bridge, the Hood Canal Floating Bridge, and the Gransville Street Bridge in Vancouver, B.C. Later in his life, Mac could be found wandering around Puget Sound in the Ted Geary designed *Blue Peter*, his 96 foot yacht. Built in 1928, the McCurdy family owned her for 54 years. Mac was instrumental in forming the Museum of History and Industry, and he donated heavily to their collections. He retired from the Puget Sound Dredging Company in 1963 after a 42 year career. He died in Seattle in 1989 after a life devoted to Northwest maritime history (www.historylink.org). The U.S. Board on Geographic Names changed the name from Middle Point in 1968 (GNIS files).

McDaniel Cove

Located on the western side of Hood Canal, it is about five miles south of Pleasant Harbor. The origin of the name is unknown.

McDermott Point

Located at the southern entrance to Filucy Bay, Wilkes named this point in 1841. It is reflected only on his chart, and unfortunately it is not clear. I shall guess at Tiye Point [7i]. The origin of the current name is unknown. According to Hale (613), *Tiye* is a Shoshone Indian term which means "dead." The Shoshones lived around the Snake River in Idaho.

McGees

Located about a mile and a half south of Beckett Point in Discovery Bay, it was named in 1905 by A. Loasby for Samuel McGee, an early settler (Hitchman 182).

McGlinn Island
Located at the southern end of the Swinomish Channel at Hole in the Wall, it was named for John McGlinn who built a hotel in La Conner in 1878. The name was first reflected on the 1892 t-sheet #2108 by the USC&GS. McGlinn arrived in the area in 1872 and was the Indian agent for the Lummi Tribe for five years (TPL website). The U.S. Board on Geographic Names selected the name over the variant McGlynn in 1941. The diked island is connected to the mainland by a causeway.

McLaughlins Island [7a] #145, 1841, Wilkes
See Lummi Island.

McLane Cove
Located on the western side of Case Inlet at the head of Pickering Passage, the origin of the name is unknown.

McMicken Island

McMicken Island [23] #6460, 1905
Located off the eastern side of Harstine Island in Case Inlet, Wilkes originally named this Stui Island in 1841 [7h]. He left no reason for the name. Wilkes did not include this name in his *Narrative*, but it is shown on his chart. The island was named for General Maurice McMicken, a railroad man, who arrived in the Northwest during the 1870s. After leaving the railroad, he became Surveyor General of the Territory. He died in Olympia in 1899 (TPL website). McMicken is a tombolo. It is connected by a sand bar to Harstine Island at low tide. The Salish name for the island was "falling on the ground" (Hilbert et. al., 295).

McNeil Island [7d] #146, 1841, Wilkes; [7i] #147, 1841, Wilkes
Located in southeastern Puget Sound, Wilkes spelled this M'Niel in his *Narrative* but McNeil on both charts in 1841. He honored William H. McNeill, Captain of the steamship *Beaver*. McNeill was born in Boston in 1803. In 1830, in command of the brig *Lama* or *Llama*, built in 1826 and owned by a Boston Trading Company, he headed to the Northwest for trade. Soon after his arrival in 1831, the Hudson's Bay Company, in need of a new trading vessel, purchased the 77 foot *Lama* and its cargo. McNeill was retained as a captain and began work for the Company. The Company sold the brig to a Honolulu merchant in 1837. The *Beaver* was launched in England in 1835, in front of the king and 150,000 onlookers. She was 101 feet in length with a 20 foot beam and an 11 foot depth of hold. Brig rigged, she sailed around the Horn to the Columbia River in 163 days where her side wheels were attached. With her steam engines already in place, she quickly began carrying cargo and collecting furs for the Hudson's Bay Company between Puget Sound and Alaska and was the first steamship in Northwest waters. The Imperial Hydrographers refitted her as a survey ship from 1863-1870, and in 1874 she was converted to a towboat. In 1883, she struck a rock and sank in Burrard Inlet. She was raised but met her final end in 1888 where she sank on the rocks at the entrance to Vancouver Harbor. The Vancouver Maritime Museum today displays many relics from the old

boat. Promoted to chief trader in 1839, McNeill held various posts in the Company at Fort Stikine, Fort George, Fort Rupert, etc. He was promoted to Chief Factor in 1856 and retired in 1863 to his 200 acre estate in Oak Bay. He died in 1875 (Meany, *Origin* 155; Kline 11, 12; Wright 15-18). Born in Ohio in 1830, Ezra Meeker grew up in Indiana. He married Eliza Jane Sumner at age 21. In 1852, the couple started out on the Oregon Trail with their month-old son. Before settling on McNeil Island, Ezra and his brother, Oliver, explored Puget Sound, looking for the best land. From Olympia they passed by Nisqually and Steilacoom. They camped in Commencement Bay and paddled up the Puyallup River. Continuing north, they visited with Charles C. Terry at Alki and Henry Yesler in Seattle. They next camped on Whidbey Island and visited Port Townsend. On the return trip, they met with Col. Isaac Ebey. Finally, they took up claims on McNeil Island, as it seemed to be near the heart of shipping in lower Puget Sound. Ezra returned to Portland and left Oliver behind to build a cabin. Upon returning with his wife and small child, Ezra found no cabin and no Oliver! But Oliver soon showed up with money in his pocket having helped load a ship at Steilacoom (Conover, C. T. "Just Cogitating: Ezra Meeker Made and Wrote Puget Sound History." *Seattle Times*. Apr. 9, 1961. Magazine Section p 6). Food was never a problem. They dug clams, had as much venison as they wanted, and ate the prolific huckleberries. Their first crop was turnips! They built an eighteen-by-eighteen-foot cabin on the southern shore of the island, very near to the prison's machine and carpenter shop. Their father, later viewing the cabin, thought the seven foot walls were a bit strange. As Ezra commented, ". . . the logs ran out, the sky was threatening and we had a race with the storm to get a roof over our heads." The Meekers were later persuaded to resettle at Steilacoom in 1855. Thus, they never filed a claim for land on McNeil even though Ezra had lived there for nine years (Meeker, *Pioneer*; Price 7, 8). J. W. McCarty settled on 160 acres of the Meeker's land. Four years later, he and his wife sold to Rominous Nix. In 1870, Nix sold to Jay Emmons Smith, and a month later Smith sold 80 acres to John M. Swan (*see also* Swantown). On January 22, 1867, the U.S.

Congress authorized a territorial jail in Washington Territory. In 1870, the U.S. Attorney General dispatched a representative to the Northwest to select a site. He arrived in Steilacoom, met with the federal judges located there, and formed a citizens committee to find a location. The group negotiated unsuccessfully with the owners of Ketron Island. Then, James Emons Smith offered 27 acres of his site on McNeil at no cost. The government accepted his offer although he was paid $100 for the land. The jail officially opened in 1875, and its first three prisoners arrived in May. The government made continual purchases of land on the island and completed the final purchase in 1936 when the remainder of the private land was condemned, including all of Pitt and Gertrude Islands (Price 7-19; McDonald, Lucile. "McNeil-Puget Sound's Forbidden Island." *Seattle Times*. June 26, 1960. Magazine Section p 4, 5). In 1846, Inskip called this Duntz Island [24] for Capt. John A. Duntz of H.M.S. *Fisgard* (Meany, *Origin* 8).

Meadow Point [19] #662, 1867, U.S. Coast Survey
Located on the eastern side of Puget Sound a mile north of Shilshole Bay, the name is perhaps descriptive of its appearance in 1867.

Meadowdale
Located on the eastern side of Puget Sound about eleven miles north of Shilshole Bay, Robert Maltby named it on April 2, 1904, ". . . because cleaned up and into grass it would be one vast meadow," (Meany, *Origin* 162, 163). The short wharf and post office were mentioned in the 1909 *Pacific Coast Pilot* (152).

Menendez, Puerto de [1] 1790, Quimper
See Point Partridge

Meridian
Located on the western end of McNeil Island, it was named for the Willamette Meridian which was the standard surveying line for the region. The post office in the logging community operated from 1890 to 1936 (TPL website).

Merrifield Cove [13m] #2689, 1904
Located in North Bay on the eastern side of San Juan Island, south of Friday Harbor, it was named by J. J. Gilbert for William Merrifield who owned the land along the cove (Wood 106). It is shown on his

Descriptive Report #2301 and t-sheet #2301 (http://riverhistory.ess.washington.edu/tsheets/reports/t2301.pdf, p 5). According to the December 31, 1896 edition of *The Islander* (p 3): "The south end boasts of the oldest man in San Juan County, to the person of Grandpa Merrifield, father of Stafford Merrifield, of this place, now in his 96th year, and still hale and hearty." Grandpa died in mid-July 1899, at his son's home (*The San Juan Islander*, July 20, 1899, p 3).

Miami Beach
Located on the eastern shoreline of Hood Canal, just south of Seabeck Bay, Charles Hall purchased the land in 1905 for delinquent taxes (Perry, *Seabeck* 190, 196). The origin of the name is unknown.

Midchannel Bank [22] #6450, 1909
It is located off the northern side of Marrowstone Point. Other than the fact that the shoal extends to the middle of the channel, the origin of the name is unknown.

Middle Bank [13a] #2689, 1859, Richards
Located southwest of Cattle Point, San Juan Island, Richards left no reason for the name.

Middle Channel [14a] #2840, 1861, Richards
See San Juan Channel.

Middle Channel [13a] #2689, 1859, Richards
Current U.S. charts and [13a] locate the channel as the preferred southern entrance from the Strait of Juan de Fuca to San Juan Channel between San Juan and Lopez Islands. The words are written vertically below the narrowing water between Cattle Point and Lopez Islands. After recording it in that location, Richards moved it in 1865 [15a] and placed it in the southern portion of San Juan Channel. The words were written between Griffin Bay and Lopez Island. According to the 1846 agreement between the U.S. and England, the boundary ". . . continued westward along the 49th parallel of north latitude to the middle of the channel which separates the continent from Vancouver's Island . . ." (Treaty between Her Majesty and the United States of America for the Settlement of the Oregon Boundary, Signed at Washington, June 15, 1846: T. R. Harrison, 1846). While this agreement resolved part of the issue, it left open to interpretation the meaning of "the middle of the channel" as there were two major channels to pick from: Haro Strait and Rosario Strait. Wood (106, 107) speculated that the reason Richards moved Middle Channel was to provide the arbitrator a third option as to the meaning of the agreement. While the British were pushing for Rosario Strait, they would have been pleased if San Juan Channel had been chosen. Wilkes on [7a] named this Little Belt Passage for the H.M.S. *Little Belt* who battled with the *President* commanded by Commodore John Rodgers in 1811. In 1841, Wilkes wrote the name from the south end of San Juan Channel nearly to the Geese Islets (Blumenthal, *Charles Wilkes* 75).

Middle Ground, The
Located in Sequim Bay, this is an intertidal shoal about a quarter mile from the entrance. That is, it is formed by currents circulating through the bay. The origin of the name is unknown.

Middle Point [10] #51, 1854, U.S. Coast Survey
See McCurdy Point.

Middle Point [7e] #158, 1841, Wilkes
Located on the eastern side of Whidbey Island in Holmes Harbor and just south of Honeymoon Bay, Wilkes left no reason for the 1841 name. Wilkes did not include this name in his *Narrative*, but it is shown on his chart. It is unnamed on current charts and not recognized by the U.S. Board on Geographic Names.

Middle Point
Located on Rich Passage, it was likely named for its location between Point Glover and Orchard Point.

Middle Point
Located in Clallam Bay, it is the "middle point" between Sekiu and Slip Point, which perhaps explains the name.

Middle Waterway
One of the waterways located on Commencement Bay, it was named for its location, halfway between the City Waterway and the Puyallup Waterway (Reese, *Origins* 75).

Midille Point [7p] #150, 1841, Wilkes
See Crane Point.

Miemois Creek
Flowing into the eastern side of Manzanita Bay on the western side of Bainbridge Island, it was named for Anders Miemois Anderson, the first settler in Manzanita. Anderson was born in Finland in 1853 where he and his wife Anna had three children. Anderson left the family in 1881 and headed to America. Working his way westward, he finally arrived on Bainbridge Island in 1883 and found work at the Port Blakely Mill. He settled in Manzanita Bay and built a cabin and sawmill powered by the creek. His family rejoined him in late 1899, and his homestead was granted in 1904. Both Anna and Anders died in 1933 at the family home. At its December 1, 2006 meeting, the Washington State Board on Geographic Names approved the name. The U.S. Board followed in 2007 (from Washington State Board Files).

Migley, Point [7d] #146, 1841, Wilkes; [7o] #157, 1841, Wilkes
See Priest Point.

Migley, Point [7a] #145, 1841, Wilkes
Located at the northern end of Lummi Island, in 1841 Wilkes spelled this Migly in his *Narrative* but reflected it as Migley on his chart. Regardless, he honored crew member William Migley (Meany, *Origin* 221). Apparently, some maps reflected the name as Midgley. The U.S. Board on Geographic Names corrected this in 1893 but used the name Migley Point. In 1977, the Board changed it to Point Migley.

Mill Bight
Located on the Nisqually Reach in Baird Cove, the origin of the name is unknown.

Mill Creek
The creek runs into Isabella Lake, south of Shelton, and continues from the lake into Hammersley Inlet, four miles east of Shelton. On the inlet, it was the site of a sawmill owned by Michael Simmons and a man named Gosnell. The entire creek on both sides of Isabella Lake was originally named Gosnell Creek [23]. The U.S. Board on Geographic Names approved that name in 1938. The name was first reflected on an 1880 USC&GS topographic survey. However, the Board reversed itself in 1968 and adopted Mill Creek for the stretch between the lake and the Hammersley Inlet (GNIS files).

Mill Point [22] #6450, 1909
Located on the western side of Discovery Bay, Wilkes first named this Helix Point [7b] in 1841. He did not include this name in his *Narrative*, but it is shown on his chart. Davidson referenced it as Point Discovery in the 1889 *Pacific Coast Pilot* (535). It was later named for the sawmill founded there in 1858 by S. B. Mastick and associates from San Francisco (Roe, *Ghost* 76, 77). Davidson referenced the sawmill in both the 1869 and 1889 *Pacific Coast Pilots* but not the new name. He also noted: "The Port Discovery mills reported for 1884 their output as 25,000,000 feet of lumber, 12,000 piles, and 8,000,000 laths, of a total value of $346,000. They have a capacity of 100,000 to 120,000 feet of lumber a day," (1889 *Pacific Coast Pilot* 535). In 1941, the U.S. Board on Geographic Names approved the current name over Wilkes'.

Miller Bay

Miller Bay
Located on the northwestern side of Port Madison, a Mr. Miller built a store and logged in the surrounding area perhaps in the 1880s. Fifty years later, some locals still remembered the "old drunk" and were disappointed that the bay would be named for him. He moved on, and the first permanent settler was Henry Willimott and his wife in 1894 (Carlson 30). It was originally named Squaib Bay [22] by a 1915 Board decision. Squaib meant "little bay branching off big bay." The U.S. Board on Geographic Names decided upon Miller Bay in 1937 (GNIS files).

Miller Bay
Located on the eastern end of Deception Pass, just west of Yokeko Point, it was apparently named after Warren E. Miller who homesteaded the property (Hamilton, Scott, Jan. 2, 2012 email to author). The name is not reflected on current charts, but it is recognized by the U.S. Board on Geographic Names.

Miller Peninsula
This is the peninsula between Discovery and Sequim Bays, named for an early settler/logger (Hitchman 188).

Miller Point
It is located on the northern side of Hammersley Inlet. According to the 1892 Mason County census, the extended family of Francis and Sarah Miller lived in the Sheldon precinct. Their relationship to Miller Point is unknown.

Miller Point
See Polnell Point.

Millers Point
See Sylvan.

Millville
Located on the western shoreline of Gig Harbor, it was the local name for the sawmill area. Arriving from Croatia, Joseph Dorotich settled in Gig Harbor and married 16-year-old Caroline Jerisich, the daughter of Samuel and Annie (see Gig Harbor). In 1877, the couple began buying waterfront property in the harbor together with Caroline's father and John and Josephine Novak. The property was subdivided into town lots. Joseph and Caroline retained four of these lots and built a home on one. It still stands at the corner of Dorotich Street and Harborview Drive (http://www.gigharbormuseum.org/PenPioneerDorotich.html)

Milwaukee Waterway
One of the waterways on Commencement Bay, it takes its name from the railroad.

Minnesota Reef
Located on the eastern side of San Juan Island, east side of the Madrona Peninsula, and opposite Turn Island, the point was named in 1898 by Professor Josephine E. Tilden from the University of Minnesota (Meany, *Origin* 167). An earlier name that didn't last was Culver Point for Fred N. Culver who bought the land from Alvin J. Paxon in 1895 for $400 (Lange). Lange also found a reference of the *Minnesota* that foundered there carrying a load of clams.

Minor Island [17] #27, 1862, U.S. Coast Survey
Located near Smith Island, the U.S. Coast Survey named the island in 1854 but left no reason for the name. According to Davidson: "A very small, low islet called Minor, exists one mile northeast of Smith's island, and at very low tides is connected with it by a narrow ridge of boulders and rocks," (*Report* 429). *See also* Smith Island.

Minter Creek
Flowing into the western shoreline of Carr Inlet, Lucinda and George Minter settled on the creek in 1882. Minter Valley is also named for the family (*A History* 60). Lucinda became the postmaster in 1885. They operated a hotel and charged $1.50-$2.00 a night (Slater 29).

Misery Point [22] #6450, 1909
Located at the eastern entrance to Seabeck Bay, Wilkes labeled this in 1841 as if there were two points. He called the outer one Scabock Point [7d], [7j], and the inner one Sanum Point [7j]. He spelled it Samum in his *Narrative* (324). Today's charts reflect the single name only, perhaps based upon difficulties faced by early pioneers.

Mission Beach
Located north of Everett, Mission Beach runs from the southern entrance of Tulalip Bay almost to Priest Point. Wilkes originally named the north end of it Bill Point [7o] in 1841 but left no reason for the name. The community of Mission, as well as the beach, was for Father Chirouse's Catholic Mission established in 1858 at Priest Point. The mission was torn down in 1904, and the community name fell into disuse (TPL website).

Mission Creek [23] #6460, 1905
Located on the northern shore of Hood Canal near Lynch Cove, the name came from the mission established by Father E. C. Chirouse (Eells, 12).

Mitchell Bay
Located off the western side of San Juan Island, the origin of the name is unknown. According to Wood (107, 108), it first appeared on U.S. chart #6381 in 1901. It also appears on the 1921 Admiralty chart [16c]. Wood related the story that an Indian fisherman named Charlie Mitchell lived there and the name gained local use. Lange found a reference to G. Mitchell, a farmer from Connecticut, age 31, as reflected on the 1860 census. He also suggested that it could have been named for J. Mitchell, the supernumery surgeon aboard the H.M.S. *Ganges* in 1859. A local name was Snug Harbor, apparently a collecting point for the Friday Harbor Labs.

Mitchell Point
Located at Annapolis in Sinclair Inlet, it was named for the early settler John Mitchell.
See also Annapolis.

Monroe, Point

Monroe, Point [7d] #146, 1841, Wilkes; [7q] #156, 1841, Wilkes
Located at the southern entrance to Port Madison, Wilkes named this in 1841 as well as Points Jefferson and Madison for the U.S. Presidents (Meany, *Origin* 221).

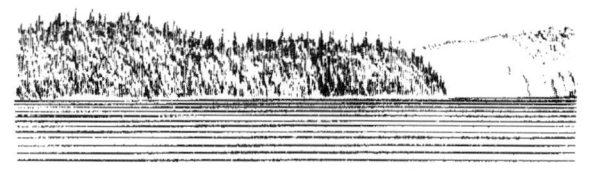

Point Monroe

Monroe Landing
Located on the eastern side of Whidbey Island on the north side of Penn Cove, opposite Coopeville, it was named for A. W. Monroe who settled on the land (Hitchman, 191). The name is not reflected on current charts.

Moody, Point [7d] #146, 1841, Wilkes; [7i] #147, 1841, Wilkes
See Johnson Point.

Moody Hills [14a] #2840, 1861, Richards
See Tiptop Hill.

Moore, Point [7d] #146, 1841, Wilkes; [7m] #160, 1841, Wilkes
See Duwamish Head.

Moore Bluff [24] #1947, 1849, Inskip
See Devils Head.

Moralesa, Isla de [3] 1791, Eliza
See Stuart Island.

Morros, Islas
See Burrows Island.

Morse Creek
Located east of Port Angeles, it flows into the Strait of Juan de Fuca. It was named for David Watterman Morse, a storekeeper, who was born on the creek in 1863 (Hitchman 193). The 1870 Clallam County census lists him as Davis Morse. In his 1907-8 survey and Descriptive Reports #2857, 2858 and 2859, W. B. Dunning wrote (http://riverhistory.ess.washington.edu/tsheets/reports/t2857.pdf, p.2): "At the first creek west of signal Bluff, at Green Point, and at Morse Point, the bluff turns sharply inland and valleys, the widest about ½ wide at Morse Point, extend inland, the shoreline in these places showing wooded instead of the bare bluff color." Morse Creek is recognized by the U.S. Board on Geographic Names but not Morse Point.

Morses Cove [7a] #145, 1841, Wilkes
See Fishing Bay.

Morses Island [7a] #145, 1841, Wilkes
See Battleship Island.

Mosquito Bay
See Manzanita.

Mosquito Bay
Located outside Mitchell Bay on the western side of San Juan Island, the name likely came from Mosquito Pass.

Mosquito Pass [13a] #2689, 1859, Richards
Located on the northwest side of San Juan Island, the pass is the southerly entrance into Roche Harbor between Henry and San Juan Islands. Richards provided no reason for the name, but Wood (108) believes it was likely descriptive.

Mouatt Reef [13b] #2689, 1861, Richards
Located in Cowlitz Bay off Waldron Island, this was one of many locations named after William A. Mouat, master mariner and trader for the Hudson's Bay Company. Mouat was born in London in 1821 and arrived on the West Coast in 1845 aboard the brigantine *Mary Dare*. He traded between the coast and Hawaii for several years, was an acting pilot at the Columbia River bar, and continued to serve in British Columbia during various periods until his death in Knight Inlet in 1871 (Walbran 344).

Mountain Lake
At 198 acres and a mile in length, it is located on Orcas Island west of Mount Pickett and south of Mount Constitution. It is part of the Moran State Park and is the primary water supply for Olga and Doe Bay. It is the largest lake in San Juan County (Lange).

Mountain View
According to the 1909 *Pacific Coast Pilot* (147), it is located "1 mile northward from Seabeck, has a landing wharf built out 100 feet, where wood and water can be obtained." The local name likely came from its view of the Olympic Mountains across Hood Canal. The name does not appear to be in use today.

Mountain View Beach
Located on Camano Island on the western shoreline of Port Susan, the name perhaps originates from the view.

Mud Bay
Located off Fossil Bay on Sucia, it was likely named for the mud flats which form at low tide.

Mud Bay
Located west of Phinney Bay in Dyes Inlet, the name may be descriptive.

Mud Bay [13h] #2689, 1888
Located on the eastern side of Lopez Island at the south end of Lopez Sound, the name is likely descriptive.

Mud Bay
Located at the southern end of Eld Inlet, the name appears on topo maps but not on charts. The name is descriptive (Palmer, 55). *See* Eld Inlet.

Mueller Park
It is located at the western end of Penn Cove, Whidbey Island, on Barstow Point. The community was platted in 1946, and a state park remains today (U.S. Board on Geographic Names, Project Ph 5905, Jan. 27, 1960). The origin of the name is unknown.

Mud Cat Point
Located in Little Skookum Inlet at The Narrows, the origin of the name is unknown.

Mukilteo
Located on the eastern shoreline of Admiralty Inlet, Jacob D. Fowler and Morris H. Frost built a trading post and primitive saloon at Elliot Point in 1858. Fowler and a fellow named Brunn previously operated a saloon and hotel at Ebey's Landing on Whidbey Island. As the operation was losing money, Fowler went into business with Frost at Mukilteo. While Frost was busy in Port Townsend as the customs inspector, Fowler ran the business. For a time, the trading post was the county seat and only voting precinct in Snohomish County. Fowler served as the county auditor. This was short-lived as he explained in a letter to Winfield Ebey dated July 21, 1861: "Our election is all over. It passed off very quiet, no fighting or drunkenness. I am a defeated candidate for auditor. Ferguson beat me 3 votes. We also lost the county seat by 3 votes. Some of our boys did not turn out and many was off at work. They gave me county commissioner instead of auditor," (McDonald). When Fowler established the post office in 1862, he became the first postmaster and named the community for the Indian word meaning "good camping ground." When Frost was ultimately

replaced as customs inspector, he moved to Mukilteo to help run the business that now included a hotel. He later served three terms as a legislator. In 1873, Mukilteo attracted a salmon saltery owned by V. T. Tull. That same year, Joseph Butterfield established a brewery that was later purchased by Frost and Fowler. They brewed 500 barrels of lager annually until it burned down in 1882. The area also attracted the first fish cannery on Puget Sound started by George T. Myers in 1877 (Humphrey 39; Meany, *Origin* 181; McDonald, Lucile. "Mukilteo's Early Trading-Post Era." *Seattle Times*. Feb. 23, 1964. Magazine Section p 2). Hilbert (344) indicated that there was no factual support for the name "good camping ground" and believes the origin of the name is truly unknown. In 1897, the U.S. Board on Geographic Names approved the name Muckilteo [22] because of predominate local usage. But in 1912, the board discarded variants including Muckilteo, Muckleteo, and Muckiltoe and decided that Mukilteo was prevalent in local use (*Decisions*).

Mulno Cove
Located on the eastern side of San Juan Island, on Griffin Bay, it was named by J. J. Gilbert for the Thomas M. Mulno family who lived there (Wood 108, 109). Mr. Gilbert surveyed in the area in 1897 and prepared Descriptive Report #2301 (http://riverhistory.ess.washington.edu/tsheets/reports/t2301.pdf, p 5). It is also shown on t-sheet #2301 from 1897 (http://kaga.wsulibs.wsu.edu/cdm-maps/sanjuantsheet.html). Plats from 1875 of San Juan County reflect the land owner as Thos. Mulne.

Mummy Rocks
See Geese Islets.

Munson Point
Located on the northern side of Hammersley Inlet across from Shelton, the origin of the name is unknown.

Murden Cove [19] #662, 1867
Located on the eastern side of Bainbridge Island, Davidson indicated that the U.S. Coast Survey named it in 1856 (1889 *Pacific Coast Pilot* 609). Harry Winchester established two logging camps along the water. The area was first settled by Dona Falk in 1876 who moved into one of the abandoned camps on the south shore. He relocated to the north shore in 1878 and built a house on the beach. He and his wife Matilda raised vegetables and berries and sold them at Port Madison. The first informal name of the bay was for him. As the community grew, it was known as Murdens Cove. The name was supposedly originated by one of the early surveyors. By 1892, town folk established the post office. They selected the name Rollins for a local beach squatter. Some, however, complained about his seedy character. Eventually, all agreed on the name of Rolling Bay, and Murden Cove was relegated to the bay in front (Marriott 68-71). The Salish name for the cove was "bad water, i.e., rough water" (Hilbert et. al., 225).

Musam Place
Referring to Jackson cove, Wilkes wrote: "At the head of the harbor is Musam Place, where a small creek enters, from which good water may be obtained." He does not show this name on his chart. Instead, he simply lists it as "watering place" (Wilkes, *Narrative* 324). The creek might be the Spencer Creek. Musam Place is not recognized by the U.S. Board on Geographic Names. According to Hale (639), it is Chinook for "to lie down or to sleep."

Mushroom Rock
Located ½ mile east of Cape Flattery, it was likely named for its shape. In its March 8, 1985 meeting, the Washington State Board on Geographic names resolved a naming issue: Mushroom vs. Mushroom Rock. The latter was approved in Docket 293. The U.S. Board followed in 1986.

Musqueti Point [7d] #146, 1841, Wilkes
Located on the eastern side of Hood Canal, at The Great Bend, Wilkes spelled this Musquiti in his *Narrative* (323) but Musqueti on his chart. The spelling on current charts is consistent with Wilkes' chart. He left no reason for the name. Bright (311) wrote that it was Twana for "having cedar trees."

Mustakumwode
It is located on the eastern side of Hood Canal, about a mile north of Musquetti Point. In the mid-1930s, the property was owned by the Wallace Young family. One afternoon, a Skokomish Indian and his wife

landed on shore and began digging for clams. The Indian's name coincidentally was Joe Young. When asked about the name of the place, Joe responded, "*Mustakumwode*" which means "land of many clams" (from Washington State Board Files, Cougar Spit). The name is not officially accepted by the state or federal government.

Mutiny Bay [22] #6450, 1909
Located off the southwestern side of Whidbey Island, north of Double Bluff, it was first settled in November 1853 by Raphael Brunns. By 1859, he built a home and a trading post on 320 acres. He and his wife raised three children. Brunns went broke about 1860, and Nathaniel Porter acquired the property. Porter was born in Boston in 1840 and shipped out by his tenth birthday. After several years at sea he joined the army. He later worked his way westward and filed for a homestead in Port Ludlow. The Puget Sound Pulp and Timber Company (Pope and Talbot) also sought the land, replete with its virgin timber. Pope and Talbot was coincidentally foreclosing on Brunns' property. They bargained with Porter to trade his homestead at Port Ludlow for the Brunns land plus some cash. Thus, only twenty years old, Porter had a sizable bank account as well as a large tract on South Whidbey. Over the years he continued to buy land, ultimately acquiring about 1,000 acres (Cherry I: 58-72, 118). The U.S. Coast Survey named it in 1855 (Davidson, *Report* 443). According to Hitchman (203), the name resulted from a group of British soldiers who deserted their ship in the cove.

Mya Cove
Located on the eastern side of Davis Bay, Lopez Island, the small cove is due east of Buck Island. The origin of the name is unknown.

Mystery Bay [22] #6450, 1909
Located off the western side of Marrowstone Island in Kilisut Harbor, it was used by early rumrunners to avoid the authorities unfamiliar with the area. When they disappeared through Kilisut Harbor and into the small bay, their location was always a mystery (TPL website). Alternatively, Hitchman (203) indicated that the name was selected by Neah Bay sealing vessels that wintered in the bay. Their reason is unknown. Paul K. Hubbs purchased 196 acres in 1863 on the northern side of Mystery Bay. Hubbs ultimately settled in Friday Harbor but hired a man by the name of Schultz to clear and live on the land. Hubbs' neighbor was J. J. Hunt, who owned the Cosmopolitan Hotel in Port Townsend. Hunt raised strawberries on his land until 1871 when he sold to James Nicholls who established a truck farm. In the 1880s, the Puget Sound Fish Preserving Company, located north of Mystery Bay, was a major employer in the area, smoking and canning up to 700 kegs of fish daily (Bean 9, 10).

Naguamos Island [7e] #158, 1841, Wilkes
See Reservation Head.

Naika Point [7j] #153, 1841, Wilkes
Located on the western side of Jackson Cove, Wilkes left no reason for the 1841 name (Wilkes, *Narrative* 324). It is neither named on current charts nor recognized by the U.S. Board on Geographic Names.

Nampa Point [7l] #159, 1841, Wilkes
It is located on the southeastern side of Point Roberts. Wilkes left no reason for the 1841 name which appeared only on his chart. Bright (311) indicated that it was a Shoshone word for "foot." It is neither named on current charts nor accepted by the U.S. Board on Geographic Names.

Narrows Bridge
The bridge spanned the three-quarter mile wide Narrows. The first bridge was known as Galloping Gertie. It collapsed November 7, 1940 in a 40 mph wind, four months after completion. The replacement took another ten years to complete.

Navy Archipelago [7a] #145, 1841, Wilkes
"Navy Archipelago is a collection of 25 islands, having the Straits of Fuca on the south, the Gulf of Georgia on the north, the Canal de Arro on the west, and Ringgold's Channel on the east," (Wilkes, *Narrative* 306). Wilkes' 1841 name for the San Juan Islands honors the U.S. Navy. The name is not currently used nor is it recognized by the U.S. Board on Geographic Names.

Seal Rock | Neah Bay W entrance | Waadah Island | Cape Flattery

Neah Bay [7b] #148, 1841, Wilkes
Located about four miles east of Cape Flattery on the Strait of Juan de Fuca, it was originally named *Nuñez Gaona* by Quimper in 1790 [1] (Wagner 126). Early fur traders called it Poverty Cove. Wilkes gave us Neah Harbour in 1841. Later in his *Narrative* and on one chart [7c], he called it Scarborough Harbor, for Capt. James Scarborough, Commander of the *Cadboro* and a Hudson's Bay Company employee who assisted Wilkes (Meany, *Origin* 184). Davidson commented: "The bay is about a mile and a quarter long S.SE. and the same in width at the entrance. The western side is high, precipitous, and bordered by craggy, outcropping rocks 300 or 400 yards from shore. The 3-fathom curve ranges about 600 yards from the foot of the bluff. The general direction of this side is SE. for one mile, when the hills suddenly cease and a low shore, with sand beach backed by woods, curves gradually to the NE. by E for a mile and a quarter to Ba-ad-dah Point, formed by a spur of the hills," (*Report* 416). The name of the bay was approved over the variant Neeah in 1896 in a U.S. Board on Geographic Names. The community of Neah Bay takes its name from the bay. The Board approved that name in 1916.

Neah Island [7b] #148, 1841, Wilkes; [7c] #144, 1841, Wilkes
See Waadah Island.

Nearns Point
Located at the northwestern end of Fox Island, Wilkes originally named this Tomos Point [7h] in 1841. He left no reason for the name. Wilkes did not include this name in his *Narrative*, but it is shown on his chart. The current name became official over Wilkes' name by a decision of the U.S. Board on Geographic Names in 1957. Based upon the recommendations of local residents, the name honors Orville J. Nearns who died in 1954. He left his estate for the purpose of operating and maintaining a DeMolay Boys Camp on the property which included the spit (GNIS files). Near the point, Augustus Lowe, Walter S. Bowen, and S.F. Sahm founded the Fox Island Brick Manufacturing Company in 1884. They located on three hundred acres of land owned by Lowe who previously worked at the Puyallup Indian Reservation as an agent and teacher. The yard employed about fifty men. In 1886, they reorganized under the name of Fox Island Clay Works. The primary market was Tacoma during its building boom. Competition in the 1890s and a declining market forced the yard out of business in 1894. Locals attempted to start it up again, but by 1911, because of an exhausted supply of clay and rising demand for concrete, the brickyard closed for good (Perish 13-17).

Neck Island [16b] #602, 1869, Pender
See Posey Island.

Neck Point [14b] #2840, 1862, Richards
It is a small neck of land located on the southeastern end of San Juan Island, north of Goose Island. Richards called it Neck Rock initially [14a] but changed the name to Neck Point on [14b], ostensibly because he later discovered it was not a rock. He likely named it for its appearance.

Neck Point [14a] #2840, 1861, Richards
Located on the western side of Shaw Island, Richards perhaps named it for its shape.

Neck Rock [14a] #2840, 1861, Richards
See Neck Point.

Ned Islet [7i] #147, 1841, Wilkes
See Eagle Island.

Neelim Point [7d] #146, 1841, Wilkes
It is located just short of the southwestern end of Hood Canal, at Potlatch. Wilkes left no reason for the 1841 name. The name is neither reflected on current charts nor recognized by the U.S. Board on Geographic Names.

Neil Bay
Neil Bay, presumably named for an early settler, is located on the northern end of San Juan Island, inside and on the eastern side of Davison Head. The name is not formally recognized, but Neil Bay Drive, which fronts it, is listed on maps. It was originally named Jeff Davis Harbor by George Gibbs who anchored there in the revenue cutter *Jefferson Davis* in 1859. The cutter was sold in 1862 to Grennan and Craney at the Utsalady mill for $2,920 (Lange found this in a 1859 Gibbs memoir; Wright 60).

Neill Point [7d] #146, 1841, Wilkes; [7g] #155, 1841, Wilkes
Located on the southeastern end of Vashon Island, Wilkes honored crew member William Neill in 1841. Wilkes did not include this name in his *Narrative*, but it is shown on his chart (Meany, *Origin* 185). The Salish name for the point was "cutting the head off" (Hilbert et. al., 238).

Nellita
Located between Tekiu Point and Seabeck on Hood Canal, it was originally known as Browns Cove after an early settler Arthur Brown. Ralph Brueger settled there and named it in 1900 for his wife Nellie (Hitchman 206).

Nelson Bay [16c] #602, 1921
Located off the southeastern side of Henry Island, it was likely named after Ole Nelson, an early settler (Wood 109). Wood found this name on [16c] as well as U.S. chart #6381 published in 1901. Lange found a reference to Edward Nelson who lived on the bay. He married Mary J. Perkins in 1888, and he jumped bail in 1904 for smuggling whiskey. T-sheet #1962 at http://kaga.wsulibs.wsu.edu/cdm-maps/sanjuantsheet.html reflects the name Christian Nelson as the owner.

Nesika Bay
It is a local name for a bay to the west of Lemolo near the entrance to Liberty Bay. Bonnie Chrey, a researcher with the Kitsap County Historical Society, uncovered a 1909 pamphlet of the Chinook jargon written by Frederic Long. Mr. Long believed the name to mean "we, us, or ours" (Mar. 11, 2011 email to author from Ms. Chrey).

Nevils Slough
See Hatt Slough.

New Channel [13a] #2689, 1859, Richards
Located immediately north of Spieden Island, Richards' reason for this name is unknown.

New Chicago
Located on the western side of Whidbey Island in Admiralty Bay, it was platted in 1890. It was to be the terminus of the Chicago & Skagit Valley Railroad, hence the name (Hitchman 2007). It is not recognized by the U.S. Board on Geographic Names.

New Market
See Tumwater.

New Georgia
When Vancouver took formal possession of the explored territory at Tulalip Bay, he named it New Georgia for the King of England. This encompassed the area from Point Arena in California to the Strait of Juan de Fuca, plus the inland waters. This name is not recognized by the U.S. Board on Geographic Names (Vancouver 289).

New Shoal
See Argyle Shoal.

Newell, Point [7b] #148, 1841, Wilkes
It is located in Neah Bay at about the western terminus of the current breakwater. The name is neither reflected on current charts nor recognized by the U.S. Board on Geographic Names. Wilkes did not include this 1841 name in his *Narrative*, but it is shown on his chart.

Newellhurst Creek
The one mile creek flows through Kingston into Appletree Cove. It runs through and is named for the Newellhurst farm. In its May 11, 2007 meeting, the Washington State Board on Geographic Names approved the name. The U.S. Board followed later in the year (from Washington State Board Files).

Newhall
See Rosario.

Newhall's Point
A small point located at the southern end of Friday Harbor, it was previously named Idlewild. Edward D. Warbass was born in New Jersey and arrived in

Washington via the California gold rush. He was the post sutler for Capt. Pickett in Bellingham and followed Pickett to San Juan Island. He later settled in Friday Harbor at what he called Idlewild. At the conclusion of the boundary dispute, Warbass disassembled one of the American Camp structures (some say it was Pickett's residence) and moved it board by board to his property. In 1860, Whatcom County citizens elected Warbass to the Territorial Legislature. In 1873, when the legislature created the County of San Juan, he served as the county auditor and clerk. Over the years, locals referred to that end of Friday Harbor as Warbass Harbor and the beach along his property as Warbass Beach. In 1906, Warbass sold his 110 acres to Andrew Newhall who had just sold his Rosario property to Robert Moran. Idlewild included a mile of shoreline on Friday Harbor. Warbass moved to Orcas, lived in a log cabin above President Channel, and mined for gold on Turtleback Mountain. He died on Christmas Eve that year at age 82 (Richardson, *Pig* 335; McDonald 45, 46, 64-69; *The San Juan Islander*, October 22, 1904, p 1). Over time, the local name for the point changed over for Andrew Newhall. Newhall sold in 1920 to Leon Little and Al Nash, the owners of the Friday Harbor Drug Co. They built a resort on the point and named it Kwan Lamah, Chinook for "glad hand" or "welcome" (Meany, *Origin* 188; Wood 166; Richardson, *Magic* 38).

Nimrod Point [7h] #154, 1841, Wilkes
Located on the eastern shore of Carr Inlet, north of Horsehead Bay, it is the present location of Kopachuck State Park. Wilkes left no reason for the 1841 name. Wilkes did not include this name in his *Narrative*, but it is shown on his chart. The name is neither reflected on current charts nor recognized by the U.S. Board on Geographic Names.

Nipple Point [7m] #160, 1841, Wilkes
See Weaverline Spit.

Nisqually
Located at the southern end of Puget Sound, the community no longer exists. Around 1880, it was called Maxfield and consisted of a few stores, a hotel, and a railroad station. Sometime later, the name changed to Sherlock. The Northern Pacific Railway finally hung a sign on its station and the community's name officially changed to Nisqually (Pearson, Hank. "Old Nisqually Just Faded Away." *Seattle Times*. Feb. 9, 1964. Magazine Section p 2).

Nisqually Bluff [7d] #146, 1841, Wilkes; [7i] #147, 1841, Wilkes
Located at the southeast end of Puget Sound, the name evidently was derived from the Hudson's Bay Company personnel. In 1824, Work wrote (211): "In the evening passed the Nisqually River which falls in from the E. into a pretty large bay. The shores are steep and bold compounded of clay, a gravel and covered with wood, principally pine, to the water's edge. In several places the wood appears pretty clear and not much chocked with underwood." Wilkes' name is now applied to the bluff, the head [23], the flats [23], the reach [23], and the river [23]. According to Meany (*Origin* 189, 190), the much used word has numerous spellings. One source reflected the word as Squally-o-bish; others spell it Nisqualli, or Askwalli, or Qualliamish, or Squalliamish. In the 1854 Medicine Creek treaty, Governor Stevens spelled it Nisqually. Davidson commented: "Nisqually, 5 miles south of Steilacoom, and on the same side of the Sound, is, at present, a place of no trade nor importance. It was one of the early posts of the Hudson Bay Company, and is still occupied by them," (Davidson, *Report* 451). In 1846, Inskip named the flats for himself [24].

Nisqually Flats [23] #6460, 1905
See Nisqually Bluff.

Nisqually River [7d] #146, 1841, Wilkes; [7i] #147, 1841, Wilkes
See Nisqually Bluff.

Nob Island [14a] #2840, 1861, Richards
Located within the Wasp Islets group off the western side of Shaw Island, Richards left no reason for the name. The U.S. Government owns the island.

Nob Point [13a] #2689, 1859, Richards
See Point Doughty.

Nodule Point [6] 1792, Vancouver
Located on the eastern side of Marrowstone Island, Vancouver provided the name for the "peculiar geological formations." Wilkes renamed this Ariel Point [7a], [7d] in 1841 for the *Ariel*, an American

Nodule Point - North Bluff

Bush Point — Double Bluff — Point No Point — Foulweather Bluff — Nodule Point

ship during the War of 1812 (Meany, *Origin* 190). Wilkes did not include this name in his *Narrative*, but it is shown on his chart. Interestingly, while it clearly was named by Vancouver, Davidson in *Report*, *Directory*, and subsequent *Pacific Coast Pilots* insisted that it was named by the U.S. Coast Survey.

Nordland
Located on Mystery Bay, Marrowstone Island, it was named for Peter F. Nordby who settled there in 1890 (Hitchman 210).

Norma Beach
It is located on the eastern side of Admiralty Inlet about twelve miles north of Shilshole Bay. The origin of the name is unknown.

North Bay [14a] #2840, 1861, Richards
Located on the northwest side of Waldron Island, Richards initially named it North Bay on [14a] but then changed it to North Road on [13c]. North Bay was ultimately retained. Eduard Graignic and Louis LaPorte, originally from Paris, jumped ship in Victoria in the late 1870s. Both married Indian women and settled in North Bay near Fishery Point. They went into the herring business. The families built bonfires on the beach at night which attracted the fish. Then, they would row out and net them. After cleaning, smoking, and packing, they sold them in Victoria. Tragedy stuck the LaPortes when two of their youngest children drowned, and soon after Louis died. Louisa remained on the island and married John Kertula from Finland. They lived about a mile southwest of Point Hammond. Together they had one child. Eduard and Lena Graignic had eleven children. The first, Frank, was born before they settled on Waldron. Their second, Peter, was the first child born on the island in 1884. He quickly learned the ways of the water and could be found sailing the family sloop alone to Victoria for supplies by age seven. Elizabeth (Lizzie) Graignic married William Chevalier (Ludwig 16, 17; Richardson, *Magic* 71).

North Bay [13a] #2689, 1859, Richards
Located off the eastern side of San Juan Island, south of Friday Harbor, Richards did not leave a reason for the name. It is home to the Friday Harbor Sand & Gravel Company.

North Bay
Located at the northern end of Case Inlet off the town of Allyn, the name is perhaps for its location to the inlet. Wilkes originally named this Paun Cove in 1841 [7h]. He did not include this name in his *Narrative*, but it is shown on his chart.

North Beach
Located on the northern end of Orcas Island, it was the site of a surly group of Whites and their Indian wives lead by Col. Enoch May. May smuggled Chinese, opium, and Canadian wool into the islands. His wildest scheme, however, was hoaxing easterners to support Lucy Bean, a supposed orphan, who needed funds to provide schooling to Indian children. Of course there was no such Lucy Bean, but before local islanders could expose the hoax, thousands of dollars rolled in (Jameson 179). It was likely named for its location.

North Beach
Located on the eastern side of Guemes Island, the origin of the name is unknown.

North Beach
Located at the northern end of Whidbey Island near the western entrance to Deception Pass, it was likely named for its location.

North Bluff [7b] #148, 1841, Wilkes; [7n] #149, 1841, Wilkes
This is the bluff to the west of the western entrance to Discovery Bay. Based upon Wilkes' chart, it appears to be the same as Diamond Point. *See* Diamond Point.

North Bluff [7e] #158, 1841, Wilkes
Located along the eastern side of Whidbey Island at the entrance to Holmes Harbor, Wilkes may have named it in 1841 for its proximity to South Bluff, about a mile to the south. Wilkes did not include this name in his *Narrative*, but it is shown on his chart. According to Meany (*Origin* 191), Wilkes honored crew member James North.

North Finger Island
Located in Echo Bay, Sucia Island, the origin of the name is unknown.

North Pacific Rock
Located in Griffin Bay, south of Halftide Rocks, it was named for a steamer which struck it in the late 1880s. Also known as North Star Rock, it was carrying a load of cattle when it struck the rock. All of the animals drowned and floated ashore (McDonald, Lucile. "Rabbit-Hunters 'Take Over' Historic Site." *Seattle Times*. Nov. 20, 1960. Magazine Section p 7). J. J. Gilbert noted the name in his 1897 survey and Descriptive Report #2301 (http://riverhistory.ess.washington.edu/tsheets/reports/t2301.pdf, p 6). He wrote: "One half mile S.S.W. of Half Tide Reef is another dangerous reef. It shows three feet above tides at lowest water. The steamer *North Pacific* struck on this rock several years ago."

North Pass [14a] #2840, 1861, Richards
Located off the southwestern end of Orcas Island, the pass between Steep Point and Reef Island leads into Deer Harbor. The name is perhaps descriptive.

North Point [7c] #144, 1841, Wilkes
See Koitlah Point.

North Road [13c] #2689, 1865
See North Bay.

Northilla
Located at the southern end of Maury Island, the Norton-Hill Company, owned by a Mr. Norton and his partner, Mr. Hill, platted it in 1909. Northilla Beach is recognized by the U.S. Board on Geographic Names. *See also* Rosehilla.

Norths Landing [7e] #158, 1841, Wilkes
Located on the eastern side of Whidbey Island in Holmes Harbor, immediately east of Freeland, in 1841 Wilkes perhaps honored crew member Lieut. James H. North who surveyed in the area. Wilkes did not include this name in his *Narrative*, but it is shown on his chart. The name is neither reflected on current charts nor recognized by the U.S. Board on Geographic Names.

Northwest Island [18] #654, 1866, U.S. Coast Survey
Located outside Deception Pass near the Fidalgo Island western shoreline, the U.S. Coast Survey provided no reason for the name.

Norwegian Point [22] #6450, 1909
Located on the western shoreline of Puget Sound, two miles south of Foulweather Bluff, it was named for the Norwegian origin of most of the settlers.

Nu-Ha-A
See Suquamish.

Nukolowap Point [7d] #146, 1841, Wilkes
See Oak Head.

Numan Point [7h] #154, 1841, Wilkes
See South Head.

Nuñez Gaona [1] 1790, Quimper
See Neah Bay.

Oak Bay [6] 1792, Vancouver
Located along the western shore of Admiralty Inlet, south of Indian and Marrowstone Islands, Vancouver named it in 1792. He wrote: "Whilst detained by this unfavorable weather, some of the young gentlemen in their excursions found several oak trees, of which they produced specimens; but stated that they had not seen any exceeding three or four feet in circumference. In consequence of this valuable discovery, the place obtained the name Oak Cove," (Vancouver 236). An interesting contrast, Davidson wrote: "Vancouver called it Oak Cove, his people having reported that the oak trees stood upon its shores. We have traversed the greater part of the shores but found none," (Davidson, *Report* 444). In 1841, Wilkes named it Port Lawrence [7d], [7p] for James Lawrence who coined the famous battle cry: "Don't give up the ship." Lawrence was killed during the 1813 battle between the *Chesapeake* and *Shannon* (Meany, *Origin* 193). In 1867, James Peter Anderson slipped over the rail of a schooner

anchored off Hadlock. Five years at sea was enough for the 20-year-old Swede, and this land reminded him of home. He hid ashore for ship three days until the departed. Then, hungry, he wandered to a cabin on Oak Bay owned by Lorens P. Hoff. His friendship with Hoff grew to the point where Hoff temporarily deeded him fifty-two of his 158 acres of land in 1869. In 1873, the deed became permanent, and the same year, Anderson received his citizenship papers. Anderson built a four-room cabin on the property, planted fruit trees and berry bushes, raised cattle for milk and meat, and worked at the Hadlock mill (*With Pride* 202, 203).

Oak Harbor
Located off the eastern side of Whidbey Island near the entrance to Penn Cove, Dr. Richard Lansdale named Oak Harbor for the Garry Oaks which grew locally. Lansdale settled at the head of Penn Cove on March 31, 1852. Charlie W. Sumner, Ulrick Freund, and Martin Taftzon were the first to settle in the harbor, filing claims on November 20, 1849. Taftzon from Hammerfest, Norway, married an Indian woman and had two children. During that time, measles were prevalent throughout the community. Before a trip to Olympia, he instructed his wife to take the children to the White man's doctor should they become ill. The children did become sick, but unable to reach the doctor, she took them to the Indian Medicine Man. Unfortunately, both children died as a result of the harsh Indian treatment, which included sweating the patients in a tent and then dipping them in the cold salt water. Upon his return, Taftzon flew into a rage and drove his wife from the cabin. He lived alone for the rest of his life, dying in 1901 (Neil 13, 27). The Salish name for the harbor was "closed mouth" (Hilbert et. al., 360).

Oak Head [22] #6450, 1909
Located at the southern end of the Toandos Peninsula in Hood Canal, Wilkes originally referenced this in his *Narrative* (324) as Nukolowap Point [7d].

Oak Island [13a] #2689, 1859, Richards
Located on the eastern side of West Sound about a mile north from the ferry landing, Richards perhaps named it for the oak trees that grew there. The U.S. Government owns the island.

Oakland & Oakland Bay [23] #6460, 1905
Located at the end of Hammersley Inlet, it was named by the first settlers, William and Elizabeth Morrow, who arrived in 1855. The Morrows claimed 320 acres and named the area and the bay after the numerous oak trees. Morrow established the post office in 1858, but it closed in 1889 (Fredson, *Oakland to Shelton* 12, 13; TPL website).

Observatory Point [9a] #1911, 1849, Kellett
It is located three miles west of Angeles Point along the Strait of Juan de Fuca. In 1790, Quimper named this *Pta de Salví* early on in his exploration. Later, he used *Salvi* to describe Stripped Peak, a couple miles further west (Meany *Origin* 194; Blumenthal, *The Early Exploration* 25). Kellett renamed it in 1847; he likely used it for surveying purposes.

Obstruction Island [7a] #145, 1841, Wilkes
Located on the eastern side of Rosario Strait, Wilkes likely named it in 1841 because it obstructs the passage between Orcas and Blakely Islands. A. P. Randolph recorded the first mining claim on the island in 1890. Conrad Behre built a cabin in 1908. He later sold to Robert Moran (McDonald 189).

Obstruction Passages [13b] #2689, 1861, Richards
Located between Orcas and Blakely Islands, on either side of Obstruction Island, it represents both Obstruction Pass and Peavine Pass. The name was likely from the island, and Obstruction Pass was eventually retained for the northernmost pass.

O'Hara Cove
See Squaw Bay.

Okho River [8a] #1917, 1847, Kellett
See Sail River.

Olalla
The bay and community are located on the western shoreline of Colvos Passage. Peter Puget first explored it in 1792. He wrote: "At the Back of this Place is a Small Lagoon & as the Tide was out the Water was perfectly fresh in it. The Entrance is sufficiently broad to admit the *Chatham*, to go in at high Water as the Tide had by the High Water Mark then fallen fourteen feet," (Puget 195).

According to Meany (*Origin* 196), the word *Olallie* means "berry" in Chinook. Hilbert indicated that *Olallie* is not an Indian word, but *Olalla* was derived from the transliteration of the Salish word meaning "place for drying salmon" (Hilbert et. al., 221). The earliest settler was Joe Fowler and his Indian wife and children. Fowler logged timber off the beach in the mid-1850s. In 1881, the first permanent homesteader arrived. L. P. Larson rowed from Tacoma and selected a homestead. Within weeks, J. B. King settled on an adjacent lot. The following year, James Anderson and his wife began homesteading, and in 1883, T. J. Westerman and Gus Nelson arrived. Locals built the first school around 1895. Prior to that, they held classes in a deserted log cabin during the late 1880s. Around 1911, they bridged across the lagoon and also constructed a dock. Arriving passengers could land rather than being rowed ashore. The town grew slowly, with the addition of a post office, bakery, hotel, garage, warehouse, blacksmith shop, lumber mill, shingle mill, and store. Most residents made their living from fishing, farming, or logging (Bowen et al., V: 124, 125).

Old Man House
See Suquamish.

Old Rock [14e] #2840, 1900
It is located southeast of Dinner Island in North Bay off the eastern side of San Juan Island. The name is neither reflected on current charts nor recognized by the U.S. Board on Geographic Names.

Old Town
See Dungeness.

Old Town Lagoon
Located on the eastern side of San Juan Island, this is the most westerly of the three lagoons. It was likely named after the community of Old Town. *See also* Jakles Lagoon.

Olele Point [7d] #146, 1841, Wilkes; [7f] #151, 1841, Wilkes; [7p] #150, 1841, Wilkes
Located three miles north of Port Ludlow, Wilkes named this in 1841 after the Chinook term meaning "berries" (Meany, *Origin* 196, 197).

Olga
Located on the eastern shoreline of East Sound, William and Sally Moore squatted on a piece of land east of Olga about 1860. William was born near Greenville, South Carolina in 1827. Raised in Georgia, he worked his way to the San Juans via California. He died in 1897, leaving his wife and nine children (*The Islander*, Feb. 25, 1897, p 3). Nearby, John Bowman settled on 160 acres. When Bowman was elected Justice of the Peace of San Juan Island in 1876, he moved to Friday Harbor. In 1890, John Ohlert opened a store, dance hall, and post office and named it for Olga Ohlert, his mother (Richardson, *Pig* 195; McDonald 120). Six years later, Ohlert sold and moved to Colville (*The Islander*, Mar. 12, 1896, p 3).

Oliver, Lake
See Deer Lagoon.

Olivine Hill
McLellan wrote: "The southeast corner of Cypress Island is formed by a symmetrical dome-shaped hill which rises to an elevation of 600 feet. For purposes of description this hill I here called Olivine Hill because it is composed largely of a fresh vitreous variety of dunite, a rock composed almost entirely of the mineral olivine." From the sketchy description, this appears to be near Richards' Broughton Point. While not reflected on current charts, it is recognized by the U.S. Board on Geographic Names.

Olo Bluff [7j] #153, 1841, Wilkes
Located on the western side of Hood Canal, perhaps near Brinnon, Wilkes left no reason for the 1841 name. The name is neither reflected on current charts nor recognized by the U.S. Board on Geographic Names.

Oluman Bluff [7p] #150, 1841, Wilkes
Located south of Port Townsend, Wilkes did not include this name in his *Narrative*, but it is shown on his chart. The name is neither reflected on current charts nor recognized by the U.S. Board on Geographic Names. According to Hale (640), it is Chinook for "old man."

Olympia [23] #6460, 1905
Located at the southern end of Budd Inlet, it was first settled by Levi Lathrop Smith and Edmund Sylvester. In 1846, the partners claimed 2½ sections of land, a portion of which was at the head of Budd Inlet. In 1848, Smith fell out of a canoe and drowned, supposedly as a result of an epileptic attack. Under Oregon Territorial laws, Sylvester inherited all of the property. According to Meany, either Colonel Isaac Ebey or Charles Hart Smith suggested the name after the Olympic Mountains. McDonald stated that it was Ebey (McDonald, Lucile. "1853 Was Year of Political Ambition, Personal Tragedy for Isaac N. Ebey." *Seattle Times*. Feb 26, 1961. Magazine Section p 10). Sylvester platted the town in 1850. (Stevenson 16, 22; Meany, *Origin* 197-199) Davidson wrote: "Olympia is situated at the head of Budd's inlet, which is 6 miles long, three-quarters of a mile wide, and runs nearly south. The shores are steep and wooded, and the head of the bay an immense mud flat, behind which is the town. It acquires prospective importance by being the capital of the Territory, but especially on account of its proximity to the Columbia river valley, and to the headwaters of the Chehalis. There is a saw-mill at New Market, 2 miles south on the Tumwater, and three others in the vicinity, besides one or two grist-mills," (Davidson, *Report* 451). Olympia was selected as the territorial capital in 1860.

Olympic Heights
See Dash Point.

Olympic Mountains
Wilkes referenced the mountain range in his *Narrative* (304). He wrote: "In entering the Strait of Fuca, it must be borne in mind that the prevailing winds are either up or down the strait. If they happen to be in the eastern quarter, they will become more easterly, and the same if in the western quarter. The cause of this is, the high lands which traverse the length of Vancouver Island, on the north, and the Olympic Range, on the south. They attain the height of several thousand feet, and act as a funnel, through which the wind draws either way." Although Wilkes did not show it on any of his charts, his reference may be the first to the name. He may have drawn from John Meares name of Mt. Olympus.

Olympic Shoal
Located in Budd Inlet, it takes its name from the town.

Olympus, Mount
Located on the Olympic Peninsula, it was named on the 4th of July, 1788, by John Meares, an English captain involved early on in the Northwest fur trade. He wrote: "In the Northern quarter it was of a great height, and covered with snow. This mountain, from its very conspicuous situation, and immense height, obtained the name of Mount Olympus," (Meares 262). Vancouver (214) also commented on Apr. 29, 1792: "The most remarkable mountain we had seen on the coast of New Albion, now presented itself. Its summit, covered with eternal snow, was divided into a very elegant double fork, and rose conspicuously from a base of lofty mountains clothed in the same manner, which descended gradually to hills of a moderate height, and terminated like that we had seen the preceding day, in low cliffs falling perpendicularly on a sandy beach; off which were scattered many rocks and rocky islets of various forms and sizes. This was generally considered, though it was not confirmed by its latitude, to be the mount Olympus of Mr. Mears; it being the only conspicuous mountain we had observed on the part of the coast he had visited."

Onamac Point
Located on the western side of Camano Island, it was a 1960s' real estate development that used Camano spelled backwards as its name (Prasse, Karen. Stanwood Area Historical Society. E-mail to author, Apr. 30, 2010).

O'Neal Island [7a] #145, 1841, Wilkes
Located in San Juan Channel, Wilkes did not include this name in his *Narrative*, but it is shown on his chart. Wilkes provided no reason for the 1841 name. Lange has an interesting theory which is consistent with Wilkes' penchant for naming adjacent places for a similar event. Such was the

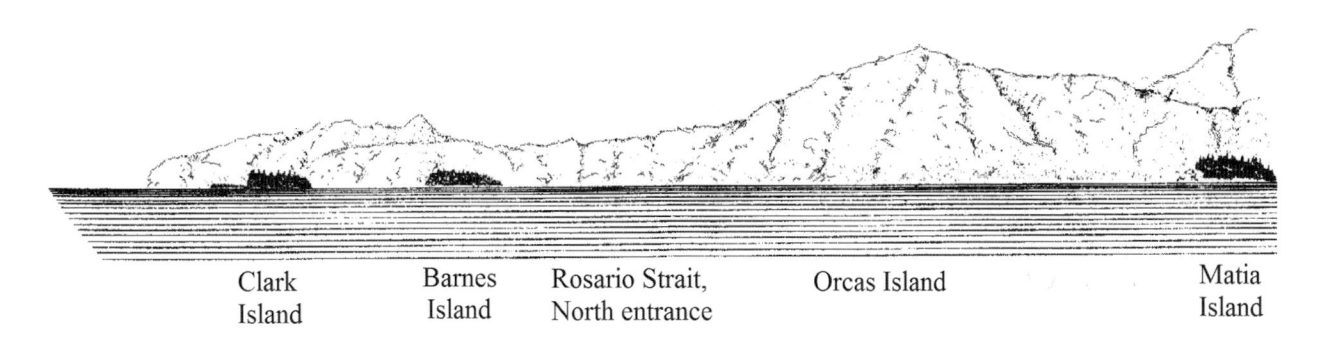

| Clark Island | Barnes Island | Rosario Strait, North entrance | Orcas Island | Matia Island |

case for John O'Neil of Havre de Grace, MD. During the War of 1812, Sir George Cockburn in command of the frigate H.M.S. *Marlborough*, two brigs, four schooners, and several gunboats, threatened Havre de Grace on May 2, 1813. He delayed attacking, and, as a result, the town militia, apparently needed elsewhere, dispersed. Soon after, Cockburn attacked and most of the town folk scattered, except an Irishman named John O'Neil. A Revolutionary War vet, he worked his way to the battery, and with the assistance of the night watchman, he fired off one cannon volley before the British overran the battery. He managed to make it to the center of town and found himself the sole defender. He was captured, while the British destroyed 40 of the 60 homes in the village. O'Neil was released after three days captivity. Commodore John Rodgers, the Commander of the *President*, had an estate in the town. Wilkes named the adjacent President Passage for the *President* and named Rodgers Island (San Juan Island) for the commodore. John Huntington quarried limestone on the island in 1892. It was named the Neal Mine Claim. In 2010, the Washington State Committee on Geographic Names received a proposal on behalf of Jerome and Ann Holbrook Moss, the current owners of the island, to change its name to Avalon Island. According to their correspondence: "Avalon is defined as *'an island paradise in the western seas to which King Arthur went to his death.'* Avalon is fitting because the island is a paradise and it is located in the western seas of the United States." In their Nov. 28, 2011 meeting, the Committee denied the proposal.

Ontario Roads [7a] #145, 1841, Wilkes
See San Juan Channel.

Open Bay [13a] #2689, 1859, Richards
Located off the south end of Henry Island, Richards likely selected the name because the bay was entirely open to southerly or southwest winds. See Henry Island.

Orcas
The community is located at the ferry landing in Harney Channel. Lange discovered that Joseph Gibson opened the first post office and named the community "Orcas Island." The name was changed to Orcas in 1898.

Orcas Island [8a] #1917, 1847, Kellett
Located in the heart of the San Juan Islands and the largest of the islands (with San Juan Island a close second), in 1841 Wilkes originally named this Hulls Island [7a] for Commodore Isaac Hull, Commander of the *Constitution* during the War of 1812. Kellett named it Orcas after the Viceroy of New Spain, whose full name was Juan Vincente de Güemes Pacheco de Padilla Horcasitas y Aguayo, Conde de Revilla Gigedo. In the very few names placed on his chart, Kellett retained the names reflected by George Vancouver and the early Spanish. With respect to a half dozen new names, in almost all cases Kellett attempted to honor the early Spanish explorers who first surveyed our inland waters (Meany *Origin* 200, 201).

Orcas Knob [13a] #2689, 1859, Richards
Located on the northwestern side of Orcas Island, Richards left no reason for the name. He spelled it "Nob." In 1791, Eliza named this *San Gil* after Francisco Gil y Lemos, then Viceroy of Peru (Blumenthal, *The Early Exploration* 47).

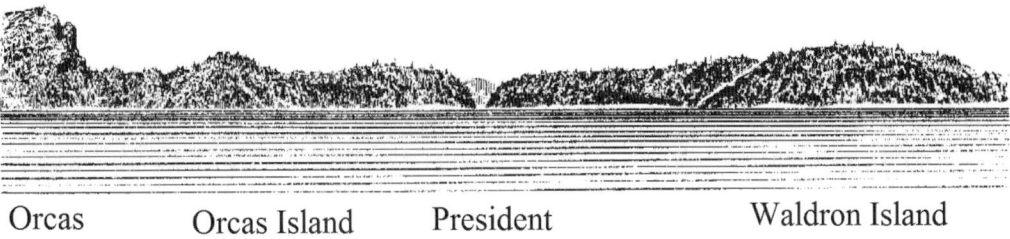

Orcas Knob — Orcas Island — President Channel — Waldron Island

Orchard, Port [6] 1792, Vancouver
Located off the western side of Bainbridge Island, Vancouver wrote (265): "From the west end of this narrow channel the inlet is divided into two branches, one extending to the S. W. about five or six miles, the other to the north about the same distance, constituting a most complete and excellent port, to all appearance perfectly free from danger, with regular soundings from 4 fathoms near the shores, to 9 and 10 fathoms in the middle, good holding ground. It occupied us the whole day to row round it, in doing which we met a few straggling Indians, whose condition seemed excessively wretched and miserable. The country that surrounds this harbour varies in its elevation; in some places the shores are low level land, in others of a moderate height, falling in steep low cliffs on the same beach, which in most places binds the shores. It produces some small rivulets of water, is thickly wooded with trees, mostly of the pine tribe, and with some variety of shrubs. This harbour after the gentleman who discovered it, obtained the name of Port Orchard." The "gentleman" was Vancouver's clerk, H. M. Orchard (Meany *Origin* 228). In his *Narrative* (317), Wilkes wrote: "Port Orchard offers all that could be desired for the safety and equipment of vessels. It will be a convenient place of resort for supplies as well as repairs. It is needless to point out any particular place of anchorage; every part of it may be used, and that resorted to will depend upon future settlements that may be formed."

Orchard, Port
The community of Port Orchard is located on the southern shoreline of Port Orchard. Sidney Stevens purchased the surrounding land from Robert Campbell in 1886. Stevens' son Frederick named the town Sidney [23] for his father when the post office

Orchard, Port

was established late that year. In 1903, townsfolk renamed it for the inlet out front (Meany *Origin* 228; TPL website).

Orchard Point [23] #6460, 1905
Located on the western entrance to Rich Passage, it likely took its name from Port Orchard. The Salish name for the point was "raccoon's water" (Hilbert et. al., 220).

Orchard Rocks [23] #6460, 1905
Located in Rich Passage east of Middle Point, it likely took its name from Port Orchard.

Oro Bay [7d] #146, 1841, Wilkes; [7i] #147, 1841, Wilkes
In his 1841 *Narrative* (322), Wilkes wrote: "On the eastern side is the Bay of Oro, lying opposite to the anchorage at Nisqually: it is nearly semicircular, and half a mile deep." Located off the southern side of Anderson Island, Wilkes left no reason for the name. According to Hale (613), the name is from the San Gabriel Indians and means "warm." The San Gabriel tribe lived in Southern California. In 1846, Inskip named this Rodd Bay [24] for John Rodd, Lieutenant of the *Fisgard* (Meany, *Origin* 202).

Osprey Hill
The hill, or bluff, is located above East Sound on Orcas Island, just north of Rosario Hill. Proponents originally selected the name Osprey Heights. But because that name had commercial connotations according to some, the word hill replaced heights. It was named for an osprey nest which had been there for 30 years. Unfortunately, while the name was under review, a windstorm took off the top ten feet of the snag and with it, the nest. In its December 12, 1997 meeting, Docket 369, the Washington State Board on Geographic Names approved the name. The U.S. Board followed in 1998 (from Washington State Board Files).

Ostrich Bay [7q] #156, 1841, Wilkes
Located off Dyes Inlet, Wilkes presumably named it in 1841 for its shape (Meany, *Origin* 203). Wilkes did not include this name in his *Narrative*, but it is shown on his chart.

Otis
Located in Mud Bay on the eastern side of Lopez Island, the post office was initially established in 1894 and was apparently named for John Edwards, who lived in Richardson but owned land in Mud Bay. Because mail was continually confused with mail for Edmonds, locals changed Edwards to Otis in 1899. Mrs. Elisa A. Sperry, wife of John Sperry (*see also* Sperry Peninsula) was the first postmistress (Lange).

Otso Point [7i] #147, 1841, Wilkes
Located at the northern end of Anderson Island, Wilkes named this in 1841. Wilkes did not include this name in his *Narrative*, but it is shown on his chart. The name comes from the Indian name *Ot sk* which is the largest of the salt water canoes used by them, generally in warfare (Reese, *Origins* 87). According to Hale (576), it is a Tahkali Indian term which means "ear." The Tahkali Tribe lived in British Columbia.

Outer Bay
Located off the southeastern end of Lopez Island, west of Watmough Head and north of Iceberg Point, the origin of the name is unknown.

Owen Point [24] #1947, 1849, Inskip
See Yoman Point.

Oyster Bay

Oyster Bay
Located at the southern end of Totten Inlet, it was named for the Olympic oysters grown there (TPL website). *See also* Totten Inlet.

Oyster Bay
Located at the south end of Ostrich Bay in Dyes Inlet, it was named for the oysters.

Pacheco, Canal de
See Hale Passage.

Padilla Bay [1] 1790, Quimper
Located off the eastern side of Fidalgo Island, Quimper named this after the Viceroy of New Spain, whose full name was Juan Vincente de Güemes Pacheco de Padilla Horcasitas y Aguayo, Conde de Revilla Gigedo. On Quimper's, Pantoja's, and Eliza's charts, it is shown as *Seno de Padilla*. Kellett in 1847 changed it to Padilla Bay [8a].

Pahrmann Creek
The creek flows into Dyes Inlet near Silverdale. H. O. Pahrmann purchased 10 acres in 1908. As of the date of the petition to name the creek, his son John (born in 1907), wife Anna, grandsons, and granddaughter lived on the property. Pahrmann was a member of the school board at Silverdale High School and helped build the Holland Road on the eastern side of Dyes Inlet in the early 1920s. He ran one of the first dairies in the area and delivered milk door to door. He raised cattle and sold produce, poultry, and beef at the Pike Place Market. In its September 28, 2000 meeting, Docket 375, the Washington State Board

on Geographic Names approved the name. The U.S. Board followed in 2001 (from Washington State Board Files).

Palela Bay
Located just south of Potlatch Point on Squaxin Island, the name means "wild cherry tree." In 1982, the Squaxin Tribe submitted the new name for consideration "to simplify navigation and to preserve the history of the tribe." At its June 11, 1982 meeting, the Washington State Board on Geographic Names approved the proposal, Docket 280 (from Washington State Board Files). *See also* Belspeox Point.

Palisi Point [7j] #153, 1841, Wilkes
Located on the western side of Hood Canal, this is the northern entrance to Pleasant Harbor. Wilkes spelled this Pasisi on his chart.

Panama Reef [13a] #2689, 1859, Richards
See Boulder Reef.

Pandora Reef [13a] #2689, 1859, Richards
Located east of Green Point on the Strait of Juan de Fuca, Richards named it for his surveying vessel, the H.M.S. *Pandora*. The name is neither reflected on current charts nor recognized by the U.S. Board on Geographic Names.

Paradise Cove
Located on the northeastern side of Sequim Bay, it is the small cove at Kiapot Point. Travis Spit and a steep cobble beach protect the cove. The source of the name is unknown.

Paradise Cove
Located on the western side of Vashon Island nearly opposite Point Richmond, the origin of the name is unknown.

Park Hill [13a] #2689, 1859, Richards
The hill is located on the eastern side of San Juan Island on the peninsula between Friday Harbor and North Bay. Richards left no reason for the name. This is likely McLellan's Bald Hill.

Park Point [7i] #147, 1841, Wilkes
See Devils Head.

Parker Reef [7a] #145, 1841, Wilkes
Located off the northern end of Orcas Island, in 1841 Wilkes originally charted this as Parkers Rock for crew member George Parker (Meany, *Origin* 208). Wilkes did not include this name in his *Narrative*, but it is shown on his chart. There were two crewmen with the name Parker: George, a captain of the top, and Thomas, a seaman. Lange noted that both deserted prior to Wilkes' arrival on the Northwest Coast. Thus, he speculated the honor actually belonged to Lt. George Parker who served aboard the U.S.S. *Constitution* under Capt. William Bainbridge.

Parks Bay [13m] #2689, 1904
Located on the southeastern side of Shaw Island, it was named for Hughie Park, an early settler who raised cattle. He was an extremely hard-working man in contrast to some of his lazy neighbors who disliked him as a result. After several years of torment, Park decided that life was no longer worth living. Before committing the ultimate act, he shot and killed one of his neighbors who had been pestering him. A short time later, another neighbor arrived to see what had become of his friend and was also killed. This was soon followed by the death of a third man. The sheriff at Friday Harbor, John Kelly, deputized fifteen or so settlers and surrounded Park's home, calling for his surrender. Park responded with gunfire. The siege lasted two days with both sides trading shots at anything that moved. Finally, the sheriff burned the house down. After it cooled, they discovered Park's body with a self-inflicted bullet wound inside (McDonald 136; Richardson, *Pig* 216, 217). In 1998, Marilyn and Fred Ellis, Sr. created conservation easements and donated more than 1,000 acres of land in Parks Bay to the University of Washington and the San Juan Preservation Trust. The head of the bay is now a biological reserve (http://www.pnwlocalnews.com/sanjuans/isw/lifestyle/84061742.html). *See also* Tharald Pond.

Parsons, Camp
See Jackson Cove.

Partridge, Point [6] 1792, Vancouver
Located on the western side of Whidbey Island at the easterly entrance to Admiralty Inlet, in 1791 Quimper named this *Menendez* [1]. Vancouver perhaps named the point for a "partridge-like" animal that he observed on shore. Eliza makes note in his journal of an abundant bird that he observed ". . . like that of

Marrowstone Point   *Point Partridge*   *Bush Point*

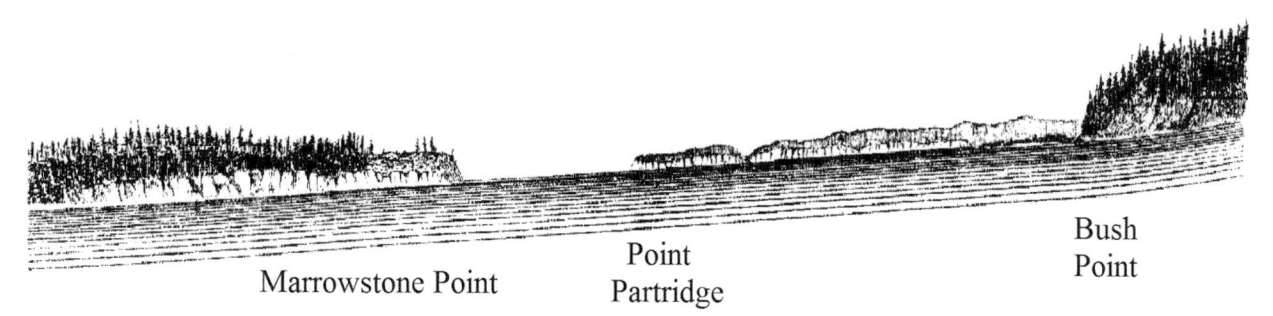

the partridge," (Wagner 184). It was apparently the grouse that Vancouver may have seen (Meany *Origin* 221, 222). More likely, Vancouver named it after his brother's wife, Martha Partridge. Davidson wrote: "Point Partridge is the western point of Whidbey island, and directly faces the Strait of Juan de Fuca. It is very steep and yellow, and flat on the summit, which is covered with spruce, fir, and cedar. The point is so rounding [sic] that it is not easily recognized on coming from the westward, but from the south and north it is well marked and prominent. Its face is composed of loose sand, which, being blown up the hill by the strong west winds, has formed a very peculiar ridge on the outer face of the top. This is so narrow that it can hardly be traveled, and in many places it is 35 feet above the ground inside, yet, being overgrown with bushes, the ridge is now permanent. The highest part of the point is about 260 feet above the water," (Davidson, *Report* 440).

Partridge Bank [17] #27, 1862, U.S. Coast Survey
Located three miles northwest of Partridge Point, the name likely came from the point. It is referenced in the 1969 *Pacific Coast Pilot*, but the name first appears on the 1862 chart.

Pass Island
Located in Deception Pass, Wilkes first named this Stam Island in 1841 [7e] (Wilkes, *Narrative* 311). According to Hale (581), *Stam* was a Coeur d'Alene Indian term which meant "bone." The current name was for Deception Pass. In 1973, the Washington State Board on Geographic Names received a proposal to rename it Canoe Island, Docket 209. In its September 10, 1976 meeting, the Board rejected the proposal. The federal database lists Stem Island (probably a misspelling) as a variant.

Pass Lake
Located on Fidalgo Island on the northern side of Deception Pass, it takes its name from the pass.

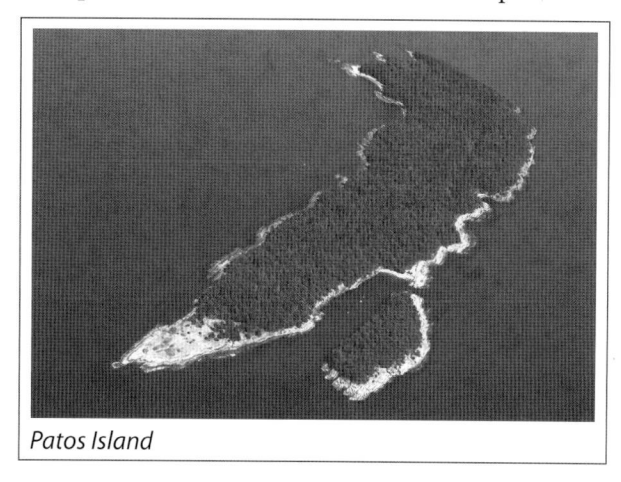

Patos Island

Patos Island [2] 1791, Pantoja
Located north of Orcas Island, Patos was named by Pantoja in 1791 for the "ducks" found there. Speaking of Patos, he said: "This we reached at 9 in the evening and anchored close to it in fine pebbles and water of 23 fathoms. Here we passed the night during all of which the wind continued very fresh. During the afternoon we had seen many gulls, seals, tunny and whales of great size," (Wagner 176). Wilkes named it Gourd Island in 1841 [7a] (Wilkes, *Narrative* 307). Kellett retained the Spanish name in the 1847 Admiralty chart [8a]. A navigational light was installed on the island in 1893. On August 15, 1905, Edward and Estelle Durgan and their family of thirteen children moved to Patos to tend the light. Their oldest daughter and her husband, appointed as assistant keepers, accompanied the family. Patos was remote and made living rugged. They frequently rowed to Bellingham for supplies, some twenty miles away. Three of the younger children died of

smallpox that first winter, a fourth child died later of appendicitis. Ed received a letter one day:

"Dear Ed:
On June 20, the fleet will pass your lighthouse. Don't fail to be on hand to receive the official salute from "Binny," our mutual friend. I have instructed him to dip three times; once for me, once for himself and once for auld lang syne.
I think of you often and, someday when I am free of my responsibility, I'll be out there to catch one of those big *tyees* you're always bragging about.
I'll be thinking of you, as the fleet goes by.
As ever, your friend,
Theodore Roosevelt."

According to one source, Ed and Roosevelt apparently had been friends in their youth. Another (Richardson, *Magic* 76) stated that Mrs. Glidden's mother was related to the President. Binny was the ship's cook. Sixteen battleships passed by that afternoon according to the story. The family moved to Bellingham in 1913 where Ed took over as light keeper at Semiahmoo. He died March 20, 1919 at the age of sixty. Estelle was promoted to keeper at Semiahmoo upon Ed's death. She died November 4, 1943 at age seventy-seven. The light on Patos was automated in 1974 (Glidden).

Patton Cove & Point
Located on the eastern side of Orcas Island, between Doe Bay and Kangaroo Point, it is a local name after the Patton family who still own most of the property. Robert Patenoster homesteaded 36 acres in 1891. Harry W. Patton (nicknamed "The Major" from his service in the Spanish-American War) purchased the property in 1907. The Major was the managing editor of the *Bellingham Daily Reville*. He named a huge fir in the front yard "Old Sentinel," which was the source of the name of Old Sentinel Road behind the property. Over the years, the property has been subdivided, transferred to family members, or sold off (Patton, Harry, Feb. 4, 2012 email to author; Harry Patton is The Major's 89 year-old grandson who lives on the property).

Patterson Point [24] #1947, 1849, Inskip
See Gibson Point.

Paul Creek
See Cascade Creek.

Paun Cove [7h] #154, 1841, Wilkes
See North Bay.

Peacock Island [7m] #160, 1841, Wilkes
See Hat Island.

Peale Passage [7d] #146, 1841, Wilkes; [7i] #147, 1841, Wilkes
Located between Squaxin and Harstine Islands, Wilkes honored crew member Titian R. Peale in 1841 (Meany, *Origin* 210).

Peapod Rocks [7a] #145, 1841, Wilkes
The two rocks are located in Rosario Strait south of Lawrence Point on Orcas Island. Wilkes named these in 1841 for their shape (Wilkes, *Narrative* 307; Meany, *Origin* 210). The U.S. Coast Survey named them Peapod #1 and Peapod #2 on their 1854 chart [10]. On the 1859 Admiralty chart [13a], Richards named them N Peapod and S Peapod. A combination of Wilkes and Richards is shown on current charts. Lange uncovered a reference to Quinlan's Rocks in the log of the H.M.S. *Cormorant* on Oct. 6, 1846.

Pear Point
Located on the eastern side of San Juan Island, east of North Bay, Wood (111) found this name on USC&GS Descriptive Report #2301, 1897 as a marginal note; it is also shown on t-sheet #2301 from 1897 (http://kaga.wsulibs.wsu.edu/cdm-maps/sanjuantsheet.html). The reason for the name is unknown. Barrel Point was the local name as a barrel was found there (McDonald, Lucile. "Rabbit-Hunters 'Take Over' Historic Site." *Seattle Times*. Nov. 20, 1960. Magazine Section p 7).

Peartree Bay
Located on the southeastern side of Burrows Island, inside Young Island, the origin of the name is unknown.

Pearl Island [7a] #145, 1841, Wilkes; [7c] #144, 1841, Wilkes
Located between San Juan and Henry Islands, it forms the north end of Roche Harbor. Wilkes did not include this 1841 name in his *Narrative*, but it is shown on his chart. He did not provide a reason for the name, nor did he name the bay (Roche Harbor).

Pearson Point
Located on the western side of Liberty Bay, Per Johan Pearson arrived in 1887 and took over the claim of his brother-in-law, S. A. Hagstron. Pearson named the adjacent point after himself (Bowen et. al., II: 165).

Peavine Pass [21] #6300, 1895
Located between Obstruction Island and Blakely Island, Peavine and Obstruction Passes (between Obstruction and Orcas Islands) collectively were originally named Obstruction Passages [13b] by Richards. To avoid confusion, it was later renamed for the native peavine growing along Blakely Island (Hitchman 227).

Pebble Beach
It is located about halfway between Camano Head and Mabana on the western side of Camano Island. The origin of the name is unknown.

Pebble Beach
This is a local name for a portion of the sand spit fronting Miller Bay in Port Madison (McDonald, Lucile. "Miller's Bay Ponders Development Plans." *Seattle Times*. Mar. 29, 1964. Magazine Section p 2, 3).

Penguin Harbor [7a] #145, 1841, Wilkes
Located off the eastern side of Guemes Island, it is the area formed by Vendovi and Jacks Islands and William Point. According to Wilkes' *Narrative* (310): "There is a connection between Penguin and Hornet Harbors on the north, through Levant Passage . . ." The *Penguin* was captured in 1812 by Capt. Lawrence in the *Hornet*. The name is neither reflected on current charts nor recognized by the U.S. Board on Geographic Names.

Penguin Island [13a] #2689, 1859, Richards
See Bare Island.

Penn Cove [6] 1792, Vancouver
Located on the eastern side of Whidbey Island, Vancouver named this for Granville Penn (1761-1844), the grandson of the founder of Pennsylvania, William Penn (1644-1718).

Penrose Point
Located on the western shoreline of Carr Inlet, Wilkes originally named this Sikwa Point [7h] in 1841. He left no reason for the name. Wilkes did not include this name in his *Narrative*, but it is shown on his chart. The point is the eastern end of a 125 acre state park named after Dr. Stephen B. L. Penrose who was the President of Whitman College in Walla Walla beginning in 1890. Penrose lived near the point during the summers (TPL website).

Pepper Corns [7i] #147, 1841, Wilkes
See Eagle Island.

Percival Group [7a] #145, 1841, Wilkes
See Sucia Islands

Percival Landing
Located at the southern end of Budd Inlet at Olympia, it was named for Capt. and Mrs. Samuel W. Percival who built a general mercantile store and sawmill on Percival Cove on Capitol Lake in 1850. In 1860, he built Percival Dock and five years later relocated it to its present site (Kline 188).

Perrys Island [7a] #145, 1841, Wilkes; [7m] #160, 1841, Wilkes
See Fidalgo Island.

Peter Point [7g] #155, 1841, Wilkes
Located on the western side of Vashon Island, Wilkes left no reason for the 1841 name. Perhaps he honored Peter Puget. Wilkes did not include this name in his *Narrative*, but it is shown on his chart. The Salish name for the point was "sleeping mats for cattails found there"; they were used for making mats (Hilbert et. al., 238). In 1983, the Washington State Board on Geographic Names reviewed the issue of Peter Point vs. Point Peter. The Board approved Peter Point in its December 9, 1983 meeting, Docket 285 (from Washington State Board Files). The U.S. Board followed in early 1984.

Peters, Point [7k] #152, 1841, Wilkes
Located near the southern end of Suquamish Harbor in Hood Canal, Wilkes left no reason for the 1841 name. Wilkes did not include this name in his *Narrative*, but it is shown on his chart. The name is neither reflected on current charts nor recognized by the U.S. Board on Geographic Names.

Phinney Bay
Located on the southern end of Dyes Inlet, it was named for Arthur Phinney. Phinney and his partner Zachariah Amos ran logging camps in numerous places around Puget Sound country, including Port

Ludlow and the eastern side of Whidbey Island. In 1861, the Amos-Phinney Company purchased the future site of the naval shipyard in Bremerton. They logged along the shoreline into Port Washington Narrows and Phinney Bay. Phinney died in 1877 (Bowen et. al. III: 2).

Phebe Lake
See Cypress Lake.

Pickering Passage [7d] #146, 1841, Wilkes; [7h] #154, 1841, Wilkes
Located on the western side of Harstine Island in Puget Sound, Wilkes honored crew member Charles Pickering in 1841 (Meany, *Origin* 212).

Pickett, Mount
Located on the eastern side of Orcas Island, it was named for Capt. George E. Pickett who was stationed around Puget Sound country, most notably at American Camp on San Juan Island. Pickett was born in Richmond, VA in 1825. Upon graduation from West Point in 1846, he saw duty in the Mexican Wars. By 1856, he was stationed in Puget Sound country. Five years later, he resigned from the U.S. Army to join the South in the Civil War. As a Confederate General, he is most famous for his failed charge on Gettysburg in 1863. He died in Norfolk, VA in 1875. The file on Morse Island from the Washington State Board on Geographic Names contains a 1925 letter from McLellan to Meany. Amongst other topics, McLellan indicates that he named the mountain: ". . . I have used the name Mount Pickett, for the second highest mountain peak in the San Juan Island area. … Up to the present time, this mountain range has not possessed even a local name," (files from the Washington State Board). Professor Meany transmitted this letter with his comments to the U.S Board on Geographic Names. The U.S. Board selected the name later that year over the variant, Doe Bay Mountain (*Decisions*).

Picnic Cove & Point
Located off the eastern side of Shaw Island, north of Canoe Island, Lange was told by an old-time resident that picnics were always held there, hence the name. Picnic Bay was perhaps first shown on t-sheet #2230 (http://kaga.wsulibs.wsu.edu/cdm-maps/sanjuantsheet.html).

Picnic Island [14d] #2840, 1872
Located on the eastern side of West Sound, Orcas Island, Richards originally named it Sheep Island [14a], as the Hudson's Bay Company apparently ran sheep there (Hitchman 270). The Admiralty changed the name to Picnic Island on [14d]. In his 1895 Descriptive Report #2229, J. J. Gilbert wrote (http://riverhistory.ess.washington.edu/tsheets/reports/t2229.pdf, p 15): "Sheep Island near the middle of White Beach Bay is a small low island with rocky shores and wooded. The underbrush has been cleared and the island is used as a picnic ground." William C. Bryant purchased the island in 1952, and the family still owns it. In 1976, the Washington State Board reviewed the name, as some government publications carried the name Flower Island, others Sheep Island. As the name Picnic Island was more in local use, and Flower Island duplicated another by the same name (off Spencer Spit), the Board chose Picnic in its March 11, 1977 meeting, Docket 216. The U.S. Board followed later in the year.

Picnic Point
Located on the eastern side of Admiralty Inlet about twelve miles north of Shilshole Bay, it was likely named because it was a good place for picnics and camping.

Pigeon Point
Located on the eastern shoreline of Samish Bay, the name is likely descriptive.

Pilash Point [7d] #146, 1841, Wilkes
See Broad Spit.

Pile Point [13a] #2689, 1859, Richards
Located on the southern side of San Juan Island, Wood claims (112) that one of Kellett's surveyors provided the name. However, it first appears on Richards' chart [13a]. The reason for the name is speculative. It may be that rocks were piled there for surveying purposes.

Pillar Point [8a] #1917, 1847, Kellett
Located along the Strait of Juan de Fuca, it was first named *Ensenada de Soto* by Quimper in 1790 [1]. In his journal, he refers to it as a bay: "I steered SW so as to approach the coast and anchor in a bay to leeward, which I named Soto Aguilar," (Meany, *Origin* 212; Wagner 120). Kellett provided its current name.

Pilot Point
Located two miles south of Point No Point, Wilkes originally named this Point Washington [7o] in 1841, perhaps after his convention of naming other nearby points after presidents (Madison, Jefferson, Monroe). *See also* Pilots Cove.

Pilots Cove [7d] #146, 1841, Wilkes; [7o] #157, 1841, Wilkes
Located along the western side of Admiralty Inlet, south of Point No Point, Wilkes wrote: "Here we anchored before sunset, and I named it Pilot's Cove from the circumstance of having been here joined by the first officer of the Hudson Bay Company's steamer, commanded by Capt. M'Niel, who on hearing of our arrival, kindly sent him down to pilot up the ship," (Meany, *Origin* 213; Wilkes, *Narrative* 303). The name is no longer in use, but the nearby Pilot Point is used. The Salish name for the point is "crabapple grove" (Hilbert et. al., 190).

Piner Point [7g] #155, 1841, Wilkes
Located at the south end of Maury Island, Wilkes honored crew member Thomas Piner. Wilkes did not include this name in his *Narrative*, but it is shown on his chart.

Piners Point [7m] #160, 1841, Wilkes
Located near the present-day Washington State ferry terminal in Elliott Bay, Wilkes likely honored crew member Thomas Piner. Wilkes did not include this name in his *Narrative*, but it is shown on his chart. The name is neither reflected on current charts nor recognized by the U.S. Board on Geographic Names. The Salish name for the point was "trash washed upon a promontory" (Hilbert et. al., 236).

Pipers Creek
The mile-long creek flows into Puget Sound about two miles north of Shilshole Bay. Because "Piper" (singular) appeared on nautical charts but the plural "Pipers" was in long-time local use, in its 1983 meeting, Docket 279, Pipers was approved by the Washington State Board on Geographic Names. The U.S. Board followed in 1984 (from Washington State Board Files).

Pippin Point [7o] #157, 1841, Wilkes
Located on the northern entrance to Appletree Cove, in 1841 Wilkes used the descriptive name for the crab apple trees he observed along the shoreline. Wilkes did not include this name in his *Narrative*, but it is shown on his chart. The name is neither reflected on current charts nor recognized by the U.S. Board on Geographic Names.

Pitship Point [7n] #149, 1841, Wilkes
Located on the western shore of Sequim Bay, Wilkes left no reason for the 1841 name. He does not include this name in his *Narrative*, but it is shown on his chart.

Pitt Island [7i] #147, 1841, Wilkes
Located off the western side of McNeil Island, in Pitt Passage, Wilkes spelled it with a single "t" in 1841. He left no reason for the name. Wilkes did not include this name in his *Narrative*, but it is shown on his chart. In 1846, Inskip named this Enriquita [24] for a daughter of Capt. John Duntze (Meany, *Origin* 214).

Pitt Passage [23] #6460, 1905
Located off the western side of McNeil Island, Wilkes named Pitt Island in 1841 but did not reference the passage. It appears on the U.S. Coast and Geodetic Survey chart #6460 [23]. In 1846, Inskip named this Crauford Channel [24].

Pleasant, Point
It is located at the southern entrance to the Swinomish Channel. Davidson referenced it in the 1889 *Pacific Coast Pilot* (602): "Point Pleasant Light.-This is a fixed red light shown from a lantern upon a white post nine feet high and six feet above high water. It is placed on a low point inside of the Hole in the Wall, and on the east side of the channel. The point is covered at high water." The name is neither reflected on current charts nor recognized by the U.S. Board on Geographic Names.

Pleasant, Point
The local name Point Pleasant was mentioned in the June 10, 1897 issue of *The Islander* (p 3) under the heading of "West Sound News." Its location was not identified. The July 22nd issue was more specific and indicated that it was on Shaw Island. It was the site of the 4th annual Farmers Co-operative Association picnic.

Pleasant Bay
It is located south of Bellingham Bay. According to the TPL website, the views across Chuckanut Bay toward Eliza and Lummi Island, the nearby mountains and forests, all provide a pleasant view and possibly explain the name.

Pleasant Beach
Located on the southern end of Bainbridge Island, on Rich Passage, Asa Fowler, who logged in the area in the early 1860s, called it Sylvan Grove. In 1896, Malcolm and Emma McDonald relocated from Port Blakely and purchased property nearby. They built a hotel with 40 rooms and a dining room that could accommodate 2,000 guests in a day. They also built a dance pavilion, a heated salt water swimming pool, a bowling alley, and a baseball field. Emma changed the name to Pleasant Beach (Mariott 99; *An Historic*; Warner 30-33). The Salish name for the area was "dancing place" (Hilbert et. al., 226).

Pleasant Harbor

Pleasant Harbor
Located on the western side of Hood Canal, in 1841 Wilkes spelled this *Tzu-sa-ted* in his *Narrative* (323) and on one chart [7j] and *Tzee-sa-ted* on another chart [7d]. According to the TPL website, an early settler, Margaret E. Felt, wrote that it was an ". . . enchanting deep water cove well named Pleasant Harbor."

Pleasure Island
The July 29, 1897 issue of *The Islander* references a picnic held by 40 people on Pleasure Island, West Sound, apparently a local name. No other information was provided about the name or location. It was perhaps Picnic Island.

Plum Point
Located in Lynch Cove at the head of Hood Canal, the name is likely descriptive. The name is not shown on current charts.

Plumper Reef [13a] #2689, 1859, Richards
See West Bank.

Poe's Point
See Post Point.

Poi Point [7h] #154, 1841, Wilkes
Located on the northern end of Reach Island, Wilkes left no reason for the 1841 name. According to Wilkes' chart, he drew Reach Island as a peninsula. He did not include this name in his *Narrative*, but it is shown on his chart. The name is neither reflected on current charts nor recognized by the U.S. Board on Geographic Names.

Pointer Island [7a] #145, 1841, Wilkes
It is located off the southeastern side of Blakely Island near Thatcher Pass. In 1841, Wilkes used the name The Pointers. Based upon the chart, it is impossible to determine which features he named. And unfortunately, he does not include this name in his *Narrative*. From looking at his chart, there are four ink blobs with the name "The Pointers" running through. Today, the names are Armitage Island, Lawson Rock, Pointer Island, and Black Rock. Which of these he intended to name is unknown. An early alternative name for Pointer Island was White Rock [13a]. The U.S. Board on Geographic Names gave it its current name in 1925 based upon a recommendation from Professor Meany and Roy McClellan (GNIS files; Washington State Board files, Morse Island).

Pole Island [16c] #602, 1921
It is located mid channel Mosquito Pass between San Juan and Henry Islands. Wilkes originally named it Gull Rock [7a]; the name was likely descriptive. He did not include this name in his *Narrative*, but it

is shown on his chart, nor did he provide a reason for the 1841 name. According to Wood (112), the name Pole Island first appeared on the 1901 U.S. chart #6381. According to J. J. Gilbert in his 1894 Descriptive Report #2194 (http://riverhistory.ess.washington.edu/tsheets/reports/t2194.pdf, p 6): "Pole Island received its name from some tall poles set up there by the Indians in early days, used for the capture of water fowl."

Pole Pass
The very narrow pass is located between Orcas and Crane Islands and is barely 500 feet wide. Indians used to hang nets on poles on either side of the pass. When Vancouver first observed these tall poles, he had no idea of their purpose. He wrote (225): "On the low land of New Dungeness were erected perpendicularly and seemingly with much regularity, a number of very tall straight poles, like flag staves or beacons, supported from the ground by spurs. Their first appearance induced an opinion of their being intended as the uprights for stages on which they might dry their fish; but this, on a nearer view, seemed improbable, as their height and distance from each other would have required spars of a greater size to reach from one to the other, than the substance of the poles was capable of sustaining. They were, undoubtedly, intended to answer some particular purpose; but whether of a religious, civil, or military nature, must be left to some future investigation." Fortunately, Charles Wilkes solved the mystery: "After passing that island, an extensive bay opened, on whose shores we saw the long poles mentioned by Vancouver, and represented in his book. The use of these he was unable to discover, but the Indians informed us that they were for the purpose of suspending nets for taking the wildfowl that frequent these shores in great numbers. On these poles the nets are set up at night, at which time the geese search these grounds for food: fires are then lighted, which alarm the birds, and cause them to fly against the nets, by which they are thrown upon the ground, where, before they have time to recover themselves, they are caught and killed," (Wilkes, *Narrative* 298). According to Archibald Fleming (*Told by the Pioneers* 51, 52): "Across this narrow waterway the Indians would place a horizontal pole at some distance above the water. Netting or sacks were hung from this pole. The Indians would hunt at night with torches and as the ducks flew against this obstruction, the Indians would kill them with their paddles."

Point No Point [7d] #146, 1841, Wilkes
Located along the western shoreline of Admiralty Inlet, Wilkes named it in 1841 for its resemblance to Point No Point on the Hudson River (Wilkes, *Narrative* 315). The Salish word for the point is "long promontory" (Hilbert et. al., 190). On some maps, the name appeared as Point-No-Point. The U.S. Board on Geographic Names approved the form of the current name in 1891. The government erected a lighthouse on the point in 1879. J. S. Maggs, the first lighthouse keeper, was replaced by F. N. Nakins in 1884. In 1914, W. H. Cary replaced Nakins. The Point No Point post office was established in 1893 with Mrs. E. Scannell as the first postmaster. Locals built a school two years later. Most of the settlers either fished or logged (Bowen et al., II: 102).

Polnell Point

Polnell Point [7a] #145, 1841, Wilkes
Located on the northeastern side of Whidbey Island, east of Oak Harbor, Wilkes honored crew member John Polnell in 1841 (Wilkes, *Narrative* 315). The Salish word for the point was "near turned" referring to the fact that the point is twisted (Hilbert et. al., 360). The U.S. Board on Geographic Names approved the name over the variants, Miller Point, Poinell Point, and Point Polnell in 1962.

Pork Hill

McLellan wrote: "The peninsula situated between Friday Harbor and Griffin Bay is composed of low rocky hills and narrow drift-covered valleys. An elevation, known as Pork Hill, is located near the center of the peninsula and its altitude is 200 feet." McLellan may have misread the 1859 chart #2689 where Admiralty Captain Richards named it Park Hill.

Porpoise Rocks Wilkes; [7m] #160, 1841, Wilkes
Located on the eastern side of Guemes Island in Padilla Bay, it is a collective name for Huckleberry, Saddlebag, and Dot Islands. In 1792, Galiano/Valdéz named it *Tres Hermanas*. Wilkes honored the *Porpoise* in 1841, one of the ships accompanying him on the exploration. Wilkes did not include this name in his *Narrative*, but it is shown on his chart (Meany, *Origin* 225; Wagner 247).

Portage

Portage

The community is located on Maury Island. Crew member George T. Sinclair of the Wilkes' expedition wrote in 1841: "Surveying as usual, one of the Boats in the harbour on Vashon Isd from which there is a portage communicating with our anchorage. It is a mere strip of sand so that Vashon is nearly two islands," (Blumenthal, *Charles Wilkes* 175). Sinclair's journal entry is likely the first formal reference to the portage. The Salish name for the area was "where one pushes a canoe over." The Indians apparently shoved their canoes over the sand spit between Tramp and Quartermaster Harbors (Hilbert et. al., 236).

Portage Bay

Located between Point Francis and the mainland at Bellingham Bay, there is a narrow sand spit referred to as The Portage connecting the mainland to Portage Island. It is covered only at the highest tides. The name comes from Indians and settlers pulling canoes over the sand spit rather than paddling the long way around Portage Island.

Portage Canal

It was originally known as the Chimacum Portage, and later the Port Townsend Canal. Located at the head of Port Townsend, it was a quarter mile in length and 150 yards wide. The Seattle Bridge and Dredging Company cut the canal through in 1915 (Bean 3, 4). As early as 1850, an army/navy commission recommended the excavation of the canal for defense purposes in time of war. The military believed that the community of Port Townsend would be more difficult to blockade with a second entrance. The idea languished until 1913 when Congress appropriated funds (McDonald, Lucile. "Canal Created 'Mysterious' Indian Island." *Seattle Times*. June 18, 1961. Magazine Section p 2). Between 1915 and 1925, Indian and Marrowstone Islanders used their own boats to get to and from the mainland. In 1925, a ferry operated to Hadlock. The bridge was constructed in 1952 (McDonald, Lucile. "Fort Flagler is Major Attraction for Marrowstone Island Visitors." *Seattle Times*. July 2, 1961. Magazine Section p 7). The U.S. Board on Geographic Names selected the current name in 1964 over variants which included Government Canal, Port Townsend Canal, and Port Townsend-Oak Bay Canal.

Portage Channel

Located at the northern end of Bellingham Bay, east of Portage Bay, this was a shoal area extending across the entire north end of Bellingham Bay where canoes could be dragged.

Portage Island

It is located on the western side of Bellingham Bay. Except for the obvious, the origin of the name is unknown but was selected by the Whatcom County Parks Department who owns it. It is possible to drive across to the island except at very high tides. In 1976, the Washington State Board on Geographic

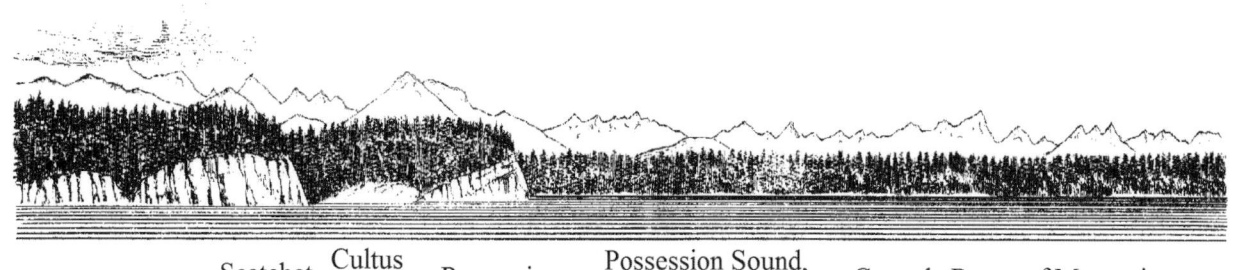

Scatchet Head | Cultus Bay | Possession Point | Possession Sound, South entrance | Cascade Range of Mountains

Names received a request to correct the spelling of the name of Point Frances to Point Francis and to apply the name to the entire island. In its March 11, 1977 meeting, Docket 210, the Board corrected the spelling (consistent with Vancouver's name) and approved the name of Portage Island for the entire island. The U.S. Board followed later in the year (based upon Washington State Board files, Point Frances).

Posey Island [16c] #602, 1921
Located off the western end of Pearl Island in Spieden Channel, it was originally reflected as Neck Island in 1869 [16b]. The Admiralty provided no reason for the change on [16c]. The U.S. Government owns the island.

Possession
Located on the southeastern end of Whidbey Island, the first settlers in the community were the Peters family. They sold to the Giant Powder Company who built a warehouse for storage and distribution of dynamite used by loggers all around Puget Sound country. The plant closed in 1935 (Cherry II: 62). The community took its name from Possession Sound.

Possession Point [19] #662, 1867, U.S. Coast Survey
Located on the southeastern end of Whidbey Island, it takes it name from Possession Sound. The Salish name for the point was "gravelly" (Hilbert et. al., 358).

Possession Sound [6] 1792, Vancouver
Located between south Whidbey Island and the mainland, Vancouver named it for the act to: ". . . take formal possession of all the countries we had lately been employed in exploring, in the name of, and for His Britannic Majesty, his heirs and successors," (Vancouver 288, 289). Archibald Menzies commented (45): "We remain here the two following days with fine pleasant weather. The latter being the King's Birth Day, Capt Vancouver landed about noon with some of the Officers on the South point of the small Bay where he took posession of the Country with the usual forms in his Majesty's name & namd it New Georgia & on hoisting the English Colours on the spot each Vessel proclaimd it aloud with a Royal Salute in honor of the Day." Vancouver did not make the boundaries of Possession Sound extremely clear. However, based upon Joseph Whidbey's exploration and the "dead end" he reached somewhere before Deception Pass, it is reasonable to believe that Vancouver named it for that body of water along the eastern side of Whidbey Island. Modern charts relegate it to the area from the south end of Whidbey into the Everett area. The balance is Saratoga Passage. *See also* Saratoga Passage.

Post Office Bay
Located to the north of Parks Bay on the western side of Shaw Island, it was the location of the Maple post office established by Bert Tift in 1886. Mrs. Cynthia Hix took over in 1890 and moved the post office to the property owned by George Griswald on the southeastern side of Blind Bay.

Post Point
It is located on the mainland south of Bellingham. According to information from the Washington State Board on Geographic Names (Point Frances file), this was originally named Poe's Point and the current name is a misspelling. Alonzo M. Poe took out a donation claim on the land in the 1850s. He was responsible for surveying the town of Whatcom in 1858.

Potlatch & Potlatch Point
Located on the western side of Squaxin Island, it was apparently named for a potlatch house on the point (Hitchman 239). The Salish name for the point was "rocky promontory" (Hilbert et. al., 289).

Poulsbo

Poulsbo
Located on the eastern side of Liberty Bay, in 1866 Harry Prescott was the first to purchase land including what is now the present site of Poulsbo. He lived across the bay at Scandia for several years and installed traps in several locations to catch the prolific dogfish. He rendered and sold the oil to local logging camps and mills. In 1877, Prescott sold the Poulsbo site to Michael Theilan who in turn sold the following year to Henry Eley and Abraham Hurdleboo (Carlson 52; Bowen et al., II: 12). Iver Moe arrived in Poulsbo in 1883. He emigrated from Norway in 1880, via Minneapolis, and settled on his 160 acre homestead near the intersection of the Lofall-Winslow highway and the old road to Kingston. He established the post office in 1886, naming the town Paulsbo (Paul's Place) after a village in Norway. Postal authorities misspelled the name. Poulsbo was incorporated in 1908, with Andrew B. Moe (Iver's son) as the first mayor. He died in 1951. The town continued to grow and prosper over the years with many descendents of the original pioneers remaining in business today (Bowen et al., II: 12-16; Kvelstad 32-40; Carlson 56). The Salish name for the area was "maple grove." The boulder at the head of the transient pier was called "filing or grinding above" by the Salish (Hilbert et. al., 199).

Poulsbo Bay
See Liberty Bay.

Poverty Bay [23] #6460, 1905
It is located on the eastern shoreline of East Passage, about five miles north of Tacoma. The origin of the name is unknown.

Poverty Cove
See Neah Bay.

Powie Point [7h] #154, 1841, Wilkes
The location is unclear. It is on the western side of Carr Inlet, south of Glencove. Wilkes left no reason for the 1841 name. He did not include this name in his *Narrative*, but it is shown on his chart. The name is neither reflected on current charts nor recognized by the U.S. Board on Geographic Names.

Pratts Bluff
Located on Whidbey Island at the northern end of Holmes Harbor near Greenbank, it was named for the Pratt family that settled in the area (Trebon, Theresa, May 25, 2010 email to author).

President Channel [7a] #145, 1841, Wilkes
It is located on the western side of Orcas Island between Orcas and Waldron Islands. However, that is not what Wilkes named it in 1841, nor is it where he placed it! Wilkes named it Presidents Passage; it was located in the northern portion of the current San Juan Channel. On his chart, the "P" in President began just west of Jones Island, and the "e" in Passage was shown to the east of Friday Harbor. Wilkes honored the U.S.S. *President*, commanded by Commodore John Rodgers. According to Richards' 1859 chart [13a], Douglas Channel was located between Orcas and Waldron Islands. He honored the Chief Factor of the Hudson's Bay Company, James Douglas (Meany, *Origin* 71). Douglas was born in 1803 in British Guiana and educated in Scotland. He joined the North West Company in 1819 and continued with the Hudson's Bay Company after the 1825 merger. At Fort St. James, he married Amelia Connolly, daughter of Chief Factor William Connolly. In 1830, he was sent to Fort Vancouver on the Columbia and promoted to chief trader in 1834. He relocated to Victoria in 1849 as the Chief Factor of the Company and, in 1851, Governor of Vancouver

Island, a position he held until 1864. Between 1858 and 1864, he was also the Premier of British Columbia. He retired in 1864 and died in 1877 in Victoria. In 1866, the U.S. Coast Survey reverted to President Channel [18] replacing Douglas Channel. The U.S. Board on Geographic Names settled the name and the location in 1892.

President Point
It is located a couple miles north of Port Madison about halfway between Point Jefferson and Appletree Cove. In 1841, Wilkes honored several former presidents with local names: Monroe, Jefferson, and Madison. As a result, according to Meany, the U.S. Coast Survey named this using the same rationale in 1856 (*Origin* 231). Davidson does in fact mention the point (1889 *Pacific Coast Pilot* 603) but does not state that the Coast Survey actually named it. It is probably a reasonable assumption, however.

Preston Point
Located at the mouth of the Snohomish River near Everett, the Indians called it *Hay-bohl-ub* (Meany, *Origin* 232). The current name came from Perrin E. and Peggy Preston who settled there and built a trading post. Their son, George W., was born on the farm in 1864 (TPL website).

Prevost
Located on Stuart Island about a quarter mile west of Charles Point in Prevost Harbor, the community name likely came from the harbor.

Prevost Harbor [13a] #2689, 1859, Richards
Located on the northern side of Stuart Island, the name honored Capt. James Charles Prevost (1810-1891), Commander of the H.M.S. *Satellite* who assisted Richards in survey activities. Prevost entered the navy in 1823 and was promoted to commander in 1845. He served on the Pacific Station from 1850-1854 and again from 1857-1860. In 1856, the British appointed Prevost as the first commissioner for settling the boundary issue. He ended his career in 1869 after a five-year tour at the Gibraltar Naval Base. In 1880, he was promoted to Admiral-retired. He died in London in 1891 (Walbran 400).

Priest Point [22] #6450, 1909
Located on the mainland, south of Tulalip Bay, Wilkes originally named this Point Migley [7d], [7o] in 1841, for crew member William Migley. Wilkes did not include this name in his *Narrative*, but it is shown on his chart. The current name honors Father E. C. Chirouse, the first Tulalip Indian agent in 1860, who spent 50 years in his missionary efforts.

Priest Point [23] #6460, 1905
Located on the eastern shoreline of Budd Inlet, north of Olympia, Father Pascal Ricard and nine other Catholic missionary priests of Oblates of Mary Immaculate started St. Joseph Mission about 1847. On a 324 acre site, they cleared the land and built a chapel and a school. They remained in the area until 1860 when they moved to British Columbia (Frost 301).

Prospect Point
Located on Colvos Passage a half mile north of Olalla, the origin of the name is unknown.

Protection Island [6] 1792, Vancouver
Located at the head of Discovery Bay, Quimper named it, in 1790, *Isla de Carrasco* for his pilot Juan Carrasco [1] (Wagner 113). In 1792, Vancouver visited the island and wrote (226): "On landing on the west end of the supposed island, and ascending its eminence which was nearly a perpendicular cliff, our attention was immediately called to a landscape, almost as enchantingly beautiful as the most elegantly finished pleasure grounds in Europe." He continued about its relationship to the bay (228): "Had this insular production of nature been designed by the most able engineer, it could not have been placed more happily for the protection of the port, not only from the N. W. winds to the violence of which it would otherwise be greatly exposed, but against all attempts of an enemy, when properly fortified; and hence I called it Protection Island." Wilkes wrote (298): "The beautiful woods and lawns of Protection Island, in particular, exist unchanged. The lawns still produce the same beautiful flowers and shrubs, and although closely surrounded by dense woods, do not seem to have been encroached upon by their luxuriant growth, although there is no apparent reason why it should not long ere this have overrun them." Davidson wrote: "The western

extremity of this island lies E. ⅔ S., distant 7½ miles from Dungeness lighthouse, and extends a little over a mile E.NE., being narrow, curved outward to the strait, and having a low point at each end, with shoal water stretching from the western. Its sides are very steep, and about 200 feet high, the seaward part covered with timber, and that towards Port Discovery undulating and covered with fern," (*Report* 422). During the late 1850s, Protection Island became home to a few squatters. Frightened from the fierce raids of northern Indians, they did not remain long. In 1860 or 1861, Alfred S. Buffington homesteaded 163 acres, almost half of the island. Paul K. Heebs settled on sixty-three acres in 1864. The following year, Henry E. Morgan homesteaded the balance and later purchased Buffington and Heebs' claims. John Power Sr., born in Warren, Ohio in 1835, arrived on the West Coast in 1859. He worked in the Seabeck and Port Madison sawmills. About 1864, he moved to Discovery Bay and found work at the Port Discovery Mill. In 1866, he married Mary Bartlett from Port Townsend, and their children, John, Stella, and Edgar were born between 1867 and 1870. During the late 1860s or early 1870s, the family began visiting and camping on the island. In 1874, Power purchased a half interest from Henry Morgan. In October of the following year, Mary Power and the children moved to the island while John continued working at the mill. In 1876, John followed the family and purchased the balance of the island from Morgan. In 1887, Power moved to Port Townsend and sold the island to a Mr. Swartout who defaulted on the loan. Power sold again to A. W. Bash and Henry Morgan for $10,000. Morgan sold his interest to James F. McNaught in 1890. Minnie Caine eventually acquired the entire island in 1909. Upon Minnie's death, her daughter Harriet inherited it. Her estate sold the island in 1953 to E. C. Tulin for $20,000. State Senator Martin J. Durkan purchased the island in 1962 for $175,000 and sold to the state the following year for $275,000 (*With Pride* 139; Power 3). Today, Protection Island is a National Wildlife Refuge (NWR) and is managed by the Washington State Department of Fish and Wildlife. About seventy percent of the nesting seabird population of Puget Sound and the Strait of Juan De Fuca make their home here. It is closed to the public.

Puffin Island [13a] #2689, 1859, Richards
Located at the eastern end of Matia Island, Richards named it for the tufted puffins which nested there (GNIS files; Meany, *Origin* 234). The U.S. Coast Survey changed the name to Matia East. Davidson wrote (1869 *Pacific Coast Pilot*, 213): "The small one on the east is called Puffin Island on the English Admiralty chart of 1859; in 1854 it was named Matia East by the U.S. Coast Survey." On the 1862 *Pacific Coast Pilot* (131), Davidson mentions that it was named by the British but does not reference the name Matia East. The original name was restored by the U.S. Coast and Geodetic Survey on chart #6380. The U.S. Board on Geographic Names approved the name in 1941.

Puget
Located on the Nisqually Reach, about halfway between the Nisqually River and Johnson Point, the community was platted by T. I. McKenny and George Barnes in 1873. By the 1890s, the name was changed to Puget, from Puget Sound. The town failed in the 1890s due to economic problems (Palmer, 68; TPL website).

Puget Sound [6] 1792, Vancouver
Puget Sound is that body of water located south of The Narrows, according to George Vancouver. Explored first by Peter Puget, Vancouver honored him with the name. Vancouver wrote (275): ". . . to commemorate Mr. Puget's exertions, the south extremity of it I named Puget's Sound." Peter Puget was born in London in 1765. He entered the navy in 1778 at the age of twelve aboard the *Dunkirk*. After serving on a number of other ships, he was transferred to the *Europa,* commanded by Vashon in 1783, where he met Vancouver and Baker. Puget was furloughed in 1787 and then assigned to the *Discovery* as a master's mate. He received his commission as lieutenant in 1790 and departed with Vancouver in 1791. In 1793, Vancouver dispatched Lieutenant Broughton, Commander of the *Chatham,* to England for additional instructions related to the Nootka issue. Vancouver promoted Puget to the command of *Chatham* following Broughton's departure. Returning to England in 1795, at the end of the voyage, Puget accepted the command of

Double Bluff   Puget Sound   Point No Point

the transport *Adelphi* early the following year. He married Hannah Elrington in 1797. During the next twenty-three years, they had seven boys and four girls. In late 1798, upon Vancouver's death, Puget assisted Vancouver's brother, John, in the completion of the final volume of the journal of the *Discovery*. For the next twenty years, Puget continued to see service on various ships. In 1821, at the age of fifty-six, he was promoted to Rear Admiral of the Blue (*see* Hood Canal for information on Admiralty ranks). He died September 14, 1849. In 1841, Wilkes wrote: "Puget's Sound embraces the extent of waters lying within the Narrows, which is the only channel by which it can be reached. The whole area comprised within its limit is about 400 square miles. Its length, northeast and southwest, is 27 miles, while its breadth extends 15 miles at right angles to the length," (Wilkes, *Narrative* 320). While Vancouver clearly intended the name to apply to the waters south of The Narrows, and Wilkes adhered to that philosophy, Puget Sound tended to grow over time — what I'll term as "The Puget Sound creep." Meany presented some interesting information on how that creep occurred. In 1836, William A. Slacum, a purser in the U.S. Navy, traveled to the Northwest. In a March 26, 1837 writing, he referenced the "Straights of Juan de Fuca and Pugitt's Sound." By implication, he extended Puget Sound to include Admiralty Inlet. In 1853, Capt. George B. McClellan wrote: "I mean here, by Puget Sound, the sheet of water made up of the sound properly so called, Admiralty Inlet, Bellingham Bay, etc." Meany humorously related an 1857 James G. Swan statement: "A strange geographical error has gained credence in the commercial world of calling all the waters on the north of Washington territory Puget Sound. This error has been principally caused by ignorant newspaper reports, particularly those of San Francisco, who always report vessels arriving from any of the different harbors in Fuca Strait as from Puget Sound." Meany continued with other examples, including a May 1, 1913 court decision by Judge Ralston of the Superior Court of Clallam County. He said that: "For the purposes of fishing laws, the Strait of Juan de Fuca is a part of Puget Sound," (*Origin* 235). Even Davidson committed the error. Writing about Port Townsend, he said: "It lies well protected just inside the entrance to Admiralty Inlet, now almost universally known as 'Puget Sound,'" (1889 *Pacific Coast Pilot* 590). All of these writings leave the precise definition of Puget Sound a bit murky, until one reviews the several decisions on the subject made by the U.S. Board on Geographic Names. In a 1917 decision, as proposed by the Coast and Geodetic Survey, the Board decided that the extent of the feature was given as "an arm of the Pacific Ocean, from the Strait of Juan de Fuca to Olympia, Wash." In 1960, the Board clarified the description because of conflicting definitions between federal and state maps, reports, and literature. The Board wrote the following under 61BGN: "Puget Sound: bay with numerous channels and branches, extending about 90 miles southward from the Strait of Juan de Fuca to Olympia; the northern boundary is formed, at its main entrance, by a line between Point Wilson on the Olympic Peninsula and Point Partridge on Whidbey Island; at a second entrance, between West Point on Whidbey Island, Deception Island, and Sares Head on Fidalgo Island; at a third entrance, at the south end of Swinomish Channel between Fidalgo Island and McGlinn Island; it was named by George Vancouver for Lieutenant Peter Puget, who explored the southern end in May 1792; Washington; 47°50' N, 122°26' W; 1961 description revised." In 1979, the Board again tweaked the boundary by substituting

"Rosario Head on Fidalgo Island" for "Sares Head on Fidalgo Island" (Yost, Louis. Executive Secretary, U.S. Board on Geographic Names. E-mail to author, June 7, 2010). So today it's clear. Puget Sound encompasses everything south of Port Townsend along with all the waters east of Whidbey Island including Deception Pass. Locals now call the "old" Puget Sound — South Sound.

Puki Cove [7h] #154, 1841, Wilkes
See Henderson Bay.

Pulali Point [7j] #153, 1841, Wilkes
Located on the eastern side of Jackson Cove, Wilkes left no reason for the 1841 name. The name is Chinook for "powder, dust or sand" (Bright 399; Hitchman 242).

Pull and be Damned Point
Located on the southern end of Fildalgo Island near the southern entrance to the Swinomish Channel, the origin of the name is unknown. It is not reflected on current charts, but Pull and be Damned Road runs behind the point.

Point Pully

Pully, Point [7d] #146, 1841, Wilkes; [7g] #155, 1841, Wilkes
See Three Tree Point

Purdy
A community located at the northern end of Carr Inlet, Joseph Purdy, William Rowland, and a Mr. Sherman erected a mill here in 1885. The town was platted the same year and named after Purdy, as he offered to donate lumber for a school (*History* I: 60).

Puyallup River
Flowing into Commencement Bay, the river is shown but not named on Wilkes' chart. There are two potential meanings of the word. The first is "shadow from the dense shade of the forest" (Reese, *Origins* 93). The second is a combination of *Pough*, meaning "generous," and *allup*, meaning "people," hence, "generous people" (Meany, *Origin* 236). Kellett called it the Sinawamis River [8a] but provided no reason for the name. The river flows into the Puyallup Waterway and then into Commencement Bay. In 1824, Work wrote (212): "Our course lay through narrow channels about ½ mile wide and some wide openings formed by traversing bays and channels formed by islands and points. Passed a channel and two bays on the W. side and two bays and a channel on the E. side, the last of the bays receives the Qualax River." The U.S. Board on Geographic Names approved the name in 1913 over the variant names including Pugallup River and Puyallop River. Interestingly, Qualax is not listed. It is possible that this is some other site. But according to the description, Work appears to be describing Commencement Bay.

Puyallup Waterway
One of the waterways on Commencement Bay, it takes its name from the river and the Indian tribe.

Pysht & Pysht River [21] #6300, 1895
It is located along the Strait of Juan de Fuca east of Pillar Point. Quimper reflected it on his chart [1] but not in his journal. While Quimper's name is difficult to read, it appears to be *Rio Carrel*. Kellett's chart [9a] is equally difficult to read, but he wrote either Canal or Canel River. Davidson referenced it (*Report* 418): "From this point the shore trends S.SE. about a mile, and receives a stream coming from the westward, called Carrel river. An Indian village exists here. The Indian name of the stream is Pisht-st meaning 'fish.'" Davidson corrected the supposed typo and later identified it as the Canal River (*Directory* 116). The name Pysht became official for both the river and community by an 1896 U.S. Board on Geographic Names decision. In 1907, the Board received a proposal to rename the river "Fish" and the community Crawford after an early settler who ran a store and post office. Subsequent to the proposal, the Board determined that Crawford was still alive but ill in a Seattle hospital. As using the name violated the policy of naming places after living persons, the proponent suggested an abeyance until the man died. In early 1908, the Board adopted the name Fish River but passed on Crawford. Subsequent to this decision, charts included the name Fish for both the river and

community. Because of continued local usage of the original name, in 1914 the Board readdressed the subject. Based upon some of the correspondence, the name does not mean fish. Instead, it was a Clallam term for "wind." The Board settled on the current name for both the community and river. This eliminated the variants Fish, Pysche, and Pyscht. Between 1917 and 1930, Merrill & Ring ran a logging camp which included a 27,000 acre tree farm. R. D. Merrill moved to Hoquiam in 1898 to run a logging operation there. With his brother-in-law (Ring) the pair began at Pysht and logged 90 million board feet of lumber annually which was towed to local mills (McDonald, Lucile. "When Pysht was Big-Tree Country." *Seattle Times*. Aug. 14, 1960. Magazine Section p 5).

Quadra, Porto de
See Discovery Bay

Qualax River
See Puyallup River.

Quarter Master Cove [7m] #160, 1841, Wilkes
See Smith Cove.

Quartermaster Harbor [7d] #146, 1841, Wilkes; [7g] #155, 1841, Wilkes
Located between Vashon and Maury Islands, in 1841 Wilkes honored the petty officers involved in survey activities. He later named nearby points for them specifically, including Piner, Neill, Sanford, Southworth, Heyer, Pully, Scott, and Henderson (Meany, *Origin* 237).

Quarters Point
Located on the western shore of Totten Inlet between the entrance to Little Skookum Inlet and Big Cove, the origin of the name is unknown.

Quatsap Point [7d] #146, 1841, Wilkes
Located on the western side of Hood Canal just south of Pleasant Harbor, Wilkes left no reason for the 1841 name. It is a Twana name for "between or end" (Bright 403).

Quiet Cove
A local name for the cove located on the northeastern side of Miller Bay at the northeast entrance to Deception Pass (Harrison, Scott, Jan. 2, 2012 email to author).

Quilcene Bay
Located on the northwestern side of Hood Canal, Wilkes originally named this Col-see-ed Harbor [7d] in 1841. He spelled it Colseed-ed on [7k]. The current name originated from the Twana Indian word *quil-ceed-o-bish*, which means "salt water people." Early on it was variously spelled Colcene, Colseed, or Quilceed (Meany, *Origin* 238, 239). During the 1860s, Hampden Cottle and a group of loggers from Maine, including his nephew Sam and son-in-law Charley Brown, settled on a claim near Wildwood Park on the Little Quilcene River. Lillie Cottle, Hampden's daughter, was the first child born in the area. Hampden's occupation was "digging ship knees." Ship knees were curved braces or ribs used inside the hull of a ship. The knee is formed where the root of a tree curves into the trunk. It was an extremely difficult job as the roots needed to be dug up and sawn out. As explained by Sam Cottle (*Told by the Pioneers* 164): "I found my first work in getting out 'knees' for vessels then being constructed at Seabeck, supplying knees for the old tug *Holyoke*, and the schooners *Sailor Boy*, *Olympus*, and *Cassandria Adams*, all built at Seabeck between 1870 and 1880. These knees were an important part of the ship construction at that time, and consisted of pieces of naturally crooked timber of such shape that they could be used in strengthening joints and fastening together different parts of the hull and structures at angles such as those formed by deck beams with the ribs." Dated 1883, t-sheet #1157 shows Sam Cottle's property along the northern and northeastern side of Quilcene Harbor.

Quimper, Bahia de [1] 1790, Quimper
See Dungeness.

Quimper Peninsula [18] #654, 1866, U.S. Coast Survey
The peninsula is located between Discovery Bay and Port Townsend Bay. It was named the Dickerson Peninsula by Wilkes in 1841 [7a] for The Honorable Mahlon Dickerson, Secretary of the Navy, responsible for outfitting the Expedition (Meany, *Origin* 239). Davidson wrote: "Between Port Discovery and Port Townshend lies a peninsula 3 miles wide, offering great advantages as a location for a town. No name

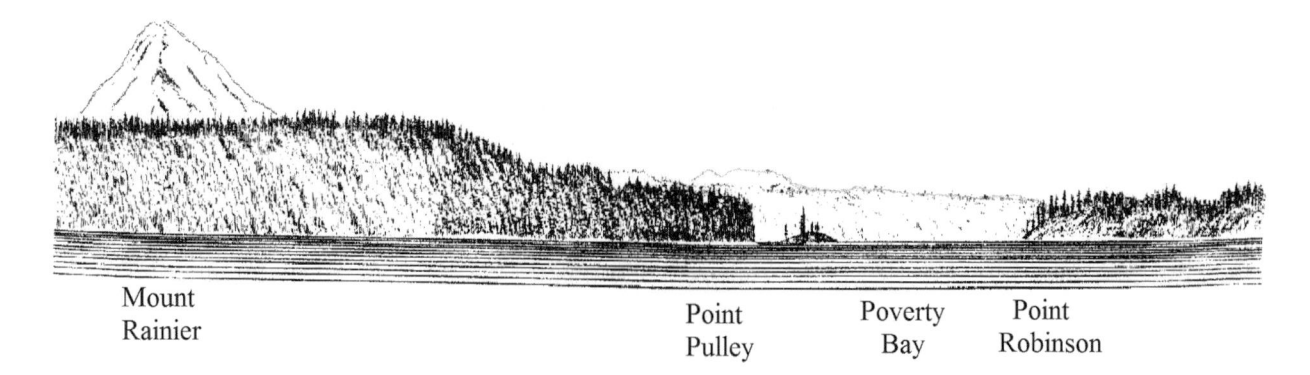

| Mount Rainier | | Point Pulley | Poverty Bay | Point Robinson |

has hitherto been applied to it, and we have ventured to designate it as the Quimper Peninsula," (Davidson, *Report* 441).

Quinlan's Rocks
See Peapod Rocks.

Qulam Point [7i] #147, 1841, Wilkes
See Gordon Point.

Rabbit Island
See Richardson Rock

Raccoon Point [13f] #2689, 1885
It is located between Points Thompson and Lawrence on Orcas Island. The name was likely for the wildlife.

Race Lagoon
Located off the eastern side of Whidbey Island two miles south of Snatelum Point, it was named for Henry Race who relocated from Australia and moved to Whidbey Island. He settled on the lagoon in 1876 (Hitchman 246).

Races Cove
Located at the eastern entrance to Hood Canal, just north of Coon Bay, it was named for Henry Race from Australia who settled in the cove in 1856 (Hitchman 246). The Hitchman entries for Race Lagoon and Races Cove are identical. It is likely that one, or perhaps both, of these entries are in error.

Rada, Punta de [1] 1790, Quimper
See Koitlah Point.

Raft Island [23] #6460, 1905
Located off the eastern shoreline in Carr Inlet, Wilkes originally named it Allshouse's Islet in 1841 [7d], [7e] for crew member Joseph Allhouse (Meany, *Origin* 240). The Stevens brothers were first to settle in 1889. In 1915, they subdivided the 160 acres into fourteen parcels and attempted to sell them with no success. In 1928, George O. Noble, from Pasadena, California, purchased the entire island and built a house. He visited sporadically for four years and then never returned. In 1942, Jess Kuhns bought the island for $30,000. He moved into Noble's house and renamed the island Kuhns Raft Island, ostensibly because it appeared like a raft from the water (Buffington 3-16).

Raindeer Point [7a] #145, 1841, Wilkes
See Fidalgo Head.

Rainier, Mount [6] 1792, Vancouver
Located south of Puget Sound in the Cascade Range, Vancouver named this "after my friend Rear Admiral Rainier." Peter Rainier (circa 1741-1808) rose to the rank of Admiral in 1805. In 1790, Quimper named this *Sierras Nevadas de San Antonio* [1]. In 1883, the director of the National Pacific Railroad who was also the president of the Tacoma Land Company changed the name to Mount Tacoma in literature for the railroad and the land company, hoping to publicize the town. Seven years later, the U.S. Board on Geographic Names addressed the name and approved Mount Rainier. Since that time, interested parties have continued to propose a name change through state legislature, Congress, and the State and U.S. Boards on Geographic Names. In 1978, the proposal was Tahhomah. The State Board denied the proposal, and the U.S. Board supported the decision in 1979. In 1983, the State Board addressed the name Mount Tahoma and decided not to reopen the issue.

Ram Island
It is located at the southern end of Lopez Sound off the eastern side of Lopez Island. Early Admiralty charts reflected it as Houston Island [13c]. E. M. Hummel, an early settler on Lopez, raised goats on the island, the possible source of its current name (McDonald 190). Hummel is definitely the source of Hummel Lake, the largest on Lopez.

Rand, Point [7d] #146, 1841, Wilkes
See Duwamish Head.

Randall Point [22] #6450, 1909
Located on the eastern side of Whidbey Island on Saratoga Passage, Roseberry Randall purchased land around the point in the early 1900s (Cherry I: 115). The Salish name for the point was "star" (Hilbert et. al., 358).

Rasmussen Creek
The two-mile long creek flows into the Strait of Juan de Fuca four or five miles southeast of Neah Bay. It was named after an early homesteader. In its March 8, 1985 meeting, Docket 292, the Washington State Board of Geographic Names changed the spelling from Rasmussan to the current, conforming to local usage. The U.S. Board followed later in the year (from Washington State Board Files).

Reach Island [23] #6460, 1905
Located off the western shoreline of Case Inlet, Joseph Pickard was the first settler on the island. He sold to Alfred W. Zizz in 1905, and Zizz lived on the island until 1952 (Bailey and Nyberg, *Gunkholing in South Puget Sound* 256). Treasure Island was a variant.

Reads Bay
Located on the southwestern side of Decatur Island, near the community of Decatur, it was named for John P. Reed who settled on Decatur Island in the 1860s and built the first house. His middle initial has been variously shown as a P. or T., and his last name has also been spelled Reid and Read. Reed was a Pennsylvania farmer who came to Bellingham about 1855. His wife Mary was an Alaska Indian. Together they raised nine children, all of whom spoke English, German, and their mother's language. According to the 1870 U.S. Census, Reed was running a shingle factory on Decatur, the island's only industry. He also had a blacksmith shop next to the house. At that time, he was 50 and Mary was 35. Reed died of pneumonia while returning home from an Alaskan prospecting trip with his oldest son Bill. Alternatively, *The Islander*, June 13, 1895, p 3 reported that he died of heart disease "about 10 days ago" while prospecting for gold on the Stikine River. His body was returned to Decatur for burial. The June 20 issue reported: "The body of John P. Reed arrived today on the *Lydia Thompson*, unheralded. He died June 4 on board the steamer *Alaska*, on the Stikine river of apoplexy or heart failure." Bill and his brother Joe founded a shipyard on the southeast corner of the bay. It opened in 1895. Henry Cayou, the son of Louis from Deer Harbor, married one of the Reed daughters. Cayou joined the business in 1903 and the name was changed to Reed and Cayou. It peaked in 1910, employing about 30 men. They built tugs, cannery tenders, and fish boats. Cayou's house, restored in 1970, is now used as a clubhouse for the Decatur Shores community. (McDonald 158, 159; McDonald, Lucile. "Decatur Island Then-Now." *Seattle Times*. July 30, 1961. Magazine Section p 10).

Red Bluff [7l] #159, 1841, Wilkes
See Birch Point

Red Bluff [7a] #145, 1841, Wilkes
See Admiralty Head.

Red Bluff [23] #6460, 1905
It is located on the eastern side of Hood Canal about two miles north of Musqueti Point. When the hillside slid, the soil appeared very red, hence the name (from Washington State Board Files, Cougar Spit).

Red Harbor
See Reid Harbor.

Redondo
Located on the eastern shoreline of East Passage about five miles north of Tacoma, it was originally called Stone's Landing, after Zacharias and Jane Stone who purchased the land in 1869 from the squatter, Timothy Lane. There are two versions of the history of the name change. Charles Betts arrived in 1904. Two years later, he renamed the community while attempting to establish a recreation area like Redondo Beach, California. Alternatively, it was

changed by Isaac Hurd and his wife when they took over the post office (Ryan, Amy M. "Redondo- It Always Will Be Called Stone's Landing by Many Old-Timers." *Seattle Times*. Jan. 6, 1963. Magazine Section p 10; TPL website).

Reef Bay
Located on the northeastern side of Johns Island, Lange found the reference in a Friday Harbor Labs publication which listed it as a collection point.

Reef Island [13a] #2689, 1859, Richards
Located near the entrance to Deer Harbor, Orcas Island, it was named for its nearby reef which is exposed at low water.

Reef Point [13a] #2689, 1859, Richards
Located on the southwestern side of Cypress Island, Richards likely named it for its rocks and shallows. Davidson wrote: "... appears the SW. point of Cypress island, off which lie rocks and foul bottom for half a mile on a line to Burrow's island," (*Report* 432).

Reef Point
Located off the eastern side of San Juan Island, south of Turn Island, the name was likely descriptive.

Reid Harbor [13a] #2689, 1859, Richards
Although listed as "Red" Harbor on this chart, Richards corrected the spelling on the 1861 chart [13b]. Located on the southeast side of Stuart Island, the name honored Capt. James Murray Reid who worked in mercantile pursuits in Victoria for most of his 28 year career with the Hudson's Bay Company. Born in 1802, he arrived on the Northwest Coast in 1852. He was Captain of the Hudson's Bay Company ship *Vancouver*. He died in 1868 (Meany, *Origin* 242; Walbran 419). Lange identified an alternative to Capt. Reid, that of George Reid, Master on the *Satellite*. Bernard Mordhorst settled in the harbor in 1876, the first to apply for a land claim on the island. His land was on the southwestern side, perhaps a quarter mile from the entrance and is marked by "2$_1$" (i.e., two fathoms, one foot) and the word "piles" on chart #18432. He and his partner Frederick Hayes fished the local waters and sold smoked herring in Seattle. Mordhorst and his wife Kate, the daughter of a Pig War soldier, had six children. Alfred Chevalier, a watchmaker born in Switzerland, migrated to

Reid Harbor

Waterloo, Iowa. After some misfortunes, the family of twelve moved from the frying pan to the fire, and to the hardships of the Dakotas. In less than a year, they decided to head west. Alfred, now fifty, with his two sons: Bert, age fifteen and Ed, age fourteen, set off for Tacoma where they found work at the coal mines at Carbonado. Alfred sent for his wife and remaining children but became despondent over the hard work and long hours in the mines and took his life early in 1891. Bert and Ed met the family in Tacoma and broke the news to Alfred's wife, Caroline Emma. The family heard of a place called Roche Harbor where jobs were readily available. They moved and worked at the lime quarry. There, Caroline Emma married James Fitch who ran sheep on Stuart Island. The family relocated to Stuart and assisted with raising sheep and fishing. Because of all the children, the Fitch home became the social center for the island. By the 1890s there were a dozen settlers, including Frank Erdmann who arrived in 1890, William Lomberg in 1890, and Joe Emanuel in 1892. When Lomberg's wife divorced him, the Chevaliers purchased his property (Richardson, *Pig* 226-230; McDonald 153, 154).

Reid Rock [20h] #1911, 1861
It is located mid San Juan Channel, just east of Friday Harbor. Meany (*Origin* 242) suggested it might have been named for Capt. James Murray Reid, an employee of the Hudson's Bay Company and for whom Reid Harbor was named. Wood (114) suggests that a more likely candidate might be George Reid, Master aboard the *Satellite*, one of the British surveying ships.

Reil Harbor [13j] #2689, 1894
Located on the southeastern side of Lummi Island, it was supposedly named for an early steamboat captain (Hitchman 249, 250). Davidson referenced it in the 1889 *Pacific Coast Pilot* (568), writing: "Reil's Harbor, towards the southeastern end of Lummi Island, is thoroughly protected with good anchorage. There is fresh water from a nice stream from a little creek during the rainy season. In summer and autumn it dwindles to a trickling stream."

Rendsland Creek
Located on the eastern shoreline of Hood Canal near Musqueti Point, it was named for the early settler Folden Rendsland. The U.S. Board on Geographic Names approved the name in 1941 over the variant names of Deer Creek and Dry Creek (*Decisions*). According to the GNIS files, the name Dry Creek first appeared in an 1884 U.S.C. & G.S. topo survey t-sheet #1650b. Rendsland first appeared on a map of Mason County prior to 1907 (the map was undated, but a later 1907 map also confirmed the name). Later maps supported the name until the 1941 decision.

Reservation Bay
See Bowman Bay.

Reservation Head
Located on the western side of Deception Pass, Wilkes originally named it Naguamos Island in 1841 [7e]. He does not include this name in his *Narrative*, but it is shown on his chart. The current name is perhaps from the nearby Reservation Bay.

Restoration Point

Restoration Point [6] 1792, Vancouver
Located on the southeastern portion of Bainbridge Island, Vancouver honored the return of Charles II after the fall of the Cromwellian Commonwealth. He wrote: "The point near our present station, forming the north point of the bay, hitherto called the Village point, I have distinguished by the name of Restoration Point, having celebrated that memorable event, whilst at anchor under it . . ." (Vancouver 279). Wilkes named it Point Gorden [7q] in 1841 for crewmember John Gorden (Hitchman 250). Wilkes did not include this name in his *Narrative*, but it is shown on his chart. Davidson wrote: "Restoration Point is in some respects very peculiar, no other in these waters, except Battery Point [Alki], presenting the same formation. For 300 yards it is flat, about 10 feet above high water, and has a good depth of soil covered with grass over a limestone rock, upheaved nearly on edge, the direction of the strata pointing

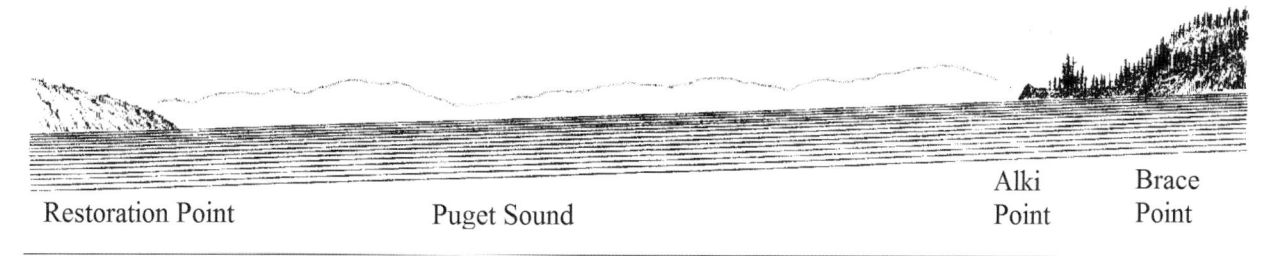

Restoration Point — Puget Sound — Alki Point — Brace Point

toward Battery or a little south of it. Inshore it rises up sharply about 100 feet, its sides covered with grass and the summit with fir trees," (*Report* 447). When Vancouver visited ashore, he met the Suquamish tribal chief, Schweabe. His son, who ultimately became Chief Seattle, was born on Blake Island. He was about seven when he met Vancouver. The Salish word for the point was "place of squeaking." There is also a reference to making fire by friction or for the fact that the wind is strong there (Hilbert et. al., 226). Theodore O. Williams, a one-time Sheriff of Kitsap County, filed a claim on Restoration Point in 1866. Eric August Sanders, aka 'Gus', was born in Sweden in 1848. He left in 1865 to meet up with his brother Charles in San Francisco. The two built a schooner and sailed to the Northwest. Gus found work at the Port Blakely Mill. In 1868, Charles bought the 108.5 acre Restoration Point claim from Theodore Williams for $200. Frustrated with farming, Charles sold out to Gus in 1875 for a pair of boots (Price 53-58). On April 16, 1891, a group of sailing enthusiasts, including George H. Heilbron, Bernard Pelly, W. A. Peters, and Edwin A. Strout, purchased five and a half acres of land on the tip of Restoration Point from Gus for about $1,000. The group soon expanded to include fifteen members who purchased the balance of Sanders' property, 102½ acres, in July 1892 for $22,500. The members incorporated under the name "Country Club" and began building homes on the property. Some spent the entire summer there. The group encountered monetary problems, and by 1894 they returned all but the original five and a half acre parcel to Sanders. During the ensuing years, members died or dropped out and were replaced by new blood. In 1904, the group again purchased the Sanders' property for $30,000. Within a few short years, because of increased usage, the lack of water became the most significant problem to the Country Club. In 1906, members purchased the 142 acre adjacent parcel, as it contained water. The price was $30,000. A three hole golf course was built in 1891, expanded to six holes in 1896, and then to nine holes in 1915 (Pelly). The clubhouse was built in 1891, and since then it has never been improved other than the plumbing.

Retsil
Located on the southeastern side of Port Orchard, opposite Bremerton, it was once part of the homestead of John and Elizabeth Mitchell who settled there in 1865. There was some difficulty arriving at a name for the community, which includes the Washington Veterans' Home. W. H. Cochran of the state Board of Control offered the suggestion of spelling the last name of the governor, Ernest Lister, backward (Meany, *Origin* 243). *See also* Annapolis.

Rich Passage [7d] #146, 1841, Wilkes; [7q] #156, 1841, Wilkes
Wilkes wrote: "The main entrance to Port Orchard is through Rich's Passage: This lies between the south end of Bainbridge Island and the Indian Peninsula, trending in a northwest direction 2 miles in length, by half a mile wide, when it takes a sharp turn to the southwest, of one mile. Properly speaking, Rich's Passage is a part of Port Orchard, but as there were so many branches, I thought it necessary to give the arms which lead into it different names, reserving the name given by Vancouver to the largest . . ." Wilkes honored crew member William Rich in 1841 (Wilkes, *Narrative* 317). Davidson wrote: "From the northwest part of the bay leads a narrow crooked pass 3 miles long to the southern part of Port Orchard, which spreads out into several arms. The pass is obstructed by rocks and is difficult of navigation. The winds are variable, light and uncertain at its narrowest part, where it makes a sharp turn, and is only a couple of hundred yards wide with a rushing swirling current. The channel generally used, although narrower than the one just mentioned, is that [Agate Passage] leading into Port Madison," (*Report* 447, 448). In a 1922 decision, the U.S. Board on Geographic Names removed the possessive form (*Decisions*).

Reynolds Bay
See Dutcher Cove.

Richards Mountain
Located on the northern end of Lummi Island, about halfway between Point Migley and Lummi Point, the source of the name for the 340 foot hill is unknown.

Richards Point [24] #1947, 1849, Inskip
See Treble Point.

Richardson [13n] #2689, 1908
Located on the southwestern side of Lopez Island, George S. Richardson settled there in 1871 followed by William Graham in 1881 who constructed a wharf and established the island's first post office. He also built a store over the pier which burned in 1990 on its 100th anniversary (Walsh 12, 13; McDonald 119; Richardson, *Pig* 63).

Richardson Bay
See Richardson. See also Jones Bay.

Richardson Rock
Located north of Jones Bay in Hidden Inlet, locals named the rock for Richardson. Of the rock, McLellan wrote: "Richardson Rock is located near the shore of Lopez Island, about 250 yards east of the boat-landing at Richardson post office. It has an area of 1.35 acres and its nearly vertical sides rise to an elevation of about 35 feet." The original name of the rock was Rabbit Island. It is mentioned at http://freepages.history.rootsweb.ancestry.com/~lopezislandhistory/Lopez%20Island%20-%20History.doc

Richmond, Point [7d] #146, 1841, Wilkes; [7g] #155, 1841, Wilkes
Located on Colvos Passage, three miles north of Gig Harbor, Wilkes honored crew member William Richmond in 1841. Wilkes did not include this name in his *Narrative*, but it is shown on his chart (Meany, *Origin* 222).

Richmond Beach [22] #6450, 1909
Located on the eastern side of Admiralty Inlet about six miles north of Shilshole Bay, it was named on October 4, 1889 by E. W. Mills and John Pappendick as a favor to John Spencer who came from Richmond, England (Meany, *Origin* 244).

Right Smart Cove
It is located immediately south of Jackson Cove on the western shoreline of Hood Canal. Back when logging was king, Ed Brown was looking for a place to dump his logs. The timber owner referred to the cove as a right smart place (Hitchman 252).

Rignal
Located on the western side of Eld Inlet south of Hunter Point, the post office opened in 1920. The origin of the name is perhaps after an early settler (Palmer, 70).

Ringgold, Point [7a] #145, 1841, Wilkes; [7d] #146, 1841, Wilkes; [7p] #150, 1841, Wilkes
See Marrowstone Point.

Ringgold's Channel [7a] #145, 1841, Wilkes
See Rosario Strait.

Rink Creek
See Massey Creek.

Ripple Island [13a] #2689, 1859, Richards
Located east of Johns Island and north of Spieden Island, Richards' reason for this name is unknown. The U.S. Government owns the island.

Roberts, Point [6] 1792, Vancouver
Located on a spit of land south of the Canadian border and isolated from the U.S. mainland, it was first named by Eliza in 1791 as the *Isla de Zepeda* [2], [3]. The early Spanish thought it was an island rather than a peninsula, but Galiano and Valdéz discovered its true form and called it *Peninsula de Cepeda* (Wagner 186, 249). Vancouver named it after Henry Roberts, his "esteemed friend and predecessor in the *Discovery*," (Vancouver 299). Vancouver and Roberts had served together under Capt. Cook during his final two voyages, 1772-1774 and 1776-1779. Roberts was selected to lead this exploration, but because of the Nootka conflicts with Spain, he was instead sent to the West Indies. Promoted to Commander, Vancouver was then chosen to lead the exploration. Speaking of the boundary markers separating the U.S. and Canada, J. J. Gilbert wrote in his 1888 survey and Descriptive Report #1874 (http://riverhistory.ess.washington.edu/tsheets/reports/t1874.pdf, p 7): "By my work, all these posts are about 250 m north of the 49th parallel."

Roberts, Point [7a] #145, 1841, Wilkes; [7d] #146, 1841, Wilkes; [7m] #160, 1841, Wilkes
See Alki Point.

Robinson, Point [7d] #146, 1841, Wilkes; [7g] #155, 1841, Wilkes
Located on the eastern side of Maury Island, Wilkes honored crew member John Robinson in 1841 (Meany, *Origin* 245). The Salish name for the point was "hollering across" (Hilbert et. al., 236). Even

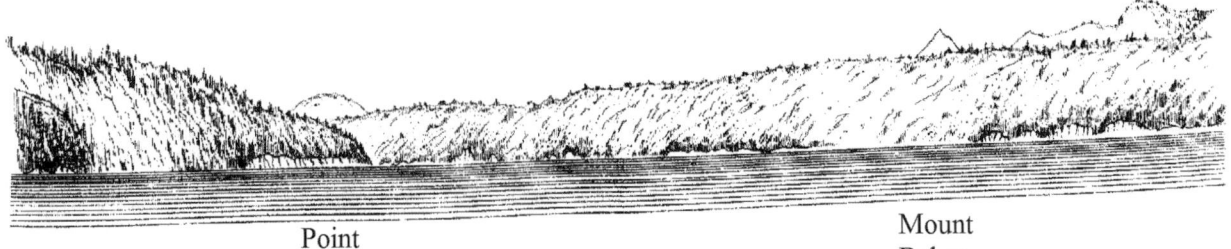

Point Robinson — *Mount Baker*

though Point Robinson is consistent with the GNIS database, current charts reflect this as Robinson Point. The difference may require resolution through the U.S. Board on Geographic Names.

Roche Harbor

Roche Harbor [13a] #2689, 1859, Richards
Located off the northwestern side of San Juan Island, Richards honored Lt. Richard Roche. Roche served as a midshipman under Capt. Henry Kellett on the H.M.S. *Herald* during Kellett's 1846-1847 survey activities in the San Juans. Roche returned ten years later and served as a lieutenant under Capt. James Prevost on H.M.S. *Satellite* (Meany, *Origin* 245). He was promoted to commander in 1864 and served in the Mediterranean from 1873-1875. He was promoted to captain-retired in 1879. The record is unclear whether Roche sounded out the harbor, but regardless, Richards named it for him. Several days after the British departed Garrison Bay, Joseph Ruff took out a preemption claim on 160 acres of land surrounding Roche Harbor, but he did not improve it or mine the lime. The Scurr brothers, Robert and Richard, visited Roche twice, once in 1871 and a second time in 1873. From England, they followed the lure of gold westward across the U.S. and apparently to the Fraser River. In 1881, they bought out Ruff for $1,000 and began production of lime (Burley 19). John S. McMillin, a lawyer in Tacoma, was born in Indiana October 28, 1855. He married Louella Hiett on June 5, 1877 and migrated to Tacoma in 1884. They had four children: John H., who died at birth on July 16, 1878; Fred, born September 16, 1880; Paul, born May 19, 1886, and Dorothy, born January 19, 1894. McMillin established the Tacoma Lime Company, holding two-thirds interest, with his wife's brother holding the remainder, and founded the town of McMillin near Orting. Hearing about lime in the San Juans, he scouted for the Company and found what he thought to be a very large and rich deposit. He purchased Roche in 1886 from the Scurrs and founded the Tacoma and Roche Harbor Lime Company. He constructed the hotel in 1887, a twenty-two room structure, around the original Hudson's Bay Company log cabin (parts of the log cabin are still visible from the top of the stairs on the second floor). A town soon grew up around the hotel, including the lime factory, barrel works, warehouses, docks, store, church, school, barns, and homes. The limestone deposit ran across the peninsula to Westcott Bay, estimated to be three quarters of a mile long by a quarter mile wide. However, it was really much larger and was reportedly the purest known to exist in the world (Burley 19-32). The Scurr brothers remained in the area for many years following the sale. Reuben Tarte, a Seattle businessman, purchased the land in 1956. It included 4,000 acres and twelve miles of shoreline. Because of antiquated equipment, it was impossible for Tarte to continue limestone operations. On October 1, 1956, the fires died for the first time in seventy-five years. A partnership of Rich Komen and Verne Howard purchased the resort in 1988. Saltchuk Resources of Seattle purchased Howard's interests in 1997. In addition to his Roche investments, Komen also owns substantial acreage on White Point.

Rock Island [10] #51, 1854, U.S. Coast Survey
See Towhead Island.

Rock Island [22] #6450, 1909
Located south of the western side of the Hood Canal Bridge, the origin of the name is unknown.

Rock Point [13a] #2689, 1859, Richards
Located on the western side of Lopez Island near the south end of San Juan Channel, it is home to a huge glacial boulder. Richards' name is descriptive.

Rockaway Beach
Located north of Onamac Point on the western side of Camano Island, the origin of the name is unknown.

Rocky Bay [13a] #2689, 1859, Richards
Located off the northeastern side of San Juan Island, inside O'Neal Island, Richards likely named it for its appearance.

Rocky Bay
Located behind Rocky Point in Case Inlet, the name was likely descriptive.

Rocky Bluff [7j] #153, 1841, Wilkes
See Jackson Cove.

Rocky Point [7d] #146, 1841, Wilkes; [7e] #158, 1841, Wilkes
Located on the eastern side of Whidbey Island at the northeast entrance to Holmes Harbor, Wilkes left no reason for the 1841 name. Wilkes did not include this name in his *Narrative*, but it is shown on his chart.

Rocky Point
Located on the Strait of Juan de Fuca, halfway between Sequim and Discovery Bay, it was likely named for its shoreline features. In 1976, the U.S. Board on Geographic Names received a proposal from James DeLao of Port Townsend to change the name to Gunstone Point. The rationale was to remove the duplicity with the other Rocky Point on Camano Island. GNIS files do not contain any information beyond the proposal, but obviously the current name endured.

Rocky Point [23] #6460, 1905
Located on the southwestern shore of Eld Inlet, it was likely named for its appearance.

Rocky Point
Located on the northwestern side of Camano Island, Wilkes originally named this Point Demock in 1841 [7a], likely for crew member John Demock. Wilkes did not include this name in his *Narrative*, but it is shown on his chart. The Salish name for the point was "big bad place at the foot of something" (Hilbert et. al., 372). Although Point Demock was used on charts and *Pacific Coast Pilots* through 1959, in 1960 the Coast and Geodetic Survey field party determined that "the name Rocky Point is in undisputed local use, and though some people said they had seen Point Demock used on maps, they had never called it by that name." The U.S. Board on Geographic Names approved the name in 1962 over Wilkes' name and another variant, Damrock Point. It appears that the name Damrock was reflected in error on a 1942 and 1948 Olympic National Forest map even though the 1932 edition correctly reflected Demock. Thus, the name Damrock was quickly discarded (GNIS files).

Rocky Point
Located between Phinney and Mud Bays in Dyes Inlet, it was named for its appearance.

Rocky Point
Located on the eastern side of Case Inlet about a mile north of Vaughn Bay, Wilkes originally named this Sota Point [7h] in 1841. He left no reason for the name. Wilkes did not include this name in his *Narrative*, but it is shown on his chart.

Rocky Point
See Cap Sante.

Rodd Bay [24] #1947, 1849, Inskip
See Oro Bay.

Rodena Beach
Located on the eastern side of Whidbey Island immediately southwest of Snatelum Point, the origin of the name is unknown. It was originally platted as Rhodena Beach which somehow morphed into Rodena Beach. Internet searches return an equal number of hits on both names, but only Rodena is recognized by the U.S. Board on Geographic Names. Access to the homes along the beach is provided by Rhodena Road.

Rodgers Island [7a] #145, 1841, Wilkes; [7c] #144, 1841, Wilkes
See San Juan Island.

Rolfe Cove

Rolfe Cove
It is located on the western side of Matia Island. Hamilton Rolfe, Jr. "fell from a cliff in the cove adjacent to our campsite and was fatally injured on August 21, 1937." His father petitioned to name the cove in his honor, and the U.S. Board on Geographic Names agreed in 1972 (GNIS files).

Rojas, Ensenada de [1] 1790, Quimper
See Clallam Bay.

Rolling Bay
See Murden Cove.

Rosario

Rosario
Located on the eastern shoreline of East Sound, Cascade Bay, Orcas Island, it was named by Robert Moran in 1906. Andrew Newhall founded the community of Newhall (local name) in 1887 around his Cascade Bay Lumber Company. The company built fruit boxes, barrels, shingles, rough lumber, windows, moldings, etc. A post office was established in 1890. In 1905, Moran purchased the lumber company along with adjoining land in Cascade Bay. He continued to buy land until he owned 7,300 acres, including most of Mount Constitution except for the summit (Richardson, *Pig* 335). Moran, originally from New York, was perhaps the most illustrious settler on Orcas. He arrived at Yesler Dock in Seattle in November 1875 with only ten cents in his pocket. The kindly Bill Gross at Our House Hash House gave the 17-year-old youngster breakfast that morning on credit. A machinist by trade, Moran found only one machine shop in the city, and that with little business. With difficulties finding work, and his debt increasing, Gross found him a job as a cook at a logging camp on Squak Slough (the Sammamish Slough). A short few days later, the men in the camp decided his food was terrible. They paid him three dollars and asked him to leave! Gross then found him a job as a deck hand on the steamer *J.B. Libby,* which ran mail weekly between Seattle and Bellingham. During the next year, Moran found additional work aboard various ships and then met Capt. George W. Bulline who was a federal boiler inspector. For reasons unknown, Bulline took Moran under his wing and tutored him in mathematics, drafting, and engineering. In 1879, Gross found Moran work on the *Cassiar* commanded by Capt. Nat H. Lane, Jr. Moran became chief engineer aboard for trade to Alaska. There he met and became good friends with John Muir. In 1881, Robert's two older brothers, Edward and Peter, arrived in the Northwest. Moran also sent for his mother and five younger brothers. The brothers started a marine repair shop: the Seattle Drydock and Shipbuilding Company, and the business prospered. In 1887, locals elected Moran to the City Council and the following year, at age thirty-one, as Mayor of Seattle. The 1889 Seattle fire destroyed the entire Moran shipyard, but within ten days, they rebuilt and were ready for business again. With a solid reputation, the services of the shipyard were in constant demand and it grew steadily. One of the largest accomplishments was the construction of the 441 foot Battleship Nebraska, launched in

1904. That same year, Moran was diagnosed with heart disease and given just a short time to live. At age forty-nine he retired. In 1905, he traveled to Orcas Island and fell in love with its tranquil life. He purchased the Newhall property renaming it Rosario. The brothers sold the shipyard to Breton, Griscom, and Jenks from the East Coast in 1906. In 1912, it became the Seattle Construction and Drydock, and in 1916 it was taken over by Todd Shipyards (Peacock 11-37). In 2011, Vigor Industrial purchased the company. Moran moved to Orcas and began construction of the mansion, completing it in 1909 at an estimated cost of $1,500,000. Surprisingly, he regained his health and lived another forty years. Generous with the islanders, he built roads and then deeded them to the county at no cost, including the machinery used in their construction. During the depression he created jobs for the locals. He built a community public water system for Olga. Ultimately, his greatest gift was to the State of Washington in the form of the Moran State Park (Richardson, *Pig* 336). Moran lived at Rosario for twenty-seven years but lost interest in the estate following the death of his wife in 1932. He sold in 1938, including 1,339 acres of land, to a California industrialist, Donald Rheem, the son of William S. Rheem, founder and Chairman of the Board of Standard Oil of California. The price was $50,000. Rheem and his wife Alice lived there part time for the next twenty years. In 1958, Rheem sold to Ralph Curton and the Falcon Corporation of Waco, Texas for $455,000. In 1960, Gilbert H. Geiser, a former Mayor of Mountlake Terrace, purchased the estate for $225,000. He began the conversion to a resort (Peacock 66-69). The property was sold again at an auction on September 30, 2008, for $5.45 million to Jerry and Jan Barto of Anacortes and owner of Signal Hill Petroleum.

Rosario Beach
Located on the southwestern side of Fidalgo Island, near Bowman Bay, it was likely named for Rosario Strait.

Rosario Head
Located on the northwestern side of Deception Pass, Wilkes originally named it Watsok Island in 1841 [7e]. Wilkes did not include this name in his *Narrative*, but it is shown on his chart. The current name was likely taken from the strait.

Rosario Hill
Located on the eastern side of Orcas Island, Richards first charted it as Stony Hill on the 1859 Admiralty chart #2689 [13a]. In 1905, the ship-builder Robert Moran purchased the Cascade Bay Lumber Company located on Cascade Bay (hence the name) and the surrounding land. Moran apparently liked the name "Rosario" from Rosario Strait and used it for his home. Subsequent U.S. Coast surveys applied the name to the nearby point and the hill. The U.S. Board on Geographic Names eliminated the variant Stony Hill in 1925 (*Decisions*). According to the GNIS files, the name was proposed by McClellan.

Rosario Island [24] #1947, 1849, Inskip
See Fox Island.

Rosario Point
See Rosario Hill

Rosario Strait [8a] #1917, 1847, Kellett
Rosario Strait forms the eastern boundary of the San Juan Islands. Originally named *Canal de Fidalgo* [1] (simply Fidalgo in his journal, Wagner 111) by Quimper in 1790, and retained in 1791 by Pantoja and Eliza [2] and [3] respectively, Wilkes renamed the strait Ringgold's Channel [7a] in 1841, honoring the Lieut. Commandant Cadwalader Ringgold,

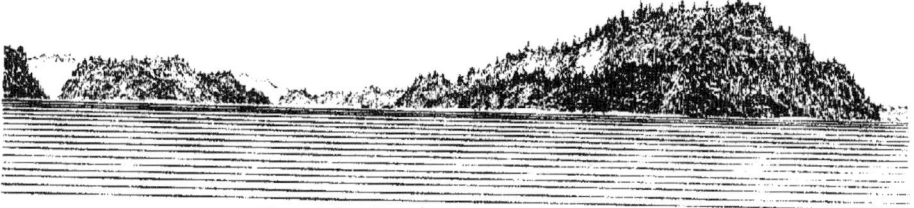

Cypress Island — Rosario Strait, North entrance — Mount Constitution

Captain of the *Porpoise* (Wilkes, *Narrative* 305). In 1791, Pantoja discovered the Strait of Georgia: "This I named El Gran Canal de Nuestra Señora del Rosario La Marinera [2], in honor of our patroness, as it was the most important place we had discovered up to the present," (Wagner 175, 176). Eliza shortened it slightly by removing "*La Marinera*" [3]. Vancouver renamed this waterway the Gulf of Georgia [6]. In 1847, recognizing these events, Kellett maintained Vancouver's name but shortened and moved Eliza's to its current location (Meany, *Origin* 248). In 1976, the Washington State Board on Geographic Names reviewed the northern and southern boundaries of Rosario Strait. In their December 10, 1976 meeting, Docket 210, the Board agreed that the boundary was "a line drawn between Sandy Point and the east end of Matia Island and then on to Pt. Thompson on Orcas Island; the southern limit is a line drawn between Iceberg Point on Lopez Island and Pt. Partridge on Whidbey Island." The Board again reviewed and revised the boundary in a June 9, 1978 meeting, Docket 222. "The northern boundary of Rosario Strait is a line between Pt. Thompson (Orcas Island) and Pt. Migley (Lummi Island). The southern boundary is a line between Pt. Colville (Lopez Island) and Rosario Head (Fidalgo Island)." The U.S. Board on Geographic Names agreed with the decision in 1979 (from Washington State Board Files).

Rose Point [7k] #152, 1841, Wilkes
See Fishermans Point.

Rose Point
Located ½ mile south of Eglon, the name was likely descriptive.

Rosedale
The community is located due east of Raft Island on the eastern shoreline of Carr Inlet. Capt. and Mrs. McLean and Walter and Willie White settled there in 1882. It was named for the wild roses that grew in the area (Meany, *Origin* 249; *History* I: 58).

Rosehilla
It is located at the southern end of Maury Island. According to the King County Plat map for Rosehilla Beach, the plat was filed in 1911 by Anton Snider and John and Mary Visell. They left no reason why they selected this name. Bo Kinney, a librarian in the special collections at the Seattle Public Library, speculated that there may be a connection between Rosehilla and Northilla. Northilla was platted in 1909 by the Norton-Hill Company. Perhaps the owners chose to maintain some consistency between the names. Laurie Tucker from the Vashon/Maury Island Heritage Association spoke with Norton's grandson who still lives on the island. She found a reference to Rosehilla in a local history by Howard Lynn. Lynn wrote: "No houses were built at Rosehilla, to the south of Manzanita, during this period either, although clearly Rosehilla was indicated as a settlement during the boom [early 1890s] because the Sawyer plat filed in 1892 indicates a Manzanita-Rosehilla Road," (May 23, 2010 email to the author). Ms. Tucker guessed that because Manzanita was named for the madrona trees there, perhaps Rosehilla was named for wild roses, prolific around our inland waters.

Ross, Point [13c] #2689, 1865
Located on the northern side of the Quimper Peninsula between McCurdy Point and Point Wilson, Richards left no reason for the name.

Ross Point
It is located in Sinclair Inlet west of the community of Port Orchard. According to Bonnie Chrey, a researcher with the Kitsap County Historical Society, the name appeared on a 1909 plat map (Mar. 25, 2011 email to author from Ms. Chrey). The 1910 Kitsap County census lists Thomas and Laura Ross plus two children as living in the Port Orchard Town precinct. Their relationship to the name of the point is unknown.

Round Head [13d] #2689, 1874
See Decatur Head.

Round Rock
Noted by McLellan, it is: "located 375 yards to the east of Charles Island" on the southwestern end of Lopez Island. The name may be descriptive.

Rowboat Cove
There are two small coves on the northern side of Davis Bay. Rowboat Cove is the more easterly. The origin of the name is unknown.

Rum Island
See Cayou Island.

Ruston
Located on the eastern shoreline of Commencement Bay, it was originally named Smelter. Locals renamed it in 1906 honoring William R. Rust, a major stockholder and manager of the Tacoma Milling & Smelting Company, which was founded in 1887. He sold in 1906 to the American Smelting and Refining Company or ASARCO. Rust died in 1928 (*A History* 81; Hitchman 258).

Ryder Channel [24] #1947, 1849, Inskip
See Balch Passage.

S West Island [11] #654, 1858, U.S. Coast Survey
See Colville Island.

Sachem Point [7m] #160, 1841, Wilkes
See March Point.

Saddle Island
See Jones Island.

Saddlebag Island [21] #6300, 1895
See Hat Island.

Sail Point [7n] #149, 1841, Wilkes
See Schoolhouse Point.

Sail River
Located two miles east of Neah Bay, Kellett first named it Okho River in 1847 [8a]. The U.S. Coast Survey changed the name to the Tocosos River on [21]. The current name perhaps came from Sail Rock.

Sail Rock [7b] #148, 1841, Wilkes; [7c] #144, 1841, Wilkes
Located east of Neah Bay, Wilkes likely named the 150 foot rock in 1841 for its appearance (Wilkes, *Journal* 108). Kellett reflected the name "Klaholoh Rock Seals" on [9a] as if it were one name. Variant names included Klahostah Rock and Seal Rock, which the U.S. Board on Geographic Names discarded in 1992 in favor of the current name.

Sail Rock Point [7b] #148, 1841, Wilkes; [7c] #144, 1841, Wilkes
See Klachopis Point.

Sakali Bluff [7j] #153, 1841, Wilkes
Located on the western side of Hood Canal outside Pleasant Harbor, Wilkes left no reason for the 1841 name. It is neither named on current charts nor recognized by the U.S. Board on Geographic Names. Wilkes did not include this name in his *Narrative*, but it is shown on his chart. An alternate spelling of Sakati may be possible, Wilkes' chart is unclear.

Salem Point
See Salmon Point.

Salish Sea
The "sea" encompasses all of inland Washington waters and the lower BC waters including the Strait of Georgia and Desolation Sound. In 1989, Professor Bert Webber, a marine biologist from Western Washington University in Bellingham suggested the name ". . . to raise consciousness about taking care of the region's waters and ecosystems." After reviewing the proposal and soliciting opinions of interested parties, the Washington State Board on Geographic Names found ". . . there did not appear to be any compelling reason to pursue the suggestion, and many strong reasons why doing so would not be worthwhile at this time," (from Washington State Board Files, 1991 file). While the first attempt at the name failed, the name grew in common usage such that when resubmitted to the Board in 2008, it was approved. The name does not replace other names, it merely overlays them. The BC Geographical Names Office approved the name in August 2009; the U.S. Board on Geographic Names similarly acted three months later (from Washington State Board Files).

Salmon Bank [13a] #2689, 1859, Richards
Located south of the southeastern end of San Juan Island, the U.S. Coast Survey reflected it in 1854 on [10] but did not name it. The size of the bank and its shallow depth made it a hazard to early shipping, but, because of its depth, salmon were forced close to the surface and were more easily caught. The Hudson's Bay Company took advantage of this during the 1850s.

Salmon Bay
Located east the locks, the Salmon Creek connected it with Shilshole Bay. The U.S. Board on Geographic Names adopted the name in 1964 over variants of Salmon Bay Waterway and Shilshole Bay. *See also* Shilshole Bay. According to the 1903 *Pacific Coast Pilot* (141): "The bight [Shilshole Bay] itself is

important only in forming the approach to the small inlet known as Salmon Bay, on which the town of Ballard is situated, and through which is the course of the proposed canal extending from deep water in Puget Sound to Lake Union. This has been partially constructed, and at low water a depth of 16 feet can be taken to the wharves at Ballard through a dredged cut 50 feet in width."

Salmon Beach
Located on the eastern side of The Narrows, the community originally was a bunch of fishing shacks. It was named for the migrating salmon (Reese, *Origins* 98).

Salmon Creek [9a] #1911, 1849, Kellett
The creek flows into the head of Discovery Bay. Davidson referenced it in *Directory* (119) as the Salmon River. It is not reflected on the U.S. Coast Survey charts until 1909 [22].

Salmon Creek
Prior to the existence of the locks, Salmon Creek flowed from Salmon Bay into Shilshole Bay. The creek was named by Arthur and David Denny for the salmon runs but was called *Cil-col* by the Indians, meaning "threading or inserting" in reference to Salmon Creek flowing into the bay (Hilbert et. al., 58).

Salmon Point
Located on the northern end of Squaxin Island, Wilkes spelled it Salom in 1841. Another variant was Salem Point. He left no reason for the name. Wilkes did not include this name in his *Narrative*, but it is shown on his charts [7h] and [7i]. According to Docket 280 of the Washington State Board on Geographic Names, the Squaxin Tribe indicated that historically the name of the point has been Salmon Point and further believes that Salom was misspelled, notwithstanding the fact that it appeared that way on two charts from Wilkes. The current name was approved by the Washington State Board on June 11, 1982 (from Washington State Board files). *See also* Belspeox Point.

Salom Point [7h] #154, 1841, Wilkes; [7i] #147, 1841, Wilkes
See Salmon Point.

Salsbury, Point [7a] #145, 1841, Wilkes
It is located on the eastern side of San Juan Island. In his hasty survey of the area in 1841, Wilkes included Turn Island as part of San Juan Island and named it Point Salsbury for crew member Francis Salsbury. Wilkes did not include this name in his *Narrative*, but it is shown on his chart. It is neither named on current charts nor recognized by the U.S. Board on Geographic Names.

Salsbury Point [7d] #146, 1841, Wilkes
Located due west of Port Gamble on the eastern side of Hood Canal, Wilkes honored crew member Francis Salsbury in 1841. He spelled the name Salisbury in his *Narrative* but Salsbury in his muster list (323, 296).

Salsbury Point [7a] #145, 1841, Wilkes; [7m] #160, 1841, Wilkes
It is the northwesterly point of Strawberry Bay, Cypress Island. In 1841, Wilkes honored crew member Francis Salsbury. Wilkes did not include this name in his *Narrative*, but it is shown on his chart. The name is neither reflected on current charts nor recognized by the U.S. Board on Geographic Names.

Salví, Pta de [1] 1790, Quimper
Early in Quimper's exploration, he referred to Observatory Point as *Salví*. Later, he changed the reference to Striped Peak. *See* Observatory Point, Striped Peak.

Samego Point [7i] #147, 1841, Wilkes
There are two points on the northern end of McNeil Island. This is the western one. Wilkes left no reason for the name in 1841. He does not include this name in his *Narrative*, but it is shown on his chart.

Samish Bay [21] #6300, 1895
Located south of Bellingham, it took its name from the local Indian tribe (Meany, *Origin* 254).

Samish Island [21] #6300, 1895
Located east of Guemes Island, it was named for the tribe of Indians that inhabited the area for centuries. Because of northern Indian raids and White diseases, tribal numbers which were estimated in the 1840s at 2,000 by some sources declined to 150 less than ten years later. Another source (*An Illustrated History*, 111) indicated that there were

again 2,000 Indians living on or around the Siwash Slough. Samish came from the Skagit Indian word *samens* meaning "hunter" (Meany, *Origin* 254; Phillips 123). The Samish Indians had permanent settlements along Chuckanut and Samish Bays, on Samish, Fidalgo, and Guemes Islands and along the Samish River. They built two longhouses on Samish Island. That on the southeast shore was said to be 600 feet in length, and the building on the west side was almost 1,000 feet long. The earliest settler was Blanket Bill Jarman (1827-1912). About 1852, with his Indian wife Alice, they moved to the island and were apparently greeted by the Samish Chief S'-yak-whom, also known as Chief Sehome. Jarman lived with the Samish Indians there at the eastern end of the island. He fished, hunted, and trapped for several years, and he carried mail by canoe between Fort Bellingham and other army posts on the sound. About 1860, Jarman migrated to an Indian camp in Bellingham Bay. According to one source, he named the shoal bay at the mouth of the Samish River after his wife; the local name continues to be used (http://www.samishisland.net/si_historytimeline.html). The Siwash Slough connected Alice Bay to Padilla Bay. Daniel Dingwall, one of the earliest and more permanent settlers, began a logging camp in 1867, a store in 1869, and a post office the following year at Fish Point. The homestead covered most of the eastern end of the island. Eventually, Col. Granville O. Haller took over the homestead. A later owner donated most of it to the Latter Day Saints. William Dean joined as a partner in the store but started a store and hotel of his own in short time. Dean later relocated to the north side of the island and built a hotel. George Washington Lafayette Allen, a Confederate veteran, platted the town of Atlanta near the east end of Samish on June 12, 1883. He intended it as a refuge for persecuted Confederates. He built the Atlanta Home Hotel in 1886; shortly thereafter, the plat was abandoned. The hotel burned down in 1933. The front door, which faced Bellingham Bay, led to a large lobby running the width of the building. A dining room was on the backside along with stairs to the upper floor. There were two rooms above the lobby with others on either side of a hallway leading to the back of the building. There were also two dormitory rooms in the attic for employees. There were living quarters in the basement, along with the kitchen, storerooms, and a workshop. Allen died in the hotel in 1903. Less than a week after he platted Atlanta, George Dean, brother of William, platted the town of Samish on the western side of the island. The southwestern point of the island carries the local name of Deans Spit. Competition ensued with each man lengthening his pier to capture the steamship trade. Ultimately, an armed battle resulted in the death of one man. The importance of Samish later declined and neither town was incorporated (Hitchman 9; Bailey and Nyberg, *San Juan Islands* 206, 207; *An Illustrated History*, 110). In the early 1900s, the quarter-mile Samish or Siwash Slough separated the island from the mainland and connected Alice and Padilla Bays. Although a wooden bridge was built over the slough, the access on either side was swampy, particularly at high tide. Skagit County filled the area to create farmland in 1932 and constructed a road along the northern side. Remnants of the slough still exist.

Samish Slough
See Samish Island.

San de Fuca
Located at the head of Penn Cove, it was originally named Coveland, presumably for the cove. Capt. Richard Holbrook, born in 1821, homesteaded on 160 acres there in 1852. Part of the homestead became San de Fuca (Cahail). The first post office in north Whidbey was located in Coveland in the county courthouse, the first courthouse on the island. The building remains today. Renamed San de Fuca in 1888 by a group of land speculators intent on building a town, the name came from the area's proximity to the Strait of Juan de Fuca (Neil 119).

San Gil
See Orcas Knob.

San José, Pta de [3] 1791, Eliza
See Drayton Harbor.

San Juan Channel [18] #654, 1865, U.S. Coast Survey
Located along the eastern side of San Juan Island, Meany (*Origin* 255) provided some evidence that Eliza named the entrance between San Juan and Lopez Islands *Boca de Horcasitas*. In 1841, Wilkes

named Griffin Bay and the southern portion of San Juan Channel Ontario Roads [7a] after Lake Ontario (Wilkes, *Narrative* 306). Richards reflected the name "Middle Channel" on [14a] in 1861. The entire name is written on his chart to the south of Cattle Point (out in the Strait of Juan de Fuca). However, he duplicated the name further north in what current charts show as San Juan Channel. The "M" in Middle began about halfway between San Juan and Jones Islands. The "l" in Channel appeared between San Juan and Shaw Islands and about halfway between Neck Point and Point George. The U.S. Coast Survey changed the name the following year and included the entire eastern side of San Juan Island.

San Juan Island [3] 1791, Eliza
Eliza's 1791 chart reflected the entry: *Isla y Archipielago de San Juan*. He encircled most of the San Juan Islands (i.e., the islands west of Rosario Strait), but it is difficult to tell if he also included Waldron or Stuart Islands. It is clear he recognized that the islands were separated by small channels, and, as such, was uninterested in exploring further. He simply used Haro and Rosario Straits as the boundaries and labeled almost everything in-between as the archipelago. Which of these islands he intended to name San Juan is also unclear. According to Pantoja: "Between Fidalgo [Rosario Strait] and Lopez de Aro [Haro Strait] there is a great archipelago of islands which was named 'San Juan'," (Wagner 187). In 1841, Wilkes [7a] named it Rodgers Island for U.S.N Commodore John Rodgers who commanded the *President* in its battle with the *Little Belt* in 1811 (Wilkes, *Narrative* 306). In the 1847 Admiralty chart, Kellett [8a] restored the Spanish name and decided that "San Juan Island" would be applied to the western-most island. The U.S. Coast Survey waffled on the name. In both [10] and [11]: "Bellevue or San Juan Island" was used in its 1854 and 1858 charts. According to John S. McMillian in a June 21, 1898 article in the *Seattle PI*, the name *Bellevue* came from the French. In the 1859 Admiralty chart [13a], Richards (and in subsequent British charts) ignored the Hudson's Bay Company name and simply used San Juan Island. The U.S. Coast Survey chart of 1862 [17] used "Bellevue or San Juan Island" but the 1866 chart [18] adopted the Admiralty name.

San Juan Islands [2] 1791, Pantoja; [3] 1791, Eliza
As noted above, Eliza's 1791 chart reflected the entry: *Isla y Archipielago de San Juan*. Pantoja's chart labeled it as simply *Archipielago de San Juan*. Both men circled the archipelago but included only the islands west of Rosario Strait. Also, it is unclear if Waldron or Stuart were included within their circle. The 1858 U.S. Coast Survey chart referenced the archipelago and surrounding waters as Washington Sound [11]. According to Davidson: "The Canal de Haro and Rosario strait were surveyed by the United States Coast Survey in 1853 and 1854, and the archipelago called Washington sound," (*Directory* 124). On [11], the "W" in Washington Sound is located about five miles due north of Protection Island. The "ton" rolls through the south end of San Juan Channel. The word "sound" crosses over Orcas Island; the "d" is located about halfway between Sucia Island and Alden Bank. A later version of the chart [18] does not reflect the name across the San Juans; it is only shown in the title of the chart. Davidson wrote in the 1889 *Pacific Coast Pilot* (556): "The Canal de Haro and Rosario Strait were surveyed by the U.S. Coast Survey in 1853 and 1854, when the name Washington Sound was applied to the whole archipelago between the mainland and Vancouver Island." In 1930, the U.S. Board on Geographic Names agreed to a boundary of the archipelago with Haro Strait on the west and Rosario Strait on the east and affirmed the name as the San Juan Archipelago. The term Washington Sound appeared on USC&GS chart #s 6380 and 6300 but disappeared from post 1930 editions, likely as a result of the U.S. Board decision. The decision was reaffirmed by the U.S. Board in 1964 and further modified the name from the San Juan Archipelago to the San Juan Islands, consistent with local usage. In 1977, the Washington Board on Geographic Names received a proposal to reinstate the name Washington Sound, and in 1978 a second proposal to name it Quimper Sound. In its March 14, 1979 meeting, the Board decided that a name for the waters surrounding the San Juan Islands was unnecessary. In their September 7, 1979 meeting, the Washington State Board also limited the name of the San Juan Islands to conform to the islands in San Juan County only (from Washington State Board files).

San Juan Town
A community that formed near the Bellevue Farm wharf in Griffin Bay; it grew after American troops were stationed at American Camp.

San Rafael, Punta de [3] 1791, Eliza
See Kwomais Point.

Sand Spit, The
Located off Nearns Point, Fox Island, it is a local name.

Sanderson Harbor
Located on the entrance to Eld Inlet, western shoreline, opposite Cooper Point, the origin of the name is unknown. It is not reflected on current charts.

Sandy Hook
Located on the southwestern side of Agate Pass near Point Bolin, the name was likely descriptive.

Sandy Hook Yacht Club Estates
Located in Cultus Bay on the southeast side of Whidbey Island, the community was formed in 1960. The name is descriptive. Developers dredged out the channel between the shore and the existing sandy berm and created building lots (http://sharepoint.sandyhookyce.org/default.aspx). Presumably the berm would be known as Sandy Hook, but according to the U.S. Board on Geographic Names, it has no formal name.

Sandy Point [7h] #154, 1841, Wilkes
Located on the eastern shoreline of Case Inlet, opposite the north end of Herron Island, Wilkes likely named this in 1841 for its appearance. Wilkes did not include this name in his *Narrative*, but it is shown on his chart. The name is neither reflected on current charts nor recognized by the U.S. Board on Geographic Names.

Sandy Point [7d] #146, 1841, Wilkes; [7o] #157, 1841, Wilkes
Located on the eastern side of Whidbey Island, Wilkes perhaps named it for its appearance in 1841. Wilkes did not include this name in his *Narrative*, but it is shown on his chart. It is locally known as Browns Point or Joe Brown Spit for Joseph Brown who settled there in 1859. Brown married a 14-year-old Indian girl, Mary, in 1865. They raised fourteen children in a large house overlooking the bluff. Joseph died in 1921 (Cherry I: 76, 77). The Salish name for the point was "scratched nose" (Hilbert et. al., 358). The U.S. Board on Geographic Names approved the name over Joe Brown in 1891.

Sandy Point [7i] #147, 1841, Wilkes
See Steamboat Island.

Sandy Point
It is located on the eastern shoreline of Anderson Island, likely named for its appearance.

Sandy Point [7a] #145, 1841, Wilkes
The point is located on the mainland, north of Lummi Island. J. J. Gilbert noted the name in his 1888 survey and Descriptive Report #1871 (http://riverhistory.ess.washington.edu/tsheets/reports/t1871.pdf, p 2). He wrote: "Sandy Point, also part of the reservation, the Indian name of which is 'Sly-ack-sèn', is a gravel spit with no sand about it. It is hard to conjecture the reason for the name by which it is universally known. I venture the supposition that it was first named by someone in a passing vessel who, at a distance, mistook the gravel for sand."

Sandy Point [7b] #148, 1841, Wilkes
See Beckett Point.

Sandy Point [7d] #146, 1841, Wilkes
See Hood Point.

Sandy Point
See West Point.

Sandy Point [13a] #2689, 1859, Richards
Located on the west end of Waldron Island, Richards likely named it for its appearance. It is one of many "sandy points" in Puget Sound country.

Sandford Point [7d] #146, 1841, Wilkes; [7g] #155, 1841, Wilkes
It is located on the western side of Vashon Island. Wilkes named this for crew member Thomas Sandford in 1841 (Meany, *Origin* 223). Wilkes does not reference the name of the point in his *Narrative*. In 1996, the Washington State Board on Geographic Names, Docket 360, formally corrected the name to Sandford Point. It had been shown on early NOAA charts as Point Sanford. Additionally, it had been

shown on other documents as Sanford Point. The U.S. Board followed later in the year (Washington State Board files).

Sanfords Cove [7a] #145, 1841, Wilkes; [7m] #160, 1841, Wilkes
See Flounder Bay.

Santa Cruz
The bluff behind Dungeness, Quimper named it in 1790. It was not shown on his chart; it was only referenced in his journal (Wagner 108).

Santa Rosa, Seno de [1] 1790, Quimper
This is the basin at the easterly end of the Strait of Juan de Fuca. When Quimper first observed it in 1790, he believed that the inlet terminated (Wagner 109).

Sanum Point [7j] #153, 1841, Wilkes
See Misery Point.

Sapip Point [7p] #150, 1841, Wilkes
Located at the northwest entrance to the Port Townsend Canal, Wilkes named this in 1841 but left no reason for the name. The name is no longer used. Wilkes did not include this name in his *Narrative*, but it is shown on his chart.

Saratoga
Located on the eastern side of Whidbey Island, the community was likely named for the passage. During the early 1900s, the area around Saratoga was full of lumbermen, mostly bachelors. For those few who were married, their families lived in Langley, three miles to the south. In 1905, Murdock McLeod moved to Saratoga with his family. His wife Lottie was the first White woman. The following year, the Goodbrandson and the Leighton families arrived along with ten more children (Cherry II: 262).

Saratoga Passage [7a] #145, 1841, Wilkes; [7e] #158, 1841, Wilkes
Located on the eastern side of Whidbey Island, Wilkes named it in 1841 for the *Saratoga* commanded by Thomas MacDonough in the War of 1812. Wilkes wrote: "Throughout Saratoga Passage the water is of sufficient depth for the largest class of vessels; it is well protected from all winds. The tides are strong, and their direction generally north and south," (Meany, *Origin* 257; Wilkes, *Narrative* 311). On [7a], Wilkes placed the "S" in Saratoga Passage off Strawberry Point on Whidbey Island. The "e" in Passage is about halfway between East Point and Sandy Point on Whidbey Island. Wilkes' intent on the boundaries of Saratoga Passage is impossible to know. Conceivably, on the north side it extended to Deception Pass. The southern boundary is more difficult. Wilkes reflected Possession Sound on [7d]; the "P" in Possession was shown at the south end of Whidbey Island. The "d" in Sound was halfway between Mukilteo and Gedney Island. How much overlap he intended between these two names is unknown. However, according to the 1903 *Pacific Coast Pilot* (149), Saratoga Passage ends and Skagit Bay begins on the line between Rocky Point on Camano Island and Polnell Point on Whidbey Island. At the southern boundary, the dividing line between Saratoga Passage and Possession Sound is the line between Camano Head and Sandy Point on Whidbey.

Sares Head [7a] #145, 1841, Wilkes; [7m] #160, 1841, Wilkes
Located on the western side of Fidalgo Island, Wilkes named this Sare's Point, in 1841, honoring crew member Henry Sares (Meany, *Origin* 142). Wilkes placed this name on his chart where Langley Point (shown as Biz Point on more current charts) is located. For whatever reason, it appears that the U.S. Coast Survey moved Wilkes' name in 1866 [18] about a mile south of Langley Point but maintained the name. "After passing Deception island on the east, the face of Fidalgo island is high, precipitous, and bare for two or three miles in a northwest direction. This is called Sares Head," (Davidson, *Report* 431, 432). The U.S. Board on Geographic Names resolved the name by eliminating the possessive form and variants of Sare Head and Sore Head in 1941 (GNIS files).

Saringa Point [7i] #147, 1841, Wilkes
Located in the far southeastern corner in Budd Inlet, Wilkes left no reason for the 1841 name. On Wilkes' chart, it is on the Olympia shoreline at East Bay. Wilkes did not include this name in his *Narrative*. The name is neither reflected on current charts nor recognized by the U.S. Board on Geographic Names.

Satellite Island

Satellite Island
It is located off the eastern shore of Stuart Island. According to GNIS files: "There are three islands in Washington Sound which hitherto have been called James. Two of these, 25 miles apart, are in San Juan County, Wash. The island here described was named in 1859, probably in honor of Capt. (later Admiral) James Charles Prevost, commanding H.M.S. *Satellite* on the Pacific Station, 1857-1860. The United States Geographic Board [1925 decision] has now named it Satellite after Prevost's ship, on recommendation of Prof. Edmond S. Meany, of the University of Washington." As noted, Richards named it James Island [13a]. Lawrence Colman purchased the island and sold it in 1947 to the Y.M.C.A., which also owns Camp Orkila on the west side of Orcas (McDonald 190).

Sawash Bluff [7n] #149, 1841, Wilkes
This represents the bluff between Kulakala Point and Port Williams, just north of Sequim. Wilkes did not include this 1841 name in his *Narrative*, but it is shown on his chart. It is neither named on current charts nor is it recognized by the U.S. Board on Geographic Names. According to Hale (639), it is Chinook for "savage."

Scabock Harbor [7d] #146, 1841, Wilkes
See Seabeck Bay.

Scabock Point [7d] #146, 1841, Wilkes
See Misery Point.

Scandia
Located on the western shore of Liberty Bay opposite Poulsbo, the property changed hands several times until John Frykholm purchased it in 1900. Originally, locals called the community Frykholm. But Frykholm felt that Scandia was a more appropriate name because of his Scandinavian heritage (Carlson 73-75).

Scarboro Shoal [24] #1947, 1849, Inskip
See Tolvia Shoal.

Scarborough Harbor [7c] #144, 1841, Wilkes
See Neah Bay.

Scarborough Point [9a] #1911, 1849, Kellett
According to Kellett's chart, this appears to be the fourth point to the east of Neah Bay and forms the easterly point of Third Beach. It is neither named on current charts nor is it recognized by the U.S. Board on Geographic Names. This may be the U.S. Coast Survey's Kashukud'dil Point.

Scatchel Point [7e] #158, 1841, Wilkes
Located on the eastern side of Whidbey Island on the east side of Holmes Harbor, Wilkes likely named it for the Skagit Indian tribe in 1841. Wilkes did not include this name in his *Narrative*, but it is shown on his chart. The name is neither reflected on current charts nor recognized by the U.S. Board on Geographic Names.

Scatchet Head [7d] #146, 1841, Wilkes
Located at the southern end of Whidbey Island, Wilkes likely named this for the Skagit Indian tribe in 1841 (Meany, *Origin* 257). Davidson added a footnote regarding the name: "The proper spelling is Skadg'-it, and the Indian name of the point, Skoolhks," (*Report* 444). The U.S. Board on Geographic Names approved the name over the variant Skagit Head in 1949.

Schoolhouse Point
Located on the western shore of Sequim Bay, Wilkes originally named this Sail Point [7n] in 1841. Wilkes did not include this name in his *Narrative*, but it is shown on his chart. The current name is apparently for a schoolhouse that was once located in the neighborhood.

Scorpus Point [7b] #148, 1841, Wilkes
It is located on the southwestern side of Discovery Bay. Wilkes left no reason for the 1841 name. Wilkes did not include this name in his *Narrative*,

but it is shown on his chart. It is neither named on current charts nor recognized by the U.S. Board on Geographic Names.

Scott Point [7d] #146, 1841, Wilkes; [7h] #154, 1841, Wilkes

Located at the entrance to Horsehead Bay, eastern shores of Carr Inlet, Wilkes honored crew member Thomas Scott in 1841 (Hitchman 266). Wilkes did not include this name in his *Narrative*, but it is shown on his chart. Although unnamed on current charts, it is a recognized name according to the U.S. Board on Geographic Names.

Scotts Point
Located on the far eastern side of Samish Island, the source of the name is unknown.

Scout Patch [16b] #602, 1869, Pender
It is located on the northeastern side of Henry Island at the entrance to Roche Harbor. It is neither named on current charts nor recognized by the U.S. Board on Geographic Names. Pender likely named it for the H.M.S. *Scout* that transported the British troops back to Esquimalt at the end of the Pig War (Wood 182). The *Scout* was on the Pacific Station in Esquimalt from 1865-1868.

Scow Bay

Scow Bay
Located at the southern end of Kilisut Harbor, a small channel used to open into Oak Bay to the south. James Johnstone of the 1792 Vancouver expedition transited the canal. He wrote: "Before daylight we were stirring and a little before 4 passed the bridge at the top of high water – a little more depth than the boat drew. Being now in a large branch of Sea which extended to the SE [Oak Bay], but was separated from the bay which the boats were in [Port Townsend Bay] by the land which in one place was so very narrow a neck that it was a stone beach without any wood. Finding no passage I hastened to return by the same channel which I had passed and was just in time to get over as the tide had fallen about a foot which was ebbing strong to the NW," (Blumenthal, *With Vancouver* 102). Davidson wrote: "At high tide this harbor communicates, by a crooked boat channel, with Oak Cove, at the south end," (Davidson, *Report* 441). In 1852, Albert Briggs drove 30 head of cattle from Portland, Oregon to Port Townsend, Washington. When he reached Tumwater, he loaded the cattle aboard a 52 foot scow. When he approached the south end of Indian and Marrowstone Islands, he passed through the narrow channel and named the small harbor at the south end of Kilisut Harbor after his craft (McCurdy, *By Juan* 30).

Sea Acre
It is located on the eastern side of Orcas Island less than a mile north of Doe Bay and includes Kangaroo Point. It was homesteaded in 1912 by S. J. Kraft. Jess and Jessie White purchased the property in 1946 and created a resort with nine cabins and a restaurant above the beach. The original Kraft home and the cabins still stand above the restaurant (Patton, Harry, Feb. 4, 2012 email to author; Mr. Patton lives just south of Kangaroo Point).

Seabeck Bay [19] #662, 1867, U.S. Coast Survey
Located on the eastern side of Hood Canal, Wilkes originally named this Scabock Harbor [7d] in 1841. He wrote (*Narrative* 324): "It is one of the most convenient anchorages in the Canal. Its shape is triangular; its shore is bordered by a sand-beach, from which the hills rise: these are well-covered with wood." Kellett reflected the name Hamhamish Harbor on his 1849 chart [9a]. Phillips (127) indicated that it was named for the hometown of Marshall Blinn — Seabeck, Maine. According to Hitchman (267), Blinn was responsible for changing the name. In early 1856, Marshall Blinn left Maine and arrived in San Francisco aboard the bark *Brontes*. With timber experience, he found sawmill partners in San Francisco, including William J.

Adams, J. R. Williamson, Bill Harmon, and W. B. Sinclair. Together they formed the Washington Mill Company. Blinn headed north in the *Brontes* and worked his way into Hood Canal, anchoring in the small cove. Over the next six months, he built the mill and began operation in July 1857 (Bowen et al., IV: 34, 35). Adams originally arrived in California in 1850 and established wholesale grocery businesses in Sacramento and San Francisco. He sold out, traveled back to his hometown of Thomaston, Maine, married Cassandra Hills, and returned to California to enter the lumber business. They built a home in Menlo Park. His grandson was the photographer Ansel Adams. Williamson, a machinist by trade, previously helped set up the mills at Port Madison and Port Gamble. In 1864, he established the mill at West Seattle. Bill Harmon was born in East Machias, Maine and arrived in the Northwest in the early 1850s. He ultimately settled on 160 acres in Steilacoom, logged, and ran the Pacific Hotel in Olympia. He died in 1899. Sinclair settled in Port Madison and married Mary Low, the town's teacher and member of the 1851 Denny party. In 1864, Blinn and Adams bought out the other partners (Perry, *Seabeck* 40-44). Blinn and Adams expanded the mill and increased production from an initial 15,000 feet of timber per day to 50,000. In 1869, Blinn sold out to his brother, Samuel, and retired to Hunts Point on Lake Washington where he died in 1888. During the 1870s, Seabeck grew to a population of 400 with four saloons, two hotels, two stores, a church, a schoolhouse, and a cemetery. In 1883, the company continued to expand by constructing a second mill with more modern equipment. On August 6, 1886, sparks from the steam tug *Richard Holyoke* blew over the dock at Seabeck. The dry lumber stacked about ignited, eventually taking with it the docks and both mills. Samuel Blinn began planning the rebuild but failed due to labor problems and the lack of good timber close at hand. The Washington Mill Company searched for a better location, finally selecting Port Hadlock. With the migration of the mill hands to Port Hadlock, Seabeck instantly became a ghost town (Newell). As a footnote, the *Brontes* saw duty carrying lumber between Puget Sound and San Francisco for years. In 1877, she carried cargo to Honolulu and was in extremely poor shape. She was condemned and sold. Her new owner left the islands and was never heard from again (Wright 70).

Seabold
Located on the western shores of Bainbridge Island, south of Agate Pass, W. R. Impett ran a logging camp there in 1859. History is unclear regarding the first permanent settlers. One story suggests that John Johnson with his sons-in-law William Bull and John Silven arrived around 1880. They originally called the community Bull Town. But in 1894, William suggested Seabold because of its proximity to the water. Albert Selland ran a store there and in 1900 moved to Manzanita and opened another store. Another story was that a Mr. Albertson along with his four sons, one of whom was Albert Selland, first settled the land. Another son, C. W. Johnson filed for the first homestead. His daughter and her husband filed on an adjacent site. Which story is correct, or perhaps a combination, is unclear. Regardless, children walked to Port Madison until a local school was constructed in 1894. (Bowen et al., VI: 100, 101; Meany *Origin* 261). The Salish name for the area was "entangling, untying something" (Hilbert et. al., 227).

Seafarm Cove
Located on the eastern side of Squaxin Island in Peale Passage, it was named for the net pen used by the Squaxin Indians in salmon rearing. The Tribe referred to the net pen as the seafarm and the cove as Seafarm Cove. The name was approved by the Washington State Board on June 11, 1982, Docket 280. The U.S. Board followed in 1983 (from Washington State Board files). *See also* Belspeox Point.

Seal Rock [7b] #148, 1841, Wilkes
Located a mile east of Neah Bay, Wilkes likely named it for the wildlife in 1841. He does not include this name in his *Narrative*, but it is shown on his chart.

Seal Rock

Kellett included a peculiar reference on [9a]. He wrote "Klaholoh Rock Seals" as if it was a single name. He also noted that it was, "150 ft high." *See also* Sail Rock.

Seal Rocks
Located in Skagit Bay off Dugwalla Bay on the northeastern side of Whidbey Island, they were likely named as a resting spot for seals.

Seattle
Meany (*Origin* 261-264) stated that Arthur Denny and Carson Boren filed a plat for Seattle on May 23, 1853, honoring Chief Seattle with the name. While very friendly to the Whites, the chief was, according to some reports: "a thorough savage." Meany quoted the Hudson's Bay Company journals. On December 6, 1837, the Chief Trader wrote: "The Chief See yat has murdered an Indian doctor, much talk about the affair amongst the Soquamish tribe. I wish they would determine on shooting the villain." On January 9, 1838, the Trader wrote: "Challicum with a party of his Indians cast up, put a few skins in the store and then left us for a visit to the Saw aye waw mish to buy some articles for the death of a So qua mish shot by the villain See yat, the latter having got a gun from the Saw aye was mish and with it committed murder." He changed his ways somewhat following his baptism. Davidson wrote: "The town of Seattle is on a small point at the NE. part of the bay [Elliott], a little over 5 miles inside of West Point. It consists of a few houses and stores, a church, and a small sawmill. It has but little trade," (*Report* 446).

Secar Rock
Located off the southwestern side of Lopez Island, the origin of the name is unknown. The U.S. Government owns the island.

Second Beach
See First Beach.

Secret Harbor [13k] #2689, 1900
Located on the eastern side of Cypress Island, inside Deepwater Bay, the origin of the name was not found. The Secret Harbor School for troubled boys was located there 1947-2008.

Sehome
See Bellingham.

Sekiu, Sekiu Point, & Sekiu River [9a] #1911, 1849, Kellett; [21] #6300, 1895
Located on the westerly side of Clallam Bay, Kellett spelled it Sekou on his chart [9a]. Davidson (*Report* 418) spelled it Sekon Point and later changed it to Sekou (*Directory* 116). In 1970 the U.S. Board on Geographic Names adopted the name Sekiu over variant names for the community of Callam and Clallam. Regarding Sekiu Point [21] and Sekiu River [21], the Board approved those names in 1896 thus resolving the differences in spelling.

Semiahmoo Bay
Located at the Washington/British Columbia border, it was named after the Indian tribe that lived in the area (Meany, *Origin* 266). The U.S. Board on Geographic Names has addressed this name three times in the past hundred years. The first in 1896 and 1897 dealt with spelling differences between charts (Semiahmoo) and tide tables (Semiamoo). Col. Granville O. Haller provided input to the Board on this question. The second in 1931 and third in 1952 reviewed the same spelling differences but with different sources. In each case, the Board approved the current name over all variants of Boundary Bay, Semiamo Bay, Semiamoo Bay, Semiamu Bay, and Simiahmoo Bay.

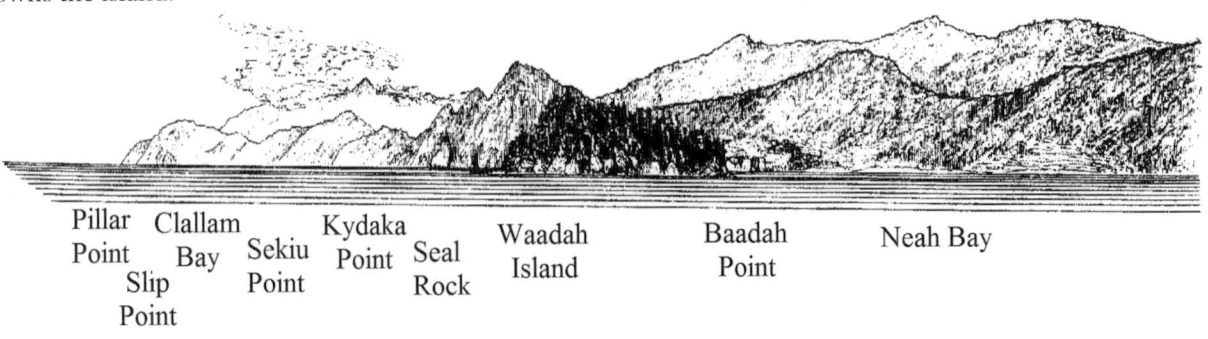

Pillar Point   Clallam Bay   Slip Point   Sekiu Point   Kydaka Point   Seal Rock   Waadah Island   Baadah Point   Neah Bay

Sentinel Island [13a] #2689, 1859, Richards
Located in Spieden Channel, Richards modified Wilkes' 1841 name (see Sentinel Rock) and applied it to the eastern island. For whatever reason, he did not name the western "rock" until 1861 [14a]. Louis Tagholm settled on the island in 1917 but did not complete his patent. Farrar (1888-1974) and June (1893-1969) Burn met in Washington DC in March 1919. They married a month later. That summer, they worked their way west. They landed at Roche Harbor where Farrar worked at the quarry. At that time, Sentinel Island was unclaimed. They rented a tent, borrowed a rowboat, and loaded their possessions and supplies aboard. That was their first experience with currents so they were unable to reach Sentinel Island, and they barely made it back to their starting point. The following morning, they tried again and were successful. Later in the fall, they dismantled an abandoned trapper's cabin on Johns Island and rowed it to Sentinel. After two weeks, they completed their eight by ten home. In the early winter, they moved in with the Chevaliers on Spieden Island, as the Sentinel accommodations were simply inadequate. June wrote a wonderful book, *Living High*, about their Northwest life and, in particular, their experiences on Sentinel Island. Today, Sentinel is owned by the Nature Conservancy.

Sentinel Rock [7a] #145, 1841, Wilkes; [7c] #144, 1841, Wilkes
On chart 145, Wilkes showed two objects in Spieden Channel and labeled both "Sentinel Rocks." On chart 144, he showed the same two objects and included the label "Sentinel R". Richards named Sentinel Island in 1859 [13a] and in 1861, used Wilkes' name but applied it simply to the small rock to the west of Sentinel Island [14a].

Seola Beach
Located on the eastern shoreline of Admiralty Inlet, south of Fauntleroy, Cardel (*About* 98) indicated that it was the winning entry in a 1910 naming contest. Originally called Kakeldy Beach after the first settler, it was renamed for the Indian word to "know the waves."

Separation Point [13j] #2689, 1894
See Humphrey Head.

Sequalitchew Creek
Located near the Nisqually Flats, the name came from the Indian word meaning "the face is marked." The reference is to the dark markings on fish in the creek (TPL website).

Sequim Bay
Located along the Strait of Juan de Fuca, between Dungeness and Discovery Bay, the name was derived from the Clallam name of *Such-e-kwai-ing* meaning "quiet water" (Meany, *Origin* 267). It was initially named Budd's Harbor by Wilkes [7n] in 1841 who wrote (*Narrative* 312): "Budd's Harbor might be designated as an extension of New Dungeness Roads, being separated from it only by a narrow tongue of land, which lies across, and renders the harbor entirely land-locked. The narrow entrance is on the west side. Vessels drawing 12 feet can pass over the bar at low water." The Admiralty named it Washington Harbor [13c]. Davidson wrote: "This harbor was surveyed first by the United States Exploring Expedition, and called Budd's harbor, but there being a sheet of water in Puget's Sound bearing a similar name, we have adopted Kellett's appellation. The Indian name of the bay is S'quim, by which it is generally known to the settlers," (*Report* 421, 422). The name and spelling of Sequim Bay became official by a 1941 decision of the U.S. Board on Geographic Names which chose the current name over Budd's Harbor, Squim Bay, or Washington Harbor (*Decisions*). According to the GNIS files, the name Sequim first appeared on an 1859 "Map of part of Wash. Terr. to accompany map of Sur. Gen." The names (excluding Budd's Harbor) were used individually on various maps and charts until the Board decision.

Seversons Bay
Located on the northern end of Waldron Island, between Fishery Point and Point Hammond, the origin of the name is unknown.

Shag Reef [14a] #2840, 1861, Richards
This is a small reef north of Spieden Island and east of Gull Reef. Richards left no reason for the name. The name is neither reflected on current charts nor recognized by the U.S. Board on Geographic Names.

Shag Rock [13h] #2689, 1888
Located near Grindstone Harbor near the southern side of Orcas Island, it was named apparently for its "ragged appearance at low tides" (Hitchman 270).

Shallow Bay [21] #6300, 1895
Located on the western side of Sucia Island, opposite Echo Bay, it was likely named because it is shallow. J. J. Gilbert noted the name in his 1888 Descriptive Report #1870 (http://riverhistory.ess.washington.edu/tsheets/reports/t1870.pdf, p 6).

Shannon Point [21] #6300, 1895, U.S. Coast Survey
Located on the eastern side of Fidalgo Island, Richards originally named it Ship Point in 1859 [13a]. It was later renamed by the U.S. Coast Survey for real estate developer E. L. Shannon (TPL website).

Shark Reef [13a] #2689, 1859, Richards
Located on the western side of Lopez Island near the south end of San Juan Channel, it was possibly named for sharks basking in the area (Hitchman 270). Lange suggested that it took the name of the *Plumper's* pinnace, *Shark*, which was caught in a storm while sounding out Griffin Bay and possibly grounded on the reef.

Sharpe Cove
Located near Deception Pass at the western entrance, on the south side of Rosario Head, it was named for the Sharpe family who settled there in 1882. James and Margaret Sharpe were born in Ireland. The family, including their three-year-old son Thomas, immigrated in 1853 and lived in New York, Ohio, Iowa, and finally Minnesota in 1861. James died there in 1879; Margaret died in 1887 in British Columbia. Thomas left home in 1865 and found work on the Mississippi for a number of years. He returned to Minnesota but again left in 1875 heading west. He landed in Port Townsend, found work on Whidbey, and then purchased land on the west side of Fidalgo Island at what became Sharpe Cove. In 1882, he married Mary J. Carr, and together they raised four children. A grandson, Lester, lived on the property until the 1970s. Part of their home and a deteriorated barn still remain. In 1977, Kathleen Sharp, daughter-in-law of Thomas, donated the family land to Skagit County, and it is now the Sharpe Park (Slotemaker, Terry, City of Anacortes, June 3, 2010 email to author; *An Illustrated History*, 612; http://www.skagitriverjournal.com/SCounty/Library/IH06/IH06Sec2Chap1-1.html).

Shaws Cove
Located on the northwestern end of Hale Passage just inside Green Point, it was the site where Peter Puget spent a night in 1792 (Puget 197). While it is recognized by the U.S. Board on Geographic Names, it is not reflected on current charts.

Shaw Island [7a] #145, 1841, Wilkes
Located south of Orcas Island, in 1841 Wilkes honored Capt. John D. Shaw who saw service in the Wars of 1812 and 1815 against Algiers (Meany, *Origin* 268).

Shawnee
Located on the western side of Quartermaster Harbor, Vashon Island, Millard F. Shaw platted it in 1907 and named it Shawnee (Haulman).

Sheep Hill [13a] #2689, 1859, Richards
See Biological Hill.

Sheep Island [14a] #2840, 1861, Richards
See Picnic Island.

Shell Point
Located on the southern shoreline of Eld Inlet, it was named for the piles of shells collected over the years by local Indians.

Shelter Bay

Shelter Bay
The harbor off Fidalgo Island is located on the western side of the Swinomish Channel, south of La Conner. The private gated residential community leases land from the Swinomish Tribe.

Shelton

It is located at the head of Hammersley Inlet. Born in 1812 in North Carolina, David Shelton migrated west and arrived at Fort Vancouver in 1847. He and his wife Frances settled on the Willamette River in what is now downtown Portland. But hearing stories of land and riches up north, Shelton packed up his family again in 1852 and boarded the Columbia River pilot ship *Mary Taylor* along with F. W. Pettygrove, L. B. Hastings, and others. They anchored in Port Townsend where the Hastings and Pettygrove families departed (*see also* Port Townsend). Shelton continued to Olympia, arriving on February 15 where he immersed himself in state politics. At various times, he was a legislator, mayor, school superintendent, and a county commissioner (Angle, Grant, and Welsh 3-7). The following year, he and his brother Tillman explored Hammersley Inlet. At that time, Michael Simmons was building a sawmill at Mill Creek, hence the name. The Shelton family moved to the inlet in April 1853 where they took up a claim of 640 acres. David chose land on the north side of the Cota Valley, away from the Indians who occupied part of the area. He built a house, cleared land, and planted rye. Their first home was on the bank of a small creek, and the site is now marked by a stone in front of the City Hall. Tillman filed a claim about three miles from David but abandoned it in 1854 and moved his family to The Dalles, Oregon. In 1854, Shelton drafted a bill to organize Swamish County, named after an Indian word meaning "drifting." The legislature approved the new county. It included Eld and Totten Inlets all the way to the coast and north to the head of Case Inlet. It was signed by Charles H. Mason, Secretary of State. The county's name was changed ten years later to honor Mason who died in 1859 at age thirty-two. Growth during this period was very slow. By 1879, Shelton had accumulated 900 acres of land. Finally, timber in the area enticed the railroads. In 1884, a group of Seattle investors drafted plans to terminate the Satsop Railroad on Shelton's homestead. Within a year, the railroad arrived and logging commenced. The Sheltonville post office was established in 1885. The postmaster, C. F. White, who was one of the original investors in the railroad and its superintendent, later shortened the name. That same year, Shelton surveyed and filed the first plat of the town. Land sold rapidly, as railroaders, loggers, and supporting enterprises joined the community. Within the next two years, two hotels, two boarding houses, four saloons, a shoe store, two general stores, two blacksmith shops, and a newspaper were established. From 1885 to 1886, the town grew from seventy-five people to more than 240. In 1889, David was elected first Mayor of Shelton and served until 1892. Francis Shelton died April 15, 1887. David followed ten years later, February 15, 1897, at age eighty-five (Fredson, *Oakland to Shelton* 4, 5, 8, 34-44).

Shelton Creek [23] #6460, 1905

The creek flows into Hammersley inlet at Shelton. It likely took its name from the community.

Sherlock

See Nisqually.

Sherwood Creek [23] #6460, 1905

Located on the western side of Case Inlet, south of Allyn, the brothers Joseph and Samuel Sherwood established a sawmill on the creek in 1854. Joe died in an 1873 logging accident (TPL website).

Shilshole Bay

Shilshole Bay

Located off Seattle on the eastern side of Admiralty Inlet, the name originated from the Duwamish word *Cil-col* which means "threading or inserting, as a thread through a bead" (Hitchman 271). Pioneers knew it as *Shul-shale*, a tribe, now extinct, who lived on the bay (Meany, *Origin* 253).

Shine

Located on the northern edge of Squamish Harbor in Hood Canal, early residents recommended the name Sunshine. When that name was rejected by postal authorities, residents submitted a second name. According to early historians, the intended name was Cheyenne, but it was misspelled Shine, which is what authorities accepted (TPL website). Alternatively, according to Hitchman (271), postal authorities simply accepted the abbreviated version of Sunshine.

Ship Bay [13a] #2689, 1859, Richards
Located at the head of East Sound, Orcas Island, it is perhaps named for its anchorage potential.

Ship Harbor [21] #6300, 1895
Located along Guemes Channel on Fidalgo Island, the harbor became home to the early shipping trade around the islands (Meany, *Origin* 269; TPL website). The name Ship Harbor was the result of the fact that the U.S.S. *Massachusetts* made the harbor its headquarters while in Puget Sound country (*An Illustrated History*, 99).

Ship Peak [13a] #2689, 1859, Richards
Overlooking West Sound on Orcas Island, Richards left no reason for the name.

Ship Point [7p] #150, 1841, Wilkes
It is located perhaps a mile north of Olele Point according to Wilkes' chart (Wilkes, *Narrative* 314). It is neither reflected on current charts nor is it recognized by the U.S. Board on Geographic Names.

Ship Point [13a] #2689, 1859, Richards
See Shannon Point.

Ship Trees [13a] #2689, 1859, Richards
Located on the west side of San Juan Island, south of Deadman Bay, the area perhaps was named because of the availability of timber for masts, spars, etc. It is neither reflected on current charts nor is it recognized by the U.S. Board on Geographic Names.

Shipwreck Point
Located on the Strait of Juan de Fuca, about halfway between Clallam Bay and Neah Bay, the origin of the name is perhaps descriptive. The name is not reflected on current charts.

Shipyard Cove Marina
Located at the southern end of Friday Harbor, next to the Jensen Marina, this name is included because of an anomaly. While the marina is formally recognized by the U.S. Board on Geographic Names, the cove is merely a local name (Soland, Leslie; Dec. 18, 2011 email to author). Early on, the local name for that end of the harbor was Warbass Cove, after the owner of the land alongside. *See also* Newhall's Point.

Shirt Tail Reef
Located between Cliff and Low Islands, and a bit south, the origin of the name is unknown.

Shoal Bay [13a] #2689, 1859, Richards
Located off the northern end of Lopez Island, it was likely named for its shallow depth.

Shoal Bay
See Snoring Bay.

Shoal Bight [17] #27, 1862, U.S. Coast Survey
Located off the southeastern side of Lopez Island near Lopez Pass, the U.S. Coast survey named it in 1854. Davidson wrote (*Directory* 129): "This bend is called Shoal bight, and has from 6 to 10 fathoms for a mile out, with level sandy bottom." Richards named it Davis Bay on the 1859 Admiralty chart [13a] for Commander Charles H. Davis, Captain of the *St. Mary* (Lange). The Coast Survey name endured. Interestingly, it is simply reflected on the 1866 U.S. Coast Survey chart [18] as "Bight," likely an error in omitting the balance of the name.

Short Bay
Located on the northern side of Burrows Island, the origin of the current name is unknown. In 1841, Wilkes named it for the British ship *Boxer* [7a], [7m] captured by the *Enterprise* commanded by Lt. William Burrows during the War of 1812 (Wilkes, *Narrative* 310). Based upon Wilkes' chart, the cove was represented as the slight indent on the northern side of Burrows Island; he left the channel between Burrows and Fidalgo Islands unnamed. While the name is recognized by the U.S. Board on Geographic Names, it does not appear on current charts.

Sidney [23] #6460, 1905
See Port Orchard.

Sierras Nevadas de San Antonio
See Mt. Rainier.

Sikwa Point [7h] #154, 1841, Wilkes
See Penrose Point.

Silipo Island [7h] #154, 1841, Wilkes
See Cutts Island.

Silver Creek
The creek flows into Puget Sound at Eglon. *See also* Eglon.

Silver Spit
Located on the western side of Budd Inlet, about a mile south of Cooper Point, the origin of the name is unknown. It is not reflected on current charts.

Silverdale
Located at the head of Dyes Inlet, William Littlewood built a cabin there in 1878. In 1888, Alexander Munson acquired the property and filed a plat for Goldendale the following year. Finding that the name duplicated another town, he renamed it Silverdale. Littlewood was allowed to remain on his original property where he died in 1895 (Bowen et. al., IV: 73; Hitchman 274). The Salish name for the area was "prairies, open spaces" (Hilbert et. al., 208).

Similk Bay [7a] #145, 1841, Wilkes; [7e] #158, 1841, Wilkes
It is located off the southern side of Fidalgo Island inside Deception Pass. Wilkes did not include this name in his *Narrative*, but it is shown on his chart. According to Hale (577), the name is from the Oregon Molele tribe and means "mouth." Phillips (130) indicated that perhaps it was an Indian word for "salmon." The Salish name for the area was "small stockade" (Hilbert et. al., 350).

Simmons Creek
Flowing into Eld Inlet on the southern shore just west of the Evergreen State College, it was named for Michael Troutman Simmons. Simmons and George Washington Bush met in 1844 on the Oregon Trail. Simmons, from Kentucky, and Bush, from Missouri, became friends on the journey. The party reached Fort Vancouver, where Bush, a mulatto, learned that the Provisional Legislative Committee had recently passed a law which prevented free Negroes or mulattoes from land ownership. As a result, Simmons, Bush, and a small group of pioneers became determined to find land in Puget Sound that was available to all. In July 1845, they headed down the Columbia to the Cowlitz where they paddled and polled up the river. When the river ran out, they walked through the forests, eventually reaching Budd Inlet. By canoe, most of the group explored Puget Sound country, but Simmons was satisfied with the land found near the Deschutes River. As the previous owner and operator of a grist mill, Simmons saw the potential. Staking claims, the group returned to Vancouver for their families. By fall, thirty men, women, and children arrived on the sound. The group constructed a single cabin where they all lived during the winter. Simmons platted a town site which he named New Market. It was later renamed Tumwater for the Indian word meaning "water." During the summer and fall of 1846, Simmons built a home and finished his gristmill. But the lure of timber was too much. Simmons erected a crude sawmill in Hammersley Inlet with machinery purchased from the Hudson's Bay Company. The first White child born in Puget Sound country was to Michael and Elizabeth Simmons in 1845. Simmons died in 1867 (Johnson 64-76; Stevenson 28, 29).

Sinahomis River [8a] #1917, 1847, Kellett
See Snohomish River.

Sinawamis River [8a] #1917, 1847, Kellett
See Puyallup River.

Sinclair Inlet [7q] #156, 1841, Wilkes
Located at the southern end of Port Orchard, Wilkes honored crew member George T. Sinclair in 1841 (Meany, *Origin* 272).

Sinclair Island [7a] #145, 1841, Wilkes
Located between Lummi and Cypress Islands, in 1841 Wilkes honored Capt. Arthur Sinclair, Sr. who commanded the *General Pike* at the beginning of the War of 1812 and later the *Argus* (Meany, *Origin* 272). Based upon an 1875 U.S. Government survey, three families lived on Sinclair Island. Mrs. J. C. Tilton lived on the southwest side, west of Urban. She ran a fishing industry, cannery, wharf, a hennery, and a warehouse. Allen C. Kittle lived on the northeast

side where he planted a fruit orchard and vegetable garden. Thomas Hogin was the third and lived on the northwest side of the island. Hogin sold to Lawrence Kelly in 1886 (*see also* Kellys Point). A post office opened at Urban in 1895, named after the postmaster's son, Urban Stenger (McDonald 180; Leach 9-15). During the 1890s, locals cut cottonwood trees. The lumber was used for barrel heads and staves at the Roche Harbor Lime Company. As a result, some referred to it as Cottonwood Island.

Sisters [7k] #152, 1841, Wilkes
Located in Suquamish Harbor, Wilkes named this Sister Rocks in 1841 (Wilkes, *Narrative* 323).

Sisters, The [7a] #145, 1841, Wilkes
Located in Rosario Strait on the eastern side of Orcas Island, south of Clark Island, Wilkes provided no reason for the 1841 name. He does not include this name in his *Narrative*, but it is shown on his chart. There are three islands in the grouping. Wilkes provided no separate names for any of them, simply Sisters. In the 1858 *Report*, Davidson wrote (433): "The course out passes on the west some small rocky islets called The Sisters, marked by one or two stunted fir trees; then Clark's Island and Barnes's Island, close under its western side, leaving a channel a mile wide between it and the north shore of Orcas Island, with very deep water and no anchorage." This statement was repeated in the 1862 *Directory* (131) as well as the 1869 *Pacific Coast Pilot* (213). In the 1889 *Pacific Coast Pilot*, Davidson altered it slightly (568): "Off the southeast end of Clark Island are two or three islets, called the Sisters. The Sisters Islets near Barnes Island are forty-two feet high. The one to the northward marked by a lone tree is twenty-six feet high." T-sheet #1869 from 1888, found at http://kaga.wsulibs.wsu.edu/cdm-maps/sanjuantsheet.html is likely the first chart to reflect the Lone Tree name. According to McLellan: "Three small rocky islands situated to the south and southeast of Clark Island make up the group known as the Sisters. These have a combined area of 8.27 acres. The largest and most northern of the Sister islands has a single conifer tree growing upon it and it is sometimes known as Lone Tree Island." Charts today reflect the northern two islands as The Sisters and the smaller southernmost island as Little Sister. Although Lone Tree Island is an accepted name according to the U.S. Board on Geographic Names, it is not reflected on current charts. The Washington State Board on Geographic Names is currently reviewing if Lone Tree should remain as a stand-alone name or simply be listed as a variant of The Sisters.

Sisters Points [7d] #146, 1841, Wilkes
Located on the northern shore of Hood Canal east of The Great Bend, Wilkes named this Sister Point in 1841 but left no reason for the name (Meany, *Origin* 273). While charts carry Wilkes' name, topos and GNIS use the name Points (plural). Apparently, in the 1980s, a government surveyor arbitrarily changed Wilkes' naming and applied it to several rocks off the point. The Washington State Board on Geographic Names is currently reviewing the discrepancy between charts and topos. Likely, the formal name will revert to what Wilkes intended.

Sinclair Inlet [7d] #146, 1841, Wilkes
Located off Bremerton, Wilkes honored crew member George T. Sinclair in 1841 (Meany, *Origin* 272).

Sitcum Waterway
One of the waterways on Commencement Bay, the name is Chinook for "half, a part, direction, middle" which refers to the small size of the waterway and its location (Reese, *Origins* 101).

Siwash Slough
See Samish Island.

Skagit Bay
Located north of Camano Island, it was named for the Indian tribe that lived on the Skagit River and parts of Camano and Whidbey Islands. The name is spelled in various ways and has been affixed to numerous place names in our waters. For example, Wilkes used Skait (Skagit) Island, Scatchel Point, and Scatchet Head. *See also* Saratoga Passage.

Skagit Head
See Scatchet Head.

Skagit Island [7e] #158, 1841, Wilkes
Located at the easterly entrance to Deception Pass, Wilkes spelled it Skait in his *Narrative* and on his

chart. It is possible that he named it for the Indian tribe in 1841 and simply misspelled it. According to Hale (581), *Skait* is a Piskwaus Indian term which means "heart." The Piskwaus Tribe lived in eastern Washington around the Wenatchee or Pisquouws Rivers.

Skiff Point [19] #662, 1867, U.S. Coast Survey
Located on the eastern side of Bainbridge Island, Davidson indicated that the U.S. Coast Survey named it in 1856 (1889 *Pacific Coast Pilot* 609), although it doesn't appear on any chart until 1867. The Peter Jacobsen family were first to homestead in the area. Jacobsen found work at the Port Madison mill in 1872. The name came from its resemblance to an overturned skiff at low tide (Meany, *Origin* 275). In 1914, Frank Moran built the Moran Junior College there, a private boy's school. Frank was the son of Robert Moran, onetime Seattle mayor, shipbuilder, and owner of Rosario on Orcas Island. In 1938, the school was purchased by the Puget Sound Naval Academy. Today, it is an elderly health care center (Marriott 72-74). The Salish name for the point was "sharp face" (Hilbert et. al., 225).

Skiou Point
Located inside Tulalip Bay on the southern shoreline, it was originally an Indian burial ground. The name originates from the Indian word *Skyu* meaning "dead body" (TPL website). A variant name was Dead Mans Point (GNIS database).

Skipjack Island [7a] #145, 1841, Wilkes
Located north of Waldron Island, there are two islands in the grouping: Skipjack and Bare. In 1841, Wilkes originally referred to both collectively as Skip Jack Islands on his chart. Wilkes did not include this name in his *Narrative*. In the U.S. Coast Survey chart of 1854 [10], the collective name Skip Jack (two words) continued to appear for both islands. On the 1858 chart, the U.S. Coast Survey [11] labeled both as Skipjack (one word) Islands but also gave names to the individual islands as Wooded and Bare. These were actually named in 1853 (*Directory* 126). On the Admiralty chart of 1859 [13a], Richards retained Skipjack for the larger western island. He renamed the eastern island Penguin. On the chart of 1888 [13h], the Admiralty reflected the name Penguin or Bare Island for the eastern island. The U.S. Coast Survey name Bare Island was later accepted.

Skokomish River
Located on the southern end of Hood Canal at The Great Bend, Wilkes named this Black Creek [7d] in 1841. He left no reason for the name. Skokomish means "river people."

Skookum Point
Located on the southern shore of Hammersley Inlet, the origin is unknown.

Skull Island
Located on the western side of West Sound, Orcas Island, Richards originally named it Skull Rock [14a] for nearby Indian battles. *See also* Haidi Point, Indian Point, Victim Island, and Massacre Bay (Meany, *Origin* 161). Splitstone (220) indicated that it received its name for the large number of skulls and bones found there. It is owned by the U.S. Government.

Skull Island
Located in Lopez Sound off the western side of the Sperry Peninsula, immediately east of Fortress Island, it was perhaps a burial ground. The name is not reflected on current charts.

Skull Rock [14a] #2840, 1861, Richards
See Skull Island.

Skunk Bay
Located on the western side of Admiralty Inlet, a mile south of Foulweather Bluff, the name is likely descriptive.

Skunk Island
Located to the southwest of Hadlock in Port Townsend, the name is likely descriptive.

Slammer Island
See Justice Island.

Slavis Point [7h] #154, 1841, Wilkes
See Ketners Point.

Sleepy Lagoon
See Carlson Bay.

Slik Point [7j] #153, 1841, Wilkes
See Black Point.

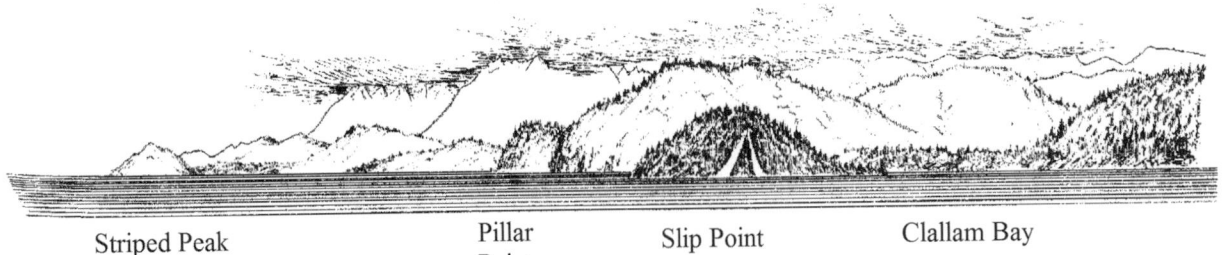

Slip Point - Smith Island

Striped Peak   Pillar Point   Slip Point   Clallam Bay

Slip Point [9a] #1911, 1849, Kellett
Located on the eastern side of Clallam Bay, Kellett provided no reason for the name.

Small Island [13a] #2689, 1859, Richards
Located off the eastern side of Lopez Island in Lopez Sound, across from Center Island, it was likely named for its size.

Smallpox Bay [21] #6300, 1895
It is located on the western side of San Juan Island, a half mile north of Bellevue Point. According to Meany who spelled it Small Pox Bay (*Origin*, 276), many Indians came down with small pox in Victoria in 1860. They then traveled to Smallpox Bay and died there. American officers doused the bodies with kerosene and burned them.

Smith Cove
Located at the northern end of Elliott Bay, Wilkes originally named the sand spit and cove behind, Tuber Point and Quartermaster Cove respectively [7m]. He likely named Quartermaster Cove for the quartermasters aboard, similar to Quartermaster Harbor. He left no reason for Tuber Point. Wilkes did not include either 1841 name in his *Narrative*, but both are shown on his chart. The current name was for Dr. Henry A. Smith. Smith was born in Ohio in 1830. He entered the Alleghany College medical school in Pennsylvania and completed his training at the Physio-Medical Institute of Cincinnati. He headed west, reached Seattle late in 1852, and homesteaded 160 acres at Smith Cove. Two years later he built a cabin, planted a fruit orchard, and became the county's first superintendent of schools. Indians torched his buildings during the Indian Wars while he was occupied as the surgeon in Company D. After the wars, he was the resident physician at the Tulalip Indian Reservation and ultimately returned to settle down in Seattle. In 1862, at age 32, he married 17-year-old Mary Ann Phelan from Portland. In 1864, the couple moved to Smith Island on the Snohomish River where he purchased 600 acres of tideland in the bay and attempted to reclaim the land by dikes. He also operated a hospital on the property. After a time, the family returned to Smith Cove where he continued to accumulate land in excess of 1,000 acres. Most of the land was sold to the Seattle Lake Shore & Eastern Railroad in 1887. He built the London Hotel on Pike Street as well as the Smith Block and other rental properties. Mary Ann Smith died in 1880. Smith, faced with raising eight young children, ultimately gave up his medical practice to spend more time with the family. He died in 1915 at age 85 (Meany, *Origin* 277; Rhodes 169, 170; Middleton 194; McDonald, Lucile. "Seattle's early-day physician, Henry A. Smith, was a Pioneer Doctor With Advanced Ideas." *Seattle Times*. Jan. 24, 1960. Magazine Section p 3).

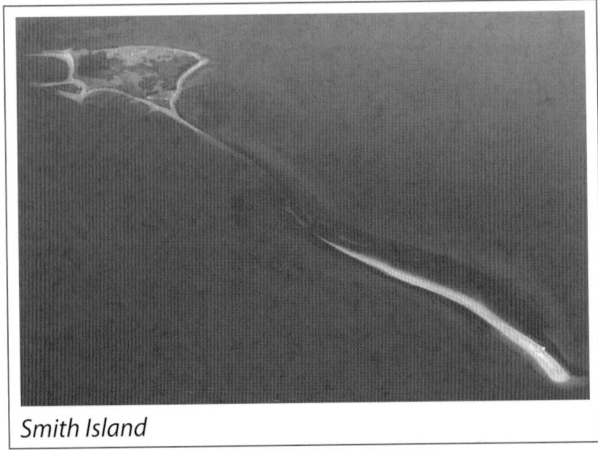

Smith Island

Smith Island [8a] #1917, 1847, Kellett
Located at the confluence of Admiralty Inlet and the Strait of Juan de Fuca, it was discovered in 1791 and appears on Eliza's chart [3] as *Islas de Bonilla*

for Antonio Bonilla, secretary to the Viceroy of New Spain. Eliza apparently recognized that there were two islands there (now Smith and Minor). In 1841, Wilkes named the larger of the two Blunts Island [7a] for crew member Simon F. Blunt but ignored Minor Island (Meany, *Origin* 277). On the 1847 Admiralty chart [8a], Kellett named it Smith Island, perhaps for a Hudson's Bay Company employee. For whatever reason, Kellett reverted to the Spanish name *Bonilla* Island on the 1849 chart [9a]. On their 1854 chart, the U.S. Coast Survey used the name Smith's Island [10]. On 1858 chart [11], the U.S. Coast Survey reflected it as "Smith's or Blunt's Island." On the 1859 Admiralty chart [13a], Richards called it "Smith's or Blunt Island." In the 1858 *Report* (429), Davidson indicated: ". . . to enter the Rosario strait, we notice, first, Smith's island, lying at the eastern termination of the Strait of Juan de Fuca, within 6 miles of Whidbey island and 7 miles broad off the southern entrance to the Rosario strait. It is quite small, not occupying half a square mile, and rises regularly from the eastern to the western extremity, where it attains a height of about 55 feet, with an almost perpendicular cliff of clay and gravel." He further states (430): "On the maps of the United States Exploring Expedition it is called Blunt's island; but it is now known by the name we have used, which is also that given on the Admiralty charts." Davidson continued to use Smith's in the *Report* as he did in the 1862 *Directory*. But in the *Pacific Coast Pilot* of 1869, he uses Smith's and Blunts interchangeably. The U.S. Coast Survey chart of 1862 [17] uses Smith's or Blunt's, but by 1866 [18] they labeled it Smith's. The lighthouse was first lit on October 18, 1858. The first keeper was DeWitt Dennison.

Smith Island [22] #6450, 1909
Located northeast of Everett, its western boundary is the Snohomish River. It was named for Dr. Henry A. Smith who settled there. *See* Smith Cove.

Smuggler Cove
It is a local name for the bay located southeast of the community of Hope on Fox Island. The origin of the name is unknown.

Smugglers Cove
Located about 1½ miles north of Bellevue Point on the western side of San Juan Island, there is only speculation as to the name. Certainly there was a great deal of smuggling going on in the mid to late 1800s. Whether or not it had anything to do with this particular cove is unknown. Wood found the name used first on chart #6379 in 1953 (118).

Smugglers Cove
Located just north of Inati Bay on the eastern side of Lummi Island, the cove was used for smuggling Chinese and liquor. A November 1, 1964 *Seattle Times* article by Whitfield Wesley Wells (Magazine Section p 10, 11) referenced the cove. Davidson referenced the name in the 1889 *Pacific Coast Pilot* (568). In late 1976, Mrs. Lloyd Niedhamer of Lummi Island proposed the name. According to her letter, the name had been locally used since 1889. In its March 11, 1977 meeting, the Washington State Board on Geographic Names approved the name, Docket 216 (from Washington State Board files, GNIS files).

Snake Rock [7f] #151, 1841, Wilkes; [7p] #150, 1841, Wilkes
Located inside Colvos Rocks about three miles north of Port Ludlow, Wilkes left no reason for the 1841 name. Wilkes did not include this name in his *Narrative*, but it is shown on his chart.

Snaklum Point
See Long Point.

Snas Point [7p] #150, 1841, Wilkes
It is located about five miles north of Port Ludlow, due west of Kinney Point. Wilkes did not include this name in his *Narrative*, but it is shown on his chart. The name is neither reflected on current charts nor recognized by the U.S. Board on Geographic Names. According to Hale (607), it is a Nasqually Indian term meaning "name." The Nasquallys (Nisqually) of course lived in southern Puget Sound. Alternatively, Hale indicated (639) that it was Chinook for "rain."

Snatelum Point
Located on the eastern side of Whidbey Island at the south entrance to Penn Cove, Wilkes originally named this Watsak Point in 1841 [7e]. He left no reason for the name. Wilkes did not include this name in his *Narrative*, but it is shown on his chart. According to Hale (600), *Watsak* originated with the Lutuami tribe from south-central Oregon and

means "dog." Meany (*Origin* 340) related that Mrs. Isaac Ebey wrote in her diary on December 27, 1852: "George Sneightlen came back from Port Townsend this evening and I had to let him and his Indians camp in the smokehouse all night." There were actually two Snatelums, Kwuss-ka-nam or George Snatelum, Sr., and Hel-mits or George Snatelum, Jr. Both signed the 1855 Point Elliott Treaty. The U.S. Board on Geographic Names chose the current name for him in 1941 eliminating variants which included Watsak Point, Snaklum Point, and Snakelum Point (GNIS files). The latter two names were simply alternative spellings by early pioneers. The Salish name for the point was "where one goes into the woods" (Hilbert et. al., 360).

Snee-oosh Point
Located on the southeastern side of Fidalgo Island inside Hope Island, it was originally named by Wilkes Hunot Point [7e] in 1841. He left no reason for the name. Wilkes did not include this name in his *Narrative*, but it is shown on his chart. According to Hale (601), *Hunot* originated with the San Juan Capistrano tribe from Southern California and means "bear." Hitchman (279) indicated simply that it was the tribal name for the point. The U.S. Board on Geographic Names reaffirmed the name Hunot Point in 1941. But because of predominant local usage, the Washington State Board on Geographic Names received a proposal in 1976 to change the name to *Snee-oosh*, an Indian word meaning "over there." At its September 10, 1976 meeting, the Board, Docket 211, approved the change. The U.S. Board followed later in the year (from Washington State Board Files).

Snohomish River
The Skykomish and Snoqualmie Rivers combine to form the Snohomish River, which flows through Everett into Port Gardner. In 1824, Work wrote (213): "Passed the Sinnahamis Bay [Port Gardner off Everett] which receives a river of the same name on the E. side, and on the same side the entrance of a bay or channel, here was also a small island on the same side in the entrance of the Sannihamis Bay." Wilkes originally named the river Freshwater Creek in 1841. He referenced it in his *Narrative* (316) but did not mark the name on any charts. Kellett attempted to maintain Work's name in his 1847 chart [8a] by calling it Sinahomis River. Meany (*Origin* 279, 280) indicated that the name was given by the Surveyor General of Washington Territory in 1857. Meany also quoted Dr. Charles M. Buchanan, a Tulalip Indian Agent, who stated that the Indian name was *Sdoh-doh-hohbsh*. Buchanan suggested that the meaning might be "the men, the warriors, the braves."

Snoring Bay
It is located on the southeastern end of Sucia Island between Fossil Bay and Echo Bay. According to the fable, a park ranger was caught napping there, hence the name. J. J. Gilbert noted the name of Shoal Bay in his 1888 Descriptive Report #1870 (http://riverhistory.ess.washington.edu/tsheets/reports/t1870.pdf, p 8).

Snug Harbor
See Mitchell Bay.

Snyder Cove
Located on the southern shoreline of Eld Inlet, on the campus of Evergreen State College, the origin of the name is unknown. The name is shown on topo maps but not on charts.

Socorro, Punta de [2] 1791, Pantoja; [3] 1791, Eliza
See Chuckanut Bay.

Solano or **Punta de Solano**
See William Point.

Solo Point
Located on the mainland near Cormorant Passage, a half mile north of Tatsolo Point, the origin of the name is unknown. It is the site of a beach and closed to all but the military.

Sore Head
See Sares Head.

Sota Point [7h] #154, 1841, Wilkes
See Rocky Point.

Soto Aguilar, Ensenada de [1] 1790, Quimper
Located along the Strait of Juan de Fuca, it was the unnamed bay behind (east of) Pillar Point. Quimper named it in 1790 [1]. In Quimper's journal, he referred to it as the Ensenada de Soto Aguilar (Wagner 120). On the chart he wrote Ens de Soto, as did Eliza [3] in 1791.

South Bay
See Henderson Inlet.

South Beach
Located a mile to the west of Restoration Point, it was named for the fact that it is located on the southern end of Bainbridge Island. It was a summer resort in the early 1900s.

South Bluff [13a] #2689, 1859, Richards
See Birch Point.

South Bluff [7e] #158, 1841, Wilkes
Located along the eastern side of Whidbey Island at the entrance to Holmes Harbor, Wilkes likely named it in 1841for its proximity to North Bluff, about a mile to the north. Wilkes did not include this name in his *Narrative*, but it is shown on his chart. It is neither named on current charts nor recognized by the U.S. Board on Geographic Names.

South Finger Island
Located in Echo Bay, Sucia Island, the origin of the name is unknown. However, along with North Finger Island and other portions of Sucia, the small island gives the appearance of a finger. The original name was South Finger Islands to accommodate two islands in the chain. When the Washington State Board on Geographic Names approved the name of Justice Island, they also received a recommendation to rename South Finger Islands to the singular. The Board approved the change in its October 8, 1992 meeting, Docket 350. The U.S. Board followed later in the year (from Washington State Board Files).

South Head [23] #6460, 1905
Located on the southwestern shoreline of Carr Inlet, a mile north of Pitt Passage, Wilkes originally named this Numan Point [7h] in 1841. He left no reason for the name. Wilkes did not include this name in his *Narrative*, but it is shown on his chart. The current name is likely for its location.

South Pass
Located at the northern end of Port Susan, it is the south pass which connects to West Pass between Camano Island and the mainland. It is the entrance to Stanwood.

South Point [7d] #146, 1841, Wilkes; [7k] #152, 1841, Wilkes
Located on the western shoreline of Hood Canal, at the south end of Suquamish Harbor, Wilkes likely named it for its location (Wilkes, *Narrative* 324).

South Sound
See Puget Sound.

Southeast Point
Located on the southeasterly side of Guemes Island, in 1841 Wilkes originally named this Sutton Head [7m], perhaps for crew member Samuel Sutton. Wilkes did not include this name in his *Narrative*, but it is shown on his chart.

Southwest Island [11] #654, 1858, U.S. Coast Survey
See Colville Island.

Southworth, Point [7g] #155, 1841, Wilkes
Located on the mainland at the northwestern entrance to Colvos Passage, Wilkes honored crew member Edward Southworth in 1841. Wilkes did not include this name in his *Narrative*, but it is shown on his chart. Southworth was a campground for local Indians. They found fish, clams, scallops, huckleberries, currants, and wild roses there at various times during the year. In 1888, George and Betsy Schultz settled on a 140 acre homestead (Bowen et al., V: 978). The community of Southworth takes its name from the point. The Salish name for the point was "a flat, overgrown with a species of grass" (Hilbert et. al., 221).

Spak Point [7n] #149, 1841, Wilkes
See Goose Point.

Spencer Lake
Located near the middle of Blakely Island, it was named for Theodore Spencer who settled on 160 acres there. In 1892, he purchased a box mill that the family operated until 1945 (TPL website). The lake drains to the west through the community of Thatcher. McLellan referenced Thatcher Lake for a name.

Spencer Spit - Spieden Island

Spencer Spit

Spencer Spit

Located on the eastern side of Lopez Island, it was originally homesteaded by Franklin Troxell and his wife Katherine. In 1860, the Troxell's purchased 162 acres which included the 130 acre state park. They sold to Rev. Isaac Dillon in 1886. In the late 1880s, Theodore Spencer purchased from Dillon and settled at the end of the spit. The Spencer family sold to the state in 1967. A replica of one of his original cabins appears on the spit (reader board on site). *See also* Blakely Island.

Sperry Point & Peninsula

It is located on the eastern side of Lopez Island, on the southern side of Lopez Pass. The point is on the north end of the peninsula. When John Kay shot and killed John Anderson, Kay was represented by Charles M. Bradshaw. Bradshaw took Kay's property, the peninsula, as payment for his fees. It was left to Sampson Chadwick, Bradshaw's son-in-law, to forcibly evict Kay's Indian wife and take possession of the house. In 1889, Bradshaw sold to John Sperry from Illinois, who farmed the land, planted orchards, and grew vegetable gardens. Frank Henderson, from Spokane, was involved in the Boy Scouts throughout his life. In 1935, he established an international camp in Westcott Bay which featured canoeing, horses, crafts, and so on. In 1938, he married Lucile Townsend who had established a similar camp for girls on Hood Canal. In 1945, Henderson lost his Westcott Bay lease and moved to the Sperry Peninsula to combine both the boys and girls camps. The Hendersons built up the area over the years with living accommodations (tents and tepees), a lodge, shower houses, and a swimming pool. The Hendersons sold the property in 1967 to a conglomerate of camping groups, and the name was changed to Nor'wester. Paul Allen purchased the 387 acre site for $8 million in 1996. Camp Nor'wester moved to the northwest corner of Johns Island (Mighetto 10-22; McDonald, Lucile. "The Pioneer Chadwicks of Lopez." *Seattle Times*. Jan. 17, 1960. Magazine Section p 5). Sperry Peninsula is a local name and is not recognized by the U.S. Board on Geographic Names.

Spieden Bluff [13a] #2689, 1859, Richards

Located on the northwestern end of Spieden Island, Richards presumably used Wilkes' 1841 Spieden Island name for the bluff.

Spieden Channel [13a] #2689, 1859, Richards

Located between San Juan and Spieden Islands, Richards presumably extended Wilkes' name for the island to the channel.

Spieden Island [7a] #145, 1841, Wilkes; [7c] #144, 1841, Wilkes

Located north of San Juan Island, Wilkes honored crew member William Spieden in 1841 (Meany, *Origin* 282). Regarding the name, J. J. Gilbert wrote the following in his Descriptive Report #2193, in 1894 (http://riverhistory.ess.washington.edu/tsheets/reports/t2193.pdf, p 10): "I was surprised at the pronunciation of Spieden. Everyone in the country calls it Spy-den while I am satisfied that the proper pronunciation is Spee-den. I understand it was named by Admiral Wilkes for one of his officers. I am not sure whether it is worthwhile to try to correct the error which is no doubt due to the first old sailor settler who could not master the diphthong and contented himself with the first vowel." Robert Smith was one of the British soldiers stationed at Garrison Bay. Rather than return home after the Pig War, Robert married an Indian woman and moved to Spieden in 1878 where he built a log cabin for his wife and her mother and raised sheep. Robert died soon after his daughter's birth. Ed Chevalier lived on Stuart Island. He worked at the barrel stave operation at Roche Harbor. One day, while out sailing, he met Robert's daughter, Mary. Ed and Mary were married in 1894. They raised sheep, turkeys, horses, and cattle, and they farmed on Spieden Island. Ed and Mary's five children soon outgrew the small cabin. Ed hauled in lumber and built another house on the top of the 114 foot hill. When the children reached school age, they attended at Stuart Island. Together, Ed and Mary were known as the King and Queen of Spieden where they lived for forty-five years. Later, they moved to Johns Island for ten years and eventually retired to Friday Harbor, surrounded by friends and family. Ed died in 1958 in Friday Harbor at the age of eighty-four (Richardson, *Pig* 233-239). Tony Sulak purchased the Spieden property in 1940. He built an airstrip on the top of the island and created a resort. The Jonas Brothers, taxidermists in Seattle, purchased the island in 1970 and renamed it Safari Island. They imported exotic animals and created a game preserve for wealthy hunters. Within a few years, because of mounting pressure from environmentalists and other islanders, the operation closed down. Alaska Airlines purchased the property next and used it as an executive retreat and recreation facility (Bailey and Nyberg, *San Juan Islands* 139; McDonald 152). In 1997, James Jannard, a resident of Orcas Island and founder of Oakley Inc., manufacturer of sun glasses, purchased the island for $22 million.

Spindle Rock
McLellan wrote: "Spindle Rock is a small rocky mass that is located about 400 yards from the northeast shore of Blakeley Island near the east entrance to Peavine Pass. It rises about 20 feet above high tide."

Split Point [16b] #602, 1869, Richards
It is located on the western end of Pearl Island. The name is neither reflected on current charts nor recognized by the U.S. Board on Geographic Names. Richards left no reason for the name.

Sportsman Lake
Mentioned by McLellan, it is located about halfway between Friday and Roche Harbors on San Juan Island.

Spring Beach [22] #6450, 1909
Located on the southwestern side of Vashon Island, 1 mile north of Point Dalco, it was named by H. B. Ritz who built a summer resort on a 200-acre parcel. It was named for the abundance of springs that surface on the beach (Hitchman 286).

Spring Beach
Located on the eastern side of Admiralty Inlet about four miles north of Shilshole Bay, it was perhaps named for springs in the area.

Spring Passage [13a] #2689, 1859, Richards
Located between Jones and Orcas Islands, Richards provided no reason for the name.

Springfield
See Wauna.

Squaib Bay [22] #6450, 1909
See Miller Bay.

Squallers Point
See Hazel Point.

Squamish Harbor [7d] #146, 1841, Wilkes; [7k] #152, 1841, Wilkes
See Suquamish Harbor.

Square Bay
See Boat Harbor.

Squaw Bay
Located on the southern end of Shaw Island near Indian Cove, it was named for the Indian village located there. The local name was O'Hara Cove after Oliver O'Hara who settled there during the 1870s. He logged and sold shingles.

Squaw Point
See Bushoowah-ahlee Point.

Squaxin Island [23] #6460, 1905
Located west of Harstine Island, Wilkes originally named this Jacks Island [7d], [7i] in 1841. Meany (*Origin* 286) related that the word comes from the Indian name *Duskwak-sin* meaning "alone." The 1854 Medicine Creek Treaty spelled it Squaxin, and it has been known by that name ever since. It is a reservation for the Squaxin Tribe.

Squaxin Passage [23] #6460, 1905
Located on the southwestern side of Squaxin Island, it was named for the island (Palmer, 80).

Squho, Point [7h] #154, 1841, Wilkes
Located on the northern side of Pickering Passage, north of Jarrells Cove, Wilkes left no reason for the 1841 name. It is neither named on current charts nor formally accepted by the U.S. Board on Geographic Names. Wilkes did not include this name in his *Narrative*, but it is shown on his chart.

St. Mary, Cape [13a] #2689, 1859, Richards
Located on the southeastern side of Lopez Island off Rosario Strait, Richards left no reason for the name. Lange speculated that it might have been named for the U.S. sloop-of-war *St. Mary*, which was built in the Washington Navy Yard in 1844.

St. Paul Waterway
One of the waterways on Commencement Bay, it was named for the St. Paul and Tacoma Lumber Company that owned property along the waterway (Reese, *Origins* 98). The lumber company was incorporated in 1888 and headed by Colonel Chauncey Griggs from St. Paul, Henry Hewitt Jr., said to be the richest man in Wisconsin, and four other partners including Griggs' son. The partners purchased 80,000 acres of mostly Douglas fir from the Northern Pacific Railroad. Davidson noted: "At Old Tacoma there is a large sawmill, and when we were there last, seven or eight large vessels were loading lumber. There are great rafts under the shore. The sawmill has an average output of two hundred and fifty thousand feet of lumber every twenty-four hours, but it has produced as high as four hundred and twenty-seven thousand feet upon a special occasion," (1889 *Pacific Coast Pilot* 617).

Stadium
Located on the western side of Case Inlet at the head of Pickering Passage, Jens Hansen established the post office in 1916. According to the TPL website, the community resembles a stadium with McLane Cove forming the field and the surrounding hills forming the seating area.

Stam Island [7e] #158, 1841, Wilkes
See Pass Island.

Stanley, Port
It is located on the eastern side of Lopez Island, at the southern end of Swifts Bay. In 1890, Frank and Sarah Baum arrived in Friday Harbor. Baum was an attorney, but with a couple of other attorneys already in town with barely enough work for one, he opened a newspaper, the San Juan County *Graphic*. Baum immediately fell into disfavor with the locals, as his prohibitionist paper conflicted wildly with a town founded on booze. Within a few months, competition ensued with a new town-supported paper, *The Islander*. Soon after, he decided it was easier to quit than fight. He joined a small group intent on building a new town that would have a higher moral character. They selected the area around Swifts Bay on Lopez Island and began buying property. The group called itself the Port Stanley Townsite Development Company. Baum selected the name after Sir Henry Stanley, whose book, *In Darkest Africa*, was very popular at the time. Port Stanley got its start in 1892 with Baum as postmaster. He built a combined post office/store/newspaper/office/home. Unfortunately, the 1893 bank panic threw the community and Baum out of business. Within a couple years, everything folded (Richardson, *Pig* 277-282).

Stanwood
Located at the northeastern end of Port Susan, it was named by Daniel O. Pearson for his wife Clara Jane Stanwood. In Lowell Massachusetts, Daniel N. Pearson (born in 1818) met Asa Mercer who was seeking to bring women to Seattle. Pearson obtained passage for himself and his two daughters, Georgiana and Josephine, two of the original Mercer girls. The three arrived in the Northwest in 1864. Daniel N. Pearson found work as a watchman at the Puget Mill in Port Gamble, while both girls taught school in Coupeville. Josie unfortunately died a few months after her arrival. Daniel N. relocated to Coupeville to join Georgia and soon found work as the keeper of the light at Admiralty Head with Georgia as his assistant. By 1866, Pearson earned enough money to send for his third daughter, Flora, age 16, his son, Daniel O., age 20, and his wife Susan (born in 1818), all of whom joined Asa Mercer on his second expedition. The balance of the family settled on Whidbey. In 1867, Georgia married Charles Townsend. Terry and Flora replaced her at the lighthouse. In 1876, Flora married Will Engle who had taken out a claim on property south of Isaac Ebey in 1852. In 1868, Daniel O. Pearson married his sweetheart Clara Jane Stanwood from Lowell. Daniel and Clara logged and farmed on Whidbey until 1877 when they moved to an area called Centerville on the Stillaguamish River. They opened a store and built a wharf on the river. Later that year, Clara gave birth to the first White child born in the area, Daniel Carlton Pearson.

The following year, the post office moved into his store. Because there were several Centervilles in Washington, Daniel re-named the town for his wife (Neil 141; *An Illustrated History*, 976). Stanwood thrived the early 1880s despite frequent floods and a declining lumber market. Logging villages extended thirty miles up the Stillaguamish. Wages were good, and locals built a store, hotel, schools, churches, and a blacksmith shop. By the late 1880s, the town added its third merchandise store, a drug store, a hardware store, and a doctor, Daniel McEachern. By this time, the population had grown to 250. In 1892, McEachern married Bertha Pearson, daughter of Daniel O. and Clara Jane. The couple headed east to live, but Bertha died in 1896 and the doctor returned to Stanwood with their two-year-old son Donald (Essex 7, 12, 13).

Starr Rock [21] #6300, 1895
Located off South Bellingham north of Post Point, the steamer *George E. Starr* hit it and sank in 1888 (Hitchman 288).

Station Cove
See Beaverton Cove.

Stau Point [7h] #154, 1841, Wilkes
Located on the northwestern side of Harstine Island, at the bend in Pickering Passage, Wilkes left no reason for the 1841 name. Wilkes did not include this name in his *Narrative*, but it is shown on his chart. The name is neither reflected on current charts nor recognized by the U.S. Board on Geographic Names.

Stavis Bay
Located off the eastern shoreline of Hood Canal, two miles south of Seabeck Bay, William and Mary Hobbs settled in the bay in 1889. As a carpenter, he soon constructed a cabin. With their five children, the family resettled in Seattle in 1906 where Hobbs worked for the Colman family (Perry, *Seabeck* 199). Peder and Severine Velde and their three children left Hanley Falls, Minnesota in May 1889. Arriving in Seattle, Peder worked as a carpenter and filed for a homestead in Stavis Bay. They departed Seattle in October, and for the next four days they rowed their belongings to the bay. Peder built a twelve by eighteen foot cabin using scrap material from the mill fire in Seabeck. They scratched out a living by selling vegetables, fruit, and eggs to Seattle merchants, and his two sons became proficient with an ax and manufactured hand-split cedar shakes. In the early 1900s, the family moved to Bremerton to better accommodate the education of the younger children born on the bay (Bowen et al., IV 59-60).

Steamboat Island

Steamboat Island [23] #6460, 1905
Located at the head of Totten Inlet, west of Hope Island, Wilkes originally named this Sandy Point [7i] in 1841. He likely named it for its appearance, as he did elsewhere in Puget Sound country. Wilkes did not include this name in his *Narrative*, but it is shown on his chart. The current name came from early settlers, who, with squinted eyes, could see some resemblance to the upper works of a steamboat (Hitchman 288). The Salish name for the island was "pushing off shore" (Hilbert et. al., 283).

Richard W. Blumenthal ♦ 243

Steep Island [13c] #2689, 1865
See Willow Island.

Steep Point [13a] #2689, 1859, Richards
Located on the southwestern side of Orcas Island, Richards likely named this for its appearance. It rises to 425 feet within a half mile from the water.

Steilacoom
It is located on the eastern shoreline of Puget Sound. In 1824, referring to Steilacoom, Work wrote (212): "Stopped at another little river where there was a village of the Nisqually Nation consisting of six houses, these are miserable habitations constructed of poles covered with mats, we were detained 1½ hours at this village, getting two men and a woman, wife to one of them, to act as interpreters and guides for us." On the return trip, he wrote (225): "Embarked a little after 4 o'clock in the morning and encamped at 2 o'clock in the afternoon at Sinoughtons, our guides' village which is called Chilacoom." Capt. Lafayette Balch (*see* Balch Passage) sailed into Steilacoom in 1850. He claimed 315.6 acres of land and established a store. He hauled timber from Puget Sound country to San Francisco and returned with merchandise to stock his store. Later in 1850, John B. Chapman filed a claim adjacent to Balch's. Both men donated land for public enterprises attempting to encourage settlement. In 1854, the towns of Balch and Chapman consolidated to become Washington Territory's first city. There are various stories on the name. One source suggested that it was named for Chief Tail-a-koom. Another suggested that it came from the local Indian village named for the Indian word *Tchil-ac-cum* meaning "pink flower." A third attributed it to either Lafayette Balch, who obtained the name from local Indians, or from John Work. Balch spelled it Cheilcoom (*A History* III: 93; Reese, *Documentary* 76, 93).

Steilacoom Creek
See Chambers Creek.

Stella Swamp
Located in the center of Cypress Island, the Washington State Board on Geographic Names received a proposal in 1993 to name it after Stella Payne who homesteaded in the area in 1919 and owned the property until 1961. Born in Newton, Illinois, Payne became a nurse and worked in Missouri for a time. She made her way west and was a cook for the Strawberry Bay fish trap camp. She married Albert Mellum who worked the fish trap, but because of the isolation the couple moved to Bellingham. Payne died in 1975, age 97. In its September 17, 1993 meeting, Docket 359, the Board approved the name. The U.S. Board followed in 1995 (from Washington State Board Files).

Stem Island
See Pass Island.

Still Harbor
Located off the northern side of McNeil Island, according to one story it was named due to the fact that the harbor is blocked from the weather by Gertrude Island (TPL website). The Salish name for the harbor was "steaming place" referring to steaming the numerous clams found on the beach (Hilbert et. al., 321).

Stockade Bay [13a] #2689, 1859, Richards
See Buck Bay.

Stoku Point [7h] #154, 1841, Wilkes
Located at the northwestern entrance to Jarrells Cove, Wilkes left no reason for the 1841 name. Wilkes did not include this name in his *Narrative*, but it is shown on his chart.

Stony Hill [13a] #2689, 1859, Richards
See Rosario Hill.

Stony Reef
See Cluster Islands.

Strawberry Bay [6] 1792, Vancouver
It is located off the western side of Cypress Island. Vancouver wrote: "On Mr. Broughton's first visit hither, he found a great quantity of very excellent strawberries, which gave it the name of Strawberry bay; but, on our arrival, the fruit season was passed," (Vancouver 296).

Strawberry Creek
The creek flows into Strawberry Bay, Cypress Island. It drains about 900 acres of land on the island including Phebe and Stella Swamp. It likely takes its name from the bay.

Strawberry Island [10] #51, 1854, U.S. Coast Survey
Located in Strawberry Bay off Cypress Island, in 1841 Wilkes named it Hautboy Islet [7a], [7m] after the common name of *Fragaria elatior*, a species of strawberry (Meany, *Origin* 293). Davidson renamed it: "On its western side and 1¼ mile from the southwest point is found a snug little harbor called Strawberry bay, which is formed by the retreating of the shore-line, and an outlying rocky islet called Strawberry or Hautboy Island," (*Report* 432).

Strawberry Island
Located on the inside of Deception Pass near Cornet Bay, Wilkes originally named it Big Tenif Island in 1841 [7e]. According to Hale (577), Tenif is a Waiilatpu name meaning "teeth." The Waiilatpu family includes the Willatpoos or Cayuse tribes who lived in eastern Washington and Oregon.

Strawberry Point
Located on the northwestern side of Whidbey Island, it was the site of the Langland farm, famous for its strawberries (Neil 241).

Stretch Island [7d] #146, 1841, Wilkes; [7h] #154, 1841, Wilkes
Located on the western side of Case Inlet, Wilkes honored crew member Samuel Stretch (Meany, *Origin* 293). Wilkes did not include this 1841 name in his *Narrative*, but it is shown on his chart.

Striped Peak [9a] #1911, 1849, Kellett
Located near the eastern entrance to Freshwater Bay, Quimper named this *Pta de Salví* in 1790 [1]. He initially used Salvi to describe Observatory Point but changed the location later (Blumenthal, *The Early Exploration* 25). Kellett provided the current name.

Stuart Island [7a] #145, 1841, Wilkes; [7c] #144, 1841, Wilkes
Located northwest of San Juan Island, Eliza named the combination of Stuart and Waldron Islands in 1791 as *Isla de Moralesa*. In 1841, Wilkes named this for crew member Frederick D. Stuart (Meany, *Origin* 294). According to Davidson: "Stuart island in many places is very high and precipitous, and covered with timber, but in some parts sparsely. Near its southwest head a perpendicular wall of rock serves also to

Stuart Island

distinguish it. After passing the western end of this island at the distance of a mile, the channel takes an abrupt turn to the eastward, and the Gulf of Georgia is seen," (*Report* 428).

Stuart Knobs
See Tiptop Hill.

Stubbs Lagoon
A small cove located in Liberty Bay with Virginia Point on its western side, it was first settled by the Ole Stubb family who built a cabin in the mid-1870s. The family emigrated from Norway to Stony Lake, Michigan in 1866. After a short time, Ole continued west, finally putting down roots in Liberty Bay. He frequently rowed to Port Madison for supplies and occasionally to Seattle (Kvelstad 32). The name is neither reflected on current charts nor recognized by the U.S Board on Geographic Names.

Stui Island [7h] #154, 1841, Wilkes
See McMicken Island.

Sucia Islands [2] 1791, Pantoja
Located north of Orcas Island, Pantoja named this grouping in 1791 *Sucia*, Spanish for dirty or foul. He referred to the reefs and rocks surrounding the islands making it a poor place to anchor (Wagner 186). Wilkes renamed the islands Percival Group [7a] in 1841 honoring Capt. John Percival, a War of 1812 hero (Meany, *Origin* 295). Kellett restored the Spanish name in the 1847 Admiralty chart [8a]. Davidson gave us an early glimpse of the islands: "A mile and a half to the westward of them [Matia group] lies the Sucia group, consisting of one large and six small

Sucia Islands

islands, with a reef off the north side of the group, and a beautiful harbor [Echo Bay] a mile long and half a mile wide, opening to the east, and carrying from 10 to 15 fathoms sticky mud bottom," (*Report* 434). It is difficult to determine what Davidson was counting and which large rocks or small islands were included. But the primary islands were Sucia, Little Sucia, Herndon, South Finger, North Finger, Justice, Ewing, and a host of other rocks and reefs. The first settler on Sucia was Charles Henry Wiggins who arrived in Mud Bay in the 1880s. He and his wife Mary raised seven boys and four girls there. The family built a house, barn, and root house. They raised foxes, cows, and sheep, tended a fruit orchard, and grew clover for the livestock. The house was located at the northwestern side of Mudd Bay. The family left the island in 1903. From the late 1800s to about 1909, workers quarried sandstone in Fossil Bay. The owners built a barracks and cookhouse in the back of Mud Bay. The operation folded when the sandstone was found to be too soft. However, enough was extracted to construct a dry dock at Bremerton (with the last shipment in 1895) and the lower five floors of the County-City Building in Seattle. The Harnden family (Harnden Island at the entrance to Mud Bay) resided on the island during the quarry days. They moved into the barracks in 1918 and lived there until a 1929 fire destroyed the buildings. After that, they built a house on a barge, anchoring it in Mud Bay. The family remained in the bay until 1942 and eventually moved to North Beach on Orcas (Cummings and Bailey 128, 129). In 1929, John G. Von Herberg, a motion picture theater owner, purchased 251 acres, almost half the island. He sold to Wilbur H. Johnston of Orcas in 1946 who established a summer camp and continued to acquire property on the main island until he owned all 551 acres. In 1958, Mr. and Mrs. Johnston contacted the Puget Sound Interclub Association founded by Everett (Ev) George Henry from Seattle, which represented thirty-six Northwest boating organizations. They worked out an arrangement for Interclub to purchase the land for $25,000. The land was turned over to the Washington State Parks and Recreation Commission in April 1960. After several additional acquisitions, the final of which occurred in 1974, the state owned the entire island. In his honor, the southwest tip of Fossil Bay carries the name Ev Henry Point. Although it is not reflected on current marine charts nor recognized by the U.S. Board on Geographic Names, it is shown on the Park and Recreation pamphlet obtainable on the island (McDonald 157; Bailey and Nyberg, *San Juan Islands* 153; McDonald, Lucile. "Sucia Island, Haven for Boaters." *Seattle Times*, July 3, 1960. Magazine Section p 5).

Sugarloaf Island
Located near the southern entrance to the Swinomish Channel off the southern end of Fidalgo Island, the origin of the name is unknown.

Sugarloaf [21] #6300, 1895
The peak is located less than a mile north of Mount Erie on Fidalgo Island. Davidson referred to it as Sugar Loaf in the 1889 *Pacific Coast Pilot* (562, 564)

Patos Island   Sucia Islands

but does not indicate who named it or why. How the name changed from Sugar Loaf to Sugarloaf is unknown, although it may be because of an aversion to two-word place names.

Sugarloaf Mountain
It is located on the western side of San Juan Island, east of Smallpox Bay, just north of Trout Lake. McLellan wrote: "At a distance of approximately one and one-half miles to the north of the summit of Mount Dallas, there is an abrupt ridge-shaped elevation known as Mount Grant which is 680 feet in altitude. Mount Grant is scantily covered with soil and conifers occur only in scattered patches." Per Kevin Loftus of the San Juan County Museum, some maps reflect the name Sugarloaf (Sept. 25, 2010 email to author), although it is not a recognized name by the U.S. Board on Geographic Names. It is not named on current charts.

Sullivan Slough
See La Conner.

Sunlight Beach
Located east of Deer Lagoon on Useless Bay at the southern end of Whidbey Island, the origin of the name is unknown.

Sunken Rock
According to the GNIS database, this is located on the western side of San Juan Island about a half mile south of Deadman Bay. It's simply a small rock unnamed on current charts. The name is likely descriptive.

Sunken Rock
According to the GNIS database, this is "a submerged bar off the S coast of Shaw Island." Based upon the latitude/longitude included in the database, it is approximately a quarter mile southeast of Hoffman Cove.

Sunny Bay
Located on the northern side of Hale Passage, west of Cromwell, the south-facing bay was likely named because it enjoyed the sunshine on clear days.

Sunny Shore Acres
Located on Camano Island on the western side of Port Susan, the origin of the name is unknown.

Sunrise Beach
Located on the western shoreline of Colvos Passage, it was named as a good location to watch the sunrise (Palmer, 81). It is directly across the passage from Sunset Beach on Vashon Island.

Sunrise Cove
Located on the eastern side of Lummi Island, it was likely named as a good location to watch the sunrise.

Sunset Beach
Located north of Onamac Point on the western side of Camano Island, the origin of the name is unknown.

Sunset Beach
Located on the western side of Vashon Island, it was likely named as a good location to watch the sunset.

Sunset Beach
Located on Eld Inlet, the name is not shown on charts but is reflected on topo maps.

Sunset Beach
Located on Fidalgo Island between Shannon and Green Points, it was likely named as a good location to watch the sunset.

Sunset Point
Located on the western side of San Juan Island between Smugglers Cove and Smallpox Bay, although it is likely descriptive, the origin of the name is unknown.

Suqaualus Point [7d] #146, 1841, Wilkes
See Hazel Point.

Suquamish
Located on the western side of Port Madison, the community was home to Chief Seattle and Old Man House. *O-le-man*, the Indian name for the dwelling is Chinook for "strong man." Whites converted this to Old Man House. When Wilkes surveyed the area in 1841, he measured it at 72 by 172 feet (Wilkes, *Narrative* 480). Hitchman (216) wrote that it was 60 by 520 feet. Chief Seattle died there in 1866 and is buried in the Saint Peter's Mission Cemetery of the Catholic Church in Suquamish (Carlson 25-28). In 1824, Work wrote (213): "On the West side we came through the Soquamis Bay from which there is a small opening to the Westward [Agate Pass]. ... We stopped at the Soquamis village situated in the bay of

the same name, it consists of 4 houses, we saw only 8 or ten men, but understand several of the inhabitants were off fishing. Our object in stopping here was to get the chief to accompany us as an interpreter, but he was not at home. The houses are build of boards covered with mats." The earliest settler was Allen Bartow and his wife. They arrived around the year 1900. Mrs. Bartow became the postmistress and named the community Bartow. As other settlers arrived, they suggested a name change to honor the Indian tribe (Bowen et al., II: 151). In 1915, the U.S. Board on Geographic Names addressed the name. Some charts and atlases reflected the name Bartow, but other documents used Suquamish. The Board opted for the latter (from U.S. Board files).

Suquamish Harbor [7d] #146, 1841, Wilkes; [7k] #152, 1841, Wilkes
Located on the opposite shoreline from Port Gamble in Hood Canal, Wilkes spelled this Suquamish for the Indian word *Suk-wa-bish* in 1841 (Wilkes, *Narrative* 323). The first three issues of the *Pacific Coast Pilot* maintained Wilkes' name. However, the 1867 chart #662 from the U.S. Coast Survey and the 1889 *Pilot* changed the name to Squamish Harbor; no reason was provided. The Salish word for the area was "clean water" referring to the fact that the water is cleaned with tidal action as opposed to a sheltered bay where the water can be more stagnant (Hilbert et. al., 198). In its March 12, 1982 meeting, the Washington State Board on Geographic Names addressed the spelling issue and approved Squamish. The U.S. Board followed in 1983 (from Washington State Board Files). In 2010, the Suquamish Indian Tribe petitioned the U.S. Board for the return of the original Wilkes' spelling. Referred back to the Washington State Board on Geographic Names, a significant controversy ensued by Klallam, S'Klallam, and other tribes adamantly opposed to this change. In its May 2012 meeting, the Washington Committee on Geographic Names approved the change. This caused the S'Klallam tribe to submit a formal request to the Board to change the name entirely to nəxʷx̣áʔəy pronounced *Nu-Ha-A*, which was the original S'Klallam name. As of this writing, neither the Washington State Board nor the U.S. Board on Geographic Names has yet approved this spelling modification from Squamish to Suquamish. Anticipating its approval however, I made the change in this text.

Suquamish Head [7d] #146, 1841, Wilkes
See Foulweather Bluff.

Susan, Port [6] 1792, Vancouver
Located north of Everett, Vancouver named it for Susanna Hyde Turner, the wife of Alan Gardner (Vancouver 289). Sailing into Port Susan, *Chatham* ran aground. Edward Bell commented: " Nothing remarkable occurred till the 2nd of June when sailing up a place called Port Gardner in Possession Sound, by the negligance of the man in the chains about one o'clock in the afternoon we run aground upon a Muddy Bank. We immediately gave the *Discovery* the alarm and at the same time made the Signal for assistance. She was astern of us and directly anchor'd and dispatched her Boats to our relief. On sounding astern of the Ship it was found that we had run a considerable distance over a Shoal and before we could carry an anchor our [out] into water sufficiently deep we veer'd away four Hawsers on end. At Highwater we hove off without any damage whatever and brought up in 9 fam. Water." As an aside, Seaman David Dorman, in charge of the lead line, received 36 lashes for neglect of duty for his failure to properly report the depth (Blumenthal, *With Vancouver* 202, 210, 211).

Sutton Head [7m] #160, 1841, Wilkes
See Southeast Point.

Swamish County
See Mason County.

Swantown
Located on the western side of East Bay in Budd Inlet, it is the local name for an area that houses the Swantown Marina, owned and operated by the Port of Olympia. John M. Swan arrived in Olympia in 1855. Among his other adventures in the Northwest, he operated the first commercial fishery on Commencement Bay, was captured by Chief Leschi during the 1855 Indian Wars, purchased property on McNeil Island (*see also* McNeil Island), and developed his claim on Budd Inlet. In 1872 he married Theresa Ann Cook.

Swifts Bay

Located off the eastern side of Lopez Island, it was named for Charles A. Swift. Born in Connecticut about 1827, he came west and settled in the bay in 1862 (TPL website). He married Ellen Chateben of Victoria in 1874 then remarried in 1885. It was reflected on Richards' 1861 chart [13b] as False Bay. Richards provided no reason for the name. Mr. Swifts' house burned to the ground in 1894.

Swindall Cove [19] #662, 1867, U.S. Coast Survey
Spelled Swindel's Cove on [23], *see* Chapman Cove.

Swinomish

See La Conner.

Swinomish Channel [21] #6300, 1895

The channel is clearly shown on Wilkes' chart [7a] but not named there or in his journal. It was named for the Indian tribe that inhabited the area. In 1824, Work (214, 215) referenced the channel, but unfortunately his description is lacking. Even if his transit was not the first White passage, it was certainly the first description: "Our course lay first round a point to one of the Scaadchet villages [perhaps Utsalady or Brown Point], then across a deep bay [Skagit Bay] and through a narrow winding channel to another larger bay [Padilla], down which we proceeded . . ." On the return trip, he wrote (224): "Embarked at 4 o'clock and after getting out of the little channel which was S.E. 6 or 7 miles, proceeded E.S.E. across a bay about 10 miles . . ." The observations of Wilkes and his men are more interesting. Wilkes wrote (*Narrative* 310): "On the east, between it and the main land, there is a marsh, which is bare at extreme low water." Alden wrote: "on the 24th Lt Maury left in charge of 3 boats with orders to pass through a passage that we had discovered a few days previous leading into Bellingham Bay . . ." Acting master George Sinclair wrote: "At 4 AM left in company with Maury to examine what appeared to be the entrance of a River on the East shore. We took with us two days provisions to survey a larger sheet of water which Maury had seen a day or so before from the top of one of the Islands. Found a communication into Bellingham Bay formed in the same manner as that between Ports Gardner & Susan by a river, emptying with a mouth in each Bay. There is a vast deal of fine land for cultivation hereabouts & on the Banks of the river we found a number of Indians living in permanent residences with a stockade close by for retreat in case of attack. They had abundance of Salmon but showed no anxcity to trade for them." And, finally, Joseph Perry Sanford wrote: "Left the Brig with Mr Maury to survey 'Bellingham' Bay and its adjacent Islands. We passed through passage of but little width of 3 or 4 miles in length. On either hand the country was low and swampy," (Blumenthal, *Charles Wilkes* 183, 210, 222). Beginning in the 1860s, settlers actively built dikes to reclaim farmland from the wetlands and sloughs and to protect the new land from high tides and flooding. By 1876, more than 2,000 acres were under cultivation, and an equal amount of land was being prepared for diking (*An Illustrated History*, 117). In 1892, J. J. Gilbert provided a description (http://riverhistory.ess.washington.edu/tsheets/reports/t2108.pdf, p 2): "The entrance from Skagit Bay, or as more familiarly known, Possession Sound, is through a narrow channel to the west of the rocky island [McGlinn Island] at the mouth of the Swinomish. This entrance is known by all steamboat-men as 'the hole in the wall.' The entrance is very narrow, and the shores are rock. There is no channel through the broad opening to the east of the island but there is water enough all over the flats at high tide for light-draught craft. After passing through the 'Hole in the Wall' the left-hand shore is a low bluff. Opposite the town of La Conner, it becomes rocky and high with a flat in front on which is an Indian Village. All the land west of the slough is Indian reservation. The point at the mouth of the unnamed slough east of the Swinomish is high rocky shore line, surrounded by marsh. Through the Swinomish Slough the border is marsh and a high dike extends the whole distance, sometimes close to the slough, sometimes a short distance back." First named Swinomish Slough on chart #6300 (1895), the U.S. Board on Geographic Names approved the name in 1897 after the Indian tribe. In 1892, Congress approved an Army Corps of Engineers dredging and diking project for the six mile slough to provide an alternative route north, bypassing Deception Pass. Although the project was completed in 1937, it continues to require additional dredging and diking every few years to preserve the channel. Thus, over time, the slough became an active channel. The 1909 *Pacific Coast Pilot* described the channel (163): "Near the upper end of the flats, and about 2 miles southward of Hope Island, is the entrance to the dredged channel leading into Swinomish Slough. This is under improvement, jetties being in course of construction and dredging operations being carried on. At its northern end the slough connects with Padilla Bay in the southern part of Washington Sound. In Swinomish Slough, near its junction with Telegraph Slough, two cut-offs have been made, eliminating two bad bends. It is used principally by light-draft vessels with local knowledge. About 4 feet can be carried through at low water, but a greater depth is contemplated; the channel is marked by several lights." In 1954, the La Conner Chamber of Commerce requested a name change, citing: "The word 'Slough' implies a dead, miry body of water, and connotes an opening at only one end of its course." The Chamber further stated: "SLOUGH is a very ugly name, and was originally mistakenly applied and continued to this day simply because no one asked officially for this name to be changed." The Board permitted the name change on June 11, 1954 (from U.S. Board files).

Swirl Island
Located off the southern end of Lopez Island, south of Aleck Rocks, perhaps it was named for the currents found nearby. The U.S. Government owns the island.

Sylopash Point [7d] #146, 1841, Wilkes
It is located on the western shoreline of Hood Canal, about two miles north of Pleasant Harbor, near the Dosewallips River. Wilkes left no reason for the 1841 name (Wilkes, *Narrative* 324). It apparently is a Twana name, but the meaning is unknown (Bright 468).

Sylvan
It is the local name for the community located on the northern side of Fox Island. Jesse B. Ball and A. Marshall were the first landowners in the area of Sylvan-Glen, that area just to the west of Ketners Point (originally named Slavis Point by Wilkes [7h]). They settled in 1870 and built a twenty-foot by twenty-foot cabin. In 1881, Ball sold ninety-seven acres to Josh M. Raines who lived in the cabin for several years. Ball moved on to found the town of Sterling in Skagit County. Raines found work at the Fox Island Brick Manufacturing Company in the mid-1880s. He sold to John Styles and built a stick house, the first on the island, in 1885. It still stands. Styles and his wife Emma lived in the cabin only a short time. They sold in 1885 to John D. Evans who also acquired Marshall's land at the same time. Andrew J. Miller and his wife and son purchased the land on the point for $1,500 in 1889. The local name Millers Point is still in use. The Millers, along with a Mr. Hutchins, were off-loaded from the steamer *Messenger* with supplies for several weeks. Looking for shelter, they discovered Jesse Ball's cabin. After much cleaning and making repairs, they moved in. Miller's neighbors from Iowa, Daniel M. and Emma Jane Booker, joined them later in the year. They established a post office in 1891, and his wife chose the name Sylvan-Glen because of the forest. Postal regulations did not permit hyphenated names, so it was shortened to Sylvan (Perisho 4, 33).

Sylvan Beach
Located on the northwestern side of Vashon Island, the developer named it in the early 1900s (Haulman).

Sylvan Cove
Located on the western side of Decatur Island, the origin of the name is unknown.

Sylvan Grove
See Pleasant Beach.

Syral Point [7f] #151, 1841, Wilkes
See Burner Point.

T'kope
See Tacoma.

Tabook Point [7d] #146, 1841, Wilkes
Located on the western side of the Toandos Peninsula, Wilkes left no reason for the 1841 name. Wilkes did not include this name in his *Narrative*, but it is shown on his chart. It apparently is a Twana name, but the meaning is unknown (Bright 469).

Tacoma
The community was founded by General Morton Matthew McCarver. He arrived in the area in 1868 seeking a terminus for the Northern Pacific Railroad.

Apparently, because the Indians called Mount Rainier by the name of Tacoma, McCarver used that name for his city (Meany, *Origin* 299-301). According to Hilbert (245, 246), Tacoma was said to be the name for Mount Rainier. However, the term was actually applied to any snow-capped mountain. It was not singularly applied to Mount Rainier. There were various other names, but that is probably attributable to the fact that there were many dialects in the region within sight of the mountain. They "knew it as white one, or good weather," meaning that when it is visible, good weather frequently followed. These are only a few of the stories as to the origin of the name. *See* Reese, *Origins of the name Tacoma* for more. The U.S. Board on Geographic Names approved the name in 1931 (from U.S. Board files). Variant names include Chebaulip, Commencement City, T'kope, and T'kopt.

Tacoma, Mount
See Mount Rainier.

Tahali Point [7h] #154, 1841, Wilkes
Located at the northern entrance to Pickering Passage, north of Point Dougal on Harstine Island, Wilkes left no reason for the 1841 name. Wilkes did not include this name in his *Narrative*, but it is shown on his chart. The name is neither reflected on current charts nor is it recognized by the U.S. Board on Geographic Names. According to Hale (593), it is a Palaihnih Indian term meaning "hail." The tribe lived in Northeastern California.

Tahlequah
Located on the south end of Vashon Island on Dalco Passage, it was the result of a $50 prize in 1920 by the Tacoma Chamber of Commerce to replace the existing name of Clam Cove. According to Cardel (*About* 105), the Indian name meant "water view." Another source (Haulman) indicated that it was named after Tahlequah, Oklahoma. The U.S. Board on Geographic Names approved the name over the variant names of Talequah and Tallequah in 1942.

Tahuya
Located near Sisters on Hood Canal, the name is derived from the Twana Indian names *ta* and *ho-i* meaning, "Some important event that occurred there," (Meany, *Origin* 301). The U.S. Board on Geographic Names approved the name of the river in 1941 over the variants which included Tahayeh Creek, Tahuya Creek, Tahuyeh Creek, Tahuyeh River, and Tahuyn Creek (*Decisions*). The spelling was adopted based upon the input of four local postmasters in the area in 1940.

Takup Point [7n] #149, 1841, Wilkes
See Hardwick Point.

Tala Point [7d] #146, 1841, Wilkes; [7f] #151, 1841, Wilkes
Located on the eastern entrance to Port Ludlow, Wilkes left no reason for the 1841 name (Meany, *Origin* 301). It is Chinook for "money," perhaps from the word "dollar" (Hale 647; Bright 474).

Tala Point [7b] #148, 1841, Wilkes; [7f] #151, 1841, Wilkes
It is located on the southeastern side of Discovery Bay. It is neither named on current charts nor is it recognized by the U.S. Board on Geographic Names. Wilkes left no reason for the 1841 name. Wilkes did not include this name in his *Narrative*, but it is shown on both charts. It is Chinook for "money," perhaps from the word "dollar" (Hale 647; Bright 474).

Talapais Point [7h] #154, 1841, Wilkes
This is the southern entrance to Vaughn Bay. Wilkes left no reason for the 1841 name. It is neither named on current charts nor is it recognized by the U.S. Board on Geographic Names. Wilkes did not include this name in his *Narrative*, but it is shown on his chart.

Talequah
See Tahlequah.

Talie Bay [7h] #154, 1841, Wilkes
See Mayo Cove.

Tanglewood Island
A small island located on the northwestern side of Fox Island in Hale Passage, the Indians called it *Tahotowa* and used it as a burial ground. Conrad Hoska, a Tacoma mortician and county coroner, purchased it in 1896 or 1897 from the State of Washington. Hoska died in 1910 at age 55. In 1934, the Hoska family sold to Dr. Alfred Schultz, a Tacoma pediatrician who ran a boy's camp there for several years. The lodge was available for church retreats,

youth camps, and other organizations (Perisho 185, Edgers 8). According to the Sylvan postmaster, local maps carried the name Grave Island, as the site was an Indian burial ground. However, it had carried the name Tanglewood Island by the Hoska family for years. This fact was supported by a 1913 news article in the *Tacoma Tribune* entitled "Tanglewood Island, a Real Fairyland." The article indicated that the island was covered by a heavy growth of timber, absolutely impenetrable. In 1946, Schultz formally proposed the name Tanglewood Island to the U.S. Board on Geographic Names, because the "huge twisting trunks of Madrona interlocking and twisted among tall cedar and fir certainly is a tangled mess." The Board approved it in 1947 (GNIS files). In addition to Grave Island, other variants included Ellen's Isle, Hoska Island, and Grant Island.

Tarboo Bay
Located at the head of Dabob Bay, the name is pronounced Tar-a-boo meaning "windy" (Hitchman 298).

Tatoosh Island

Tatoosh Island
"This island lies W.NW. half a mile from the point of Cape Flattery. It is composed of small islets connected by reefs, is quite flat-topped, and without trees. The surface is 100 feet above high water, and the sides are perpendicular; the entire mass being composed of coarse sandstone conglomerate with an outcrop of basalt on one of the reefs." Davidson went on to say: "This island, with its outlying reef, is the most western portion of the United States," (*Report* 412, 413). Meares named this in 1788 for the Indian chief Tatooche, although he spelled it Tatootche (Meany, *Origin* 302; Meares 251). Seemann (95) wrote: "Off Cape Classet lies Tatooche Island, which, having no trees, forms a great contrast to the mainland. The shores are lined with rocks in curious shape, with edges as sharp as if in a newly-cut quarry. The island is divided into two parts, and covered with houses."

Tatsolo Point [7i] #147, 1841, Wilkes
Located on the eastern shoreline of Puget Sound a couple miles north of the Nisqually Flats, Wilkes left no reason for the 1841 name. Wilkes did not include this name in his *Narrative*, but it is shown on his chart.

Tatugh
Located on the eastern side of Blake Island, Davidson indicated that was the Indian name for the point (*Report* 448). It is unnamed on current charts, but the name Tatugh is included in the U.S. Board on Geographic Names database. The name shows on the 1876-1877 t-sheet #1452a.

Taylor Bay
Located on the western side of the Key Peninsula at the entrance to Case Inlet, it was named after, "old man Taylor, who came to this coast as a sailor on an English ship and settled by this bay," (Meany, *Origin* 303).

Tchinom Point [7d] #146, 1841, Wilkes
See Chinom Point.

Waadah Island   Tatoosh Island Lighthouse   Cape Flattery

Teekalet Bluff
Located at the western entrance to Port Gamble, it was originally the site of an Indian village which was moved to Point Julia as Port Gamble developed. In 1853, Josiah P. Keller (*see also* Port Gamble) established a village where the community of Port Gamble is now located. Keller arrived on the *L.P Foster* and with Cyrus Walker assisted in building the mill at Port Gamble. Keller's wife was the first White woman in the area. In naming the village, he used *Teekalet*, a transliteration of the Indian word for "brightness of the noon-day sun." Keller died in Victoria in 1862 at age 50 (Meany, *Origin* 226, 227; Wright 114). The Salish word means "skunk cabbage" (Hilbert et. al., 190).

Teelan
See Eagledale.

Tekiu Point [7d] #146, 1841, Wilkes
Located on the eastern side of Hood Canal about seven miles south of Seabec, Wilkes left no reason for the 1841 name. Wilkes did not include this name in his *Narrative*, but it is shown on his chart. The Indian name is for "elk" (TPL website). However, Bright (486) believed it was Twana for "horse" or perhaps Lushootseed for "wolf." The area was originally logged by one of the many companies supplying timber to the Washington Mill Company. In the late 1930s, Col. Julian Willcox and his wife Constance built the old mansion. The 7,800 square-foot home included the most modern conveniences available at that time and cost $250,000. The house became the entertainment center on the canal for years. At one time, Erle Stanley Gardner nearly purchased it, but Constance felt that his offer was too low (Bowen et al., IV: 64).

Teko Point [7h] #154, 1841, Wilkes
The precise location is unclear. Wilkes' chart places it on the western side of Carr Inlet, south of Glencove. Wilkes left no reason for the 1841 name. He did not include this name in his *Narrative*, but it is shown on his chart. It is neither named on current charts nor recognized by the U.S. Board on Geographic Names.

Telegraph Bay [13h] #2689, 1888
Located on the southeastern side of Lopez Island, south of Cape St. Mary, it was the location of the telegraph which went into service in 1866 between Vancouver Island and the Washington mainland. The other end, Telegraph Bight, is on Fidalgo Island, just south of Langley Point. The line was authorized by Vancouver Island Parliament in 1864 (two years before the island joined British Columbia). The Lopez-Fidalgo Island section was laid first and then the San Juan Island-Victoria section. The final portion connected San Juan and Lopez Islands. All of this work was completed in 1866. Soon after completion, a band of Indians landed in Telegraph Bay to dig for clams. While working, they uncovered and cut into the telegraph cable. Gold fever was rampant in those days. The Indians, believing that the copper in the cable was actually gold, began cutting out sections. The cable operator on Lopez observed these activities and rushed to the beach to chase them away. Threatened with his life, he quickly returned to Sampson Chadwick's home for help. By the time the men returned, the Indians had departed, heading in the direction of Fidalgo Island. The operator quickly repaired the cable and sent a message to the office on Fidalgo explaining the events. As he assumed that the Indians were headed to the Anacortes assay office, the telegraph office quickly sent someone to intercept them. By the time the Indians arrived, they were surprised that the news of their "gold strike" reached Fidalgo before they had. They were further surprised and disappointed to learn that their samples were worthless. Breaks in the line were common. New ones occurred almost before old ones could be repaired. By the early 1870s, the San Juan Island to Victoria route was relocated.

Telegraph Bight
See Telegraph Bay.

Termination Point [7d] #146, 1841, Wilkes; [7k] #152, 1841, Wilkes
It is located on the western side of Hood Canal and marks the spot where the floating bridge connects to land. Meany (*Origin* 305) believed the name to be descriptive. That is, it represented the northern end of Hood Canal.

Terrill Beach
Located on the northern end of Orcas Island, it was named for Benj and Sarah Terrill who settled there. According to the 1885 San Juan County census, Benj, from England, was 69, and Sara, from Ireland, was 63. No children were listed.

Tesi Point
See Lone Tree Point.

Tetusi Bay [7i] #147, 1841, Wilkes
See Filucy Bay.

Tharald Pond
The man-made pond is located near Parks Bay on the western side of Shaw Island. Theodore (1851-1926) and Thomas Tharold (1854-1923) homesteaded the 150 acre property. Born in Norway, the brothers came to the U.S. in 1870. By 1885, they were farming and running sheep on Shaw Island, where they built a log cabin which still stands today. Both are buried on the island. Robert H. Ellis MD and his wife Blanche purchased the homestead from Earl and Margery Hofman in 1935. The Ellis' son Fred and his wife Marilyn have lived in the cabin since their marriage in 1954. The Ellis' had an Orcas Island man excavate the pond in 1988 as a place for waterfowl. The pond occupies about eight acres and is 25 feet deep at the deepest point. In 1993, Fred Ellis petitioned the Washington State Board on Geographic Names to name the pond after the Tharold brothers. At its December 10, 1993 meeting, the Board approved the name (from Washington State Board files). For whatever reason, the U.S. Board on Geographic Names failed to act on the name. As such, it is not yet "official." This oversight is currently under review by the Washington Board. The Ellis' eventually placed all of their Shaw Island property into a conservation easement with the San Juan Preservation Trust.

Thatcher & Thatcher Bay
The community and bay are located on the western shore of Blakely Island. The names come from Thatcher Pass.

Thatcher Lake
See Spencer Lake.

Thatcher Pass [13a] #2689, 1859, Richards
Located between Blakely and Decatur Islands, Richards provided no reason for the name. Davidson noted (1869 *Pacific Coast Pilot* 211): "Northwest of James Island is an opening on the west between Decatur Island and Blakely Island, with twenty-five fathoms in it, but with a rock, covered at a quarter flood, exactly in the middle of the entrance. It is called Thatcher Pass."

The Brothers
See Fauntleroy Cove.

The Narrows [7d] #146, 1841, Wilkes
Located at the original entrance to Puget Sound, Wilkes wrote (*Narrative* 304): "…and finally, towards evening, anchored just below the narrows leading into Puget Sound, within a few yards of the shore and under a high perpendicular bank, in sixteen fathoms." Wilkes continued with the following description: "The scenery about this pass becomes very fine: on all sides are high projecting bluffs of sandstone, rising almost perpendicularly from the water, with a great variety of shrubs along their base. The tide, which runs through the narrows with great velocity, causes many eddies and whirlpools, through which a ship is carried with extraordinary rapidity, while the danger seems to be imminent." Fifty years before Wilkes, Peter Puget wrote: "A Most Rapid Tide from the Northward hurried us so fast past the Shore that we could scarce land – In Mid Channel we found 30 fths water – soft Bottom – " (Puget 196).

The Narrows
Located to the east of The Great Bend on Hood Canal, this represents the narrowing of the canal off Sisters Point. The name is likely descriptive. It is not reflected on current charts.

The Narrows
Located on the Little Skookum Inlet, the name is descriptive.

The Twins
The two small islands (or large rocks) are located in the back of Port Ludlow and protect the entrance to the inner bay.

Thea Foss Waterway
Located on Commencement Bay, Arthur and Thea Foss, originally from Norway, lived on a houseboat in Commencement Bay. In 1889, Thea bought a rowboat

for five dollars and sold it for fifteen. She then bought two more and rented them out to settlers interested in fishing. From this experience, Arthur, a carpenter by trade, began building rowboats, ultimately reaching more than 200, which the family continued to rent. The business expanded as did the size of the boats to include launches and ultimately tugs. Soon, they founded the Foss Tug and Launch Company (Bailey and Nyberg, *South Puget Sound* 184). Born in 1857, Thea died in 1927 from pancreatic cancer. In 1988, the Washington State Board on Geographic Names received and approved the proposal to change the name of City Waterway to the Thea Foss Waterway, Docket 343. The U.S. Board on Geographic Names followed in 1990 (from Washington State Board files).

Third Beach
See First Beach.

Third Lagoon
Located on the eastern side of San Juan Island, this is the most easterly of the three lagoons. *See also* Jakles Lagoon.

Thompson, Point [7a] #145, 1841, Wilkes
Located nearly at the northern tip of Orcas Island, in 1841 Wilkes honored crew member Matthew Thompson. Wilkes did not include this name in his *Narrative*, but it is shown on his chart.

Thompson Cove [24] #1947, 1849, Inskip
Located off the southeastern side of Anderson Island, it was named by Capt. R. N. Inskip in 1846 for the Rev. Robert Thompson, chaplain of the H.M.S. *Fisgard* (Meany, *Origin* 308).

Thorndyke Bay
Located off the eastern side of the Toandos Peninsula on Hood Canal, four miles south of Suquamish Harbor, it was named for John. R. Thorndyke who built a sawmill in the bay in 1852 (TPL website).

Thorndyke Lake
Located at the northern end of Thorndyke Bay, it was named for the bay.

Three Tree Point
Located on the eastern side of Puget Sound, about halfway between Alki Point and Commencement Bay, the name was perhaps descriptive. It was originally named Point Pully by Wilkes [7d], [7g] in 1841 for crew member Robert Pully (Meany, *Origin* 222). Wilkes did not include this name in his *Narrative*, but it is shown on his chart. The Indian name for the point is "loading things into a canoe." According to the legend, a young girl married a Squally man. Because she didn't like him, she ran away and returned home. Wearing a marmot skin robe, he followed. To run faster, he threw his robe over a boulder. The girl saw her father and mother from afar. They were loading their belongings into a canoe to move. The girl hollered for them to wait. Instantly, according to Indian lore, the transformer turned all of them into stone. The canoe became the point. The girl became a white rock at Redondo. The surface of the rock is wrinkled as if her husband's robe still covered it. It is referenced as blanket rock by the Indians (Hilbert et. al., 69). In 1974, members of the Three Tree Point Garden Club wrote to the Washington State Board on Geographic Names to point out the confusion of Point Pully on nautical charts and Three Tree Point on other maps. In its June 13, 1975 meeting, the Board approved Three Tree Point, Docket 201. The U.S. Board followed later in the year (from Washington State Board Files).

Tide Point [13c] #2689, 1865
Located on the western side of Cypress Island, Richards left no reason for the name. Davidson commented: "In this narrow part of the strait the depth of water is about 60 fathoms and the current goes through with a roar like the sound of a gale of wind through a forest. When at anchor in 10 fathoms, under the low point [Tide Point] 1½ mile north of Strawberry island, we found the current four miles per hour, and swirling so much that the vessel had to be steered to prevent her breaking her sheer," (*Report* 432, 433). Wilkes originally named it Point Somerndyke [7m]; he left no reason for the 1841 name.

Tift Rocks
Located on the western side of Shaw Island, south of Neck Point, they were named after Bert Tift who ran the first post office on Shaw Island (McDonald 136; Richardson, *Pig* 216, 217).

Tillicum Beach
Located on Camano Island on the western side of Port Susan, the origin of the name is unknown. *Tillicum* is the Chinook word for "friend."

Tiptop Hill
Located on the southwestern side of Stuart Island, Richards originally named this Moody Hills [14a] after Col. Richard Clement Moody, R.E. who commanded a company of sappers and miners. He arrived in Esquimalt in 1858. When his detachment disbanded in 1883, he returned to England. He died in 1887 (Lange). J. J. Gilbert observed these hills in 1894. Accompanying Descriptive Report #2193, he wrote (http://riverhistory.ess.washington.edu/tsheets/reports/t2193.pdf, p 1): "The highest of these ridges is that between Reid Harbor and Haro Strait and culminates in two knobs of nearly equal height, just east of the head of Reid Harbor. The height is about 650 feet. I have designated these hills as Stuart knobs." McLellan referred to the formation as: "an elongated dome called Tiptop Mountain, which is 640 feet high." Based upon McLellan's observations, the U.S. Board on Geographic Names renamed the dome in 1925. Current charts show the height as 640 feet.

Tit Point [7f] #151, 1841, Wilkes
See Burner Point.

Titusi Bay [7i] #147, 1841, Wilkes
See Filucy Bay.

Tiye Point [7i] #147, 1841, Wilkes
See McDermott Point.

Toandos Peninsula [7d] #146, 1841, Wilkes
Located in the northern portion of Hood Canal, Wilkes named this in 1841 for the Twana Indian name *tu-an-hu* which means "portage" (Meany, *Origin* 311).

Tocosos River [21] #6300, 1895
See Sail River.

Toe Point [13a] #2689, 1859, Richards
Located on the east end of Patos Island, Richards perhaps named it for its shape, like the toes of a foot (Meany, *Origin* 311). McLellan wrote: "At the east end of Patos Island there are three long points, composed of resistant material, that extend out far beyond the intervening spaces due to differential erosion. Since these long narrow parallel points of land extend out from the end of the island like the toes on the foot, this end of Patos Island is called Toe Point."

Tolo Beach
Located on the western side of Bainbridge Island between Battle Point and Fletcher Bay, it was named by Martin Andreason for the Chinook word "to earn" or "to gain." After losing all he owned in the great Chicago fire of 1871, Andreason moved to Seattle and found work in Clairmont & Co. cabinet shop located in the Pontius Building at the corner of Front and Madison Streets. The June 6, 1889 Great Seattle Fire was initially blamed on an overturned glue pot in Jimmie McGough's paint shop on the first floor. But, in fact, it was Andreason's glue pot in the basement. He moved to Tolo the following year and settled on 160 acres (Warner 60; Mariott 105).

Tolvia Shoal [7d] #146, 1841, Wilkes; [7i] #147, 1841, Wilkes
Located east of McNeil Island, this name appears on Wilkes' chart but is not referenced in his *Narrative*. He left no reason for the 1841 name. In 1846, Inskip named this Scarboro Shoal [24] for Capt. James Scarborough of the Hudson's Bay Company schooner *Cadboro* (Meany, *Origin* 312).

Tom Islet [7i] #147, 1841, Wilkes
See Eagle Island.

Tomos Point [7h] #154, 1841, Wilkes
See Nearns Point.

Tongue Point [9a] #1911, 1849, Kellett
Located on the Strait of Juan de Fuca, on the eastern side of Crescent Bay, west of Port Angeles, Kellett provided the current name, perhaps for its shape.

Tongue Point
See Madrona Point.

Tongue Point (Semiamoo)

Tongue Point [7a] #148, 1841, Wilkes; [7l] #159, 1841, Wilkes
Located in Semiamoo Bay, Wilkes named it for its appearance in 1841. Wilkes did not include this name in his *Narrative*, but it is shown on his chart. Davidson referenced it as Tongue Spit (1889 *Pacific Coast Pilot* 576).

Tonkon Islands [7e] #158, 1841, Wilkes
Located off the southern end of Fidalgo Island, Wilkes originally named these Tokano Islets; he left no reason for the 1841 name. Wilkes did not include this name in his *Narrative*, but it is shown on his chart. Somehow the spelling evolved into Tonkon. According to Hale (588, 589), *Tokano* was a western Shoshonee name which means "night or darkness." The Shoshonees lived in Oregon and Western Idaho. *See also* Deadman Island.

Tosi Point [7e] #158, 1841, Wilkes
It is located on Fidalgo Island, east of Hope Island. Wilkes did not include this name in his *Narrative*, but it is shown on his chart. According to Hale (601), *Tosi* was a Palaiks Indian name meaning "deer." The Tribe lived in Northeastern California. The Salish name for the point was "single tree standing" (Hilbert et. al., 350). *See also* Lone Tree Point.

Totten Inlet [7d] #146, 1841, Wilkes; [7i] #147, 1841, Wilkes
Located at the southwestern side of Puget Sound, Wilkes honored crew member George M. Totten in 1841 (Meany, *Origin* 314). The U.S. Board on Geographic Names approved the current name over an early local name, Oyster Bay, in 1937 (GNIS files). *See also* Henderson Inlet.

Totten's Point [7f] #151, 1841, Wilkes
Located at the western entrance to Port Gamble, Wilkes named this for crew member George M. Totten in 1841, who was working under Lieut. Augustus Case during the survey of Hood Canal (Wilkes, *Narrative* 323). It is neither named on current charts nor accepted by the U.S. Board on Geographic Names.

Towhead Island
Located off the northern shore of Fox Island, it is used as a support for the bridge to the mainland. According to 1947 correspondence from the postmaster of Sylvan, the name was Tow Head Island (GNIS files, Tanglewood Island). A toehead, as popularized by Huck Finn, is a small islet or sandbar in a river. Twain wrote in the third paragraph in chapter XII: "When the first streak of day begun to show we tied up to a towhead in a big bend on the Illinois side, and hacked off cottonwood branches with the hatchet, and covered up the raft with them so she looked like there had been a cave-in in the bank there. A towhead is a sand-bar that has cottonwoods on it as thick as harrow-teeth." The name likely originated from this definition.

Towhead Island
Located off the northern shore of Cypress Island, the U.S. Coast Survey named this Rock Island [10] in 1854, but no reason was provided. According to Davidson: "Half a mile off the north end of Cypress island is a small islet covered with trees and called Rock island. NW. of it are some sunken rocks, but their exact position is not accurately known," (*Report* 433). In the 1868 *Pacific Coast Pilot* (212), the name was changed to Cypress Rock. Davidson indicated that the U.S. Coast Survey named it in 1854. That name was adopted by the U.S. Board of Geographic Names in 1893, but the Board changed it to Towhead Island in 1925 (*Decisions*). According to the GNIS files, McClellan discovered a "G.L.O. Plat" from 1875 which referenced Towhead. Accordingly, McClellan proposed the name change. A note in the file indicated that the 1893 decision was overlooked.

Townsend, Port [6] 1792, Vancouver
It is located at the western head of Admiralty Inlet. Vancouver wrote: "To this port I gave the name of Port Townshend, in honor of the noble Marquis of that name," (233). Born February 28, 1724, one of Townshend's sponsors at his baptism was King George I. Throughout his life, he saw increasingly important military assignments, reaching Brigadier General in 1759. In addition, he received more titles, including the Marquis Townshend of Rainham in 1786. He died in 1807. Wilkes wrote: "Port Townsend is a fine sheet of water, three miles and a quarter in length, by one mile and three quarters in width. Opposite to our anchorage is an extensive table-land, free from wood, and which would afford a good site for a town," (Wilkes, *Narrative* 302, 303). Vancouver spelled the name TownsHend (my emphasis). Townsfolk in the small community became increasingly bitter with the British as a result of the Pig War and boundary dispute. In 1852, they convened and discussed the idea of changing the name. One of the early leaders recommended simply removing the "h" from the name and leaving the balance alone. The other community leaders agreed, and shortly thereafter they drafted a plat for Port Townsend (McCurdy, *By Juan* 41). Davidson wrote: "The town numbers a few houses, and in the vicinity are some good farms. The place is noted for the rough character of its 'beach combers,'" (*Report* 441). The U.S. Board on Geographic Names approved the name for the bay and the community in 1899 by eliminating the "h" as was still reflected on some maps. Variant names for the bay included Port Townsend Bay and Port Townsend Harbor. Alfred A. Plummer was born March 3, 1822, in Alfred, Maine. At age eighteen, he traveled to Boston and entered the saddlery and harness making business. With the news of a gold strike in California, the West Coast beckoned. Being without funds, he joined the U.S. Quartermaster's Department as a saddler. In 1849, he left for El Paso, resigned, and then continued working toward the West Coast. His path took him to Mazatlan where he boarded the bark *Phoenix* (a bark is a ship with three or more masts, rigged with square sails on the forward masts, and a fore and aft sail on the aft mast) and reached San Francisco in May 1850. There, he opened the Plummer Hotel where he met Capt. Lafayette Balch who became a frequent patron. Balch spun yarns about the wonderful opportunities on the Northwest Coast and trading excursions aboard his brig, *George Emery*. (A brig is a two-masted ship, square-rigged on both masts.) In December, the 29-year-old Plummer closed his hotel and along with another friend, Charles Bachelder, booked passage with Balch and headed north. The captain was destined for Steilacoom where he owned a general store. As the ship entered Admiralty Inlet, Balch pointed out the Port Townsend area, describing its potential for an excellent town site. The two friends worked for the captain that year at Steilacoom. There they met Henry C. Wilson who had already filed a claim in Port Townsend Harbor and reaffirmed everything Balch had said. Finally, Plummer and Bachelder acquired a canoe and paddled from Steilacoom to Port Townsend, arriving on April 24, 1851. They found several hundred Indians camped in the area. Plummer and Bachelder provided some trinkets and were permitted to remain. The day after their arrival, Plummer filed a claim for 158 acres on either side of Point Hudson. Bachelder filed a claim as well but failed to perfect his title. With assistance from the Indians, the two immediately constructed a fifteen by thirty foot cabin on what is now the northeast corner of Water and Tyler Streets (McCurdy, *By Juan* 11-17).

Townsend Canal, Port
See Portage Canal.

Toy Point
Located on the southeast end of Fox Island, halfway between Fox Point and Gibson Point, the origin of the name is unknown.

Tracyton [23] #6460, 1905
Located on the southeastern side of Dyes Inlet, the name honored Benjamin Franklin Tracy who was the Secretary of the Navy under President Benjamin Harrison (Meany, *Origin* 315, 316).

Tramp Harbor [23] #6460, 1905
Located off the southeastern side of Vashon Island, a portage exists between the harbor and Quartermaster Harbor. Settlers carried their boats or pushed them across the sand to avoid rowing all the

way around Maury Island. It was apparently quite a tramp (i.e., an effort to hike across while pulling or pushing the boat) unless there were people to assist (TPL website). Davidson referenced the name in the 1889 *Pacific Coast Pilot* (615). He wrote: "Under the south side of Point Heyer is a broad open bight, called Tramp Harbor, with a very low shore on the southern part and nearly connected with the head of Quartermaster's Harbor. In this bight there is anchorage in fifteen to eighteen fathoms of water, over fine gray sand, with deep water, of more than sixty fathoms, on the line between Point Heyer and Point Robinson." Trump Harbor was a variant. The U.S. Board on Geographic Names approved the current name in 1897.

Travis Spit
The spit covers the mouth of Sequim Bay. The 1871 Clallam County census lists Robert Travers from Ireland, age 36, along with his daughter Maggie, as living in the Sequim precinct. They were not shown in the 1870 census. Travis Spit is perhaps named for the Travers family.

Treasure Island
See Reach Island.

Treasure Island
Located in Port Madison, it was originally called Dead Man's Island as it was used as a burial ground for local Whites and perhaps the Suquamish Indians as well. The name was changed by its first settler in the early 1900s, according Luke May. May was an independent criminal forensic specialist and detective from Seattle. Based on his story, for which there was apparently never any supporting evidence, he found gold coins on the island (May 13, 2010 email to author, Kitsap Regional Library). In 1931, Mr. May wrote to the U.S. Board on Geographic Names suggesting the name. The Board enlisted the opinion of Edmund Meany, who responded: "Mr. May is an interesting man, a professional criminologist whose services are called into play in various parts of the Pacific Northwest. It may be that he knows about some hidden history of that little island. What ever his reasons may be, I would favor his suggestion. I feel that he is dependable." The Board approved the name over the variant in 1931 (GNIS files).

Treble, Point [7d] #146, 1841, Wilkes; [7i] #147, 1841, Wilkes
Located on the western side of Anderson Island, Wilkes honored crew member George Treble in 1841 (Meany, *Origin* 223). Wilkes did not include this name in his *Narrative*, but it is shown on his chart. In 1846, Inskip named this for Lieut. Fleetwood J. Richards [24] who served on the *Fisgard* (Reese, *Origins* 91). The chart entry is a bit strange, as it is clearly printed as "Richard2 Pt". The entry might have been a typo, as the gentleman's name was definitely Richards.

Tree Bluff [8a] #1917, 1847, Kellett
Located five miles east of Pillar Point on the Strait of Juan de Fuca, Kellett provided no reason for the name.

Tres Hermanas
See Porpoise Rocks.

Triangle Cove [7a] #145, 1841, Wilkes; [7o] #157, 1841, Wilkes
Located on the eastern side of Camano Island, Wilkes likely named it for its shape in 1841 (Wilkes, *Narrative* 315).

Trimble Island
See Blake Island.

Trincas Island
The rock is located to the northeast of Picnic Island in West Sound. It was named by William C. Bryant for his daughter. Mr. Bryant purchased Picnic Island in 1952 and the family still owns it (from files of Washington State Board, Picnic Island). The name is neither reflected on current charts nor recognized by the U.S. Board on Geographic Names.

Triton Cove [23] #6460, 1905
Located on the western side of Hood Canal about five miles south of Pleasant Harbor, it likely took its name from the adjacent head.

Triton Head [7d] #146, 1841, Wilkes
Located on the western side of Hood Canal about five miles south of Pleasant Harbor, Wilkes left no reason for the 1841 name (Wilkes, *Narrative* 322). The TPL website suggested that it was named for Triton, the Greek god of the sea.

Trout Lake
It is located on the western side of San Juan Island, east of Smallpox Bay. The origin of the name is unknown. The name is shown on the 1894 t-sheet #2194 (http://kaga.wsulibs.wsu.edu/cdm-maps/sanjuantsheet.html). McLellan wrote: "Between Mount Grant and Mount Dallas Range there is a low divide which contains Trout Lake, the source of the water supply for the village of Friday Harbor."

Trump Harbor
See Tramp Harbor.

Trump Island
McLellan wrote: "Trump Island is located in Lopez Sound near the western shore of Decatur Island. It has an area of 29.4 acres, and its greatest elevation, which is located at its eastern margin, is 120 feet." The origin of the name is unknown. In 1976, Phillip and Peggy Yeager purchased the island and submitted a name change of Eagle Island to the Washington State Board on Geographic Names. In discussing the subject, the Board was unable to locate the origin of Trump but determined that the name had been used for at least 100 years. Landis noted the name in his 1917 *Geographic Dictionary of Washington*. Accordingly, the Board denied the change and thus affirmed the current name (from Washington State Board Files, GNIS files).

Tsiko Point [7h] #154, 1841, Wilkes
It is located on the eastern entrance to Wollochet Bay. Wilkes did not include this 1841 name in his *Narrative*, but it is shown on his chart. It is neither named on current charts nor accepted by the U.S. Board on Geographic Names. According to Hale (580, 581), *Tsiko* is a Palaihnih Indian term meaning "foot or toes." The Palaihnih Tribe lived in Northeastern California.

Tskutsko Point [7d] #146, 1841, Wilkes
It is located on the southwest side of the Toandos Peninsula. Spelled Tskutska in Wilkes' *Journal* and Tskulusco in his *Narrative* (324), he spelled it Tskulsko on his chart. Wilkes left no reason for the 1841 name.

Tuber Point [7m] #160, 1841, Wilkes
See Smith Cove.

Tuckapahwox Point
Located on the western side of Squaxin Island, half mile south of Salmon Point, the word is a transliteration of the Squaxin word meaning "crane." The current name was requested by the Squaxin Island Tribe and approved by the Washington State Board in its June 11, 1982, Docket 280. The U.S. Board followed in 1983 (from Washington State Board Files). *See also* Belspeox Point.

Tucksel Point
Located at the southern end of Squaxin Island, in 1841 Wilkes named it Unsal Point. He left no reason for the name. Wilkes did not include this name in his *Narrative*, but it is shown on his charts [7d], [7i]. According to Hale (610), *Unsul* is a Tahkali Indian term which means "small." The Tahkali Tribe lived in British Columbia. It is shown as both Tucksel and Unsal on some older charts. The Squaxin Tribe believed that the name is an attempted transliteration of the Skwaks-namish Indian word *Txels* meaning "rocks arranged like a man lying on his stomach." The tribe proposed the name Tucksel because it was closer to the original name. A variant name was Tueksel Point. The current name was approved by the Washington State Board on June 11, 1982 (from Washington State files). The U.S. Board followed with their approval the following year and listed Unsal as a variant. *See also* Belspeox Point.

Tukey [22] #6450, 1909
The small community is located on the eastern shoreline of Discovery Bay. John F. Tukey arrived in Discovery Bay in 1850 or 1851. Part of a crew digging ships knees (*see* Quilcene Bay), he fell in love with the country, jumped ship, and settled on the east side of Discovery Bay. In 1880, he and his wife Linnie Ackley Chase built an inn, naming it Saints Rest. By the late 1890s or early 1900s, Linnie operated the inn as a summer resort for children of well-off parents. Linnie died in 1912 at the age of 61; John died the following year at age 83. The Chase family roots were from the Cheviott Hills in England. A friend who was familiar with the famous golf course in Maryland suggested combining these names. Thus, it gained the new name of Chevy Chase (Easton, Lois Chase. "History of Chevy Chase." Unpublished

paper, November 28, 1978. Presented to author by Andi Meucci). Tukey was listed on the 1857 Clallam County census as age 26.

Tulalip Bay

Tulalip Bay [22] #6450, 1909
Located four miles north of Everett, it was here that Vancouver took possession of the Northwest Coast. Mr. Menzies wrote: "We remaind here the two following days with fine pleasant weather. The latter being the King's Birth Day, Capt Vancouver landed about noon with some of the Officers on the South point of the small Bay where he took posession of the Country with the usual forms in his Majesty's name & namd it New Georgia & on hoisting the English Colours on the spot each Vessel proclaimd it aloud with a Royal Salute in honor of the Day," (Menzies 45). Wilkes originally named this Duck Harbor [7o] in 1841. Wilkes did not include this name in his *Narrative*, but it is shown on his chart. According to Meany (*Origin* 317, 318), the Indian word for the bay is *Duh-hlay-lup* which means "a bay almost landlocked, or having a small mouth." A corruption of this is suspiciously close to Wilkes' name, but unfortunately he left no reason for the name. The current name was used in the 1855 treaty negotiations between the various tribes and Governor Isaac I. Stevens. Today, the Tulalip Indian Reservation surrounds the bay. Some early settlers, John Gould and Peter Goutre, established a sawmill at Tulalip Bay. Because of the treaty, their claims were voided and the equipment moved (Humphrey 16, 17). Above the marina is the St. Anne's Catholic Mission, constructed in 1904. It is well maintained with white horizontal cedar siding and a composition roof. The original mission, destroyed by fire in 1902, was built by Father E. C. Chirouse in 1867 where the cemetery is currently located. The bell of the first church was the only item salvaged.

Tulare Beach
It is located along the eastern shore of Port Susan. The origin of the name is unknown.

Tule Point [7h] #154, 1841, Wilkes
Located on the western side of Case Inlet about a mile south of Allyn, Wilkes left no reason for the name. The name is neither reflected on current charts nor is it recognized by the U.S. Board on Geographic Names. Wilkes did not include this name in his *Narrative*, but it is shown on his chart.

Tumwater
Located near Olympia, it was first settled by Michael Simmons in 1845. When he platted the town, the settlers named it New Market. They later renamed it Tumwater from the Chinook jargon. The Indians called it "throb of a beating heart tumtum." That sound is similar to the sound of falling water, hence Tumwater (Meany, *Origin* 318). Simmons' fluency in the Chinook language made him useful during treaty negotiations with the Indians. He was the first Indian agent. A. B. Rabbeson settled in Tumwater the year after Simmons. With several other men, Rabbeson built the first sawmill on Puget Sound. It had a daily capacity of 1,000 board feet of lumber.

Turku Point [7i] #147, 1841, Wilkes
See Lyle Point.

Turn Island [13a] #2689, 1859, Richards
Located east of San Juan Island, Meany (*Origin*, 319) speculated that Richards' reason for the name was that it marks a turning point while navigating through San Juan Channel. In 1841, Wilkes named it Point Salsbury for crew member Francis Salsbury [7a]. Today, it is a 35 acre state marine park.

Turn Point [13a] #2689, 1859, Richards
Located on the north end of Stuart Island, Richards named it because it was the logical "turn point" for ship traffic navigating through Haro Strait (Meany, *Origin* 319). The lighthouse was installed on the point

in 1893 and automated in 1974. The first keeper was Edward Durgan. The 74 acre parcel of land on the point is owned by the U.S. Government.

Turn Rock [14a] #2840, 1861, Richards
Located to the east of Turn Island in San Juan Channel, it was likely named for the island.

Turner, Point [7d] #146, 1841, Wilkes; [7q] #156, 1841, Wilkes
Located at Bremerton, Wilkes honored crew member Henry Turner. Wilkes did not include this name in his *Narrative*, but it is shown on his chart.

Turners Bay
Located at the northern end of Similk Bay, the origin of the name is unknown.

Turnours Bay [24] #1947, 1849, Inskip
See Filucy Bay.

Turtleback Mountain [13a] #2689, 1859, Richards
Located on the northwestern side of Orcas Island, Richards likely named this for its appearance. At about 1,500 feet high, it looks like the back of a turtle with Orcas Knob as the turtle's head. McLellan wrote: "To the northward a dome-shaped hill known as Orcas Knob (the head of the 'turtle') rises abruptly to an elevation of 1050 feet." In 1976, the Washington State Board on Geographic Names addressed variants including Turtle Back Range and Turtleback Range used on official charts and maps. At its September 10, 1976 meeting, the Board opted for the name most used by locals, Turtleback Mountain, Docket 209. The U.S. Board on Geographic Names followed later in the year (from Washington State Board Files). Beginning in the 1950s, Weyerhaeuser executive Norton Clapp amassed most of Turtleback's 1,578 acres. After Clapp's death in 1995, the property was granted to his Medina Foundation who put the mountain on the market in 2005. It was sold in 2006 to a partnership of conservation organizations, including the San Juan Preservation Trust, for $18.5 million.

Twin
Located about seven miles east of Pillar Point, this small community is named for its location between the West Twin [21] and East Twin rivers [21] (TPL website). In 1941, the U.S. Board on Geographic Names addressed the variant Twin Rivers and settled on the current name (GNIS files).

Twin Lakes
Mentioned by McLellan, the two small lakes are located about a mile north of Mountain Lake, east of Mount Constitution, on Orcas Island.

Twin Rocks [13b] #2689, 1861, Richards
McLellan wrote: "Twin Rocks are located on the west side of East Sound, directly opposite the village of Olga. They have a combined area of a little more than an acre and both have elevations of about 15 feet. They owe their presence to a spur of rock that projects out from the shore of Orcas Island, Twin Rocks being remnants of erosion. The inner rock is almost connected by a land bridge with Orcas Island at low tide." Richards likely named it because there are two rocks.

Twin Spits
Located on the eastern side of Foulweather Bluff, the name is descriptive.

Tyee Beach
Located on Camano Island on the western shoreline of Port Susan, the origin of the name is unknown.

Tyee Shoal
Located on the eastern side of Bainbridge Island between Blakely and Eagle Harbors, it is Chinook jargon for "chief, ruler, or leader."

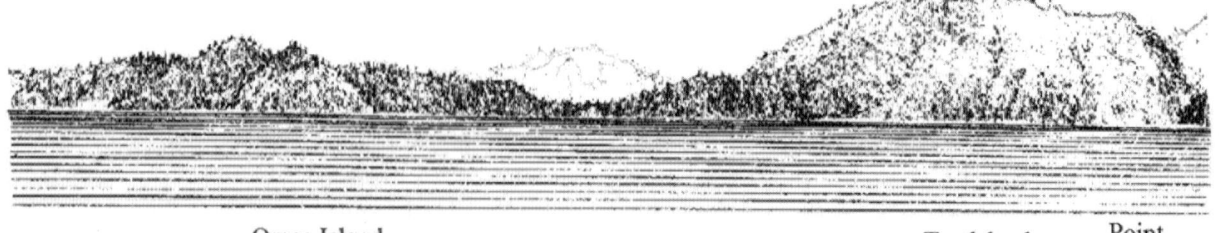

Orcas Island   Turtleback Mountain   Point Hammond

Ty Kels Cove
See Big Tykel Cove.

Tzu-sa-ted Cove [7d] #146, 1841, Wilkes; [7j] #153, 1841, Wilkes
See Pleasant Harbor.

Undertakers Reef
Located at the northwestern end of Decatur Island, the origin of the name is unknown.

Union [23] #6460, 1905
Located at the southern end of Hood Canal at The Great Bend, a Mr. Perrin settled in the area in the early 1850s but soon moved on. Mr. Anderson and E. A. Willson followed in 1858 and built a trading post. Willson also built a cottage and then a house containing a tavern on the lower floor and six bedrooms above. Anderson died from small pox. A short time later, Franklin C. Purdy purchased part of the business and ultimately bought out Willson (Eells 12-16). John McReavy became an important citizen on Hood Canal. Like Pope and Talbot, he was born in East Machias, Maine. He left at age twenty-one and arrived in Puget Sound in 1862. While logging near Point No Point, he broke his arm which never healed properly and was of little use. He took a job for a short time as a cook but did poorly. He finally convinced Cyrus Walker to sell him a logging camp in North Bay, near the head of the canal, for $7,000 with no money down. Within a year, McReavy paid off the debt and then built a railroad to Clifton which was renamed Belfair in 1925. The railroad expanded logging opportunities. He moved to Union in 1864, established the post office, and purchased part of Purdy's business. In 1870, he filed a plat for the town site and built a Masonic Lodge and church. Three years later, he bought the other half of Franklin Purdy's interests which by then included a hotel, saloon, and store. By the late 1880s, Union began to boom. McReavy's properties now included a sawmill, another hotel, a second store, and three logging camps. Growth continued with reports that the Union Pacific Railway would terminate a line there. Additional stores for drugs, grocery, dry goods, and hardware were built until 1890 when the boom failed (Eells, 15). McReavy ultimately became the school superintendent of Mason County, a state senator, and was instrumental in establishing colleges at Pullman (Washington State University) and the normal schools at Ellensburg, Cheney, and Bellingham. He died in 1918 (Fredson 22-25). It was named Union City in 1890 presumably after the railroad. "City" was dropped in 1895 (TPL website).

University Point
Located immediately south of Gilberton on the eastern side of Port Orchard, the origin of the name is unknown.

University of Washington Oceanographic Lab
Located at the north end of Friday Harbor, H. R. Foster and Trevor Kincaid founded the University of Washington Oceanographic Lab in 1903. UW owns 475 acres along Friday Harbor and Point Caution, the largest single parcel of land in the San Juans.

Unsal Point [7d] #146, 1841, Wilkes; [7i] #147, 1841, Wilkes
See Tucksel Point.

Upper Lynch Cove
Located on the northern shoreline of the Little Skookum Inlet, the origin of the name is unknown. It is about a mile to the west of Lower Lynch Cove.

Upright Channel [13a] #2689, 1859, Richards
Located between Shaw and Lopez Islands, Wilkes originally named this Frolic Straits [7a] in 1841 after the H.M.S. *Frolic* which was captured by the U.S.S. *Wasp*, commanded by Capt. Jacob Jones, during the War of 1812 (Meany, *Origin* 322). According to Wood (120), Upright Hill is shown on the log of H.M.S. *Plumper* for April 22, 1858, which ultimately became Upright Point on [13b]. No reason for the name was provided, although perhaps it was for its steep appearance. Meany added that the head received its name from the channel, although maybe the reverse was really true.

Upright Head [13b] #2689, 1861, Richards
Reflected as Upright Point on [13b], it is located on the northern end of Lopez Island. In 1841, Wilkes named this Point Lloyd honoring crew member William Lloyd [7a]. Wilkes did not include this name in his *Narrative*, but it is shown on his chart. *See also* Upright Channel.

Urchin Rocks
Located near Deception Pass, west of Rosario Head, it was likely named for the wildlife there.

Useless Bay [7d] #146, 1841, Wilkes
Located at the southern end of Whidbey Island, Wilkes named it for its lack of shelter (Meany, *Origin* 322).

Utah Rock
Located off the western side of San Juan Island south of False Bay, Hitchman (316) indicated that it was named by the Puget Sound Marine Station at Friday Harbor and honored the State of Utah.

Utsalady, Utsalady Bay, & Utsalady Point
Located on the northern end of Camano Island, Meany (*Origin* 323) indicated that the name comes from the Indian word for "land of berries." Another source insists that the name was a corruption of the Salish name *Atsula'di* meaning "pointing corner" referring to the angle formed by the island as it points toward Whidbey Island. A favorite fable of mine was that the name originated from a Scottish settler whose wife was expecting. The morning after the stork visited, a neighbor hollered out, "What is it?" The Scotsman replied, "Uts-a-laddy!" Lawrence Grennan, Marshall Campbell, and a third man named Thompson founded a spar camp in 1853. A ship carrying their machinery from San Francisco became stranded on the Columbia Bar. The captain threw everything overboard to lighten his load, and the spar camp went bankrupt (Hilbert et. al., 372; Dean 11). Because of the quality lumber in the area, mill work grew over the years. In 1857, Capt. Isaac Parker financed a mill at Utsalady. The new partnership of Grennan and Thomas Cranney (husband of Sarah Coope) took over the mill and began delivering spars and lumber early the following year. The mill had a capacity of 64,000 board feet a day. By 1860, there were fifty-six men, most working at the mill or spar camp, one woman (married), and her child (Joergenson VII; Dean 15). As was true in other seaports, Utsalady had its share of mariners who tired of onboard duties and jumped ship. One night, four young men tried. Three of them, Peter Frostad, Andrew Olsen, and Hans Boreson were successful. Frostad settled on Whidbey Island southwest of the Strawberry Point area. Olsen settled elsewhere on Whidbey. Boreson worked at the mill and homesteaded near Rocky Point. In 1899, he sold and settled in Livingston Bay. Locals in Puget Sound country well remember his grandson, Stan (Dean 20). Utsalady Bay and Utsalady Point are both named for the community. Davidson wrote: "There is a very extensive saw-mill located here, capable of a daily output of a hundred thousand feet of lumber; there is deep water close to the wharves, and capital protection in all weathers. Vessels reach it by the south entrance to possession Sound, through Port Gardner, and Saratoga Passage to Point Demock [Rocky Point]" (1889 *Pacific Coast Pilot* 601). In 1957 and again in 1969, the spelling was questioned. In both cases, the U.S. Board on Geographic Names agreed to the current name over the variant Utsaladdy (GNIS files).

Valerianos, Mount
There are two peaks south of Mount Dallas on San Juan Island. The Washington State Board entertained an attempt in 1991 to name them for Juan de Fuca's Greek name, Apostolos Valerianos. The taller of the two would be Mount Valerianos and the shorter Mount Apostolos. Proponent suggested these were seemingly unnamed but then later identified them as Richards' Little Mountain and Mount Little. The proposal to rename these places failed, but the Washington State Board indicated that they would entertain an alternate location. Somehow, the proponent selected an unnamed peak in a wilderness area in the Olympic Mountains. In late 1992, the Washington State Board approved the name. Federal guidelines do not permit naming features in wilderness areas unless there is a substantial need for the name. As such, this is one of those rare instances where the name is officially recognized by Washington State but is not an accepted name by the U.S. Board on Geographic Names. Thus, it cannot appear on any documents created by the federal government (e.g., charts, topo maps, etc.) but may appear on documents created by Washington State.

Van Asselt
See Alki Point.

Vanderfords Harbor [7d] #146, 1841, Wilkes; [7h] #154, 1841, Wilkes
See Wollochet Bay.

Vashon, Point [7d] #146, 1841, Wilkes; [7g] #155, 1841, Wilkes

Located at the northern end of Vashon Island, Wilkes likely honored James Vashon. Wilkes did not include this name in his *Narrative*, but it is shown on his chart. The Salish name for the point was "wide or split" (Hilbert et. al., 236).

Vashon Island [6] 1792, Vancouver

It is located in the southerly portion of Admiralty Inlet. Vancouver wrote: "The land composing the eastern shore of this channel, and the western shore of that we had pursued on saturday morning, was now ascertained to be the most extensive island we had yet met with in our several examinations of this coast; which after my friend Capt. Vashon of the navy, I have distinguished by the name of Vashon's Island," (Vancouver 274, 275). Born in 1742, Vashon entered the navy in 1755. He was ultimately promoted to admiral in 1814. He died in 1827. James Tilton began to survey Vashon Island in 1855. By 1864, numerous claims were filed including Pope and Talbot from Port Gamble as well as George A. Meigs from Port Madison (Carey 5-8).

Vaughn Bay

Vaughn, Vaughn Bay [23] #6460, 1905, & **Vaughn Creek**

Located on the western side of the Key Peninsula, the community, bay, and creek were named after William Vaughn who settled on the south side of the bay and built a log cabin in 1852. In 1851, Vaughn joined a wagon train in Virginia. He reached Oregon by October and spent the following spring prospecting in the Queen Charlotte Islands. With no success, he returned to Olympia and then to Vaughn. In later years, as his health failed, he eventually resettled in Steilacoom and died in 1920 at age 89. The Critchfield family hailed from Iowa. They arrived in Tacoma June 16, 1882, lived for two years in Puyallup, and then settled in Vaughn. Critchfield rowed to Olympia, purchased lumber, and hired a barge to deliver it to the bay. He built a home, store, and post office. About the same time, the Alverson family also settled in the bay. In 1885, the W. F. Wright family arrived. Mrs. Wright and Mrs. Critchfield were sisters. The Wright's established the first school in their home that year with fifteen children attending. The area prospered throughout the 1880s and settlers continued to arrive. Most men logged but turned to oyster farming in the late 1890s as the timber industry declined (Meany, *Origin* 326; Davison 1-5, 22). The Salish name for the area was "where there is a lake." The sand spit protecting the bay was known as "downstream promontory" (Hilbert et. al., 268). The name of the creek was not formalized until a 1992 decision by the Washington State Board on Geographic Names. The U.S. Board followed in 1994 (from Washington State Board Files).

Vega Bay

Vega Bay

Located off the southern side of Anderson Island, inside Oro Bay, it was named by Bengt Johnson after his birthplace, Vegatorp, Sweden. Johnson and his wife Anna, the third settlers on the island, arrived in 1881 and settled near Eagle Island. Bengt Johnson built a wharf and supplied cord wood to the steamers. He became "Keeper of the Eagle Island Post Light" in 1887 and was paid $12 per month. In 1903, his salary was increased to $15. When he died in 1917, his son Ben took over, who was also responsible for the lights at Gibbons Point, Fox Island, and Devils Head (Heckman 84; Cammon 216, 217).

Vendovi Island [7a] #145, 1841, Wilkes
Located between Lummi and Guemes Islands, in 1841 Wilkes named this for the Fiji chief Vendovi who was involved in the massacre of Wilkes' nephew, Wilkes Henry, on July 24, 1840. As a result of the massacre and his participation, Wilkes took Vendovi hostage. Interestingly, Vendovi died several days after the Exploring Expedition returned to the East Coast. His skull became part of the artifacts which were eventually displayed in Washington D.C. (Meany, *Origin* 327). The Hopely family owned Vendovi in the 1880s. Wilbur ran sheep on the island and his sister Georgia, homesteaded the balance. Wilbur, with his brother George who tended the sheep, found a market for the mutton in Anacortes and Bellingham, and they shipped the wool to Seattle. The Hopelys were followed by Bert and Al March who logged on the north shore. They sold to Vendovi Island Fur Farm, who attempted to raise foxes during the mid-1920s. Father Divine's religious cult purchased the island in the early 1930s (McDonald 191). The Fluke family bought the island in 1966 for $225,000 and sold in 2010 for $6.4 million to the San Juan Preservation Trust.

Venice
Located on the western side of Bainbridge Island about a mile south of Manzanita, locals named Venice for its counterpart in California (Warner 61).

Victim Island [14a] #2840, 1861, Richards
Located on the western side of West Sound, Orcas Island, Richards named it for nearby Indian battles. It is owned by the U.S. Government.

Victor
It is a community across from Allyn in Case Inlet. The origin of the name is unknown. Settled early in the 1900s, there was no road. Thus, homesteaders built a community dock as well as a community center, firehouse, post office, school, and a store. Of all these features, only the community center and firehouse remain today (from Washington State Board Files, Point Victor).

Victor, Point
The small point juts into North Bay at the head of Case Inlet, across from Allyn. It was originally named after the community by the land owner, who also petitioned for the name,. In its June 12, 1981 meeting, Docket 272, the Washington State Board on Geographic Names approved the name. The U.S. Board followed in 1982 (from Washington State Board Files).

Victory Island
See Indian Island.

View Park
The community is located on the western shoreline of Colvos Passage.

Village Point [7b] #148, 1841, Wilkes; [7c] #144, 1841, Wilkes
See Baada Point.

Village Point [17] #27, 1862, U.S. Coast Survey
Located on the northwestern side of Lummi Island, the U.S. Coast Survey named it in 1854: ". . . the large Indian village is now deserted," (Davidson, *Report* 434). The village housed split-board huts where during the summers Indian women prepared and dried salmon that the men caught (McDonald, Lucile. "Lummi Island Is Synonymous With Reef-Netting." *Seattle Times*. June 25, 1961. Magazine Section p 10, 11).

Vincente, San [2] 1791, Pantoja; [3] 1791, Eliza
See Cypress Island.

Vinland
Located on the eastern side of Hood Canal nine miles north of Seabeck Bay, it was first settled in 1888 by the Nel Oens, the Halvor Swensons, and the Chris Lakeness families. When the post office was established in 1902, Mrs. Lakeness suggested the name Vineland from the large number of blackberry vines. Postal authorities misspelled it and it became Vinland (Carlson 37). The U.S. Board on Geographic Names reaffirmed Vinland over Vineland in 1943 (GNIS files).

Violet Point [7b] #148, 1841, Wilkes; [7n] #149, 1841, Wilkes

Located on the eastern side of Protection Island, Wilkes likely named it for the flower. Wilkes did not include this name in his *Narrative*, but it is shown on his chart.

Virginia Point

Located on the western side of Liberty Bay, S. A. Hagstron filed a claim for Virginia Point next to the Ole Stubb claim. The two were friends, and it was Stubb who encouraged Hagstron to move from Seattle. Hagstron built the first floating dock which was visited weekly by the steamer *Augusta*. Hagstron's brother-in-law, Per John Pearson, arrived in 1887 and took over the homestead. Pearson built a store and post office and named the adjacent point after himself. A school house was constructed later that year a couple miles from the shoreline. Pearson donated land for the Baptist church which stands today (Bowen et. al., II: 165; Kvelstad 32-35).

Viti Rocks [7a] #145, 1841, Wilkes

Located south of Lummi Island and north of Vendovi Island, in 1841 Wilkes named this for one of the Fiji Islands, home to Vendovi (Meany, *Origin* 328). *See also* Vendovi Island.

Von Geldern Cove [23] #6460, 1905

Located on the western side of Carr Inlet, it was the site where Peter Puget and his party stopped for a midday meal and encountered some difficulties with the local population. Thomas Manby of the party reported: "The tribe of savages eyed our preparations with serious attention. They had been for some time slyly slipping on their quivers and placing their spears so as to be grasped in a moment. Old one eye gave a signal which occasioned every Indian to string his bow and rise up. A party of twenty then attempted to gain our rear by flying off to the woods. These we stopped, forced them to set down, tho' much against the will of the diabolical old chief. I had shown the chief the external destructive beauties of my double barreled gun, filled with a sliding bayonet and fortunately got an opportunity of shewing its effect in the midst of our party by bringing down a crow that was flying above my head. In an instant wonder and silent astonishment ensued. I advanced to them with the dead bird and evidently saw their confused surprise. Some shook with fear and terror hung on every visage. To continue the alarm this event had occasioned, we fired a barrel loaded with bullets. Its report and the distant skipping balls completely cooled their courage. Some dropped on the ground and others jumped to their canoes and paddled in haste from the cove," (Blumenthal, *With Vancouver* 192, 193). The cove appeared as Joes Bay on some early charts, apparently named for Joe Faulkner who settled there in 1870. He later drowned in the bay (Meany, *Origin* 115, 124; Slater 19). Puget named it Alarm Bay, a name that was not carried forward by Vancouver. According to the TPL website, the current name honored an early settler.

Wa Wa Point [7h] #154, 1841, Wilkes

Located on the Indian Peninsula along the western shoreline of Case Inlet opposite McMicken Boulder, Wilkes' reason for the name is not known. The name is neither reflected on current charts nor recognized by the U.S. Board on Geographic Names. Wilkes did not include this name in his *Narrative*, but it is shown on his chart.

Waadah Island

Located in Neah Bay, Wilkes originally provided the name Neah Island (Wilkes, *Narrative* 485). In 1847, Kellett changed it to utilize the Makah Indian name, Wyadda Island. By the time the U.S. Coast Survey was in the neighborhood during the 1850s, they changed the spelling to Wa-addah [20f], very close to today's spelling (Meany, *Origin* 328). Davidson wrote: "This island is a narrow, high ridge, about 250 yards wide and half a mile long, covered with trees, and having a direction SE. ¼ E. pointing toward Ba-ad-dah Point," (*Report* 417). The U.S. Board on Geographic Names approved the name Waada Island in 1934 and Waadah Island in 1959, apparently believing the latter spelling was more appropriate (GNIS files). Interestingly, in 1934, the Board also corrected the spelling of Baada Island over the variant Baadah. Although this fact was pointed out to them in 1959, they did not see fit to change it back.

Walan Entrance [7p] #150, 1841, Wilkes
This is the entrance to Kilisut Harbor from Port Townsend. Wilkes named it in 1841 but left no reason for the name. The name is neither reflected on current charts nor recognized by the U.S. Board on Geographic Names.

Walan Point
Located on the northwestern side of Indian Island, Wilkes named this Flag Point [7p] in 1841. He left no reason for the name. Wilkes did not include this name in his *Narrative*, but it is shown on his chart. This was the location where Vancouver discovered human heads in 1792. He wrote: "In our way thither, we found on one of the low points projecting from the eastern shore, two upright poles set in the ground, about fifteen feet high, and rudely carved. On the top of each was stuck a human head, recently placed there. The hair and flesh were nearly perfect; and the heads appeared to carry the evidence of fury or revenge, as, in driving the stakes through the throat to the cranium, the sagittal, with part of the scalp, was borne on their points some inches above the rest of the skull," (Vancouver 233). For whatever reason, when the U.S. Coast Survey was in the neighborhood [20g], they eliminated the name Flag Point, replaced it by Walan Point, and eliminated the name Walan Entrance. Its first appearance on a chart is likely [20g].

Waldron Island [7a] #145, 1841, Wilkes
Located west of Orcas Island, Wilkes likely named it in 1841 for either (or both) crew member Thomas W. Waldron, Captain's clerk on the *Porpoise* or R. R. Waldron, purser on the *Vincennes* (Meany, *Origin* 330). In 1791, Eliza named this island Lemos (Blumenthal, *The Early Exploration* 47). James Cowan was reputedly the first settler on the island. He lived in a shanty near Sandy Point in Cowlitz Bay. In March 1868, friends visited his shack, concerned that he had not been seen for several days. They opened the house and found it deserted. The ashes in the fireplace were cold. They then heard Cowan's dog whimpering nearby. They followed the dog through the woods to Cowan's body, buried under a pile of brush, shot in the back. His murderer was never discovered. John T. Oldham purchased Cowan's place. George Dingmans lived near the center of the island and started the first post office in 1880 naming the community Waldron. He rowed to Orcas each week and walked into East Sound to gather the mail (Ludwig 3, 4, 15). During the early 1880s, William "Blanket Bill" Jarman (1820-1912) lived on the island with several other men. Jarman, an ex-British soldier, sailed aboard an Australian ship in 1846 to trade with the Indians at Nootka Sound. While he was ashore, his ship was attacked and departed, leaving him behind. Jarman was captured by the Indians and later ransomed by James Douglas of the Hudson's Bay Company in 1848 or 1849 for a stack of Company blankets, hence his name. From Nootka, Jarman paddled to Port Townsend preceding the founding settlers, where he remained until around 1852. He apparently met the new settlers, but rather than joining the group he moved on (Richardson, *Pig* 243). See www.skagitriverjournal.com for the most complete biography. Jarman lived the balance of his life near Sedro-Woolley on the Jarman Prairie, a name that was approved by the Washington State Board on Geographic Names in 1991, Docket 348 (from Washington State Board Files).

Walkers Landing
Locating on the western side of Pickering Passage, the origin of the name is unknown.

Wapato Waterway
See Blair Waterway.

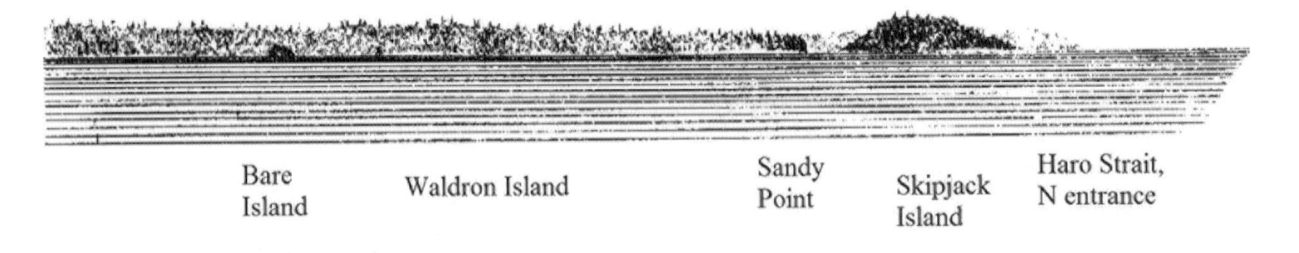

| Bare Island | Waldron Island | Sandy Point | Skipjack Island | Haro Strait, N entrance |

Warmhouse Beach
Located 2½ miles east of Cape Flattery, the origin of the name is unknown.

Warren
Located on the Great Peninsula on the northern side of Hale Passage, it was named for Freeman Warren who settled there in 1905. By 1913, his son Charles was running the family store and had built the wharf (TPL website). It was first mentioned in the 1909 *Pacific Coast Pilot* (158) which noted it as "a village of about 25 houses."

Warrenville
Located on the eastern side of Hood Canal, almost two miles north of Seabeck, the origin of the name is unknown. It is not reflected on current charts.

Washington, Point [7o] #157, 1841, Wilkes
See Pilot Point.

Washington Harbor
See Sequim Bay.

Washington Narrows, Port

Washington Narrows, Port [23] #6460, 1905, U.S. Coast Survey
Located on the western side of Port Orchard, the channel connects Sinclair Inlet to Dyes Inlet.

Washington Rock
Located on a cliff in Mackaye Harbor, Lange found a reference to this local name which apparently looked like George Washington.

Washington Sound [11] #654, 1858, U.S. Coast Survey
See San Juan Islands.

Wasp Island
See McConnell Island.

Wasp Islets [7a] #145, 1841, Wilkes
Located essentially between Orcas and Shaw Islands, Wilkes named these islands for the *Wasp*, commanded by Commodore Jacob Jones during the War of 1812. Jones captured the 22-gun British ship *Frolic* on Oct. 18, 1812 (Meany, *Origin* 339). Wilkes did not include this name in his *Narrative*, but it is shown on his chart. There are seven islands in the grouping, including Reef, Yellow, Low, Coon, Cliff, McConnell, and Nob. Richards named the first three [13a].

Wasp Passage [13a] #2689, 1859, Richards
Located between the northern end of Shaw Island and Crane Island, Richards likely lifted Wilkes' 1841 name from the Wasp Islets [7a] and used it for the passage.

Waterman Point
Located on the southeastern side of Port Orchard opposite Bremerton, it was named for Delos Waterman who purchased 300 acres of land in 1882 (Meany, *Origin* 339).

Watmough Bay [13a] #2689, 1859, Richards
Located on the southeastern side of Lopez Island off Rosario Strait, Richards transferred Wilkes' name from the head to the bay. The evolution of the spelling of the name is intriguing. In 1841, Wilkes named the head for John Goddard Watmough, a lieutenant in the U.S. Army wounded at Fort Erie in the War of 1812. However, Wilkes spelled it as Watmaugh in his *Narrative* (305) and chart [7a]. In 1854, the U.S. Coast Survey attempted to correct the error but reflected the head as Walmough [10]. They finally got it right in 1858 [11]. Enter Richards in 1859 who derived an entirely new spelling with Walmouth Head on [13a]. He similarly errored with the bay by naming it Walmouth Bight. The U.S. Coast Survey returned and corrected both names on the charts of 1862 [17] and 1866 [18]. At that point, the two places were named Watmough Bight and Watmough Head. Subsequent Admiralty charts maintained their original errors. The U.S. Board on Geographic Names formalized the spelling of the head in 1891,

and the bight became a bay in 1959 (*Decisions*, GNIS files). Lange provided some additional biography on Watmough. Resigning from the Army in 1816, he returned to Philadelphia where he served as a U.S. Representative from 1831-1835. In 1836, he was High Sheriff of Philadelphia, and in 1841 he was a surveyor of the Port of Philadelphia. He died in that city in 1861. Apparently Wilkes knew Watmough while both were in Washington.

Watmough Head [7a] #145, 1841, Wilkes
See Watmough Bay.

Watsak Point [7e] #158, 1841, Wilkes
See Snatelum Point.

Watsak Point
See Long Point.

Watsok Island [7e] #158, 1841, Wilkes
See Rosario Head.

Wauna
Located on the western side of Carr Inlet, the community was platted and named Springfield by George McCormick and James and Deborah Wickersham when the first post office was established in 1890. A later postmistress, Mary F. White, renamed it on May 17, 1906. She and her husband William built a store and large house which they named the Wauna Lodge. The store and post office remained in the family for three generations. The store was finally demolished in 2006. The Indian word means "mighty or strong" (Meany, *Origin* 340; Slater 29).

Wawa Point [7j] #153, 1841, Wilkes
Located on the western side of Jackson Cove, Wilkes spelled it Weewa in his *Narrative* (324) and Wawa on his chart. According to Hale (609), *Wawa* was a Palaihnih Indian term which means "great." The Palaihnih Tribe lived in Northeastern California. Hale (639) also indicated that it was a Chinook term for "to speak or talk."

Weaver Point
Located north of Eagle Point on the west side of San Juan Island, Lange uncovered a reference to it as a collection point for the Friday Harbor Labs. The name is neither reflected on current charts nor recognized by the U.S. Board on Geographic Names.

Weaverline Spit
Located on the western side of Fidalgo Bay, on the eastern side of Fidalgo Island (west of March Point), Wilkes' 1841 chart [7m] placed Nipple Point at about where Weaverline Spit is currently located. Wilkes did not include Nipple Point in his *Narrative*. According to the TPL website, the current name is for James and Francis Weaverling who arrived on Fidalgo in 1872. A portion of the point was removed with explosives in 1920. Davidson referenced it in the 1889 *Pacific Coast Pilot* (564): "The southern point of the entrance is known as *Weaverline Spit*, and a *fixed red light*, lens lantern, is shown from the top of a white post nine feet high and eight feet above the water. It has been placed about fifty yards from the extremity of the spit."

Weh Weh Point [7p] #150, 1841, Wilkes
Located south of Port Townsend, Wilkes named this in 1841. Wilkes did not include this name in his *Narrative*, but it is shown on his chart. The name is neither reflected on current charts nor recognized by the U.S. Board on Geographic Names.

Wells, Point [7d] #146, 1841, Wilkes
Located along the mainland two miles south of Edmonds, Wilkes honored crew member William Wells. Wilkes did not include this name in his *Narrative*, but it is shown on his chart (Meany, *Origin* 224).

Wepusec Inlet [7i] #147, 1841, Wilkes
See Gull Harbor.

Werner
See Eureka Beach.

West Bank [11] #654, 1858, U.S. Coast Survey
Located west of Sucia Island, the U.S. Coast Survey named this in 1858. It is possibly named for Sub-Assistant P. C. F. West who assisted James Lawson in 1858. Apparently West, assigned to the brig *Fauntleroy*, discovered the reef while moving his long boat from one station to another. According to Davidson: "West's reef lies S. 66 W., one mile from the SW. point of Sucia; it has less than two fathoms upon it, and is marked by a large mass of kelp," (*Directory* 126). On the Admiralty chart of 1859 [13a], Richards named it for his Steam Sloop

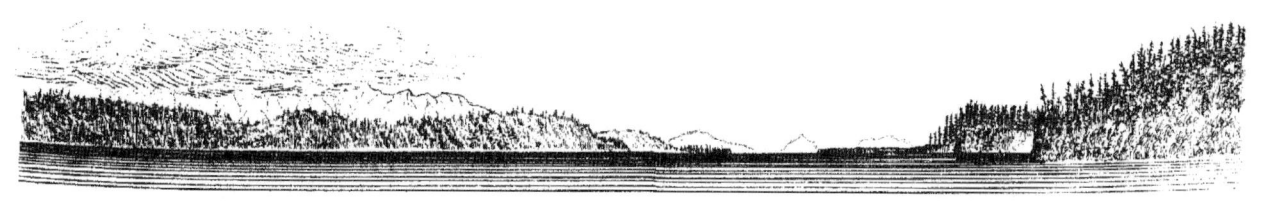

> West Point   Alki Point   Point Robinson   Point Jefferson   Appletree Point

H.M.S. *Plumper*, however, West Bank survived. According to Lange, the *Plumper* grounded on the reef on May 1, 1858. Thus, the Admiralty referred to it as Plumper reef. *Plumper* was an auxiliary steam sloop, barque rigged, 484 tons, and made 6 knots under steam. She was launched in Portsmouth, England in 1848. She arrived on the Northwest Coast in 1857 and remained until replaced by the H.M.S. *Hecate* in 1861. Anthony H. Hoskins brought the *Hecate* out and returned to England in the *Plumper* (Walbran 384).

West Bay
Located on the western side of Budd Inlet, it was named for its location. The Washington State Board on Geographic Names adopted this name in their April 11, 1985 meeting, Docket 292. The U.S. Board followed later in the year (from Washington State Board Files).

West Beach
Located on the northwestern side of Orcas Island, about two miles south of Point Doughty, the origin is unknown.

West Blakely
Located on the southern end of Bainbridge Island on Rich Passage, Andrew Gus Anderson was first to settle on an 80 acre tract of land in 1890. Other Scandinavians followed, and most worked at the Port Blakely Mill, a short one-mile walk through the woods (Bowen et al., VI: 88).

West Pass
See South Pass.

West Passage
See Colvos Passage.

West Point
Located on the northwestern side of Whidbey Island, Wilkes originally named this Maurys Point in 1841 [7e], likely for crew member William L. Maury. Wilkes did not include this name in his *Narrative*, but it is shown on his chart. The Salish word for the point was "thrust far out," referring to the fact that the point juts into the Strait of Juan de Fuca (Hilbert et. al., 61). Davidson noted the local name of Sandy Point (1889 *Pacific Coast Pilot* 606). Somehow, that name gained local usage by steamboat captains. The U.S. Board on Geographic Names retained West Point in 1891 over the variant (from U.S. Board files).

West Point

West Point [7d] #146, 1841, Wilkes; [7m] #160, 1841, Wilkes
Located at the northerly entrance to Elliott Bay off Seattle, Wilkes named this perhaps because it points due west (Meany, *Origin* 342).

West Reef
See West Bank.

West Rock [13c] #2689, 1865
See Halftide Rocks.

West Sound [13a] #2689, 1859, Richards
There are two large inlets which scar the southern portion of Orcas Island, one of which is West Sound. In 1841, Wilkes named it Guerriere Bay [7a] for the British frigate *Guerriere*, captured by the *Constitution* during the War of 1812 (Meany, *Origin* 342, 343). Richards renamed it for its position on Orcas (TPL website). Wilkes' naming scheme is interesting in that he named East Sound for the *Constitution*, and he named Orcas Island for the Captain of the *Constitution*, Commodore Isaac Hull. The British of course changed all of these names!

West Sound
Located on the eastern shoreline of West Sound, the community takes its name from the water.

West Waterway
See Harbor Island.

Westcott Bay
Located on the northwestern side of San Juan Island, south of Roche Harbor, Richards used the name Westcott Creek [13a] for George Blagdon Westcott, the paymaster aboard H.M.S. *Bacchante* (Meany, *Origin* 343; Walbran 526). In observing Richards' label, the "W" in Westcott is near Bell Point on the western side of the bay. The "k" in Creek is near the head of the bay. Although there is a creek flowing into the bay, Richards' name actually applies to the bay because of a different interpretation of the word creek. While Americans generally accept it as a stream or brook, to the British, it is a small harbor or inlet that may dry at low tide. It originates with the Old Norse word *kriki* for nook. Wood noted (121) that the word Bay replaced Creek in 1938, although Meany reported that chart #6381, corrected to June 25, 1921, reflected the name Westcott Bay. In their March 14, 1991 meeting, Docket 348, the Washington State Board on Geographic Names addressed the spelling of the name: Westcot vs. Westcote vs. Wescott vs. Westcott and accepted the longstanding current name. The U.S. Board on Geographic Names followed in 1992 (from Washington State Board Files).

Westcott Creek [13a] #2689, 1859, Richards
See Westcott Bay.

Weyer Point
Located between Chapman and Woodard Bays in Henderson Inlet, it was named for Weyerhaeuser for the log boom operation there (Palmer 96). The name is not recognized by the U.S. Board on Geographic Names.

Whale Rocks [14a] #2840, 1861, Richards
Located off the southwestern side of Lopez Island, it was one of the islands in the grouping which Wilkes named as the Geese Islets [7a]. Richards left no reason for the current name.

Whatcom
Located on the shores of Bellingham Bay, it was a Nooksack word for "noisy water" and also the name of the local chief (http://www.historylink.org). In 1903, it became part of Bellingham. According to the 1887 survey and Descriptive Report #1798 (http://riverhistory.ess.washington.edu/tsheets/reports/t1798.pdf, p.234), J. J. Gilbert wrote: "Whatcom was settled in Dec. 1852 by Mr. R. V. Peabody and Capt. Henry Roeder who built a sawmill in 1853 at the mouth of Whatcom Creek. And a town site was laid out in 1854 and named Whatcom which was the Indian name for the creek."

Whiskey Rock
It is located south of Bellingham, immediately north of Wildcat Cove. In 1981, the Washington State Department of Fisheries suggested the name to the State Board. Previously unnamed, the Fisheries Department utilized the local name as a fishing area boundary and wished to make it formal. In its March 12, 1982 meeting, the Washington State Board agreed with the name. The U.S. Board followed in early 1983 (from Washington State Board Files).

Whiskey Spit
See Point Hannon.

Whisper Creek
The 1½ mile creek flows through Kingston into Appletree Cove. In its May 11, 2007 meeting, the Washington State Board on Geographic Names approved the name. The U.S. Board followed later in the year (from Washington State Board Files).

White, Point [7d] #146, 1841, Wilkes; [7q] #156, 1841, Wilkes
Located on the northern side of Rich Passage, Wilkes honored crew member James White (Meany, *Origin* 224). Wilkes did not include this name in his *Narrative*, but it is shown on his chart. The Salish name for the point was "goose droppings" (Hilbert et. al., 226). Jack Nibbe was born in Germany in 1847. He went to sea at age 14 for a short tour of duty on merchant ships between Hamburg and New York. In 1863, he joined the U.S. Navy, and the following year he found action aboard the U.S.S. *Peteral* in the Yazoo River near Vicksburg. Confederates blew up the Union ship, landing Nibbe in a southern prison for a short time. He was discharged from the navy in 1865. Three months later, at the end of the war, Jack was awarded a Medal of Honor for his acts of heroism aboard *Peteral*. Nibbe opened a store at Point White in 1867. He married an Indian woman, Jennie, and later, Georgianna Porter, a widow. Nibbe was the postmaster of Nibbeville, as the area was originally known, from 1885 to 1890. Recognizing settlers' needs for goods, he seemed one step ahead of early pioneers with moves to Mitchell's Point, Sidney, and ultimately Bremerton, opening a general merchandise store in each location. During that period, Nibbe owned and operated several different boats which he used to transport merchandise to his stores. Nibbe left his job as the Bremerton Postmaster in 1901, retired from his business in 1902, and died the following year.

White Beach
Located north of Diamond Point in East Sound, Orcas Island, the name was likely descriptive.

White Beach Bay [13a] #2689, 1859, Richards
It is located on the western side of West Sound, Orcas Island. In his 1895 Descriptive Report #2229, J. J. Gilbert wrote (http://riverhistory.ess.washington.edu/tsheets/reports/t2229.pdf, p 14): "The name is due to two or three patches of whitish gravel beach."

White Bluff
Located at the southern end of Gedney Island, it was likely named for its appearance. The bluff rises steeply 280 feet from the water.

White Bolder [13a] #2689, 1859, Richards
Located on the eastern side of Lopez Island, south of Spencer Spit, it was apparently named for its appearance.

White Cliff [13c] #2689, 1865
Located on the southwestern side of Decatur Island, it was likely named for its appearance.

White Cliffs [13a] #2689, 1859, Richards
Located on the western side of Lopez Island near the south end of San Juan Channel, it was likely named for its appearance.

White Point
See Hardwick Point.

White Point
Located on the southern shoreline of Eld Inlet, the origin of the name is unknown.

White Point [16b] #602, 1869, Pender
It is located at the northern entrance to Garrison and Westcott Bays. Wood (121) suggested several possibilities for the name. Charles W. White was surgeon on the H.M.S. *Phaeton* in 1853. A shipmate was Lieut. Mountford S. L. Peile who was a surveying officer aboard the *Satellite* in 1857-1860. This is consistent with the naming of Bell and Hanbury Points after medical officers. Alternatively, it could have been named for James T. A. White, a surveyor aboard the *Zealous* in 1869. Also aboard were shipmates for whom other nearby points were named, e.g., Hanbury, Beadon, Delacombe, and Inman.

White Rock [22] #6450, 1909
Located off the eastern shoreline of Hood Canal, just north of Hood Head, it was likely named for its color.

White Rock [10] #51, 1854, U.S. Coast Survey
Located off the southeastern side of Blakely Island in Rosario Strait, it was named in 1854 (*Directory* 130), likely for its appearance. The name Pointer Island was later moved to this location. *See also* Pointer Island.

White Rock [13a] #2689, 1859, Richards
Located off the southern end of Waldron Island, it was named likely because of its color.

Whitehorn, Point [7a] #145, 1841, Wilkes; [7l] #159, 1841, Wilkes
Located at the southerly entrance to Birch Bay, Wilkes honored crewmember Daniel Whitehorn. Whitehorn had a terrible accident at Nisqually on the 4th of July. According to Wilkes' *Narrative* (412, 413): "At this time the salute was fired, when one of the men, by the name of Whitehorn, had his arm most dreadfully lacerated from the sudden explosion of the gun. This accident put a momentary stop to the hilarity of the occasion. Dr. Fox, who was on the ground, thought that amputation of the arm above the elbow would be necessary, but it was deemed better to delay it for a time." Whitehorn survived but never recovered the use of his hand.

Whiteman Cove
Located on the western side of the Key Peninsula, a man named Reed settled there with his Indian wife. He was the only White man in the neighborhood, thus the name (Meany, *Origin* 347). The U.S. Board on Geographic Names adopted the current name in 1941 over the variants Whitemans and Whitmans.

Whitney Point
Located on the western side of Hood Canal near the entrance to Quilcene Bay, it was named for Robert Whitney who arrived in the area in 1874. In 1883, Whitney married Anne, the daughter of John Clements from Dosewallips (Bailey, *Brinnon* 102).

Whulj
In 1987, the Washington State Board on Geographic Names received a petition from Harvey Manning, author of hiking and climbing books, to use this name for inland Washington waters. Mr. Manning later withdrew his proposal for various reasons. But with his withdrawal, he suggested that the Board convene a committee to search for a name describing these waters and incorporate Canadian representation as well. While the name has floated around for years, Mr. Manning's suggestions are likely satisfied with the adoption of the Salish Sea. Unfortunately, Mr. Manning died before that occurred.

Wiggins Head
Located on the east entrance of Fossil Bay, it was named for Charles Henry Wiggins who settled on Sucia in the 1880s. By 1892, the family developed a house, barn, root house, orchard, and a garden. Henry and his wife Mary had 11 children. The family lived there for 30 years. In 1983, Eugene A. Wiggins proposed the name to the Washington State Board on Geographic Names to honor his grandfather. The State Board approved the name at its Dec. 9, 1983 meeting (from Washington State Board Files). The U.S. Board approved the name in 1984. *See also* Sucia Island.

Wiggins Reef
Located on the north side of Echo Bay off Sucia, it was named for Charles Henry Wiggins, the earliest settler on Sucia. McLellan wrote: "Near the north shore of Echo Bay, to the south of Ewing Island and the north arm of Sucia Island, there are a number of knob-shaped islands and reefs called the Cluster Islands, some of which are covered at high tide. The most western member of the Cluster Islands is known as Wiggins Reef. The most eastern member is called Stony Reef." *See also* Sucia Island.

Wikat Point [7j] #153, 1841, Wilkes
Located on the eastern entrance to Seabeck Bay, Wilkes spelled this *Wikat* in his *Narrative* (324) but Wikut on the chart. He left no reason for the name. The name is neither reflected on current charts nor recognized by the U.S. Board on Geographic Names. According to Hale (650), *Wikat* is Chinook for "way or path."

Wildcat Cove [21] #6300, 1895
Located on the mainland south of Bellingham Bay, the origin of the name is unknown.

Wildcat Cove [23] #6460, 1905
It is located at the southern entrance to Little Skookum Inlet off Totten Inlet. The origin of the name is unknown. In its September 11, 1981 meeting, the Washington State Board on Geographic Names addressed a difference between some charts and maps: cove vs. harbor as it appeared on [23]. The Board ultimately approved the term cove. The U.S. Board followed later in the year (from Washington State Board Files).

William Point [6] 1792, Vancouver
Located at the western end of Samish Island, at the southerly entrance to Bellingham Channel, Vancouver honored Sir William Bellingham. In 1791, Eliza named this Solano [3] (Meany, *Origin* 224; Wagner 247). Vancouver noted the point on his chart but did not reference it in his journal. In 1973, the Washington State Board on Geographic Names addressed the location of the point. There are two points involved; the more westerly has a beacon on it. There is a second point to the northeast as well. The Board found that the name should include both points in their March 11, 1977 meeting, Docket 210. The U.S. Board followed later in the year (from Washington State Board Files).

William Spit [13a] #2689, 1859, Richards
Located on the southwestern end of Samish Island, south of William Point, Richards likely took the name from the nearby point. The name is neither reflected on current charts nor recognized by the U.S. Board on Geographic Names.

Williams, Point [7d] #146, 1841, Wilkes
Located on the mainland three miles south of Alki Point, Wilkes honored crew member Samuel Williams. Wilkes did not include this name in his *Narrative*, but it is shown on his chart (Meany, *Origin* 224, 225). The Salish name for the point was "crowded, tight" (Hilbert et. al., 69).

Williams, Point [7e] #158, 1841, Wilkes
It is located on the eastern side of Whidbey Island in Holmes Harbor, about two miles north of Scatchel Point. He left no reason for the name. Wilkes did not include this name in his *Narrative*, but it is shown on his chart. The name is neither reflected on current charts nor recognized by the U.S. Board on Geographic Names.

Williams, Port
Located on the Strait of Juan de Fuca, north of Sequim, the town was named after developer Thomas Williams who attempted unsuccessfully to encourage settlement in the 1890s (TPL website). The 1903 *Pacific Coast Pilot* (133) mentions the port: "Port Williams is a post office and an open landing about 4½ miles southeastward from New Dungeness lighthouse and near the entrance to Washington Harbor. Some shingles and salmon are exported and general merchandise imported. A wharf has been built out northeastward from the shore for about 500 feet, with a width of 25 feet; the outer end is about 100 feet on the face and about 80 feet wide. There is 15 feet alongside the outer face."

Williamson Rocks [7a] #145, 1841, Wilkes; [7m] #160, 1841, Wilkes
Located south of Burrows and Allan Islands, in 1841 Wilkes honored crew member John G. Williamson (Meany, *Origin* 350).

Willow Island
Located off the western side of Blakely Island, the Admiralty named it Steep Island on [13c]. In his 1889 survey and Descriptive Report #1953, (http://riverhistory.ess.washington.edu/tsheets/reports/t1953.pdf, p 9), J. J. Gilbert wrote: "Willow Island is a bold rock, with a few willow trees in one sag and a few scattering firs." This perhaps explains the name. The U.S. Government owns the land.

Wilson, Point

Wilson, Point [6] 1792, Vancouver
Located at the easterly end of the Strait of Juan de Fuca, the point marks the westerly entrance to Admiralty Inlet. Vancouver wrote: ". . . the west point of Admiralty inlet, which after my much esteemed friend Capt. George Wilson of the navy, I distinguished by the name of Point Wilson . . ." (Vancouver 291).

Wilson Creek
Flowing into Colvos Passage, the creek is about a mile south of Point Southworth. Wilkes named it the Kosa River [7g] but left no reason for the name. Wilkes did not include this name in his *Narrative*, but it is shown on his chart. According to Hale (610), *Kosa* is an Oregon Molele Indian name which means "small." Its current name came from an early settler (Phillips 160).

Wilson Point [7d] #146, 1841, Wilkes; [7i] #147, 1841, Wilkes
Located on the eastern side of Harstine Island, Wilkes honored crew member Thomas Wilson (TPL website). Wilkes did not include this name in his *Narrative*, but it is shown on his chart.

Windy Bluff
Located on the eastern side of Case Inlet, north of Vaughn Bay, the origin of the name is unknown. It was originally named Bald Bluff ". . . because of its high barren and bald appearance standing . . . a stern and unrelenting guard over the narrow channel . . ." (Reese, *Origins* 16).

Windy Point
Located on the eastern side of Dyes Inlet, it was possibly named for weather conditions.

Windy Point
Located on the eastern side of Samish Bay, the name is likely descriptive.

Wing Point [7q] #156, 1841, Wilkes
Located on the northerly entrance to Eagle Harbor, Wilkes may have named this for eagles in the area. Wilkes did not include this name in his *Narrative*, but it is shown on his chart. The Salish word for the point was "gradually falling promontory" (Hilbert et. al., 226).

Winslow
It is located on Eagle Harbor, east side of Bainbridge Island. Although it had an early logging history, it was not settled until 1877. *See* Hawley. In 1890, Charles and Cynthia Williams established a post office out near Wing Point and named the entire Winslow area Madrone, for the trees. William Finch became postmaster in 1902. His house still stands in downtown Winslow. Also in 1902, the Hall brothers relocated their shipyard from Port Blakely to Winslow (Marriott 77-80). The town was ultimately renamed in 1903 for Winslow Hall (TPL website). The Halls sold the shipyard in 1916, and the Washington State ferry terminal and repair facilities now occupy what was the Hall Brothers shipyard (Marriott 77-80). *See also* Blakely Harbor.

Wollochet & **Wollochet Bay** [23] #6460, 1905
Located west of the southern entrance to The Narrows, Wilkes originally named this Vanderfords Harbor [7d], [7h] honoring crew member Benjamin Vanderford who died at sea on March 23, 1842 (Meany, *Origin* 348). The current name is Indian in origin and has two meanings, one of which is "squirting clams." The second is "cut throat." According to the legend, a young brave, unable to marry the woman of his choosing, took his life by cutting his throat (from Washington State Board Files). Upon first seeing the bay, Peter Puget wrote: "About a Mile from the Dinner Point [Point Fosdick] we found a Small Cove at the head of which were a Party of Seventeen or Eighteen Indians in temporary Habitations drying Clams Fish &c which they readily parted with for Buttons Trinkets &c they did not appear the least Alarmed at our Approach but immediately offered their Articles for Sale—In their Persons these People are slenderly made they wear their Hair long which is quite Black and exceeding Dirty—Both Nose & Ears are perforated, to the which were affixed Copper Ornaments & Beads, the whole Party was Naked," (Puget 196, 197). The first settler was Miles B. Hunt in 1876. The following year, his wife and children joined him. The oldest of their seven children was Forrest, nineteen; followed by Emmett, eighteen; Lillie, sixteen; Arthur, ten; Arda, five; and the twins, Lloyd and Floyd, two. Miles claimed 160 acres about a mile from the head of the bay. He established a post office in 1878 and called it Artondale. Forest and Emmett filed nearby claims as well. By 1888, Artondale had two brickyards and a lumber mill. Forrest worked in Steilacoom as a store clerk while Emmett opened a school in Artondale in 1878. Emmett purchased the mail contract between Artondale and Steilacoom in 1881 and rowed in a 13 foot skiff once a week. With his younger brother, Arthur, eight years his junior, he built a second skiff and soon moved on to a third, twenty-six feet in

length and steam powered, called *Baby Mine*. Within a couple of years, he was constructing his fourth boat, thirty-one feet and eleven tons gross weight. At age thirty-six, he married Henrietta Middleton, twenty-two, from Victoria. Emmett continued with his boat building business but lost all interest when Henrietta died in 1907. He remarried, began to develop rental properties in the area, and died in 1933. All of the brothers worked together at various times building boats and hauling freight on Puget Sound. Arda's son, Reed Hunt, started as a laborer in the Port Townsend area and rose to Chairman of the Board of Crown Zellerback Company in 1963 (Evans 12-16). The U.S. Board on Geographic Names approved the name of Wollochet for the community in 1942 over the variants Berg and Bergs Landing. Additionally, the Board approved Wollochet Bay over the variant Whollochet. According to a letter from the County Road Engineer in the GNIS files: "The Indian name and the one used and shown on early maps was spelled Whollochet Bay, but the later records and general public know it as Wollochet Bay, and is so shown on county and state maps."

Wollochet Creek
In 1989, the Washington State Board on Geographic Names received a proposal from the Artondale Elementary School to name the creek which flows into Wollochet Bay. The Board approved the proposal.

Woodard Bay & Creek
Located in Henderson Inlet in Puget Sound, the State DNR and Nature Conservancy of Washington agreed to a ten acre conservation lease of the submerged lands in the bay for ten years beginning in 2005. The intent was to restore the habitat for Olympia oysters and provide a habitat for birds, otters, seals, etc. The bay and creek were named after Harvey R. and Solome Woodard who arrived in Oregon in 1852. After the winter, they settled on Henderson Inlet in 1853. In its September 7, 1979 meeting, Docket 254, the Washington State Board on Geographic Names clarified the spelling. This correction altered a 1941 decision by the U.S. Board which spelled it Woodward. The U.S. Board accepted this correction in 1980 (from Washington State Board Files).

Wooded Island #654, 1858, U.S. Coast Survey
See Skip Jack Island.

Woodmans
Located on the eastern side of Discovery Bay, it was named for James O. Woodman from Portsmouth, England, who settled on the Bay in 1850. He lived there for nearly 60 years (Meany, *Origin* 353). *See* Adelma Beach.

Woodward Bay
See Woodard Bay.

Woolard, Mount
The 1,180 foot peak is located on the peninsula between West Sound and East Sound, Orcas Island. It was named after George W. Woolard, a logger who settled in the area (Lange). The name is referenced in McLellan's text along with the Mount Woolard Range. He wrote: "The highest elevation in the southern part of the peninsula is found on Mount Woolard, which is 1180 feet in height. On its north and east sides, Mount Woolard is steep and precipitous, but it slopes more gently towards the southwest." The U.S. Board on Geographic Names approved the name over the variant Mount Woodard in 1925.

Worden, Fort
Located at Point Wilson, the name honored Admiral John Lorimer Worden, commander of the *Monitor*. As a lieutenant, Worden was wounded in the Civil War battle with the *Merrimac* in March 1862. He died in 1897 at the age of seventy-nine. By the time troops arrived in 1902 and were quartered in tents, construction of the fort had already begun and the improvements continued for several years. H. M. Chittenden, later responsible for the construction of the Seattle locks, directed the building of gun emplacements from 1906 to 1908. In June 1953 the post was closed. First converted to a state juvenile treatment center, the site later became a state park in 1973 (*With Pride* 243-248).

Wyckoff Shoal [23] #6460, 1905
Located off the northern side of McNeil Island, it was named for Ambrose B. Wyckoff who took command of the Naval Shipyard at Bremerton on September 16, 1891 (Reese, *Origins* 125).

Yakso, Point [7k] #152, 1841, Wilkes
Located about halfway up the eastern shoreline of Quilcene Bay, Wilkes left no reason for the name (*Narrative* 324). The name is neither reflected on current charts nor recognized by the U.S. Board on Geographic Names. According to Hale (647), it is Chinook for "hair."

Yawa Island [7h] #154, 1841, Wilkes
This nonexistent island was reflected on Wilkes' chart between Stretch Island and the mainland. He left no reason for the name. Wilkes did not include this name in his *Narrative*, but it is shown on his chart.

Yellow Bluff [13a] #2689, 1859, Richards
Located on the southwestern side of Guemes Island, Richards left no reason for the name.

Yellow Bluff Reef
Located off the southwestern side of Guemes Island, it likely takes its name from the bluff.

Yellow Island [13a] #2689, 1859, Richards
It is located between Orcas and Shaw Islands. McLellan wrote: "Yellow Island, so-called because of its arid nature and the typical color of its vegetation, is located 350 yards to the southwest of McConnell Island. It has an area of 10.27 acres, is thinly covered with glacial materials, and its low rolling hills reach a maximum elevation of 40 feet. Rocky masses of land are tied to the north end, and also to the south end of Yellow Island, by means of sand spits. A species of prickly cactus occurs in abundance on Yellow Island." Lewis E. and Tib Dodd purchased the island from F. B. Townsley, and in 1947 they moved in. They lived in a tent for two years while collecting driftwood from the beach to build a cabin. Lew Dodd died in the small cabin in 1960. Tib moved to the mainland, returning to Yellow Island for six months each year. She died in 1978. The Nature Conservancy purchased the island in 1980 and created a nature preserve. It is open to the public on a limited basis. The Dodd cabin sits on the southern shore and is used by the caretaker (Richardson, *Pig* 273; McDonald 78, 169, 187).

Yeomalt & Yeomalt Point
Located on the eastern shoreline of Bainbridge Island, the point was originally known as Finch Point. The Ebersold family settled there in the 1880s. The Finch family arrived in 1890 (Marriott 74: *An Historic* 12). Yeomalt is a corruption of the Salish word meaning "fighter's home." It was based upon the legend of the battles between the South Wind and the North Wind. When the South Wind chased the North Wind from the Duwamish Valley, the North Wind crossed the sound to Yeomalt Point. There, the two fought again (Hilbert et. al., 12, 225). The community of Yeomalt took its name from the point.

Yokeko Point [7e] #158, 1841, Wilkes
Located on the eastern side of Deception Pass, south end of Fidalgo Island, Wilkes left no reason for the name. Wilkes did not include this name in his *Narrative*, but it is shown on his chart. According to Hale (571), *Yokeko* is a San Raphael Indian name which means "infant or child." The San Raphael Tribe lived north of San Francisco. In 1913, Fred Finson established a ferry service in Deception Pass between Yokeko and Hoypus Points. In 1924, the Olson family constructed the ferry *Deception Pass*. At 68 feet in length and 24 feet wide, she carried auto as well as passenger traffic. Ferry service ended in 1935 with the construction of the Deception Pass Bridge. The bridge was declared a National Historical Monument in 1982 (Bailey and Nyberg, *San Juan Islands* 177, 180).

Yoman Point [7i] #147, 1841, Wilkes
Located on the northeastern side of Anderson Island, it was named by Charles Wilkes in 1841. Wilkes did not include this name in his *Narrative*, but it is shown on his chart. He left no reason for the name. Inskip named it Owen Point [24].

Young, Mount [13a] #2689, 1859, Richards
See Young Hill.

Young Cove
Located on the western shore of Eld Inlet, it was named for Volney Young, a local steamboat captain on the sound. He was born in Olympia in 1881 and ultimately formed the Capital Tug Company where he worked until his death in 1926 (TPL website).

Young Hill

Located on the northwestern side of San Juan Island, just south of Roche Harbor, it was named Mount Young by Richards [13a]. According to Wood (122), Richards perhaps honored William A. G. Young who was involved in survey activities under Richards and for a time was loaned to Governor Douglas in 1858 as a Colonial Secretary. The U.S. Board on Geographic Names approved the name in 1925 over Mount Young (*Decisions*). Based upon the GNIS files, the logic used to change the name from Mt. Young to Young Hill is unclear.

Young Island [7a] #145, 1841, Wilkes; [7m] #160, 1841, Wilkes

A small island located off the southeastern side of Burrows Island, Wilkes called it Young Islet. He honored Ewing Young, a fur trapper who later turned to farming and cattle. Wilkes visited Young's farm in Oregon (Meany, *Origin* 356).

Yukon Harbor [23] #6460, 1905

Located south of Bainbridge Island off the mainland, Wilkes named it Barrons Bay [7q] for Commodore Samuel Barron who served in the Tripolitan War of 1805. The harbor was renamed for the Yukon River in the 1890s (Meany, *Origin* 356, 357).

Yulkat Bluff [7k] #152, 1841, Wilkes

Located on the northern edge of Suquamish Harbor in Hood Canal above Shine, Wilkes left no reason for the name. Wilkes did not include this name in his *Narrative*, but it is shown on his chart. The name is neither reflected on current charts nor recognized by the U.S. Board on Geographic Names.

Zangle Cove

Located on the eastern side of Dover Point northeast of Boston Harbor, Martin and Annie Sangle settled there. Somehow, the "S" became a "Z".

Zelatched Point [7d] #146, 1841, Wilkes

Located on the southwestern end of the Toandos Peninsula, Wilkes left no reason for the name. He does not include this name in his *Narrative*, but it is shown on his chart.

Zenith

The small area is now part of the city of Des Moines. Cardel (*King County* 118) indicated that when the post office was established, it was named for its location on top of a hill.

Zepeda, Isla de [2] 1791, Pantoja; [3] 1791, Eliza

See Point Roberts.

APPENDIX A - CHARTS

Some charts are listed more than once. Duplicate listings represent a different area of that chart.

Chart 1 - [1] 1790, Quimper
Chart 2 - [2] 1791, Pantoja
Chart 3 - [3] 1791, Eliza
Chart 4 - [6] 1792, Vancouver
Chart 5 - [6] 1792, Vancouver
Chart 6 - [7a] #145, 1841, Wilkes
Chart 7 - [7a] #145, 1841, Wilkes
Chart 8 - [7d] #146, 1841, Wilkes
Chart 9 - [7d] #146, 1841, Wilkes
Chart 10 - [7e] #158, 1841, Wilkes
Chart 11 - [7i] #147, 1841, Wilkes
Chart 12 - [7p] #150, 1841, Wilkes
Chart 13 - [8a] #1917, 1847, Kellett
Chart 14 - [10] #51, 1854, U.S. Coast Survey
Chart 15 - [10] #51, 1854, U.S. Coast Survey
Chart 16 - [11] #654, 1858, U.S. Coast Survey
Chart 17 - [11] #654, 1858, U.S. Coast Survey
Chart 18 - [13a] #2689, 1859, Richards
Chart 19 - [13a] #2689, 1859, Richards
Chart 20 - [14a] #2840, 1861, Richards
Chart 21 - [14a] #2840, 1861, Richards
Chart 22 - [15a] #611, Richards
Chart 23 - [16a] #602, 1865, Richards
Chart 24 - [17] #27, 1862, U.S. Coast Survey
Chart 25 - [17] #27, 1862, U.S. Coast Survey
Chart 26 - [18] #654, 1866, U.S. Coast Survey
Chart 27 - [18] #654, 1866, U.S. Coast Survey
Chart 28 - [19] #662, 1867, U.S. Coast Survey
Chart 29 - [19] #662, 1867, U.S. Coast Survey
Chart 30 - [19] #662, 1867, U.S. Coast Survey

Appendix A - Charts

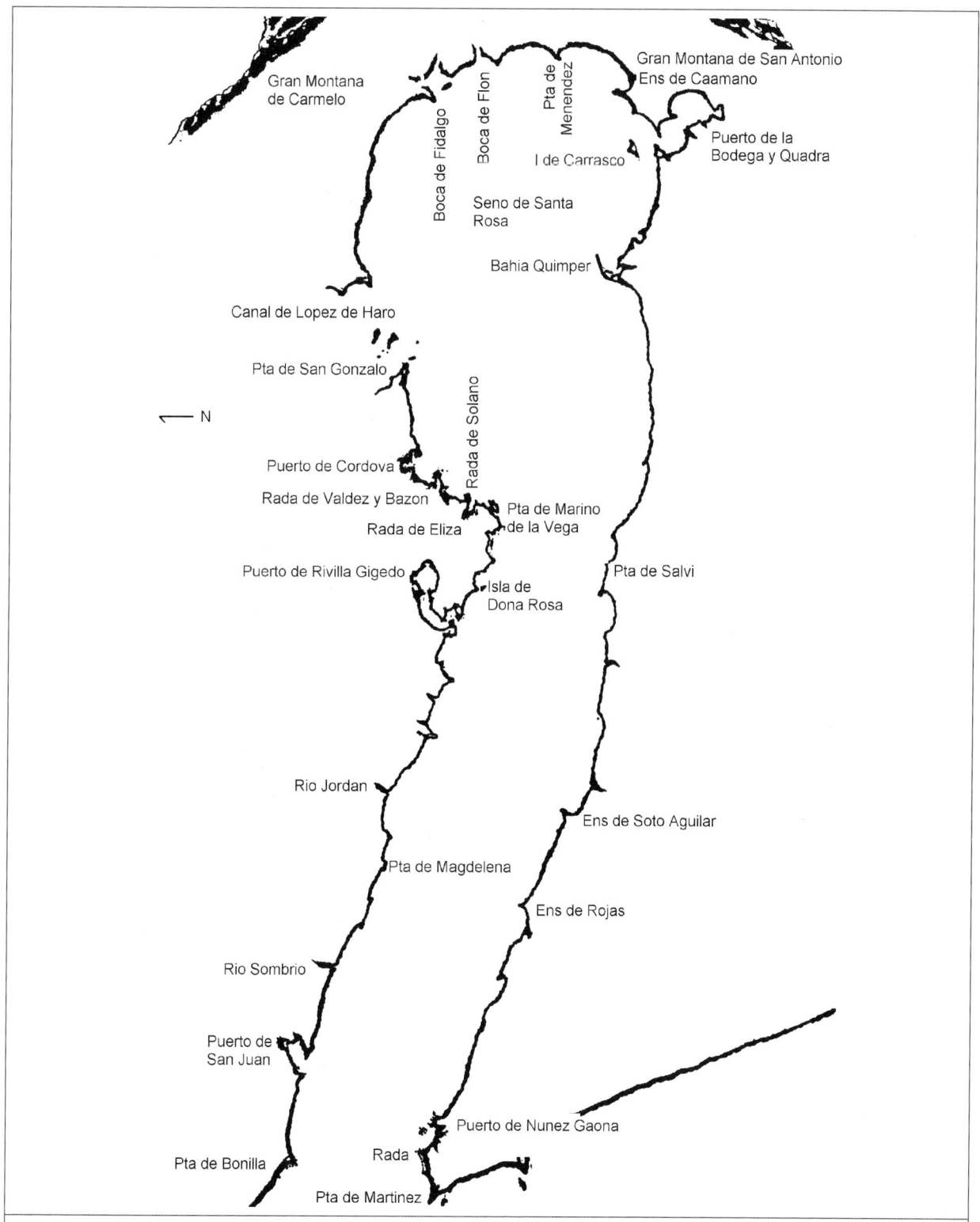

Chart 1 - [1] 1790, Quimper. Because of the poor quality of this chart, I took the liberty of cleaning it up by removing the names and reentering more readable replacements, while retaining the outline of the original chart.

Appendix A - Charts

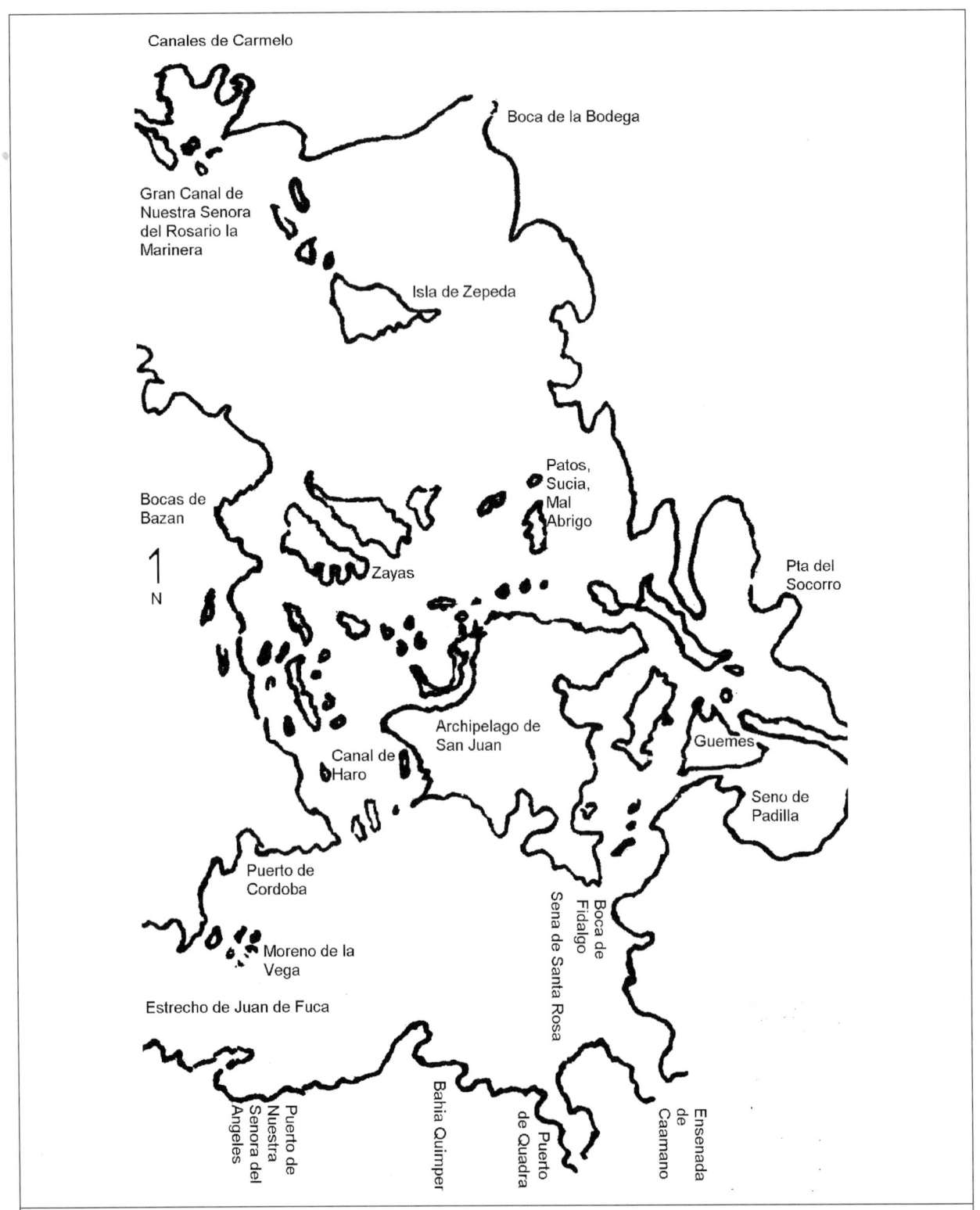

Chart 2 - [2] 1791, Pantoja. Because of the poor quality of this chart, I took the liberty of cleaning it up by removing the names and reentering more readable replacements, while retaining the outline of the original chart.

284 ♦ Maritime Place Names - Inland Washington Waters

Appendix A - Charts

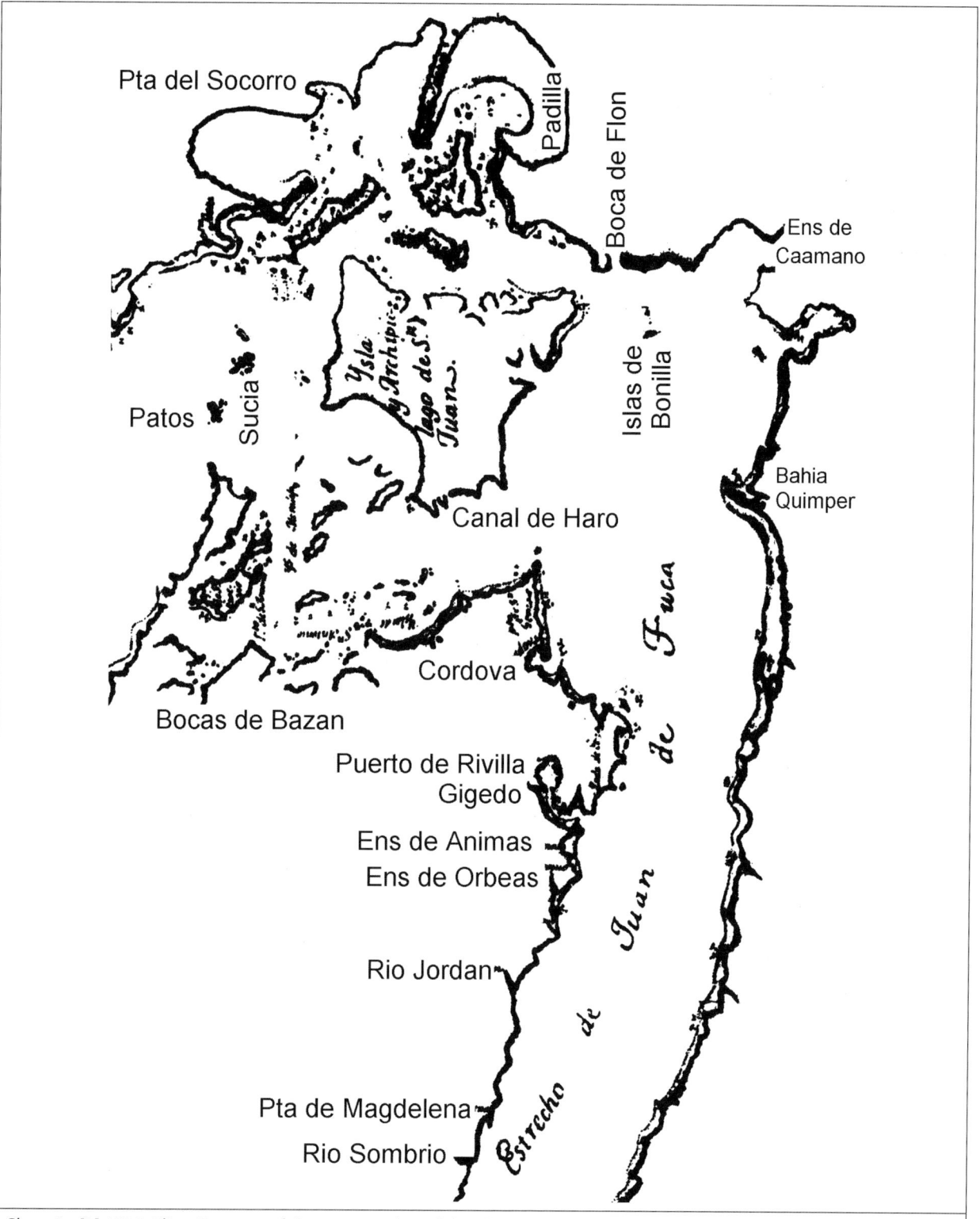

Chart 3 - [3] 1791, Eliza. Because of the poor quality of this chart, I took the liberty of cleaning it up by removing the names and reentering more readable replacements, while retaining the outline of the original chart.

Appendix A - Charts

Chart 4 - [6] 1792, Vancouver

Appendix A - Charts

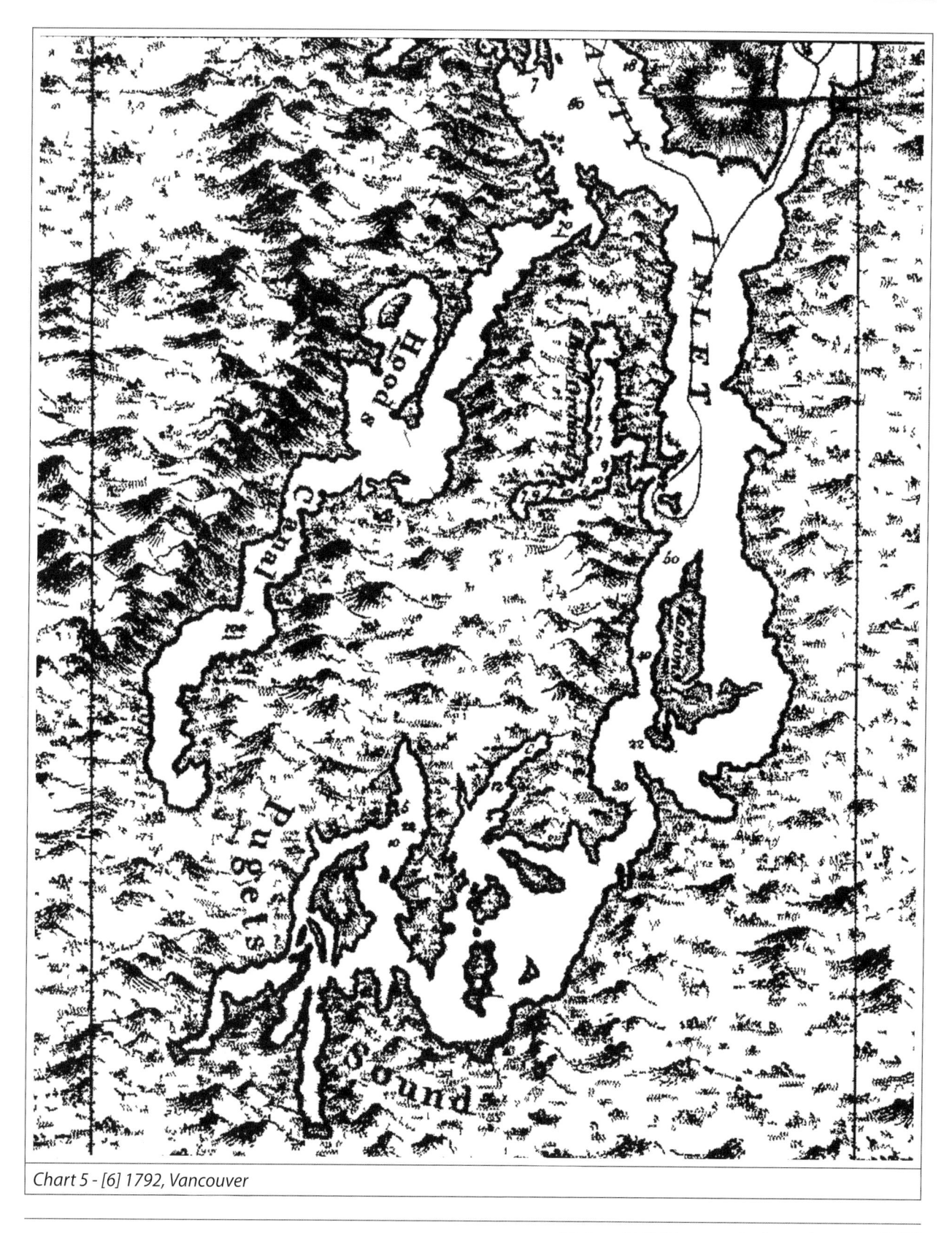

Chart 5 - [6] 1792, Vancouver

Appendix A - Charts

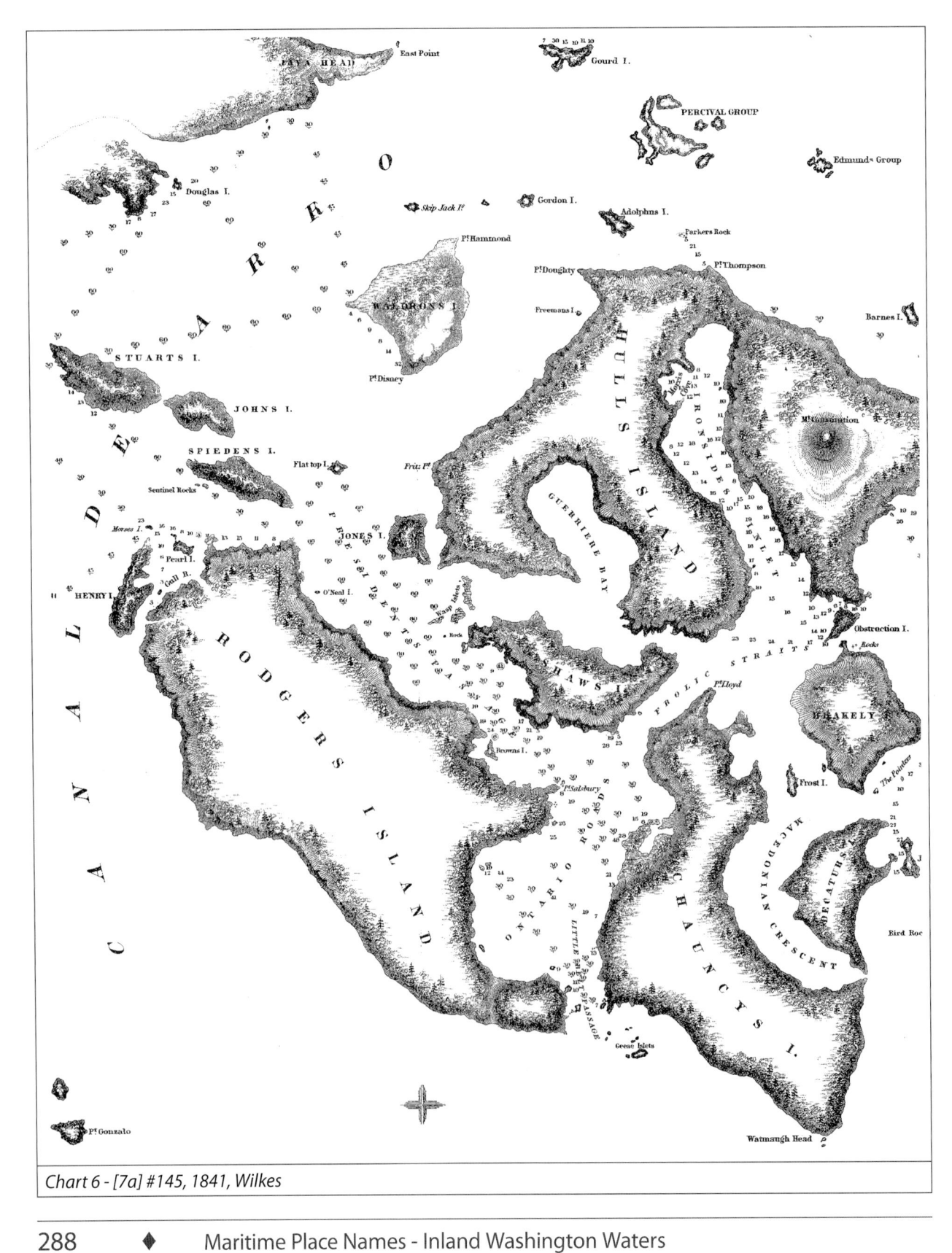

Chart 6 - [7a] #145, 1841, Wilkes

Chart 7 - [7a] #145, 1841, Wilkes

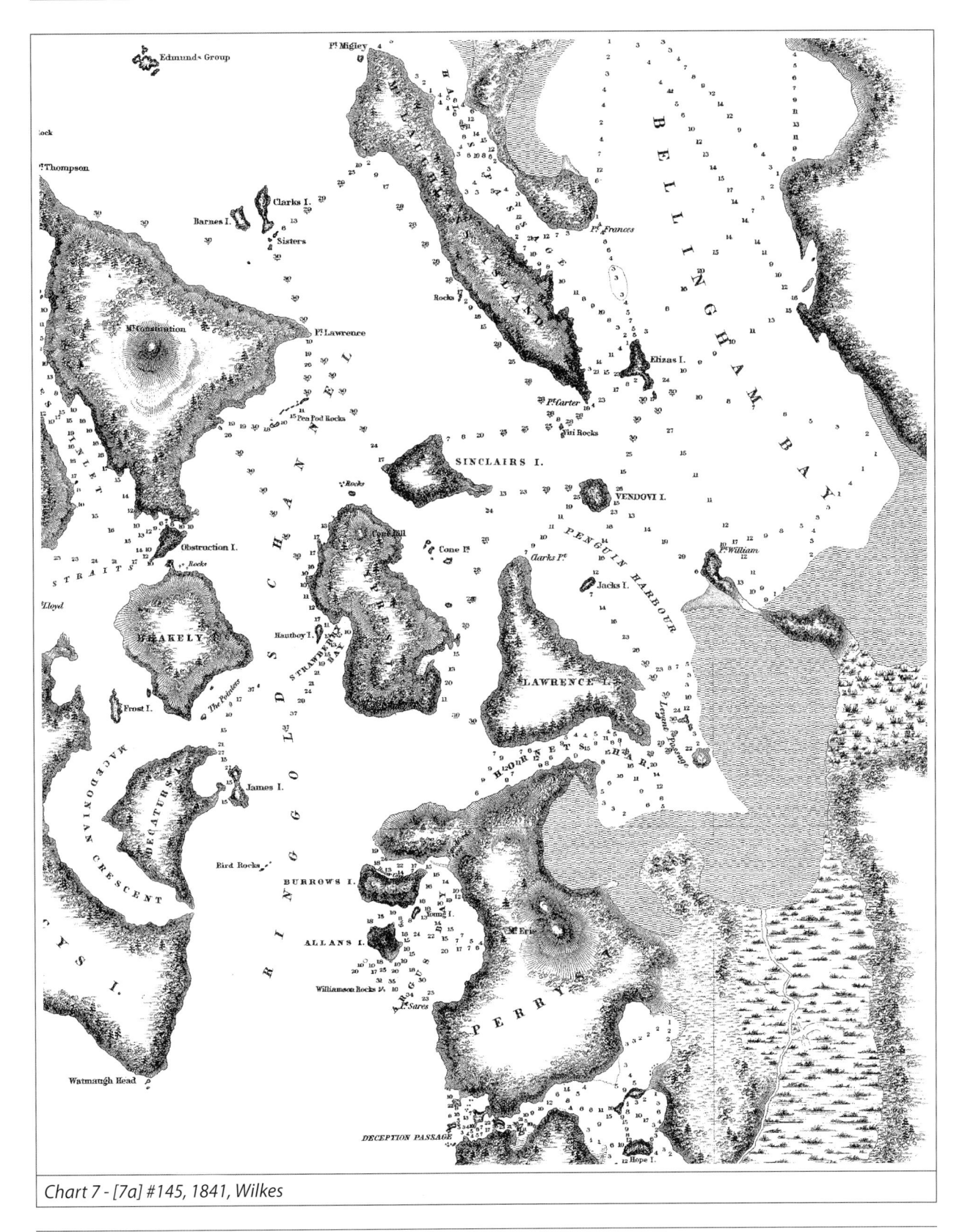

Appendix A - Charts

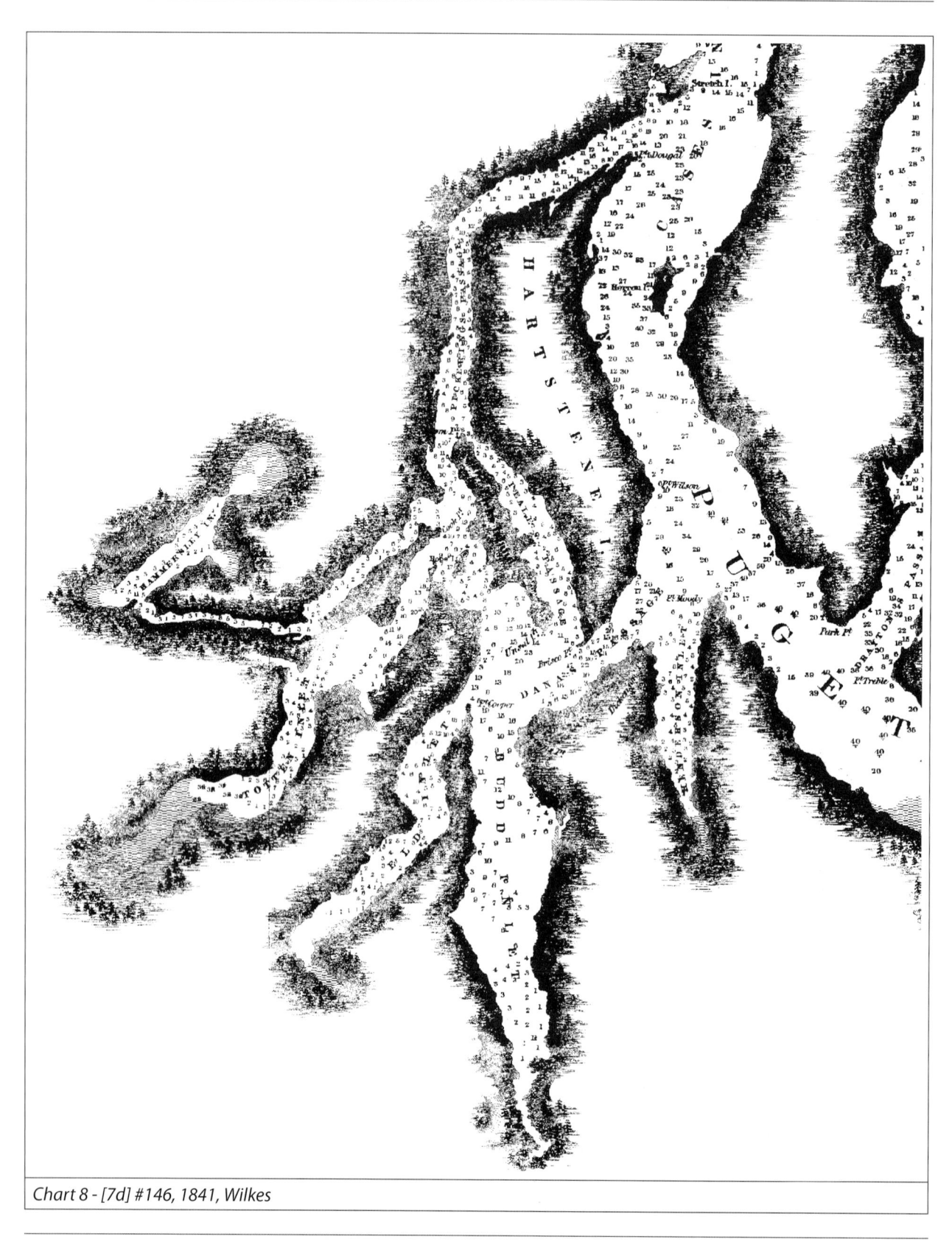

Chart 8 - [7d] #146, 1841, Wilkes

Chart 9 - [7d] #146, 1841, Wilkes

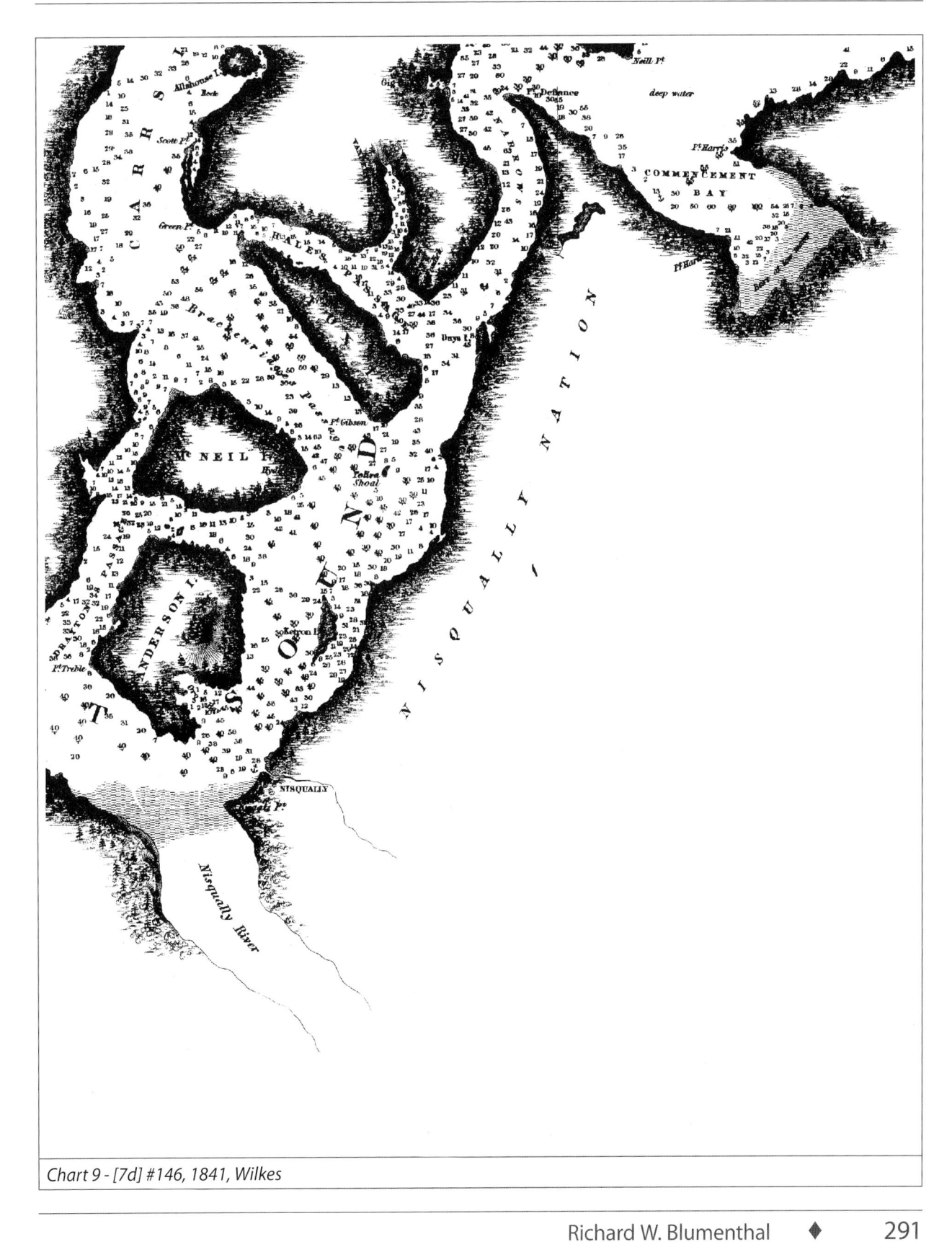

Appendix A - Charts

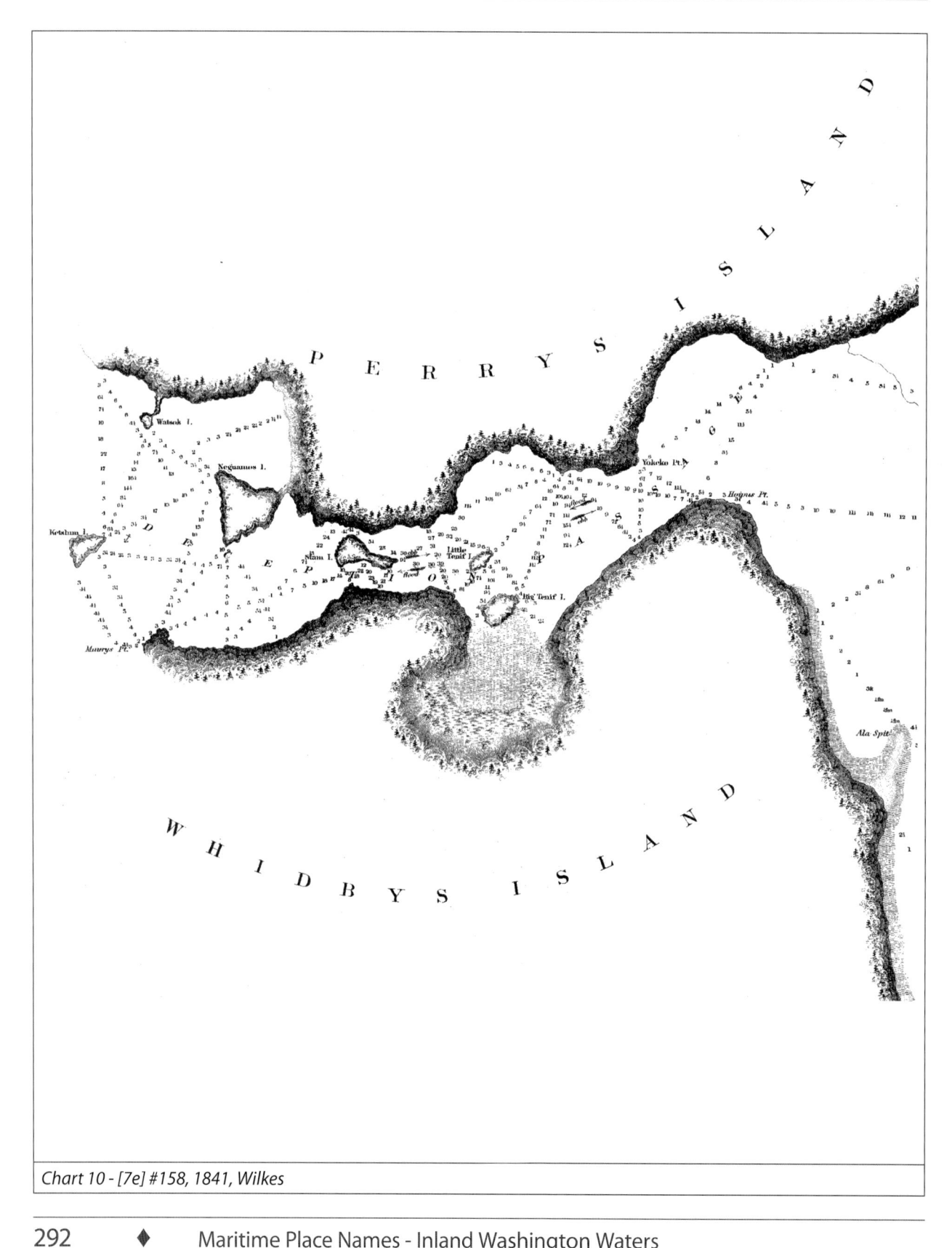

Chart 10 - [7e] #158, 1841, Wilkes

Maritime Place Names - Inland Washington Waters

Appendix A - Charts

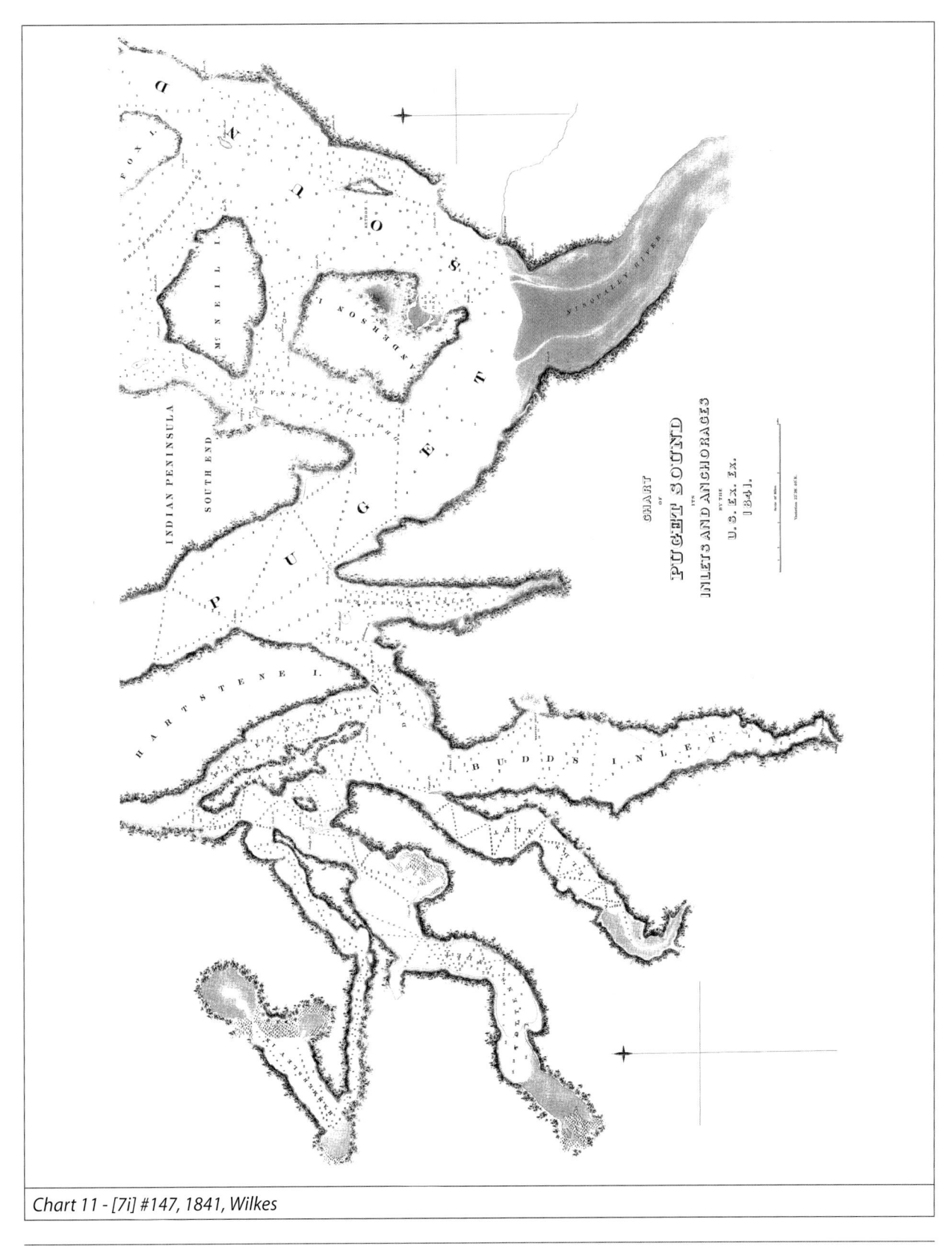

Chart 11 - [7i] #147, 1841, Wilkes

Appendix A - Charts

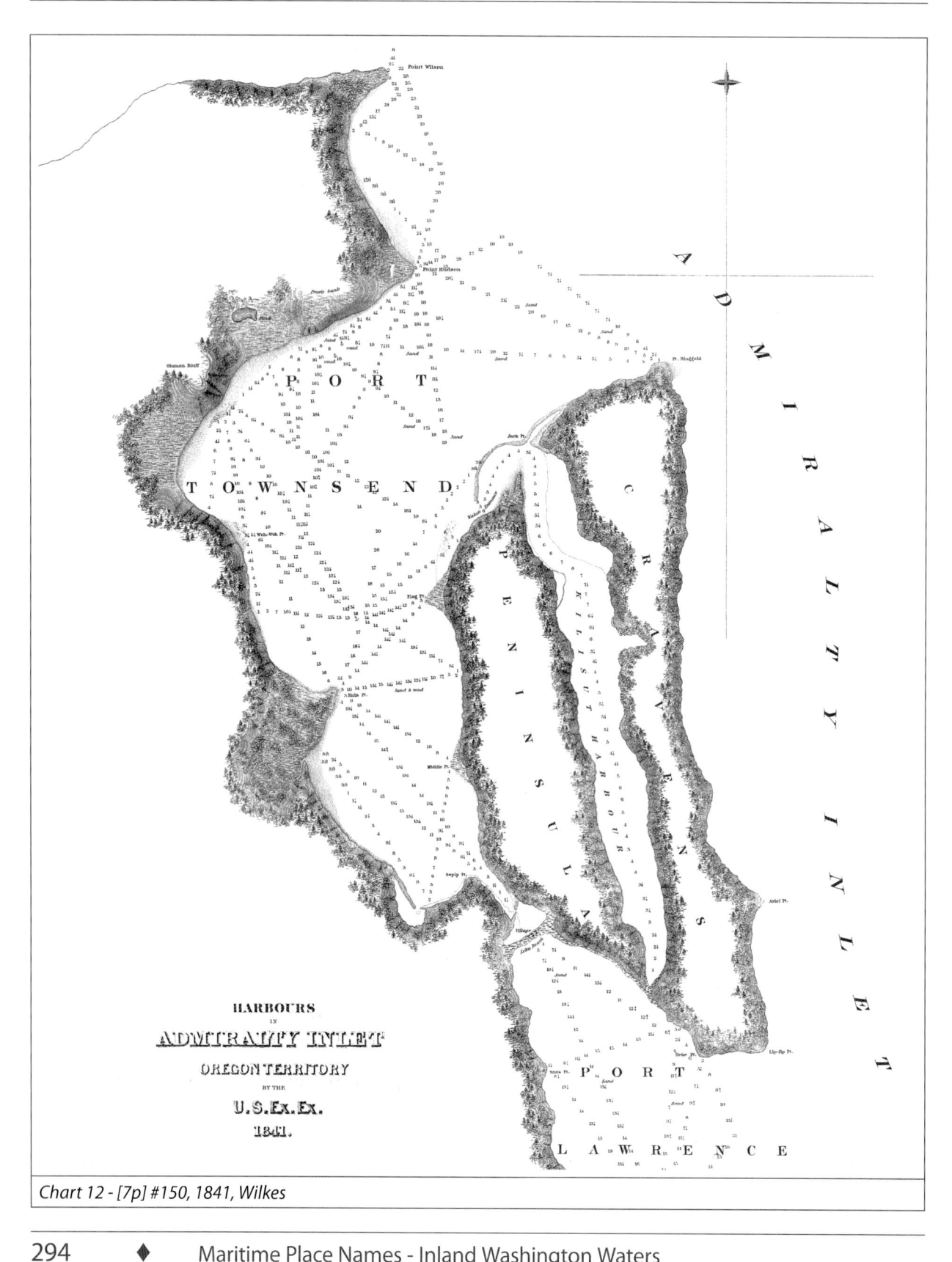

Chart 12 - [7p] #150, 1841, Wilkes

Chart 13 - [8a] #1917, 1847, Kellett

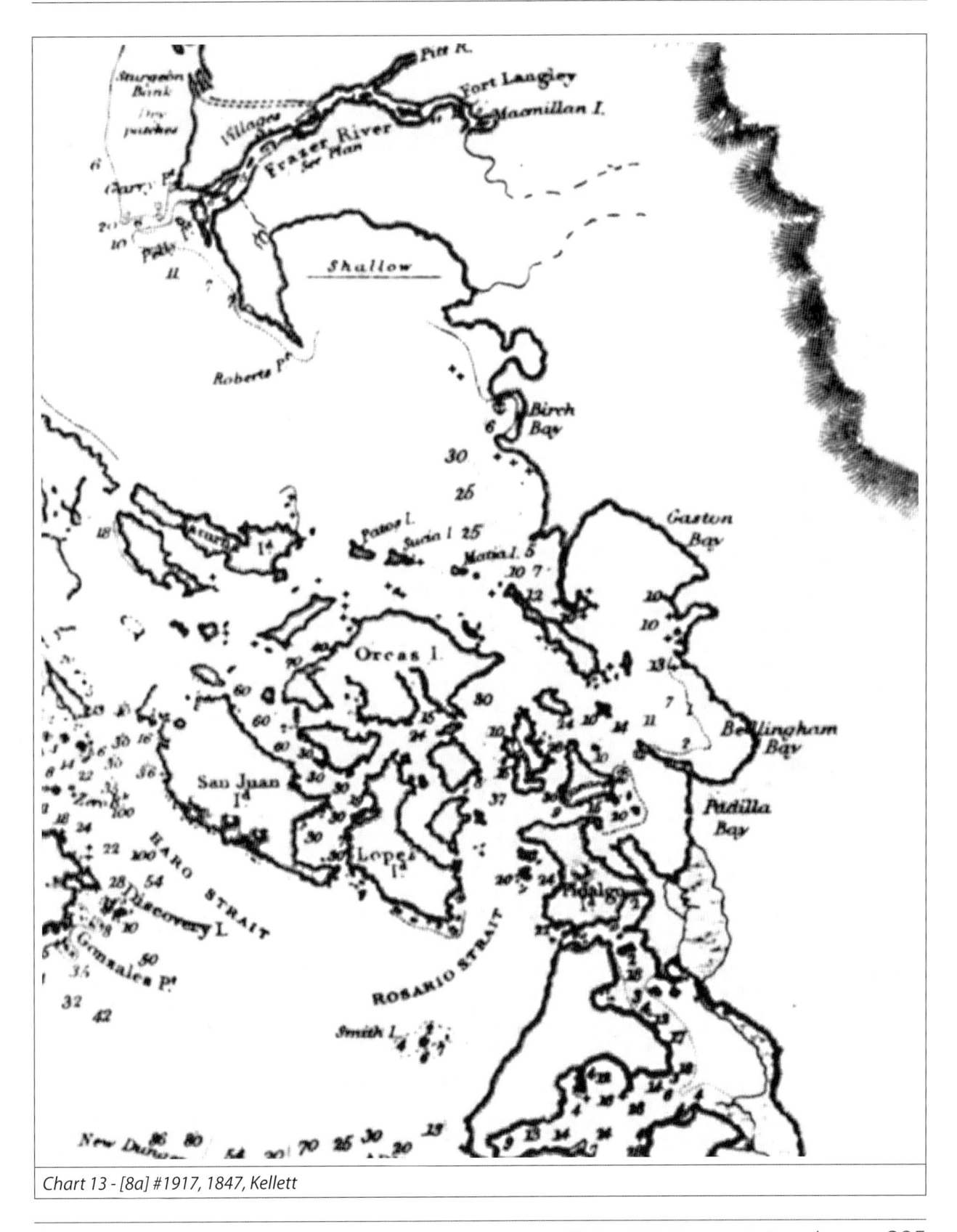

Appendix A - Charts

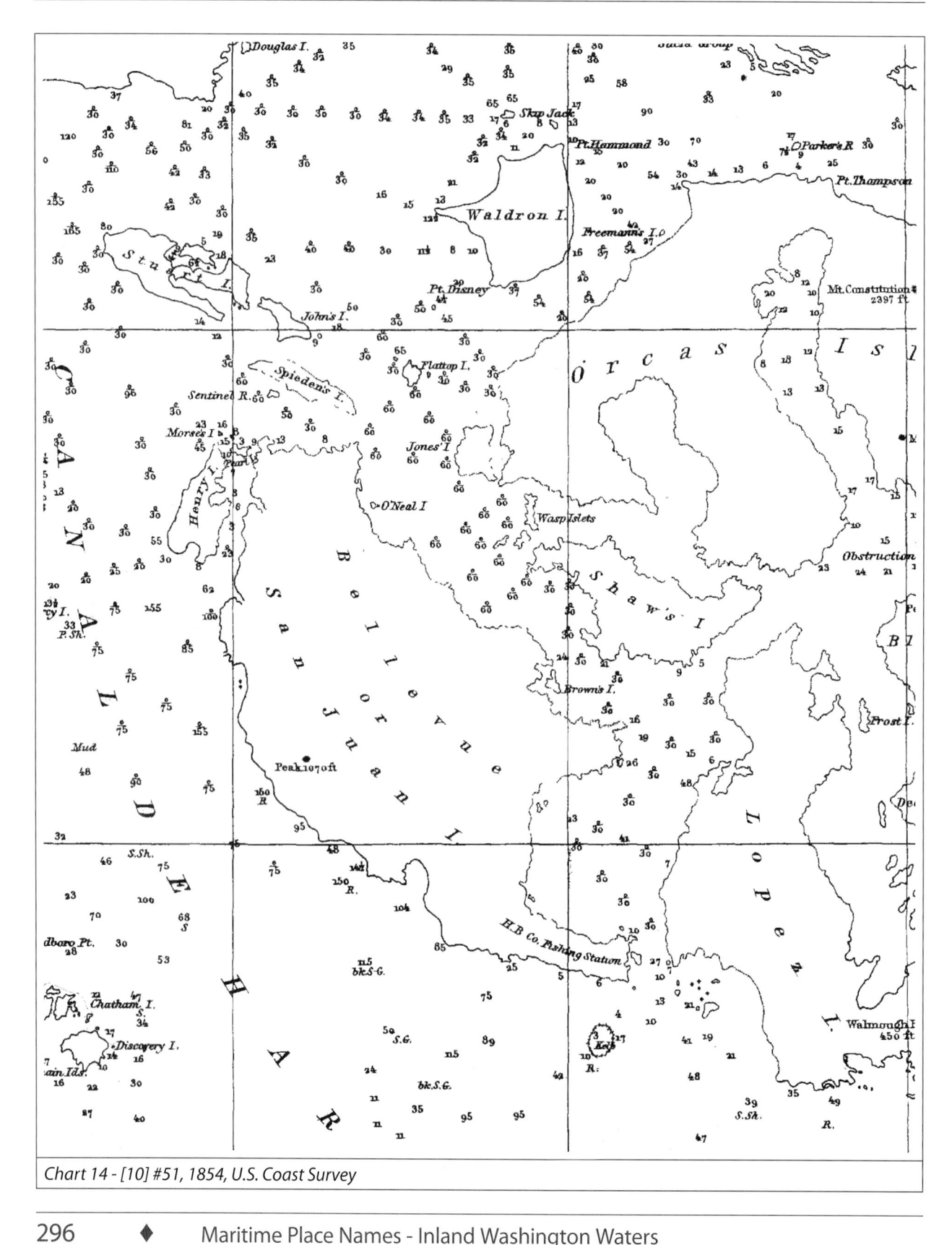

Chart 14 - [10] #51, 1854, U.S. Coast Survey

Chart 15 - [10] #51, 1854, U.S. Coast Survey

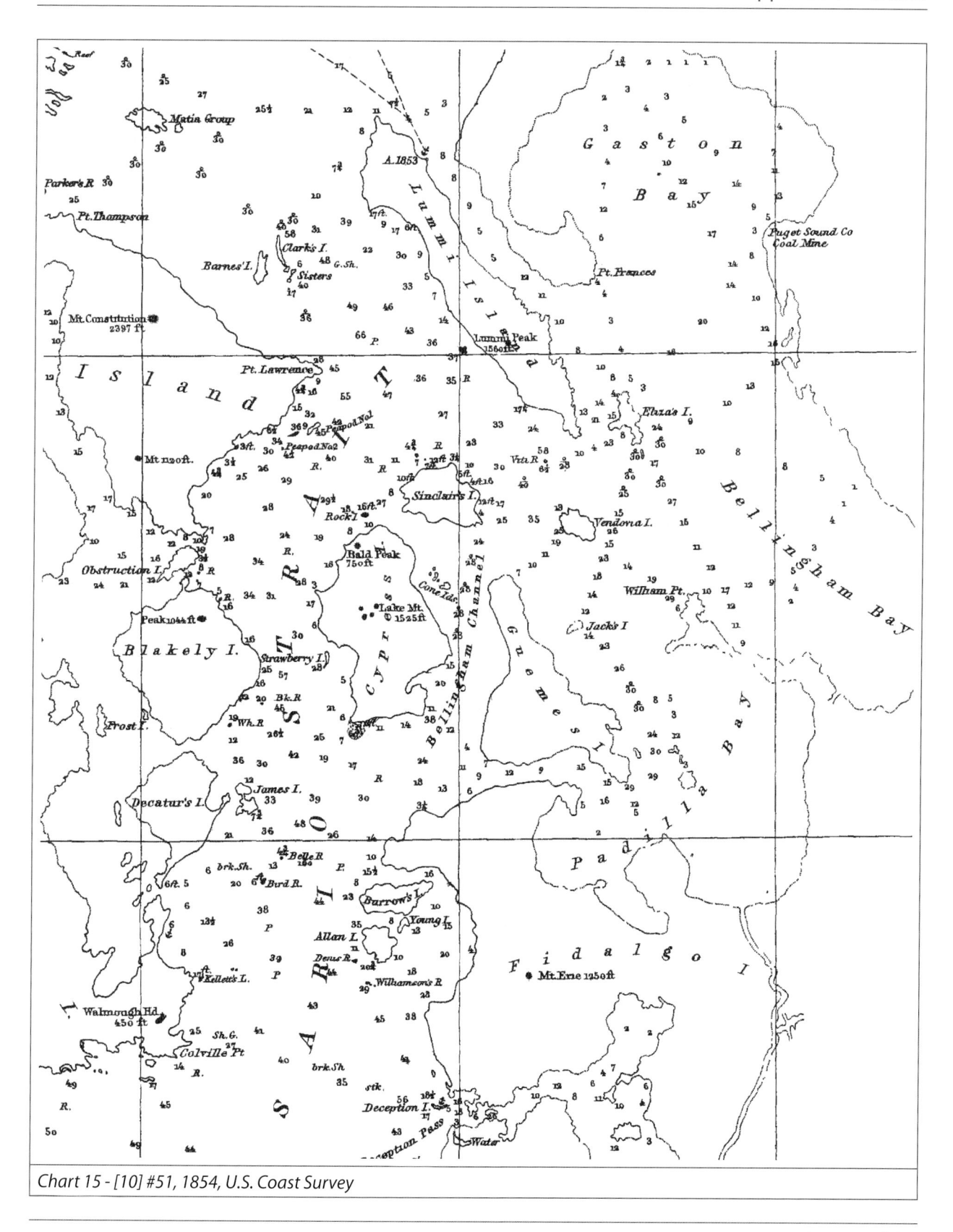

Appendix A - Charts

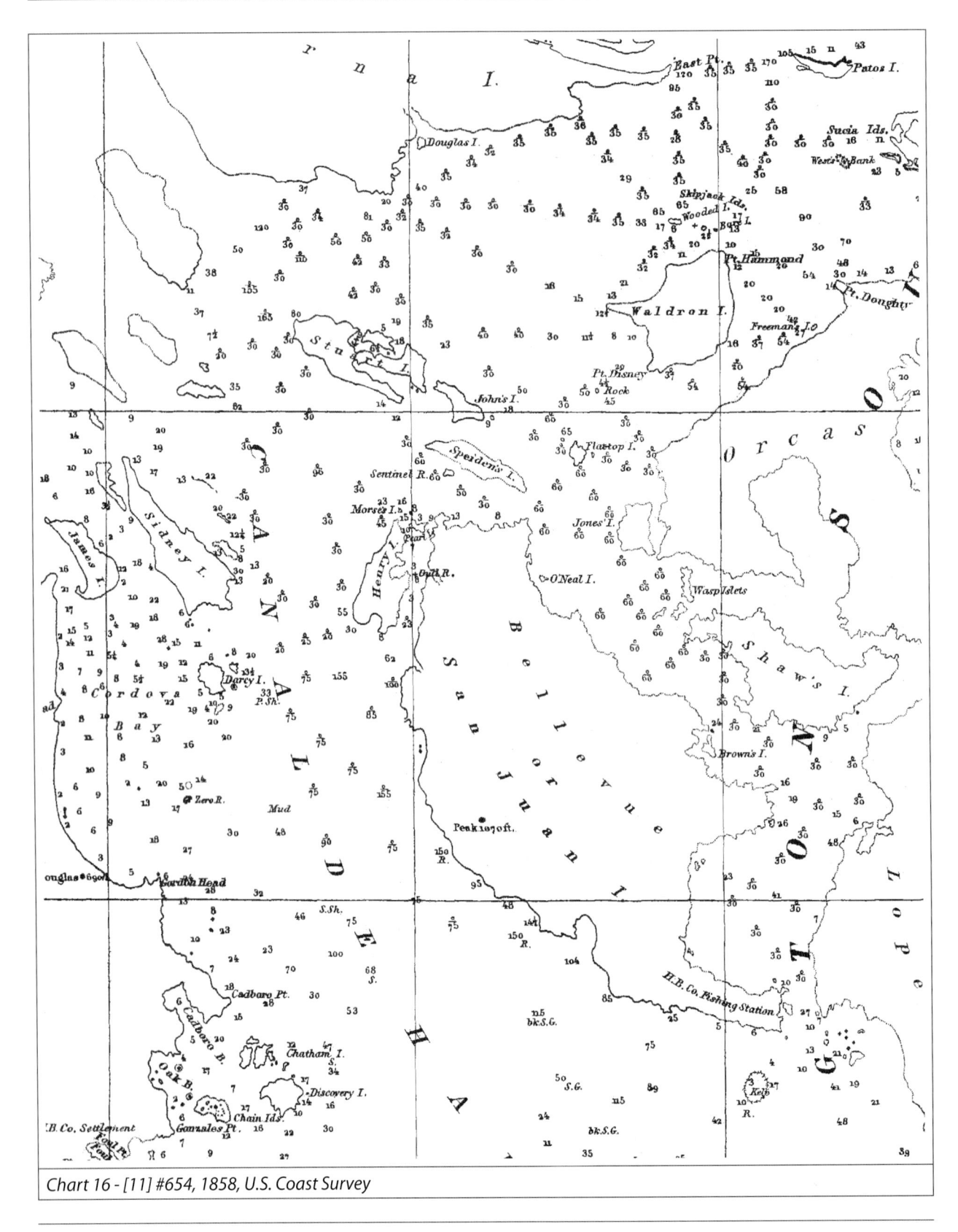

Chart 16 - [11] #654, 1858, U.S. Coast Survey

Chart 17 - [11] #654, 1858, U.S. Coast Survey

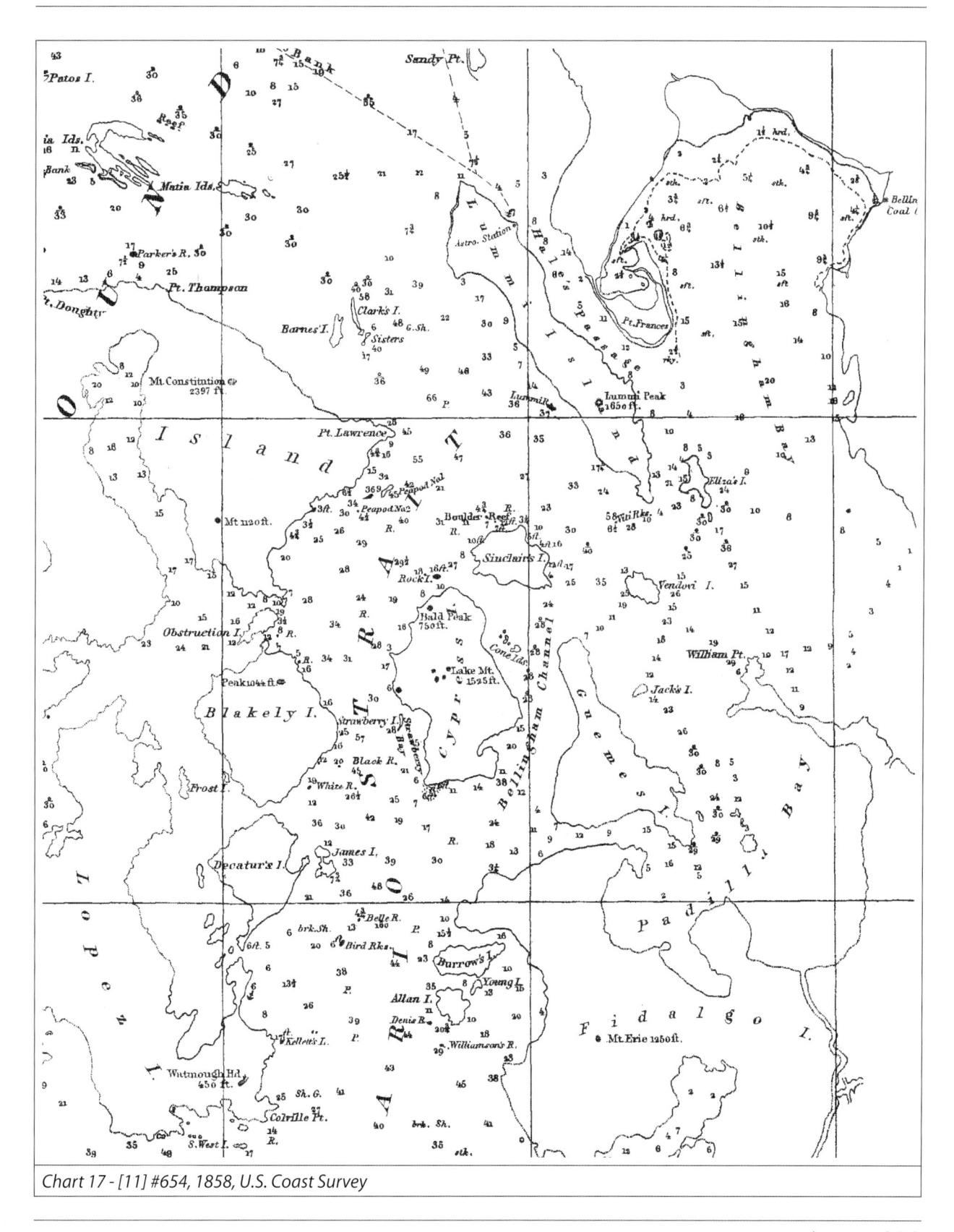

Appendix A - Charts

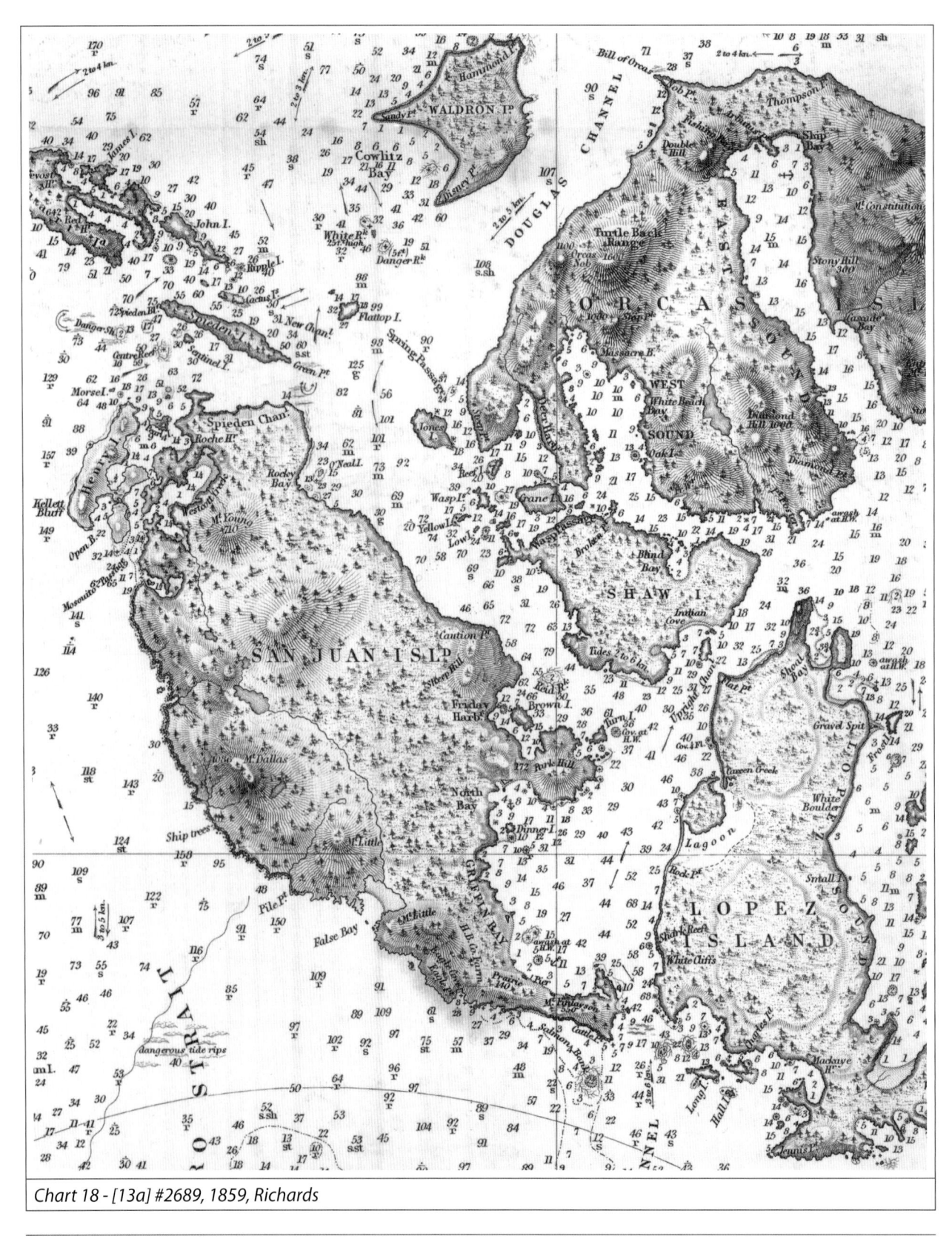

Chart 18 - [13a] #2689, 1859, Richards

Appendix A - Charts

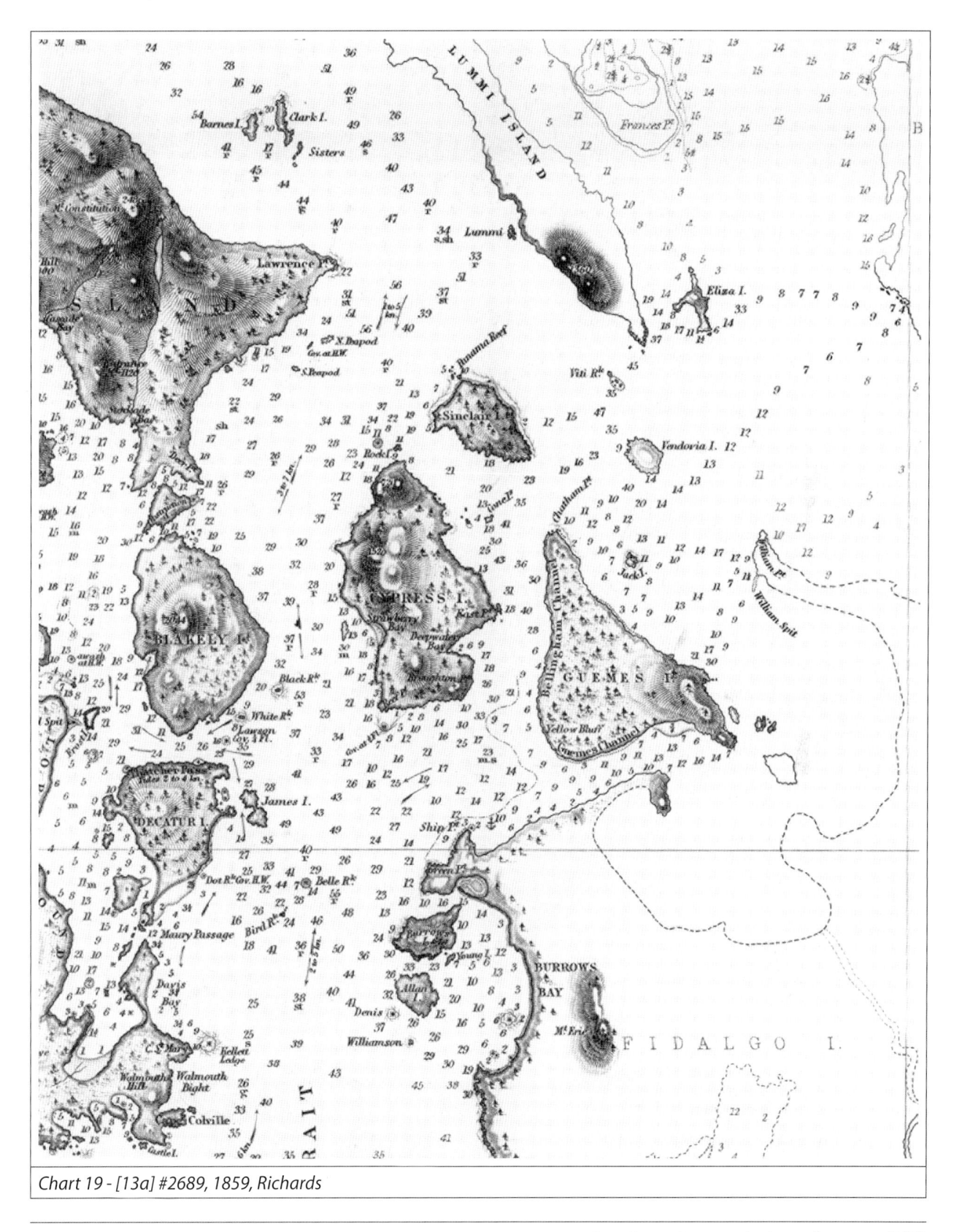

Chart 19 - [13a] #2689, 1859, Richards

Appendix A - Charts

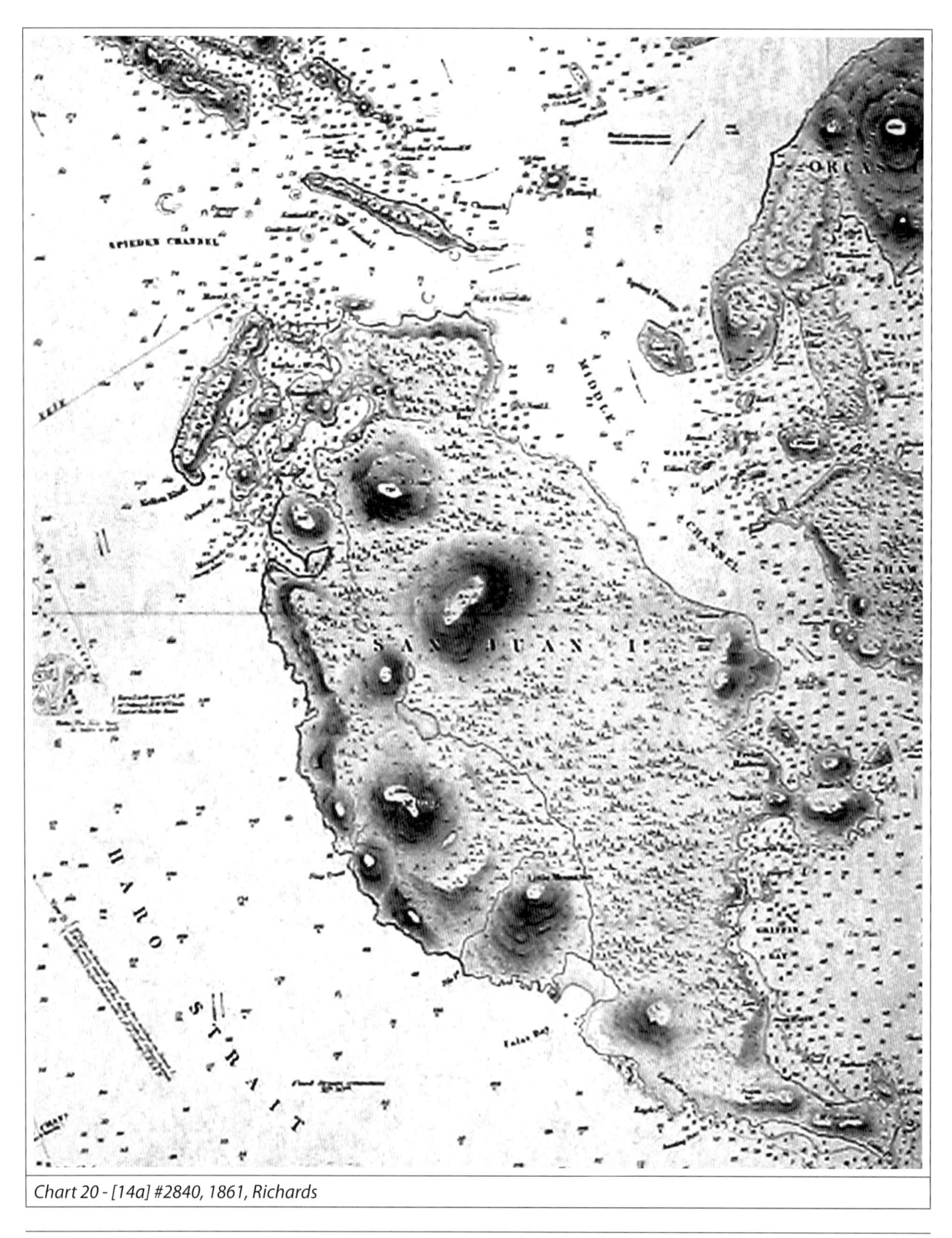

Chart 20 - [14a] #2840, 1861, Richards

Chart 21 - [14a] #2840, 1861, Richards

Appendix A - Charts

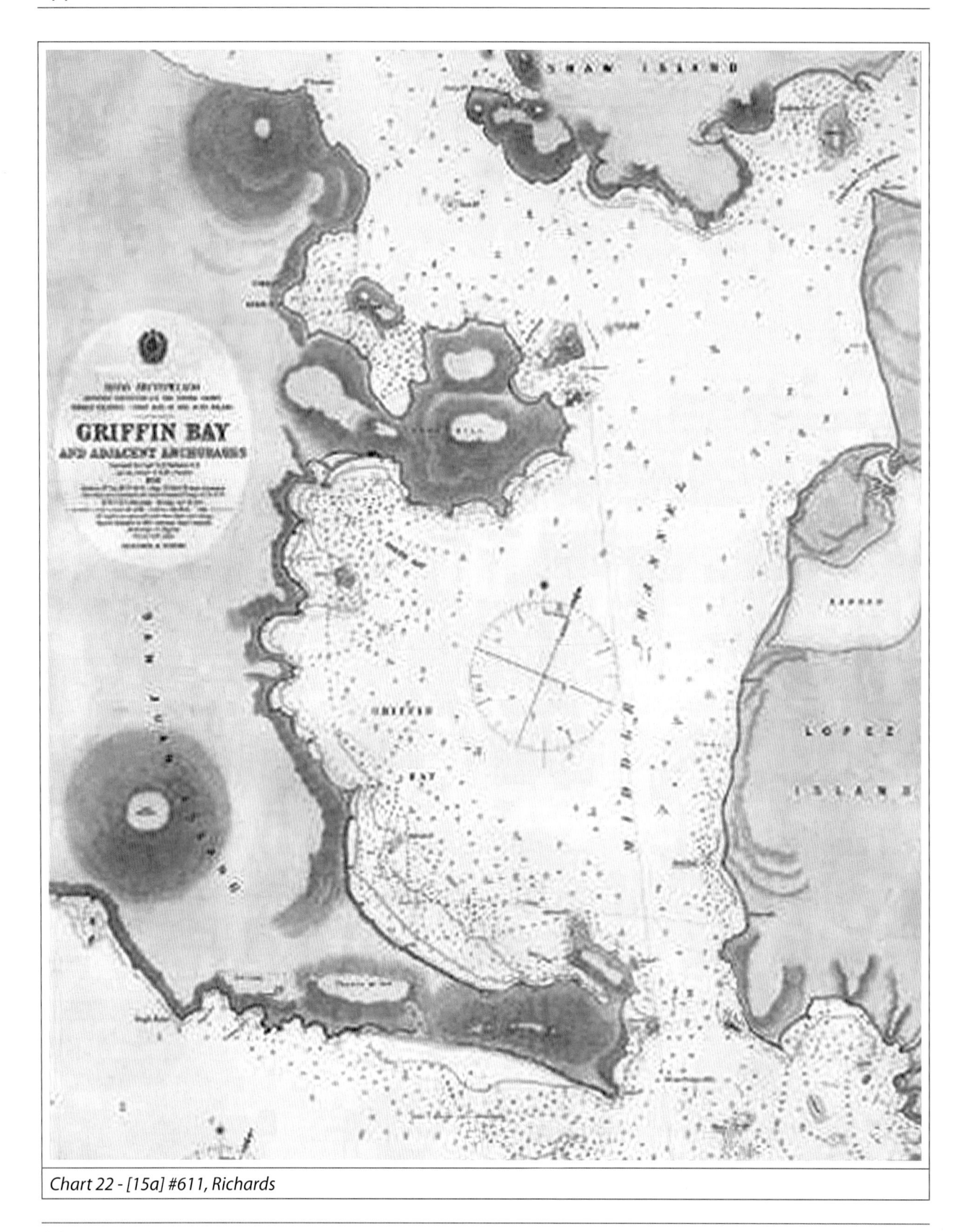

Chart 22 - [15a] #611, Richards

Chart 23 - [16a] #602, 1865, Richards

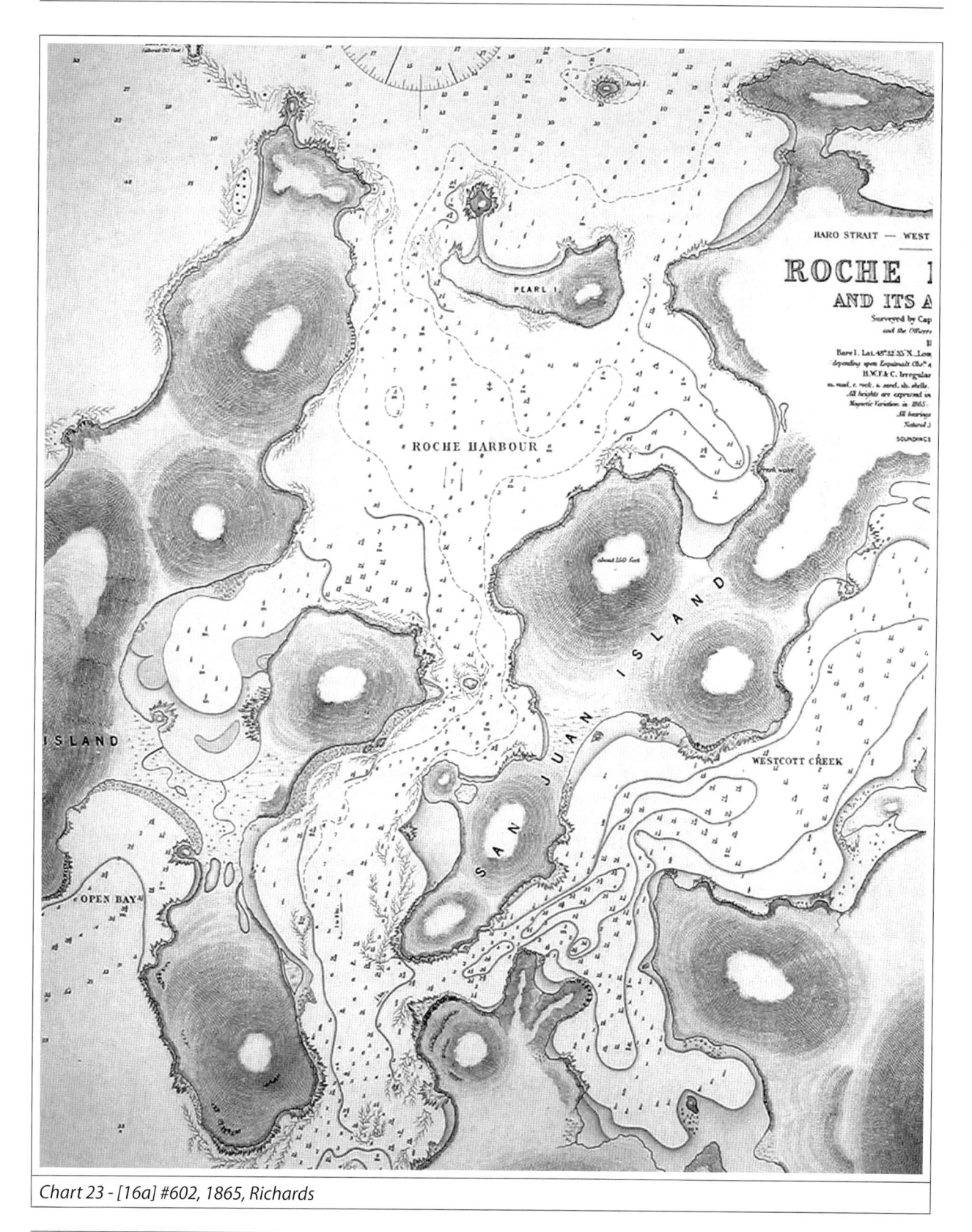

Appendix A - Charts

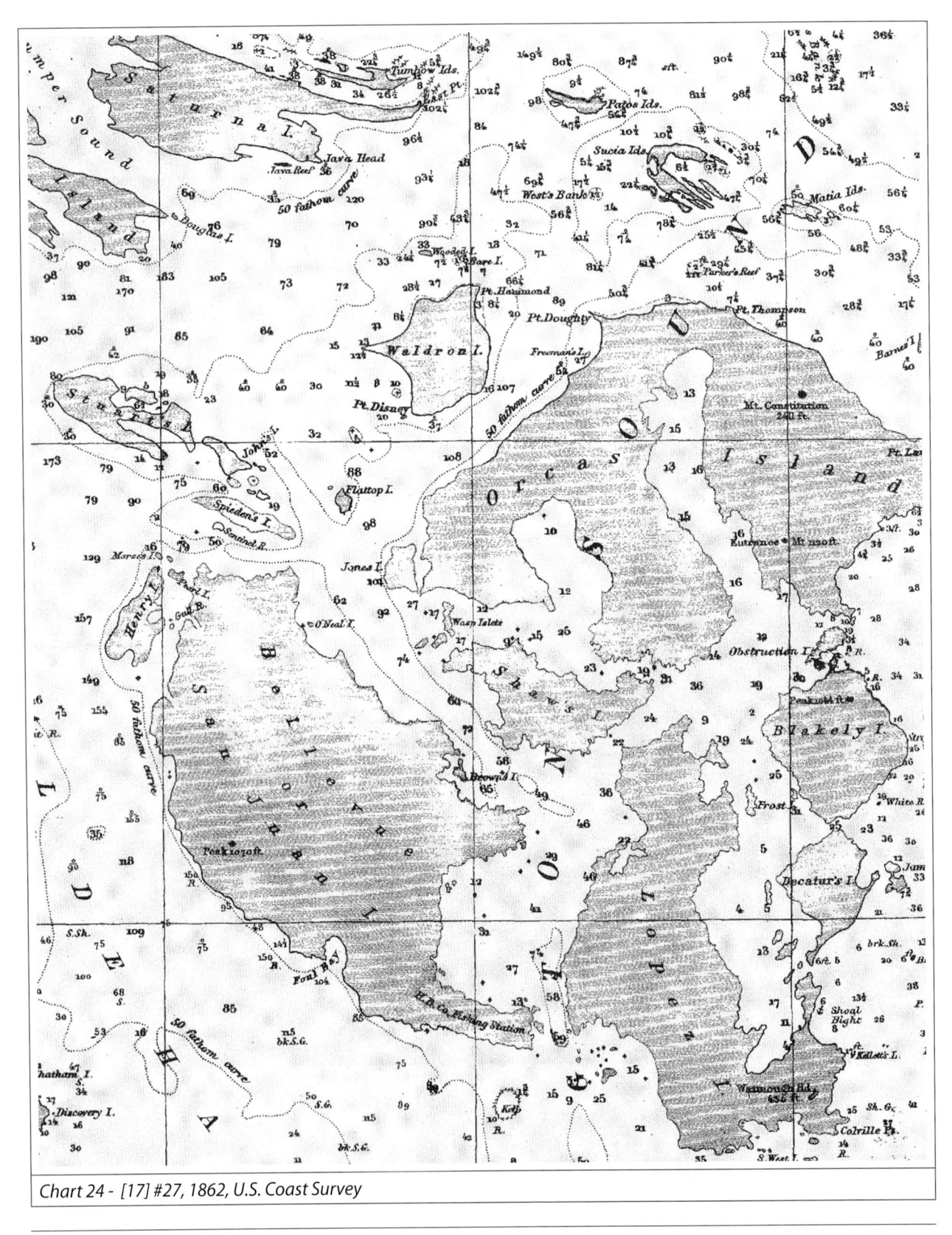

Chart 24 - [17] #27, 1862, U.S. Coast Survey

Chart 25 - [17] #27, 1862, U.S. Coast Survey

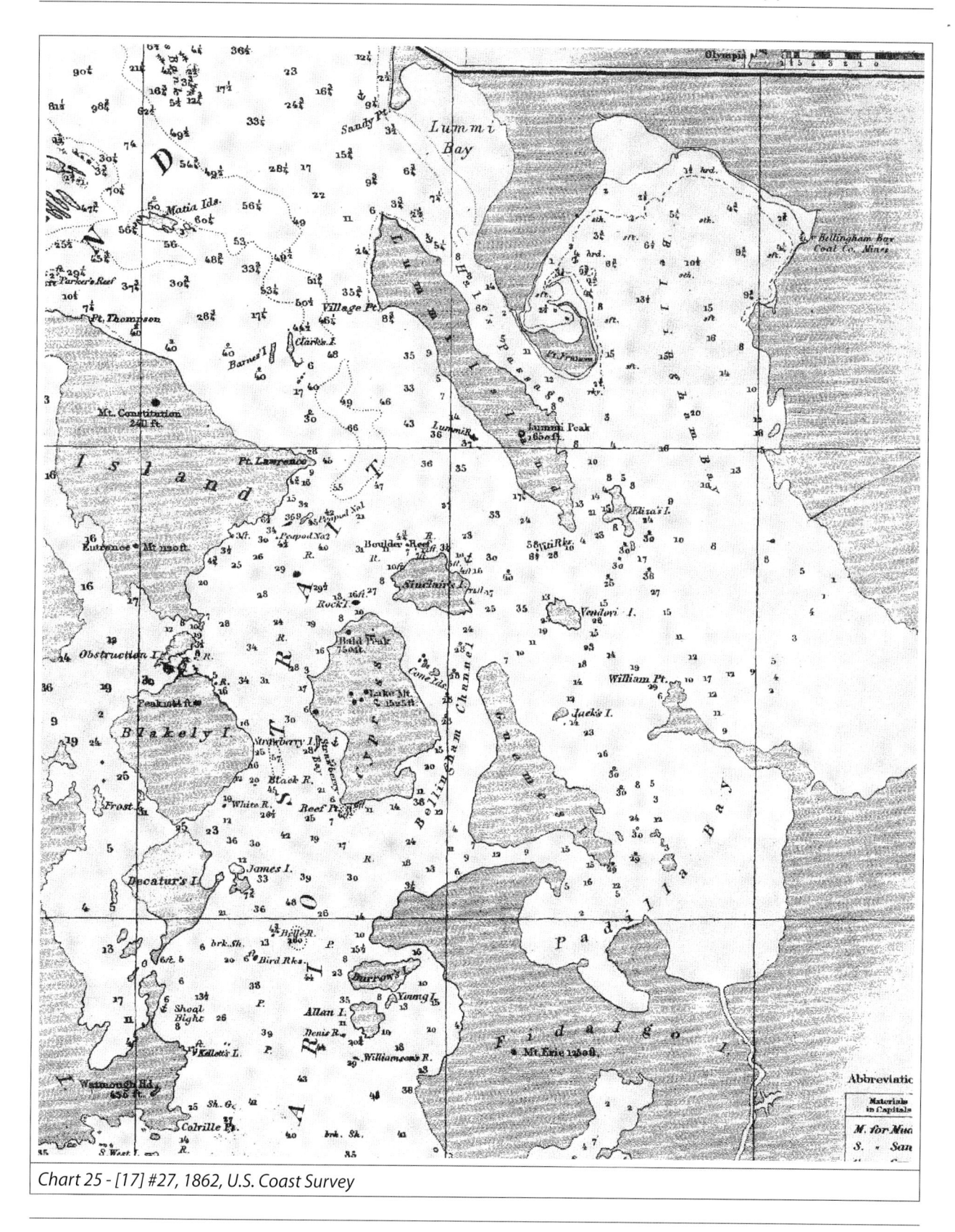

Appendix A - Charts

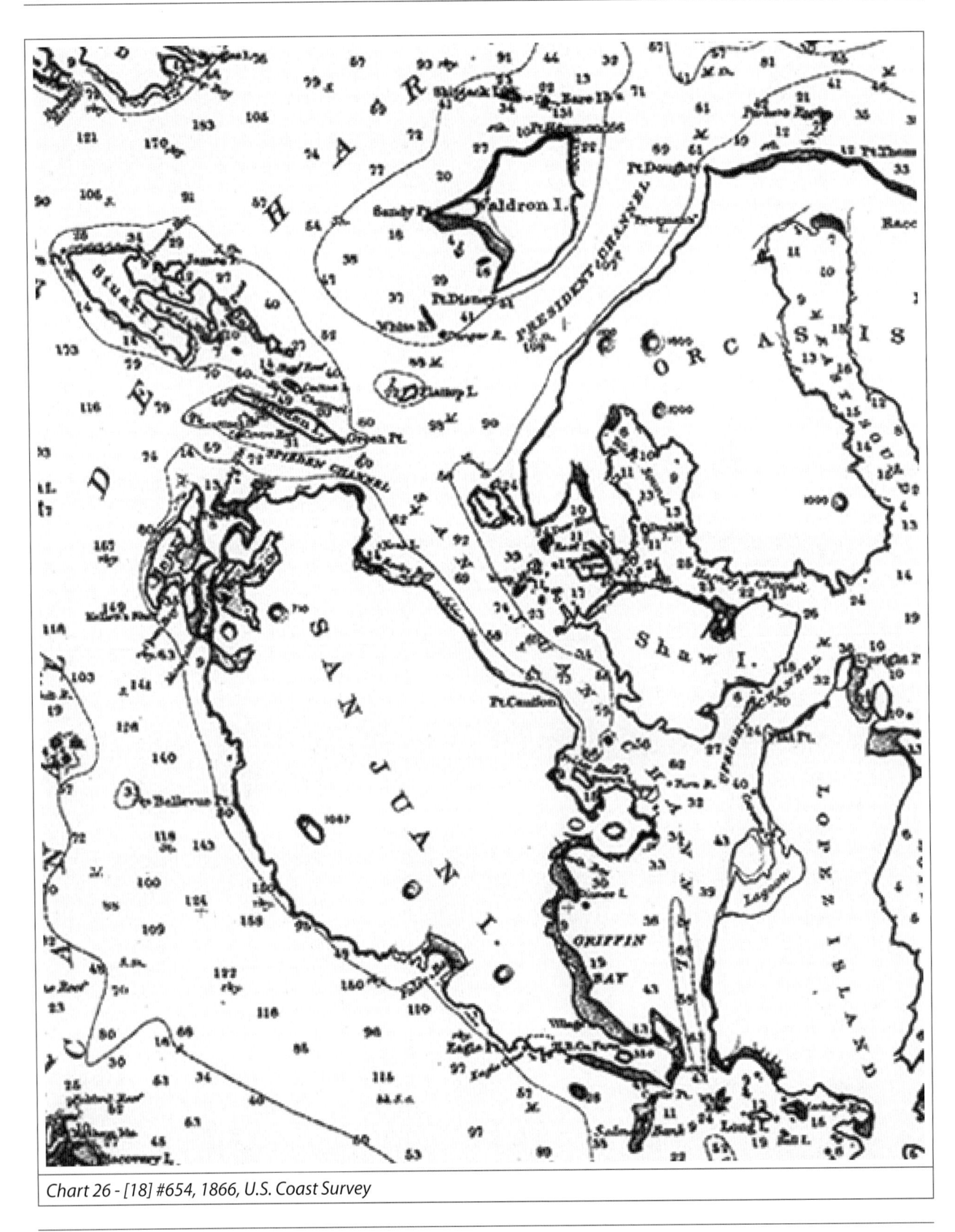

Chart 26 - [18] #654, 1866, U.S. Coast Survey

Appendix A - Charts

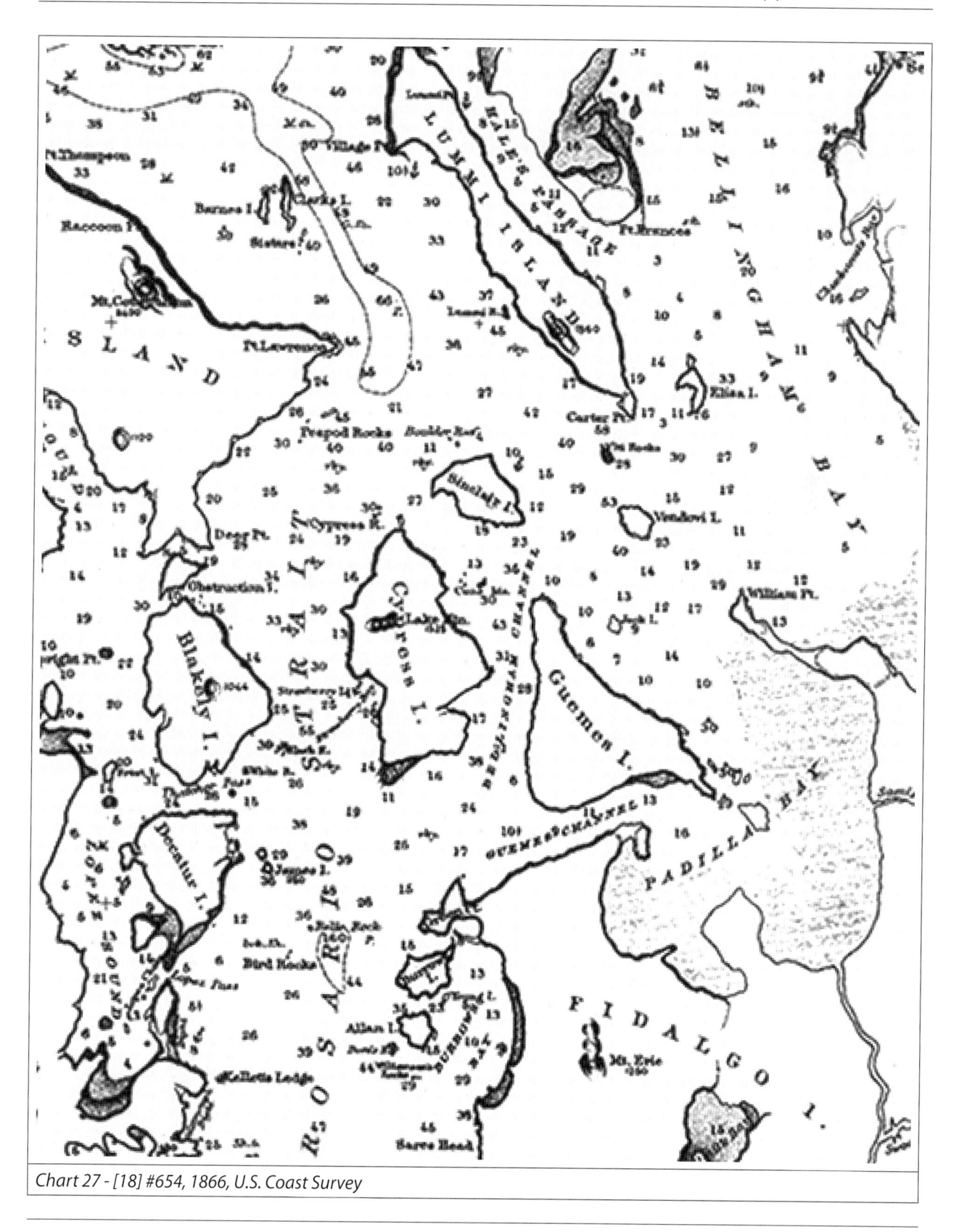

Chart 27 - [18] #654, 1866, U.S. Coast Survey

Appendix A - Charts

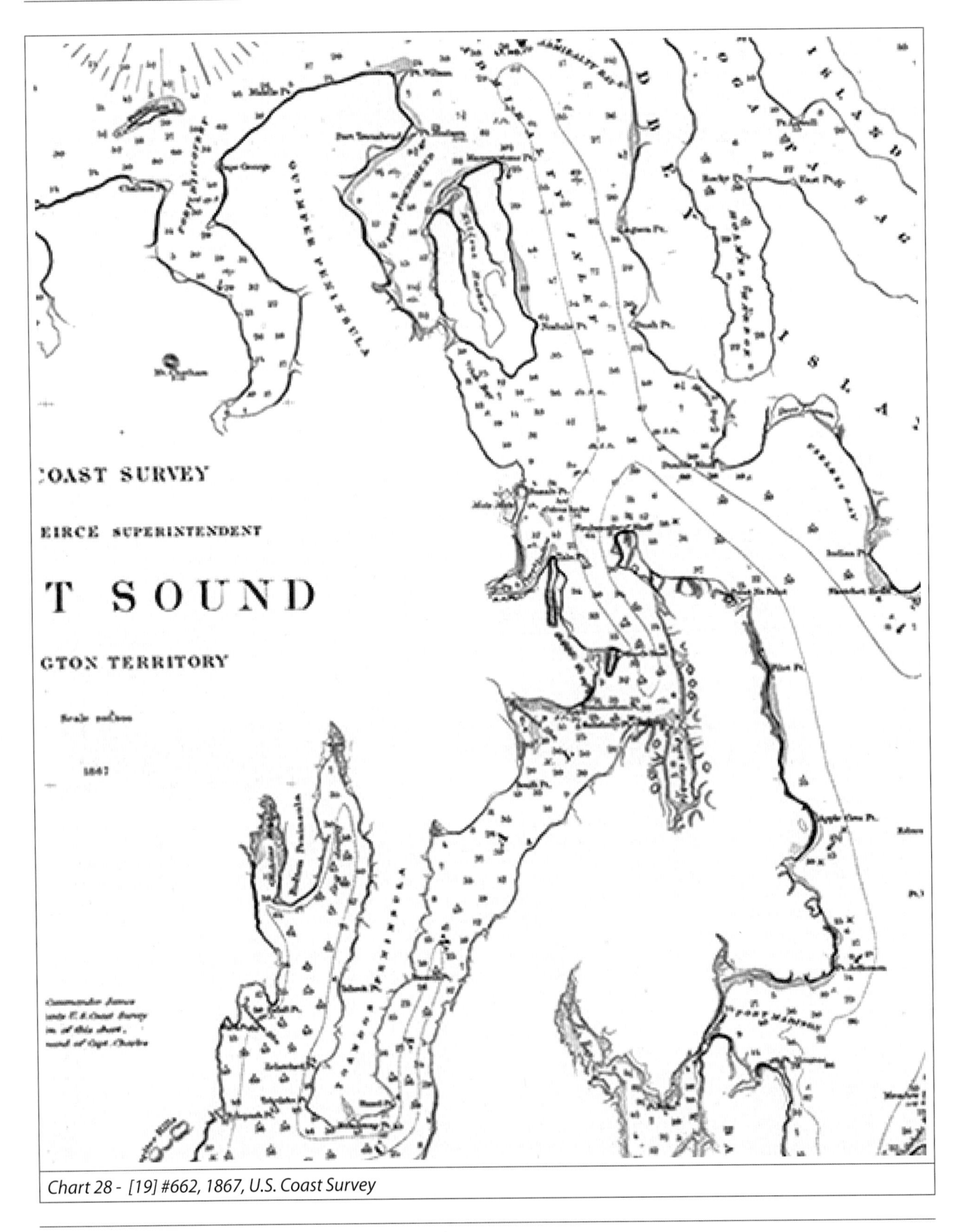

Chart 28 - [19] #662, 1867, U.S. Coast Survey

Appendix A - Charts

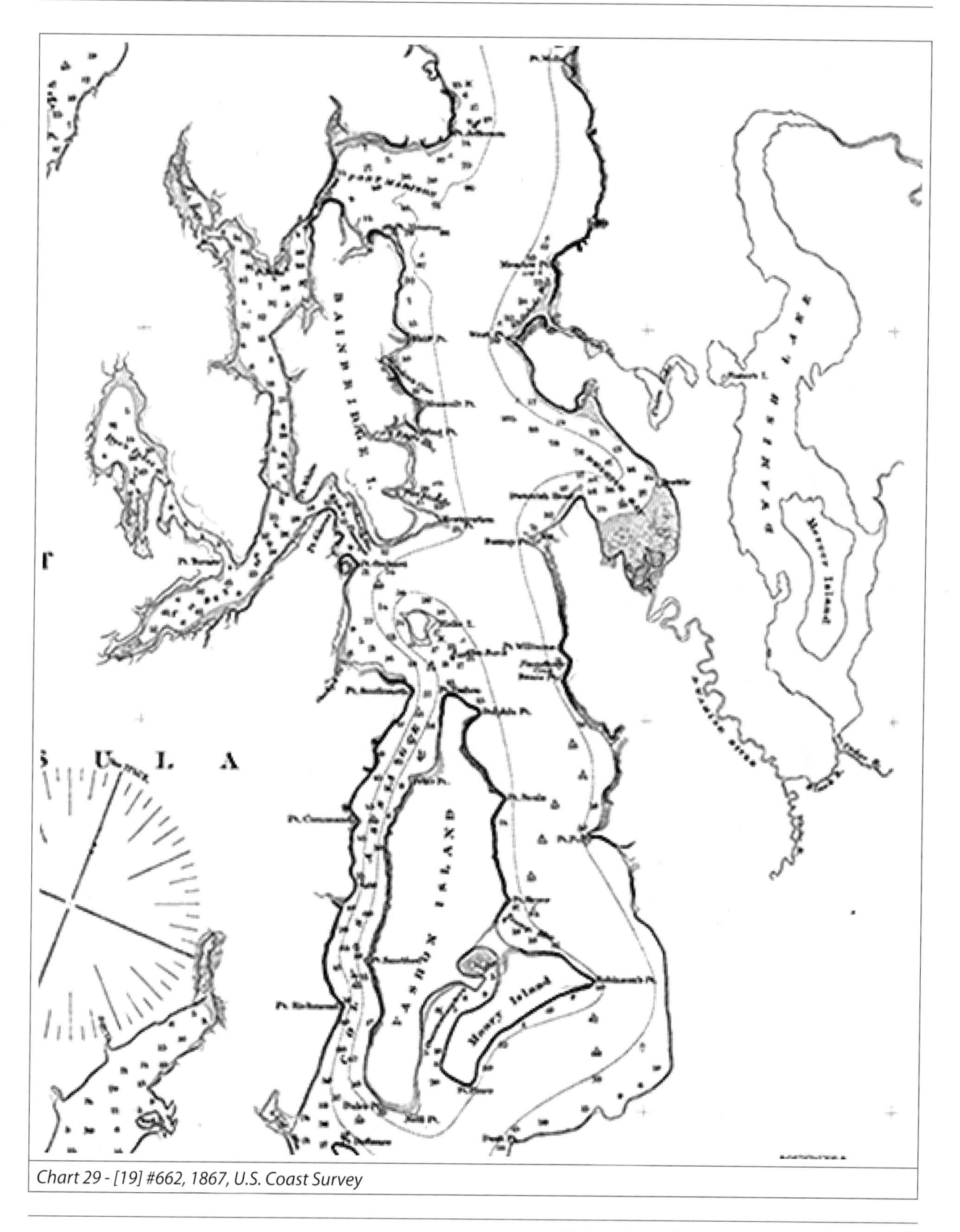

Chart 29 - [19] #662, 1867, U.S. Coast Survey

Appendix A - Charts

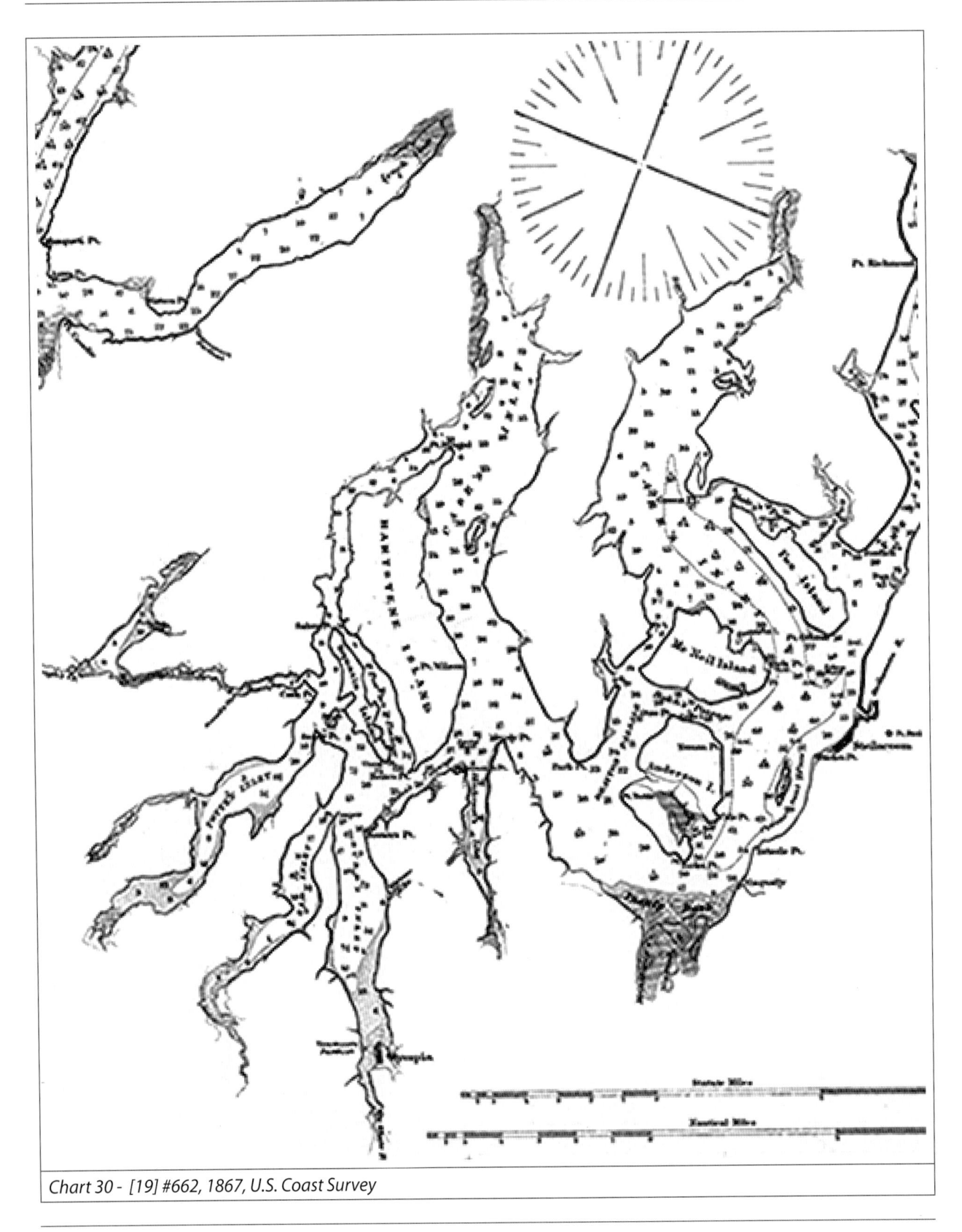

Chart 30 - [19] #662, 1867, U.S. Coast Survey

312 ♦ Maritime Place Names - Inland Washington Waters

APPENDIX B - LIST OF CHARTS

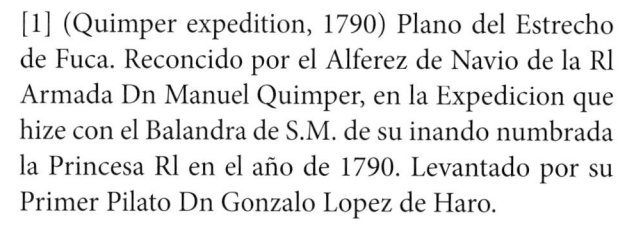

[1] (Quimper expedition, 1790) Plano del Estrecho de Fuca. Reconcido por el Alferez de Navio de la Rl Armada Dn Manuel Quimper, en la Expedicion que hize con el Balandra de S.M. de su inando numbrada la Princesa Rl en el año de 1790. Levantado por su Primer Pilato Dn Gonzalo Lopez de Haro.

[2] (Pantoja, Eliza expedition, 1791) Pequeñia Costa que comprehende los interiors, 7 veril de la Costa des de los 48 gs de Latd N Hasta los 50, examinados los expresados interiors con las prolixidad possible per los Pilotos del Port de su Magd, el Sn Carlos y Goleta Sta Saturnina mandordos ambos por el Teniente de Navis de la Rl Armada Dn Franco Eliza y descubierto el Gran Canal de Ntra Señora del Rosario por los mismos en la Goleta y Lancha del Pagt en este año de 91.

[3] (Eliza chart, 1791) Carta que comprehende los inteniones 7 veril de la Costa desde los 48° de Latitud N hasta los 50° examinados esciulosa mente por el Teniente de Navio de la Rl Armada Dn Franco Eliza Comandante del Pamicbot des SM Sn Carlos del porte 16 Cañones 7 Golita Sta Saturnina (Alias Orcacitas).

[4] Carta Reducida de una parte del Estrecho de Juan de Fuca y Canales Assembier tas en el por los Oficiales de Marina y Pilotos Españoles e Yngleses, que han navegado sobre la costas al N O de este America desde el año pasado de 1790 hasta el presente de 1793.

[5] Carta Esferica de los Reconocimientos Hechos En La Costa No. De America desde la parta en que empiezan á angostar Los Canales de la Entrada De Juan de Fuca hasta la salida de las Goletas Sutil y Mexicana. Año de 1793.

[6] A Chart shewing part of the Coast of N.W. America, with the tracks of His Majesty's Sloop Discovery and Armed Tender Chatham; Commanded by George Vancouver Esqr. And prepared under his immediate inspection by Lieut Joseph Baker, in which the continental Shore has been traced and determined from Lat 45.30°N and Long 236.12°E to Lat 52.15°N and 232.40°E at the different periods shewn by the Tracks. The parts not shaded are taken from Spanish Authorites.

[7a] #145, Archipelago of Arro, Gulf of Georgia, Ringgolds Channel and Straits of Fuca Oregon Territory, by the U.S. Ex. Ex. 1841.

[7b] #148, (3 separate charts) San Juan Harbor, Straits of Fuca, Vancouver Island by the U.S. Ex. Ex. 1841; Scarborough Harbor, Straits of Fuca, Oregon Territory by the U.S. Ex. Ex. 1841; Port Discovery. Straits of Fuca, Oregon Territory by the U.S. Ex. Ex. 1841.

[7c] #144, Straits of Juan de Fuca, Oregon Territory. From Surveys of the U.S. Ex. Ex. and Spanish and English Authorities. 1841.

[7d] #146, Chart of Admiralty Inlet, Puget Sound and Hoods Canal, Oregon Territory by the U.S. Ex. Ex. 1841.

[7e] #158, (3 separate charts) Deception Passage, Oregon Territory by the U.S. Ex. Ex. 1841; Penns Cove, Whidbys Island, Oregon Territory by the U.S. Ex. Ex. 1841; Holmes Harbour, Whidbys Island, Oregon Territory by the U.S. Ex. Ex. 1841.

[7f] #151, (2 separate charts) Port Ludlow, Hoods Canal, Oregon Territory by the U.S. Ex. Ex. 1841; Port Gamble, Hoods Canal, Oregon Territory by the U.S. Ex. Ex. 1841.

[7g] #155, The Narrows at the Entrance of Puget Sound with Commencement Bay, Colvos Passage and a part of Admiralty Inlet, Oregon Territory by the U.S. Ex. Ex. 1841.

[7h] #154, (2 separate charts) Case's Inlet, Puget Sound, Oregon Territory by the U.S. Ex. Ex. 1841; Carrs Inlet, Puget Sound, Oregon Territory by the U.S. Ex. Ex. 1841.

Appendix B - List of Charts

[7i] #147, Chart of Puget Sound, its Inlets and Anchorages by the U.S. Ex. Ex. 1841.

[7j] #153, (2 charts), Hooetzen Harbour, Hoods Canal, Oregon Territory by the U.S. Ex. Ex. 1841; Scabock Harbour, Hoods Canal, Oregon Territory by the U.S. Ex. Ex. 1841.

[7k] #152, (2 charts), Colsee-ed Harbour, Hoods Canal, Oregon Territory by the U.S. Ex. Ex. 1841; Suquamish Harbour, Hoods Canal, Oregon Territory by the U.S. Ex. Ex. 1841.

[7l] #159, (3 charts), Anchorage at Point Roberts, Oregon Territory by the U.S. Ex. Ex. 1841; Birch Bay, Oregon Territory by the U.S. Ex. Ex. 1841; Draytons Cove, Oregon Territory by the U.S. Ex. Ex. 1841.

[7m] #160, (4 charts), Hornets Harbour, Archipelago of Arro, Oregon Territory by the U.S. Ex. Ex. 1841; Argus Bay, Perry's Island, Oregon Territory by the U.S. Ex. Ex. 1841; Strawberry Bay, Archipelago of Arro, Oregon Territory by the U.S. Ex. Ex. 1841; Elliott Bay, Admiralty Inlet, Oregon Territory by the U.S. Ex. Ex. 1841.

[7n] #149, New Dungeness Roads and Budds Harbour, Straits of Fuca, Oregon Territory by the U.S. Ex. Ex. 1841.

[7o] #157, (4 separate charts) Pilot Cove, West Side Admiralty Inlet, Oregon Territory by the U.S. Ex. Ex. 1841; Port Gardner, Admiralty Inlet, Oregon Territory by the U.S. Ex. Ex. 1841; Apple Cove, West Side, Admiralty Inlet, Oregon Territory by the U.S. Ex. Ex. 1841; Port Susan, Oregon Territory by the U.S. Ex. Ex. 1841.

[7p] #150, Harbours in Admiralty Inlet, Oregon Territory by the U.S. Ex. Ex. 1841.

[7q] #156, Ports Orchard and Madison including the inlets and passages between them in Admiralty Inlet, Oregon Territory by the U.S. Ex. Ex. 1841.

[8a] #1917, North America. West Coast. Vancouver Island and the Gulf of Georgia from the Surveys of Captain G. Vancouver R.N. 1793 [sic], Captains D. Galiano and C. Valdéz 1792, Captain H. Kellett R.N. 1847. Pub Feb 28, 1847.

[8b] #1917, North America. West Coast. Vancouver Island and the Gulf of Georgia from the Surveys of Captain G. Vancouver R.N. 1793 [sic], Captains D. Galiano and C. Valdéz 1792, Captain H. Kellett R.N. 1847. Pub Feb 28, 1849 with corrections to 1858.

[8c] #1917, North America. West Coast. Vancouver Island and the Gulf of Georgia from the Surveys of Captain G. Vancouver R.N. 1793 [sic], Captains D. Galiano and C. Valdéz 1792, Captain H. Kellett R.N. 1847, Captain G. H. Richards R.N. 1859-61. Pub Feb 28, 1849 with corrections to 1859-61, June 1862.

[8d] #1917, North America. West Coast. Vancouver Island and adjacent shores of British Columbia surveyed by Captn. G. H. Richards, R.N. assisted by Lieut R. C. Mayne; J. A. Bull, D. Pender, E. P. Bedwell, Masters; J. T. Gowlland & G. A. Browning, Sec. Masters & E. Blunden, Mast. Asst. 1859-64. Juan de Fuca Strait from Capt. Henry Kellett's Survey of 1847. Shores of Washington Territory from the United States Coast Survey. Pub Sept. 25, 1865.

[8e] #1917, North America. West Coast. Vancouver Island and adjacent shores of British Columbia surveyed by Captn. G. H. Richards, R.N. assisted by Lieut R. C. Mayne; J. A. Bull, D. Pender, E. P. Bedwell, Masters; W. Blackney, Paymaster, J. T. Gowlland & G.A. Browning, Sec. Masters, & E. Blunden, Mast. Asst. 1859-65. Juan de Fuca Strait from Capt Henry Kellett's Survey of 1847. Shores of Washington Territory from the United States Coast Survey. Pub Sept. 25, 1865. Corrections to Aug 66, Dec 66.

[8f] #1917, North America. West Coast. Vancouver Island and adjacent shores of British Columbia surveyed by Captn. G. H. Richards, R.N. assisted by Lieut. R. C. Mayne; J.A. Bull, D. Pender, E. P. Bedwell, Masters; W. Blakeney, Paymaster, J. T. Gowlland & G. A. Browning, Sec. Masters, & E. Blunden, Mast. Asst. 1859-65. Juan de Fuca Strait from Capt Henry Kellett's Survey of 1847. Shores of Washington Territory from the United States Coast Survey. Pub Sept. 25, 1865. Corrections to Aug 66, Dec 66, Nov 71. Small corrections I 71, IV 71, II 72, V 74, VIII 74, III 75.

[8g] #1917, North America. West Coast. Vancouver Island and adjacent shores of British Columbia Surveyed by Captn. G. H. Richards, R.N. assisted by Lieut. R. C. Mayne; J. A. Bull, D. Pender, E. P. Bedwell, Masters; W Blakeney, Paymaster, J. T. Gowlland & G. A. Browning, Sec. Masters, & E. Blunden, Mast. Assist. 1859-65. Juan de Fuca Strait from Capt. Henry Kellett's Survey of 1847. Shores of Washington Territory from the United States Coast Survey. Pub Sept 25, 1865. Corrections to Aug 66, Dec 66, Nov 71. Small corrections I 71, IV 71, II 72, V 74, VIII 74, III 75, IV 76.

[8h] #1917, North America. West Coast. Vancouver Island and adjacent shores of British Columbia Surveyed by Captn. G. H. Richards, R.N. assisted by Lieut. R. C. Mayne; J. A. Bull, D. Pender, E. P. Bedwell, Masters; W Blakeney, Paymaster, J. T. Gowlland & G.A. Browning, Sec. Masters, & E. Blunden, Mast. Assist. 1859-65. Juan de Fuca Strait from Capt. Henry Kellett's Survey of 1847. Shores of Washington Territory from the United States Coast Survey. Pub Sept 25, 1865. Corrections to Aug 66, Dec 66, Nov 71. Small corrections I 71, IV 71, II 72, V 74, VIII 74, III 75, IV 76, XII 79.

[8i] #1917, North America. West Coast. Vancouver Island and adjacent shores of British Columbia Surveyed by Captn. G. H. Richards, R.N. assisted by Lieut. R. C. Mayne; J. A. Bull, D. Pender, E. P. Bedwell, Masters; W Blakeney, Paymaster, J. T. Gowlland & G. A. Browning, Sec. Masters, & E. Blunden, Mast. Assist. 1859-65. Juan de Fuca Strait from Capt. Henry Kellett's Survey of 1847. Shores of Washington Territory from the United States Coast Survey. Pub Sept 25, 1865. Small corrections III 75, IV 76, XII 79, I 83, VII 85, V 86, VI 86, XI 87, II 88, IX 88.

[8j] #1917, North America. West Coast. Vancouver Island and adjacent shores of British Columbia Surveyed by Captn. G. H. Richards, R.N. assisted by Lieut. R. C. Mayne; J.A. Bull, D. Pender, E. P. Bedwell, Masters; W Blakeney, Paymaster, J. T. Gowlland & G. A. Browning, Sec. Masters, & E. Blunden, Mast. Assist. 1859-65. Juan de Fuca Strait from Capt. Henry Kellett's Survey of 1847. Shores of Washington Territory from the United States Coast Survey. Pub Sept 25, 1865. Small corrections III 75, IV 76, XII 79, I 83, VII 85, V 86, VI 86, XI 87, II 88, IX 88, II 90, V 90.

[8k] #1917, North America. West Coast. Vancouver Island and adjacent shores of British Columbia Surveyed by Captn. G. H. Richards, R.N. assisted by Lieut. R. C. Mayne; J. A. Bull, D. Pender, E. P. Bedwell, Masters; W Blakeney, Paymaster, J. T. Gowlland & G. A. Browning, Sec. Masters, & E. Blunden, Mast. Assist. 1859-65. Juan de Fuca Strait from Capt. Henry Kellett's Survey of 1847. Shores of Washington Territory from the United States Coast Survey. Pub Sept 25, 1865. Large corrections Nov 1890. Small corrections III 75, IV 76, XII 79, I 83, VII 85, V 86, VI 86, XI 87, II 88, IX 88, II 90, V 90.

[8l] #1917, North America. West Coast. Vancouver Island and adjacent shores of British Columbia Surveyed by Captn. G. H. Richards, R.N. assisted by Lieut. R. C. Mayne; J. A. Bull, D. Pender, E. P. Bedwell, Masters; W Blakeney, Paymaster, J. T. Gowlland & G. A. Browning, Sec. Masters, & E. Blunden, Mast. Assist. 1859-65. Juan de Fuca Strait from Capt. Henry Kellett's Survey of 1847. Shores of Washington Territory from the United States Coast Survey. Pub Sept 25, 1865. Large corrections Nov 1890. Small corrections III 75, IV 76, XII 79, I 83, VII 85, V 86, VI 86, XI 87, II 88, IX 88, II 90, V 90, I 91, VII 91, VIII 91, IX 91.

[8m] #1917, North America. West Coast. Vancouver Island and adjacent shores of British Columbia Surveyed by Captn. G. H. Richards, R.N. assisted by Lieut. R. C. Mayne; J. A. Bull, D. Pender, E. P. Bedwell, Masters; W Blakeney, Paymaster, J. T. Gowlland & G. A. Browning, Sec. Masters, & E. Blunden, Mast. Assist. 1859-65. Juan de Fuca Strait from Capt. Henry Kellett's Survey of 1847. Shores of Washington Territory from the United States Coast Survey. Pub Sept 25, 1865. Large corrections Nov 1890. Small corrections III 75, IV 76, XII 79, I 83, VII 85, V 86, VI 86, XI 87, II 88, IX 88, II 90, V 90, I 91, VII 91, VIII 91, IX 91, V 92, IX 92.

[8n] #1917, North America. West Coast. Vancouver Island and adjacent shores of British Columbia Surveyed by Captn. G. H. Richards, R.N. assisted by Lieut. R. C. Mayne; J. A. Bull, D. Pender, E. P. Bedwell, Masters; W Blakeney, Paymaster, J. T. Gowlland & G. A. Browning, Sec. Masters, & E. Blunden, Mast. Assist. 1859-65. Juan de Fuca Strait from Capt.

Appendix B - List of Charts

Henry Kellett's Survey of 1847. Shores of Washington Territory from the United States Coast Survey. Pub Sept 25, 1865. Large corrections to Nov 1890. Small corrections III 75, IV 76, XII 79, I 83, VII 85, V 86, VI 86, XI 87, II 88, IX 88, II 90, V 90, I 91, VII 91, VIII 91, IX 91, V 92, IX 92, III 93, IX 93.

[8o] #1917, North America. West Coast. Vancouver Island and adjacent shores of British Columbia Surveyed by Captn. G. H. Richards, R.N. assisted by Lieut. R. C. Mayne; J. A. Bull, D. Pender, E. P. Bedwell, Masters; W Blakeney, Paymaster, J. T. Gowlland & G. A. Browning, Sec. Masters, & E. Blunden, Mast. Assist. 1859-65. Juan de Fuca Strait from Capt. Henry Kellett's Survey of 1847. Shores of Washington Territory from the United States Coast Survey. Pub Sept 25, 1865. Large corrections to Nov 1890. Small corrections III 75, IV 76, XII 79, I 83, VII 85, V 86, VI 86, XI 87, II 88, IX 88, II 90, V 90, I 91, VII 91, VIII 91, IX 91, V 92, IX 92, III 93, IX 93, X 94, VIII 95.

[8p] #1917, North America. West Coast. Vancouver Island and adjacent shores of British Columbia Surveyed by Captn. G. H. Richards, R.N. assisted by Lieut. R. C. Mayne; J. A. Bull, D. Pender, E. P. Bedwell, Masters; W Blakeney, Paymaster, J. T. Gowlland & G. A. Browning, Sec. Masters, & E. Blunden, Mast. Assist. 1859-65. Juan de Fuca Strait from Capt. Henry Kellett's Survey of 1847. Shores of Washington Territory from the United States Coast Survey. Pub Sept 25, 1865. Large corrections to Nov 1890. Small corrections VI 96, VII 96, IX 96, X 97, XII 97, III 98, IV 98, V 98, VI 98, VIII 98, IX 98, X 98, XI 98, V 99, VIII 99.

[8q] #1917, North America. West Coast. Vancouver Island and adjacent shores of British Columbia Surveyed by Captn. G. H. Richards, R.N. assisted by Lieut. R. C. Mayne; J. A. Bull, D. Pender, E. P. Bedwell, Masters; W Blakeney, Paymaster, J. T. Gowlland & G. A. Browning, Sec. Masters, & E. Blunden, Mast. Assist. 1859-65. Juan de Fuca Strait from Capt. Henry Kellett's Survey of 1847. Shores of Washington Territory from the United States Coast Survey. Pub Sept 25, 1865. Large corrections to Nov 1890 and Feb 1900. Small corrections VI 96, VII 96, IX 96, X 97, XII 97, III 98, IV 98, V 98, VI 98, VIII 98, IX 98, X 98, XI 98, V 99, VIII 99, 00IX 00.

[9a] #1911, America. N.W. Coast. Strait of Juan de Fuca. Surveyed by Captain Henry Kellett, R.N. 1847. Admiralty Inlet and Puget Sound by the U.S. Ex. Ex 1841. Pub Jan. 18, 1849.

[9b] #1911, America. N.W. Coast. Strait of Juan de Fuca. Surveyed by Captain Henry Kellett, R.N. 1847. Haro & Rosario Straits by Captain G. H. Richards, R.N. 1858. Admiralty Inlet and Puget Sound by the United States Exploring Expedition, 1841. Pub Jan 18, 1849. Corrections to 1861.

[9c] #1911, America. N.W. Coast. Strait of Juan de Fuca. Surveyed by Captain Henry Kellett, R.N. 1847. Haro & Rosario Straits by Captain G. H. Richards, R.N. 1858. Admiralty Inlet and Puget Sound by the United States Exploring Expedition, 1841. Pub Jan 18, 1849. Corrections & Additions Aug 1861, Feb 65.

[9d] #1911, America. N.W. Coast. Strait of Juan de Fuca. Surveyed by Captain Henry Kellett, R.N. 1847. Haro & Rosario Straits by Captain G. H. Richards, R.N. 1858. Admiralty Inlet and Puget Sound by the United States Exploring Expedition, 1841. Pub Jan 18, 1849. Corrections & Additions Aug 1861, Feb 65. Small corrections X 66, V 67, II 68.

[9e] #1911, America. N.W. Coast. Strait of Juan de Fuca. Surveyed by Captain Henry Kellett, R.N. 1847. Haro & Rosario Straits by Captain G. H. Richards, R.N. 1858. Admiralty Inlet and Puget Sound by the United States Exploring Expedition, 1841. Pub Jan 18, 1849. Corrections & Additions Aug 1861, Feb 65. Small corrections I 71, IV 71, XII 71, II 72.

[9f] #1911, America. N.W. Coast. Strait of Juan de Fuca. Surveyed by Captain Henry Kellett, R.N. 1847. Haro & Rosario Straits by Captain G. H. Richards, R.N. 1858. Admiralty Inlet and Puget Sound by the United States Exploring Expedition, 1841. Pub Jan 18, 1849. Corrections & Additions Aug 1861, Feb 65. Small corrections I 71, IV 71, XII 71, II 72, VII 74.

[9g] #1911, North America-West Coast. Juan de Fuca Strait from the latest Admiralty surveys 1883. Additions & corrections from United States' Charts to 1889. Pub July 12, 1883. Large corrections Oct 1890. Small corrections XI 85, V 86, VI 86, IX 88, V89, V90, XI 90.

[10] #51 U.S. Coast Survey. A. D. Bache Supdt. Reconnaissance of Canal de Haro & Strait of Rosario and Approaches. Geographical positions & triangulation by G. Davidson Assist. Hydrography by the Party under the command of Lieut J. Alden U.S.N. Assist. 1854.

[11] #654 U.S. Coast Survey. A. D. Bache Superintendent Coast Survey. Reconnaissance of Washington Sound and approaches, Washington Territory. Triangulation and topography by G. Davidson Asst. and J. S. Lawson Sub-Assistant. Hydrography by the Parties under the command of Comdr. J. Alden and Lieut. R. M Cuyler U.S.N. Assists. 1858. (Note: This chart is actually unnumbered. However, I assume it should carry #654 as it has a similar title and covers the same area as its counterpart [18].)

[12] North America West Coast. Haro and Rosario Straits. Surveyed by Captn. G. H. Richards, & the Officers of the H.M.S. Plumper. 1858-9. The shores of Juan de Fuca Strait to Admiralty Inlet from Captn. H. Kellett's Survey, 1847. (This chart was apparently re-engraved in the United States but carries no publishing date.)

[13a] #2689 North America. West Coast. Haro and Rosario Straits. Surveyed by Captn. G. H. Richards & the Officers of H.M.S. Plumper 1858-9. The shores of Juan de Fuca Strait to Admiralty Inlet from Captn. H. Kellett's Survey, 1847. Pub July 28, 1859.

[13b] #2689 North America. West Coast. Haro and Rosario Straits Surveyed by Captn. G. H. Richards & the Officers of H.M.S. Plumper 1858-9. The shores of Juan de Fuca Strait to Admiralty Inlet from Captn. H. Kellett's Survey, 1847. Pub July 28, 1859. Corrections to 1861.

[13c] #2689 North America. West Coast. Haro and Rosario Straits Surveyed by Captn. G. H. Richards & the Officers of H.M.S. Plumper 1858-9. The shores of Juan de Fuca Strait to Admiralty Inlet from Captn. H. Kellett's Survey, 1847. Pub July 28, 1859. Corrections to Septr. 1864. Feb 65.

[13d] #2689 North America. West Coast. Haro and Rosario Straits Surveyed by Captn. G. H. Richards & the Officers of H.M.S. Plumper 1858-9. The shores of Juan de Fuca Strait to Admiralty Inlet from Captn. H. Kellett's Survey, 1847. Pub July 28, 1859. Corrections to Septr. 1864. Feb 65. Small corrections to V 70, XI 70, I 71, IV 71, XII 71, XI 72, VII 74.

[13e] #2689 North America. West Coast. Haro and Rosario Straits. Surveyed by Captn. G. H. Richards & the Officers of H.M.S. Plumper 1858-9. The shores of Juan de Fuca Strait to Admiralty Inlet from Captn. H. Kellett's Survey, 1847. Pub July 28, 1859. Corrections to Septr. 1864. Feb 65. Small corrections to V 70, XI 70, I 71, IV 71, XII 71, XI 72, VII 74. (From all appearances, this is a duplicate of [13d].)

[13f] #2689 North America. West Coast. Haro and Rosario Straits. Surveyed by Captn. G. H. Richards & the Officers of H.M.S. Plumper 1858-9. The shores of Juan de Fuca Strait to Admiralty Inlet from Captn. H. Kellett's Survey, 1847. The East Coast of Rosario Strait from Bellingham Bay to Admiralty Inlet from U.S. Surveys to 1856. Pub. Aug 22, 1882. (The lower left corner of this chart is torn. Thus, it is impossible to read the small corrections. It is likely 1885 as it was published in 1882 and [13g] carries small corrections to 1886.)

[13g] #2689 North America-West Coast. Haro and Rosario Straits. Surveyed by Captn. G. H. Richards, H.M.S. Plumper, 1858-9. assisted by Lieutt. R. C. Mayne; J. A. Bull, & D. Pender, Masters; E. P. Bedwell, J. Gowlland & G.A. Browning and E. Blunden, Secd. Masters, R.N. additions to 1882. Pub Aug 22, 1882. Small corrections VII 85, XI 85, V 86, VI 86.

[13h] #2689 North America-West Coast. Haro and Rosario Straits. Surveyed by Captn. G. H. Richards, H.M.S. Plumper, 1858-9. assisted by Lieutt. R. C. Mayne; J. A. Bull, & D. Pender, Masters; E. P. Bedwell, J. Gowlland & G. A. Browning and E. Blunden, Secd. Masters, R.N. additions to 1882. Pub Aug 22, 1882. Small corrections VII 85, XI 85, V 86, VI 86, XI 87, II 88.

[13i] #2689 North America-West Coast. Haro and Rosario Straits. Surveyed by Captn. G. H. Richards, H.M.S. Plumper, 1858-9. assisted by Lieutt. R. C. Mayne; J. A. Bull, & D. Pender, Masters; E. P. Bedwell, J. Gowlland & G. A. Browning and E. Blunden, Secd. Masters, R.N. additions to 1882. Pub Aug 22, 1882.

Appendix B - List of Charts

Large corrections to Jan 1892. Small corrections VII 85, XI 85, V 86, VI 86, XI 87, II 88, VIII 89, XII 89, V 90, IX 90, X 90, VIII 91. (Due to the fragility of the copy at Victoria Archives, this chart was unavailable to me. Thus, I was unable to check on several place names.)

[13j] #2689 North America-West Coast. Haro and Rosario Straits. Surveyed by Captn. G. H. Richards, H.M.S. Plumper, 1858-9. assisted by Lieutt. R. C. Mayne; J. A. Bull, & D. Pender, Masters; E. P. Bedwell, J. Gowlland & G. A. Browning and E. Blunden, Secd. Masters, R.N. additions to 1882. Pub Aug 22, 1882. Large Corrections May 1891, Jan 1892, June 1893, May 1894. Small corrections VII 85, XI 85, V 86, VI 86, XI 87, II 88, VIII 89, XII 89, V 90, IX 90, X 90, VIII 91, IV 92, V 92, VII 92, I 93, II 93, III 93, VIII 93, IX 93, X 93, XI 93, III 94.

[13k] #2689 North America-West Coast. Haro and Rosario Straits. Surveyed by Captn. G. H. Richards, H.M.S. Plumper, 1858-9. assisted by Lieutt. R. C. Mayne; J. A. Bull, & D. Pender, Masters; E. P. Bedwell, J. Gowlland & G. A. Browning and E. Blunden, Secd. Masters, R.N. additions to 1889. Pub Aug 22, 1882. Large Corrections May 1891, Jan 1892, June 1893, May 1894, Dec 1896, and Feb 1900. Small corrections VII 94, VIII 94, I 95, II 95, III 95, IV 95, VII 95, X 95, IV 96, VII 96, IX 96, X 96, V 97, VI 98, IX 98, X 98, XI 98, I 99, V 99, VI 99, VIII 99, I 00, III 00.

[13l] (In the Victoria Archive index, this is listed as c.2 or copy 2. It has the identical fiche number and thus is a duplicate of [13k] even though it is listed as a separate entry.)

[13m] #2689 North America-West Coast. Haro and Rosario Straits. Surveyed by Captn. G. H. Richards, H.M.S. Plumper, 1858-9. assisted by Lieutt. R. C. Mayne; J. A. Bull, & D. Pender, Masters; E. P. Bedwell, J. Gowlland & G. A. Browning and E. Blunden, Secd. Masters, R.N. additions to 1889. Pub Aug 22, 1882. Large Corrections May 1891, Jan 1892, June 1893, May 1894, Dec 1896, Feb 1900, Dec 1900, Jan 1904. Small corrections VII 94, VIII 94, I 95, II 95, III 95, IV 95, VII 95, X 95, IV 96, VII 96, IX 96, X 96, V 97, VI 98, IX 98, X 98, XI 98, I 99, V 99, VI 99, VIII 99, I 00, III 00, IV 00, VI 00, IX 00, V 01, VI 01, IX 01, II 02, VI 02, VI 03, XII 03, III 04, V 04, VII 04.

[13n] #2689 North America-West Coast. Haro and Rosario Straits. Surveyed by Captn. G. H. Richards, H.M.S. Plumper, 1858-9. assisted by Lieutt. R. C. Mayne; J. A. Bull, & D. Pender, Masters; E. P. Bedwell, J. Gowlland & G. A. Browning and E. Blunden, Secd. Masters, R.N. additions to 1889. Pub Aug 22, 1882. Large Corrections May 1891, Jan 1892, June 1893, May 1894, Dec 1896, Feb 1900, Dec 1900, Jan 1904. Small corrections VII 94, VIII 94, I 95, II 95, III 95, IV 95, VII 95, X 95, IV 96, VII 96, IX 96, X 96, V 97, VI 98, IX 98, X 98, XI 98, I 99, V 99, VI 99, VIII 99, I 00, III 00, IV 00, VI 00, IX 00, V 01, VI 01, IX 01, II 02, VI 02, VI 03, XII 03, III 04, V 04, VII 04, XI 04, II 05, V 05, VII 05, VIII 05, IX 05, X 05, XII 05, I 06, III 06, IV 06, V 06, VII 06 X 06, XI 06, I 07, III 07, IV 07, VI 07, VIII 07, X 07, XI 07, XII 07, I 08, V 08, VI 08, VII 08, VIII 08.

[14a] #2840 North America West Coast. Haro Strait and Middle Channel. Surveyed by Captn. G. H. Richards & the Officers of HMS Plumper 1858-60. Additional to 1861. Pub November 26, 1861. (This chart has been particularly elusive. It was not available at the British Columbia Archives in Victoria or the University of British Columbia collection in Vancouver. It was also not available from the Canadian Hydrographic Office or the National Archives in Ottawa. The United Kingdom Hydrographic Office reported that they do not have the first issue. The British Library, the National Archives, the National Maritime Museum, and the Royal Geographic Society, all of London, did not have the first issue. Dr. Andrew S. Cook from the Dalrymple Research Institute checked the collections of Cambridge University Library, the Bodleian Library at Oxford, the National Library of Scotland and the Bibliotheque Nationale de France in Paris, all without success. NOAA Central Library historians and archivists have no idea where to obtain a copy. It is not available at the Geography and Map Division of the Library of Congress, the American Geographical Society Library, the Naval Observatory Library, the Smithsonian Institution Libraries, the U.S. Geological Survey Library, the Navy Department Library, the National Library of Australia, Deutsche Nationalbibliothek, or the Russian National Library.

The second edition of this chart was dated June 1862 and is readily available. Dr. Cook speculated that with the second edition coming just seven months after the first, that perhaps there was no public issue of the November 1861 edition. And that might explain why a copy cannot be found. Just as all hope was nearly lost, Mr. Guy Hannaford of the United Kingdom Hydrographic Office located a copy. As Mr. Hannaford noted: "It is heavily annotated with secondary surveying activities and referenced [in hand] as 'Additional to 1861.'")

[14b] #2840, North America West Coast. Haro Strait and Middle Channel surveyed by Captn. G. H. Richards & the Officers of H.M.S. Plumper 1858-60. Published November 26, 1861. Corrections to June 1862.

[14c] #2840, North America West Coast. Haro Strait and Middle Channel. Surveyed by Captn. G. H. Richards & the Officers of H.M.S. Plumper 1858-60. With additions and corrections to 1861. Pub November 26, 1861. Corrections to Sept 1864, Feb 1865, June 69, May 70. Small corrections IV 9, XI 66, XII 66, V 70.

[14d] #2840, North America West Coast. Haro Strait and Middle Channel. Surveyed by Captn. G. H. Richards & the Officers of H.M.S. Plumper 1858-60. With additions and corrections to 1861. Pub November 26, 1861. Corrections to Sept 1864, Feb 1865, June 69, May 70, Nov 72.

[14e] #2840, North America West Coast. Haro Strait and Middle Channel. Surveyed by Captn. G. H. Richards. Assisted by Lieutt. R. C. Mayne; J. A. Bull & D. Pender, Masters; E. P. Bedwell, 2nd Master. H.M.S. Plumper 1858-60. with corrections by D. Pender Navg Lieutt 1868. Pub Nov 26, 1861. Large corrections Nov 1872, June 1893, May 1896, Dec 99, May 1900, Dec 1900, Aug 1902, Oct 1903, Aug 1904, Oct 1906. Small corrections VII 85, V 86, VI 86, XI 87, II 88, VIII 89, XII 89, V 90, IX 90, VIII 91, VII 92, I 93, VIII 93, IX 93, XI 93, IV 95, X 95, VI 96, IX 96, X 96, I 99, V 99, VIII 99, I 00, III 00, IV 00, VI 00, XII 00, V 01, VI 01, IX 01, II 02, VI 02, XII 02, VI 03, XI 03, III 04, II 05, VII 05, VIII 05, IX 05, X 05, XII 05, IV, 06, V 06, VII 06, X 06.

[15a] #611, Haro Archipelago between Vancouver I. & the United States. Middle Channel – East Side of San Juan Island. Griffin Bay and Adjacent Anchorages. Surveyed by Captn. G. H. Richards, R.N. and the officers of H.M.S. Plumper. 1858. Pub Aug. 30, 1865.

[15b] #611, Haro Archipelago between Vancouver I. & the United States. Middle Channel – East Side of San Juan Island. Griffin Bay and Adjacent Anchorages. Surveyed by Captn. G. H. Richards, R.N. and the officers of H.M.S. Plumper. 1858. Pub Aug. 30, 1865. Small correction III 81.

[16a] #602, Haro Strait – West Side of San Juan Island. Roche Harbour and its Approaches. Surveyed by Captn. G. H. Richards, R.N. and the Officers of H.M.S. Plumper 1857. Pub Sept. 30, 1865.

[16b] #602, Haro Strait – West Side of San Juan Island. Roche Harbour and its Approaches. Surveyed by Captn. G. H. Richards, R.N. and the Officers of H.M.S. Plumper 1857. Additions by Staff Comr. Pender R.N. 1869. Pub 1865 with corrections to 1869.

[16c] #602, North America-West Coast. Haro Strait – San Juan Island. Roche Harbour and Approaches. From the United States Government Survey, 1894-5. Pub Nov 21, 1902. Small corrections VI 08, XI 11, 1919-1921.

[17] #27, Reconnaissance of Washington Sound and Approaches. Washington Territory. 1862.

[18] #654, Washington Sound and Approaches. Washington Territory. 1866.

[19] #662, Puget Sound. Washington Territory. 1867
U.S. Coast Survey Harbor Charts

[20a] #6376, Reconnaissance of Bellingham Bay, Washington by the Hydrographic party under the command of Lieut. Comdg. J. Alden U.S.N. Asst. 1856.

[20b] #655, Reconnaissance of Blakely Harbor, Washington Ter. By the Hydrographic party under the command of Lieut. Comdg. J. Alden U.S.N. Asst. 1856.

[20c] #651, Reconnaissance of Duwamish Bay and Seattle Harbor, Washington Ter. By the Hydrographic party under the command of Lieut. Comdg. J. Alden U.S.N. Asst. 1854.

Appendix B - List of Charts

[20d] #35, Port Gamble, Washington Ter. From a Trigonometrical Survey under the direction of A. D. Bache Superintendent of the Survey of the Coast of the United States. Triangulation by G. Davidson Assistant. Topography by J.S. Lawson Sub Assistant. Hydrography by the party under the command of Comdr. James Alden U.S.N. Assist. 1859.

[20e] #53, Reconnaissance of False Dungeness Harbor, Washington. By the Hydrographic Party under the command of Lieut. James Alden U.S.N. Assist. 1853.

[20f] #654, Cape Flattery and Neé-ah Harbor, Washington. Topography by G. Davidson Assistant USCS. Hydrography by the Party under the command of Lieut. James Alden U.S.N Assistant. 1853.

[20g] #647, Port Townsend, Washington. From a Trigonometrical Survey under the direction of A. D. Bache Superintendent of the Survey of the Coat of the United States. Triangulation by G. Davidson Asst. Topography by J.S. Lawson Sub Asst. Hydrography by the party under the command of Comdr. James Alden U.S.N. Asst. undated (The chart indicates that triangulation occurred in 1855, base measured in 1856, topography in 1856 and hydrography in 1854.)

[20h] #653, Reconnaissance of Olympia Harbor, Washington Ter. By the Hydrographic Party under the command of Lieut, Comdg. J. Alden U.S.N. Assist. 1856.

[20i] #6410, Preliminary Survey of Port Ludlow, Washington. Triangulation by G. Davidson Assistant. Topography by J.S. Lawson Sub-Asst. Hydrography by the Party under the command of Lieut. Comdg. James Alden U.S.N. Asst. 1856.

[20j] #6399, Reconnaissance of Semi-ah-moo Bay, Washington. By the Hydrographic Party under the command of Lieut. Comdg. R. M. Cuyler U.S.N. Asst. 1857.

[21] #6300, Gulf of Georgia and Strait of Juan de Fuca. United States Coast and Geodetic Survey. 1895.

[22] #6450, Admiralty Inlet and Puget Sound to Seattle. United States Coast and Geodetic Survey. Feb. 1905 with additions through 1909. (Note: I have identified in the text that certain place names first appeared on this 1909 chart. As I was unable to locate a copy of the 1905 chart, I was unable to confirm if the place names also appeared there.)

[23] #6460, Puget Sound to Olympia. United States Coast and Geodetic Survey. 1891 corrected to 1905. (Note: I have identified in the text that certain place names first appeared on this 1905 chart. As I was unable to locate a copy of the 1891 chart, I was unable to confirm if the place names also appeared there.)

[24] #1947, America. West Coast. Puget Sound by R. M. Inskip N.I. 1846. Pub Oct 11, 1849.

APPENDIX C - LIST OF NAMES

After completing this book, I concluded that it could be improved as a reference tool. If one stumbled across a place name, the alpha order of the book allows easy access to the name. However, it may be of interest to the reader, while looking at inland charts or maps or while wandering around our waters, to wonder if there is a "hidden" name between two identified locations, perhaps one that is not reflected on the chart either because there was not enough room, because it was a local name, or because the name was simply not recognized by the U.S. Board on Geographic Names. This book provides no help as one needs to know the name first before learning more about it. Thus, this appendix.

I have generally sequenced all of the major names (variants are excluded) in the order that they would be encountered while cruising our inland waters. The list starts at the entrance of the Strait of Juan de Fuca, continues eastward, then southward into Admiralty Inlet, Hood Canal, and counterclockwise through the remainder of Puget Sound. The list continues to the north into Saratoga Passage and along Whidbey Island. It then jumps to San Juan County followed by Island County. The final section starts at the Canadian Border and runs past Bellingham into Padilla Bay.

This "reverse directory" hopefully provides easy access to all of the names.

Strait of Juan de Fuca
Fuca Pillar
Tatoosh Island
Hole in the Wall
Jones Rock
Cape Flattery
Mushroom Rock
Chibahdehl Rocks
Warmhouse Beach
Kydikabbit Point
Neah Bay
Koitlah Point
Point Newell
Waadah Island
Point Lewhough
Baada Point
First Beach
Dtokoah Point
Second Beach
Klachopis Point
Third Beach
Kashukud'dil Point
Scarborough Point
Seal Rock

Sail Rock
Sail River
Bird Rock
Rasmussen Creek
Shipwreck Point
Sekiu River
Hoko River
Kydaka Point
Sekiu Point
Eagle Point
Hygedith
Clallam Bay & River
Middle Point
Slip Point
Pillar Point
Ketsoth
Pysht
Tree Bluff
W Twin River
Twin
E Twin River
Lyre River
Low Point
Gettysburg

Agate Bay
Crescent Rock
Crescent Head
Crescent Bay & Port
Tongue Point
Stripped Peak
Observatory Point
Freshwater Bay
Coville Creek
Elwha River
Angeles Point
Port Angeles
Ediz Hook
Morse Creek
Morse Point
Green Point
Pandora Reef
Dungeness Bay
Dungeness
Dungeness Shoal
Santa Cruz
Old Town
Dungeness Spit
Graveyard Spit

Dungeness River
Cline Spit
Jamestown
Kulakala Point
Sawash Bluff
Bertodano Cove
Grays Marsh
Port Williams
Gibson Spit
The Lagoon
Washington Harbor
Sequim Bay
The Middle Ground
Pitship Point
Johnson Creek
Schoolhouse Point
Blyn
Goose Point
Hardwick Point
Paradise Cove
Kiapot Point
Travis Spit
Miller Peninsula
Rocky Point

321

Appendix C - List of Names

Thompson Spit
Diamond Point
Protection Island
Daisy Bluff
Violet Point
Discovery Bay
Eagle Creek
Gardiner
Contractors Point
Contractors Creek
Kalset Point
Mill Point
Mount Chatham
Port Discovery
Scorpus Point
Maynard
Salmon Creek
Discovery Junction
Fairmont
Tala Point
Camp Point
Woodmans
Quimper Peninsula
Adelma Beach
Chinook
Tukey
Double Point
McGees
Beckett Point
Cape George
McCurdy Point
Point Ross
Point Wilson

Port Townsend, Marrowstone area
Point Wilson
Fort Warden
Port Townsend
Chetzemoka Park
Point Hudson
Oluman Bluff
Glen Cove
Weh Weh Point
Kala Point
Kuhn Spit

Chimacum Creek
Irondale
Port Hadlock
Skunk Island
Sapip Point
Port Townsend Canal
Portage Canal
Chimacum Portage
Craven Peninsula
Indian Island
Crane Point
Walan Point
Walan Entrance
Kilisut Harbor
Bishops Point
Jorgenson Hill
Scow Bay
Mystery Bay
Nordland
Griffiths Point
Jack Point
Marrowstone Point
Midchannel Bank
Fort Flagler
Craven Rock
Nodule Point
Liplip Point
Kinney Point
Oak Bay
Leku Beach

Port Ludlow area
Oak Bay
Snas Point
Olele Point
Mats Mats
Klas Rock
Basalt Point
Colvos Rocks
Snake Rock
Jones Bluff
Port Ludlow
Burner Point
Tit Point
Hallets Cove
The Twins

Bulls Head
Tala Point

Hood Canal
Tala Point
White Rock
Hood Head
Point Hannon
Bywater Bay
Termination Point
Rock Island
Sisters
Suquamish Harbor
Yulkat Bluff
Shine
Case Shoal
Kakua
Bridgehaven
South Point
Thorndyke Lake
Thorndyke Bay
Toandos Peninsula
Brown Point
Hazel Point
Coyle
Fisherman Harbor
Oak Head
Tskutsko Point
Dabob Bay
Long Spit
Broad Spit
Zelatched Point
Tabook Point
Camp Harmony
Camp Discovery
Long Point
Tarboo Bay
Broad Spit
Bolton Peninsula
Red Bluff
Fishermans Point
Quilcene Bay
Point Yakso
Little Quilcene River
Big Quilcene River
Frenchmans Point

Bramblebluff
Whitney Point
Pulali Point
Jackson Cove
Rocky Bluff
Double Heads
Musam Place
Camp Parsons
Naika Point
Marple Point
Jackson Creek
Wawa Point
Right Smart Cove
Turner Creek
Seal Rock
Sylopash Point
Dosewallips River
Jupiter Hills
Brinnon
Olo Bluff
Palisi Point
Pleasant Harbor
Pasisi Point
Slik Point
Boston Point
Sakali Point
Black Point
Quatsap Point
Duckabush
McDaniel Cove
Fulton Creek
Triton Cove
Triton Head
Cummings Point
Hamma Hamma River
Eldon
Ayock Point
Eagle Creek
Lilliwaup Bay & River
Sund Creek
Miller Creek
Clark Creek
Hoodsport
Potlatch
Neelim Point
The Great Bend

322 ♦ Maritime Place Names - Inland Washington Waters

Appendix C - List of Names

Point Crowlie
Annas Bay
Indian Hole
Skokomish River
Union
Alderbrook
Shady Beach
Sunset Beach
Lynch Cove
Belfair
Union River
Mission Creek
Sunbeach
Stimpson Creek
Lake Tahuya
The Narrows
Sisters Point
Tahuya
Ayres Point
Musqueti Point
Rendsland Creek
Mustakumwode
Cougar Spit
Red Bluff
Long Point
Dadah Point
Dewatto Bay
Little Dewatto
Capstan Rock
Chinom Point
Holly
Anderson Cove
Tekiu Point
Nellita
Frenchmans Cove
Boyce Creek
Hood Point
Stavis Bay
Maple Beach
Scenic Beach
Miami Beach
Seabeck
Misery Point
Makak Point
Wikat Point
Mountain View

Little Beef Harbor
Big Beef Harbor
Warrenville
Lone Rock
Bangor
King Spit
Vinland
Breidablik
Lofall
Salsbury Point
Teekalet Bluff
Totten's Point
Port Gamble
Little Boston
Point Julia
Coon Bay
Races Cove
Twin Spits
Foulweather Bluff

Admiralty Inlet, W side
Foulweather Bluff
Skunk Bay
Hansville
Norwegian Point
Point No Point
Pilot Point
Eglon
Rose Point
Applecove Point
Blossom Point
Appletree Cove
Kingston
Whisper Creek
Kingston Creek
Fukuzawa Creek
Carpenter Creek
Crabapple Creek
Kingfisher Creek
President Point
Landmark
Point Jefferson
Indianola
Miller Bay
Hyland Spit
Clam Island

Suquamish
Agate Passage
Agate Point
West Port Madison
Port Madison
Treasure Island
Point Monroe
Hedley Spit
Rolling Bay
Skiff Point
Murden Cove
Ferncliff
Yeomalt Point
Wing Point
Eagle Harbor
Hawley
Hornbecks Spit
Winslow
Eagledale
Creosote
Bill Point
Tyee Shoal
Blakely Harbor
Port Blakely
Blakely Rock
Restoration Point
Decatur Reef
Bainbridge Reef
South Beach
Beans Point
Fort Ward
Rich Passage
Orchard Rocks
Pleasant Beach
West Blakely
Lynwood Center
Point White
Point Glover
Wautauga Beach
Middle Point
Clam Bay
Point Tatugh (Blake I.)
Orchard Point
Manchester
Colchester
Yukon Harbor

Colby
South Colby
Curley Creek
Harper
Southworth
Blake Island
Point Southworth
Colvos Passage
Wilson Creek
Driftwood Cove
View Park
Fragaria
Command Point
Anderson Point
Prospect Point
Olalla
Maplewood
Point Richmond
Sunrise Beach
Gig Harbor
Millville
Jerisich Park
Point Evans

Port Orchard
Agate Pass
Seabold
Manzanita
Miemois Creek
Arrow Point
Venice
Battle Point
Tolo
Fletcher Bay
Issei Creek
Gazzam Lake
Crystal Springs
Point White
Point Glover
Waterman Point
Sinclair Inlet
Retsil
Annapolis
Port Orchard
Ross Point
Gorst

Richard W. Blumenthal ♦ 323

Appendix C - List of Names

Bremerton
Point Turner
Port Washington
Narrows
Dyes Inlet
Anderson Cove
Phinney Bay
Bass Point
Rocky Point
Mud Bay
Ostrich Bay
Madrona Point
Oyster Bay
Elwood Point
Erlands Point
Chico Bay
Chico
Silverdale
Pahrmann Creek
Windy Point
Fairview
Tracyton
Manette
Point Herron
Enetai & Enetai Creek
Illahee
University Point
Gilberton
Burke Bay
Brownsville
Keyport
Liberty Bay
Virginia Point
Pearson
Scandia
Poulsbo
Nesika Bay
Bjorgen Creek
Lemolo
Point Bolin
Sandy Hook
Agate Pass

Vashon, Maury Islands
Allen Bank
Point Vashon
Dolphin Point
Aquarium
Glen Acres
Point Beals
Dilworth
Point Heyer
Ellisport
Portage
Tramp Harbor
Luana Beach
Maury
Point Robinson
Magnolia Beach
Piners Point
Rosehilla
Quartermaster Harbor
Manzanita
Hongking
Dockton
Judd Creek
Burton
Shawnee
Magnolia Beach
Indian Point
Harbor Heights
Dalco Passage
Neill Point
Tahlequah
Point Dalco
Colvos Passage
Spring Beach
Sunset Beach
Camp Sealth
Paradise Cove
Point Sanford
Christenson Cove & Creek
Lisabuela Cove
Point Peter
Colvos
Cedarhurst
Fern Cove
Sylvan Beach
Biloxi

Southern Puget Sound
The Narrows
Narrows Bridge
Point Evans
Evans Rock
Hale Passage
Point Fosdick
Wollochet Bay
Artondale
Bay View
East Cromwell
Cromwell
Sunny Bay
Warren
Arletta
Green Point
Shaws Cove
Carr Inlet
Horsehead Bay
Scott Point
Nimrod Point
Cutts Island
Raft Island
Rosedale
Lay Inlet
Allen Point
Henderson Bay
Goodnough Creek
Purdy
Burley Lagoon
Burley
Wauna
Elgin
Powie Point
Teko Point
Minter Creek
Glencove
Home
Von Geldern Cove
Amah Point
Mayo Cove
Lakebay
Penrose Point
Delano Beach
South Head
Wyckoff Shoal

Pitt Passage
Mahnckes Point
Filucy Bay
Longbranch
McDermott Point
Drayton Passage
Devils Head
Case Inlet
Taylor Bay
Whiteman Cove
Joemma Beach State Park
Wa Wa Point
Herron Island
Herron
Sandy Point
Dutcher Cove
Kalila Point
Talapais Point
Vaughn Bay
Vaughn & Vaughn Creek
Sunshine Beach
Windy Bluff
Rocky Bay
Rocky Point
Victor
Point Victor
North Bay
Coulter Creek
Allyn
Devereaux Lake
Tule Point
Sherwood Creek
Grapeview
Reach Island
Mane Cove
Fair Harbor
Stretch Island
Yawa Island
McLane Cove
Stadium
Point Squho
Tahali Point
Pickering Passage
Walkers Landing
Grant

Appendix C - List of Names

Graham Point	Carylon Beach	Weyer Point	
Hungerford Point	Squaxin Passage	Woodard Creek	**McNeil Island**
Hammersley Inlet	Hunter Point	Johnson Point	Samago Point
Cape Horn	Eld Inlet	Poncin Cove	Manhait Point
Libby Point	Rignall	Baird Cove	Still Harbor
Church Point	Sanderson Harbor	Mill Bight	Baldwin Point
Hoballa	Frye Cove	Puget	Gertrude
Miller Point	Young Cove	Dogfish Bight	Gertrude Island
Munson Point	Sunset Beach	Big Slough	Brackenridge passage
Oakland Bay	Flapjack Point	Butterball Cove	Hyde Point
Chapman Cove	Rocky Point	De Wolf Bight	Bee
Bay Shore	Mud Bay	Hogum Bay	Hogan Point
Shelton	Shell Point	Kwaatz Point	Meredian
Shelton Creek	Simmons Creek	Loa Point	Wykoff Shoal
Goldsborough Creek	White Point	Nisqually	Floyd Cove
Eagle Point	Snyder Cove	Sequalitchew Creek	
Skookum Point	Bushoowah-ahlee Point	DuPont	**Anderson Island**
Mill Creek	Green Point	Tatsolo Point	Balch Passage
Cannery Point	Cooper Point	Solo Point	Higgens Cove
Cape Cod	Budd Inlet	Cormorant Passage	Otso Point
Arcadia	Silver Spit	Ketron Island	Eagle Island
Totten Inlet	Tykle Cove	Gordon Point	Yoman Point
Windy Point	Butler Cove	Heath Bay	Sandy Point
Baron Point	Olympia Shoal	Steilacoom	Cole Point
Little Skookum Inlet	Marshville	Chambers Creek	Oro Bay
Deer Harbor	West Bay	Kosa Point	East Oro Bay
The Narrows	Olympia	Sunset Beach	Mailman Point
Mud Cat Point	East Bay	Days Island	Vega
Lower Lynch Cove	Swan Town	Salmon Beach	Lyle Point
Upper Lynch Cove	Saringa Point		Thompson Cove
Brown Cove	Ellis Cove Creek	**Fox Island**	Treble Point
Wildcat Cove	Priest Point	Nearns Point	Carlson Bay
Kamilche Point	Gull Harbor	Towhead Island	Amsterdam Bay
Quarters Point	Dofflemyer Point	Echo Bay	
Big Cove	Boston Harbor	Tanglewood Island	**Herron Island**
Deepwater Point	Jeal Point	Millers Point	Coopers Point
Hurley Cove	Dover Point	Sylvan	Bung Bluff
Bowman Cove	Dana Passage	Ketners Point	
Burns Landing	Zangle Cove	Cedrona Bay	**Harstine Island**
Oyster Bay	Little Fishtrap	Hope	Dougall Point
Burns Point	Big Fishtrap	Smuggler Cove	McMicken Boulder
Burns Cove	Dickenson Point	Fox Point	Ballow
Hudson Cove	Henderson Inlet	Toy Point	Buffingtons Lagoon
Cougar Point	Itsami Ledge	Gibson Point	Fudge Point
Camp Point	Cliff Point	Castlenook	Wilson Point
Gallagher Cove	Chapman Bay	Macklin	Briscoe Point

Richard W. Blumenthal ♦ 325

Appendix C - List of Names

Peale Passage
Stau Point
Stoku Point
Jarrell Cove
Indian Cove

Squaxon Island
Salmon Point
Seafarm Cove
Tucksel Point
Squaxon Passage
Belspeox Point
Palela Bay
Potlatch Point
Tuckapahwox Point

Admiralty Inlet, E side
Salmon Beach
Point Defiance
Commencement Bay
Ruston
Point Harmon
Thea Foss Waterway
Middle Waterway
St. Paul Waterway
Puyallup Waterway
Puyallup River
Milwaukee Waterway
Sitcum Waterway
Blair Waterway
Hylebos Waterway
Browns Point
Caledonia
Dash Point
Dumas Bay
Adelaide
Poverty Bay
Lakota
Redondo
Poverty Bay
Zenith
Des Moines
Zenith
Massey Creek
Three Tree Point
Seola Beach

Brace Point
Fauntleroy Cove
Point Williams
Alki Point
Elliot Bay
Duwamish Head
West Waterway
Harbor Island
East Waterway
Duwamish Waterway
Kellog Island
Georgetown
Seattle
Smith Cove
Magnolia Bluff
Fourmile Rock
West Point
Shilshoal Bay
Fort Lawton
Chittendon Locks
Salmon Bay & Creek
Meadow Point
Pipers Creek
Spring Beach
Richmond Beach
Point Wells
Edwards Point
Edmonds
Meadowdale
Norma Beach
Browns Bay
Lunds Gulch
Norma Beach
Picnic Point
Big Gulch
Mukilteo
Elliot Point

Possession Sound, Saratoga Passage, E side
Gedney Island
White Bluff
Mukilteo
Port Gardner
Edgewater
Darlington

East Waterway
Everett
Jetty Island
Preston Point
Snohomish River
Smith Island
Union Slough
Steamboat Slough
Ebey Slough
Marysville
Quilceda Creek
Priest Point
Mission Beach
Tulallip Bay
Skiou Point
Tulallip
Hermosa Beach & Point
Port Susan
Tulare Beach
Sunny Shores
McKees Beach
Kayak Point
Warm Beach
Hat Slough
South Pass
Stillaguamish River
Stanwood
Leque Island
Davis Slough
Juniper Beach
Livingston Bay
Lona Beach
Barnum Point
Triangle Cove
Driftwood Shores
Cavelero Beach
Bretland
Sunny Shores Acres
Tillicum Beach
Tyee Beach
Camano Head
Pebble Beach
Mabana
Elger Bay
Lowell Point
Breezy Point

Cama Beach
Indian Beach
Camano
Onamac Point
Camp Lagoon
Woodland Beach
Rockaway Beach
Sunset Beach
Madrona Beach
Camp Grande
Rocky Point
Maplegrove Beach
Utsalady Point
Utsalady
Brown Point

Arrowhead Beach
English Boom
Skagit Bay
Tom Moore Slough
South Fork Skagit River
North Fork Skagit River
Bald Island
Hawk Point
Ikia Island
Goat Island

Whidbey Island
Deception Pass
Strawberry Island
Ben Ure Island
Coronet Bay
Goose Rock
Hoypus Point
Ben Ure Spit
Dugualla Bay
Seal Rocks
Strawberry Point
Mariners Cove
Polnell Point
Crescent Harbor
Forbes Point
Maylor Point
Oak Harbor
Klootchman Rock
Scenic Heights

326 ♦ Maritime Place Names - Inland Washington Waters

Appendix C - List of Names

Blowers Bluff
Monroe Landing
Penn Cove
San de Fuca
Coveland
Kennedys Lagoon
Barstow Point
Mueller Park
Port Arthur
Coupeville
Lovejoy Point
Long Point
Rodina Beach
Snatelum Point
Rodena Beach
Harrington Lagoon
Race Lagoon
North Bluff
Pratts Bluff
Greenbank
South Bluff
Holmes Harbor
Dines Point
Honeymoon Bay
Middle Point
Freeland
Norths Landing
Point Williams
Scatchel Point
Beverly Beach
Rocky Point
Baby Island
East Point
Bells Beach
Saratoga
Langley
Sandy Point
Maple Cove
Clinton
Randall Point
Columbia Beach
Glendale
Possession
Possession Point
Cultus Bay
Sandy Hook Yacht Club

Estates
Scatchet Head
Indian Point
Maxwelton
Useless Bay
Deer Lagoon
Bayview
Sunlight Beach
Lake Oliver
Double Bluff
Mutiny Bay
Austin
Bush Point
Lagoon Point
Admiralty Bay
Keystone Harbor
Admiralty Head
Fort Casey
Ebeys Landing
Point Partridge
West Beach
Rocky Point
West Point
Deception Island
North Beach
Gun Point
Macs Cove

Fidalgo Island
Anacortes
Cap Sante
Fidalgo Bay
Weaverline Spit
Crandall Spit
March Point
Swinomish Channel
La Conner
Hole in the Wall
Craft Island
Ika Island
McGlinn Island
Sugarloaf Island
Goat Island
Dot Island
Marthas Bay
Pull and be Damned

Point
Tonkon Islands
Little Deadman Island
Deadman Island
Snee-oosh Point
Hope Island
Lang Bay
Tosi Island
Lone Tree Point
Kiket Bay & Island
Flagstaff Point
Skagit Island
Similk Bay
Turners Bay
Fidalgo City
Gibraltar
Dewey
Yokeko Point
Kingfisher Cove
Miller Bay
Quiet Cove
Deception Pass
Pass Lake
Bowman Hill
Canoe Pass
Lottie Bay & Point
Lighthouse Point
Reservation Head
Bowman Bay
Deception Island
Gull Rock
Coffin Rock
Northwest Pass
Sharpe Cove
Rosario Head
Rosario Beach
Urchin Rocks
Northwest Island
Sares Head
Telegraph Bight
Biz Point
Williamson Rocks
Langley Point & Bay
Mount Erie
Sugarloaf Mountain
Edith Point

Burrows Bay
Allen Pass
Allen Island
Dennis Shoal
Young Island
Burrows Island
Burrows Pass
Alice Bight
Short Bay
Peartree Bay
Short Bay
Alexander Beach
Anaco Beach
Flounder Bay
Fidalgo Head
Green Point
Sunset Beach
Shannon Point
Ship Harbor
Guemes Channel
City of Seattle Rock

Matia Island
Puffin Island
Rolfe Cove
Eagle Point

Sucia Islands
Clements Reef
Sucia Island
Ewing Island & Cove
Cluster Islands
Wiggins Reef
Stony Reef
Echo Bay
South Finger Island
North Finger Island
Justice Island
Johnson Point
Snoring Bay
Wiggins Head
Fossil Bay
Herndon Island
Mud Bay
E.V. Henry Point
Fox Cove

Appendix C - List of Names

Little Sucia Island
Shallow Bay
Lawson Bluff

San Juan Island
Davison Head
Neil Bay
Lonesome Cove
Limestone Point
O'Neal Island
Rocky Bay
Sportsman Lake
Eureka Beach
Point Caution
Biological Hill
Reid Rock
Friday Harbor
Shipyard Cove
Brown Island
Beaverton Cove
China Cove
Fridays Creek
Newhall's Point
Madrona Peninsula
Madrona Point
Turn Island
Point Salsbury
Kansas Cove
Boat Channel
Minnesota Reef
Turn Rock
Reef Point
Danger Rock
Pear Point
Park Hill
Bald Hill
North Bay
Little Island
Argyle Creek
Argyle Shoal
Argyle Lagoon
Argyle
Dinner Island
Old Rock
Griffin Bay
Merrifield Cove

Mulno Cove
Jensen Bay
Low Point
Halftide Rocks
Hope Reef
North Pacific Rock
Old Town Lagoon
Jakles Lagoon
Third Lagoon
Mount Finlayson
American Camp
Forth of July Beach
San Juan Town
Fish Creek
Harbor Rock
Neck Point
Goose Island
Cattle Point
Inner Passage
Chicken Rock
Bellevue Prairie
Grandmas Cove
Landing Place
Eagle Cove
Eagle Point
Weaver Spit
Point Joe
Little Mountain
Utah Rock
False Bay
Enterprise Bay
Kanaka Bay
Fleming Beach
Pile Point
Little Mountain
Deadman Bay
Sunken Rock
Ship Trees
Mount Dallas
Lime Kiln Point
Lime Kiln
Bellevue Point
Trout Lake
Sugarloaf Mountain
Smallpox Bay
Low Island

Andrews Bay
Sunset Point
Smugglers Cove
Mitchell Bay
Mosquito Bay
Mosquito Pass
Hanbury Point
Delacombe Point
Horseshoe Bay
Garrison Bay
Guss Island
English Camp
Young Hill
Bell Point
Westcott Bay
White Point
Bazalgette Point
Roche Harbor
Pearl Island
Barren Island
Posey Island

Henry Island
McCracken Point
Inman Point
Scout Patch
Nelson Bay
Cooper Point
Open Bay
Kellett Bluff
Battleship Island

Spieden Island
Gull Reef
Cactus Islands
Ripple Island
New Channel
Gull Rock
Flattop Island
Spieden Bluff
Green Point

Stuart Island
Boundary Pass
Turn Point
Charles Point

Prevost Harbor
Prevost
Satellite Island
Johns Pass
Johns Island
Reef Bay
Gossip Islands
Reid Harbor
Tiptop Hill

Waldron Island
Skipjack Island
Bare Island
Point Hammond
Limberry Point
Mail Bay
Point Disney
Mount Cement
Danger Rock
White Rock
Mouatt Reef
Sandy Point
North Bay
Seversons Bay
Fishery Point
Skipjack Island
Bare Island
Gordon Island

Orcas Island
Parker Reef
Point Thompson
Day Lake
Buckhorn Lodge
Buck Mountain
Raccoon Point
Barnes Island
Clark Island
The Sisters
Little Sister
Mount Pickett
Twin Lakes
Mountain Lake
Kangaroo Point
Lawrence Point
Kangaroo Point

Appendix C - List of Names

Patton Cove
Patton Point
Doe Bay
Peapod Rocks
Doe Island
Granite Beach
Buoy Bay
Deer Point
Lydia Shoal
Obstruction Island
Obstruction Pass
Buck Mountain
Brown Rock
Barnacle Rocks
Barnacle Rock Beach
Buck Bay
Port Langdon
Olga
East Sound
Entrance Mountain
Cascade Lake
Cascade Creek
Summit Lake
Paul Creek
Cascade Bay
Rosario Point
Rosario Hill
Giffin Rocks
Coon Hollow
Ship Bay
Buck Mountain
Eastsound
Osprey Hill
Crescent Beach
Madrona Point
Fishing Bay
Indian Island
Judd Bay
Lookout Hill
Dolphin Bay
Twin Rocks
White Beach
Diamond Point
Shag Rock
Guthrie Bay
Foster Point

Harney Channel
Grindstone Harbor
Killebrews Lake
Elwha Rock
Orcas
West Sound
Oak Island
White Beach Bay
Picnic Island
Haidi Point
Harbor Rock
Ship Peak
Massacre Bay
Skull Island
Indian Point
Victim Island
Double Island
Alegria Island
Evans Cove
Caldwell Point
Evans Cove
Pole Pass
Deer Harbor
Cayou Cove
Fawn Island
Steep Point
North Pass
Spring Passage
Fritz Point
Orcas Knob
Turtleback Mountain
Lovers Cove
West Beach
Kimple Point & Beach
Beach Haven
Freeman Island
Camp Orkila
Point Doughty
North Beach
Terrill Beach

Wasp Islands
Reef Island
Bird Rock
Crane Island
Bell Island

Cliff Island
Harbour Rock
Knob Island
Shirt Tail Reef
Low Island
Yellow Island
Coon Island
McConnell Island

Shaw Island
Ben Nevis
Broken Point
Blind Island
Blind Bay
Griswold
Hudson Bay
Point Hudson
Hankin Point
Upright Channel
Picnic Cove
Picnic Point
Indian Cove
Canoe Island
Squaw Bay
Sunken Rock
Hoffman Cove
Hicks Bay
Reid Rock
Point George
Parks Bay
Tharald Pond
Post Office Bay
Maple
Tift Rocks
Neck Point
Wasp Passage

Lopez Island
Upright Head
Shoal Bay
Humphrey Head
Leo Reef
Swifts Bay
Port Stanley
Flower Island
Spencer Spit

Frost Island
Lopez Sound
White Boulder
Small Island
Lopez Hill
Jasper Bay
Hunter Bay
Islandale
Crab Island
Fortress Island
Skull Island
Mud Bay
Otis
Sperry Point & Peninsula
Lopez Pass
Shoal Bight
Kellett Ledge
Cape St. Mary
Telegraph Bay
Chadwick Hill
Watmough Bay
Watmough Head
Boulder Island
Point Colville
Davidson Rock
Colville Island
Castle Island
Blind Island
McArdle Bay
Hughes Bay
Aleck Bay
Aleck Rocks
Swirl Island
Flint Beach
Barnacle Rock
Iowa Rock
Iceberg Point
Iceberg Island
Outer Bay
Agate Beach
Johns Point
Mackaye Harbor
Washington Rock
Barlow Bay
Jones Bay
Richardson

Richard W. Blumenthal

Appendix C - List of Names

Hidden Inlet
Richardson Rock
Round Rock
Charles Island
Secar Rock
Hall Island
Long Island
Mummy Rocks
Buck Island
Davis Bay
Mya Cove
Rowboat Cove
Davis Point
Deadman Island
Kings Point
White Cliffs
Shark Reef
Rock Point
Big Rock
Fisherman Bay
Careen Creek
Lopez
Hummel Lake
Flat Point & Creek

Blakely Island
Peavine Pass
Spindle Rock
Horseshoe Lake
Blakely Peak
Black Rock
Pointer Island
Armitage Island
Lawson Rock
Thatcher Pass
Willow Island
Thatcher Bay
Thatcher
Spencer Lake
Bald Bluff
Blakely Island Shoal

Decatur Island
Fauntleroy Point
Decatur Head
James Island

White Cliff
Dot Rock
Lopez Pass
Lopez Chain
Ram Island
Cayou Island
Rim Island
Center Island
Reads Bay
Decatur
Trump Island
Brigantine Bay
Sylvan Cove
Undertakers Reef

Cypress Island
Cypress Reef
Towhead Island
Cone Islands
Buttonhole Island
Eagle Harbor
Duck Lake
Cypress Lake
Cypress Head
Stella Swamp
Deepwater Bay
Secret Harbor
Broughton Point
Reef Point
Strawberry Bay & Creek
Strawberry Island
Salsbury Point
Tide Point
Eagle Cliff

Sinclair Island
Buckeye Shoal
Boulder Reef

Guemes Island
Clark Point
Jack Island
North Beach
Boat Harbor
Southeast Point
Levant Passage

Porpoise Rocks
Huckleberry Island
Long Bay
Saddlebag Island
Dot Island
Hat Island
Guemes Channel
Cooks Cove
Deadman Bay
Kellys Point
Yellow Bluff
Yellow Bluff Reef
Indian Village

Lummi Island
Point Migley
Richards Mountain
Lummi Point
Lane Spit
Echo Point
Beach
Bumstead Spit
Sunrise Cove
Smugglers Cove
Inati Bay
Reil Harbor
Carter Point
Lummi Peak
Lummi Rocks
Lovers Bluff
Legoe Bay
Village Point
Carlisle
Fern Point

Canadian Border-Bellingham Bay
Boundary Bay
Semiahmoo Bay
Blaine
Drayton Harbor
Tongue Point
Birch Point
Kiowo Point
Birch Bay
Point Whitehorn

Cherry Point
Neptune Beach
Sandy Point
Lummi Bay
Hale Passage
Gooseberry Point
Fisherman Cove
Portage Island
Brant Point
Point Francis
Portage Bay
Brant Island
Bellingham Bay
Portage Channel
Fish Point
Bellingham Bay
Bellingham
Whatcome
Starr Rock
Post Point
Chuckanut Bay
Chuckanut Rock
Chuckanut Island
Pleasant Bay
Governors Point
Whiskey Rock
Wildcat Cove
Samish Bay
Dogfish Point
Blanchard
Edison
Samish Island
Alice Bay
Scotts Point
Fish Point
Atlanta
William Point
William Spit
Padilla Bay
Joe Leary Slough
Bay View

BIBLIOGRAPHY

Anderson, Helen McReavy. *How When and Where on Hood Canal.* Puget Press. 1960.

Angle, Grant C. and William D. Welsh. *A Brief History of Shelton Washington.* 2nd printing, July 1841.

Bailey, Joanne I., and Carl O. Nyberg. *Gunkholing in the San Juan Islands.* Seattle: San Juan Enterprises, Inc., 2000.

—. *Gunkholing in South Puget Sound.* Seattle: San Juan Enterprises, Inc., 1997.

Bailey, Ida and Vern. *Brinnon.* Bremerton: Perry Publishing, 1997.

Baird, Dorothy Peterson. *Island Memories. Vashon-Maury Island.* Seattle, WA. 1955.

Baker, Joseph, 3rd Lieutenant. *A Log of His Majesty's Ship Discovery from 22nd December 1790 to 27 November 1792.* Microfilm copy #A49. Seattle: University of Washington. 1792.

Baker, Loren. *Washington's Pioneers.* Pioneer Bank. 1986.

Bave, Emelia L. *San Juan Saga. A Unique History of the Pig War and the San Juan Islands.* Friday Harbor: 1976.

Bean, Jeanne and Karen Russell. *Marrowstone.* Port Townsend: Port Townsend Publishing Co., Inc., 1978.

Bell, Edward. "A New Vancouver Journal on the Discovery of Puget Sound". Ed. Edmond S. Meany, *Washington Historical Quarterly*, Vol. V, nos 2, 3, 4; Vol. VI, no. 1 (April, July, October 1914; January 1915).

Blumenthal, Richard W. Ed. *The Early Exploration of Inland Washington Waters. Journals and Logs from Six Expeditions, 1786 – 1792.* Jefferson, NC: McFarland & Co., 2004.

—, *With Vancouver in Inland Washington Waters. Journals of 12 Crewmen, April – June 1792.* Jefferson, NC: McFarland & Co., 2006.

—, *Charles Wilkes and the Exploration of Inland Washington Waters. Journals from the Expedition of 1841.* Jefferson, NC: McFarland & Co., 2009.

Bowen, Evelyn T., et al. *Kitsap County History, A story of Kitsap County and its Pioneers.* Seattle: Dinner & Klein, 1977.

Bright, William. *Native American Placenames of the United States.* Norman: University of Oklahoma Press, 2004.

Britton, Diane F. *The Iron and Steel Industry in the Far West. Irondale, Washington.* University Press of Colorado, 1991.

Brokenshire, Doug. *Washington State Place Names. From Alki to Yelm.* Caldwell, Id: Caxton, 1993.

Broughton, William R. "Broughton's Log of a Reconnaissance of the San Juan Islands in 1792," Ed. J. Neilson Barry, *Washington Historical Quarterly*, Vol. XXI (January, 1930) p. 55-60

—, *Journal* (untitled). Microfilm copy #A137. Seattle: University of Washington. 1792.

—, *A Voyage of Discovery to the North Pacific Ocean: In Which the Coast of Asia, from the Lat of 35° North, the Island of Insu, (Commonly Known Under the Name of the Land of Jesso,) the North, South, and East Coasts of Japan, the Lieuchieux and the Adjacent Isles, As Well As the Coast of Corea, Have Been Examined and Surveyed.* 1804.

Brunjes, Robert A. *Hat Island History.* http://www.hatisland.org/library/community/HAT_ISLAND_HISTORY.pdf

Buffington, Andy. "The History of Raft Island". Self published, 26pp. May 1998. (High school project) http://www.raftisland.org/images/RaftIslandHistory.pdf

Burley, George and Lynette Evans. *Roche Harbor. A Saga in the San Juans.* Everett: B & E Enterprises, 1972.

Burn, June. *Living High.* 3rd ed. Friday Harbor: 1992.

Bibliography

Cahail, Alice Kellogg. *Sea Captains of Whidby Island*. 1901. http://files.usgwarchives.net/wa/island/history/whidcapn.txt

Cammon, Betsey Johnson. *Island Memoir. A Personal History of Anderson and McNeil Islands*. Puyallup: The Valley Press, Inc.

Campbell, Patricia. *A History of the North Olympic Peninsula*. Port Angeles: The Daily News, 1977.

Cardel, Doug. *About Those King County Place-Names*. WA: Coastal Press, 1989.

—, *Who the Hell Was San Juan? Examining the Roots of San Juan Islands Place Names*. Lopez Island, WA: Coastal Press, 1982.

Carey, Roland N. *Van Olinda's History of Vashon – Maury Island*. Seattle: Alderbook Publishing Company, 1985.

Carlson, Joan. *Tall Timber and the Tide*. Poulsbo: Kitsap Weeklies, 1971.

Cherry, Lorna (author and editor). *South Whidbey and Its People*. Volume I. South Whidbey Historical Society, 1983.

—, *South Whidbey and Its People*. Volume II. South Whidbey Historical Society, 1985.

—, *South Whidbey and Its People*. Volume III. South Whidbey Historical Society, 1986.

Clark, Normal H. *Mill Town. A Social History of Everett, Washington, from Its Earliest Beginnings on the Shores of Puget Sound to the Tragic and Infamous Event Known as the Everett Massacre*. Seattle: University of Washington Press, 1970.

Clayson, Edward. *Historical Narratives of Puget Sound Hood's Canal, 1865-1885*. Fairfield: Ye Galleon Press, 1969.

Cloud, Ray V. *Edmonds. The Gem of Puget Sound*. Edmonds Tribune-Review Press, 1953.

Cook, James. *A Voyage to the Pacific Ocean Undertaken, By the Command of His Majesty, for Making Discoveries in the Northern Hemisphere. To Determine the Position and Extent of the West Side of North America; its Distance from Asia; and the Practicability of a Northern Passage to Europe. Performed Under the Direction of Captains Cook, Clerke, and Gore, in his Majesty's Ships the Resolution and Discovery. In the Years 1776, 1777, 1778, 1779, and 1780*. London: Published by Order of the Lords Commissioners of the Admiralty. Printed by W. and A. Strahan, 1784.

Craig, Paula M. *The Early History of Silverdale*. Revised 1974.

Cummings, Al and Jo Bailey. *Gunkholing in the San Juans*. Edmonds: Nor'westing, Inc., 1984.

Davidson, George. *Report: The Superintendent of the Coast Survey showing the progress of the Survey during the Year 1858*. Washington: William A. Harris, Printer. 1859.

—, *Directory for the Pacific Coast of the United States, report to the Superintendent of the U.S. Coast Survey*. printed in 1862.

—, *Pacific Coast, Coast Pilot of California, Oregon, and Washington Territory*. Washington: Government Printing Office. 1869.

—, *Pacific Coast, Coast Pilot of California, Oregon, and Washington. Fourth Edition*. Washington: Government Printing Office. 1889.

Davis, Jeff & Al Eufrasio. *Weird Washington*. New York: Sterling Publishing. 2008.

Davison, Bertha M. (Gabrielson). *A History of the Early Days of Vaughn, Washington*. Printed by the Peninsula Gateway, 1961.

Dean, John and Art Kimball. *Camano Island. Life and Times in Island Paradise*. Pub by John Dean and Art Kimball. Stanwood/Camano NEWS Printing, 1994.

Denny, Arthur Armstrong. *Pioneer Days on Puget Sound*. Fairfield: Ye Galleon Press, 1979.

Denny, Emily Inez. *Blazing the Way*. Seattle: Rainier Printing Company, Inc., 1909.

DeShaw, William. Personal papers. UW Northwest Collection.

Dilgard, David. *Everett Chronology*. Everett: Lowell Printing & Publishing, 1992.

Douglas, David. *Journal Kept by David Douglas 1823-1827*. Printed by Spottiswoode and Co. Ltd., Colchester, London and Eton. Available at http://www.sos.wa.gov/history/publications_detail.aspx?p=56

—, *Journal kept by David Douglas during his travels in North America 1823-1827: together with a particular description of thirty-three species of American oaks and eighteen species of Pinus, with appendices containing a list of the plants introduced by Douglas and an account of his death in 1834.* W. Wesley & Son under the direction of the Royal Horticultural Society. Available online through the Washington State Library's Classics in Washington History collection.

Edgers, Don. *Fox Island.* Charleston: Arcadia Publishing, 2008.

Eells, Myron. "The History of Hood Canal, Mason County". (hand typed, no date)

Elmore, Helen Troy. *This Isle of Guemes.* Anacortes, 1973.

Essex, Alice. *The Stanwood Story.* Stanwood: *The Stanwood News*, in 3 volumes, 1971-1997

Evans, Jack R. *Little History of Gig Harbor, Washington.* Seattle: SCW Publications, 1988.

Firth, Lila Hannah. "Early Life on San Juan Island". self typed. 1945.

Fish, Harriet U. *Fish Tales of Port Gamble and Port Ludlow.* (undated ms)

—, *Tales of Port Hadlock.* 1985.

—, *Tracks, Trails, and Tales in Clallam County, State of Washington.* Port Angeles: Olympic Printers, Inc., 1983.

Fredson, Michael. *Log Towns.* West Olympia: Minuteman Press, 1993.

—, *Oakland to Shelton. The Sawdust Trail.* Belfair: Mason County Historical Society, 1976.

Frost, Nell. "The Early History of Priest Point Park". (4 hand typed pages, no date)

Glidden, Helene. *The Light on the Island. Tales of a Lighthouse Keeper's Family in the San Juan Islands.* 2nd ed. Woodinville: San Juan Publishing, 2001.

Hale, Horatio. *Ethnography and Philology.* Philadelphia: Printed by C. Sherman, 1846. found at http://www.sil.si.edu/digitalcollections/usexex/navigation/ScientificText/usexex19_07b.cfm?start=14

Haller, Col. Granville O. *San Juan and Secession.* Facsimile Reproduction 1967, The Shorey Book Store, Seattle, WA.

Hansen, Kenneth C. *The Maiden of Deception Pass. A Spirit in Cedar.* Anacortes: Samish Experience Productions, 1983.

Hanson, Howard A. "The Naming of Elliott Bay". *Pacific Northwest Quarterly*, Vol. 45, January 1954.

Haulman, Dr. Bruce. *Vashon History. Vashon-Maury Place Names.* http://www.vashonhistory.com/vashonplacenames.htm. 2008

Hayden, Mary Jane. *Pioneer Days.* San Jose: Murgotten's Press, 1915.

Heckman, Hazel. *Island in the Sound.* Seattle: University of Washington Press, 1967.

Hermanson, James and Peter Simpson. *Port Townsend: Years That Are Gone.* Port Townsend: Quimper Press, a division of Port Townsend Publishing Co.

Hilbert, Vi; Jay Miller, and Zalmai Zahir. *Puget Sound Geography. Original Manuscript from T. T. Waterman.* Federal Way: Lushootseed Press, 2001.

Hitchcock, Beula, and Helen Wingert. *The Island Remembers. A History of Harstine Island and its People.* Harstine: Harstine Women's Club, 1979.

Hitchman, Robert. *Place Names of Washington.* Washington State Historical Society. 1985. While I hesitate to disparage a well-known and respected text on place names, I must alert readers that I discovered better than an 18% substantive error rate with respect to maritime names, which unfortunately leaves the entire manuscript suspect.

Holt, Carole Rambo. "Poncin Estate, Johnson Point, the Camp Set in Clover". 1989 (hand typed)

Humphrey, Robert M. *Everett and Snohomish County: A Pictorial History.* Norfolk: The Donning Company, 1984.

Hunt, Herbert and Floyd C. Kaylor. *Washington, west of the Cascades.* Vol 3. Seattle: S.J. Clark, 1917.

Jameson, Elizabeth and Susan Hodge Armitage Eds. *Writing the range: race, class, and culture in the women's West.* Norman: University of Oklahoma Press, 1997.

Bibliography

Joergenson, Gustav B. *History of the Twin Cities. Twin City News.* Series of articles beginning April 1, 1948.

Johnson, Jalmar. *Builders of the Northwest.* New York: Dodd, Mead & Company, 1963.

Johnstone, James. *Journal* (untitled). London: Public Record Office Ref: Adm 53/339. 1792.

Keeting, Virginia, ed. *Dungeness: The Lure of a River.* Port Angeles: Sequim Bicentennial Committee and *The Daily News.* Olympic Printers, 1976.

Keith, Gordon, and Roderic Marble Olzendam. *It Came to Pass in the San Juan Islands.* Portland: Binfords & Mort, 1978.

—, *The James Francis Tulloch Diary. 1875 – 1910.* Portland: Binfords & Mort, 1978.

King County Journal, August 29, 2005.

Kline, M. S. and G. A. Bayless. *Ferryboats. A Legend on Puget* Sound. Seattle. Bayless Books, 1983.

Kvelstad, Rangvald, ed. *Poulsbo. Its First Hundred Years.* Silverdale: Silverdale Printer, 1986.

Landes, Henry. *A Geographic Dictionary of Washington.* Olympia. Frank M. Lamborn, Public Printers, 1917. This text contains a gazetteer which lists place names and their locations, but it does not include history on any of the locations.

Lange, Greg. Research notes collected between 1960 to present on 3x5 cards for place names in San Juan County.

Leach, Mary March. *Cottonwood Collection. History of Sinclair Island.* Snohomish: Snohomish Publishing Co., 1988.

Lovering, Frances K. *Island Ebb & Flow. A Pioneer's Journal of Life on Waldron Island.* Friday Harbor: Masterworks, Inc., 1985.

Ludwig, Charles H. *A Brief History of Waldron Island.* self pub 1959.

Manby, Thomas. *Journal of the Voyages of the H.M.S. Discovery and Chatham.* Fairfield: Ye Galleon Press, 1988.

Marriott, Elsie Frankland. *Bainbridge Through Bifocals.* Seattle: Gateway Printing Company, 1941.

Martin, Paul J. *Port Angeles, Washington: A History.* Port Angeles: Peninsula Publishing, Inc., 1983.

Mason, Beryl Troxell. *John Franklin Troxell, fish Trap Man. Puget Sound and San Juan Islands, Washington. A Collection of Facts and Memories by his Daughter.* Watmough Publishing, Oak Harbor, WA. 1991.

McCurdy, James G. *By Juan de Fuca's Strait. Pioneering Along the Northwestern Edge of the Continent.* Portland: Binfords & Mort, 1937.

—, "Criss-Cross Over the Boundary". *The Pacific Monthly*, Volume 23, January to June 1910.

McDonald, Lucile S. *Making History: The People Who Shaped the San Juan Islands.* Friday Harbor: Harbor Press, 1990.

McLellan, Roy Davidson. *The Geology of the San Juan Islands.* Seattle: University of Washington Press. 1927. http://www.nps.gov/history/history/online_books/geology/publications/state/wa/uw-1927-2/contents.htm (without page numbers) A note on this text: McLellan wrote it as part of a doctoral dissertation at the University of Washington. In the process of his studies, he unwittingly named a number of features in the San Juans. Some, he obviously chose himself (Olivine Hill), others were likely provided to him by people living in the area. As such, the manuscript is extremely useful from the standpoint of the origin of place names. He unfortunately provided no reasons for any.

Meany, Edmond S. *Origin of Washington Geographic Names.* Seattle: University of Washington Press, 1923.

—, *Vancouver's Discovery of Puget Sound.* Portland: Binsfords & Mort, 1957.

—, *Indian Geographic Names of Washington.* Seattle: The Hyatt-Fowells School, 1908.

Meares, John, Esq. *Voyages Made in the Years 1788 and 1789 from China to the N. W. Coast of America: with an Introductory Narrative of a Voyage Performed in 1786, from Bengal, in the Ship Nootka to which are annexed, Observations on the Probable Existance of a North West Passage.* Vol. 1. London: Logographic Press, 1791.

Meeker, Ezra. *Pioneer Reminiscences of Puget Sound.* Seattle: Lowman & Hanford Stationary and Printing Co., 1905.

—, *The Tragedy of Leschi*. 1905.

Menzies, Archibald. *Menzies' Journal of Vancouver's Voyage*. Edited with Botanical and Ethnological Notes, by C. F. Newcombe, M.D., and a Biographical Note by J. Forsyth. Victoria, B.C.: William H. Cullin, 1923.

Middleton, Lynn. *Place Names of the Pacific Northwest Coast*. Victoria: Elldee Publishing, 1969.

Mighetto, Lisa & Goetz, Linda Naoi. *Inventory of Historical Resources on the Sperry Peninsula Lopez Island, Washington*. Presented for Kona Residence Trust and the Paul Allen Family. Historical Research Associates, Inc. Seattle, WA. 1997.

Minnick, Benjamin. *Daily Journal of Commerce*. January 7, 2007.

Morgan, C. T. *The San Juan Story*. 15th ed. Friday Harbor: San Juan Industries, 1966.

Morrison, Homer P. "Origins of Place Names Point Julia, Port Gamble and Annas Bay". 6 pgs, unpublished letter dated 3/30/2010.

Murray, Keith A. *The Pig War*. Tacoma: Washington State Historical Society, 1968.

Neil, Dorothy, and Lee Brainard. *By Canoe and Sailing Ship They Came*. Oak Harbor: Spindrift Publishing Company, 1989.

Newell, Gordon. *Town Where Time Stood Still. The Story of Seabeck*. Seattle: Seabeck Christian Conference, 1958.

Nokes, J. Richard. *Almost a Hero: The Voyages of John Meares, R.N., to China, Hawaii, and the Northwest Coast*. Washington State University. 1998.

Osborne, Harold F. *Little City by the Sea*. Kingston: Apple Tree Press, 1990.

Palmer, Gayle and Shanna Stevenson, Eds. *Thurston County Place Names: A Heritage Guide*. Olympia, Thurston County Historic Commission, November 1992.

Parratt, Smitty. *Gods and Goblin s. A Field Guide to Place Names of Olympic National Park*. Port Angeles: CP Publications. 1984.

Peacock, Christopher M. *Rosario Yesterdays. A Pictorial History*. Rosario Productions, 1985.

Pelly, T.M. *The Story of Restoration Point and the Country Club*. Seattle: Lowman & Hanford Co., 1931.

Perisho, Caroline. *Fox Island. Pioneer Life on Southern Puget Sound*. Echo Bay Press, 1990.

Perry, Fredi. *Port Madison, Washington Territory. 1854-1889*. Bremerton: Perry Publishing, 1989.

—, *Seabeck. Tide's Out. Table's Set*. Bremerton: Perry Publishing, 1993.

—, Ed. Kitsap County. *The Year of the Child*. Silverdale: The Silverdale Printer, 1979.

Phillips, James W. *Washington State Place Names*. Seattle: University of Washington Press, 1971.

Power, Edward Allen. *Protection Island and the Power Family*. Self published. 1978.

Praase, Karen. *Camano Island. Images of America*. Charlston: Arcadia Publishing. 2006.

Price, Andrew, Jr. *Port Blakely. The Community Captain Renton Built*. Port Blakely Books, 1990.

Price, Lester K. *McNeil (History of a Federal Prison)*. McNeil Island: Vocational Training Duplication Department, 1970.

Puget, Peter. *The Vancouver Expedition: Peter Puget's Journal of the Exploration of Puget Sound, May 7 – June 11, 1792*. Ed. Bern Anderson. *Pacific Northwest Quarterly*, Vol. XXX, Nos. 1 thru 4, 1939.

Reese, Gary Fuller. *A Documentary History of Fort Steilacoom*. Tacoma Public Library, 1978.

—, *Origins of Pierce County Place Names*. Tacoma: R&M Press, 1989.

Retherford, Sylvia E. (assembled the material). *Compilation of Writings and Photos Concerned with the History of Home, Washington*. Vol. I, 1985.

Rhodes, Marjorie. *Biography Notes on Pioneers of Puget Sound*. 1992. Appears to be self printed.

Richardson, David. *Magic Islands. A Treasure-Trove of San Juan Islands Lore*. self pub. 1964.

—, *Pig War Islands. The San Juans of Northwest Washington*. Eastsound: Orcas Publishing Company, 1990.

Roe, JoAnn. *Blakely. Island in Time*. Bellingham: Montevista Press, 2005.

Bibliography

—, *Ghost Camps & Boom Towns.* Bellingham: Montevista Press, 1995.

Sanford, Joseph Perry. *Journal* (untitled). Microfilm U.S. National Archives (Seattle), Box 91, Records Group 39, M-75, roll 19.

Satterfield, Archie. *Edmonds The First Century.* The City of Edmonds, 1990.

Scott, Andrew. *The Encyclopedia of Raincoast Place Names. A Complete Reference to Coastal British Columbia.* Madiera Park, BC: Harbour Publishing. 2009.

Seemann, Berthold. *Narrative of the Voyage of the H.M.S. Herald during the years 1845-1851, under the Command of Captain Henry Kellett, R.N., C.B.* London: Reeve and Co. 1853.

Sebring, Al. *Sebring's Skagit County Illustrated.* Skagit County: Al Sebring, 1902.

Shaw, George C. *The Chinook Jargon and How to Use It.* Seattle: Rainier Printing Company, Inc, 1909.

Sinclair, George T. (Untitled). Microfilm U S National Archives (Seattle), Box 91, Records Group 39, M-75, roll 21.

Slater, Colleen A. *Images of America. The Key Peninsula.* Charleston: Arcadia, 2007.

Splitstone, Fred John. *Orcas. Gem of the San Juans.* 2nd ed. Bellingham: Cox Brothers, 1954.

Stevenson, Shanna B. *Lacey, Olympia, and Tumwater. A Pictorial History.* Norfolk/Virginia Beach: The Donning Company/Publishers, 1985.

Strevey, Tracy Elmer. *Pickett on Puget Sound.* A thesis submitted for the degree of Master of Arts. University of Washington. 1925.

Sundberg, Trudy James. *Portrait of an Island.* Oak Harbor: Whidbey Press, 1961.

Swift, Joan. *Brackett's Landing. A History of Early Edmonds.* Everett: The Printers, 1975.

—, *Historic Coupeville. A Sketchbook.* 1978.

Tacoma Public Library "TPL website" Washington Place Names database edited by Gary Fuller Reese http://search.tacomapubliclibrary.org/wanames/wpnv2.asp

Thomas, Berwyn B. *Shelton Washington. The First Century. 1885 – 1985.* Belfair: Mason County Historical Society, 1985.

Thompson, Pat, Ed. *In and Around Port Ludlow.* Olympic Publishing, Inc., 1987.

Turner, Erin, Ed. *Rotgut Russlers. Whiskey, Women and Wild Times in the West.* Morris Book Publishing, 2009.

U.S. Board on Geographic Names website, http://geonames.usgs.gov/

van Cleve, F. H. *Friday Harbor then and now.* Friday Harbor: Long House Printcrafters and Publishers, 1979.

Vancouver, George. *A Voyage of Discovery to the North Pacific Ocean, and Round the World in Which the Coast of North-West America Has Been Carefully Examined and Accurately Surveyed.* 4 vols. London: Printed for G.G. and J. Robinson, Paternoster-Row and J. Edwards, Pall-Mall, 1798. Unless otherwise noted, cites to Vancouver are to Vol. IV.

Vouri, Michael. *The Pig War. Standoff at Griffin Bay.* Friday Harbor: Griffin Bay Bookstore, 2006.

—, *Images of an American San Juan Island.* Charleston, SC: Arcadia, 2010.

Wagner, Henry R. *Spanish Explorations in the Strait of Juan de Fuca.* Santa Ana: Fine Arts Press, 1933.

Walbran, Captain John T. *British Columbia Coast Names, 1592-1906. Their Origin and History.* Seattle: University of Washington Press, 1972.

Walsh, Sophie. *History and Romance of the San Juan Islands.* Anacortes: Anacortes American Press, 1932.

Warner, Katy. *A History of Bainbridge Island.* Bainbridge Island: Bainbridge Island Public Schools, 1968.

Welsh, William D. *A Brief Historical Sketch of Port Townsend, Washington.* 6th ed. Port Townsend Chamber of Commerce, 1956.

—, *A Brief History of Port Angeles Washington Sketching the Highlights of Discovery and Development of the "Second National City" of the United States.* 10th ed. Port Angles Newsprint Division of Crown Zellerbach Corporation, 1960.

Bibliography

Whitebrook, Robert B. "From Cape Flattery to Birch Bay. Vancouver's Anchorages on Puget Sound". Seattle: University of Washington Press, *Pacific Northwest Quarterly*, 44 (3): 115-128.

Wilkes, Charles U.S.N. *United States Exploring Expedition During the years 1838, 1839, 1840, 1841, 1842*. Vol. 4. Philadelphia: Lea & Blanchard, 1845. Cites to this material are referenced as "Narrative".

—, *Journal Kept by Charles Wilkes Commanding the Exploring Expedition*. handwritten between 1838-1842.

—, *United States Exploring Expedition During the years 1838, 1839, 1840, 1841, 1842*. Vol. 23, Ch 16, Philadelphia: Lea & Blanchard, 1845.

—, *Diary*. Microfilm U S National Archives (Seattle) Box 91, Records Group 39, M-75, roll 9. 1841.

Wing, Robert C. *Joseph Baker: Lieutenant on the Vancouver Expedition for whom Mt. Baker was named*. Seattle: Grey Beard Publishing, 1992.

Wing, Robert C. with Gordon Newell. *Peter Puget: Lieutenant on the Vancouver Expedition, fighting British naval officer, The man for whom Puget Sound was named*. Seattle: Grey Beard Publishing, 1979.

Wood, Bryce. *San Juan Island. Coastal Place Names and Cartographic Nomenclature*. Ann Arbor MI: University Microfilms International, 1980.

Work, John. *The Journal of John Work. January to October 1835*. Victoria, B.C.: Printed by Charles F. Banfield, Printer to the King's Most Excellent Majesty. 1945.

—, Work, John. Ed. By T.C. Elliott. *Journal of John Work, November and December 1824. Pacific Northwest Quarterly*. Vol. 3, No. 3. July 1912. pp 198-228.

Wright, E. W. (Ed). *Lewis & Dryden's Marine History of the Pacific Northwest*. Portland: The Lewis & Dryden Printing Company. 1895.

The following are sources without authors:

A History of Mariners' Cove, Whidbey Island Washington. Undated ms.

A History of Pierce County Washington 1990. Volume I. Dallas: Taylor Publishing Company, 1990.

A History of Pierce County Washington 1992 Volume II. Dallas: Taylor Publishing Company, 1992.

A History of Pierce County Washington 1992 Volume III. Dallas: Taylor Publishing Company, 1992.

An Historic Resources Survey of Bainbridge Island, Washington. Prepared by Boyle Wagoner Architects. March 1987.

An Illustrated History of Skagit and Snohomish Counties. Their People, Their Commerce and Their Resources With an Outline of the Early History of the State of Washington. Interstate Publishing Company. 1906. available online at http://www.archive.org/details/illustratedhisto00inte

Decisions of the United States Geographic Board by the United States Geographic Board. Available online at http://books.google.com/books?id=F40tAAAAMAAJ&pg=RA8-PA44&lpg=RA8-PA44&dq=who+named+%22mount+woolard%22&source=bl&ots=o3I_mkPEwY&sig=iknYq4D0lGYoBBXYUBkV70n_qIQ&hl=en&ei=38NATJ2PK4X0tgOM0o3XDA&sa=X&oi=book_result&ct=result&resnum=9&ved=0CDEQ6AEwCA#v=snippet&q=clallam%20bay&f=false. Because this is comprised of several volumes, each individually numbered, I have excluded page numbers from the manuscript. In addition to this online site, other U.S. Board decisions were found at the Hathi Trust Digital Library from the University of Michigan.

Edmonds: 100 Years for the Gem of Puget Sound. The Edmonds Paper. 1990.

English Camp. San Juan Island NHP. Historic Structures Report – Part I. June 1969.

History of the Pacific Northwest: Oregon and Washington. Vol 1–1889. Compiled and Published by the North Pacific History Co., Portland, OR.

History of the Pacific Northwest: Oregon and Washington. Vol 2–1889. Compiled and Published by the North Pacific History Co., Portland, OR.

Bibliography

Indianola: A Community Memoir. Published by the Indianola Beach Improvement Club, 1998.

Northwest Boat Travel, Vol 16, No 2. Ed. Phil & Gwen Cole. Published by Hugo & Rachel Anderson. 1993.

Port Gardner Neighborhood. History to Share. Published by City of Everett, 1983.

Port Gamble Story, 1853 – 1953. No publisher or date.

Seattle Times. July 28, 2008. p. A1.

Seattle Times. Magazine Section, various editions.

Seattle Times. September 28, 2001. p. B7.

The Duwamish Diary. 1849 – 1949. Seattle: Cleveland High School, 1949.

The Islander. Issues from 1891 to 1898 available at http://chroniclingamerica.loc.gov/lccn/sn88085189/issues/. From 1898 to 1914 available at http://chroniclingamerica.loc.gov/lccn/sn88085190/issues/. Note: *The Islander* became *The San Juan Islander* with the February 24, 1898 issue. However, after this date, it continued to refer to itself simply as *The Islander.*

The San Juan Dispute. A Thrilling Period in U.S. History. 1852 – 1872. Friday Harbor, Journal Print.

Told By the Pioneers. Vol III. Printed under W.P.A. Sponsored Federal Project No. 5814. 1938.

http://geonames.usgs.gov/ for U.S. Board on Geographic Names decisions.

United States Coast Pilot, Pacific Ocean. California, Oregon, and Washington. Washington: Government Printing Office. 1903.

United States Coast Pilot, Pacific Ocean. California, Oregon, and Washington. Washington: Government Printing Office. 1909.

United States Coast Pilot, Pacific Ocean. California, Oregon, and Washington. Washington: Government Printing Office. 1917.

United States Coast Pilot, Pacific Ocean. California, Oregon, and Washington. Washington: Government Printing Office. 1919.

United States Coast Pilot, Pacific Ocean. California, Oregon, and Washington. Washington: Government Printing Office. 1934.

United States Coast Pilot, Pacific Ocean. California, Oregon, and Washington. Washington: Government Printing Office. 1942.

Washington State census data at http://www.digitalarchives.wa.gov/

With Pride in Heritage. History of Jefferson County. Port Townsend: Edited and published by the Jefferson County Historical Society, 1966.